# THE COMPLETE GUIDE TO IMMIGRATION AND SUCCESSFUL LIVING IN THE UNITED STATES

## Access USA, Inc.

All inquires should be addressed to:
Access USA, Inc.
1761 Long Hill Road
Millington, NJ 07946-1344
USA
Phone 1-908-647-2334     Fax  1-908-604-4801

Library of Congress Catalog Card No. 94-079290

International Standard Book No. 0-9639667-2-3

Published in the United States of America by
L.K. Graphic Communications
R.D.5, Box 7
Belle Vernon, PA 15012

This book is dedicated to the tens of millions of immigrants who have struggled to enter this country and become productive citizens. Their participation in this great experiment in democracy has contributed to what the United States of America is today. This nation is rooted in the concept of individual freedom and the right to life, liberty, and the pursuit of happiness. We hope that succeeding generations of immigrants will strengthen our shared future by adhering to those principles.

Welcome and good luck!

# ACKNOWLEDGMENTS

This book was developed in conjunction with professionals from a wide variety of fields. They were selected for their credentials and for their knowledge of particular aspects of law or life in the United States. We wish to recognize their contributions and thank them for a job well done.

Special thanks to:
Cathy Baszczewski

Thanks also to:

Tony Adams
Paul C. Amatangelo
AT&T
Barbara H. Brackett
Na Mi Baszczewski
Beneficial Management Corporation
Berlitz Schools of Languages
Louis Brooks, C.P.A.
Dr. Raymond K. Brown
Shannon Brown
Paul Cappelli
Joann Cardinal
Carlson Wagonlit Travel
Audrene S. Chakmakjian
Anthony Cocuzza
Joseph M. Colombo
Dr. Robert Corcetti
William G. Cowan
Diane Dunay
Rene Débray
A. Michael Del Duca, G.R.I.
Arnold E. Eagle
Rick Famely, C.P.A.
Ramiro Fandino
Robin Flowers
Dean Foster
Joel Hill
Hsin-cha Hsu
Henry "Pete" Hoke III

Kenneth L. Kaimin
Gregory Labuza, R.P.
Michael Leber
Gil A. Lebron
Jack C. Leonard
John S. Longstaff, C.F.P.
Larry Marchiony
Dan McDaniels
Georgia McDaniels
Maura E. McLaughlin
Dr. Amadee B. Merbedone
MetLife
Brian Nakai
J. Patrick Rau
Chief Robert Re
Dennis Regenye
Chris Reynolds
Sandoz Consumer Pharmaceuticals
Aron D. Scharf
Florence Starita
Dirk Smith
Edwin P. Soriano
Patricia Sze
Robert L. Townsend
Alex Virvo
Betty B. Weber, G.R.I.
Joanne Wrba, R.N.
Joseph M. Wrba
Martin Wahoske, C.T.C.

# CONTENTS

## SECTION H: HEALTH CARE

*Preventative and curative care, where to go for medical attention, medication, staying well, living wills, what to do in case of an emergency, medical professionals, immunization schedule, and fire safety tips.*

## SECTION I: COMMUNICATIONS

*Telephone, mail, telegraph, and services.*

## SECTION J: EDUCATION

*Pre-school, primary and secondary education, technology in the class-room, post-secondary education, adult education, what to look for in a school, library services, and learning English.*

## SECTION K: RECREATION AND TRAVEL

*Entertainment; sports, activities, organizations, religion, holidays, travel: by car, plane, train or recreational vehicle, climate, the United States; a brief tour, and state departments of tourism.*

## MISCELLANEOUS

**Section L:** *Time zones, metric conversions, state chambers of commerce, embassies and consulates abroad, INS offices,*
**Section M:** *sample immigration forms*
**Section N:** *glossary and index.*

*Plus:*
*Special services questionnaire, Access USA Club International application and green card lottery registration.*

## EDITORIAL BOARD

*Walter A. Baszczewski*
*L. Hale Sims, M.P.I.A., M.S.H.*
*Linda K. Gush*
*Frank B. McLaughlin, J.D.*
*Jane H. Yates*
*Kevin Wolfe, Esq.*
*Sara J. McLaughlin*
*Donald M. Kobaly*

# PREFACE

This book is designed to:

- Provide you with an understanding of the way immigration law works. It will enable you to work better with an immigration attorney and improve your chances of obtaining citizenship.

- Provide you with the information on day-to-day life essential to your smooth transition to life in the United States.

It consists of two parts:

- **The immigration law section** which gives an overview and detailed information on the different types of visas available. It also contains samples of the required U.S. Immigration and Naturalization Service forms.

- **The successful living section** which gives a picture of American life and information you will need on how to adjust to it.

Also included are:

- Enrollment forms for the *Access USA Club International* which provides members with special services such as money saving discounts, immigration law updates, telephone information helpline, educational scholarship programs, quarterly newsletters, and access to appropriate attorneys and *Green Card Lottery* submission (where appropriate). Club membership guarantees that your application for the Green Card Lottery will be properly submitted. You will even receive a notarized certification that your application has been properly submitted.

- An enrollment information questionnaire, the first step in continuing our relationship with you. The information you give us is used solely to provide services to make your adjustment easier. **It is not available to any government agency.**

Review the materials in the book and send in your enrollment form and completed questionnaire as soon as possible.

# ADVISORY

No one can guarantee you a green card. People promising inside help or low prices can be very persuasive but are likely to disappear, leaving you with expensive legal bills and a loss of valuable time in your immigration process.

Applications received by the U.S. Immigration and Naturalization Service are kept as permanent record. All documents submitted are added to your file. Nothing is removed from it. Therefore, it is advisable to be as accurate as possible when submitting information.

Do not purchase or attempt to purchase false documents. You may be able to go undetected for a while, however the government can now cross-check your information by computer and may eventually find and prosecute you.

This book is designed to provide you with the latest information on immigration law and life in the United States. Neither the authors, nor the publisher, can accept responsibility for changes to the law or immigration process that occur after printing. Some details may change over time. To get the most up-to-date information we recommend you send in your membership in the *Access USA Club International*.

This book is not intended to be used as a do-it-yourself legal text. It is meant to supply comprehensive explanations of the immigration process in lay terms, not to render professional legal advice. Such legal advice or other assistance should be sought only from a competent professional.

# TABLE OF CONTENTS

# SPECIAL CONSIDERATIONS IN THE IMMIGRATION LAW

# THE NATURALIZATION PROCESS

# LISTING OF IMMIGRATION FORMS

# INTRODUCTION

As a new arrival, you might feel overwhelmed. This is a big country with over 260 million people. What are they like? Are any of them from your old country? How can you legally come to the United States? Where will you live? How can you find an apartment or a house? What kind of work can you find? How can you start your own business? How will you manage your money? How can you get a driver's license or mail a letter or call home? How can you learn English? Where can you or your children get an education? Where can you get medical help? Where can you worship? What will you do for recreation? You will find the answers you need in this book.

This book was written for the new or prospective immigrant to the United States of America. It provides both an overview and an in-depth look at the country. Although designed for the newcomer, it can also help others – persons making frequent or prolonged stays, established immigrants wanting to relocate, foreign students, and corporate transferees, – understand the process of daily life and work in America. Read the whole book now or just the parts you need.

## THE EVOLUTION OF IMMIGRATION LAW

Immigration law deals with the movement of people from one country to another for the purpose of permanent residence. It is influenced by changing global, social, and political realities. Conversely, those realities are influenced by immigration law.

Most of the early colonists in pre-revolutionary America came in hope of economic opportunity and the promise of religious freedom. Some, however, paid their way as indentured servants, others were sent by London as convicts, or sold out of Africa as slaves. There was an early attempt at immigration control, an effort designed to reduce the number of criminals coming in, but the lack of a centralized authority prevented any such control.

After the Revolution in 1776, the United States experienced essentially unrestricted immigration for a period of about 100 years. Although there was some minimal legislative work to regulate naturalization and expel "dangerous aliens," the demand for labor in the huge frontier prevented any strict immigration controls.

Only in 1820 did the federal government start recording immigration data. Although some states in the midwest had established agencies to foster immigrant settlement, by the mid-1800s the general public began to fear that too many immigrants were not good for the economy or the fabric of American society. These fears led to the 1875 passing of legislation to impose "quality controls," barring the entrance of convicts and prostitutes.

In 1882, responding to a belief that Chinese immigrant laborers were depressing the U.S. wage scale, Congress enacted the first openly racist restrictive law, suspending all immigration of Chinese laborers for ten years. This Chinese Exclusion Act also imposed a head tax on every newly arriving immigrant, in order to raise revenue and to exclude immigrants with no economic means. It also excluded convicts and the mentally ill.

During the 1890s, immigration continued to be perceived by a majority of Americans as a threat to the U.S. economy. In response, Congress expanded the list of excludable foreigners to include the pauper, the diseased, and the polygamist. Foreign publication advertisements encouraging immigration to the U.S. were forbidden. In 1903, responding to the assassination of President McKinley, the anarchist was added to the list of excludables, along with the epileptic, the insane, and the beggar.

In 1917, Congress enacted a literacy requirement, raised the head tax, and prohibited the immigration of Asians from countries within specific latitudes and longitudes. The then newly formed National Association for the Advancement of Colored People (NAACP) halted attempts to bar entrance of blacks.

After World War I, concern arose that displaced Bolshevists arriving from Europe would undermine the country. Congress passed the Immigration Act of 1924, implementing numerical controls. Immigration from each nation was limited to three percent of the number of foreign-born individuals residing in the U.S. under the 1910 census. This national-origins system was rooted in the conviction that the "foreigner balance" of the 1920s had to be preserved. It discriminated against countries with only a small proportion of the U.S. population (Japan, among others, was totally excluded) and favored those already well represented. Ireland, Great Britain, and Germany, for instance, were allotted 70 percent of the quota. In 1929, the annual quota of all immigrants was set at 150,000.

Immigration to the U.S. dropped dramatically during the depression of the 1930s when emigration far exceeded immigration. No major new controls were devised during this time period.

World War II imposed new economic realities upon the United States. Workers were needed to fulfill war-related needs. The U.S. made agreements with Mexico to establish a temporary workers program. The ban on Chinese immigration was repealed.

The plight of war refugees led to the admission of thousands of displaced persons.

The Immigration and Naturalization Act of 1952 (the McCarren-Walter Act), while continuing the national origins formula, did set small quotas for admission of previously excluded nationalities and established preference levels.

Liberalized in 1965 in response to the civil rights movements, the national-origins system was eliminated in 1968. A first-come, first-served policy was instituted with annual ceilings: originally 170,000 immigrant visas for nations outside the Western hemisphere; 120,000 within. These ceilings were equalized in 1978; raised to a 700,000 total in 1990.

Three reasons were recognized as the basis for immigration visas:

- Kinship to a U.S. citizen or a legal alien
- Job skills
- Demonstratable status as a political refugee.

## REFUGEES

A major problem has been the influx of refugees from Southeast Asia and the Caribbean that began in the 1970s. The 1980 Refugee Act broadened the definition of eligibility but by no means stemmed the tide. The fact that Cubans were once accorded virtual automatic asylum while Haitians were not has aroused much concern in the U.S.

## ILLEGAL IMMIGRATION

There is concern as well over illegal immigration, because of its impact on the American job market and social services, including health care and education. An estimated five million illegal immigrants settled in the U.S. in the 1970s and 1980s.

## THE 1990 IMMIGRATION ACT

Today, immigration law is primarily regulated by the 1990 amendments to the Immigration and Nationality Act (INMACT 90). These amendments increased the quota for worldwide immigration to 700,000 per year for a period of three years, after which it is reduced to 675,000 per year. If the additional quota for refugees is included, the total is 800,000 per year.

INMACT 90 set new quotas for all the different preference levels. For family-sponsored immigration, 465,000; for employment-related, 140,000; the diversity program; 55,000. Special considerations are given to inhabitants of Hong Kong, and four new immigrant visa categories were added to the original 13 categories.

# CHAPTER 1

# CATEGORIES BY WHICH FOREIGN NATIONALS MAY LEGALLY ENTER THE U.S.

Foreign nationals may legally enter the U.S. in on of two basic categories: immigrants or nonimmigrants.

An **immigrant** intends to reside permanently in the U.S. He is issued an **Alien Registration Receipt Card** or **green card** certifying his permanent residence.

A **nonimmigrant** intends to remain only temporarily in the U.S. Here for a specific purpose, he is issued a nonimmigrant visa, valid for a specified length of time.

An important distinction between these visas is the annual number of each available. Most types of immigrant visas are limited in number to an annual quota; most types of nonimmigrant visas are not.

There are several classifications within each category. What follows is a brief overview of the material described in more detail in subsequent chapters.

## IMMIGRANT VISAS: KEYS TO PERMANENT RESIDENCE

Immigrant visas may or may not be subject to a quota.

### Immigrant visas not subject to quotas

Foreign individuals who are immediate relatives of U.S. citizens may obtain visas not subject to annual quota. The following categories of people may apply:

- Spouses of U.S. citizens, including recent widows and widowers

- Parents of U.S. citizens

- Unmarried children under 21 years old: this includes non-marital and marital children, stepchildren, adopted children, orphans adopted abroad or orphans coming to the United States to be adopted.

## *Immigrant visas subject to quotas*

These are issued to foreign nationals who qualify for one of three types of visas: family-sponsored, employment-related, or diversity immigrant.

**FAMILY-SPONSORED VISAS** have four preference levels:

- **First preference:** unmarried sons and daughters, over 21 years of age, of U.S. citizens

- **Second preference:** spouses, unmarried children under 21 years of age, and unmarried sons and daughters of lawful permanent residents (green card holders)

- **Third preference:** married sons and daughters of U.S. citizens

- **Fourth preference:** brothers and sisters of U.S. citizens.

## EMPLOYMENT-RELATED VISAS

Since the passage of the Immigration Act of 1990, more attention has been paid to meritorious foreign individuals who wish to immigrate to the U.S. While family-sponsored visa applications are still favored in preference level over employment related applications, the educational background and skills of prospective immigrants play a greater role than ever before. There are five preference levels:

- **First preference:** priority workers defined as:
  - Persons of extraordinary ability in the sciences, arts, education, business, or athletics
  - Outstanding professors and researchers
  - Executives and managers of multinational corporations.

- **Second preference:** professionals holding advanced degrees or persons of exceptional ability in the sciences, arts, or business.

- **Third preference:** skilled workers in short supply, professionals holding baccalaureate degrees, and certain other workers in short supply.

- **Fourth preference:** special immigrant categories including:
  - Ministers of recognized religious denominations, their spouses and their children
  - Former employees of the U.S. government and international organizations
  - Foreign medical graduates in the U.S. since 1978
  - Foreign workers employed by the U.S. Consulate in Hong Kong for at least three years.

- **Fifth preference:** employment creation visas are now available for investors in new American businesses that will employ at least ten full-time American workers. The required minimum investment is usually $1 million. If the business is located in a rural area or in an area of high unemployment, the minimum investment is $500,000. Chapter 3 discusses this category in more detail.

## DIVERSITY IMMIGRANT VISAS

The ethnic diversity category was established by the Immigration Act of 1990. Through a program popularly called the Green Card Lottery, individuals from countries deemed under-represented in the U.S. are eligible for one of 55,000 visas allocated annually beginning in October 1994. (Chapter 4 explores the lottery program in more detail.)

### Hong Kong residents

In expectation of Hong Kong's return to the People's Republic of China in 1997, the U.S. has increased the number of visas allocated to employees working for American corporations doing business in Hong Kong.

Under the Immigration Act of 1990, visas may be issued to Hong Kong residents until January 1, 2002, giving them the opportunity to immigrate to the U.S.

# NONIMMIGRANT VISAS

Nonimmigrant visas are issued for temporary residence to perform a specific activity. These visas authorize a foreign national to enter the U.S. to perform a specific activity. These visas are categorized A through R in accordance with the laws relating to that category. Within each lettered category, a number is assigned establishing priority within the category. Each of the eighteen status types (A through R) has different privileges, restrictions, and requirements; serves a particular purpose; and differs in the length of stay permitted in the U.S. (These details can be found in Chapter 7.)

## How long does it take to receive a visa?

The answer may depend upon several factors:

- The type of visa for which you are applying

- Your category of immigrant or nonimmigrant status

- The current quotas for your type of visa

- The experience of the attorney handling your case.

# ADVISORY

The information contained in this section is of a distinctly legal nature. This material is designed and provided to serve as a useful overview and guide to the immigration process. This section does not constitute a do-it-yourself guide to the complicated realm of immigration law and procedure. We recommend that anyone seeking to immigrate first consult an immigration attorney. This will help expedite your immigration process and avoid potential costly errors. Although we have taken every measure to ensure the accuracy of this section, it must be remembered that immigration law is in a continuous state of change. The required forms and filing fees associated with such forms should be confirmed with your attorney or local INS office prior to filing.

# NONIMMIGRANT VISA CATEGORIES

| | |
|---|---|
| **A-1, A-2, A-3** | Career diplomats |
| **B-1, B-2, B-1/B-2** | Temporary visas for business and pleasure |
| **C-1, C-2, C-3** | Foreign nationals in transit |
| **D-1, D-2** | Crew members |
| **E-1, E-2** | Treaty traders, investors and their children |
| **F-1, F-2** | Students |
| **G-1, G-2, G-3, G-4, G-5** | International organization representatives |
| **H-1A** | Temporary workers performing services as Registered Nurses |
| **H-1B** | Temporary professional workers |
| **H-2A, H-2B** | Temporary workers performing agricultural services |
| **H-3** | Trainees |
| **H-4** | Spouses and children of any H category visa holder |
| **I** | Foreign media representatives |
| **J-1, J-2** | Exchange visitors |
| **K-1, K-2** | Fiance(é)s of U.S. citizens, or their children |
| **L-1, L-2** | Intercompany transferees |
| **M-1, M-2** | Students in non-academic institutions |
| **N** | Parents and children of special immigrants |
| **O-1, O-2** | Foreign nationals with extraordinary abilities |
| **P-1, P-2, P-3, P-4** | Entertainers |
| **Q-1, Q-2** | Cultural exchange program participants |
| **R-1, R-2** | Religious workers |

# VISAS SUBJECT TO NUMERICAL LIMITATIONS (QUOTAS)

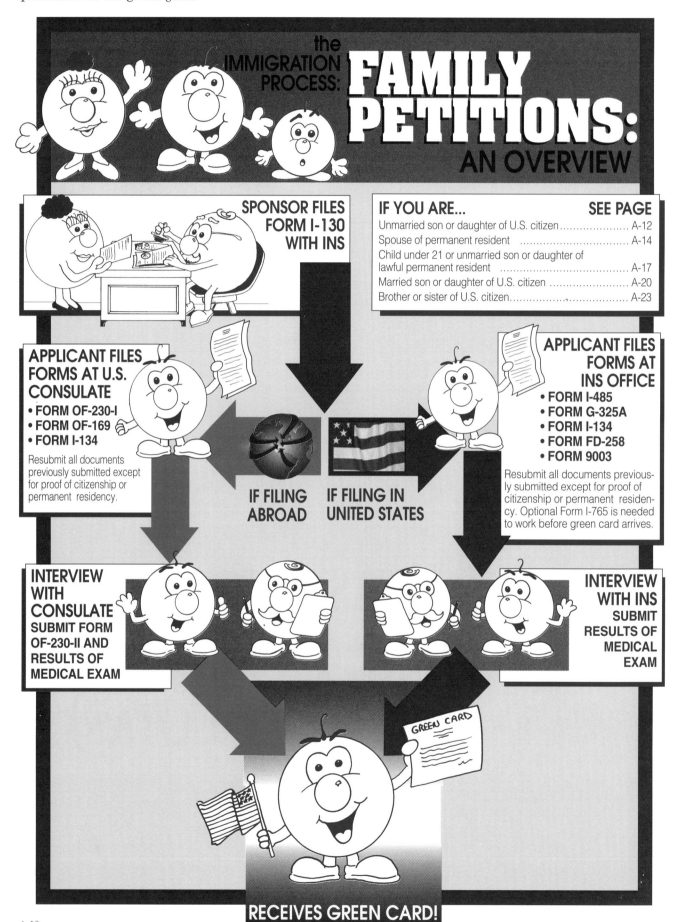

the
IMMIGRATION
PROCESS: **FAMILY PETITIONS:** AN OVERVIEW

**SPONSOR FILES FORM I-130 WITH INS**

**IF YOU ARE...**                         **SEE PAGE**

Unmarried son or daughter of U.S. citizen.....................A-12

Spouse of permanent resident ...............................A-14

Child under 21 or unmarried son or daughter of
lawful permanent resident .......................................A-17

Married son or daughter of U.S. citizen .......................A-20

Brother or sister of U.S. citizen...................................A-23

**APPLICANT FILES FORMS AT U.S. CONSULATE**
• **FORM OF-230-I**
• **FORM OF-169**
• **FORM I-134**

Resubmit all documents
previously submitted except
for proof of citizenship or
permanent residency.

**APPLICANT FILES FORMS AT INS OFFICE**
• **FORM I-485**
• **FORM G-325A**
• **FORM I-134**
• **FORM FD-258**
• **FORM 9003**

Resubmit all documents previously submitted except for proof of
citizenship or permanent residency. Optional Form I-765 is needed
to work before green card arrives.

**IF FILING ABROAD**      **IF FILING IN UNITED STATES**

**INTERVIEW WITH CONSULATE SUBMIT FORM OF-230-II AND RESULTS OF MEDICAL EXAM**

**INTERVIEW WITH INS SUBMIT RESULTS OF MEDICAL EXAM**

GREEN CARD

**RECEIVES GREEN CARD!**

# CHAPTER 2

# OBTAINING A VISA UNDER THE FAMILY-SPONSORED CATEGORY

You may petition for a family-sponsored visa provided you fall into one of these categories:

- Unmarried sons and daughters (over 21 years of age) of U.S. citizens
- Spouses, children, and unmarried sons and daughters of lawful permanent residents
- Married sons and daughters of U.S. citizens
- Brothers and sisters of U.S. citizens.

Remember that the family-sponsored visa is limited by annual quota. At left is an overview of the process, but the details to the process are in this chapter. Refer directly to the section in this chapter that pertains to your circumstance and follow those specific directions. All forms needed for the process are listed with their corresponding pages in section M of the appendix.

The application process depends on the foreign national's place of residence. If living in his country of origin or some other country, he must file at a U.S. consulate. If legally residing in the United States, he must file at the appropriate INS office.

In addition, recent changes in immigration law have made it possible for many illegal aliens, who would have otherwise been eligible for an immigration visa abroad, to adjust their status to that of lawful permanent resident. Applicants who would not otherwise qualify for adjustment status are required to pay an additional fee of $650 (U.S.). This provision is scheduled to expire on October 1, 1997. It is always recommended that the applicant seek professional legal advice when seeking to adjust their alien status.

Regardless of residence, two elements are essential to the process:

- The petition, which is filed by the sponsor, and
- The application, which is filed by the foreign national. (Upon filing the application he is officially called "the applicant.")

# FIRST PREFERENCE: UNMARRIED SONS AND DAUGHTERS OF U.S. CITIZENS

A U.S. citizen can petition for an unmarried son or daughter over 21 years old. The waiting period is usually short for this category, except for people born in Mexico or in the Philippines where the number of nationals admitted has exceeded their respective quotas.

## Stage one: the petition

The sponsor should submit the petition (Form I-130) to the INS at either a local office or a regional service center. The petition will be assigned a priority date, the date when the petition is received and filed by the INS. The official waiting period for the green card begins on this date. To file the petition, follow the chart below.

### PETITIONER (SPONSOR) COMPLETES FORM I-130 (See page M-5).
*The sponsor must attach the following to Form I-130:*

☐ **Evidence of U.S. Citizenship**

    Birth certificate

    Certificate of citizenship

    Naturalization certificate

    U.S. consular record of birth abroad

    Valid U.S. passport

☐ **Long form birth certificate of the unmarried son or daughter**

### IN ADDITION, IF YOU ARE THE FOLLOWING SPONSOR YOU MUST SUBMIT:

| Father | Father of Non-marital Child | Stepparent | Adoptive Parent (non-orphan*) |
|---|---|---|---|
| The beneficiary's parents' marriage certificate | **Evidence of paternity:** Birth certificate with father's name on it<br><br>OR<br><br>**Evidence of legitimization:** Affidavit showing father acknowledges paternity<br><br>Affidavit from someone who knows sponsor and beneficiary<br><br>Income statement showing son or daughter resides in the same house as the sponsor | Proof that parent and the stepparent were married before the 18th birthday of the stepchild | Proof that adoption took place before child's 16th birthday<br><br><br><br>* *A special procedure must be followed if the child falls into the category of orphan.* |

**Attach check or money order** for $80.00 (U.S.) and return to the INS office.

## *Stage two: the application process*

Once the sponsor receives approval of the petition, the beneficiary should begin the application process for an immigration visa (green card).

 **APPLICATION PROCESS AT A U.S. CONSULATE** *The applicant must submit the notice of petition approval together with the following forms and documents to a U.S. consulate:*

| Form # | Description | Use |
|---|---|---|
| **OF-230-I**<br>*See page M-10* | Biographical Information | Used to perform a security check on the applicant. |
| **OF-169**<br>*See page M-12* | Certification of Documents | Certifies that the applicant possesses all documents needed to complete the application and to attend the immigration interview with a consulate officer. |
| **OF-230-II**<br>*See page M-18* | Application for Immigration Visa | *This form must be submitted only at the time of the immigration interview.* It should not be mailed or filed with other forms. |
| **I-134 or OF-167**<br>*See page M-22 or M-91* | Proof of Financial Support | Certifies that the applicant will not become a public charge. |

**IN ADDITION, THE APPLICANT MUST SUBMIT THE FOLLOWING:**

- **All documents previously submitted by the sponsor EXCEPT the sponsor's proof of citizenship.**
- **Applicant's valid passport from country of origin.**
- **Police clearance certificate.**
- **Military records of applicant.**
- **Three photographs of applicant.**
- **Results of applicant's required medical exam.**
- **Filing fee of $100.00 (U.S.).**

**Applicant must attend an interview with a consulate officer. The period of time for acceptance of the petitioner's application varies greatly. See your local consulate for more information.**

 **APPLICATION PROCESS AT A U.S. INS OFFICE** *The applicant must submit the notice of petition approval together with the following forms and documents to the INS local office nearest to his place of residence:*

| Form # | Description | Use |
|---|---|---|
| **I-485**<br>*See page M-25* | Application for Permanent Residence and Adjustment of Status | Used to adjust status to that of permanent resident. |
| **I-485**<br>**Supplement-A**<br>*See page M-87* | Application for Permanent Residence and Adjustment of Status | Determines whether applicant is legally residing in the United States. If he is not, he is required to pay an additional fee of $650 (U.S.) for applicants over the age of 17 (certain exceptions may apply). |

*Process Continues on Next Page* ▶

## APPLICATION PROCESS AT A U.S. INS OFFICE, *Continued from page A-13.*

| Form # | Description | Use |
|---|---|---|
| G-325-A *See page M-31* | Biographical Data Form | Used to compile personal background information. |
| I-134 or OF-167 *See page M-22 or M-91* | Proof of Financial Support | Certifies that the applicant will not become a public charge. |
| F-258 | Fingerprint Card | For the purpose of identification. |
| I-94 *See page M-32* | Departure Record | Records foreign national's entrances and departures to and from the U.S. |
| I-765 Optional *See page M-33* | Application for Employment Authorization | Used to obtain approval to work prior to applicant's green card approval. Must be submitted with filing fee of $70.00 (U.S.). |

### IN ADDITION, THE APPLICANT MUST SUBMIT THE FOLLOWING:

- **IRS (Internal Revenue Service) Form 9003 to determine whether applicant owes taxes for previous periods of employment in the U.S. Applicants who have not worked in the U.S. should mark the form "Not Applicable."**
- **All documents previously submitted by the sponsor EXCEPT the sponsor's proof of citizenship.**
- **Three photographs of applicant.**
- **Results of all required medical exams.**
- **Filing fee of $130 (U.S.) for applicants 14 years of age or older, $100 (U.S.) if applicant is under 14.**

**Applicant must attend an interview with an INS official. The period of time for acceptance of the application will vary greatly. See your local INS office.**

# SECOND PREFERENCE: SPOUSES, CHILDREN, AND UNMARRIED SONS AND DAUGHTERS OF LAWFUL PERMANENT RESIDENTS

## *Spouses of permanent residents*

A permanent resident (green card holder) of the United States may petition for (sponsor) his or her spouse. The waiting period for this category may be up to three years regardless of the beneficiary's country of origin. When petitioning for a spouse, the beneficiary's unmarried children under age 21 may automatically obtain green cards as accompanying relatives (derivative status) without filing separate petitions.

Regardless of residence, two elements are essential to the process:

- The petition, which is filed by the sponsor, and
- The application, which is filed by the foreign national. (Upon filing the application he is officially called "the applicant.")

## Stage one: the petition

The sponsor should submit the petition (Form I-130) to the INS at either a local office or a regional service center. The petition will be assigned a priority date, the date when the petition is received and filed by the INS. The official waiting period for the green card begins on this date. To file the petition, follow the chart below.

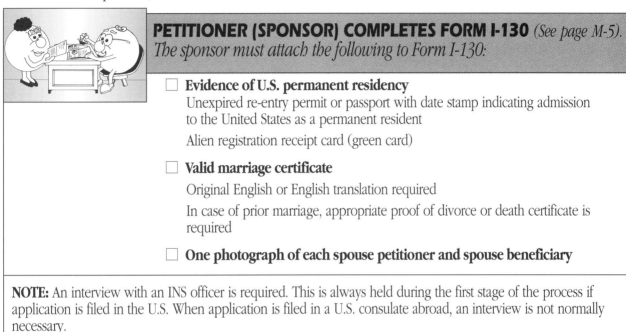

**PETITIONER (SPONSOR) COMPLETES FORM I-130** *(See page M-5).* *The sponsor must attach the following to Form I-130:*

☐ **Evidence of U.S. permanent residency**
   Unexpired re-entry permit or passport with date stamp indicating admission to the United States as a permanent resident
   Alien registration receipt card (green card)

☐ **Valid marriage certificate**
   Original English or English translation required
   In case of prior marriage, appropriate proof of divorce or death certificate is required

☐ **One photograph of each spouse petitioner and spouse beneficiary**

**NOTE:** An interview with an INS officer is required. This is always held during the first stage of the process if application is filed in the U.S. When application is filed in a U.S. consulate abroad, an interview is not normally necessary.

**Attach check or money order** for $80.00 (U.S.) and return to the INS office.

## Stage two: the application process

Once the sponsor receives approval of the petition, the beneficiary should begin the application process for an immigration visa (green card).

**APPLICATION PROCESS AT A U.S. CONSULATE** *The applicant must submit the notice of petition approval together with the following forms and documents to a U.S. consulate:*

| Form # | Description | Use |
|---|---|---|
| **OF-230-I**<br>*See page M-10* | Biographical Information | Used to perform a security check on the applicant. |
| **OF-169**<br>*See page M-12* | Certification of Documents | Certifies that applicant possesses all documents needed to complete the application and to attend the immigration interview with a consulate officer. |
| **OF-230-II**<br>*See page M-18* | Application for Immigration Visa | *This form must be submitted only at the time of the immigration interview.* It should not be mailed or filed with other forms. |
| **I-134 or OF-167**<br>*See page M-22 or M-91* | Proof of Financial Support | Certifies that the applicant will not become a public charge. |

*Process Continues on Next Page*▶ A-15

## APPLICATION PROCESS AT A U.S. CONSULATE, *continued from page A-15.*

**IN ADDITION, THE APPLICANT MUST SUBMIT THE FOLLOWING:**

- All documents previously submitted by the sponsor EXCEPT the sponsor's proof of permanent residency.
- Applicant and accompanying relatives' valid passports from country of origin.
- Police clearance certificates for applicant and each accompanying relative.
- Military records of applicant and each accompanying relative if applicable.
- Three photographs of applicant and each accompanying relative.
- Results of required medical exams for applicant and each accompanying relative.
- Filing fee of $100.00 (U.S.).

Applicant must attend an interview with a consulate officer. The period of time for acceptance of the petitioner's application varies greatly. See your local consulate for more information.

## APPLICATION PROCESS AT A U.S. INS OFFICE *The applicant must submit the notice of petition approval together with the following forms and documents to the INS local office nearest to his place of residence:*

| Form # | Description | Use |
|---|---|---|
| **I-485**<br>*See page M-25* | Application for Permanent Residence and Adjustment of Status | Used to adjust status to that of permanent resident. |
| **I-485**<br>**Supplement-A**<br>*See page M-87* | Application for Permanent Residence and Adjustment of Status | Determines whether applicant is legally residing in the United States. If he is not, he is required to pay an additional fee of $650 (U.S.) for applicants over the age of 17 (certain exceptions may apply). |
| **G-325-A**<br>*See page M-31* | Biographical Data Form | Used to compile personal background information. |
| **I-134 or OF-167**<br>*See page M-22 or M-91* | Proof of Financial Support | Certifies that the applicant will not become a public charge. |
| **F-258** | Fingerprint Card | For the purpose of identification. |
| **I-94**<br>*See page M-32* | Departure Record | Records of foreign national's entrances and departures to and from the U.S. |
| **I-765**<br>Optional<br>*See page M-33* | Application for Employment Authorization | Used to obtain approval to work prior to applicant's green card approval. Must be submitted with filing fee of $70.00 (U.S.). |

## APPLICATION PROCESS AT A U.S. INS OFFICE *Continued*

### IN ADDITION, THE APPLICANT MUST SUBMIT THE FOLLOWING:

- IRS (Internal Revenue Service) Form 9003 to determine whether applicant owes taxes for previous periods of employment in the U.S. Applicants who have not worked in the U.S. should mark the form "Not Applicable."
- All documents previously submitted by the sponsor EXCEPT the sponsor's proof of permanent residency.
- Three photographs of applicant and each accompanying relative.
- Results of required medical exams for applicant and each accompanying relative.
- Filing fee of $130 (U.S.) for applicants 14 years of age or older, $100 (U.S.) if applicant is under 14.

Applicant must attend an interview with an INS official. The period of time for acceptance of the application will vary greatly. See your local INS office.

## Special circumstances

It should be noted that if the green card application is based on a marriage of less than two years, the green card is conditional for two years. To have this condition removed before the expiration of the green card, both beneficiary and spouse must apply to the INS using **Form I-751** *(See page M-73)*. If the marriage ended in divorce or if the permanent resident spouse refuses to join on the petition, the beneficiary of the conditional green card must prove that the original marriage was in good faith, that deportation would cause extreme hardship, or that the spouse was abusive. If the marriage ended because of death, the widow or widower must file Form I-751 before the expiration of the conditional period, but no more than two years after the death of the spouse.

A permanent resident spouse who obtained a green card through marriage of a previous spouse cannot petition for a new foreign spouse:

- Unless five years have passed since the petitioner obtained his permanent residence or
- Unless the previous marriage ended with the death of the previous spouse.

## Children and unmarried sons / daughters of lawful permanent residents

A permanent resident who claims to be the parent of a child under age 21 or an unmarried son or daughter over 21 must file a petition on Form I-130.

Regardless of residence, two elements are essential to the process:

- The petition, which is filed by the sponsor, and
- The application, which is filed by the foreign national. (Upon filing the application he is officially called "the applicant.")

## Stage one: the petition

The sponsor should submit the petition (Form I-130) to the INS at either a local office or a regional service center. The petition will be assigned a priority date, the date when the petition is received and filed by the INS. The official waiting period for the green card begins on this date. To file the petition, follow the chart below.

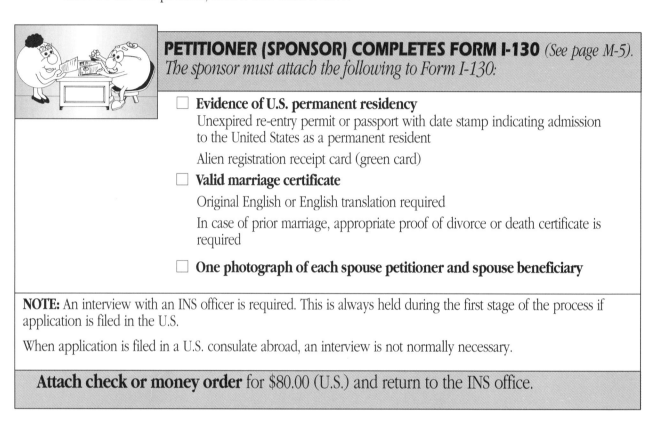

**PETITIONER (SPONSOR) COMPLETES FORM I-130** *(See page M-5).*
*The sponsor must attach the following to Form I-130:*

- ☐ **Evidence of U.S. permanent residency**

  Unexpired re-entry permit or passport with date stamp indicating admission to the United States as a permanent resident

  Alien registration receipt card (green card)

- ☐ **Valid marriage certificate**

  Original English or English translation required

  In case of prior marriage, appropriate proof of divorce or death certificate is required

- ☐ **One photograph of each spouse petitioner and spouse beneficiary**

**NOTE:** An interview with an INS officer is required. This is always held during the first stage of the process if application is filed in the U.S.

When application is filed in a U.S. consulate abroad, an interview is not normally necessary.

**Attach check or money order** for $80.00 (U.S.) and return to the INS office.

## Stage two: the application process

Once the sponsor receives approval of the petition, the beneficiary should begin the application process for an immigration visa (green card).

**APPLICATION PROCESS AT A U.S. CONSULATE** *The applicant must submit the notice of petition approval together with the following forms and documents to a U.S. consulate:*

| Form # | Description | Use |
|---|---|---|
| **OF-230-I** *See page M-10* | Biographical Information | Used to perform a security check on the applicant. |
| **OF-169** *See page M-12* | Certification of Documents | Certifies that applicant possesses all documents needed to complete the application and to attend the immigration interview with a consulate officer. |
| **OF230-II** *See page M-18* | Application for Immigration Visa | *This form must be submitted only at the time of the immigration interview.* It should not be mailed or filed with other forms. |
| **I-134 or OF-167** *See page M-22 or M-91* | Proof of Financial Support | Certifies that the applicant will not become a public charge. |

**IN ADDITION, THE APPLICANT MUST SUBMIT THE FOLLOWING:**

- **All documents previously submitted by the sponsor EXCEPT the sponsor's proof of permanent residency.**
- **Applicant's valid passport from country of origin.**
- **Police clearance certificate.**
- **Military records of applicant.**
- **Three photographs of applicant.**
- **Results of applicants required medical exam.**
- **Filing fee of $100.00 (U.S.).**

**Applicant must attend an interview with a consulate officer. The period of time for acceptance of the petitioner's application varies greatly. See your local consulate for more information.**

**APPLICATION PROCESS AT A U.S. INS OFFICE** *The applicant must submit the notice of petition approval together with the following forms and documents to the INS local office nearest to his place of residence:*

| Form # | Description | Use |
|---|---|---|
| **I-485** *See page M-25* | Application for Permanent Residence and Adjustment of Status | Used to adjust status to that of permanent resident. |
| **I-485 Supplement-A** *See page M-87* | Application for Permanent Residence and Adjustment of Status | Determines whether applicant is legally residing in the United States. If he is not, he is required to pay an additional fee of $650 (U.S.) for applicants over the age of 17 (certain exceptions may apply). |

*Process Continues on Next Page* ▶

## APPLICATION PROCESS AT A U.S. INS OFFICE, *Continued from page A-19.*

| Form # | Description | Use |
|--------|-------------|-----|
| **G-325-A** <br>*See page M-31* | Biographical Data Form | Used to compile personal background information. |
| **I-134 or OF-167** <br>*See pages M-22 or M-91* | Proof of Financial Support | Certifies that the applicant will not become a public charge. |
| **FD258** | Fingerprint Card | For the purpose of identification. |
| **I-94** <br>*See page M-32* | Departure Record | Records of foreign national's entrances and departures to and from the U.S. |
| **I-765** <br>Optional <br>*See page M-33* | Application for Employment Authorization | Used to obtain approval to work prior to applicant's green card approval. Must be submitted with filing fee of $70.00 (U.S.). |

### IN ADDITION, THE APPLICANT MUST SUBMIT THE FOLLOWING:

- IRS (Internal Revenue Service) Form 9003 to determine whether applicant owes taxes for previous periods of employment in the U.S. Applicants who have not worked in the U.S. should mark the form "Not Applicable."
- All documents previously submitted by the sponsor EXCEPT the sponsor's proof of permanent residency.
- Three photographs of applicant.
- Results of all required medical exams.
- Filing fee of $130 (U.S.) for applicants 14 years of age or older, $100 (U.S.) if applicant is under 14.

**Applicant must attend an interview with an INS official. The period of time for acceptance of the application will vary greatly. See your local INS office.**

Finally, it is important to note that the petition for an unmarried son or daughter will end if the beneficiary marries before the issuance of the immigrant visa. Also, if the beneficiary obtains permanent residence and subsequently marries or has a child, the new spouse or child is not given permanent status and must apply separately under this second preference category.

## THIRD PREFERENCE: MARRIED SONS AND DAUGHTERS OF U.S. CITIZENS

A U.S. citizen can sponsor a married son or daughter over the age of 21. (A permanent resident, as previously explained, can sponsor only an unmarried son or daughter over 21 years old.)

Regardless of residence, two elements are essential to the process:

- The petition, which is filed by the sponsor, and
- The application, which is filed by the foreign national. (Upon filing the application is officially called "the applicant".)

## Stage one: the petition

The sponsor should submit the petition (Form I-130) to the INS at either a local office or a regional service center. The petition will be assigned a priority date, the date when the petition is received and filed by the INS. The official waiting period for the green card begins on this date. To file the petition, follow the chart below.

**PETITIONER (SPONSOR) COMPLETES FORM I-130** *(See page M-5)*.
*The sponsor must attach the following to Form I-130:*

☐ **Evidence of U.S. Citizenship**

Birth certificate

Certificate of citizenship

Naturalization certificate

U.S. consular record of birth abroad

Valid U.S. passport

☐ **Long form birth certificate of the unmarried son or daughter**

**IN ADDITION, IF YOU ARE THE FOLLOWING SPONSOR YOU MUST SUBMIT:**

| Father | Father of Non-marital Child | Stepparent | Adoptive Parent (non-orphan*) |
|---|---|---|---|
| The beneficiary's parents' marriage certificate | **Evidence of paternity:** Birth certificate with father's name on it<br><br>OR<br><br>**Evidence of legitimization:** Affidavit showing father acknowledges paternity<br><br>Affidavit from someone who knows sponsor and beneficiary<br><br>Income statement showing son or daughter resides in the same house as the sponsor | Proof that parent and the stepparent were married before the 18th birthday of the stepchild | Proof that adoption took place before child's 16th birthday<br><br><br>* A special procedure must be followed if the child falls into the category of orphan. |

**Attach check or money order** for $80.00 (U.S.) and return to the INS office.

## Stage two: the application process

Once the sponsor receives approval of the petition, the beneficiary should begin the application process for an immigration visa (green card).

**APPLICATION PROCESS AT A U.S. CONSULATE** *The applicant must submit the notice of petition approval together with the following forms and documents to a U.S. consulate:*

| Form # | Description | Use |
|--------|-------------|-----|
| **OF-230-I**<br>*See page M-10* | Biographical Information | Used to perform a security check on the applicant. |
| **OF-169**<br>*See page M-12* | Certification of Documents | Certifies that applicant possesses all documents needed to complete the application and to attend the immigration interview with a consulate officer. |
| **OF-230-II**<br>*See page M-18* | Application for Immigration Visa | *This form must be submitted only at the time of the immigration interview.* It should not be mailed or filed with other forms. |
| **I-134 or OF-167**<br>*See page M-22 or M-91* | Proof of Financial Support | Certifies that the applicant will not become a public charge. |

### IN ADDITION, THE APPLICANT MUST SUBMIT THE FOLLOWING:

- **All documents previously submitted by the sponsor EXCEPT the sponsor's proof of citizenship.**
- **Applicant and accompanying relatives' valid passport from country of origin.**
- **Police clearance certificate for applicant and each accompanying relative.**
- **Military records of applicant and each accompanying relative if applicable.**
- **Three photographs of applicant and each accompanying relative.**
- **Results of required medical exam for applicant and each accompanying relative.**
- **Filing fee of $100.00 (U.S.).**

**Applicant must attend an interview with a consulate officer. The period of time for acceptance of the petitioner's application varies greatly. See your local consulate for more information.**

**APPLICATION PROCESS AT A U.S. INS OFFICE** *The applicant must submit the notice of petition approval together with the following forms and documents to the INS local office nearest to his place of residence:*

| Form # | Description | Use |
|--------|-------------|-----|
| **I-485**<br>*See page M-25* | Application for Permanent Residence and Adjustment of Status | Used to adjust status to that of permanent resident. |
| **I-485 Supplement-A**<br>*See page M-87* | Application for Permanent Residence and Adjustment of Status | Determines whether applicant is legally residing in the United States. If he is not, he is required to pay an additional fee of $650 (U.S.) for applicants over the age of 17 (certain exceptions may apply). |
| **G-325-A**<br>*See page M-31* | Biographical Data Form | Used to compile personal background information. |

## APPLICATION PROCESS AT A U.S. INS OFFICE, *Continued*

| Form # | Description | Use |
|---|---|---|
| **I-134 or OF-167** *See page M-22 or M-91* | Proof of Financial Support | Certifies that the applicant will not become a public charge. |
| **F-258** | Fingerprint Card | For the purpose of identification. |
| **I-94** *See page M-32* | Departure Record | Records of foreign national's entrances and departures to and from the U.S. |
| **I-765** Optional *See page M-33* | Application for Employment Authorization | Used to obtain approval to work prior to applicant's green card approval. Must be submitted with filing fee of $70.00 (U.S.). |

### IN ADDITION, THE APPLICANT MUST SUBMIT THE FOLLOWING:

- **IRS (Internal Revenue Service) Form 9003 to determine whether applicant owes taxes for previous periods of employment in the U.S. Applicants who have not worked in the U.S. should mark the form "Not Applicable."**
- **All documents previously submitted by the sponsor EXCEPT the sponsor's proof of citizenship.**
- **Three photographs of applicant and each accompanying relative.**
- **Results of required medical exams for applicant and each accompanying relative.**
- **Filing fee of $130 (U.S.) for applicants 14 years of age or older, $100 (U.S.) if applicant is under 14.**

**Applicant must attend an interview with an INS official. The period of time for acceptance of the application will vary greatly. See your local INS office.**

# FOURTH PREFERENCE: BROTHERS AND SISTERS OF U.S. CITIZENS

The petitioner, a U.S. citizen, sister or brother, must be at least 21 years old. Half-brothers and half-sisters can petition since the only requirement is that the petitioner and beneficiary have at least one common parent. The marital status of the brother or sister is irrelevant, therefore, if the spouse or child (under 21 years old) of the brother or sister cannot otherwise obtain an immigrant visa, the spouse or child is admitted in this preference category with the same priority as the beneficiary brother or sister. Again, to obtain this "derivative status", the spouse or child must be "accompanying" or "following to join" the beneficiary brother or sister.

Regardless of residence, two elements are essential to the process:

- The petition, which is filed by the sponsor, and
- The application, which is filed by the foreign national. (Upon filing the application is officially called "the applicant".)

## *Stage one: the petition*

The sponsor should submit the petition (Form I-130) to the INS at either a local office or a regional service center. The petition will be assigned a priority date, the date when the petition is received and filed by the INS. The official waiting period for the green card begins on this date. To file the petition, follow the chart below.

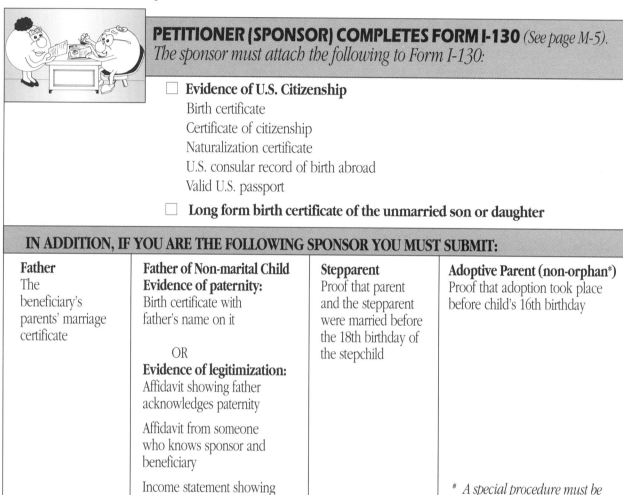

**PETITIONER (SPONSOR) COMPLETES FORM I-130** *(See page M-5).*
*The sponsor must attach the following to Form I-130:*

☐ **Evidence of U.S. Citizenship**
Birth certificate
Certificate of citizenship
Naturalization certificate
U.S. consular record of birth abroad
Valid U.S. passport

☐ **Long form birth certificate of the unmarried son or daughter**

### IN ADDITION, IF YOU ARE THE FOLLOWING SPONSOR YOU MUST SUBMIT:

| Father | Father of Non-marital Child | Stepparent | Adoptive Parent (non-orphan*) |
|---|---|---|---|
| The beneficiary's parents' marriage certificate | **Evidence of paternity:** Birth certificate with father's name on it<br><br>OR<br><br>**Evidence of legitimization:** Affidavit showing father acknowledges paternity<br><br>Affidavit from someone who knows sponsor and beneficiary<br><br>Income statement showing son or daughter resides in the same house as the sponsor | Proof that parent and the stepparent were married before the 18th birthday of the stepchild | Proof that adoption took place before child's 16th birthday<br><br><br><br>* *A special procedure must be followed if the child falls into the category of orphan.* |

**Attach check or money order** for $80.00 (U.S.) and return to the INS office.

## *Stage two: the application process*

Once the sponsor receives approval of the petition, the beneficiary should begin the application process for an immigration visa (green card).

**APPLICATION PROCESS AT A U.S. CONSULATE** *The applicant must submit the notice of petition approval together with the following forms and documents to a U.S. consulate:*

| Form # | Description | Use |
|---|---|---|
| **OF-230-I** *See page M-10* | Biographical Information | Used to perform a security check on the applicant. |
| **OF-169** *See page M-12* | Certification of Documents | Certifies that applicant possesses all documents needed to complete the application and to attend the immigration interview with a consulate officer. |
| **OF-230-II** *See page M-18* | Application for Immigration Visa | *This form must be submitted only at the time of the immigration interview.* It should not be mailed or filed with other forms. |
| **I-134 or OF-167** *See page M-22 or M-91* | Proof of Financial Support | Certifies that the applicant will not become a public charge. |

**IN ADDITION, THE APPLICANT MUST SUBMIT THE FOLLOWING:**

- All documents previously submitted by the sponsor EXCEPT the sponsor's proof of citizenship.
- Applicant's and accompanying relatives' valid passport from country of origin.
- Police clearance certificate for applicant and each accompanying relative.
- Military records of applicant and each accompanying relative if applicable.
- Three photographs of applicant and each accompanying relative.
- Results of required medical exam for applicant and each accompanying relative.
- Filing fee of $100.00 (U.S.).

Applicant must attend an interview with a consulate officer. The period of time for acceptance of the petitioner's application varies greatly. See your local consulate for more information.

## APPLICATION PROCESS AT A U.S. INS OFFICE *The applicant must submit the notice of petition approval together with the following forms and documents to the INS local office nearest to his place of residence:*

| Form # | Description | Use |
|---|---|---|
| **I-485**<br>*See page M-25* | Application for Permanent Residence and Adjustment of Status | Used to adjust status to that of permanent resident. |
| **I-485 Supplement-A**<br>*See page M-87* | Application for Permanent Residence and Adjustment of Status | Determines whether applicant is legally residing in the United States. If he is not, he is required to pay an additional fee of $650 (U.S.) for applicants over the age of 17 (certain exceptions may apply). |
| **G-325-A**<br>*See page M-31* | Biographical Data Form | Used to compile personal background information. |
| **I-134 or OF-167**<br>*See page M-22 or M-91* | Proof of Financial Support | Certifies that the applicant will not become a public charge. |
| **F-258** | Fingerprint Card | For the purpose of identification. |
| **I-94**<br>*See page M-32* | Departure Record | Records of foreign national's entrances and departures to and from the U.S. |
| **I-765**<br>Optional<br>*See page M-33* | Application for Employment Authorization | Used to obtain approval to work prior to applicant's green card approval. Must be submitted with filing fee of $70.00 (U.S.). |

### IN ADDITION, THE APPLICANT MUST SUBMIT THE FOLLOWING:

- **IRS (Internal Revenue Service) Form 9003 to determine whether applicant owes taxes for previous periods of employment in the U.S. Applicants who have not worked in the U.S. should mark the form "Not Applicable."**

- **All documents previously submitted by the sponsor EXCEPT the sponsor's proof of citizenship.**

- **Three photographs of applicant and each accompanying relative.**

- **Results of required medical exam for applicant and each accompanying relative.**

- **Filing fee of $130 (U.S.) for applicants 14 years of age or older, $100 (U.S.) if applicant is under 14.**

**Applicant must attend an interview with an INS official. The period of time for acceptance of the application will vary greatly. See your local INS office.**

# CHAPTER 3:

# EMPLOYMENT-RELATED VISAS

Since the passage of the Immigration Act of 1990, great emphasis has been placed on the procedure of immigrating through employment. Close attention is paid to the educational background and skills of prospective foreign employees intending to immigrate. There is an annual quota of 140,000 immigrant visas for all five preference levels, each of which is allocated a specific percentage. The preferences are:

- Priority workers
- Members of the professions holding advanced degrees or persons of exceptional ability
- Skilled workers, professional workers, and unskilled workers
- Special immigrants (some of these types are not employment related)
- Employment creation visas.

The employer often acts as the petitioner for the foreign national. If you intend to apply for an employment-related visa, choose the preference that best suits your circumstances and refer directly to that part of this chapter. On the next page there is an overview of the process, but the details are in each chapter section. All forms needed for the process are listed with their corresponding pages in section M of the appendix.

## FIRST PREFERENCE: PRIORITY WORKERS

28.6 percent of employment-related visas, plus any visas not issued from the fourth and fifth preferences are allocated annually.

Included in this category are:

- Persons of extraordinary ability in the sciences, arts, education, business, or athletics
- Outstanding professors and researchers
- Executives and managers of multinational corporations.

**Unlike workers obtaining visas under the second and third preferences, priority workers are not required to have a job offer or to go through the selective and difficult labor certification process.** This is also true when it is deemed in the national interest to qualify a person as having exceptional abilities under the employment-related second preference. There are two stages in the immigration process for priority workers: the petition and the application.

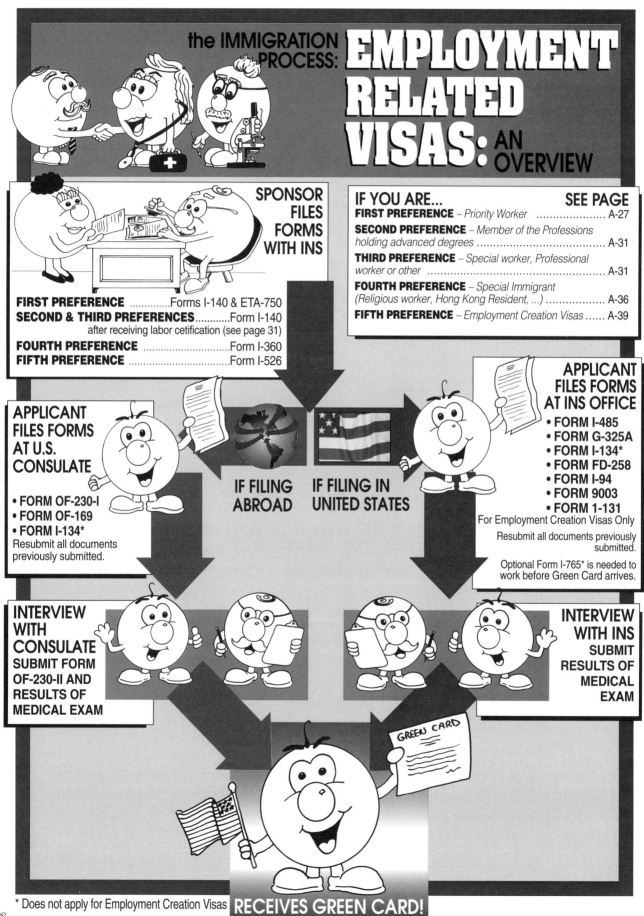

the IMMIGRATION PROCESS: **EMPLOYMENT RELATED VISAS:** AN OVERVIEW

**SPONSOR FILES FORMS WITH INS**

**FIRST PREFERENCE** .............Forms I-140 & ETA-750
**SECOND & THIRD PREFERENCES**...........Form I-140
after receiving labor cetification (see page 31)
**FOURTH PREFERENCE** .............................Form I-360
**FIFTH PREFERENCE** ...................................Form I-526

**IF YOU ARE...**       **SEE PAGE**
**FIRST PREFERENCE** – Priority Worker ....................A-27
**SECOND PREFERENCE** – Member of the Professions
holding advanced degrees .......................................A-31
**THIRD PREFERENCE** – Special worker, Professional
worker or other ......................................................A-31
**FOURTH PREFERENCE** – Special Immigrant
(Religious worker, Hong Kong Resident, ...) .................A-36
**FIFTH PREFERENCE** – Employment Creation Visas ......A-39

**APPLICANT FILES FORMS AT INS OFFICE**
• **FORM I-485**
• **FORM G-325A**
• **FORM I-134***
• **FORM FD-258**
• **FORM I-94**
• **FORM 9003**
• **FORM 1-131**
For Employment Creation Visas Only

Resubmit all documents previously submitted.

Optional Form I-765* is needed to work before Green Card arrives.

**APPLICANT FILES FORMS AT U.S. CONSULATE**
• **FORM OF-230-I**
• **FORM OF-169**
• **FORM I-134***
Resubmit all documents previously submitted.

**IF FILING ABROAD**

**IF FILING IN UNITED STATES**

**INTERVIEW WITH CONSULATE** **SUBMIT FORM OF-230-II AND RESULTS OF MEDICAL EXAM**

**INTERVIEW WITH INS** **SUBMIT RESULTS OF MEDICAL EXAM**

GREEN CARD

* Does not apply for Employment Creation Visas **RECEIVES GREEN CARD!**

## Stage one: the petition

The petitioner (U.S. employer) should submit the petition (**Form I-140,** *page M-77*) to the Immigration and Naturalization Service (INS) regional service center having jurisdiction in his area. He must also submit **Form ETA-750,** (a Labor Certification Application, *page M-94*). Although the petitioner does not follow the labor certification procedures, the paperwork is still required.

If the priority worker is a person of extraordinary ability, an outstanding professor or researcher, an executive or manager of a multinational corporation, the following should be submitted as relevant:

- Documents showing national or international awards or prizes recognizing the person's extraordinary ability, research, and contributions

- Publications or other materials which include contributions by the person with extraordinary ability or samples of professor's or researcher's scholarly work

- Documentation proving that the person has been an executive or manager of a multinational corporation for one of the past three years.

It should be noted that a specific job offer is not required for an applicant in this preferred group, provided that the applicant is in the United States to continue work in his chosen field. Thus, an applicant may file his own petition with the INS, rather than having an employer file, as described above. The cost for filing the petition is $75 (U.S.). If the employer files the petition, he must include the company's tax return from the previous year to prove his ability to pay a salary to the beneficiary.

## Stage two: the application

Once the petitioner receives petition approval, the beneficiary should begin the application process for an immigrant visa ("green card").

The application process depends on the foreign national's place of residence. If living in his country of origin or some other country, he must file at a U.S. consulate. If legally residing in the United States, he must file at the appropriate INS office.

In addition, recent changes in immigration law have made it possible for many illegal aliens, who would have otherwise been eligible for an immigration visa abroad, to adjust their status to that of lawful permanent resident. Applicants who would not otherwise qualify for adjustment status are required to pay an additional fee of $650 (U.S.). This provision is scheduled to expire on October 1, 1997. It is always recommended that the applicant seek professional legal advice when seeking to adjust their alien status.

**APPLICATION PROCESS AT A U.S. CONSULATE** *The applicant must submit the notice of petition approval together with the following forms and documents to a U.S. consulate:*

| Form # | Description | Use |
|---|---|---|
| **OF-230-I**<br>*See page M-10* | Biographical Information | Used to perform a security check on the applicant. |
| **OF-169**<br>*See page M-12* | Certification of Documents | Certifies that applicant possesses all documents needed to complete the application and to attend the immigration interview with a consulate officer. |
| **OF-230-II**<br>*See page M-18* | Application for Immigration Visa | *This form must be submitted only at the time of the Immigration Interview.* It should not be mailed or filed with other forms. |
| **I-134 or OF-167**<br>*See page M-22 or M-91* | Proof of Financial Support | Certifies that the applicant will not become a public charge. If the applicant has a job offer in the U.S., this form does not need to be filed. |

**IN ADDITION, THE APPLICANT MUST SUBMIT THE FOLLOWING:**

- **All documents previously submitted by the sponsor must be resubmitted at this time.**
- **Long form birth certificate of the applicant and each accompanying relative.**
- **Valid passports from country of origin for applicant and each accompanying relative.**
- **Police clearance certificates for applicant and each accompanying relative.**
- **Military records of applicant and each accompanying relative if applicable.**
- **Three photographs of applicant and each accompanying relative.**
- **Letter from petitioner certifying that job offer is still open.**
- **Results of required medical exam for applicant and each accompanying relative.**
- **Filing fee of $100.00 (U.S.) per applicant.**

**Applicant must attend an interview with a consulate officer. The period of time for acceptance of the petitioner's application varies greatly. See your local consulate for more information.**

**APPLICATION PROCESS AT A U.S. INS OFFICE** *The applicant must submit the notice of petition approval together with the following forms and documents to the INS local office nearest to his place of residence:*

| Form # | Description | Use |
|---|---|---|
| **I-485**<br>*See page M-25* | Application for Permanent Residence and Adjustment of Status | Used to adjust status to that of permanent resident. |
| **I-485**<br>**Supplement-A**<br>*See page M-87* | Application for Permanent Residence and Adjustment of Status | Determines whether applicant is legally residing in the United States. If he is not, he is required to pay an additional fee of $650 (U.S.) for applicants over the age of 17 (certain exceptions may apply). |

## APPLICATION PROCESS AT A U.S. INS OFFICE *Continued*

| Form # | Description | Use |
|---|---|---|
| **G-325-A** *See page M-31* | Biographical Data Form | Used to compile personal background information. |
| **I-134 or OF-167** *See pages M-22 or M-91* | Proof of Financial Support | Certifies that the applicant will not become a public charge. If the applicant has a job offer in the U.S., this form does not need to be filed. |
| **FD-258** | Fingerprint Card | For the purpose of identification. |
| **I-94** *See page M-32* | Departure Record | Records of foreign national's entrances and departures to and from the U.S. |
| **I-765** Optional *See page M-33* | Application for Employment Authorization | Used to obtain approval to work prior to applicant's green card approval. Must be submitted with filing fee of $70.00 (U.S.). |

### IN ADDITION, THE APPLICANT MUST SUBMIT THE FOLLOWING:

- **IRS (Internal Revenue Service) Form 9003 to determine whether applicant owes taxes for previous periods of employment in the U.S. Applicants who have not worked in the U.S. should mark the form "Not Applicable."**
- **Long form birth certificate of the applicant and each accompanying relative.**
- **Letter from petitioner certifying that job offer is still open.**
- **Three photographs of applicant and each accompanying relative.**
- **Results of required medical exams for applicant and each accompanying relative.**
- **Filing fee of $130.00 (U.S.) for applicants 14 years of age or older, $100.00 (U.S.) if applicant is under 14.**

**Applicant must attend an interview with an INS official. The period of time for acceptance of the application will vary greatly. See your local INS office.**

## SECOND AND THIRD PREFERENCES

The immigration process is essentially the same for these preferences. The only differences are that the second preference has priority handling over the third and that an employer must file Form I-140 to petition for it.

### Second preference: members of the professions holding advanced degrees or persons of exceptional ability

28.6 percent of employment-related visas, plus any visas from the first preference are allocated annually. Persons included in this category are:

- Professionals holding postgraduate degree

- Professionals holding a baccalaureate degree plus at least five years' experience in their field

- Individuals who have excelled in the sciences, arts, and business without reaching the level of "extraordinary ability" but who are considered more skilled than the average person.

### Third preference: skilled workers, professional, and other workers

28.6 percent of employment-related visas, plus any visas not issued from the first and second preferences, are allocated annually.

Persons included in this category are:

- Professionals holding a baccalaureate degree with less than five years work experience

- Skilled workers without baccalaureate degree

- Unskilled workers.

Individuals wishing visas under the second and third preferences must have a job offer, show proof of professional qualifications and expertise, and obtain labor certification.

## Stage one: labor certification

A foreign national wishing to immigrate through the second or third preference must first obtain a job offer. Once a job has been offered, the labor certification process can begin. The U.S. government uses the labor certification to:

- Determine that there is an insufficient number of American workers qualified for the job desired by the foreign national

- Ensure that the wage and working conditions proposed by the employer will be in line with prevailing standards of similarly employed U.S. workers

- Determine that the foreign national's educational and other qualifications meet the requirements for the preference level and the job being offered.

### The labor certification process is as follows:

1. Employer files Form **ETA-750,** Parts A and B *(see page M-94)* with the state employment agency. Priority date for application is established.

2. State employment agency reviews forms and documents.

3. Employer advertises job offer according to guidelines issued by the state department of labor.

4. State employment agency establishes that no American workers are available for the desired job and forwards labor certification materials to the U.S. Department of Labor regional office who reviews application and issues a notice of findings.

5. If certification is approved, sponsoring employer is notified.

## Stage two: the petition

Once the labor certification is approved, the petition process can begin:

1. Employer files **Form I-140** *(see page M-77)* with the INS service center having

jurisdiction over the place of employment.

2. Petitioner must attach the following to Form I-140:

- Labor certification notice of approval

- All documents previously submitted in stage one, including diplomas, transcript from colleges and universities, and other professional certificates

- Financial statements and tax returns of the petitioner's company for the past two years.

The cost for filing this petition is $75. Once the petition is approved and the priority date is "current" (valid, based on the previously assigned priority date), the application for an immigrant visa can begin.

## Stage three: the application

Once the petitioner receives petition approval, the beneficiary should begin the application process for an immigrant visa ("green card").

The application process depends on the foreign national's place of residence. If living in his country of origin or some other country, he must file at a U.S. consulate. If legally residing in the United States, he must file at the appropriate INS office.

In addition, recent changes in immigration law have made it possible for many illegal aliens, who would have otherwise been eligible for an immigration visa abroad, to adjust their status to that of lawful permanent resident. Applicants who would not otherwise qualify for adjustment status are required to pay an additional fee of $650 (U.S.). This provision is scheduled to expire on October 1, 1997. It is always recommended that the applicant seek professional legal advice when seeking to adjust their alien status.

**APPLICATION PROCESS AT A U.S. CONSULATE** *The applicant must submit the notice of petition approval together with the following forms and documents to a U.S. consulate:*

| Form # | Description | Use |
|---|---|---|
| **OF-230-I**<br>*See page M-10* | Biographical Information | Used to perform a security check on the applicant. |
| **OF-169**<br>*See page M-12* | Certification of Documents | Certifies that applicant possesses all documents needed to complete the application and to attend the immigration interview with a consulate officer. |
| **OF-230-II**<br>*See page M-18* | Application for Immigration Visa | *This form must be submitted only at the time of the immigration interview.* It should not be mailed or filed with other forms. |
| **I-134 or OF-167**<br>*See pages M-22 or M-91* | Proof of Financial Support | Certifies that the applicant will not become a public charge. If the applicant has a job offer in the U.S., this form does not need to be filed. |

**IN ADDITION, THE APPLICANT MUST SUBMIT THE FOLLOWING:**

- **All documents previously submitted must be resubmitted at this time.**
- **Long form birth certificate of the applicant and each accompanying relative.**
- **Valid passports from country of origin for applicant each accompanying relative.**
- **Police clearance certificates of applicant and each accompanying relative.**
- **Military records of applicant and each accompanying relative if applicable.**
- **Three photographs of applicant and each accompanying relative.**
- **Letter from petitioner certifying that job offer is still open.**
- **Results of required medical exam for applicant and each accompanying relative.**
- **Filing fee of $100.00 (U.S.) per applicant.**

**Applicant must attend an interview with a consulate officer. The period of time for acceptance of the petitioner's application varies greatly. See your local consulate for more information.**

## APPLICATION PROCESS AT A U.S. INS OFFICE
*The applicant must submit the notice of petition approval together with the following forms and documents to the INS local office nearest to his place of residence:*

| Form # | Description | Use |
|---|---|---|
| **I-485**<br>*See page M-25* | Application for Permanent Residence and Adjustment of Status | Used to adjust status to that of permanent resident. |
| **I-485**<br>**Supplement-A**<br>*See page M-87* | Application for Permanent Residence and Adjustment of Status | Determines whether applicant is legally residing in the United States. If he is not, he is required to pay an additional fee of $650 (U.S.) for applicants over the age of 17 (certain exceptions may apply). |
| **G-325-A**<br>*See page M-31* | Biographical Data Form | Used to compile personal background information. |
| **I-134 or OF-167**<br>*See pages M-22 or M-91* | Proof of Financial Support | Certifies that the applicant will not become a public charge. If the applicant has a job offer in the U.S., this form does not need to be filed. |
| **FD-258** | Fingerprint Card | For the purpose of identification. |
| **I-94**<br>*See page M-32* | Departure Record | Records of foreign national's entrances and departures to and from the U.S. |
| **I-765**<br>Optional<br>*See page M-70* | Application for Employment Authorization | Used to obtain approval to work prior to applicant's green card approval. Must be submitted with filing fee of $70.00 (U.S.). |

### IN ADDITION, THE APPLICANT MUST SUBMIT THE FOLLOWING:

- IRS (Internal Revenue Service) Form 9003 to determine whether applicant owes taxes for previous periods of employment in the U.S. Applicants who have not worked in the U.S. should mark the form "Not Applicable."
- Long form birth certificate of the applicant and of each accompanying relative.
- Letter from petitioner certifying that job offer still exists.
- Three photographs of applicant and each accompanying relative.
- Results of required medical exams for applicant and each accompanying relative.
- Filing fee of $130.00 (U.S.) for applicants 14 years of age or older, $100.00 (U.S.) if applicant is under 14.

Applicant must attend an interview with an INS official. The period of time for acceptance of the application will vary greatly. See your local INS office.

# FOURTH PREFERENCE: SPECIAL IMMIGRANTS

This category includes:

- Religious workers from recognized religious organizations

- Foreign employees of the U.S. government

- Employees of Panama Canal Zone

- Retired employees of the U.S. Consulate in Hong Kong who have worked no less than three years

- Foreign nationals declared dependent in U.S. juvenile courts. *(Not employment-related, these are nevertheless classified in this category)*

- Foreign medical graduates who have practiced medicine in the U.S. since January 9, 1978.

Applying for a special immigrant visa involves two parts: the petition and the application.

## *Stage one: the petition*

**File petition Form I-360** *(see page M-62)* **with qualifying documents,** which depend on the special immigrant category. Mail the petition to INS regional service center in the U.S. with jurisdiction over the beneficiary's place of work or residence.

Examples of these qualifying documents include:

### Religious Workers
- Letter from the U.S. religious organization explaining the operations of the organization in the U.S. and abroad

- Documents proving the beneficiary's religious qualifications

- Verification of work within the same religious organization abroad in the past two years

- Letter from the U.S. religious organization describing the job offer and salary to be paid.

### Foreign Employees of the U.S.
- Recommendation letter from the U.S. Secretary of State

- Written verification of U.S. government employment for at least 15 years

- Recommendation letter from officer in charge of office where employee worked.

### Former Employees of the Panama Canal Zone
- Proof of employment with the Canal Zone government or Panama Canal Company on or before October 1, 1979

- Evidence that the beneficiary was a resident of the Canal Zone or Panama national on April 1, 1979.

### Retired Employees of International Organizations
- Evidence of G-4 or N-visa

- Written evidence from the international organization of period of employment

- Income tax returns for the past 15 years.

### Foreign Medical Graduates
- I-94 card showing admission to the United States prior to January 9, 1978, under a J or H nonimmigrant visa classification

- Copy of U.S. medical license obtained before January 9, 1978

- Evidence of continuous residence in the United States since entry.

### Foreign national declared dependent on a juvenile court
- Copy of the decree declaring the child dependent on the court

- Letter from the court stating that the juvenile has been deemed eligible by the court for long-term foster care

- Letter from the court stating that it would be in the foreign national juvenile's best interest to be returned to his country of nationality or last national residence.


## *Stage two: the application*

Once the petitioner receives petition approval, the beneficiary should begin the application process for an immigrant visa ("green card").

The application process depends on the foreign national's place of residence. If living in his country of origin or some other country, he must file at a U.S. consulate. If legally residing in the United States, he must file at the appropriate INS office.

In addition, recent changes in immigration law have made it possible for many illegal aliens, who would have otherwise been eligible for an immigration visa abroad, to adjust their status to that of lawful permanent resident. Applicants who would not otherwise qualify for adjustment status are required to pay an additional fee of $650 (U.S.). This provision is scheduled to expire on October 1, 1997. It is always recommended that the applicant seek professional legal advice when seeking to adjust their alien status.

## APPLICATION PROCESS AT A U.S. CONSULATE *The applicant must submit the notice of petition approval together with the following forms and documents to a U.S. consulate:*

| Form # | Description | Use |
|---|---|---|
| **OF-230-I** <br> *See page M-10* | Biographical Information | Used to perform a security check on the applicant. |
| **OF-169** <br> *See page M-12* | Certification of Documents | Certifies that applicant possesses all documents needed to complete the application and to attend the immigration interview with a consulate officer. |
| **OF-230-II** <br> *See page M-18* | Application for Immigration Visa | *This form must be submitted only at the time of the Immigration Interview.* It should not be mailed or filed with other forms. |
| **I-134 or OF-167** <br> *See pages M-22 or M-91* | Proof of Financial Support | Certifies that the applicant will not become a public charge. If the applicant has a job offer in the U.S., this form does not need to be filed. |

### IN ADDITION, THE APPLICANT MUST SUBMIT THE FOLLOWING:

- **All documents previously submitted by the sponsor must be resubmitted at this time.**
- **Long form birth certificate of the applicant and each accompanying relative.**
- **Valid passports from country of origin for applicant and each accompanying relative.**
- **Police clearance certificates for applicant and each accompanying relative.**
- **Military records of applicant and each accompanying relative if applicable.**
- **Three photographs of applicant and each accompanying relative.**
- **Letter from petitioner certifying that job offer is still open.**
- **Results of required medical exam for applicant and each accompanying relative.**
- **Filing fee of $100.00 (U.S.) per applicant.**

**Applicant must attend an interview with a consulate officer. The period of time for acceptance of the petitioner's application varies greatly. See your local consulate for more information.**

## APPLICATION PROCESS AT A U.S. INS OFFICE
*The applicant must submit the notice of petition approval together with the following forms and documents to the INS local office nearest to his place of residence:*

| Form # | Description | Use |
|---|---|---|
| **I-485** *See page M-25* | Application for Permanent Residence and Adjustment of Status | Used to adjust status to that of permanent resident. |
| **I-485 Supplement-A** *See page M-87* | Application for Permanent Residence and Adjustment of Status | Determines whether applicant is legally residing in the United States. If he is not, he is required to pay an additional fee of $650 (U.S.) for applicants over the age of 17 (certain exceptions may apply). |
| **G-325-A** *See page M-31* | Biographical Data Form | Used to compile personal background information. |
| **I-134 or OF-167** *See pages M-22 or M-91* | Proof of Financial Support | Certifies that the applicant will not become a public charge. If the applicant has a job offer in the U.S., this form does not need to be filed. |
| **FD-258** | Fingerprint Card | For the purpose of identification. |
| **I-94** *See page M-32* | Departure Record | Records of foreign national's entrances and departures to and from the U.S. |
| **I-765** Optional *See page M-33* | Application for Employment Authorization | Used to obtain approval to work prior to applicant's green card approval. Must be submitted with filing fee of $70.00 (U.S.). |

### IN ADDITION, THE APPLICANT MUST SUBMIT THE FOLLOWING:

- IRS (Internal Revenue Service) Form 9003 to determine whether applicant owes taxes for previous periods of employment in the U.S. Applicants who have not worked in the U.S. should mark the form "Not Applicable."
- Long form birth certificate of the applicant and of each accompanying relative.
- Letter from petitioner certifying that job offer is still open.
- Three photographs of applicant and each accompanying relative.
- Results of required medical exams for applicant and each accompanying relative.
- Filing fee of $130.00 (U.S.) for applicants 14 years of age or older, $100 (U.S.) if applicant is under 14.

Applicant must attend an interview with an INS official. The period of time for acceptance of the application will vary greatly. See your local INS office.

## FIFTH PREFERENCE: EMPLOYMENT CREATION VISAS

These visas are issued to those who, for the purpose of benefiting the U.S. economy, will invest at least $1 million in a new enterprise and employ no fewer than ten full-time American workers. Should the business be located in a rural area or an urban area deemed by the government to have an unemployment rate of 150 percent greater than the national average, the investment requirement could be reduced to $500,000. The quota set for this category is 7.1 percent of the employment-related visas.

Immigrating through monetary investment involves two stages: the petition and the application.

## Stage one: the petition

**Petitioner submits to the INS regional service center Form I-526** (Immigrant Petition by Alien Entrepreneur, *see page M-68*), which must be accompanied by documents evidencing the business investment in the U.S., (proof of having invested at least $1,000,000 or $500,000, whichever is the case). Examples of these documents include:

- Comprehensive business plans with cash flow projections
- Contracts and bills of sale
- Bank transfer memos showing amount of money sent to the U.S.
- Letters of credit
- Articles of incorporation or copies of stock certificates showing ownership
- Business licenses or any other documentation showing the investment is real.

A filing fee of $155 (U.S.) is required.

## Stage two: the application

The application process depends on the foreign national's place of residence. If living in his country of origin or some other country, he must file at a U.S. consulate. If legally residing in the United States, he must file at the appropriate INS office.

In addition, recent changes in immigration law have made it possible for many illegal aliens, who would have otherwise been eligible for an immigration visa abroad, to adjust their status to that of lawful permanent resident. Applicants who would not otherwise qualify for adjustment status are required to pay an additional fee of $650 (U.S.). This provision is scheduled to expire on October 1, 1997. It is always recommended that the applicant seek professional legal advice when seeking to adjust their alien status.

The application forms (sent to the investor by the Transitional Immigrant Visa Processing Center) will include:

- **Form OF-230-I** (Biographical Information, *see page M-10*).
- **Form OF-169** (Affirmation that investor is in possession of documents necessary to complete the application, *see page M-12*).
- **Form OF-230-II** (Application for Immigrant Visa, *see page M-18*).

Again, the investor must resubmit to the U.S. consulate all documents submitted during Stage One of the process. In addition to the notice of approval of petition, long-form birth certificate and birth certificate of each accompanying relative are required. Also, police clearance, military records, three photographs, and valid passports are needed for the applicant and all accompanying relatives.

After a medical exam (to determine if the applicant is medically excludable) and the interview process, which involves verification of all information furnished by the applicant, the investor passport will be stamped allowing the entrance to U.S. with an immigrant visa. The green card will be mailed months after the investor and accompanying relatives have entered the U.S.

If the application is submitted in the U.S. at the local INS office, the application basic form is **INS Form I-485** (Application for Permanent Residence – Adjustment of Status, *see page M-25*), **Form I-485 Supplement A** (verifying applicant is legally residing in the U.S., *see page M-87*), and **Form G-325-A** (biographical data, *see page M-31*). A separate application must be filed for each accompanying relative. Once the application is filed, if the applicant leaves the U.S. before approval, it is viewed as a termination of that application for a green card. If the investor has to leave due to an emergency an advance parole should be requested, and **Form I-131** completed *(see page M-58)*. In a different situation, when the investor wants to work before the application for a green card is approved, he must file **Form I-765** separately *(see page M-33)*. Both of these forms must be filed at the same local INS office where Form I-485 was filed.

When step two of this process is filed in the U.S., the documents to submit are:

• Notice of action showing petition approval

• Long-form birth certificate of applicant's and any accompanying relatives

• Proof of marital status of applicant and spouse, if any (marriage certificate, divorce decree)

• I-94 card

• Fingerprints of applicant and accompanying relatives

• Results of required medical examination of applicant and accompanying relatives.

If the application is approved, the applicant is issued a conditional green card for two years. The investor must file a petition for removal of that condition. The INS investigates whether the investment was made. If so, the condition is removed.

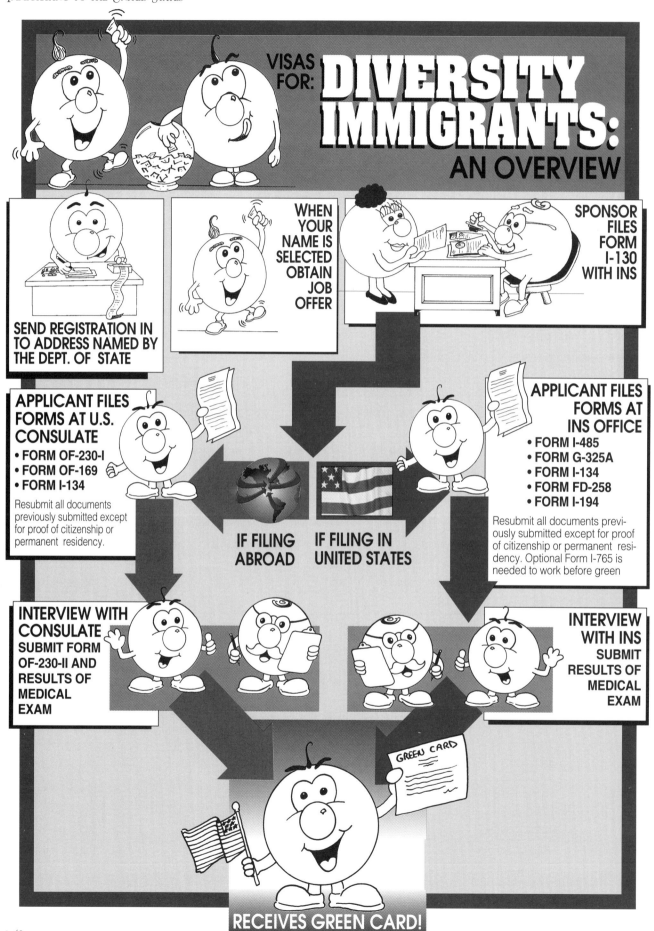

VISAS FOR: **DIVERSITY IMMIGRANTS: AN OVERVIEW**

WHEN YOUR NAME IS SELECTED OBTAIN JOB OFFER

SPONSOR FILES FORM I-130 WITH INS

SEND REGISTRATION IN TO ADDRESS NAMED BY THE DEPT. OF STATE

**APPLICANT FILES FORMS AT U.S. CONSULATE**
• FORM OF-230-I
• FORM OF-169
• FORM I-134

Resubmit all documents previously submitted except for proof of citizenship or permanent residency.

**APPLICANT FILES FORMS AT INS OFFICE**
• FORM I-485
• FORM G-325A
• FORM I-134
• FORM FD-258
• FORM I-194

Resubmit all documents previously submitted except for proof of citizenship or permanent residency. Optional Form I-765 is needed to work before green

IF FILING ABROAD    IF FILING IN UNITED STATES

**INTERVIEW WITH CONSULATE** SUBMIT FORM OF-230-II AND RESULTS OF MEDICAL EXAM

**INTERVIEW WITH INS** SUBMIT RESULTS OF MEDICAL EXAM

GREEN CARD

**RECEIVES GREEN CARD!**

# CHAPTER 4

# DIVERSITY IMMIGRANTS

The Diversity Program, popularly known as "The Lottery", was introduced with the Immigration and Nationality Act of 1990, making visas available to people from countries with disproportionately low emigration to the United States. The program allows selective applicants, with spouse, and children under age 21 to immigrate to the United States. Applicants may apply for this program only once a year. They are chosen randomly by computer and are notified of their selection.

## THE PERMANENT DIVERSITY PROGRAM

As of October 1994, the Permanent Diversity Program allocates 55,000 visas yearly to qualified applicants. To participate, applicants must prove that their country of origin had fewer than 50,000 emigrants to the U.S. during the previous five years. Applicants must either have a high school education or its equivalent or have worked for at least two years in an occupation requiring two years of training or experience.

| Countries Eligible for Participation in the Diversity Program | | | |
|---|---|---|---|
| Albania | Estonia | Indonesia | Netherlands |
| Algeria | Finland | Ireland | New Caledonia |
| Argentina | France | Italy | Northern Ireland |
| Austria | Germany | Japan | Norway |
| Belgium | Gibraltar | Latvia | Poland |
| Bermuda | Great Britain | Liechtenstein | San Marino |
| Canada | Guadeloupe | Lithuania | Sweden |
| Czechoslovakia | Hungary | Luxembourg | Switzerland |
| Denmark | Iceland | Monaco | Tunisia |

There are two stages to immigration through both programs: registration and application.

## *Stage One: Registration*

1. Only one registration per year is accepted. Mail it to the address specified by the Department of State (DOS). This address changes from year to year. Contact the DOS at (202) 663-1600 for information.

2. The registration form must be typed or legibly handwritten in the Roman alphabet on a plain sheet of paper and must include the following information:
   - Full name, date and place of birth
   - Current mailing address
   - Last city and country of residence.
   - Name of the U.S. consulate where the case, if selected, is to be processed
   - Name, dates, and places of birth of spouse and children under 21 years of age expecting to immigrate.

3. No registration fee is required.
   The registration must be mailed in an envelope between 6 and 10 inches long (15.24 and 25.4 cm.) by between 3 1/2 and 4 1/2 inches wide (8.89 and 11.43 cm.). The upper left hand corner of the envelope must state the applicant's country of origin and current address. The address of the appropriate INS office depends on the applicant's country of origin as follows:

**Region 1 (Africa)**
D-V 1 Program
National Visa Center
Portsmouth, NH 11213
U.S.A.

**Region 2 (Asia)**
DV-1 Program
National Visa Center
Portsmouth, NH 11210
U.S.A.

**Region 3 (Europe)**
D-V 1 Program
National Visa Center
Portsmouth, NH 11212
U.S.A.

**Region 4 (North America other than Mexico)**
D-V 1 Program
National Visa Center
Portsmouth, NH 11215
U.S.A.

**Region 5 (Oceania)**
D-V 1 Program
National Visa Center
Portsmouth, NH 11214
U.S.A.

**Region 6 (South America including Mexico, Central America and the Caribbean**
D-V 1 Program
National Visa Center
Portsmouth, NH 11211
U.S.A.

**Envelopes which fail to conform to these specifications will be rejected and disqualified.**

## *Stage two: application*

Because the INS ultimately grants fewer visas than the number of applicants chosen in the lottery, it is imperative that applicants begin the application process as quickly as possible after notification of selection.

The application process depends on the foreign national's place of residence. If living in his country of origin or some other country, he must file at a U.S. consulate. If legally residing in the United States, he must file at the appropriate INS office.

In addition, recent changes in immigration law have made it possible for many illegal aliens, who would have otherwise been eligible for an immigration visa abroad, to adjust their status to that of lawful permanent resident. Applicants who would not otherwise qualify for adjustment status are required to pay an additional fee of $650 (U.S). This provision is scheduled to expire on October 1, 1997. It is always recommended that the applicant seek professional legal advice when seeking to adjust their alien status.

**APPLICATION PROCESS AT A U.S. CONSULATE** *The selected applicant must submit the notice of registration approval together with the following forms and documents at a U.S. consulate:*

| Form # | Description | Use |
| --- | --- | --- |
| **OF-230-I** *See page M-10* | Biographical Information | Used to perform a security check on the applicant. |
| **OF-169** *See page M-12* | Certification of Documents | Certifies that the applicant possesses all documents needed to complete the application and to attend the immigration interview with a Consulate officer. |
| **OF-230-II** *See page M-18* | Application for Immigration Visa | This form must be submitted only at the time of the immigration interview. It should not be mailed or filed with other forms. |
| **I-134 or OF-167** *See pages M-22 or M-91* | Proof of Financial Support | Certifies that the applicant will not become a public charge. If the applicant has a job offer in the U.S., this form does not need to be filed. |

**IN ADDITION, THE APPLICANT MUST SUBMIT THE FOLLOWING:**

- **High school diploma or its equivalent or proof that applicant has worked in an occupation requiring at least two years of training or experience.**
- **Long form birth certificate of the applicant and of each accompanying relative.**
- **Marriage records, if applicable.**
- **Valid passports of applicant and each accompanying relative from country of origin.**
- **Police clearance certificates of applicant and each accompanying relative.**
- **Three photographs of applicant and each accompanying relative.**
- **Military records of applicant and each accompanying relative if applicable.**
- **Results of all required medical exams for applicant and each accompanying relative.**
- **Filing fee of $100.00 (U.S.) per applicant is required.**

**Applicant must attend an interview with a consulate officer. The period of time for acceptance of the petitioner's application varies greatly. See your local consulate for more information.**

## APPLICATION PROCESS AT A U.S. INS OFFICE  *The selected applicant must submit the notice of registration approval together with the following forms and documents to the INS local office nearest to his place of residence:*

| Form # | Description | Use |
|---|---|---|
| **OF-230-I** *See page M-10* | Biographical Information | Used to perform a security check on the applicant. Send this form with a money order for $25.00 to the appropriate U.S. consulate. Make a notation on this form that you are adjusting status in the U.S. Obtain receipt of money order from consulate. |
| **I-485** *See page M-25* | Application for Permanent Residence and Adjustment of Status | Used to adjust status to that of a permanent resident. |
| **I-485 Supplement-A** *See page M-87* | Application for Permanent Residence and Adjustment of Status | Determines whether applicant is legally residing in the United States. If he is not, he is required to pay an additional fee of $650 (U.S.) for applicants over the age of 17 (certain exceptions may apply). |
| **G-325-A** *See page M-31* | Biographical Data Form | Used to compile personal background information. |
| **I-134 or OF-167** *See pages M-22 or M-91* | Proof of Financial Support | Certifies that the applicant will not become a public charge. If the applicant has a job offer in the U.S., this form does not need to be filed. |
| **FD258** | Fingerprint Card | For the purpose of identification. |
| **I-94** *See page M-32* | Departure Record | Records of entrances and departure to and from the U.S. |
| **I-765** Optional *See page M-33* | Application for Employment Authorization | If applicant wishes to work before his green card has been approved, he must submit this form along with a filing fee of $70.00 (U.S.). |

### IN ADDITION, THE APPLICANT MUST SUBMIT THE FOLLOWING:

- IRS (Internal Revenue Service) Form 9003 to determine whether the applicant owes taxes for previous periods of employment in the U.S. Applicants who have not worked in the U.S. should mark the form "Not Applicable."
- High school diploma or its equivalent or proof that the applicant worked in an occupation that requires at least two years of training or experience.
- Birth certificates of applicant and each accompanying relative.
- Valid passports of applicant and each accompanying relative from country of origin.
- Three photographs of applicant and each accompanying relative.
- Results of required medical exams for applicant and each accompanying relative.
- Filing fee of $130.00 (U.S.) per applicant over age 14, $100.00 (U.S.) for applicants under the age of 14.

**Applicant must attend an interview with an INS official. The period of time for acceptance of the application will vary greatly. See your local INS office.**

# CHAPTER 5

# IMMIGRANT VISAS FOR HONG KONG RESIDENTS

Special consideration is given to inhabitants of Hong Kong in expectation of its return to Chinese rule in 1997. The United States treats Hong Kong as an independent country rather than a dependent colony where immigration is concerned.

There is a special immigrant category for employees of the U.S. Consulate in Hong Kong. (See chapter *Employment-Related Visas.*)

The U.S. has established three other provisions allowing Hong Kong residents immigration.

1. Since September 30, 1993, Hong Kong has been entitled to the allotment given to all independent countries – seven percent of the worldwide quota, or approximately 25,000 green cards annually. Prospective Hong Kong immigrants are subject to the same requirements and must follow the same procedures as any other green card applicant.

2. A limited number of green cards will be issued to qualified employees (executives, managers, officers, supervisors, and other individuals with special qualifications) working in Hong Kong for American companies. Again, prospective immigrants are subject to the same requirements and procedures as any other applicants in the category of employment related visas. (See chapter *Employment-Related Visas.*) Applicants qualifying under this provision fall under the first preference; hence, labor certification is not required. However, a letter from the employer must be included. This letter must show that:

   • The American company employer has no fewer than 100 people working in the U.S. and no fewer than 50 individuals employed abroad

   • The company has a gross annual income of no less than $50 million

   • The Hong Kong employee has a job offer in the U.S. from the same company in a similar position valid until the employee immigrates.

3. The last provision lengthens the period of validity of immigrant visas issued to Hong Kong residents after November 29, 1990, and before September 1, 2001. (The usual time period of immigrant visa validity is 120 days.) Hong Kong residents in need of an extension to September 1, 2002, may request one at the U.S. consulate.

# VISAS NOT SUBJECT TO NUMERICAL LIMITATIONS (QUOTAS)

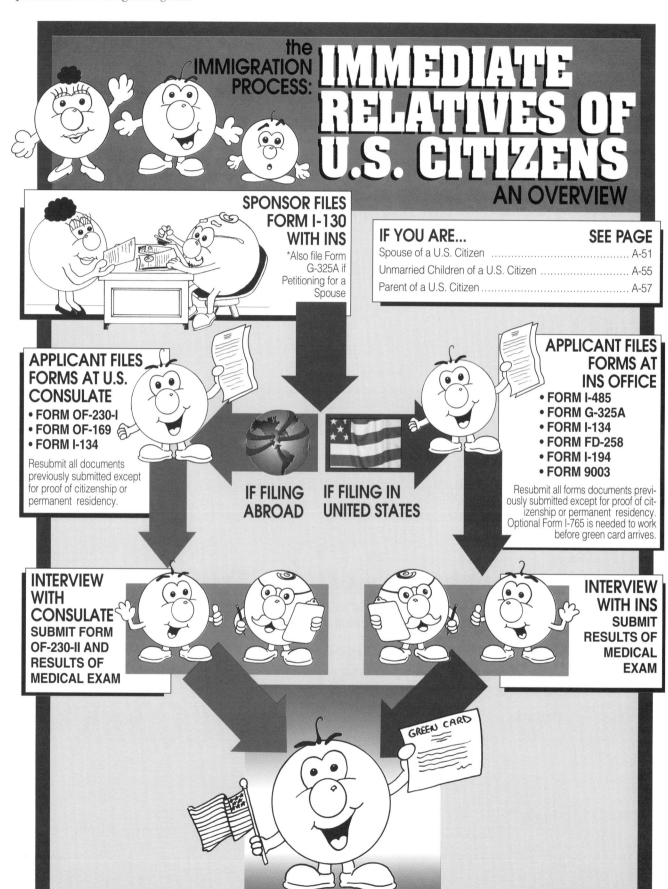

the IMMIGRATION PROCESS: **IMMEDIATE RELATIVES OF U.S. CITIZENS**

AN OVERVIEW

**SPONSOR FILES FORM I-130 WITH INS**

*Also file Form G-325A if Petitioning for a Spouse

| IF YOU ARE... | SEE PAGE |
|---|---|
| Spouse of a U.S. Citizen | A-51 |
| Unmarried Children of a U.S. Citizen | A-55 |
| Parent of a U.S. Citizen | A-57 |

**APPLICANT FILES FORMS AT U.S. CONSULATE**
• FORM OF-230-I
• FORM OF-169
• FORM I-134

Resubmit all documents previously submitted except for proof of citizenship or permanent residency.

**APPLICANT FILES FORMS AT INS OFFICE**
• FORM I-485
• FORM G-325A
• FORM I-134
• FORM FD-258
• FORM I-194
• FORM 9003

Resubmit all forms documents previously submitted except for proof of citizenship or permanent residency. Optional Form I-765 is needed to work before green card arrives.

**IF FILING ABROAD**

**IF FILING IN UNITED STATES**

**INTERVIEW WITH CONSULATE** SUBMIT FORM OF-230-II AND RESULTS OF MEDICAL EXAM

**INTERVIEW WITH INS** SUBMIT RESULTS OF MEDICAL EXAM

GREEN CARD

**RECEIVES GREEN CARD!**

# CHAPTER 6

# OBTAINING VISAS FOR IMMEDIATE RELATIVES OF U.S. CITIZENS

To be eligible to receive a visa not subject to quotas the beneficiary must be an immediate relative of a U.S. citizen, defined as:

- Spouse of a U.S. citizen

- Widow or widower of a deceased U.S. citizen when married to that citizen for at least two years and the citizen has died within two years of the petition filing.

- Unmarried children (under age 21) of a U.S. citizen.

- Parent of a U.S. citizen over age 21.

At left is an overview of the process, but the details to the process are in this chapter. Refer directly to the section in this chapter that pertains to your circumstance and follow those specific directions. All forms needed for the process are listed with their corresponding pages in section M of the appendix.

The application process depends on the foreign national's place of residence. If living in his country of origin or some other country, he must file at a U.S. consulate. If legally residing in the United States, he must file at the appropriate INS office.

In addition, recent changes in immigration law have made it possible for many illegal aliens, who would have otherwise been eligible for an immigration visa abroad, to adjust their status to that of lawful permanent resident. Applicants who would not otherwise qualify for adjustment status are required to pay an additional fee of $650. This provision is scheduled to expire on October 1, 1997. It is always recommended that the applicant seek professional legal advice when seeking to adjust their alien status.

## SPOUSE OF A U.S. CITIZEN

Special restrictions have been imposed on those who attempt to immigrate through the marriage of a U.S. citizen. The Immigration Marriage Fraud Amendment of 1986 and the Immigration Act of 1990 make it a criminal offense to file a visa petition based on a sham or fraudulent marriage. A sham marriage is defined as one entered into by an American citizen and a foreign national with the purpose of circumventing immigration laws.

As a result of that legislation, foreign nationals immigrating through a marriage in existence less than two years first acquire a **conditional permanent resident** status before any unconditional permanent status is given.

Regardless of residence, two elements are essential to the process:

- the petition, which is filed by the sponsor, and
- the application, which is filed by the foreign national. (Upon filing the application he is officially called "the applicant.")

## Stage one: the petition process

The sponsor (U.S. citizen) should follow this petition process:

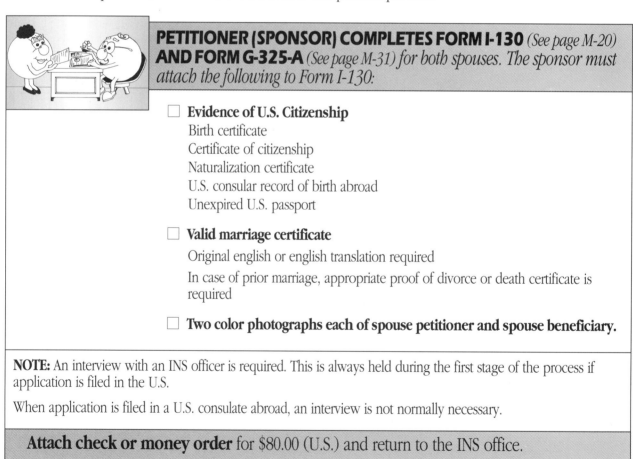

**PETITIONER (SPONSOR) COMPLETES FORM I-130** *(See page M-20)* **AND FORM G-325-A** *(See page M-31) for both spouses. The sponsor must attach the following to Form I-130:*

☐ **Evidence of U.S. Citizenship**
Birth certificate
Certificate of citizenship
Naturalization certificate
U.S. consular record of birth abroad
Unexpired U.S. passport

☐ **Valid marriage certificate**
Original english or english translation required
In case of prior marriage, appropriate proof of divorce or death certificate is required

☐ **Two color photographs each of spouse petitioner and spouse beneficiary.**

**NOTE:** An interview with an INS officer is required. This is always held during the first stage of the process if application is filed in the U.S.

When application is filed in a U.S. consulate abroad, an interview is not normally necessary.

**Attach check or money order** for $80.00 (U.S.) and return to the INS office.

## Stage two: the application process

Application will be filed by the beneficiary of the approved petition, (the foreign national spouse), in either a U.S. consulate of the foreign national or in the U.S. at an INS office.

**APPLICATION PROCESS AT A U.S. CONSULATE** *The applicant must submit the notice of petition approval together with the following forms and documents to a U.S. consulate:*

| Form # | Description | Use |
|---|---|---|
| **OF-230-I**<br>*See page M-10* | Biographical Information | Used to perform a security check on the applicant. |
| **OF-169**<br>*See page M-12* | Certification of Documents | Certifies that applicant possesses all documents needed to complete the application and to attend the immigration interview with a consulate officer. |
| **OF-230-II**<br>*See page M-18* | Application for Immigration Visa | *This form must be submitted only at the time of the Immigration Interview.* It should not be mailed or filed with other forms. |
| **I-134 or OF-167**<br>*See pages M-22 or M-91* | Proof of Financial Support | Certifies that the applicant will not become a public charge. |

### IN ADDITION, THE APPLICANT MUST SUBMIT THE FOLLOWING:

- **All documents previously submitted by the sponsor EXCEPT the sponsor's proof of citizenship.**
- **Long form birth certificate of the applicant.**
- **Valid passport from applicant's country of origin.**
- **Police clearance certificate.**
- **Military records of applicant if any.**
- **Three photographs of applicant.**
- **Results of required medical exam for applicant.**
- **A filing fee of $100 (U.S.) is required.**

**Applicant must attend an interview with a consulate officer. The period of time for acceptance of the petitioner's application varies greatly. See your local consulate for more information.**

 **APPLICATION PROCESS AT A U.S. INS OFFICE** *The applicant must submit the notice of petition approval together with the following forms and documents to the INS local office nearest to his place of residence:*

| Form # | Description | Use |
|---|---|---|
| **I-485**<br>*See page M-25* | Application for Permanent Residence and Adjustment of Status | Used to adjust status to that of permanent resident. |
| **I-485**<br>**Supplement-A**<br>*See page M-87* | Application for Permanent Residence and Adjustment of Status | Determines whether applicant is legally residing in the United States. If he is not, he is required to pay an additional fee of $650 (U.S.) for applicants over the age of 17 (certain exceptions may apply). |

*Process Continues on Next Page* ▶

## APPLICATION PROCESS AT A U.S. INS OFFICE *Continued from page A-53.*

| Form # | Description | Use |
|---|---|---|
| **G-325-A** <br> *See page M-31* | Biographical Data Form | Used to compile personal background information. |
| **I-134 or OF-167** <br> *See pages M-22 or M-91* | Proof of Financial Support | Certifies that the applicant will not become a public charge. |
| **FD-258** | Fingerprint Card | For identification purposes. |
| **I-94** <br> *See page M-32* | Departure Record | Records of foreign national's entrances and departures to and from the U.S. |
| **I-765** <br> Optional <br> *See page M-33* | Application for Employment Authorization | Used to obtain approval to work prior to applicant's green card approval. Must be submitted with filing fee of $70.00 (U.S.). |

### IN ADDITION, THE APPLICANT MUST SUBMIT THE FOLLOWING:

- **IRS (Internal Revenue Service) Form 9003 to determine whether applicant owes taxes for previous periods of employment in the U.S. Applicants who have not worked in the U.S. should mark the form "Not Applicable."**
- **All documents previously submitted by the sponsor EXCEPT the sponsor's proof of citizenship.**
- **Long form birth certificate of the applicant.**
- **Three photographs of the applicant.**
- **Results of required medical exam for applicant.**
- **Filing fee of $130 (U.S.) for applicant.**

**Applicant must attend an interview with an INS official. The period of time for acceptance of the application will vary greatly. See your local INS office.**

## Special circumstances

It should be noted that if the green card application is based on a marriage of less than two years, the green card is conditional for two years. To have this condition removed before the expiration of the green card, its beneficiary and spouse must apply to the INS together using **Form I-751** *(see page M-73)*. If the marriage ended in divorce or because the U.S. citizen spouse refuses to join on the petition, the beneficiary of the conditional green card must prove that the original marriage was in good faith, or that deportation would cause extreme hardship, or that the spouse was abusive. If the marriage ended in death, the widow or widower must file Form I-751 before the expiration of the conditional period, but no more than two years after the death of the spouse.

A permanent resident spouse who obtained a green card through marriage of a previous spouse cannot petition for a new foreign spouse

- Unless five years have passed since the petitioner obtained his or her permanent residence or
- Unless the previous marriage ended with the death of the previous spouse.

# UNMARRIED CHILDREN (UNDER AGE 21) OF A U.S. CITIZEN

To immigrate through this category, a child must be unmarried and under 21 years old. The child may be legitimate, a non-marital, a stepchild, or an adopted child. Children under age 21 are assumed to be dependent upon their parents. U.S. Immigration laws treat them in the same manner as spouses. From a legal standpoint, it is necessary to distinguish among types of children: legitimate, non-marital, stepchild, adopted child.

Regardless of residence, two elements are essential to the process:

• The petition, which is filed by the sponsor, and

• The application, which is filed by the foreign national. (Upon filing the application he is officially called "the applicant.")

## Stage one: the petition process

The sponsor (U.S. citizen) should follow this petition process:

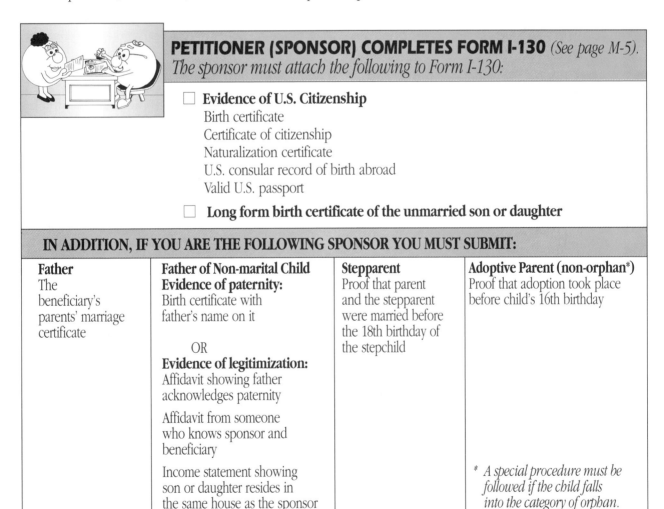

**PETITIONER (SPONSOR) COMPLETES FORM I-130** (*See page M-5*). *The sponsor must attach the following to Form I-130:*

☐ **Evidence of U.S. Citizenship**
Birth certificate
Certificate of citizenship
Naturalization certificate
U.S. consular record of birth abroad
Valid U.S. passport

☐ **Long form birth certificate of the unmarried son or daughter**

### IN ADDITION, IF YOU ARE THE FOLLOWING SPONSOR YOU MUST SUBMIT:

| **Father** | **Father of Non-marital Child** | **Stepparent** | **Adoptive Parent (non-orphan\*)** |
|---|---|---|---|
| The beneficiary's parents' marriage certificate | **Evidence of paternity:** Birth certificate with father's name on it<br><br>OR<br>**Evidence of legitimization:** Affidavit showing father acknowledges paternity<br><br>Affidavit from someone who knows sponsor and beneficiary<br><br>Income statement showing son or daughter resides in the same house as the sponsor | Proof that parent and the stepparent were married before the 18th birthday of the stepchild | Proof that adoption took place before child's 16th birthday<br><br><br><br>\* *A special procedure must be followed if the child falls into the category of orphan.* |

**Attach check or money order** for $80.00 (U.S.) and return to the INS office.

## Stage two: the application process

If the sponsor receives approval of the petition, the beneficiary of the petition should begin the application process for an Immigration Visa ("green card").

 **APPLICATION PROCESS AT A U.S. CONSULATE** *The applicant must submit the notice of petition approval together with the following forms and documents to a U.S. consulate:*

| Form # | Description | Use |
|---|---|---|
| **OF-230-I**<br>*See page M-10* | Biographical Information | Used to perform a security check on the applicant. |
| **OF-169**<br>*See page M-12* | Certification of Documents | Certifies that applicant possesses all documents needed to complete the application and to attend the immigration interview with a consulate officer. |
| **OF-230-II**<br>*See page M-18* | Application for Immigration Visa | *This form must be submitted only at the time of the Immigration Interview.* It should not be mailed or filed with other forms. |
| **I-134 or OF-167**<br>*See pages M-22 or M-91* | Proof of Financial Support | Certifies that the applicant will not become a public charge. |

**IN ADDITION, THE APPLICANT MUST SUBMIT THE FOLLOWING:**

- **All documents previously submitted by the sponsor EXCEPT the sponsor's proof of citizenship.**
- **Long form birth certificate of the applicant.**
- **Valid passport from applicant's country of origin.**
- **Police clearance certificate.**
- **Military records of applicant if any.**
- **Three photographs of applicant.**
- **Results of required medical exam for applicant.**
- **A filing fee of $100 (U.S.) is required.**

**Applicant must attend an interview with a consulate officer. The period of time for acceptance of the petitioner's application varies greatly. See your local consulate for more information.**

## APPLICATION PROCESS AT A U.S. INS OFFICE *The applicant must submit the notice of petition approval together with the following forms and documents to the INS local office nearest to his place of residence:*

| Form # | Description | Use |
|---|---|---|
| **I-485**<br>*See page M-25* | Application for Permanent Residence and Adjustment of Status | Used to adjust status to that of permanent resident. |
| **I-485 Supplement-A**<br>*See page M-87* | Application for Permanent Residence and Adjustment of Status | Determines whether applicant is legally residing in the United States. If he is not, he is required to pay an additional fee of $650 (U.S.) for applicants over the age of 17 (certain exceptions may apply). |
| **G-325-A**<br>*See page M-71* | Biographical Data Form | Used to compile personal background information. |
| **I-134 or OF-167**<br>*See pages M-22 or M-91* | Proof of Financial Support | Certifies that the applicant will not become a public charge. |
| **FD-258** | Fingerprint Card | For the purposes of identification. |
| **I-94**<br>*See page M-4* | Departure Record | Records of foreign national's entrances and departures to and from the U.S. |
| **I-765**<br>Optional<br>*See page M-61* | Application for Employment Authorization | Used to obtain approval to work prior to applicant's green card approval. Must be submitted with filing fee of $70.00 (U.S.). |

### IN ADDITION, THE APPLICANT MUST SUBMIT THE FOLLOWING:

- **IRS (Internal Revenue Service) Form 9003 to determine whether applicant owes taxes for previous periods of employment in the U.S. Applicants who have not worked in the U.S. should mark the form "Not Applicable."**
- **All documents previously submitted by the sponsor EXCEPT the sponsor's proof of citizenship.**
- **Three photographs of applicant.**
- **Results of required medical exams for applicant.**
- **A filing fee of $130 (U.S.) for applicants 14 years of age or older, $100 (U.S.) if applicant is under 14.**

**Applicant must attend an interview with an INS official. The period of time for acceptance of the application will vary greatly. See your local INS office.**

# PARENT OF A U.S. CITIZEN

Only a U.S. citizen son or daughter who is over 21 years old may petition for his or her parent(s). Separate petitions must be filed for each parent.

Regardless of residence, two elements are essential to the process:
- The petition, which is filed by the sponsor, and

- The application, which is filed by the foreign national. (Upon filing the application is officially called "the applicant".)

## *Stage one: the petition process*

The sponsor (U.S. citizen) should follow this petition process.

**PETITIONER (SPONSOR) COMPLETES FORM I-130** *with the Immigration and Naturalization Service in the United States (See page M-5). The sponsor must attach the following to Form I-130:*

☐ **Evidence of U.S. Citizenship**
Birth certificate by U.S. government
Certificate of citizenship
Naturalization certificate
U.S. consular record of birth abroad
Unexpired U.S. passport

☐ **Long Form Birth Certificate of the Son or Daughter.**

**IN ADDITION, PETITIONERS FOR THE FOLLOWING BENEFICIARIES MUST SUBMIT:**

| **Father** | **Non-marital Parent, Stepparent or Adoptive Parent** |
|---|---|
| Sponsor must submit a copy of the marriage certificate to the sponsor's mother | Sponsor must introduce evidence by documents or by other proof of the validity of the claimed relationship with beneficiary. |

**Attach check or money order** for $80.00 (U.S.) and return to the INS office.

## *Stage two: the application process*

Once the sponsor receives approval of the petition, the beneficiary should begin the application process for an immigration visa (green card).

**APPLICATION PROCESS AT A U.S. CONSULATE** *The applicant must submit the notice of petition approval together with the following forms and documents to a U.S. consulate:*

| Form # | Description | Use |
|---|---|---|
| **OF-230-I**<br>*See page M-10* | Biographical Information | Used to perform a security check on the applicant. |
| **OF-169**<br>*See page M-12* | Certification of Documents | Certifies that applicant possesses all documents needed to complete the application and to attend the immigration interview with a consulate officer. |
| **OF-230-II**<br>*See page M-18* | Application for Immigration Visa | *This form must be submitted only at the time of the Immigration Interview.* Forms should not be mailed or filed with other forms. |
| **I-134 or OF-167**<br>*See pages M-22 or M-91* | Proof of Financial Support | Certifies that the applicant will not become a public charge. |

## APPLICATION PROCESS AT A U.S. CONSULATE *Continued*

### IN ADDITION, THE APPLICANT MUST SUBMIT THE FOLLOWING:

- All documents previously submitted by the sponsor EXCEPT the sponsor's proof of citizenship.
- Long form birth certificate of the applicant.
- Valid passport from applicant's country of origin.
- Police clearance certificate.
- Military records of applicant if any.
- Three photographs of applicant.
- Results of required medical exam for applicant.
- A filing fee of $100 (U.S.) is required.

Applicant must attend an interview with a consulate officer. The period of time for acceptance of the petitioner's application varies greatly. See your local consulate for more information.

## APPLICATION PROCESS AT A U.S. INS OFFICE *The applicant must submit the notice of petition approval together with the following forms and documents to the INS local office nearest to his place of residence:*

| Form # | Description | Use |
|---|---|---|
| **I-485**<br>*See page M-25* | Application for Permanent Residence and Adjustment of Status | Used to adjust status to that of permanent resident. |
| **I-485**<br>**Supplement-A**<br>*See page M-87* | Application for Permanent Residence and Adjustment of Status | Determines whether applicant is legally residing in the United States. If he is not, he is required to pay an additional fee of $650 (U.S.) for applicants over the age of 17 (certain exceptions may apply). |
| **G-325-A**<br>*See page M-31* | Biographical Data Form | Used to compile personal background information. |
| **I-134 or OF-167**<br>*See pages M-22 or M-91* | Proof of Financial Support | Certifies that the applicant will not become a public charge. |
| **FD-258** | Fingerprint Card | For the purpose of identification. |
| **I-94**<br>*See page M-32* | Departure Record | Records of foreign national's entrances and departures to and from the U.S. |
| **I-765**<br>Optional<br>*See page M-33* | Application for Employment Authorization | Used to obtain approval to work prior to applicant's green card approval. Must be submitted with filing fee of $70.00 (U.S.). |

*Process Continues on Next Page* ▶

## APPLICATION PROCESS AT A U.S. INS OFFICE *Continued from page A-59.*

**IN ADDITION, THE APPLICANT MUST SUBMIT THE FOLLOWING:**

- IRS (Internal Revenue Service) Form 9003 to determine whether applicant owes taxes for previous periods of employment in the U.S. Applicants who have not worked in the U.S. should mark the form "Not Applicable."
- All documents previously submitted by the sponsor EXCEPT the sponsor's proof of citizenship.
- Three photographs of applicant.
- Results of required medical exams for applicant.
- Filing fee of $130 (U.S.) for applicants 14 years of age or older, $100 (U.S.) if applicant is under 14.

Applicant must attend an interview with an INS official. The period of time for acceptance of the application will vary greatly. See your local INS office.

# CHAPTER 7

# NONIMMIGRANT VISAS

Nonimmigrant visas are temporary each serving a particular purpose and offer different privileges. They are issued by the U.S. government through its embassies and consulates abroad and are divided into eighteen categories (A through R).

## A VISAS – DIPLOMATS

- **A-1 visas** are issued to ambassadors, public ministers, career diplomats, consular officers, and members of their immediate families.

- **A-2 visas** are given to other officials and foreign government employees and their immediate families.

- **A-3 visas** are given to the personal employees, attendants, and servants of individuals holding A-1 and A-2 visas.

U.S. working privileges are given to holders of A-1 or A-2 visas.

A-1, A-2 and A-3 visas are valid as long as the holder remains officially recognized by the U.S. Secretary of State, but no longer than three years plus any authorized extension.

## B VISAS – BUSINESS AND PLEASURE

- **B-1 visas** are issued to business visitors.

- **B-2 visas** are issued to tourists.

- **B-1/B-2 visas** are multi-purpose and are issued for both business and tourism.

B visas are normally valid for at least one year and may carry no expiration date. However, each visit must not last longer than six months. Six-month extensions are available. Visitors for business or pleasure may enter the U.S. any number of times.

Holders of B visas are prohibited from accepting employment while in the U.S. Visitors here on business cannot be paid by any source located in the United States. Visitors here for pleasure must not engage in any business activities.

While visitor visas are issued at all U.S. embassies and consulates, it is advisable to apply in the home country.

The application process is as follows:

File **Form OF-156** *(see page M-36)* at any embassy or consulate chosen to submit the application. Attach the following:

- Documents evidencing the intention of the visitor to return to his home country

- Documents proving that the visitor has sufficient financial support during the visit to the United States. Bank statements, financial statements, or **INS Form I-134** (Affidavits of Support from a U.S. relative – *see page M-22*) can be adequate proof.

## C VISAS – FOREIGN NATIONALS IN TRANSIT

- **C-1 visas** are issued to foreign nationals who travel repeatedly through the U.S. (Travel includes maximum layovers of eight hours and a two transfer limit.)

- **C-2 visas** are issued to foreign nationals permitted transit to the United Nations.

- **C-3 visas** are issued to foreign government officials in transit.

These visas are valid for a maximum of 29 days without possibility of renewal or adjustment of nonimmigrant status. Holders of C visas are prohibited to work in the United States.

## D VISAS – CREW MEMBERS

These visas are issued to foreign nationals working on board international vessels and aircraft.

- **D-1 visas** are issued to workers needed to remain on board.

- **D-2 visas** are issued to employees dismissed from one ship to work on another.

These visas are valid for a maximum of 29 days without possibility of renewal or adjustment of nonimmigrant status. Holders of D visas are prohibited to work in the United States.

## E VISAS – TREATY TRADERS, TREATY INVESTORS, THEIR SPOUSES AND CHILDREN

These nonimmigrant visas are issued to nationals of countries that have trade or investor treaties with the United States. It is possible to be eligible for an E visa if a foreign country extends the same benefit to U.S. nationals even if no treaty exists. Canada and Australia are examples.

- **E-1 visas** are issued to treaty traders, their spouses and children.

- **E-2 visas** are issued to treaty investors, their spouses and children.

To obtain either of these visas an application must be filed at a U.S. embassy or consulate using **Form OF-156.** Foreign nationals legally present in the U.S. may file **Form I-129** with an **E supplement** at the appropriate INS office. *(See pages M-36, M-46, and M-48 for samples of forms.)*

The basic documents to be included for the E-1 visa must evidence:

- That the foreign national is a citizen of a country with a trade treaty with the U.S.

- That the applicant is coming to the U.S. to work in a company which he either owns or which is at least 50 percent owned by citizens of his home country, and in which he is a key employee

- That more than 50 percent of the company's total trade occurs between the U.S. and the applicant's home country, and

- That the applicant intends to return to his country once his business in the U.S. is completed.

The basic documents to be included for the E-2 visa must show:

- Proof that the foreign national is citizen of a country with an investor treaty with the U.S.

- That the applicant is coming to the U.S. to work in a company which he either owns or which is no less than 50 percent owned by citizens of his home country and in which he is a key employee

- That the company has made a substantial cash investment in a U.S. business actively engaged in trade or services, and

- That the applicant intends to return to his country once his business in the U.S. is completed.

E-1 and E-2 visas are valid for a maximum of one year with possibility of renewal for an indefinite period of time, as long as the holder of the visa continues the activity for which it was issued.

In addition, holders of E-1 or E-2 visas are permitted to work in the U.S. only for the purpose for which it was issued; however, their spouses and children are not permitted to be employed.

# F VISAS – ACADEMIC STUDENTS, THEIR SPOUSES AND CHILDREN

- **F-1 visas** are issued to students who enter the U.S. to study at academic high schools, colleges, universities, language schools, conservatories, or seminaries.

- **F-2 visas** are issued to the spouses and unmarried children under age 21 of such students.

F visas are valid for the duration of studies, plus sixty days within which student and family must leave the U.S.

To apply for a F-1 visa, the student must have been previously accepted by the institution in which he wishes to study. The academic institution must complete **Form I-20 A-B** (Certificate of Eligibility for Nonimmigrant Student Status – *see page M-37*) and send it to the student.

**IF THE STUDENT IS ABROAD** *he fills out the following forms at a U.S. consulate in his home country:*

| Form # | Description | Use |
|---|---|---|
| **OF-156**<br>*See page M-36* | Biographical Information | Used to perform a security check on the applicant. |
| **I-20 A-B**<br>*See page M-37* | Certificate of Eligibility for Nonimmigrant (F-1) Student Status | Certifies that the applicant possesses all documents needed to complete the application. |
| **I-134**<br>*See page M-22* | Affidavit of Financial Support | Certifies that someone will assume financial responsibility for the applicant. |

**IN ADDITION, THE APPLICANT MUST HAVE THE SPONSORING INSTITUTION SUBMIT THE FOLLOWING:**

- Documents showing proof of the student's intent to return to his country after completion of studies in the U.S. These documents may include, but are not limited to:
    - Proof that a job is waiting once the student returns to his country.
    - Proof of ownership of real estate.
    - Proof of ownership of other property.

**IF THE STUDENT IS IN THE U.S.** *he must file the following forms:*

| Form # | Description | Use |
|---|---|---|
| **I-539**<br>*See page M-40* | Application to Extend/Change Nonimmigrant Status | Used to perform a security check of the applicant. |
| **I-20 A-B**<br>*See page M-37* | Certificate of Eligibility for Nonimmigrant (F-1) Student Status | Certifies that the applicant possesses all documents needed to complete the application. |
| **I-134**<br>*See page M-22* | Affidavit of Financial Support | Certifies that someone will assume financial responsibility for the applicant. |

**IN ADDITION, THE APPLICANT MUST HAVE THE SPONSORING INSTITUTION SUBMIT THE FOLLOWING:**

- Documents showing proof of the student's intent to return to his country after completion of studies in the U.S. These documents may include, but are not limited to:
    - Proof that a job is waiting once the student returns to his country.
    - Proof of ownership of real estate.
    - Proof of ownership of other property.

An F-1 visa holder wishing to work while pursuing studies may do so only in the case of economic necessity or required student practical training.

If during the course of studies his economic circumstances change unexpectedly the student will be allowed to work only if:

- the student has kept F-1 status for no less than one year, and

- he does not work more than 20 hours per week while studying on a full-time basis.

**The student must file Work Permission Based on Economic Need Form I-538 Parts A and B, together with Form I-765.** These forms and documents supporting the basis of economic necessity must be submitted to the local INS office with jurisdiction over the area in which the school is located. *(See page M-33 for form I-765).*

When employment authorization is required for practical training to fulfill an academic requirement prior to graduation (curricular practical training) or after graduation (post-completion practical training) the F-1 student must show proof of enrollment on a full-time basis for no less than nine consecutive months.

The application must include Form I-538, endorsed by the designated school official authorizing the practical training, and Form I-765. If the application is for post-completion practical training, a letter from the prospective employer must be included.

In either case, the forms and documents supporting the application must be submitted to the local INS office with jurisdiction over the area in which the school is located.

F-2 visa applicants (the spouse or unmarried children under age 21 accompanying the F-1 student), must introduce a copy of the original I-20 A-B given to the student. F-2 visa holders are not authorized to work.

# G VISAS – INTERNATIONAL ORGANIZATION REPRESENTATIVES

- **G-1 visas** are issued to principal government representatives of international organizations, their staff, and their immediate families.

- **G-2 visas** are issued to other government representatives of international organizations and their immediate families.

- **G-3 visas** are issued to non-government representatives of international organizations and their immediate families.

- **G-4 visas** are issued to international organization officers or employees and their immediate families.

- **G-5 visas** are issued to the attendants, servants, or personal employees, and immediate families of holders of visas G-1 through G-4 .

Except for the immediate family of G-2 visa holders, family members of G visa holders are not allowed to work in the United States. G visas are valid for one year plus renewals.

# H VISAS – TEMPORARY WORKERS

This category includes only temporary visas available to qualified employees filling a temporary need of American employers.

**H-1A visas** are issued to temporary workers performing services as Registered Nurses. They must be licensed in the U.S. state where they intend to work, or certified by the Commission of Foreign Nursing Schools (CGFNS) after passing the required examination.

The U.S. institution seeking to hire foreign nurses because of a critical nursing shortage must file an attestation with the U.S. Department of Labor (**Form ETA 9029** – *see page M-44* ). After approval, the U.S. prospective employer must file petition **Form I-129** and **H supplement**, *(see pages M-46 and M-49)* together with the following supporting documents:

- Working credentials of the foreign nurse

- Nursing diploma and transcripts

- License from the country where the foreign national attended nursing school

- Written employment agreement between institution and nurse.

After petition approval, foreign nurses still in their home country must apply at a U.S. consulate, using **Form OF-156** *(see page M-36)*. This application must also be filed for each accompanying immediate relative.

Foreign nurses legally present in the U.S. need not file any additional forms. However, **Form I-539** must be filed separately for the spouse and/or each child accompanying the applicant. *(See page M-40)*

H-1A visas are valid for an initial period of not more than three years and cannot be held for more than six years.

**H-1B visas** are issued to temporary workers of distinguished merit and ability performing services other than a registered nurse. This visa category has a quota of 65,000 per year.

The prospective employer must file an attestation with the U.S. Department of Labor (**Form ETA 9035** – *see page M-55*). After attestation acceptance, the prospective U.S. employer must file petition **Form I-129** and **H supplement** *(see pages M-46 and M-49)*, together with the following supporting documents:

- An employment contract (job duties, salary, and hours)

- Description of the job function

- Employer tax return for the past two years

- Bank statements showing the capital of the corporation

- Documents showing the proof that the beneficiary of the H-1B visa is a professional (diplomas and transcripts)

- Documents showing that the beneficiary of the H-1B visa holds a degree equivalent at least to a Bachelor's degree. An academic credential evaluation service recognized by the INS is essential.

Once the petition is approved foreign nationals must apply at a U.S. consulate in the home country using Form **OF-156** *(see page M-36)*. This application must also be filed for each accompanying immediate relative.

Foreign nationals legally present in the U.S. need not file any additional forms. However, **Form I-539** must be filed separately for the spouse and/or each child accompanying the applicant. *(See page M-40)*

H-1B visa, are valid for an initial period of not more than three years and cannot be held for more than six years.

**H-2A visas** cover temporary workers performing agricultural services for which workers are unavailable in the United States. Agricultural workers already in the U.S. illegally cannot benefit from these visas. H-2A visas are part of a major recruitment effort for domestic agricultural workers. The procedures required are extremely complex and time-consuming. Prospective employers are advised not to initiate this process unless a large number of workers are involved.

**H-2B visas** are issued to temporary workers performing other services for which workers are unavailable in the United States. These services generally require skilled or unskilled workers with no college education.

H-2B visas are limited to 25,000 annually. To obtain a visa within this category, the prospective employer must file for temporary labor certification with the state department of labor.

The prospective employer must submit **Form ETA 750, Part A** *(see page M-94)* together with documents showing that he has advertised the job offer in a newspaper or journal chosen by the state department of labor and exhausted other recruitment efforts. He must establish that no other workers are available to take the job.

Once the temporary labor certification is approved, the prospective employer must file a petition using:

- Form **I-129** and **H supplement**, *(see pages M-46 and M-49)* together with the same documents submitted to the Department of Labor,

- Written employment contract

- Employer financial statements

- Tax returns and bank statements

- Diplomas and transcripts from prospective employee

- All other documents necessary to prove the qualifications of the prospective employee.

After petition approval, foreign nationals must apply for H-2B visas at a U.S. consulate in the home country using **Form OF-156** *(see page M-36)*. If the applicant is already legally present in the U.S., no additional form is required. However, **Form I-539** *(see page M-40)* must be filed separately for the spouse and/or each child accompanying the applicant.

H-2B visas are valid for an initial period of one year with additional one year extensions, but cannot be held for more than three years.

**H-3 visas** are issued to trainees. Trainees are foreign nationals who come to the U.S. to receive training other than graduate medical training not available in their home country. These visas are valid for the duration of the training program, normally up to a maximum of 18 months. Extension of a year may be permitted when the training program has not been completed.

**H-4 visas** cover the spouses and children of foreign nationals classified H-1 A/B, H-2A/B, or H-3. H-4 visa holders may not work in the United States.

## I VISAS – FOREIGN MEDIA REPRESENTATIVES

This visa category covers representatives of the foreign media, (press, radio, film, TV) their spouses and children on the condition that the foreign national's country grants reciprocal treatment to U.S. citizens in the media industry. These visas are valid for the duration of employment.

## J VISAS - EXCHANGE VISITORS

• **J-1 visas** are issued to exchange visitors.

• **J-2 visas** are issued to the spouse and/or children of exchange visitors.

To obtain a J-1 visa, the foreign national must have been accepted in an exchange visitor program in the role of student, scholar, teacher, trainee, professor, medical graduate, or research assistant. These programs are approved by the United States Information Agency.

**J-1 visa** holders are legally permitted to work if the work is part of the respective program or the visa holder has received authorization from the sponsor of the exchange program. Immediate relatives of the exchange visitor can request work authorization from the INS.

**J-2 visas** are valid as long as the holder is participating in the requisite exchange program. A two-year foreign residency requirement applies to some exchange visitors after their participation in such a program if:

• The program was financed by the U.S. government or the foreign national's country

• the exchange visitor came to the U.S. to receive graduate medical training or

• the exchange visitor came from a country designated by the U.S. as needing the services of people with certain skills or special knowledge.

## K VISAS - FIANCÉ(E) OF A U.S. CITIZEN AND THEIR CHILDREN

• **K-1 visas** are issued to foreign nationals who intend to marry a U.S. citizen.

• **K-2 visas** are issued to the children of fiancé(e)s.

These visas are valid for 90 days. The reason for this short period is that the only purpose for coming to the U.S. is to marry a U.S. citizen.

To obtain a K-1 visa, both the petitioner and beneficiary must submit petition **Form I-129F** and **Form G- 325A** (Biographical Information – *See pages M-97 and M-31*). The petitioner (U.S. citizen) must file at the INS service center with jurisdiction in his district of residence. Documents must be submitted with the petition showing proof of the petitioner's U.S. citizenship, the parties' freedom to get married, and the foreign national's intent to marry the petitioner.

Once the petition is approved, the fiancé(e) must apply at a U.S. consulate in his or her home country for a K-1 visa. This application process can be done only abroad.

The fiancé(e) must submit the same documentation already provided by the petitioner in the U.S. together with **Forms OF-230-I or OF-179** (Biographical Information – *pages M-10 or M-56*), **Form OF-156** (Nonimmigrant Visa Application – *page M-36*) and **Form I-134** (Affidavit of Support – *page M-22*).

The application is approved only after the fiancé(e) and any accompanying children have been interviewed and have passed the required medical examination.

K-visa holders may apply to work in the U.S., but this authorization is valid only for the 90-day period of the visa.

# L VISAS – INTERCOMPANY TRANSFEREE, SPOUSES AND CHILDREN

The L-1 visa covers employees working for a foreign corporate subsidiary, affiliate, or joint venture partner of a U.S. corporation who are being temporarily transferred to the U.S.

**To obtain an L-1 visa, the employee must have worked with the corporation abroad for at least one year. The purpose of his transfer must be to aid business operations in the U.S. in the same managerial or executive capacity.**

**L-1 visas** are valid for three years, with extensions of two years, up to a total maximum of seven years.

**L-2 visas** holders (immediate relatives (spouse and children) of transferees) are not allowed to work in the U.S.

# M VISAS – VOCATIONAL STUDENTS OR OTHER NON-ACADEMIC STUDENTS, THEIR SPOUSES AND CHILDREN

• **M-1 visas** are issued to vocational or other non-academic students.

• **M-2 visas** are issued to the spouses and unmarried children under age 21 of such student.

M visas are valid only for the duration of studies plus 30 days or a maximum of one year, whichever is less. These visas can be renewed.

The same application process for the F-1 visa must be followed if the foreign national intends to come to the U.S. to enter a vocational or non-academic program. Once the student has been accepted the school must complete the certificate of eligibility for nonimmigrant student status (F-1), **Form I-20 A-B** (*page M-37)* and send it to the student.

Following this, the student must apply for the vocational student visa by presenting the I-20A-B form to a U.S. consulate, together with the necessary accompanying documents. These must show proof of financial support and intent to return to the country of origin.

Temporary employment is available for M-1 students depending on circumstances. M-2 visa holders cannot legally work in the United States.

# O, P, Q AND R VISAS

These temporary visas created by the Immigration Act of 1990 are aimed at certain outstanding foreign nationals with special abilities in the arts, entertainment, sciences, education and athletics.

- **O-1 visas** cover foreign nationals of "extraordinary ability" in the arts, athletics, business and sciences, business, and education.

- **O-2 visas** are issued to the support staff of the O-1 visa holders.

- **O-3 visas** are issued to the accompanying relatives of O-1 and O-2 visa holders.

- **P-1 visas** are given to outstanding athletes, athletic teams, and entertainment companies.

- **P-2 visas** are given to artists or entertainers who participate in regional exchange programs.

- **P-3 visas** include individual or groups of artists or entertainers considered "culturally unique."

- **Q visas** are given to those participating in an international exchange program.

- **R visas** are given to religious workers (R-1) and their accompanying relatives (R- 2).

To obtain a visa in one of these categories, it is necessary to have a job offer from a prospective U.S. employer. The U.S. employer must submit a petition using Form **I-129,** with **supplements O, P, Q, R,** as appropriate. (See *pages M-46, M-52, and M-53.*)

If the INS service center finds the petition and its accompanying documents in order, it is approved.

If abroad, the applicant must then file **Form OF-156** (*page M-36)* at any U.S. consulate. If the applicant is already legally present in the U.S., no additional form is required. However, **Form I-539** must be filed for the spouse and/or any children accompanying the applicant. (See *page M-40).*

The visa permits the applicant to work only for the petitioner (sponsor). Accompanying relatives may not legally work in the U.S.

# SPECIAL CONSIDERATIONS IN THE IMMIGRATION LAW

# CHAPTER 8

# EXCLUSION AND DEPORTATION

The U.S. government reserves the right to bar entry to (exclude) or remove from the country (deport) any foreign national who does not comply with existing restrictions and regulations.

## EXCLUSIONS

The U.S. government may lawfully bar the entry of foreign nationals to the U.S. when they fall within certain preestablished grounds for exclusion. These apply whether the foreign national intends to reside permanently or temporarily. Four of the most common grounds for exclusion follow.

### Ground one: health-related exclusion

The Secretary for Health and Human Services determines the grounds for this exclusion. It applies to foreign nationals with communicable diseases that threaten the public health. Today, tuberculosis (TB), human immune deficiency virus (HIV) or acquired immune deficiency syndrome (AIDS) are the most common grounds.

Individuals with physical or mental disorders whose behavior may pose a threat to others are also considered excludable. It is important to note that the 1990 Immigration and Nationality Act eliminated within this subdivision the exclusion of gay men and lesbians.

Evidence of drug addiction or abuse is also grounds for exclusion.

### Ground two: crime-related exclusion

Foreign nationals are considered excludable for crimes of moral turpitude. Crimes of moral turpitude are acts demonstrating "baseness, vileness, or depravity" including prostitution and commercialized vice; or for multiple criminal convictions for two or more crimes involving moral turpitude. Foreign nationals under age 18 will not be excluded because of minor criminal violations, provided any convictions occurred at least five years prior to application for entry.

### Ground three: security-related exclusion

The Secretary of State determines security-related grounds for exclusion. Terrorist activities, espionage, sabotage, export control violations, and communist or totalitarian party membership are all cited.

Note that with respect to the communist or totalitarian party membership, exclusion is only applicable to those who intend permanent residence in the United States. Those who became members of such parties involuntarily are not considered excludable. Intellectual interest in communist ideology does not constitute affiliation with a communist party unless there has been positive and voluntary action.

### Ground four: previous immigration violations or exclusion for misrepresentation

If during the immigration process, the applicant has made false representations or lied, has been previously excluded or deported, or has been a smuggler of foreign nationals, he may be excludable.

### Waivers

Any grounds for exclusion, including those not covered here, may be legally waived. The fact that particular grounds may apply does not necessarily mean that a foreign national will be excluded. He may be able to obtain a waiver of excludability.

## DEPORTATION

The United States government may lawfully deport a foreign national who has already entered the country if he fits into one of these five preestablished grounds.

### Ground one: immigration violations

This applies to any foreign national excludable at the time of entry to the United States. Deportation proceedings are initiated under the applicable grounds of excludability existing at the time of entry.

If a foreign national fails to comply with the conditions and restrictions of nonimmigrant or immigrant status, he will be deported. A classic example of this is the foreign national given nonimmigrant status prohibiting employment within the U.S. who then takes a job. Another example of violation is marriage fraud.

### Ground two: criminal offenses

This subdivision includes crimes of moral turpitude (acts demonstrating "baseness, vileness, or depravity"); multiple criminal convictions (for two or more crimes involving moral turpitude); aggravated felonies (murder, illicit traffic in drugs and/or firearms, addiction to narcotic drugs, and money laundering).

### Ground three: document-related violations

Foreign nationals in the U.S. must register with the INS and report any change of address within ten days. Deportation proceedings can be initiated for failure to comply.

Foreign nationals are deportable if they have committed fraud or made misrepresentations on the INS registrations forms, permits, or other documents related to their status in the U.S.

### Ground four: national security risk

Terrorist activities, espionage, sabotage, export control violations, and communist or totalitarian party membership are grounds for deportation, constituting national security risk.

The communist or totalitarian party membership deportation ground is applicable only to those intending permanent residence. Those who became members of such parties involuntarily are not considered deportable. Mere intellectual interest in communist ideology does not constitute affiliation with a communist party unless there has been positive and voluntary action.

## Ground five: public charge

If the foreign national becomes a public charge, he is deportable. To be considered a public charge the national's income must have fallen below poverty level guidelines within five years of entering the U.S.; he must have received public assistance (which by law imposes a debt for services rendered and demands payment), and have refused to pay back the government agency provider.

# CHAPTER 9

# REFUGEES AND POLITICAL ASYLUM*

U.S. immigration law has special programs to protect foreign nationals from political persecution.

- Refugee status may be applied for by foreign nationals still in their native countries

- Political asylum may be applied for by foreign nationals currently in the United States

- Both refugee status and political asylum allow immigration to the U.S. without any family or employment requirements.

## REFUGEES

To be eligible for refugee status, the foreign national:

- Must seek refugee status from outside the United States

- Must show a "well-founded fear of persecution because of race, religion, nationality, membership in a particular social group, or political opinion"

- Must be subject to a quota imposed on different regions of the world

- Must be subject to the grounds of excludability imposed on all other foreigners. However, normal requirements of economic sufficiency and valid entry documents are not considered

- Must be sponsored by a person or an organization willing to guarantee the costs of the trip and resettlement in the United States.

Following application, the foreign national must undergo a medical examination and an interview by an INS officer. If the application is approved the refugee is allowed to enter the United States. After one year of holding this status the refugee may apply for adjustment of status to that of lawful permanent resident. This requires an INS inspection and examination to determine admissibility.

---

*At the time of printing, legislative changes in this area of immigration law are expected.*

# POLITICAL ASYLUM

A political asylee is a foreign national who may be persecuted if returned to his country of origin.

To qualify as a political asylee the following conditions must be met:

- The foreign national must be already present in the United States or at its borders

- The foreign national applying for asylum must be unable to return to his country of origin because of persecution or "well-founded fear of persecution on account of race, religion, nationality, membership in a particular social group, or political opinion"

- While not subject to quotas, the asylum applicant is subject to the grounds of excludability imposed on all other foreigners, except that grounds which require showing economic sufficiency and the validity of entry documents are not considered.

The foreign national, unless in exclusion or deportation proceedings, must submit forms and documents to the INS district director who forwards them on to an asylum officer.

Copies of the application and documents are studied and sent to the Office of Refugees, Asylum, and Parole (CORAP) and the Department of State.

Interview by the asylum officer is part of the application proceeding. It is possible during it to submit affidavits and have the assistance of legal counsel.

Based on the information compiled by the asylum officer, a determination is made conferring or denying asylum. If the determination is favorable, asylum status is granted for an indefinite period. Employment authorization is also granted.

The applicant's spouse and/or children may be granted asylum as well. Applicants granted asylum and remaining in the country for a year may apply for an adjustment of status to that of lawful permanent resident.

If the determination to grant asylum is negative, there is no right to appeal the decision. However, during deportation or exclusionary proceedings, the application for asylum can be renewed.

# THE NATURALIZATION PROCESS

# CHAPTER 10

# THE NATURALIZATION PROCESS

Thousands of immigrants become American citizens each year. Their reasons may often be personal since legal permanent residents and U.S. citizens are entitled to many of the same benefits.

There are a few privileges afforded only to U.S. citizens.

- Citizens can vote, serve on juries, and qualify for all government jobs. Green card holders cannot

- Citizens travel freely. Green card holders are subject to time limits on travel abroad

- Citizens can sponsor the entrance of more relatives to the United States. Green card holders cannot sponsor parents or siblings. Relatives of citizens are processed faster.

Immigrants can acquire U.S. citizenship through naturalization. Requirements are as follows:

## RESIDENCY REQUIREMENTS

A petition must be filed by the lawful permanent resident who wishes to become a citizen.

- Residency must have been for a continuous period of no less than five years

- The applicant must have been physically present in the U.S. for at least half of that time (or 30 months plus one day during the five years prior to filing)

- The applicant must have been a resident of the district in which he or she filed the petition for at least three months.

Note that temporary absence (less than six months) from the U.S. does not interrupt the continuity of an applicant's residence. However, if the absence is for more than six months, the applicant must prove he did not abandon residence in the U.S.

## LINGUISTIC AND KNOWLEDGE REQUIREMENTS

The INS must determine whether the applicant can speak and write the English language. In addition, the applicant must prove knowledge of the fundamentals of American history, government and other aspects of the U.S. Constitution. He must pass an examination designed to test that knowledge. Exceptions are made for individuals unable to hear or see or for people over 55 years of age who have legally resided in the U.S. for at least 15 years.

## OTHER REQUIREMENTS

The applicant must be eighteen years of age or older. Parents can file petitions on behalf of children under 18.

In addition, proof of good moral character, attachment to the principles of the Constitution of the U.S., and an oath of allegiance to the United States are required.

## PART FOUR: THE APPLICATION

Application for Naturalization is filed on Form N-400. Applicants must also provide information regarding their family history, periods of residency in the U.S., and the names of people who will support the petition for naturalization (witnesses).

A fingerprint chart, three identical photographs, and record of the applicant's alien registration number must be attached to the application.

An interview at an INS office is the final step.

Once a favorable determination is reached, the federal district court with jurisdiction in the locality where the applicant resides administers the oath of allegiance to the now U.S. citizen.

"We hold these truths to be self evident, that all men are created equal, that they are endowed by their Creator with certain unalienable Rights, that among these are Life, Liberty and the pursuit of Happiness.–

That to secure these rights, Governments are instituted among Men, deriving their just powers from the consent of the governed,–

That whenever any Form of Government becomes destructive of these ends, it is the Right of the People to alter or to abolish it, and to institute new Government, laying its foundation on such principles and organizing its powers in such form, as to them shall seem most likely to effect their Safety and Happiness."

From The Declaration of Independence, July 4, 1776

THE UNITED STATES OF AMERICA: FOR THE PEOPLE

# TABLE OF CONTENTS

# A NATION OF IMMIGRANTS

Although 94 percent of today's Americans were born here, almost all can trace their families back to a relative who first landed on these shores. Even the Native Americans are thought to have migrated centuries ago from Asia. Once referred to as "Indians", an estimated one million were here when the colonists arrived.

## THE PEOPLE: WHO ARE THEY

Among today's Americans (about 20 million of foreign birth) are people from every continent, speaking almost every language, practicing almost every religion. They have often come in waves from a single region for a single reason and settled near each other. In such ethnic neighborhoods, especially in the larger cities,

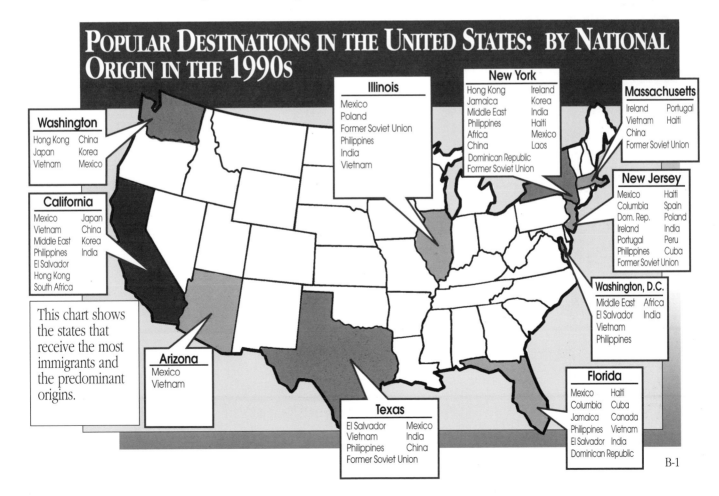

## POPULAR DESTINATIONS IN THE UNITED STATES: BY NATIONAL ORIGIN IN THE 1990s

**Illinois**
Mexico
Poland
Former Soviet Union
Philippines
India
Vietnam

**New York**
| Hong Kong | Ireland |
| Jamaica | Korea |
| Middle East | India |
| Philippines | Haiti |
| Africa | Mexico |
| China | Laos |
| Dominican Republic | |
| Former Soviet Union | |

**Massachusetts**
| Ireland | Portugal |
| Vietnam | Haiti |
| China | |
| Former Soviet Union | |

**Washington**
| Hong Kong | China |
| Japan | Korea |
| Vietnam | Mexico |

**California**
| Mexico | Japan |
| Vietnam | China |
| Middle East | Korea |
| Philippines | India |
| El Salvador | |
| Hong Kong | |
| South Africa | |

**New Jersey**
| Mexico | Haiti |
| Columbia | Spain |
| Dom. Rep. | Poland |
| Ireland | India |
| Portugal | Peru |
| Philippines | Cuba |
| Former Soviet Union | |

**Washington, D.C.**
| Middle East | Africa |
| El Salvador | India |
| Vietnam | |
| Philippines | |

This chart shows the states that receive the most immigrants and the predominant origins.

**Arizona**
Mexico
Vietnam

**Texas**
| El Salvador | Mexico |
| Vietnam | India |
| Philippines | China |
| Former Soviet Union | |

**Florida**
| Mexico | Haiti |
| Columbia | Cuba |
| Jamaica | Canada |
| Philippines | Vietnam |
| El Salvador | India |
| Dominican Republic | |

Immigration patterns to the United States reflect both home country pressures and changes in U.S. law.

Once predominantly European in origin, the large majority today come from developing countries.

you can find their regional food, clothing, language, and customs.

Patterns of immigration to the New World have always been greatly influenced by Old World circumstances. Many of the original colonists came seeking religious, political, and economic freedom. Some were sent as indentured servants or convicts from Europe, or as slaves from Africa. Slaves, comprising an estimated one-fifth of the population under the first American president, were not declared free until the sixteenth president, Abraham Lincoln.

Persecution, economic crisis, war, and national chaos are longtime factors in migration which continue today. Famine triggered the wave of Irish immigrants that arrived in the 1840s. Persecution in Russia forced over two million Jews to flee for shelter here by World War I. Economic depression brought six million Germans between 1820 and 1940. More than a million more have entered since World War II. While Germany has sent the most immigrants, other European nations are not far behind. Over five million immigrants each have entered from Italy and Great Britain; over four million from Ireland. With the break-up of the former Soviet Union, thousands of refugees are arriving from Eastern Europe.

But this European picture has changed. After the Vietnam War, almost a million refugees entered the U.S. from Vietnam, Laos, and Cambodia. Some 10.5 million people have arrived in the last 20 years, reflecting a pattern of immigration far less European in origin than in the past. (See Table 1 at the end of this chapter for detail.) In 1992, for example, 44 percent of new immigrants came from Latin America and the Caribbean; 37 percent from Asia; and 15 percent from Europe. Almost 80 percent of these settled in seven states. (See Table 2 for the most popular cities.)

Immigration law also greatly influences who comes. New laws allow immigrant visas to families of U.S. citizens and permanent residents, to certain kinds of refugees, and to workers with particular job skills. (Table 3 shows the countries sending the most immigrants and their categories of admission.)

New laws also welcome investor immigrants. In 1991, Congress designated 10,000 visas a year for immigrants willing to invest $1 million in a business employing at least ten people.

## THE IDEAL: FREEDOM UNDER LAW

Americans come from many backgrounds. Diversity is common here. What holds us together is an ideal: individual freedom. What makes it work is tolerance: mutual respect.

Whatever your birthplace, American freedom probably plays a part in your decision to emigrate. Here you can choose where and how you want to live, what you want to do, how you want to worship or work or spend your time. Freedom to act is also freedom to fail. There are no guarantees of success. The right to choice is basic – but not unlimited. One's liberty to act, you might say, stops at the next person's nose. Our freedom is both defined and protected by a complex system of law and government.

*Rung July 4, 1776 in Philadelphia to proclaim U.S. Independence. The Liberty Bell is a symbol of the freedom Americans enjoy today.*

# THE STATUE OF LIBERTY

The Statue of Liberty was conceived and designed by Frédéric-Auguste Bartholdi (with Gustave Eiffel's help). It was given to the United States by France in honor of the 1876 centennial of American Independence. Funded by subscriptions from the French people, it was dedicated by President Grover Cleveland in 1886 and declared a national monument in 1924.

151 feet (46m) tall, it still stands at the entrance to New York harbor, the inscription on its base is a touching reminder of the American vision:

"…Give me your tired, your poor,

Your huddled masses yearning to breathe free,

The wretched refuse of your teeming shore.

Send these, the homeless, tempest-Tost to me,

I lift my lamp beside the golden door!"

–Emma Lazarus, *"The New Colossus"*

# Table 1: Immigration to U.S. by Country of Origin

| COUNTRIES | 1820-1990 | 1990 | 1981-90 | 1971-80 | 1961-70 | 1951-60 | 1941-50 | 1820-1940 |
|---|---|---|---|---|---|---|---|---|
| **Europe** | | | | | | | | |
| Albania | 3,090 | 78 | 479 | 329 | 98 | 59 | 85 | 2,040 |
| Austria | 2,661,318 | 675 | 4,636 | 9,478 | 20,621 | 67,106 | 24,860 | 2,534,617 |
| Belgium | 209,196 | 682 | 5,706 | 5,329 | 9,192 | 18,575 | 12,189 | 158,205 |
| Bulgaria | 70,484 | 428 | 2,342 | 1,188 | 619 | 104 | 375 | 65,856 |
| Czechoslovakia | 150,074 | 1,412 | 11,500 | 6,023 | 3,273 | 918 | 8,347 | 120,013 |
| Denmark | 370,422 | 666 | 5,380 | 4,439 | 9,201 | 10,984 | 5,393 | 335,025 |
| Estonia | 1,294 | 20 | 137 | 91 | 163 | 185 | 212 | 506 |
| Finland | 37,346 | 369 | 3,265 | 2,868 | 4,192 | 4,925 | 2,503 | 19,593 |
| France | 778,358 | | 23,124 | 25,069 | 45,237 | 51,121 | 38,809 | 594,998 |
| Germany | 7,061,615 | 7,493 | 70,111 | 74,414 | 190,796 | 477,765 | 226,578 | 6,021,951 |
| Great Britain | 5,102,100 | 15,928 | 142,123 | 137,374 | 213,822 | 202,824 | 139,306 | 4,266,561 |
| Greece | 694,657 | 2,742 | 29,130 | 92,369 | 85,969 | 47,608 | 8,973 | 430,608 |
| Hungary | 1,60,979 | 1,655 | 9,764 | 6,550 | 5,401 | 36,637 | 3,469 | 1,609,158 |
| Ireland | 4,725,987 | 10,333 | 32,823 | 11,490 | 32,966 | 48,362 | 14,789 | 4,580,557 |
| Italy | 5,338,478 | 3,287 | 32,894 | 129,368 | 214,111 | 185,491 | 57,661 | 4,719,223 |
| Latvia | 2,981 | 45 | 359 | 207 | 510 | 352 | 361 | 1,192 |
| Lithuania | 4,418 | 67 | 482 | 248 | 562 | 242 | 683 | 2,201 |
| Luxembourg | 3,166 | 31 | 234 | 307 | 556 | 684 | 820 | 565 |
| Netherlands | 373,952 | 1,424 | 11,958 | 10,492 | 30,606 | 52,277 | 14,860 | 253,759 |
| Norway | 753,456 | 524 | 3,901 | 3,941 | 15,484 | 22,935 | 10,100 | 697,095 |
| Poland | 620,474 | 20,537 | 97,390 | 37,234 | 53,539 | 9,985 | 7,571 | 414,755 |
| Portugal | 500,850 | 4,035 | 40,020 | 101,710 | 76,065 | 19,588 | 7,423 | 256,044 |
| Romania | 212,947 | 4,647 | 39,963 | 12,393 | 1,039 | 1,076 | 156,945 | |
| Spain | 280,413 | 1,886 | 15,698 | 39,141 | 44,659 | 7,894 | 2,898 | 170,123 |
| Sweden | 1,391,428 | 1,196 | 10,211 | 6,531 | 17,116 | 21,697 | 10,665 | 1,325,208 |
| Switzerland | 357,666 | 845 | 7,076 | 8,235 | 18,453 | 17,675 | 10,547 | 295,680 |
| U.S.S.R. | 3,470,110 | 25,524 | 84,081 | 38,961 | 2,465 | 671 | 571 | 3,343,361 |
| Yugoslavia | 136,691 | 2,828 | 19,182 | 30,540 | 20,381 | 8,225 | 1,576 | 56,787 |
| Other Europe | 60,920 | 195 | 2,661 | 4,049 | 4,904 | 9,799 | 3,447 | 36,060 |
| Total Europe | 37,045,140 | 112,401 | 705,630 | 800,368 | 1,123,492 | 1,325,727 | 621,147 | 32,468,776 |
| | | | | | | | | |
| **ASIA** | | | | | | | | |
| China | 4,257,851 | 16,812 | 119,204 | 169,939 | 413,310 | 377,952 | 171,718 | 3,005,728 |
| India | 466,771 | 30,667 | 261,841 | 164,134 | 27,189 | 1,973 | 1,761 | 9,873 |
| Israel | 129,620 | 4,664 | 36,353 | 37,713 | 29,602 | 25,476 | 476 | |
| Japan | 458,407 | 5,734 | 43,248 | 49,775 | 39,988 | 46,250 | 1,555 | 277,591 |
| Turkey | 409,937 | 2,468 | 20,843 | 13,399 | 10,142 | 3,519 | 798 | 361,236 |
| Other Asia | 3,677,389 | 248,082 | 2,042,025 | 1,198,831 | 285,957 | 66,374 | 15,729 | 44,053 |
| Total Asia | 6,098,449 | 338,581 | 2,066,449 | 1,588,178 | 427,642 | 153,249 | 37,028 | 1,074,926 |
| | | | | | | | | |
| **America:** | | | | | | | | |
| Canada | 4,257,851 | 16,812 | 119,204 | 169,939 | 413,310 | 377,952 | 171,718 | 3,005,728 |
| Central America | 810,293 | 146,202 | 458,753 | 134,640 | 101,330 | 44,751 | 21,665 | 49,154 |
| Mexico | 3,886,136 | 679,068 | 1,653,250 | 640,294 | 453,937 | 299,811 | 60,589 | 778,255 |
| South America | 1,244,433 | 85,819 | 455,977 | 295,741 | 257,954 | 91,628 | 21,831 | 121,302 |
| West Indies | 2,723,518 | 115,065 | 892,392 | 741,126 | 470,213 | 123,091 | 49,725 | 446,971 |
| America | 111,020 | 411 | 1,352 | 995 | 19,630 | 59,711 | 29,276 | 56 |
| Total America | 13,033,251 | 1,043,377 | 3,580,928 | 1,982,735 | 1,716,374 | 996,944 | 354,804 | 4,401,466 |
| | | | | | | | | |
| **Africa** | 349,464 | 35,893 | 192,212 | 80,779 | 28,954 | 14,092 | 7,367 | 26,060 |
| **Australia & New Zealand** | 143,627 | 2,583 | 20,169 | 23,788 | 19,562 | 11,506 | 13,805 | 54,437 |
| **Pacific Islands** | 57,460 | 3,599 | 21,041 | 17,454 | 5,560 | 1,470 | 746 | 11,089 |
| **Countries not specified** | 266,623 | 49 | 196 | 12 | 93 | 12,491 | 142 | 253,689 |
| | | | | | | | | |
| **Total of all countries** | 56,994,014 | 1,536,483 | 7,338,062 | 4,493,314 | 3,321,677 | 2,515,479 | 1.035.039 | 38,290,443 |

*Source: Department of Justice, Immigration and Naturalization Service*

# Table 2: Top 20 Metropolitan Areas of Intended Residence for U.S. Immigrants, 1992

| U.S. Metropolitan Area of Intended Residence | Number | Percent | U.S. Metropolitan Area of Intended Residence | Number | Percent |
|---|---|---|---|---|---|
| Los Angeles-Long Beach, CA | 129,266 | 13.3 | Oakland, CA | 17,187 | 1.8 |
| New York, NY | 127,875 | 13.1 | Riverside-San Bernardino, CA | 16,535 | 1.7 |
| Chicago, IL | 37,236 | 3.8 | Newark, NJ | 13,734 | 1.4 |
| Anaheim-Santa Ana, CA | 34,417 | 3.5 | Bergen-Passaic, NJ | 12,405 | 1.3 |
| Miami-Hialeah, FL | 31,627 | 3.2 | Dallas, TX | 12,312 | 1.3 |
| Washington, D.C.-MD-VA | 27,387 | 2.8 | Philadelphia, PA-NJ | 11,882 | 1.2 |
| Houston, TX | 27,067 | 2.8 | Nassau-Suffolk, NJ | 11,415 | 1.2 |
| San Jose, CA | 23,537 | 2.4 | Seattle, WA | 9,855 | 1.0 |
| San Francisco, CA | 21,276 | 2.2 | Sacramento, CA | 9,564 | 1.0 |
| San Diego, CA | 20,936 | 2.1 | Other | 290,200 | 29.8 |
| Boston, MA[1] | 18,259 | 1.9 | Rural | 65,594 | 7.1 |

1. Includes Essex, Middlesex, Norfolk, Plymouth, and Suffolk counties. Source: U.S. Dept. of Justice, 1992 Statistical Yearbook of the Immigration and Naturalization Service (1993).

# Table 3: Top 20 Countries of Birth for U.S. Immigrants and Major Categories of Admission, 1992

| Country of Birth | Total Immigrants[1] | Percent | Category of Admission | | | | |
|---|---|---|---|---|---|---|---|
| | | | Relative Preferences | Occupational Preferences | Immediate Relatives | Refugees and Asylees | IRCA Legalization[2] |
| All countries | 973,977 | 100.0% | 213,123 | 116,198 | 235,484 | 117,037 | 163,342 |
| Mexico | 213,802 | 22.0 | 33,361 | 3,226 | 24,440 | 29 | 122,470 |
| Vietnam | 77,735 | 8.0 | 12,133 | 142 | 11,306 | 32,155 | 7 |
| Philippines | 61,022 | 6.3 | 14,435 | 9,708 | 30,572 | 221 | 1,843 |
| Dominican Republic | 41,969 | 4.3 | 26,463 | 298 | 13,077 | 27 | 1,129 |
| China, mainland | 38,907 | 4.0 | 12,198 | 11,058 | 11,443 | 884 | 172 |
| India | 36,755 | 3.8 | 14,468 | 9,686 | 9,796 | 34 | 2,126 |
| El Salvador | 26,191 | 2.7 | 6,735 | 2,978 | 2,449 | 743 | 5,081 |
| Poland | 25,504 | 2.6 | 7,054 | 1,575 | 3,174 | 1,512 | 667 |
| United Kingdom | 19,973 | 2.1 | 1,322 | 7,572 | 7,358 | 7 | 216 |
| Korea | 19,359 | 2.0 | 6,270 | 4,712 | 7,559 | – | 376 |
| Jamaica | 18,915 | 1.9 | 8,996 | 1,482 | 5,446 | 1 | 2,095 |
| Taiwan | 16,344 | 1.7 | 4,610 | 8,368 | 2,812 | 10 | 112 |
| Canada | 15,205 | 1.6 | 1,545 | 6,304 | 6,172 | 5 | 247 |
| Ukraine3 | 14,383 | 1.5 | 45 | 101 | 670 | 13,347 | – |
| Iran | 13,233 | 1.4 | 1,682 | 2,434 | 4,582 | 3,093 | 425 |
| Columbia | 13,201 | 1.4 | 3,667 | 1,273 | 4,956 | 74 | 1,357 |
| Ireland | 12,226 | 1.3 | 180 | 712 | 908 | 2 | 59 |
| Cuba | 11,791 | 1.2 | 1,261 | 22 | 471 | 9,919 | 37 |
| Japan | 11,028 | 1.1 | 288 | 3,203 | 2,550 | 5 | 53 |
| Haiti | 11,002 | 1.1 | 680 | 78 | 1,422 | 16 | 8,591 |

1. Total includes Amerasians, Soviet and Indochinese parolees, foreign government officials, special immigrants, and admissions from nonpreference "underrepresented countries," suspension of deportation, and private law. 2. Under the Immigration Reform and Control Act (IRCA) of 1986, illegal aliens with temporary resident status became eligible for permanent legal residence. 3. If the former Soviet Union were counted as one country, it would have 43,614 immigrants (fourth overall) to the U.S. Source: U.S. Dept. of Justice, 1992 Statistical Yearbook of the Immigration and Naturalization Service (1993).

# GOVERNMENT

The foundation of American government is a single document, the **Constitution of the United States of America,** in effect since 1788. It developed in part out of the British system that held power here from 1607 to 1776.

## BACKGROUND

Each British colony in America had a royal governor, its own legislature and a structure of local government similar to that in England. The focus was local, the problems immediate and unprecedented. Final authority lay far away in Britain. This was no help to the colonists in the ongoing wars against France and the native "Indians." Early settlers had to rely on themselves. In accordance with British tradition, they assumed they had the right to elect a representative government, to assemble when they wanted, and to petition the government. For some 170 years, they paid the king no formal taxes. They resented it when asked to support a Parliament where they had no representation. By 1774, they had formed a Continental Congress to discuss this and other issues. They held another Congress in 1775: this time they took the position that they could govern on their own. An army was formed led by George Washington, who would become the new nation's first president. Fighting had already begun against the British in Lexington and Concord, Massachusetts.

After decades of self sufficiency tempered by war, the colonists felt it was time to assert their independence. The Founding Fathers believed they had a right to self-determination and to representation in government. King George III of England disagreed. Although the first battle of the Revolutionary War began in Massachusetts on April 19, 1775, Independence was only formally declared on July 4, 1776. Fighting ceased October 19, 1781 with the surrender of the British General Cornwallis at Yorktown. The official treaty to end the war, The Treaty of Paris, was signed September 3, 1783.

*The real power in the U.S. lies with the people, who exercise it by voting. The right to vote is afforded to any U.S. citizen over the age of 18 who has registered to vote, unless convicted of a **felony** (major crime).*

July 4, 1776, the Second Continental Congress voted for the **Declaration of Independence,** the document that proclaimed freedom from Britain. Now the colonies declared themselves to be individual states, part of the United States of America. Over the next four years, each state organized its own system of government – a fact reflected in the structure of today's government.

In 1777, the Continental Congress adopted and sent to each state for **ratification** (approval) the **Articles of Confederation.** A forerunner of the Constitution, this loosely organized the former colonies into a "Confederation of States" with equal representation in a single legislative assembly. The states deliberately limited that assembly, wanting to retain their own power.

They did allow the government to create currency – but the new money did not reflect actual market value and was, in fact, worthless. The old phrase "not worth a continental" reflected that early economic fact. Concerned businessmen, landowners, and lawyers held conferences in 1785 and 1786, calling for a stronger central government to regulate the economy. At the Constitutional Convention in Philadelphia in 1787, they abandoned the Articles of Confederation and wrote the new law of the land, the Constitution of the United States of America. It is still in effect today.

### Federalism

The delegates chose federalism, the concept of a strong national government that allows the states to retain those powers that do not require central authority. The Constitution establishes and defines the federal system of government: certain powers are **delegated** (granted) to the national government; all others belong to the states. This balance between the states' rights and those of the federal government keeps either from becoming too powerful. The American Civil War (1861-1865) was fought over the issue of states' rights as well as slavery. The seceding southern states were denied the right to leave the Union and lost the war that followed.

Ten amendments, called the **Bill of Rights,** were adopted shortly after the Constitution was ratified by the states. These specify the rights of individuals. The Constitution can be **amended** (changed) only if three-quarters of the states and two-thirds of both Houses of Congress approve. There have been only sixteen amendments since the Bill of Rights went into effect in 1791. Among the most important are: the 13th, 14th, and 15th (these, in turn, abolished slavery, declared former slaves to be citizens, and gave them the right to vote), and the 19th (which gave women the right to vote).

### Separation of powers

Out of the same concern that created the demand for federalism, the delegates incorporated the doctrine of separation of powers into the Constitution. The separation of powers divides the national government into three separate branches (the executive, the legislative, and the judicial), each able to prevent abuse of power by the others through a system of **checks and balances.**

# THE EXECUTIVE BRANCH

The executive branch, headed by the president and employing several million people in its departments and agencies, **executes** (carries out) the laws of the United States.

### The president

The president (who, incidentally, cannot be an immigrant) must be at least 35 years old and have been residing in the U.S. at least 14 years. The president has a four-year term of office, limited to two elected terms. He is elected by the people (through the electoral college system which reflects state population) with a vice president whom he chooses himself (usually on the advice of his political party). Inauguration is on January 20th, following November elections.

The president is the chief executive and head of state. With the Secretary of State, he carries on official business with foreign nations and appoints representatives to them. He negotiates treaties (which are binding only when approved by two-thirds of the Senate). He is the commander-in-chief of the armed forces, including the state units of the National Guard.

He has judicial power in that he appoints federal judges, including the justices of the Supreme Court (again, subject to Senate confirmation). He can grant pardon to anyone convicted of federal crime (except in a case of impeachment or removal from office).

He has great legislative power: he is the chief maker of public policy and a major influence on public opinion. He recommends legislation to Congress and may veto what it passes. He can call Congress into special session as needed.

### The vice president

The vice president assists the president, succeeding him in the event of his resignation, death or inability to function. He also serves as presiding officer of the Senate (voting only in case of a tie).

The president can name a vice president when that office is vacated. The new vice president must then be confirmed by Congress.

### The executive departments and agencies

The president appoints his own cabinet: the secretaries of the executive departments of: State, Treasury, Defense, Justice (headed by the attorney general, this Department also includes

## Electoral College System

The people do not vote directly in presidential elections. The names of the candidates (president and vice president) appear on the ballot, but the voter actually selects a slate of electors, one for every senator and representative in each state (a total of 538). The candidate with the highest number of popular votes (one per citizen voting) wins all the electoral votes of that state. To be elected, the president must get 270 votes. If no candidate has a majority, the final decision is made by the House of Representatives with each state getting one vote.

## Military Service

All men between the ages of 18 and 26 are required to register with the Selective Service System. Provision is made for conscientious objectors, the handicapped, and others. Women are admitted to the military but not required to register. Their participation in all branches of all services is not yet universal; some sections are still restricted to men. Military service is no longer compulsory. Since the 1970s, the armed forces - the army, navy, marines, air force, and coast guard - have been completely volunteer. All come under the umbrella of the Department of Defense, headquartered at the Pentagon in Arlington, Virginia. (During peace time, the coast guard reports to the Department of Transportation). Each of these forces also maintains reserve troops.

## Transition of Executive Power

The Constitution, modified in 1967 by the 25th Amendment, describes the specific conditions for presidential succession if the president becomes incapacitated; and for resumption of office in the event of recovery. After the vice president, presidential power goes to the speaker of the House of Representatives, then to the president *pro tempore* of the Senate (a senator elected by that body to preside in the absence of the vice president). Cabinet officers follow in a designated order.

An example from recent history: October 10, 1973, Vice President Spiro T. Agnew resigned (pleading no contest to charges of income tax evasion). Two days later, President Richard M. Nixon appointed Gerald R. Ford, approved by Congress December 6, 1973. Ford, in turn, took over as president when Nixon resigned August 9, 1974. He nominated New York Governor Nelson A. Rockefeller as Vice President August 20th. Vice President Rockefeller was confirmed by Congress December 19, 1974.

the Federal Bureau of Investigation), Interior, Agriculture, Commerce, Labor, Health and Human Services, Housing and Urban Development, Transportation, Energy, Education, and Veterans' Affairs. These are all appointed on the advice and consent of the Senate.

The president also appoints the heads of all other executive agencies which handle the daily administration and enforcement of federal law in their specific areas as defined by Congress.

## THE LEGISLATIVE BRANCH

Congress makes the national laws. It consists of two elected bodies: the House of Representatives (with proportional representation based on state population) and the Senate (with equal representation – two senators per state). The Constitution requires a national census every ten years and a redistribution of House seats according to population shifts. Each house of Congress has its own terms of office and areas of specialization.

Congress decides its own rules of procedure, seating, and disciplining its members. In accordance with the first article of the Constitution, Congress has the power to: levy and collect taxes; borrow money for the public treasury; regulate interstate commerce and trade with other nations; coin money, state its value, punish counterfeiters; establish federal courts, rules of naturalization, national bankruptcy laws, post offices, standards for weights

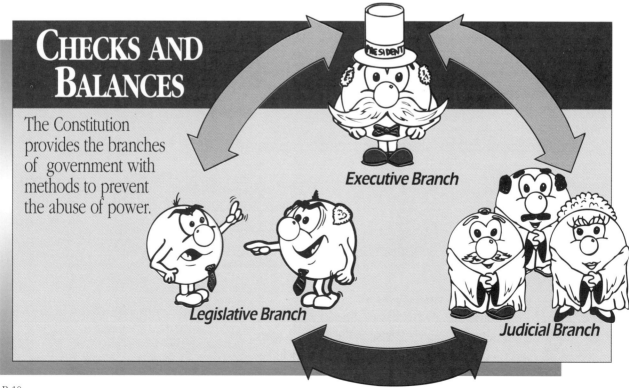

# CHECKS AND BALANCES

The Constitution provides the branches of government with methods to prevent the abuse of power.

*Executive Branch*

*Legislative Branch*

*Judicial Branch*

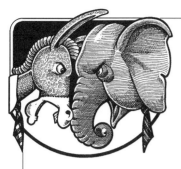

*In political cartoons, the Democratic party is symbolized by a donkey and the Republican party by an elephant.*

# Congress in Brief

Congress reflects a compromise made some two hundred years ago. At the Constitutional Convention in 1787, the large states wanted the "Virginia Plan" calling for a bicameral (two-house) legislature with representation based on population or taxes. The small states wanted the "New Jersey Plan," which proposed a single-chambered legislature, one state having one vote. Thanks to a solution proposed by Connecticut, both won.

## POLITICAL PARTIES

The U.S. has two major political parties, the Republican and the Democratic. Each has liberal and conservative wings and a network of power based, at the local level, on municipal districts or precincts. The parties designate majority and minority floor leaders and party whips who manage the flow of legislation in Congress.

| Congressional Make-Up | House of Representatives | Senate |
|---|---|---|
| Total membership... | 435 | 100 |
| Number of members for each state... | According to population | 2 |
| Elected by... | Voters of congressional district | Voters of the entire state |
| Term of office... | 2 years | 6 years. Senate terms are staggered; one-third of members are elected every two years |
| Vacancy... | Filled by special election or at next general election | Special election or temporary appointment by state governor until special or regularly scheduled election |
| Session (regular)... | Meets Jan. 3 of each year | Meets Jan. 3 of each year |
| Presiding officer... | Speaker of the House | Vice president of the United States |
| Exclusive powers of each house... | (1) Originates revenue bills<br>(2) Initiates any impeachment proceedings<br>(3) Elects a president if no candidate has a majority of the electoral vote | (1) Approves or rejects treaties<br>(2) Tries impeached government officials<br>(3) Confirms or rejects appointments made by the president<br>(4) Elects a vice president if no candidate has a majority of the electoral vote |

and measures; issue patents and copyrights; make all laws necessary to enforce the Constitution and for the District of Columbia (which is not a state); provide for an army and navy; call out militia; and declare war.

# THE JUDICIAL BRANCH

The judicial branch of government interprets both the Constitution and the laws made by Congress. It is led by the Supreme Court. The court has nine members appointed for life by the president (with the advice and consent of the Senate).

The judicial branch can declare both actions of the president and laws passed by Congress to be unconstitutional and therefore null and void (in violation of the Constitution and therefore no longer in effect).

Below the Supreme Court are other courts with specific responsibilities. Each state has at least one federal district court and federal judge (appointed for life by the president, with Senate consent).

## Lawmaking

This chart follows a bill originating in the House of Representatives. Bills (proposed laws) other than revenue (taxes) can be introduced in either chamber, be suggested by committees, the president or other citizens and organizations. All follow a similar path.

| HOUSE OF REPRESENTATIVES | SENATE |
|---|---|
| 1. Bill is introduced, numbered, printed... | 4. The bill, now called an "act," is delivered to the Senate; here too, it is assigned to a committee... |
| 2. ... and referred to a standing committee which studies it and issues a report to the full House. The committee can ignore, revise, kill or approve a bill for full consideration "on the floor"... | 5. ...debated and voted on, killed or approved, perhaps with amendments. Since Senate and House versions must be identical, if amended it is referred to ... |
| 3...where the bill is debated and voted "for" or "against" passage. | |

### ...A CONFERENCE COMMITTEE

6...composed of equal numbers of members from each house. When differences have been resolved, the new bill goes back to both houses for approval...

7...and then to the president who may either sign it into law or veto it. Reapproval by two-thirds vote in each house overrides the veto. If the president does nothing, the proposed law takes effect 10 days later – unless Congress adjourns. Adjournment negates the entire legislative process and is called a "pocket veto."

# THE UNITED STATES COURT SYSTEM

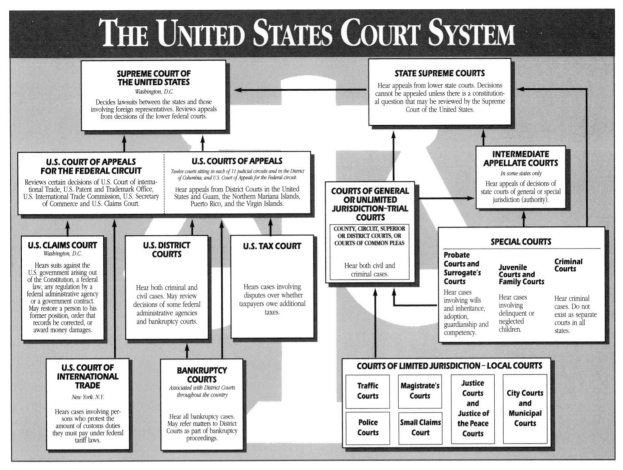

**SUPREME COURT OF THE UNITED STATES**
*Washington, D.C.*
Decides lawsuits between the states and those involving foreign representatives. Reviews appeals from decisions of the lower federal courts.

**STATE SUPREME COURTS**
Hear appeals from lower state courts. Decisions cannot be appealed unless there is a constitutional question that may be reviewed by the Supreme Court of the United States.

**U.S. COURT OF APPEALS FOR THE FEDERAL CIRCUIT**
Reviews certain decisions of U.S. Court of international Trade, U.S. Patent and Trademark Office, U.S. International Trade Commission, U.S. Secretary of Commerce and U.S. Claims Court.

**U.S. COURTS OF APPEALS**
*Twelve courts sitting in each of 11 judicial circuits and in the District of Columbia; and U.S. Court of Appeals for the Federal circuit.*
Hear appeals from District Courts in the United States and Guam, the Northern Mariana Islands, Puerto Rico, and the Virgin Islands.

**INTERMEDIATE APPELLATE COURTS**
*In some states only*
Hear appeals of decisions of state courts of general or special jurisdiction (authority).

**COURTS OF GENERAL OR UNLIMITED JURISDICTION–TRIAL COURTS**
COUNTY, CIRCUIT, SUPERIOR OR DISTRICT COURTS, OR COURTS OF COMMON PLEAS
Hear both civil and criminal cases.

**U.S. CLAIMS COURT**
*Washington, D.C.*
Hears suits against the U.S. government arising out of the Constitution, a federal law, any regulation by a federal administrative agency or a government contract. May restore a person to his former position, order that records be corrected, or award money damages.

**U.S. DISTRICT COURTS**
Hear both criminal and civil cases. May review decisions of some federal administrative agencies and bankruptcy courts.

**U.S. TAX COURT**
Hears cases involving disputes over whether taxpayers owe additional taxes.

**SPECIAL COURTS**

**Probate Courts and Surrogate's Courts**
Hear cases involving wills and inheritance, adoption, guardianship and competency.

**Juvenile Courts and Family Courts**
Hear cases involving delinquent or neglected children.

**Criminal Courts**
Hear criminal cases. Do not exist as separate courts in all states.

**U.S. COURT OF INTERNATIONAL TRADE**
*New York, N.Y.*
Hears cases involving persons who protest the amount of customs duties they must pay under federal tariff laws.

**BANKRUPTCY COURTS**
*Associated with District Courts throughout the country*
Hear all bankruptcy cases. May refer matters to District Courts as part of bankruptcy proceedings.

**COURTS OF LIMITED JURISDICTION – LOCAL COURTS**

| Traffic Courts | Magistrate's Courts | Justice Courts and Justice of the Peace Courts | City Courts and Municipal Courts |
| Police Courts | Small Claims Court | | |

## STATE GOVERNMENT

All state governments are designed along the same lines as the federal, with a constitution, an executive branch (headed by a governor), a bicameral or two-chambered legislature (except for Nebraska), and a judiciary.

Constitutions and patterns of organization differ but, in general, matters lying within its borders are the exclusive concern of each state. Matters that cross state lines generally become federal concerns. No state may adopt laws that contradict or violate federal law. No state has the power to conduct foreign affairs.

State services, paid for by state taxes, include: public health, education, welfare, and unemployment; conservation; highways; motor vehicles; corrections; professional licensing; regulation of agriculture, business, and industry. Protection of life and property is usually provided by a state militia (the National Guard, which can be called into federal service as necessary), state police force, and state highway patrol. State laws vary – what is legal in one state may not be in another. State laws take precedence over county, city, and municipal government laws.

## TRIAL BY JURY

The legal system is based on the belief that a person is innocent until proven guilty. No one may be convicted of a crime or made to satisfy a civil claim except by a jury of his peers. Almost all American citizens of legal age can be called to serve on a jury in federal, state, or local court.

There are two types of jury: grand and petit. The grand jury investigates and decides whether there is sufficient evidence for trial. If so, it indicts (formally accuses the person). The case then passes on to (petit) court for a trial by jury of 12 ordinary citizens.

If found guilty, the accused has the right to appeal. The case is then heard at the next higher court. The appeal process can continue up to the Supreme Court, which decides whether or not to hear the case. If it refuses, the most recent ruling stands. The decision of the Supreme Court is final.

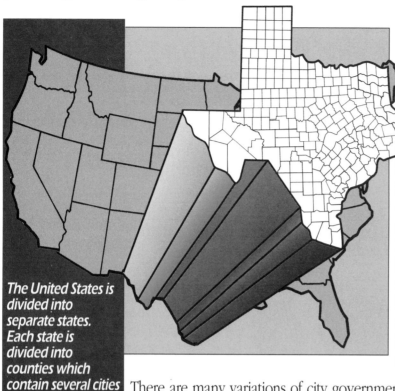

The United States is divided into separate states. Each state is divided into counties which contain several cities and municipalities. For example, the state of Texas has 254 counties.

# COUNTY, CITY, AND MUNICIPAL GOVERNMENTS

Counties are subdivisions of states, usually containing two or more cities, townships, or villages. Most have one town or city designated as the county seat, where county government offices are located. Two notable exceptions are the state of Louisiana and the city of New York. Louisiana's state law evolved as a result of French rule. For example, instead of counties they have parishes. New York City is so large that it has five subdivisions called boroughs, each of which is a separate county.

There are many variations of city governments. However, almost all have an elected council that acts as legislature (passing city ordinances or laws that must conform to state and national constitutions), an elected executive (mayor), and a court system.

Thousands of smaller town and village governments exist to meet local needs: water supply; street lighting and paving; police and fire protection; sanitation; health; schools; and taxes.

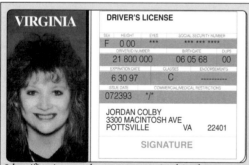

Identification cards are not required in this country, but some form of personal identification is often necessary. A passport or papers from the INS can be used for important matters (like signing a lease or opening bank accounts). A driver's license or a student identification card from a college is often all that is needed for routine purposes (such as cashing a personal check).

# LICENSES

Most licensing comes under state jurisdiction.

### Driver's license and vehicle registration

Each state has a Department of Motor Vehicles responsible for all automotive licensing and registration of both cars and drivers. Local branches are listed in the phone book.

A basic driver's license is generally available to anyone of age who can pass a written test on traffic law and a road test proving driving ability. Chauffeur (for private cars such as taxis and limousines) and commercial (for trucks and buses) licenses are available to drivers who pass the qualifying tests. Privately owned and operated driving schools will provide instruction for a fee if you meet state minimum age requirements (usually sixteen or seventeen). Driver's education courses are frequently available to students in high school.

Generally, a vehicle must be registered in the state where the owner resides. Many states require annual safety and pollution inspections. These inspections are available at local service stations, car dealers, or state-operated facilities. Most states also require insurance coverage. (See chapter *Insurance*)

*Note: Wearing seat belts not only saves lives but is required by law in many states. Children are often required to use state-approved child car seats. While the laws may vary, good judgment dictates that the driver and passengers wear their seat belts.*

*In addition, you may be fined, have your license suspended or go to jail for driving under the influence of alcohol.*

### Marriage licenses/family matters

Each state has its own laws and licensing regulations pertaining to marriage, separation, divorce, adoption, division of marital property, child custody, child support responsibilities, and related matters. Requirements for marriage licenses vary. The minimum age is usually 18. Anyone younger requires parental permission. Typically, the wedding must be performed by an authorized member of the clergy or a justice of the peace.

### Gun licenses

Many states require a license to own or carry a gun. Regulations vary with the type of weapon. Under federal law, guns may never be carried on planes, trains, or buses.

### Hunting and fishing licenses

Again regulated by states, these are seasonal permits varying with the type of game. They are available at municipal offices and often at stores selling hunting and fishing equipment. In many states, you must take a course and pass a test to get a hunting license. There are regulations (enforced by game wardens) as to the land and waters where you can hunt or fish, and the kind, size, and number of game animals, birds, or fish you can take.

### Pet licenses

Many states require owners to get their dogs or cats licensed and vaccinated against transmission of such diseases as rabies. Licenses are not required for most other pets, but annual vaccinations are recommended where appropriate.

Pets coming in from other countries are usually quarantined for a period of time to ensure that they are not transmitting disease.

### Liquor licenses

Liquor licenses are granted to restaurants, bars, and stores, authorizing them to sell alcoholic beverages.

Laws on the sale and the age of consumption of alcoholic beverages are regulated by states, counties, and municipalities. The most common legal age is 21. Liquor license holders are penalized for selling alcohol to minors drinking.

For papers and questions regarding immigration and citizenship, call your local Immigration and Naturalization Services office or speak with an attorney who specializes in immigration law. There are over 3,000 of them. Most belong to the American Immigration Lawyers Association (AILA).

For questions concerning your home country (passport, travel documents, tax liability), seek advice from your embassy or consulate. Virtually every country maintains an embassy in Washington, D.C. as well as consulates in some cities. (See Page L-7 for listings.)

## Notary Public

A notary public is a person licensed by the state to administer certain oaths, certify certain types of documents, and perform other similar acts regarding business and legal matters. They are not trained in the law and can not give any legal advice.

# YOUR RIGHTS AS AN IMMIGRANT

As an immigrant, you generally have the same basic rights under the Constitution as an American citizen – and the same obligation to obey the law. Federal law is universal, in effect throughout the nation, but there are variations in state and municipal laws and regulations. What is legal in one state or city may be illegal in another, especially where licenses are concerned. It is a good idea to learn something about laws and regulations that affect you.

Your right to sue in civil court, to correct or collect damages for a wrong done to you, physical or financial, is not affected by your citizenship. You can also be sued. Deportation, getting sent back to your native country, is not generally an issue in either civil matters or conviction of minor offenses (such as drunkenness, disturbing the peace, or petty theft).

If you are convicted of a major crime (burglary, robbery, rape, murder, or an illegal drug offense), you may be deported. Whatever the case, you do have a right to a hearing before deportation.

If you are involved in any litigation or charged with any crime, you have a right to a lawyer. You are not required to answer questions without one.

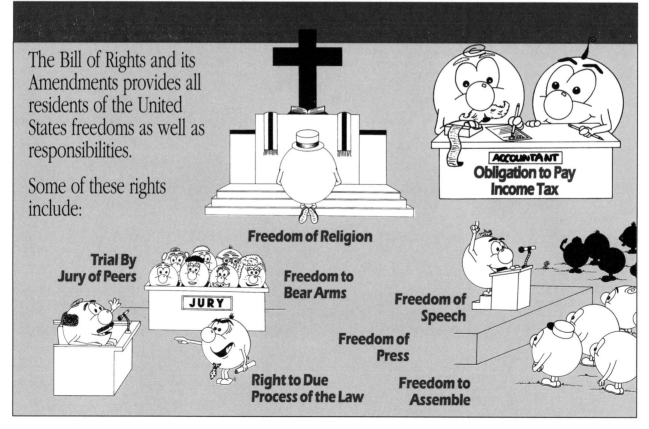

The Bill of Rights and its Amendments provides all residents of the United States freedoms as well as responsibilities.

Some of these rights include:

Freedom of Religion

Obligation to Pay Income Tax

Trial By Jury of Peers

Freedom to Bear Arms

Freedom of Speech

Freedom of Press

Right to Due Process of the Law

Freedom to Assemble

# ATTORNEYS

The United States has more attorneys than the rest of the world combined. Why so many? There is no one answer. Perhaps it is because we have so many laws to protect the individual or because life in this country has become fast - paced and complicated, or because our system provides a guarantee that each person can have their day in court.

Almost 600,000 attorneys, (also called lawyers or counselors) practice law here. About half are in "single" practice (without partners). The others are in law firms of two to 100 or more attorneys. Over 3,000 attorneys specialize in immigration law, and most of these belong to A.I.L.A. (The American Immigration Lawyers Association).

## When to use an attorney

Almost everyone needs an attorney at some point. General reasons to consult one includes:

### Buying a home

While not all states require you to use an attorney when you buy a home, it is advisable to do so, given the large number of legal documents involved. See chapter *Housing*.

### Starting a business

It is recommended that you have an attorney review any business documents before you sign them. An attorney can file incorporation papers; explain technical legal terms such as the differences between a corporation and a partnership, and advise you on relevant government regulations. See chapter *Starting a Business*.

### Marital situations

Legal advice is necessary in matters of divorce, separation, child custody and support, alimony, property settlements, and other marital problems. It is also advised for pre-marital contracts involving property rights and financial obligations.

### Significant financial matters

Consultation with a reputable attorney is advised any time you are involved in lending or borrowing large sums of money or filing for bankruptcy. It may not be necessary when taking out a small bank loan.

### Will preparation

While generally not required by law, an attorney is strongly recommended in the making of your will. This document

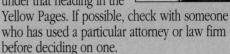

## How do you get an attorney?

Attorneys, (lawyers or counselors) are listed under that heading in the Yellow Pages. If possible, check with someone who has used a particular attorney or law firm before deciding on one.

Fees and methods of payment vary. Routine cases may be handled on a flat fee basis (a set amount to carry out a specific service). Attorneys may request a retainer (a fee to engage them) and subsequent payment by the hour, including time spent talking to you. In some civil cases, attorneys may charge you on a contingency basis requiring payment for services only if they recover damages (money) for you. You may still have to pay some expenses.

If you are accused of a crime, an attorney may be appointed for you by the court. There are federally funded lawyers to help in civil cases; you may be eligible. University students can often get legal assistance through their schools. There are also agencies that specialize in providing legal help to immigrants in deportation, housing, and divorce issues.

### Attorney qualifications

In virtually all cases, an attorney is required to have the following background:

- Completed four years of college and received a degree (diploma).

- Taken a special entrance exam for law school and completed an approximate three-year program at an accredited law school (recognized by the American Bar Association).

- Taken and passed a special state bar examination. This test takes two to three days to complete and is strictly monitored. The degree of difficulty varies from state to state.

- Passed a committee evaluation on their character and professional ethics for the practice of law.

- Received a license from the supreme court of the state in which they passed the bar exam. Attorneys can practice only in those states in which they are admitted to the bar.

## What are your legal rights if you are arrested?

The Supreme Court has ruled that immigrants, both legal and illegal, have the same rights as citizens.

If arrested you are entitled to:

- Receive written notice of your rights.
- Talk with a lawyer.
- Contact a diplomatic officer of your country.
- Make a phone call. It is advisable to call someone who can, in turn, make additional calls to obtain legal representation and money for bail. Bail is a bond paid as security to the authorities for your release from custody. It is retained when you comply with the legal process. Bail is generally granted if a judge decides you are not a danger to the community.
- Request a list of legal services.
- Get a hearing before an immigration judge prior to deportation.

provides for the allocation of all your assets (what you own, also known as estate) in the case of your death. Regulations and taxes vary by state. If you die without a will, the courts appoint an executor to manage the distribution of your estate. The cost involved may be deducted from your assets. In your will, you may also specify your funeral arrangements. You may also write a **living will** specifying your wishes if you are placed on artificial life support. (See chapter *Health Care*.)

### Personal injury

If you are injured in an accident, have had your property damaged by another person, or think that the actions of another person have harmed you, consider getting legal advice.

### Tax questions

Laws regarding the taxation of income, inheritances, sales of homes or businesses, stock market profits and losses, and medical expenses are complex. You and the Internal Revenue Service (IRS) may disagree on what you owe. Consider discussing any such questions with an attorney and/or an accountant.

### Criminal matters

Seek legal counsel if you are detained by the police or other government official.

### Immigration

The immigration process can be long and confusing. There are many people who are not attorneys who will tell you that they can do it cheaper, or offer to provide you with the papers you need, or have a friend at INS (Immigration and Naturalization Service), or have done immigration work for hundreds of people. It is considered much wiser to discuss matters with an immigration attorney rather than a non-professional.

## POLICE

There is no national police force in the United States. However, there are a number of federal agencies that deal with specific areas of crime and crime prevention. The Federal Bureau of Investigation (FBI) deals with certain federal crimes, including interstate crime, kidnapping, federal civil rights violations, and such domestic crimes against the United States as bombings. The Secret Service, part of the Treasury Department, has two primary roles: guarding the president and dealing with certain crimes such as counterfeiting. Other agencies, such as the Bureau of Alcohol, Tobacco, and Firearms, Drug Enforcement Agency (DEA) and U.S. Marshall's Department, serve other specialized functions.

Each state has its own police which serves under the direction of the governor. State

police are used in special investigations which cross county and city lines. They provide police protection in rural areas that may not have their own police force. They also assist local police with technology and manpower.

County police and sheriffs serve on a county basis. They work closely with local police and assist in intercity matters within the county.

Local police operate within an individual city. They are employed by the city and usually work under the direction of a chief of police who reports to the mayor or city council.

### The Role Of The Local Police

The average person has few dealings with the police, other than on a local level. The role of the police officer is to protect and serve. Policemen are often community members. They receive on-going training in both police work and social issues. The local police station generally provides information on adverse weather conditions, travel directions, and guidance in some areas of the law (but not legal advice).

### What To Do If Stopped By The Police

Police officers may stop and ask you a question or two only if they have specific reason.

If you are driving and a police car behind you puts on its red roof lights, the officer wants you to pull over. If this happens, DO NOT PANIC. Simply slow down and turn on your right directional signal. This will let the officer know that you realize he wants you to stop. Do not stop in the middle of the road. Pull to the right side of the road, as far as possible, and stop where it is safe.

Once you have stopped, REMAIN IN YOUR CAR. He will stop behind you. He will leave the police car and come to you. The officer will ask you for your driver's license and the registration (proof of ownership) of the car. If you are in a state that requires automobile insurance, you will also be asked for an insurance card, (see chapter *Insurance*). If you are driving a rented car, the rental company will have provided you with the necessary registration and papers, (usually stored in the glove compartment).

Be friendly and polite. Give the officer the necessary papers and advise him that you are a visitor from another country. If you do not understand what he is saying to you, ask him to please repeat his instructions.

If you are involved in an accident, do not leave. Remain at the scene of the accident. Ask someone to call the police for you. The police will come to the scene, provide all necessary assistance and write a report. Again, (see chapter *Insurance*).

## FIRE-FIGHTERS

Fire-fighters, men and women specially trained in fire-fighting and rescue techniques are prominent in every community. There are generally two types of fire departments:

• Those which come under the jurisdiction of local government and are supported by tax dollars, and

• Volunteer services, people in the community donate their time to the needs of maintaining the fire department. The funds needed for support come from private donations and fund raising projects.

Fire-fighters actively train in the latest fire-fighting and rescue techniques. They have knowledge in and practice CPR and advanced first aid. The equipment that fire-fighters use is specially designed to protect them from intense heat and smoke inhalation. (Boots and oxygen masks in particular were developed as a result of the equipment created by NASA for astronauts.)

In addition, fire-fighters participate in community functions and educate the public, particularly children on fire safety. See page H-12 for tips on fire safety.

Rapid changes in technology have permanently and radically altered not only the way that business is conducted in the United States, but the type of work available. Many new fields of opportunity have developed.

The face of the workplace itself has changed with increased computerization. Familiarity with the use of computers has become important at virtually all types and levels of employment.

Included in this section are techniques on finding employment in this new job market and essential information on starting your own business.

# TABLE OF CONTENTS

## LOOKING FOR WORK

## STARTING A BUSINESS

# LOOKING FOR WORK

You might arrive in the United States with company-guaranteed employment or sponsored by family. However, what about later on? What about your spouse? How can he or she find work? What if your job turns out to be less secure than you thought? What if you want to move on to better pay and more responsibility – or just to move on?

## EMPLOYMENT OUTLOOK

The changes in the way we do business have created many new fields of opportunity. In the employment opportunities section of any newspaper you will find dozens of new categories of employment that did not exist a few years ago. Positions with good wages are readily available in such fields as computer programming, electronics, telecommunications, film production, health care, travel, private education, data base

## Doing Business...American-Style:

• Americans believe in the value of hard work for work's sake, and are proud to show it. Demonstrate your willingness to make extra effort, to put in extra time at work, to participate in problem-solving. You will be rewarded. On the other hand, people who do not contribute to solutions, work only the hours they are assigned, and do not appear to be making extra effort are not valued, and are considered a burden to the company.

• Americans like to think that everyone should be equal; it is written in their Declaration of Independence, and laws exist in an effort to insure that everyone, despite the circumstances of their birth, has equal opportunity. While this is far from a reality, at work this means that differences in rank, gender, age, race, ethnicity, religion, etc., as well as special relationships between individuals, should never prevent individuals from demonstrating their competence to get the job done.

• Americans make a clear distinction between personal and professional performance. Your co-worker or manager may criticize your work, but then invite you out to lunch. You are expected not to take things personally at work. Professional criticism does not mean Americans do not like you personally.

• Work is a race against time. There are winners and losers. You are always expected to be a winner. Time is the one thing that must never be wasted: the one who does the most the best in the least amount of time wins.

• Americans can appear very friendly and easy to get to know at first, this is due to a combination of the immigrant background, the vast distances, and current advanced technology, which together makes for a very mobile and diverse population. Therefore, Americans have learned the value of casual relationships, often expressed by up-front familiarity and friendliness. Such behavior at work is not usually an invitation to a close, personal relationship, which, for Americans, takes just as long to develop as for anyone else. Casual friendliness, referring to everyone by their first names, disregard for formal respect of titles, etc. is merely an efficient way for Americans to get the job done.

For more information on Berlitz's Cross-Cultural Training Division see page C-5 or call 1-800-528-8908.

management, computer repair, accounting, and office management. There are good opportunities for unskilled and semiskilled workers in areas such as retailing, security, maintenance, manufacturing, transportation, and temporary services. Temporary services are positions that will last several months to several years. They are often good places to get exposure to employment and they can lead to a permanent position.

The new technology and economy have also caused a permanent change in the way people become and stay employed. Up until the early 1980s, the average person secured a position in a company and stayed with that company for most of his working life. Nowadays, most employees understand that they will probably have at least two careers. If you think about it, it is more stimulating to have two or three areas of achievement over 40 years of employment than one that lasts a lifetime. This also means that you will need to be retrained at some point in your career. Many large employers now understand this better than they did during the 1980s. In fact, career employment counselling and retraining are growing industries.

Another employment opportunity point to consider is geographic location. The United States is large and the employment situation in any one region may be different from that of another region. For example, the state of New Jersey has many corporations that deal in health care products and pharmaceuticals. Northern California, Massachusetts, and New Jersey have many computer industry-related companies. Many new automobile manufacturing plants have opened in states such as Tennessee, North Carolina, Ohio, and Kentucky.

## Who may work?

Immigrants who have become permanent residents of the U.S., identified by the Green Card issued by the INS, are allowed to obtain work legally; so are foreign nationals with visas that permit temporary employment. If you want to change jobs while on an employment-related visa, your new employer must take over sponsorship of your visa.

Other foreign nationals (non-immigrants) legally present in the U.S. may apply (using Form I-765) for employment authorization. An interview with an INS official is required in each case.

You will need a Social Security card in order to be legally employed. (See chapter *Taxes* for information on applying for a Social Security card.) Employers must file INS Form I-90 for all potential employees who are non-citizens to verify their eligibility for employment.

Women represent almost half of all employees. Many progressive companies and local communities offer services such as day care for children of working parents. (See chapter *Education.*) Increasingly, women are moving up the ranks of corporations and building successful businesses of their own. There are also many women who stay at home either to care for children in a traditional manner or for cultural reasons. However, the benefit of a second paycheck to finance a vacation or purchase a home or other luxuries is often welcomed.

## FINDING EMPLOYMENT

Getting work can be difficult. There are no guarantees of employment or success. We suggest a number of techniques, resources, and employment services that can be useful in your search. Basic to these is the proper authorization to work. During the job interview process, you will probably be asked to show a Green Card or a Social Security card and to fill out INS Form #I-9.

English is essential to your job search – and to any work outside your ethnic community. (See chapter *Learning English.*)

## TECHNIQUES

**Resume:** A resume is a brief description (usually one or two pages) of your work history and education. You will need to have a resume to apply for most jobs. For professional work (office, management, sales, and most skilled workers), it is a must. All prospective employers will require you to fill out an employment application. The same information that you would include in a resume will also be needed to fill out an employment application.

(For translation and evaluation of academic and professional credentials, diplomas and certificates, see chapter *Education.*)

**Cover letter:** It is important to send a cover letter with your resume. It is used as an informal way to introduce yourself. It also provides an opportunity to stress any important information you want to communicate. Match your skills to the job you are seeking. When possible, use the wording in the advertisement. (For example, "I have a background in..." or, "I have experience in...")

**References:** You will also need at least three and sometimes five personal references who have known you for several years. No matter what type of work you are applying for, you will be asked for these. References can include teachers, family

## Equal Rights Under the Law

The law prohibits employers from discriminating against anyone based on age, sex, religion, nationality, or any factors that do not impair the applicant's performance of the work for which they are applying.

## Blue-collar and White-collar Workers

**Blue-collar worker** refers to someone who performs manual labor rather than office work. It can apply to both skilled and unskilled workers.

**White-collar worker** is a general term for someone who works in an office. It refers to office workers who were once restricted to wearing dress white shirts while manual workers generally wore blue work shirts.

The terms are not considered offensive but are not used in employment advertisements.

## Newspapers, Journals, and Directories

Almost all local and regional Sunday newspapers have an employment opportunities section. Although you should check the newspapers daily, you should never miss the Sunday edition. The section is often in two parts, the professional opportunities and the general opportunities. Some newspapers have special days or sections for different areas of employment, such as accounting, computer-related employment, health care, or sales.

Trade and professional journals sometimes list positions available and specialized employment agencies and services.

Business and trade periodicals often publish directories of companies on a broad national and industry specific basis.

Check with your local library for journals and directories, such as the *Encyclopedia of Associations*, the *Directory of Directories*, *Polk's City Directories*, *State Industrial Directories*, and *Standard and Poors Industrial Surveys and Register of Corporations, Directors and Executives*.

friends, personal friends, previous employers, and colleagues. Family members are not accepted as references. Recommendations from previous employers are important. A good recommendation from someone who knows your work can be essential; a bad one disastrous.

**Job interview:** Let's say you wrote a good cover letter and sent it with your resume. What happens next? Very often, nothing at all. You might get a letter acknowledging the fact that you wrote. This is why you must send out several resumes each day. However, eventually, you should get a telephone call or a letter inviting you to an interview. The interview is a critical tool; how you present yourself, how you dress, the way you explain how your skills fit the job – all are important.

In many cases you will be sending your papers to a human resources manager (also known as personnel manager). In almost all cases you will be required to meet with the human resources manager. His opinion of you will weigh heavily in the hiring decision. During the interviewing process, you may also meet with several other employees to see how well you would fit within the company. While individual competence is important, the ability to work well with others at all levels is needed to succeed.

**Thank you note:** Always write a thank you note, no matter how well or poorly you feel you did during the interview. In a good interview it enhances your chances for success. In a weak interview it may earn you a second chance. It can give you an opportunity to call the Human Resources Manager or any other persons that you met during the interview process for advice. Even if you don't get an employment offer, it can be used as part of your networking efforts. Send the thank you note out as soon as possible to make the best use of it.

**Networking:** There is a saying that, "The best jobs go unadvertised." There is a good bit of truth in that statement. When you start looking for work, you will hear the term "networking." It simply means informally asking social friends or work-related acquaintances to provide the names of anyone they recommend you speak with for advice or help.

It is important to understand that you are not asking them to get personally involved. When you ask for the names of personal contacts you must communicate that, *"Of course, I won't use your name,"* or *"I'm not looking for your involvement."* In many cases, however, people will give you permission to use their name.

Networking works well because it doesn't put pressure on your social or work friends to help you. You must also respect the fact that they may be unable to help you for a variety of reasons. However, even if they can't help you right away, they may call you in the future with useful information.

**Cold calling:** Calling up personnel offices or places where you might want to work is another technique. Do not use it unless your English is fluent and you are confident you can do a good job of selling yourself.

**Employment offers:** If you have done your research, you should have a good idea of what the position you are seeking pays. Do not let a few dollars stand in your way of acceptance. Salary offers are usually quite firm. Overtime pay, while generally not given in management positions, is legally required for overtime work done by employees paid by the hour. Health care benefits are also a factor to consider. Many employers make at least a contribution toward health care insurance. This can be important when one considers the cost of private health insurance. (See chapter *Insurance*.)

## CROSS-CULTURAL TRAINING

For most people, learning to communicate in a new country means learning the native language – pure and simple. You will certainly find this to be true of your new life in the United States, where learning English well is essential to your personal and professional success. (See chapter *Learning English*.)

Real communication, however, is about more than just learning a new vocabulary. As the saying goes, it is not only what you say, but how you say it that matters. For example, expected levels of formality versus informality, gender roles, and business protocol vary from country to country.

All these cultural values and customs affect the way one communicates. To be an effective communicator in your new country, then, you should compare the culture and customs of your native country with those in the United States. You may even want to consider a cross-cultural training program. Berlitz, for example, offers programs entitled "Living and Working in the U.S.," which are custom-designed to reflect the viewpoint of any country of origin.

A good cross-cultural program will help alleviate the "culture shock" normally associated with moving to a new country. It should be general enough to help all mem-

### Suggested Readings

There are many good books available at book stores or libraries that have excellent examples of different types of resumes, cover letters, approaches to finding a job, and career opportunities.

We suggest the following to begin:

J. Michael Farr, *America's Fastest Growing Jobs,* JIST Works, Inc., 1994.

John W. Wright, *The American Almanac of Jobs and Salaries,* Avon Books, 1993.

Bob Adams, *The Adams Jobs Almanac,* Bob Adams, Inc., 1994.

Jeffrey G. Allen, *The Complete Q & A Job Interview Book,* Wiley, Inc., 198).

Asa Fisk, *You're Hired! A Complete Guide for Conducting a Successful Job Search,* Merechip Publishing Company, 1992.

bers of the family adjust to daily life, and specific enough to address the concerns of those entering the world of U.S. business. Such key functions as management and marketing, for example, may be carried out very differently in the U.S. than in your home country. (See *Doing Business...American Style* on page C-1.)

## EMPLOYMENT SERVICES

**Executive search firms** are retained by companies to find candidates for management positions. Some search firms specialize in specific areas, such as advertising, accounting, or engineering. Other search firms have a broader array of positions. Virtually all executive search firms are "fee paid." This means that the employer pays the search firm. It is very rare that the prospective employee pays the fee.

**Employment agencies** provide professional job search services. They match your abilities to potential positions. Some concentrate on local jobs, important if you want to stay in the same town. Others have a wider range. If you are willing to relocate, consider an agency with a national network. In some cases, the prospective employee pays the fee. It is not recommended to pay any fee in advance of starting a job. Be sure never to sign any agreement unless you have an attorney or someone who has experience in these matters advise you on what to do.

**College placement services** have lists of job openings of relevance to their students. Look for the *College Placement Annual.* It reviews occupational needs in business and government for college graduates.

**Computerized clearinghouse systems** listing job openings may be available through your library or local college.

**Specialized agencies** focus on particular types of jobs (domestic help, for example). Many recruit for office work. These will test your office skills (such as typing, computer data entry, and word processing).

**Temporary "temp" agencies** specialize in temporary employment. In this case, you are paid by the agency, not the company where you work. You are usually paid by the hour but do not get any benefits (such as health insurance) or job security. Depending on your contract with the agency, a permanent job may become available.

# RESUME WRITING

The resume is used primarily to screen employment applicants for meeting the basic mandatory requirements an employer needs to fill a position. It is also used as a fact sheet and as a reference to ask you questions about yourself during the interview.

A resume typically contains the following information: your name, address, a phone number where you can be reached, educational background, and your work history. Work history includes the month and year you started working and the month and year you stopped working for each employer. Your work title and a brief description of each position in which you worked are also needed. Be sure to include several examples of any important contributions you made during your employment. You should include any other different positions you filled in the same company if they are relevant. Examples of this include a promotion or transfer to a position that required supervisory work or a change in responsibility.

**Denise E. Burk**

96 Bastine Avenue • Donora, PA  15033  (412) 555-2116

**SUMMARY/EMPLOYMENT OBJECTIVE**

Hardworking, dedicated employee with more than 15 years of experience in various office positions.  Frequently promoted and assigned to positions of greater responsibility. Qualified in every aspect of business operation. Excellent phone, interpersonal, and organizational skills. Seeking hands-on, challenging work in secretarial capacity or office management. Willing to receive additional training.

**EMPLOYMENT HISTORY**

Store Manager - August, 1992 to present
Ripepi Winery, Monongahela, PA
  • Sold and marketed wine and related products. Handled all aspects of shipping, invoicing, and inventory.
  • Maintained detailed records in compliance with state and federal regulations.
  • Scheduled and hosted wine-tasting events for groups of all sizes.

Dental Assistant/Secretary/Receptionist - July, 1988 to July, 1992
Drs. Gardner and McCreary, Donora, PA
  • Assisted with all dental procedures.
  • Greeted patients; scheduled appointments; updated patient charts; ordered supplies; handled billing.

Front Desk Clerk - July, 1986 to June, 1988
Mon Valley YMCA, Charleroi, PA
  • Promoted from volunteer to paid full-time position.
  • Greeted incoming members and guests; booked facilities.

Clerk/Switchboard Operator - June, 1984 to June, 1986
The Valley Independent, Monesson, PA
  • Performed all general office duties including filing, typing, bookkeeping, etc.

**EDUCATION**

Diploma, June, 1984, Mon Valley Catholic High School, Monongahela, PA
Currently attending Pittsburgh Junior College, evening classes. Anticipated graduation date June, 1995.

**REFERENCES**

Harry Milch - Pharmacist
64 McKean Street
Donora, PA  15033
(412) 555-3050

Albert Hondler - Business Owner
822 McKean Street
Donora, PA  15033
(412) 555-5605

Try to be concise in describing your work experience. You will have ample time to emphasize your background during the interview. No more than three sentences should be used to describe what your work involved in any position. This, added to any specific achievements, is more than enough. Try to avoid too many technical terms as the interviewer may not know what you are trying to communicate. Be sure to include any awards or honors you have received.

You will also need to list your educational background. This includes any technical certificates or diploma's. If you are currently enrolled in any educational programs, you should include them and the date you anticipate completing the program.

You may include one or two hobbies or special interests at the end of the resume.  For example, playing a musical instrument, playing a sport, woodworking, or gardening.

In general, the resume should be no longer than two pages if you have five to ten years work experience.  If you are a recent university graduate or do not have much work experience, the resume should be only one page.

The printing of a resume is important.  There are many small printing stores that can produce several dozen high quality copies of your resume for ten to twenty dollars.  Many of them will store your resume on computer so you can create different versions of it, tailored toward particular positions.

There are numerous resume preparation services available, but their services may be expensive and unnecessary. It is not difficult to find several people who can help. There are many community programs that offer this type of information at evening classes in local schools. You can also find help at the local library, community center, or through volunteer groups.  We suggest you make a few calls if you are not sure what to do next.

# TIPS FOR A SUCCESSFUL INTERVIEW

**Dress:** Proper attire is a must. In management, a business suit and tie are required. Proper attire is also important for blue-collar work. Always make sure your clothes are neat, clean, and conservative. A good interviewer will notice your shoes and personal appearance.

**Practice interviews:** You will be asked many questions during the interview process. We suggest you rehearse for the interview. Many of the books on the recommended reading list have samples of questions you will be asked. Be sure you review them and have an appropriate answer ready.

**Research the company:** You should prepare for the interview by learning as much about the company as you can. The reference section of any local public library can assist you. If you are looking for work in a small company or trade, prepare yourself to discuss different aspects of the type of work you are seeking. Again, try the library for trade journals.

**Act interested:** Don't be afraid to get up and look at such things as charts, product samples, or anything that seems appropriate. Ask questions. Show a positive attitude. It is important in both the interview and the search for employment.

**Etiquette:** When you are introduced to the interviewer, make sure you:

- Stand up and firmly but gently shake their hands. This applies to women as well as men.

- Smile. A pleasant smile, not forced, helps set the tone of the interview.

- Look directly at the interviewer's eyes or face.

- Introduce yourself in a friendly and simple manner. If you didn't hear the interviewer's name properly, ask him to repeat it.

- When you sit down, be aware of your posture.

- Relax. The interviewer is a person and may be a bit nervous, too. He probably has a busy schedule to return to. Remember that the interview is a positive step toward a position. You would not have been called if they were not interested.

- Try to avoid answers that are very long or very short. Twenty-five words to answer a question is about right.

**Review what happened:** After each interview, think about what you and the interviewer did and said. Ask the interviewer if you may take notes during the interview. (A good interviewer will also take notes.)

# OCCUPATIONS EXPECTED TO GROW SUBSTANTIALLY OVER THE NEXT TEN YEARS

**Accounting and Bookkeeping:** This profession has historically had good growth as changes in tax laws, financial reporting standards, and investment analysis occur routinely. Accounting requires at least a college degree and ongoing training for advancement. As international trade continues to grow it is an advantage to be knowledgeable about international accounting practices.

**Computers, Computer Programming, and Computer Systems Analyst:** These areas continue to show incredibly strong growth as the demand for more, faster, and cheaper information continues to increase. There is a great demand for computer-related specialists in telecommunications, data communications, networking, health care, office management, factory automation, software development, accounting, scientific research, and many other fields. In large companies a college degree is required. Smaller companies tend to be less concerned about formal degrees and more interested in hands-on experience.

**Construction:** Carpenters, plumbers, masons, electricians, roofers, heavy equipment operators, ceramic tile installers, and other trades involved in both heavy construction and home building and repair are in strong demand. Tradespeople are traditionally very well paid. There are four good reasons for this solid growth.

- First, there is much new government investment in rebuilding or replacing bridges, roads, subways, sewage systems, water systems, airports, schools, and other major works needed to improve or maintain commerce.

- Second, there is a growing demand for new offices and factories that are "smart." "Smart buildings" are those designed with new materials and techniques that make them more energy efficient, functional, and able to meet the needs of the next generation. These buildings are also designed to include the latest electronics and computers that make them both more versatile and cheaper to maintain.

- Third, during the past few years the United States suffered a number of natural disasters. Buildings and other structures that were made using the newer methods and materials did not suffer much damage. The older buildings were not so fortunate. The repair and replacement of these homes and buildings continue today and will take at least several more years to finish.

- Fourth, as the economy moves forward, there is an increasing demand for new homes as families outgrow their homes.

**Education:** Good growth in employment opportunities for pre-school, primary, secondary school teachers and teacher aides is evident. Changes in child care responsibilities and arrangements are fueling this growth. Computer technology in the classroom has also created new and unique opportunities for both technically and non-technically oriented teachers.

**Engineers:** Demand for engineers depends on the area of specialty. Computer, chemical, civil, electrical, electronic, and aerospace engineers will experience good to very good growth. Other areas such as mining, nuclear, petroleum, and industrial engineering will not grow as fast. A college degree is required for advancement. It is also important to note that the number of engineers needed in the future is forecasted to increase while fewer students are enrolling in the engineering field.

**Health Care:** Demand for employees in all aspects of nursing, and X-ray technology, and as medical assistants, surgical technicians, dental hygienists, physical therapists, home health aides, EEG technicians, health services managers, and many other fields is strong. Professionals such as nurses, technicians, and other workers involved in the new technologies are in high demand and are well compensated. The population of the United States now has a large and growing segment of people older than sixty-five. For the next twenty years there will be a strong demand for persons that are trained in the health care field. Also, new techniques such as laser surgery have created a demand for more trained nurses and technicians. The way medical services are delivered is also changing. Hospital stays are becoming shorter as patients can receive their treatments at home where they are more comfortable. This means continued demand for nurses and technicians who will visit the patient at home. A college degree is not required for many entry level positions. There are also a number of technical schools that provide the appropriate certification. A college degree is often required for advancement. However, good wages can still be earned without a degree. Degree requirements vary based on the needs of the area. In some areas there are serious shortages of trained personnel.

**Hotel Employment:** The term "Hospitality Industry" is used for this field of employment. Both business travel and tourism continue to increase. This growth is expected to continue for the next seven to ten years. More hotels, motels, and restaurants are in the planning and building stages. This should continue to keep up the demand for all types of employment. While a college degree is very helpful, many managers and owners worked their way up from the ranks of clerks, housekeepers, waiters, and chefs. Wages of managers and workers vary widely. It should not go unnoticed that the tips a waiter receives can make for an outstanding wage.

**Landscaping:** Good growth is expected in this area as new construction of homes and offices continues to grow. Frequently, households with more than one wage earner do not have the time to take care of lawns and gardens. A substantial income can be made providing these services. In snowfall areas, landscapers can provide snow plowing as an off-season service, generating a significant income during the winter months.

**Life Sciences (agriculture, biology, environmental engineering, and chemistry):** These areas are expected to experience good growth in career opportunity. They all require a college degree for advancement. The increasing concern for the environment and new laws to protect and restore ecological balance are key reasons these professions are growing.

**Real Estate Management and Maintenance:** Good growth is evident in this type of work. The country's total of buildings and homes continues to grow. This creates a demand for managers, maintenance workers, and supervisors. Many small apartment complexes employ a custodian who lives rent free and may earn extra money for doing minor repairs. Large office buildings require skilled managers and well-paid maintenance workers to keep the equipment running.

**Restaurant and Food Service:** Employment in this industry varies from unskilled workers who earn a minimum salary to highly paid managers of sophisticated systems that prepare and serve millions of meals in as little as a week. A degree is helpful to enter the managerial ranks. Work experience and ability, however, can offset the need for formal education. Many owners and managers started at the lower levels. Even though wages are not high at the lower level, it has always been thought of as an ideal place to learn and earn. There are many success stories about people who came to this country, started out at the entry level, and now own several restaurants. Many people, now highly skilled and well-paid professionals, got their start serving fast food hamburgers. The restaurant and food service industry is expected to grow at a strong rate. Among the many factors in this growth, are working couples, the fast pace of life, and the demand for the meals prepared and eaten away from home.

**Visual Arts and Graphics:** Increases in the demand for more written and visual information, new consumer products and services, the rapidly growing number of television stations, and many other factors are contributing to the strong growth of this industry. Employment for both freelance and in-house artists is readily available. Here again, computer technology has taken a strong lead. The same factors that are causing the increase in demand also require computer skills to meet that demand. Even though the demand for computer-driven graphics is strong, there is still opportunity for the traditional artist. While earnings for individual artists vary widely, the average pay is considered good.

# STARTING A BUSINESS

The United States is a nation of corporations. Each year over a million new corporations are formed. Some have only one, two, or three owners, others have thousands of shareholders who each own a piece of the company. Owning your own business is considered another part of the "Great American Dream." Many successful American businesses, large and small, have been founded by immigrants. It is interesting to note that once a person has been in business for himself, he will rarely go back to work in a traditional employment position.

## WHAT IS A CORPORATION?

In simple terms, a corporation is a legal entity which allows the person or persons incorporating to act on behalf of the company rather than as individuals. The company is like a person; and they are its representatives or employees. This is done to help protect the persons as individuals. The individuals are not held liable if the business fails or if it is sued for damages by another person or corporation. The corporate structure, it should be noted, will not protect individuals from the consequences of any criminal actions. Without this protection from business problems or failures, no one would be able to conduct business affairs. They would be risking everything they own every time they made a decision.

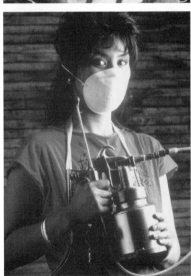

### How do you incorporate (establish a corporation)?

The best way is to consult an experienced attorney. Incorporation fees are not expensive. A simple incorporation should cost no more than three-to-five hundred dollars. (See chapter *Government* for information on how to select an attorney.) You will need to notify certain federal, state, and in some cases, local government offices that you are in business. You will also need a **Federal Identification Number**. (See page C-16 *"Banking Services for Business."*)

## THE BASICS OF STARTING A BUSINESS

There are a number of different ways to start a business and a number of well-written books, magazines, and periodicals available on the subject. All good sources should provide you with questions to ask

yourself and others before making any decisions that involve investing money; in particular, your money. Most books agree that the first step is to develop a plan. It should be kept in writing because there are too many details to remember. It can be written in a notebook you carry, produced on a computer, or be developed by a professional plan writer.

A plan is a road map of where you want to go. It does not need to be fancy. It needs to contain the questions you should be asking and any answers you have. You may have different answers from several sources to any one question. It is important to understand that not all the answers are available – this is part of the risk involved in starting a business.

Before you start working on your business plan you should do the following:

• **A personal assessment** to help you understand your goals and evaluate them to see if they are reasonable. This often consists of a series of questions to ask yourself. There are no right or wrong answers. Questions in this phase include: Why do you want to be in business for yourself? What are your qualifications? and What is your definition of success?

• **A general business assessment** to help you evaluate what is going on in the type of business or industry you wish to establish. Questions in this area deal with finding out if the business outlook is favorable or unfavorable in the area in which you want to compete. There are numerous government reports on the growth trends of almost every type of business. They are available to read or photocopy for a few dollars at almost any public library. Ask the reference librarian, who will be happy to assist you.

• **A general financial assessment** to evaluate how much money you need to invest in the business. How much money is usually required to start the business is an important question. This answer will come from several different sources: the reference library, industry publications and discussions with trade associations. Consider what will happen to you if you lose all your money. Financial caution is advised. A major reason that businesses fail is because they run out of money too quickly.

Once your overall assessment is complete, begin development of your plan. It should help you understand many of the details that need to be considered before opening your business. Keep the plan in writing: there are too many things to remember. Some plans take weeks to develop; others may take a year. It depends on your level of business and the complexity of the business you wish to enter.

### *Points to consider when preparing your plan*

#### *What is the market potential for your business?*

This area deals with the general need or demand for the product or service you intend to offer. Products (goods) are manufactured items such as dishes or paintbrushes. Service refers to work that is done for someone, like painting a house or a restaurant providing a meal. Consider the number of people already providing similar products and services, what they are charging their customers, and if the demand is growing or shrinking.

#### *Exactly what is your product or service?*

What does it do and how is it different from other things already available? Why will people buy from you and not someone else? Examples of some reasons are: your product or service may be cheaper or better quality, faster, more dependable, save the customer time and trouble, be easier for customers to find, or too difficult for customers to do by themselves.

#### *What major steps must you take before you can open your business?*

Are there any licenses or permits you will need to obtain from any government agencies? Your attorney, accountant, and local trade association can help you get started here. Will you need to purchase inventory or equipment, hire people, rent an office, store, or factory before you open the business?

#### *How will the company operate?*

What needs to be done to run the business? Consider all important activities and how you will take care of them: days and hours of operation, your sources of supply for equipment and inventory; the amount of merchandise needed; the length of time it takes to order and receive supplies, and, importantly, the steps you will take if anything goes wrong in any of these areas (contingency plan).

#### *How will the business be staffed and managed?*

In this section you will need to identify the people needed to work in the business. You will need to understand what their responsibilities will be, what qualifications are required, and what you will pay them.

## TYPES OF BUSINESS

There are more types of businesses in the United States than any one person can think of listing. For example, government publications available in any library have several thousand pages of types of businesses. Trade shows and expositions on business and self-employment are abundant. A visit to the library to look at the *"Directory*

## Be Cautious!

Franchising swindles (scams) do exist. Contact the Better Business Bureau and your state Attorney General's office for information on them.

Never sign anything until you have discussed it with your attorney and your accountant. Make sure you understand what legal rights you have before you sign the contract or any other document.

If you do not follow this rule, you are almost certain to become a victim.

*Many people start businesses in their homes. This is an excellent way to minimize expenses during the beginning months.*

*of Trade Shows,"* is recommended as there are 1,500 pages of shows covering every topic from baby care to funeral services. Three popular ways to get started in business are:

• **Part-time:** If you are working elsewhere but want to learn how a particular business operates, a good way is to work for someone in that field on a part-time (evenings or weekends) basis. You will gain hands-on experience and make some extra money you can save to start your own business.

• **Start a small business:** Many multi-million dollar businesses started out in someone's basement or garage, a small store, or even on a kitchen table. There are books and monthly magazines available that explain how to get started in areas such as: automotive care and maintenance, services to other businesses, food, retailing, personal services, publishing, sports, beauty and cosmetics, clothing, entertainment, home maintenance and repair, cleaning, landscaping and several hundred more types of small businesses you can start without having a large amount of money to invest.

• **Buy a franchise:** This is a popular way to start a business when you have some money available but lack experience in the industry. Franchising generally means buying the "rights" to an existing type of business such as a restaurant, beauty salon, car wash, employment agency, clothing store, or automobile repair shop. There are several thousand different types of business franchises available. Generally speaking, in a franchised business you pay for: the rights to use the company's name, advice on selecting a location, access to equipment and supplies you will need to open and maintain the business, the design and layout of the location, initial management and employee training, advertising and merchandising support and materials (you are required to pay for many of these), standard operations instructions and procedures, and purchase of supplies cheaper than you could get them yourself.

In exchange for these benefits, you generally pay a fee of anywhere from several thousand dollars (substantially more if you are buying a well-known franchise). You sign contracts that obligate you to maintain the business according to the company's specifications and to purchase virtually all your materials from them. Many companies (the franchisors) also charge you a percentage of your sales.

Both individuals and corporations buy franchises because they offer a good chance for success in many areas of business.

## When Buying a Franchise, Consider:

• **The risks involved.** Some franchises carry a greater degree of risk than others. Well-established, well-managed, and financially secure franchises are more expensive to purchase. Talk to other franchisees (people who have already bought a franchise from the same franchisor in a different location). Check with state agencies that monitor business complaints. Read the books available to help you evaluate your opportunity.

**What you are getting for your money.** Make sure you understand the materials you are given to review. There are laws that a franchisor must follow in providing much of the information you need to make your decision. Do not believe anything that is not in writing. It is advisable to ask any questions in writing and require written answers.

### Recommended Readings

The Editors of Entrepreneur, *Entrepreneur Magazine's 184 Businesses Anyone Can Start and Make a Lot of Money*, Bantam Books,1990.

*Franchise Opportunities 22nd Edition,* Sterling Publishing Co., 1991.

Greg Straughn and Charles Chickadel, *Building A Profitable Business 2nd Edition,* Bob Adams, Inc., 1994.

*Franchise Opportunities Guide,* The International Franchise Association, 1994.

## CUSTOMER CREDIT SERVICES

If you start your own business, it can be very helpful to extend credit to your customers so they can use it to purchase your merchandise, and afford larger purchases. Companies such as Beneficial Credit Services℠, can act as your credit department to provide credit for your customers, and to provide your customers with charge cards with your store's name on them.

The advantage of this type of program include:
- Increased sales for you.
- Charge cards that can be used only in your store.
- Additional credit that does not tie up your customers' other credit cards
- A better chance of getting credit approved than at a bank
- Added convenience for your customers, who might not be able to afford to make certain purchases without this additional credit.

Beneficial Credit Services also provides you with sales support materials and marketing programs, at no cost to you as a business owner, to help you increase your sales.

In order to receive more information on these types of business services, you can call your local Beneficial Credit Services office. They are listed in the white pages of your local telephone directory under *Beneficial.*

# BANKING SERVICES FOR BUSINESSES

**Checking Accounts:** Business checking accounts are similar to those for individuals but use the company name rather than the individual. Separate business and personal accounts are essential and particularly helpful when it comes to figuring out whether you made a profit or a loss and what you owe in taxes.

**Identification Numbers:** Banks and the government require businesses to have a identification number. If you are a sole proprietor with no employees, your social security number may be used as the Tax Identification Number (TIN). Sole proprietors, who employ people, partnerships, and corporations must apply for an Employer's Identification Number (EIN). To obtain any of these numbers, you or your accountant must contact the IRS and ask for form number SS4. The IRS will issue your number after receiving the completed form. For more detailed information call the IRS at 1-800-829-1040.

**Business Loans:** Financial terms for loans and credit lines vary from bank to bank. To get credit, you will have to clearly establish that your business will be able to repay the funds. The interest payments on business loans, in contrast to personal, are tax deductible.

**Merchant Credit Cards:** Ask your bank to authorize merchant credit card service for your retail business. It enables you to collect Visa and MasterCard credit card charges from your customers. You must obtain Discover and American Express card services directly from those companies rather than a bank. A small percentage of your customer receipts goes toward such services. It is well worth the investment for the extra customers the service will attract.

You may consider extending credit to your customers with your store's own credit card, which has your store's name on it. Companies, such as Beneficial Credit Services$^{SM}$ can act as your credit department, providing your customers with credit and a charge card. To apply, call the Beneficial office listed in the white pages of your phone book.

**Cash Management:** Some banks offer cash management services to their business accounts. For example, Overnight Investment Service, invests any excess cash you have in your account yet keeps that money available for your use. Access to your account through your personal computer is another example.

# Loans You Can Afford. Service You Can Rely On.

$500 to $500,000

Home Equity Loans

Credit Line Accounts

Personal Loans

Fast Service

Products listed above may not be available in all states.

The consumer finance subsidiaries of Beneficial Corporation have over 75 years experience, and over 1,000 local offices throughout the United States, United Kingdom, Canada, and Germany. Look in the white pages of your telephone directory for the Beneficial office nearest you.

## Beneficial®

Loans You Can Afford. Service You Can Rely On. ℠

# TABLE OF CONTENTS

# BANKING

American banking differs from that in most countries. There are several types of banks offering a variety of services. Their financial reserves and the national money supply are regulated through the U.S. Federal Reserve System which was created to avoid a concentration of financial power in any single central bank.

## TYPES OF ACCOUNTS

### Savings accounts

Several types of **savings** (deposit) accounts are available. With each, you deposit your money in the bank because it is protected there, usually insured by the **Federal Deposit Insurance Corporation** (FDIC), and because it earns interest – money paid to you by the bank for the use of your deposit money. The U.S. government regards that interest, if earned on a regular savings account, as taxable. How much interest you earn depends on the bank. Rates vary from bank to bank and on the type of savings account you choose. Before you decide on your savings account, ask about the interest rates and about any service fees that might be charged. Some banks require you to maintain a minimum balance in order to earn interest.

- With a **passbook savings account**, you are given a booklet (passbook) where your deposits and withdrawals are recorded.

- With a **statement savings account**, you are simply sent a regular record (monthly or quarterly statement) of your transactions.

- **Holiday savings clubs**, which require the weekly deposit of a specific amount to be made (supposedly for holidays), may pay rates comparable to your normal savings account – or may pay no interest, offering only a systematic savings plan.

- A **money market account** requires a higher minimum

## Protecting your money

The Federal Deposit Insurance Corporation (FDIC) is a government corporation that insures virtually all deposits at commercial and savings banks in this country.

All personal checking, savings, money market, NOW and CD accounts held in a single institution by the same owner are added up and insured for a maximum of $100,000.

IRAs and Keogh accounts (savings accounts used for the purpose of saving money for retirement) held in a single institution are also added up and insured up to $100,000. (See chapter *Investments*.)

For further information, call the FDIC Consumer Affairs Hotline: 1-800-934-3342.

## Minimum Balance

Maintaining a certain minimum balance (the smallest amount of money required to be kept on deposit) can reduce your bank fees and qualify you for free checking and other services. Depending on the bank, it is usually based on the average monthly amount in a single account or in some combination of your accounts at that bank. Some banks charge if the total account balance drops below a specified required amount at any point in the month.

## Interest and Penalty Fees

**Annual Percentage Rate (APR)** is the amount of simple interest you will have to pay on a loan. In many cases, a lender is required by law to inform you in writing the APR of the loan.

**Simple interest** pays a simple percentage. ($1000 at 8% annual interest earns $80.00.)

**Compound interest** pays more, adding the interest you earn to your first investment and then paying interest on that combined sum.

Interest can be compounded at various intervals - daily, monthly, quarterly, semi-annually. $1000 at 8% interest compounded quarterly would be $1020.00 at the end of the first quarter and $1082.44 at the end of the year.

**Annual effective yield** is the total amount earned, expressed as a percentage of your investment.

**Penalty fees** are fees that you may pay for withdrawing your money from a CD or IRA before the scheduled maturity date. Penalty fees are charged against the interest and should never be charged against the principal.

balance, but pays a higher rate of interest than the typical no-minimum-required savings account. There are also tax-free money market accounts, usually not FDIC-insured, where the interest earned may not be taxed by the government.

• Generally paying an even higher interest rate than a money market or a savings account is a **Certificate of Deposit** (CD). You buy it from a bank or a broker, usually depositing a minimum of $500. You commit to leaving it there for a specific length of time to earn the rate specified. You incur penalty fees on the interest if you withdraw your money early. Standard times for a CD are three months, six months, nine months, a year, and longer. If you do not notify the bank in writing when the CD **matures** (at the end of the time period), the bank can roll over (reinvest) the amount in another CD for the same length of time at the current rate of interest - which may be different.

Usually, the longer you commit your money to the bank, the higher the interest rate (special short term, high-interest CD's may be available). CD's are insured up to $100,000; interest on them is taxable.

• Taxes on the interest earned in an **Individual Retirement Account (IRA)**, on the other hand, are deferred until you reach age 59 1/2 or older. Specifically designed to help you save some of your present assets for retirement, there are various types of IRA. Some have fixed interest rates; others have investment options. All have tax penalties for early withdrawal. (See chapter *Investments.)*

### Checking accounts

A **regular checking account** earns no interest and has standard fees for services. These fees can be waived if you keep a minimum balance in the bank. You establish the account with a FDIC-insured deposit. Because you can get that money out on demand, it can also be called a **demand deposit account.** You write checks against it, authorizing the bank transactions you specify. A checking account, therefore, is also called a **transaction account.**

Checks are a convenient way to pay bills and far safer to use than cash. It is the bank's obligation to verify the endorsement signature before cashing it. Notify the bank immediately if your checkbook is lost or stolen – but if a forged check slips through, the bank is responsible for the loss. You can also ask the bank to stop payment on a check you have written to a person or company. There are usually some restrictions and a fee for this service.

**Overdraft protection** may be available depending on your credit standing with the

# CHECK WRITING

A check is a written order (today, a standardized form) to the bank to transfer an amount of money you specify to a person or business you specify. It must have:

- a date (stale checks, six months or more old, may not be honored by the bank)
- the name of the individual or business, written after the words "Pay to the order of." If you write "cash", the check can be used by anyone
- the amount, in both words and numbers
- your signature, corresponding to the signature verification card you signed when you opened the account.

Your account number, check number, and a check routing number are pre-printed in Magnetic Image Character Recognition (MICR) digits so the check can be scanned by bank computers. You may also order checks pre-printed with your name and address. This is convenient because most stores require that information on the check before they will accept it.

A person (or company) receiving a check must endorse (sign) it on the back, on the top left side. For safety reasons, he may also note "for deposit only" and his account number if he is depositing the entire amount of the check.

# TIPS ON BALANCING YOUR CHECKBOOK

RECORD ALL CHARGES OR CREDITS THAT AFFECT YOUR ACCOUNT

| NUMBER | DATE | DESCRIPTION OF TRANSACTION | PAYMENT/DEBIT (-) | √ T | FEE (IF ANY) (-) | DEPOSIT/CREDIT (+) | BALANCE |
|--------|------|---------------------------|-------------------|-----|------------------|---------------------|---------|
| | | | | | | | 829. 72 |
| 372 | 8/21 | Jones Real Estate Rent Aug | 250. 00 | | | | -250. 00 |
| | | | | | | | 579. 72 |
| | 8/22 | Mac. Withdrawal | 20. 00 | | | | -20. 00 |
| | | | | | | | 559. 72 |
| | 8/23 | Deposit paycheck | | | | 429. 70 | +429. 70 |
| | | | | | | | 989. 42 |
| 373 | 8/24 | Columbia Gas utilities | 47. 93 | | | | -47. 93 |
| | | | | | | | 941. 49 |
| | 8/25 | Bank Fee checks | 14. 00 | | | | -14. 00 |
| | | | | | | | 927. 49 |

REMEMBER TO RECORD AUTOMATIC PAYMENTS/DEPOSITS ON DATE AUTHORIZED.

- Make sure you enter every transaction – deposit or withdrawal. Do not forget your ATM transactions.

- Keep all deposit receipts until your monthly statement comes from the bank.

- When your statement arrives, it will show the transactions for the month. Check off each one carefully, making sure all transactions were properly recorded.

- Check all cancelled (processed) checks that return with your statement. Keep the cancelled checks as proof of payment in case of any dispute.

- Make sure the balance you show agrees with that of the bank. Take into account any checks that have yet to be processed. If the balances differ, try again. If you have any questions or problems with balancing your checkbook, your bank will be happy to assist you.

bank and if your bank offers it. With it, if you bounce a check (write one without the money to cover it), the bank will still honor it (pay the amount of the check). Without overdraft protection, the bank returns the check to the payee (person to whom you gave the check) and charges you and them an **insufficient funds** processing fee. Bouncing checks can seriously affect your credit reputation. It is also a crime to knowingly **issue** (write) **bad checks** (not covered by money in the account). People often bounce checks because they do not keep track of the checks they write. Keep your checkbook balanced.

A **Negotiable Order of Withdrawal (NOW)** account is a higher interest-paying checking account requiring a higher minimum balance than a checking account. Fees can also be higher than those in regular checking if that balance is not maintained.

An **investment account** allows you to write checks against the money in that account. While interest rates on these accounts can fluctuate (vary), they are usually higher than those in the accounts above.

Popular types of these accounts include:

• **Bank money market deposit accounts** require a large minimum balance. They may charge high fees if you fall below that balance and often limit you to three checks per month.

# ELECTRONIC BANKING

Enter ATM Card into machine.

Answer questions that follow.

Remove money and card from machine.

Electronic Funds Transfer (EFT) is a computerized way to automatically transfer money between accounts. It is used for:

• Direct deposit into your account of items such as paychecks, pension checks, investment earnings, or Social Security checks.

• Automatic withdrawals or payment of regular bills.

• Wire money transfers (including the American Express Moneygram, the Western Union Money Transfer, bank wires, and postal money orders) which can move funds within minutes, even internationally.

• The **Automated Teller Machine** (ATM) which gives you access to your account outside normal banking hours and locations. ATMs are found in or next to banks, supermarkets, shopping malls, and many other convenient locations. They enable you to withdraw cash, make deposits, transfer funds between accounts, and perform other banking operations. To use the machine, you need an ATM card (issued by your bank) or a major credit card (approved by the credit card company). ATM cards require a secret password, called a Personal Identification Number (PIN). A fee may be charged for ATM use. Check with your bank.

There are several ATM networks. Most banks belong to one of the two largest, Plus Systems or Cirrus. Other networks are Honor, Star, and NYCE. Citibank, part of Cirrus, has linked all its ATMs internationally.

*For personal safety, do not visit an isolated ATM alone.*

- **Money market funds** usually allow unlimited check-writing, but may require a minimum amount per check – $500, for example. These accounts, also subject to market rates, are available through hundreds of mutual fund companies, including MetLife. (See chapter *Investments.*)

- **Asset management accounts** require the highest minimum balance (usually $5,000 or more) and charge annual fees and investment fees. They offer unlimited check-writing and are available at many large banks and brokerage firms and include many other services.

### Special checks

The following checks can be purchased for a fee:

**Cashier's checks** (bank checks) are purchased from and guaranteed by the bank because they are drawn against its own account, not that of the individual. They are often recommended or required when large sums of money change hands (for example, an automobile or real estate purchase). An officer of the bank writes the check after you provide the valid funds (cash or direct withdrawal from an account at that bank).

**Certified checks** are personal checks guaranteed by a bank. You must have the amount of the check available in your account. The bank puts a hold on your account for that amount and stamps the check certified.

**Traveler's checks** are available from travel associations, credit card companies, and banks. They are issued in various amounts and currencies. You actually buy them from the issuer, signing each separate check before a witness. You sign each check again when you cash it. They are more widely accepted than personal checks and safer to carry than cash, because they can be replaced by the issuer if they are lost or stolen.

Banks also sell **money orders.** Used like checks, they are issued and guaranteed like traveler's checks. You buy them outright for amounts specified, plus a fee. Regarded as cash, money orders are accepted in some places where personal checks are not. You can also buy **international money orders** from the bank and mail them yourself.

**International money transfer service** may be of particular interest. Your bank wires the amount you request to an affiliated bank in the country you specify. That bank

### What to look for in a bank

Look at **services and interest rates.** They vary. Where branch banking exists you can get the same services at any branch of that bank - a significant convenience.

**Consider fees** such as ATM charges and checking account services.

**Consider location.** Where do you expect to utilize the bank most, nearer your home or your workplace?

**Bank hours** are also a factor. Most banks are open 9 AM to 3 PM weekdays. Some banks offer drive in window service until 6 PM. Some banks are also open Saturdays and selective evenings. Also, find out if the bank offers ATM (Automated Teller Machine) access after their regular business hours.

### Documents Needed To Open A Bank Account

To open a bank account, a passport and Alien Registration Receipt Card (green card) are essential. You also may need two additional forms of identification such as a driver's license, credit card, or other identity documents (school or employee identification card).

A Social Security card is often required. To get one, visit any Social Security Administration office or call 1-800-772-1213. (See chapter *Taxes.*) The Social Security number also serves as the bank's Taxpayer Identification Number (TIN). This number is required by the government for reporting earned interest.

*Exchanging foreign currency for American money can be done at most larger banks. See page D-9 for exchange rates.*

converts your dollars into local currency and makes it available to the person you designated. You pay a fee for this service (usually about $25). It generally takes a few days to complete the transaction.

# OTHER BANK SERVICES

### Loans

Banks have a variety of loans available. They will not let you borrow unless you are considered a good credit risk. You will have to prove sufficient income and collateral (assets) to be able to handle the loan. The bank will establish your amortization schedule (repayment plan, including the interest rate and the time period).

You can take out a personal loan to pay for education or to buy a car. If you own a home, you can borrow against it with a home equity loan.

Banks, investment, and finance companies, like Beneficial are all good sources of capital to the borrower. (See chapter *Credit and Credit Cards.*)

### Trust services

Available at many banks, trust services establish and manage trust funds (legal entities that manage money, securities or other property for the benefit of heirs, minors, or others unable to handle their own affairs).

### Safety deposit boxes

Banks rent locked boxes kept in a vault for the secure storage of important valuables or papers. They make rooms available to renters to put in or take out what they want in privacy. Larger storage vaults are also available from private companies.

# TYPES OF BANKS

Distinctions between banks and other financial institutions have blurred in recent years. Many banks now offer similar banking, insurance, and securities services.

**Commercial banks** typically offer the most complete service for the highest fees. They serve businesses and individuals from many convenient branches. Accounts are FDIC-insured for up to $100,000 per depositor.

**Savings banks** do not perform all the functions of commercial banks. Because their purpose is to encourage saving, they are also known as **thrift institutions** or **thrifts.** Usually state chartered, they pass on any profits to depositors as interest. Depositors have no power to elect officials. Individual accounts are FDIC-insured to a maximum of $100,000.

**Savings and loan associations (S & L's)**, also called **cooperative banks** or **mutual loan associations,** were originally set up to help people purchase houses. At one time, they were the major source of home mortgages. Today they offer a larger range of services. Most are federally chartered, insure accounts up to $100,000 through the Federal Savings and Loan Insurance Corporation (FSLIC), and are owned by their depositors. Once you deposit, you become a shareholder. You get your profit as interest on your account. In some cases, you may also help elect a board of directors which manages the bank.

**Credit unions** are **thrift associations** rather than banks. They are formed by groups of people with some common interest (such as working for the same company). They generally pay higher interest than banks, as they lack a profit motive. They pool their resources and make loans available (by law to members only) at low rates of interest. Many provide share drafts, written like checks, to pay bills. Individual accounts are insured for up to $100,000 by the National Credit Union Share Insurance Fund.

## Before you sign your name...

Almost all financial institutions (banks, credit card companies, investment houses, and insurance companies) are required by law to provide detailed information on the mutual rights and obligations involved.

When you sign your name, you guarantee that you understand what you are signing. It is important not to sign anything unless you do fully understand it. Do not depend on verbal statements. Only written material is valid in court.

Any complicated financial transaction should be done with legal advice. Simple matters can be explained by a financial planner or an experienced friend. However, even in simple matters, never sign anything if you have any question about it.

# U.S. CURRENCY

These illustrations of common U.S. currency are not actual size. They are presented for informational purposes only.

└ 1.9 cm. ┘

**Penny (1¢)** = *One Cent*

└ 2.1 cm. ┘

**Nickel (5¢)** = *Five Cents*

└ 1.8 cm. ┘

**Dime (10¢)** = *Ten Cents*

└ 2.4 cm. ┘

**Quarter (25¢)** = *Twenty Five Cents*

**One Dollar bill ($1.00)** = *100 Cents*

**Five Dollar bill ($5.00)** = *500 Cents*

**Ten Dollar bill ($10.00)** = *1,000 Cents*

**Twenty Dollar bill ($20.00)** = 2,000 Cents

**Fifty Dollar bill ($50.00)** = 5,000 Cents

**One Hundred Dollar bill ($100.00)** = 10,000 Cents

## How much is the American dollar worth?

The value of the American dollar fluctuates daily, as is the case with all currency. A specific comparison follows. For current exchange rates check with a bank or in the financial section of a newspaper.

### Exchange Rates for October 14, 1994

| Country | Currency | U.S. dollar equivalent |
|---|---|---|
| Argentina | Peso | 1.01 |
| Australia | Dollar | .7377 |
| Austria | Schilling | .09224 |
| Belgium | Franc | .03166 |
| Brazil | Cruzeiro Real | 1.2034 |
| Britain | Pound | 1.5855 |
| Canada | Dollar | .7401 |
| Czech. Rep. | Koruna | .035955 |
| Chile | Peso | .002464 |
| China | Renminbi | .115221 |
| Columbia | Peso | .001198 |
| Denmark | Krone | .1662 |
| Finland | Markka | .21059 |
| France | Franc | .19020 |
| Germany | Mark | .6515 |
| Greece | Drachma | .004259 |
| Hong Kong | Dollar | .12942 |
| India | Rupee | .03212 |
| Indonesia | Rupiah | .0004602 |
| Ireland | Punt | 1.5726 |
| Israel | Shekel | .3298 |
| Italy | Lira | .0006410 |
| Japan | Yen | .010048 |
| Jordan | Dinar | 1.4620 |
| Kuwait | Dinar | 3.3585 |
| Mexico | Peso | .2932981 |
| Netherlands | Guilder | .5817 |
| New Zealand | Dollar | .6057 |
| Phillipines | Peso | .03960 |
| South Africa | Rand | .2792 |
| South Korea | Won | .0012491 |
| Sweden | Krona | .1361 |
| Switzerland | Franc | .7823 |
| Taiwan | Dollar | .038153 |
| Venezuela | Bolivar | .00590 |

# INVESTMENT

When you save money by putting it in a bank you know your money is generally safe. However, over time, inflation will reduce the purchasing power of your money. Also, the interest earned in savings accounts can be significantly reduced by taxes and bank charges.

When you **invest**, you commit money for a period of time in order to earn a financial return. You also risk losing the money (capital) you commit. So why invest? To earn more money (get greater return) than you would through a savings account. The idea is to have a risk-and-return strategy consistent with your personal financial goals.

## FINANCIAL PLANNING

Before you invest, you need to analyze your present situation and your future goals. A good financial plan is a strategy to meet both your short-term and long-term goals and takes into account your current financial situation, future requirements and expected changes.

It should enable you to maximize your earning potential, help reduce your taxes, leave resources available for both expected and unexpected expenses, provide for your retirement, and address other personal issues.

To start, you should calculate your net worth, cash flow, and personal circumstances. **Net worth** is what you own (assets) less what you owe (liabilities). **Assets** may include money in savings and checking accounts, your home, car, and cash value of insurance policies among others. **Liabilities** include all debt such as mortgages, credit card balances, and car or personal loans.

What is your income and where does it go (**cash flow**)? Make a budget, estimating what you spend on essentials such as housing, food, transportation, utilities, telephone, clothing, medical expenses, and entertainment.

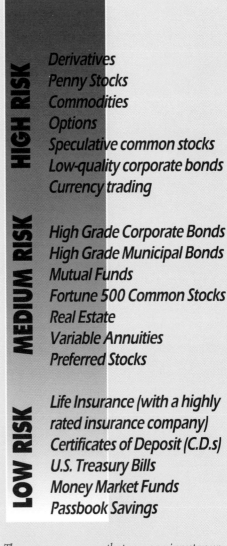

**HIGH RISK**

*Derivatives*
*Penny Stocks*
*Commodities*
*Options*
*Speculative common stocks*
*Low-quality corporate bonds*
*Currency trading*

**MEDIUM RISK**

*High Grade Corporate Bonds*
*High Grade Municipal Bonds*
*Mutual Funds*
*Fortune 500 Common Stocks*
*Real Estate*
*Variable Annuities*
*Preferred Stocks*

**LOW RISK**

*Life Insurance (with a highly rated insurance company)*
*Certificates of Deposit (C.D.s)*
*U.S. Treasury Bills*
*Money Market Funds*
*Passbook Savings*

*There are many ways that you can invest your money. The amount of return (profit) you make on your investment generally corresponds with the amount of risk involved.*
***Note:*** *Diversify. This means you should choose some low risk, some medium risk and some high risk investments.*

Then examine your personal circumstances. What are your current responsibilities and what will they be later on? What about your job security and your future prospects? How old are you? Have you planned for retirement? What personal factors (illness in the family or up-coming education expenses) might affect your resources? How much liquidity (immediate access to your invested money) do you need?

A cash reserve of two to six months is recommended to meet unexpected expenses. You might put it in short-term cash-equivalent investments like CD's or a bank account.

Before you invest, make sure you have a good idea of the balance you need between liquidity, safety, and the return you want to earn.

*Stock certificates, written records of company ownership, may soon be replaced by computer records. This has already happened to bonds in the U.S. as well as to both stocks and bonds in Europe.*

# SECURITIES

There are two basic kinds of investment: **debt instruments,** where you loan money in exchange for a promise of repayment with interest, and **equity instruments,** which represent some form of ownership.

## Stocks

**Common stocks** are equity instruments, small shares you own in a company. Their value fluctuates with the actual and perceived success of that business and with the general economy. You earn money through dividend payments received while you own the stock or by selling the stock for a **profit.** Your **return** (profit) is the amount of money you made from the sale plus any dividend payments (less any brokerage fees or commissions and the price you paid for the stock). A company may share part of its annual profit as dividends to you, but there is no guarantee that your investment will earn anything. You may lose the money you invested, even with honest professional advice.

**Preferred stocks** pay fixed dividend interest regardless of the market or value of the stock. While you may not earn as much as with common stock if the company does well, you get paid first and you may recover more of your investment than with common stock if the company fails.

Stock prices are based on their market value; what investors will pay. **Blue chip stocks** is the term for stocks of the biggest and best companies that have shown consistent profit. The term comes from the most valuable color of poker chip. The investor should be aware that companies dominant in industry attract competition. The competitors may become the blue chips of the future.

**Income stocks** show a pattern of regular high-dividend payment (useful for the investor's current income). They pay high dividends to attract investors and tend to be older (mature slower) in their growth. They tend to attract investors more interested in high cash flow than capital appreciation.

**Growth stocks** are the opposite. Growth companies generally reinvest most of their profits to expand their own business. They reward their **shareholders** (owners) through capital appreciation (long-term capital gains). Capital gains taxes are due only when the stocks are sold and the profits consummated (made by you selling your stock).

**Penny stocks** generally sell for under $5 a share. They are frequently start-up companies or those in a major period of change. Hence, penny stocks are considered speculative.

## STOCK BROKERAGES

You can only buy stocks through a registered broker. You pay a transaction commission for every purchase or sale regardless of whether or not you make a profit. The fee schedule must be disclosed to you.

**Full-service brokerage** firms have research departments and have investment executives to advise you.

**Discount brokerages** may charge 20 to 70 percent less on commissions than full-service houses, but generally do not give you investment advice.

## BONDS

All **bonds** are debt instruments, loans to (rather than ownership in) corporations or government. Ordinary bank accounts, money market accounts, and CD's are also debt instruments. Regular interest is paid on the bond for that loan. How much depends on the general economic climate and the perceived future of the borrower. If the company you invest in fails, you may lose your money.

**Corporate bond** interest is taxable but is a higher rate of interest than government bonds. Like stocks, they must be bought through a broker. Payment of interest and principal is the obligation of the bond issuer.

### STOCK SPLITS

A company may decide to split its stock to create more liquidity (more shares outstanding) and to reduce the price to put it in a more comfortable range for the average investor. A 2 for 1 split, for example, means you get two shares for every one you have at half the previous price. If the price goes back up again, so does the individual share value.

### MARGIN ACCOUNTS

A margin account uses leverage which allows you to purchase more dollar value of securities than you could with a cash dollar deposit. Your brokerage firm uses the securities as collateral to borrow the funds it is lending to you. Interest is charged on this loan.

This leverage allows you to control more securities. It increases your profit or loss depending on the outcome of the investment.

You can also use a margin account to borrow stocks before you own them to **sell short**, speculating you will sell at a higher price than you actually pay on the agreed date - you keep the difference as profit. These accounts are clearly not advised for inexperienced investors.

**Municipal bonds** (issued by state, county, or city governments) generally have less risk but pay at lower rates. Interest is federal income tax-free and can also be state and city tax-free.

**Junk bonds** are very low-rated corporate or municipal bonds that offer both high current income and high risk.

**U.S. savings bonds** give you a guaranteed rate of interest based on market rates if held five years. Buy them from banks or through payroll deductions. **Series EE bonds**

*U.S. Savings Bond*

are sold at a price lower than the full face value printed on them. At the time of maturity, you redeem them (turn them in) for the face value. They are usually purchased through a bank. There are no fees for the purchase or redemption of savings bonds.

**U.S. Treasury bills** are issued for 13, 26, or 52 weeks in lots of $10,000. Purchase may be made directly from the Federal Reserve Bank or through a broker or local bank. They are purchased at a discount to face value which is your interest received at maturity.

**U.S. Treasury notes,** are issued for two to 10 years. U.S. treasury bonds are long-term (10-30 years). They pay semi-annual interest which is taxable on your federal income tax return, but not your state income tax return.

**Federal agency bonds** are issued by specific agencies of the federal government in $1,000 investments. **"Ginnie Maes"** for example, are backed by the Government National Mortgage Association. They are sold at minimums of $25,000.

All treasury bonds are backed by the "full faith and credit" of the U.S. government and are sold directly (without any commission) by the Federal Reserve Bank or through your broker.

## MUTUAL FUNDS

Mutual funds offer the greatest diversity in investment. The money contributed by shareholders is combined and invested by expert fund managers. The prospectus information on the fund will state which types of investments are included in the port-folio. You, as an investor, are paid regular dividends and/or capital gains in proportion to how many shares you own in the fund. You can automatically reinvest your dividends back into the fund.

Individual mutual funds are widely advertised and can be purchased without going through a full service broker. You can simply call the given telephone number and buy shares. A registered broker, while not charging you a fee for advice, is still work-ing behind the scene. ($500 or more is usually required to start.) **No-load** funds charge no commission. However, there may still be fund management fees to pay. If you use a broker, expect to pay a commission (or **load**; **front-end** on purchase, **back-end** on sale of your shares). Brokers like MetLife Securities offer a wide variety of funds and can assist you in selecting the right funds for your goals.

Overall, mutual funds have a good record of safety, but they do range from very safe to very risky depending on the quality of stocks or bonds held. Some mutual fund companies specialize in one kind of security, others include literally hundreds of different investments. You should be able to read and understand the prospectus before you invest.

# FUTURES

Investing in the **futures market** (where trade in raw materials and financial investments occurs) is only recommended for experienced investors of high net worth. Types of commodities may include farm products, precious metals, petroleum – and financial instruments like stocks, bonds, and currencies.

**Options** on futures and on stocks are also traded. They are the right to buy or sell other **futures contracts** or stocks at a specified date and price. As the expiration date nears, the time premium declines. Hence, your entire investment is at risk.

**Trading** (buying and selling) in both futures and options is done through regulated options and futures exchanges. Investment futures and options trading can be only done through registered brokers.

**Hedgers** (people who produce or use particular commodities or investors who have big investment portfolios) trade in this market because they are interested in ensuring a future price, or the delivery of particular commodity, or because they want to lower the volatility of their investment portfolios. Speculators get involved because they consider the possible gain worth the risk.

# RETIREMENT PLANNING

### Individual Retirement Accounts (IRAs)

These are available to almost anyone earning income. They are opened through brokerages, mutual funds, insurance companies, and banks. As an incentive to save for retirement, the federal government defers taxes on IRA earnings until you reach age 59 1/2. You are first allowed to withdraw money without paying a penalty at age 59 1/2. At age 70 1/2, the government forces you to withdraw funds by placing a 50 percent tax penalty on the amount that should have been withdrawn according to **actuarial** (life expectancy) charts. You decide where your money is invested. You can transfer the account elsewhere if you do not like the **yield** (interest rate or return on investment) you are getting. There are restrictions:

• You are allowed to deposit up to $2,000 a year in an

## FINANCIAL PLANNERS

Professional financial planners advise individuals on personal financial analysis and investment strategies. Some are employed by banks, money management firms and insurance companies. Others are independent. Some are Certified Public Accountants (CPAs) or Certified Financial Planners (CFPs). CFPs are licensed by the International Board of Standards and Practices for Certified Financial Planners, Inc. (IBCFP).

### Do you need a financial planner?
Not if you fully understand your own circumstances and how investments work.

### How are financial planners paid?
Fee-only planners charge flat fees or hourly rates. Commission-only planners are paid a sales commission on the financial products they sell. Some planners are paid a combination of fees and commissions. It is important that you ask for and receive complete information on the compensation the planner will earn including incentives or bonuses for recommendations.

### How do you find one you can trust?
Here are three associations that will provide you a list of financial planners in your area.

**The Institute of Certified Financial Planners** They will also send you a pamphlet titled Selecting A Qualified Financial Planning Professional: Twelve Questions to Consider. Call 1-800-282-7526.

**The International Association of Personal Financial Planners.** Call 1-800-945-4237

**The National Association of Personal Financial Planners.** This association provides the names of fee-only planners. Call 1-708-537-7722.

### Check references
Check with people a planner has advised. Also check with the SEC (Securities and Exchange Commission), appropriate state agencies, the Better Business Bureau or IBCFP to determine if complaints have been filed against the planner.

IRA (or 100 percent of your income if it is less than $2,000 per year). Whether or not this sum is tax deductible depends on whether you or your spouse participate in another qualified pension plan and your income. Tax laws change frequently; as of this writing, income limits are $25,000 for single tax payers; $40,000 for married. You are responsible for knowing when you reach the maximum contribution. If you go over it, there is a penalty.

- If you make withdrawals from the account before age 59 1/2, you must pay a 10 percent penalty to the federal government - and taxes on the amount withdrawn.

- If you do not start withdrawing from the IRA by age 70 1/2, you must pay a tax penalty.

### Retirement plans

Similar to the IRA are several retirement plans that let you defer taxes on some of your salary until you retire or reach age 59 1/2 or in the event of permanent disability.

**401(k) Plans** are company-sponsored. Plans vary but are available to all qualified employees regardless of salary. The company establishes a separate account for this purpose and controls the investment options. The employee chooses from investment options offered in the plan. The plan itself may be administered by the employer. However, the funds invested are not available to the employer. Also, you make the investment decisions as to the type of investment option (stocks, bonds, savings plan). You contribute up to 10 percent of your pay up to a set amount. That amount is changed annually to keep pace with inflation. Your contribution may be matched by one from your employer.

**403(b) Plans** for employees of the government or tax-exempt organizations are virtually identical. (However, your contribution is limited to 25% of your salary, up to $9,500.)

**Keogh Plans** provide tax-deductible, tax-deferred savings for the self-employed. They can be complicated to set up. Professional advice is recommended.

Less complicated and serving the same purpose for owners of small businesses and the self-employed are **Simplified Employee Pension Plans** (SEP's).

## ANNUITIES

Savings plans, sold mainly by insurance companies such as MetLife, provide retirement income called annuities. A fixed annuity yields (pays) regular payments in a set amount to the purchaser (or annuitant).

If you buy a **life annuity,** payments stop when you die. If you buy a **life annuity with installments certain,** payments continue for your lifetime or for a specified number of years, whichever is longer. Your beneficiaries receive the payments if you die during the course of the policy.

**Variable annuities,** invested in stocks or mutual funds, can help protect you against inflation. Payments, rather than being fixed, depend on stock performance.

If you work for a public school system or a non-profit organization, you can buy another type of **tax-deferred annuity.** Its advantage is that you do not usually pay taxes on the income you contribute to the annuity until retirement.

## SOCIAL SECURITY

The Social Security System was established in 1935 as a response to the economic depression of the 1930s. Intended to help retired workers, the system requires paycheck contributions of all workers, Today, almost all Americans over 65 collect Social Security benefits. The retirees either contributed to the system through their own paychecks or are the dependents or spouses of someone who did. Divorced people can collect on the benefits of the ex-spouse if they were married for at least 10 years.

The amount received depends on the average of the contributor's 35 highest salary years, adjusted for cost-of-living increases. You can collect full benefits at age 65; 80 percent at age 62, but benefits increase the longer you work. You can continue to work even while you are collecting Social Security, but your benefits may be taxed.

### Recommended Reading

Ken and Daria Dolan, *The Smart Money Family Financial Planner,* Berkely Books, New York, 1992.

Janet Bamford, Jeff Blyskal, Emily Card and Eileen Jacobson, *The Consumer Reports Money Book,* ed. Consumers Reports Books, Consumers Union, Yonkers, New York, 1992.

Editors of Money Magazine, *Making the Most of Your Money Now,* Money Books, New York, 1994.

Patrick Naylor, *A Beginners Guide to Savings and Investing ,* Edition q, Inc., Carol Steam, Illinois, 1994.

# INVESTMENT TEST

The following is a list of some of the terms you should fully understand before investing your money in the stock market.

- ☐ American Stock Exchange
- ☐ Annual Report
- ☐ Annuities
- ☐ Arbitrage
- ☐ Ask
- ☐ Back Loaded
- ☐ Barron's
- ☐ Bid
- ☐ Broker
- ☐ Brokerage House
- ☐ Call
- ☐ Capital Appreciation
- ☐ Chapter 11
- ☐ Commodity
- ☐ Common Stock
- ☐ Consumer Price Index
- ☐ Discount Broker
- ☐ Diversify
- ☐ Dow Jones Average
- ☐ Dun and Bradstreet
- ☐ Economic or Investment Newsletters
- ☐ Federal Reserve Board
- ☐ Front Loaded
- ☐ Growth Cycle
- ☐ Leveraging
- ☐ Liquidity

- ☐ Margin Buying
- ☐ Moody's
- ☐ Mutual Funds
- ☐ NASDAQ
- ☐ New York Stock Exchange
- ☐ Over-the-Counter Stock
- ☐ Preferred Stock
- ☐ Price earning ratio
- ☐ Programmed buying and selling
- ☐ Put
- ☐ Return on investment
- ☐ Scams
- ☐ Securities and Exchange Commission (SEC)
- ☐ Selling Short
- ☐ Speculative
- ☐ Standard and Poors
- ☐ Tax Free Municipal Bond
- ☐ Wall Street Journal
- ☐ Warrant

# CREDIT AND CREDIT CARDS

**C**redit (the borrowing and repayment of money in small monthly installments over a period of time) is an important part of day-to-day life in the United States. Your **credit history**, the record of your own borrowing and repayment, is essential in this process. Anyone you bank or do business with becomes a part of your credit history. Information on how you pay your bills is provided to national credit bureaus which, in turn, give out the information to other businesses as requested.

There are three nationwide credit bureaus (TRW, Equifax, and Trans Union) and over a thousand local ones. Under the *Fair Credit Reporting* and *Fair Credit Billing* acts you have a right to know what they say about you. You can call the credit bureaus (telephone numbers are below) to see if you are listed and get a copy of your credit rating. Correct any errors you find in these reports as they can adversely affect your credit rating. The credit bureau will provide you with the instructions you need to resolve any discrepancies.

If you have had a serious problem with bankruptcy, financial court judgments or failure to pay taxes in the U.S., there will be a public record of it that affects your credit standing.

## HOW TO CHECK YOUR CREDIT

If you are planning a large purchase on credit, such as a car or home, it is advisable to check your credit rating to avoid any unpleasant surprises. It is not uncommon to find small errors on your credit history. However, a large error may cause you needless problems.

If you are rejected for credit because of information in your credit history, you have the right to look at your record within 30 days of your denial. Sometimes there is a small fee for this service, usually under $10.00.

The credit bureau must investigate and remove any item that cannot be substantiated. If a correction is required, you should also write to the two other major bureaus to be sure their records are accurate.

If a matter is not resolved and deleted from your record, you have the right to have a 100-word explanation placed in your file.

If a negative item is removed from your record, you have the right to have the credit bureau inform all credit grantors who received a report on you within the last six months.

The major credit bureaus will provide you a copy of your credit history regardless of the reason. To get a copy of your report, call them for instructions.

| | |
|---|---|
| TRW Credit Report Request | 1-214-390-9191 |
| Equifax Credit Information Services | 1-800-685-1111 |
| Trans Union Credit | 1-216-779-7200 |

Name of Credit Card Holder
Period card is valid through
Account Number
Bank Name Card is Issued Through

Type of Card

Decorative Holograph
for security purposes

## How do you choose a credit card?

Consider annual fee, grace period, finance charges (interest rates), acceptability and extra features. Cards are evaluated periodically by a number of reputable consumer magazines (*Consumer Reports* and *Money* for example).

Read the disclosure statement sent with every card–it must spell out the details of its financial arrangement with you. You are protected against billing errors and paying for faulty products if you report them within the time specified in the disclosure statement.

If your card is lost or stolen, report it immediately to the credit card company. You are usually not responsible for any charges. If you fail to report the card missing, you will have to dispute unauthorized charges in writing. Protection plans are available for a small fee that will cover any charges that result from a lost or stolen card.

### Extra features may include:

- Some offer additional cards for family members with no extra charges.
- Some automobile companies allow you to credit five percent of your bill toward the price of a new car. You can also earn frequent flier miles on certain airlines.
- Some cards give you automatic collision insurance and the lowest rates on rental cars.
- Some give you travel insurance and discounts guaranteeing the lowest prices on hotels and air fare or other additional benefits.
- Some offer shopping discounts, extended warranty, and even replacement of lost or stolen purchases made with your card.

## CREDIT CARDS

A credit card is a personalized plastic card which allows you to buy now and pay later. You cannot get a card without a good credit history. You use the card instead of cash or a check to pay for goods and services. Almost all businesses accept credit cards; some may require a minimum purchase amount.

Credit card use has become so widespread in this country that it is very difficult to carry out certain transactions without one (renting a car, reserving a hotel room by telephone, or buying an airplane ticket for example).

Four major credit cards are available to consumers through a number of separate providers. Visa and MasterCard are internationally marketed cards issued by individual banks directly to consumers. In addition, some credit cards are issued by companies such as Sears (the Discover Card) and American Express (Optima).

You can get cash advances with credit cards at an Automatic Teller Machine (ATM) or by using special checks supplied by the credit card company. You must request these special services. Cash advances may be charged interest at a higher rate than purchases. If you need to borrow a lot of money you will probably pay less interest with a bank than with a credit card.

Issuing banks have different annual fees and interest rates. You are sent a separate monthly bill for each credit card you have, detailing the charges for that month. You can pay the **balance** (amount owed) in full, or pay the specified minimum payment. A finance charge is applied to any unpaid balance and it is carried forward to the next month. The finance charge is based on the interest rate that the card carries. If you do not make the minimum payment on time, you are charged a late fee. Late fees can be costly and hurt your credit rating. If you are having difficulty in making your payments, you should seek help from a financial or credit advisor.

The **grace period** is the length of time between billing and payment due, before a finance charge is applied. It can vary, as do annual fees. Some cards charge an annual fee; some charge an annual fee only after the first year; some have none. Some "no-annual-fee" cards have no grace period. They begin finance charges at the time of purchase rather than after a month, even though they send you a monthly bill.

## TRAVEL AND ENTERTAINMENT (T&E) CARDS

American Express, Carte Blanche, and Diners Club are not actually credit cards. You can charge most of the same goods and services on these cards, however, you cannot carry a balance. You must pay off your charges completely every month. This has two advantages – you avoid all interest charges and you cannot overspend.

## SECURED CREDIT CARDS

If you have not established credit but want the convenience credit cards offer, a secured credit card is a good choice. Secured credit cards require a separate savings account which you draw against when you use the card. You must keep a balance in the savings account equal to your **credit line** (the maximum amount you can charge).

### Safety Tips

- Do not tell anyone your Personal Identification Number (PIN) - and do not write it where someone might find it. With some cards you are allowed to select your own PIN, which makes it easier to remember.

- Do not tell your credit card number to anyone unless you are placing an order.

- Make sure you get your card back after a salesperson uses it - and destroy all carbons to prevent use of your number.

- Personally destroy all cards when they expire and you get a new one.

- Keep a record of all credit cards you carry in case you have to report them missing.

### Credit Card Shopping – The Fair Credit Billing Act

This law allows you to withhold payment for unsatisfactory goods or services. Three conditions that apply are:

- You must show that you tried to resolve the dispute with the seller. This can often be done by letter.

- The purchase must have been made in your home state or within 100 miles of your billing address. In many states, mail order sales fall into the category of purchasing from your home.

- The item or service must cost more than $50.00.

This type of protection is another reason why credit card purchases are a wise way to shop.

### Unsolicited Goods

Federal law states that if you receive something by mail which you did not order, you may either refuse it or keep it as a gift. However, to avoid any potential problems, you should notify the company in writing that you did not order the merchandise and are keeping it.

# DEBIT CARDS

Some banks offer cards that work like checks. At the time of purchase, your account is **debited** (the amount of each purchase is deducted from it) and the money credited to the seller's account.

# OTHER CARDS

**Charge cards** are also offered by many retailers for exclusive use with that particular company. Department store and oil company cards are most common.

**Check-cashing cards** are not credit cards. They act as a form of identification for local stores such as a supermarket. They are necessary if you want to either cash a check or pay for your purchases at that store by check. You apply directly to each store for its card.

# LOANS

Virtually everyone needs to borrow money at different times and for different reasons throughout their lifetime. Where can you go? How much can you borrow? It depends on your credit rating, the type of loan you want and the purpose of the loan.

If you have a good credit rating, a bank will generally lend you money for education, personal use, home improvement or the purchase of a car or a home. You can also borrow money from a credit union which may be more flexible and offer lower interest rates than banks. However, by law, you must belong to the credit union before you can borrow money.

In addition to banks and credit unions, finance companies are one of the most popular places to borrow money. To be able to obtain credit, you will often need to establish a credit history (record of borrowing and repaying money). If you do not have a credit history, or if you have a high debt ratio (debts/income), you have a better chance of getting approved for a loan at a finance company such as your local Beneficial* consumer loan company.

The following are examples of good ways to establish credit and borrowing money that you should consider. If you would like any additional information you can call the Beneficial office nearest you. They are listed in the white pages of your telephone directory under Beneficial.

## Personal credit line

It is always advisable to have at least a small line of credit available in case of emergency or unexpected opportunity. This is the convenience that a personal credit line offers. In many cases, you can receive an approval the same day you apply for a personal line of credit. Once approved, you will receive an initial cash advance, and a special checkbook to use up to the limit of your personal credit line, which is usually about $3,000. There are usually no fees or charges for checks. And you pay interest on

*Beneficial is a registered service mark used by the consumer finance companies offering the services described in this section.*

your outstanding balance only, while the rest of your credit line remains available for you to use as soon as you need it.

### Personal loan

There may be a time when you will need a loan fast and cannot wait to visit with a bank to get the loan application forms, fill them out, and wait perhaps a week or more for an approval. In these cases, you can call a finance company such as your local Beneficial consumer loan company and apply for a loan over the phone. If you apply in the morning, you can often have your check by late afternoon. They can offer you a personal loan from $1,000 to $5,000 with a low monthly repayment plan. There are no application fees in most cases.

### Bill consolidation loan

Regardless of how careful you are, at some point in time you may have too many bills piling up. This is the time to consider a bill consolidation loan. By combining all your bills into one loan, with lower monthly payments, you can often pay noticeably less each month.

If you wish, an employee of a finance company such as Beneficial will review your current income and bills and discuss your future plans and credit needs. They can also explain how you can get a loan to pay off all your bills and lower your monthly payments. This way, instead of not having enough money to pay your bills each month, you may have extra money for your other expenses at the end of the month.

### Home equity borrowing

As time goes by, the value of your home generally increases. You can use this additional **equity** as security to borrow money. You may want to borrow money to repair or remodel your home. You may want to pay off your higher-interest credit cards, car loans or other bills at a lower interest rate saving you money on the interest you pay. You may want to borrow money for any reason. This can often be done by obtaining a **Home Equity Loan** or a **Home Equity Credit Line Account.** Because these loans are secured by your home, they generally offer a lower interest rate than other types of credit.

**A Home Equity Loan** often has a fixed interest rate based on the rates in effect on the date you borrow the money, and fixed monthly payments for the **term** (repayment period) of the loan. You receive the full amount of the loan immediately, at a competitive interest rate that is guaranteed not to go up. You can choose the monthly payment that best fits your budget. Your monthly repayment amount remains the same for the full term of the loan.

With a **Home Equity Credit Line Account,** you receive an initial cash advance and a special checkbook so you can write checks, up to the full amount of your credit line, as you need the money. Your interest rate and monthly payments will vary, based on the current interest rate at the time you use the money and how much money you use from the credit available in your account (your outstanding balance).

PHOTO COURTESY BENEFICIAL

# HOME EQUITY LOAN VS. HOME EQUITY CREDIT LINE – WHICH ONE IS RIGHT FOR YOU?

*Knowing the differences between a home equity loan and a home equity line of credit can save you money. Listed below are the features to consider.*

## Home Equity Loan

- You have expenses to pay immediately.

- You want the full amount of the loan immediately.

- You want a fixed interest rate and fixed monthly payments. This means your interest rate and monthly payments will be the same throughout the entire time of the loan.

## Home Equity Credit Line

- You want money available as you need it. You may use some of it now and more of it at a later date.

- You write checks from a special account when you need the money.

- You pay interest only on the amount of money you use. Your monthly payment is based on how much money you use.

For further information on these types of loans, call the Beneficial office nearest you.

# A SAMPLE OF CREDIT CARDS AVAILABLE THROUGH BANKS

Many banks offer Visa and MasterCard credit cards. There are five different categories of cards you may want to consider. The ones you select should be based on your personal circumstances. All of these banks offer a 25-day grace period for purchases. Some have annual fees. Some charge a fixed interest rate; others a variable rate. The interest rates that follow are as of September, 1994.

## Low interest rate standard cards

These bank cards are used when you will be carrying a balance (not paying off your bill in full on a month to month basis).

| Bank | Interest Rate | Annual Fee | Telephone Number |
|---|---|---|---|
| Citibank Choice | 6.9% | None | 1-800-462-4642 |
| Wachovia Bank | 7.25% | $18.00 | 1-800-842-3262 |
| Central Carolina Bank | 9.75% | $29.00 | 1-800-577-1680 |

## No fee standard cards

These are designed for persons who will be paying off their bill in full each month. They offer special benefits and discounts for using their card in addition to no annual fee. These benefits can include a percentage of whatever you charge and pay for being allocated toward the purchase price of a car (up to a limit) or free gasoline.

| Bank | Interest Rate | Annual Fee | Telephone Number |
|---|---|---|---|
| General Motors/HH Bank | 17.65% | None | 1-800-846-2273 |
| GTE Assoc. Bank | 9.9% | None | 1-800-638-3673 |
| Shell Oil/Chemical Bank | 16.4% | None | 1-800-373-3427 |

## Secured credit cards

These are designed for persons with no credit history or poor credit. They require a minimum deposit in a savings account for security. Your credit limit is restricted to that amount. There may also be additional fees for processing an application and other service charges. Also, you receive interest on your security money kept in the savings account.

| Bank | Interest Rate | Interest on Savings | Annual Fee | Telephone Number |
|---|---|---|---|---|
| Beneficial National Bank USA | 19.9% | 2.13% | $45.00 | 1-800-533-6234 |
| Bank One | 18.5% | 3.25% | $35.00 | 1-800-395-2555 |
| Signet Bank | 19.8% | 5.0% | $20.00 | 1-800-333-7116 |

## Gold cards

These are for persons with an excellent credit history. They usually require a minimum annual income and can offer special benefits.

| Bank | Interest Rate | Annual Fee | Telephone Number |
|---|---|---|---|
| Wachovia Bank | 7.25% | $28.00 | 1-800-842-3262 |
| Amalgamated Trust | 9.75% | $45.00 | 1-800-365-6464 |
| AFBA Industrial Bank | 9.75% | $35.00 | 1-800-776-2265 |

## No fee gold cards

These are also for persons with an excellent credit history and require a minimum annual income. They are for persons who will be paying off their monthly balance in full each month.

| Bank | Interest Rate | Annual Fee | Telephone Number |
|---|---|---|---|
| USAA Federal Savings | 12.5% | None | 1-800-922-9092 |
| Oak Brook Bank | 16.15% | None | 1-800-536-3000 |
| Bank of NY | 14.15% | None | 1-800-235-3343 |

# TAXES

Public taxes in the U.S. are not a new concept. The Office of the Commissioner of Internal Revenue was established by an act of Congress in 1862. Under the Sixteenth Amendment to the Constitution in 1913, the U.S. government can directly tax both personal and corporate income.

## FEDERAL INCOME TAX

Today's Internal Revenue Service (IRS) is responsible for administering and enforcing the internal revenue laws and statutes (except for those relating to alcohol, tobacco, firearms, and explosives). Headquartered in Washington, D.C., it stretches across the country through seven regional offices, 62 district offices, 10 service centers, and a compliance center in Austin, Texas. Part of its job is to educate the public and advise

## HOW ARE TAXES WITHHELD FROM A PAYCHECK?

TOTAL COMPANY
Myrtle Beach, South Carolina

PAY STATEMENT

| Social Security No. | Name | | | | | Pay Period | Pay Date |
|---|---|---|---|---|---|---|---|
| 100-00-0000 | BEARDON, JANE | | | | | ENDING 2/21/94 | 2/28/94 |

| Hours/Unit | Rate | Earnings | Type | Deduction | Type | Deduction | Type |
|---|---|---|---|---|---|---|---|
| 76 00 | 8 0000 | 608 00 REG | | 19 13 INSURANCE | | | |
| 8 90 | 12 0000 | 106 80 O/T | | | | | |

| | This Pay | Gross Pay | Federal Income Tax | Soc. Sec. Tax | Medicare Tax | State Income Tax | Local Income Tax | SUI/SDI | NET PAY |
|---|---|---|---|---|---|---|---|---|---|
| This Pay | | 714 80 | 70 58 | 44 32 | 10 36 | 20 01 | 7 15 | 1 07 | 542 18 |
| YTD | | 2274 00 | 231 18 | 140 99 | 32 97 | 63 67 | 22 74 | 3 41 | |

TEAR HERE

TEAR HERE

**Year to Date**

Pay stubs, such as the sample above, are usually attached to your paycheck. The style of pay stubs varies from company to company but carries the same basic information. The sample above demonstrates the information printed on a typical pay stub.

The employer withholds the money to prepay your federal and state taxes from every paycheck and distributes it to the proper government agencies. Local taxes may also be withheld from your paycheck; more commonly you are responsible for paying them yourself.

If you have questions on the way your pay was calculated or about the taxes withheld, speak to the bookkeeper or personnel department of your company.

Independent contractors (self-employed) pay a quarterly estimated tax; in effect, paying their own withholding.

## HOW TO GET A SOCIAL SECURITY CARD

Apply in person at a Social Security Administration (SSA) office. The address and telephone number can be found in telephone book white pages or by calling: 1-800-772-1213.

### Take:

- your original birth certificate or passport, and/or

- the **original documents** given to you by the Immigration and Naturalization Service (INS). Examples of INS documents are the Alien Registration Receipt Card (Form I-151 or I-551 and Form I-94.) Photocopies will not be accepted.

### Types of Social Security Card

- For U.S. citizens and permanent resident aliens, the card shows only the individual's name and Social Security number. It allows the person to work with no restriction.

- For foreign nationals admitted to the U.S. on a temporary basis, not for work reasons, the card is marked "NOT VALID FOR EMPLOYMENT."

- For people admitted to the U.S. on a temporary basis under INS authorization, the card is marked "VALID FOR WORK ONLY WITH INS AUTHORIZATION." These cards have only been issued since 1992.

Many hospitals help parents get Social Security cards for their newborn children. This is done for children of citizens and both legal and illegal immigrants. Most children born in the United States acquire their Social Security number this way.

taxpayers of their rights and their responsibilities. It encourages voluntary compliance with the Internal Revenue Code – and enforces it as needed.

By far the most important source of tax revenue is the individual federal income tax. You must pay it on all income – wages, profits, tips, and interest. You also may have to pay a **capital gains tax** from the sale of any property, including stocks and real estate.

Resident aliens are taxed like citizens; non-resident aliens are usually taxed only on income earned in the United States. The U.S. has special tax agreements with a number of other nations under which their citizens residing here are either taxed at a reduced rate or exempt from tax. Consult the local IRS office for assistance or call: 1-800-424-1040.

## STATE AND CITY TAXES

Some states and cities have income taxes that follow the same pattern as federal income tax and are also subject to prepayment through **withholding**.

When you get your first pay check, you will see that a portion of your income has been withheld (deducted). This is called withholding. This money has gone directly for federal income tax, any other applicable income tax, and Social Security tax (also called FICA – Federal Insurance Contributions Act). The percentage depends on how much money you make and how many dependents you have. You record the number of your dependents on a W-4 form when you first start working for an employer.

State and any city income tax returns are due at the same time as federal but filed on different forms. These forms are available at local libraries, post offices, and state and city offices. The tax rates vary from state to state and city to city.

## SOCIAL SECURITY

Social Security is a form of social insurance financed by both an employee and an employer tax.

Under the Social Security Administration; Social Security and Medicare taxes are deducted from the pay of about 95 percent of workers in America – and matched dollar-for-dollar by their employers. Your Social Security liability (what you owe) is based on your earned (wages and salary) income only. The tax rate in 1994 was 6.2 percent of gross salary on wages up to a limit of $60,600. Beyond that, you pay only the Medicare portion of the tax (1.5 percent of salary with no wage limit). Self-employed people pay a combined employee-employer tax rate. Interest and capital gains are not subject to Social Security taxation.

Social Security is not considered charity. It is the right of every working person. It provides these coverages:

- **retirement** – benefits paid monthly as early as age 62.

- **disability** – benefits paid monthly to workers of all ages who have a severe qualifying disability.

- **family** – benefits paid monthly to spouses, children, and dependent adults of retired and disabled workers.

- **survivors** – benefits paid monthly to the widow or widower and children of deceased workers.

- **Medicare** – for virtually all Americans over age 65, provides help with hospital bills and some nursing facility stays. You are also eligible if you have been on social security disability for 24 months.

## FILING YOUR INCOME TAX RETURN

April 15th each year is the deadline for filing income tax returns. In January or soon after, you receive a W-2 form

### How much tax should I have removed from my pay?

When you start a new job, you will be asked to fill out a W-4 form. This will determine how much tax is withheld from your pay. It is important to be sure that enough is withheld each pay period to prevent your owing tax at the end of the year.

The scale is based on your marital status and number of dependents. You can claim yourself as a dependent if you want less tax withheld, but this may not be enough to cover your liability for the year.

**EXAMPLE:**
M-1: Married with one dependent
M-0: Married with no dependents
S-1: Single with one dependent

### *What if I have too much tax withheld?*

You will get a refund on any overpayment of taxes when you file your federal, state, or local tax returns. Many people use this as a method of forced savings.

---

## W-2 Form

### W-2 Federal Copy

Form W-2 Wage and Tax Statement 1994 OMB No. 1545-0008
Copy to be filed with employee's Federal Income Tax Return.
Employee's and Employers's copy compared.

| 1 Control Number 001999 TX1 | Dept. 700 | Corp. | Employer use only A 27 |
|---|---|---|---|

2 Employer's name, address and ZIP code

ABC COMPANY
ANY STREET
ANYTOWN, PA 15000-1383

| 3 Employer's ID Number 25-1000000 | | |
|---|---|---|
| 4 Employer's State ID Number 251000000 | 5 Employer's SSA Number 100-00-0000 | |
| 6 Stat Emp. | Deceased | Pension Plan | Legal rep. | 942 emp. | Deferred Comp. |
| 7 Allocated Tips | 8 Advance EIC Payment |
| 9 Federal Income Tax Withheld 1939.22 | 10 Wages, tips, other comp. 24661.20 |
| 11 Social Security Tax Withheld 1529.02 | 12 Social Security Wages 24661.20 |
| 13 Social Security Tips | 14 Medicare Wages and Tips 24661.20 |
| 15 Medicare Tax Withheld 357.62 | 16 Nonqualified Plans |
| 17 See Instructions for Box 17 | 18 Other |

19 Employee's name, address and ZIP code

JANE DOE
MAIN STREET
SAMETOWN, PA 15000-1428

| 22 Dependant Care Benefits | 23 Benefits included in Box 10 | |
|---|---|---|
| 24 State Income Tax 655.58 | 25 State Wages, Tips 24661.20 | 26 Name of State PA W-2 |
| 27 Local Income Tax 246.66 | 28 Local Wages, Tips 24661.20 | 29 Name of Locality ANYTOWN |

You will receive a W-2 from your employer stating how much money you earned and how much tax was withheld from your pay.

The W-2 form comes in four parts. You must:

- Attach one part to your Federal Income Tax Return.

- Attach one part to your State Income Tax Return.

- Attach one part to your City or Local Income Tax Return.

- Keep the last copy for your files.

It is advised that you keep copies of all of your tax returns for seven years.

from your employer summarizing your earned income for the previous year (January 1 to December 31) and the amount of money withheld for taxes. You must make every effort to file your federal, state and local tax returns by April 15th. Mail them to the appropriate government office listed in the instructions provided with the tax returns. Be sure your envelopes are **postmarked** April 15th. (See chapter *Mail Service* for a sample of postmarked letters). If you cannot file your federal tax return on this date you must file for an extension by April 15th using IRS form 4868. You are allowed up to two extensions to submit your income tax. (first extension is for 120 days – August 15th; second extension is for the 60 days following the first one – October 15th). Interest is charged on any tax due during the extension period. Taxes due should be estimated and paid at the time the extension is filed to avoid interest and penalty charges.

You will also be sent 1099 Forms by your banks and investment companies summarizing banking and investment gains and losses.

Tax forms for use in filing are available at libraries, post offices, IRS offices – and by written and telephone request to the IRS. If you filed the previous year, the IRS automatically mails you forms.

The IRS will answer questions and assist you in getting forms and preparing your tax return. However, it is not responsible for any mistakes in that help or advice. Call: 1-800-424-1040.

Private accountants, lawyers, and specialized tax return firms (listed in the phone book) can be hired to help you get all your tax returns filed on time.

## SALES TAX

Federal, state, and municipal governments also raise revenue by taxing sales of certain consumer goods, especially gasoline, alcohol, and tobacco. Some states use a sales taxes instead of an income tax; others use both. Sales taxes may already be included in the price displayed or may be added at the check out counter.

Sales tax rates vary regionally within states and from state to state. Certain items (food bought outside a restaurant, for example) are frequently not taxed.

## PROPERTY TAX

In every community, land and the buildings on it are assessed (valued) for tax purposes. Rates on these assessments vary greatly across the country; generally, commercial property is assessed at a higher rate than residential. Property taxes are the usual source of support for public school education and services such as police, fire, sewage, and roads.

# CHECK LIST OF EXPENSES TO KEEP RECORDS OF THROUGH THE YEAR.

The following is a list of expenses that may be deducted on your federal income tax return. It is advisable to keep track of these expenses throughout the year. For further details you should consult an income tax professional or the IRS.

| *EXPENSE* | *PERCENT/AMOUNT DEDUCTIBLE* |
| --- | --- |

## MEDICAL EXPENSES
☐ Doctor bills, dentist bills, hospital bills, insurance premiums, eyeglasses, and medication . . . . . . . . . . . . . . . . . . . . .Any amount exceeding 7 1/2 percent of gross income

## TAXES
☐ Real Estate Taxes, Occupational Tax, or Personal Property Taxes. . . . . . . . . . . . . . . . . . . . . . . . 100 percent

## INTEREST
☐ Interest on mortgages and equity loans on homes . . . . . . . . . . . . . . . . . . . . . . . . . . . . . . . . . . . 100 percent

## CHARITY EXPENSES
☐ Charitable contributions (cash or property) . . . . . . . . . . . . . . . . . . . . . . . . . . . . . . . . . . . . . . . .100 percent
☐ Travel for charitable functions . . . . . . . . . . . . . . . . . . . . . . . . . . . . . . . . . . . . . . . . . . . . . . . . .2¢ per mile

## EMPLOYEE BUSINESS EXPENSES
☐ Employee travel (excluding regular commute to and from work). . . . . . . . . . . . . . . . . . . . . . . . 29¢ per mile
☐ Union dues . . . . . . . . . . . . . . . . . . . . . . . . . . . . . . . . . . . . . . . . . . . . . . . . . . . . . . . . . . . . . . . 100 percent
☐ Uniforms and Protective clothing (if not able to be used as regular apparel) . . . . . . . . . . . . . . . 100 percent
☐ Parking and tolls for business travel. . . . . . . . . . . . . . . . . . . . . . . . . . . . . . . . . . . . . . . . . . . . . . 100 percent
☐ Lodging for business travel . . . . . . . . . . . . . . . . . . . . . . . . . . . . . . . . . . . . . . . . . . . . . . . . . . . . 100 percent
☐ Meals during business travel . . . . . . . . . . . . . . . . . . . . . . . . . . . . . . . . . . . . . . . . . . . . . . . . . . . 50 percent
☐ Moving expenses (provided you stay with the same employer and the move is greater than 50 miles) . . . . . . . . . . . . . . . . . . . . . . . . . . . . . . . . .100 percent

## INVESTMENT EXPENSES
☐ Safety Deposit Box . . . . . . . . . . . . . . . . . . . . . . . . . . . . . . . . . . . . . . . . . . . . . . . . . . . . . . . . . . 100 percent
☐ Annual Fees charged by investment company if paid separately . . . . . . . . . . . . . . . . . . . . . . . . . 100 percent
☐ Investment interest deductions. . . . . . . . . . . . . . . . . . . . . . . . . . . . . . . . . . . . . . . . . . . . . . . . . . 100 percent

## MISCELLANEOUS
☐ Tax return preparation fees . . . . . . . . . . . . . . . . . . . . . . . . . . . . . . . . . . . . . . . . . . . . .100 percent deductible
☐ Casualty and theft losses . . . . . . . . . . . . . . . . . . . . . . . . . . . . . . . . . . . . . . . . . . . . . . .100 percent deductible
☐ Day care expenses . . . . . . . . . . . . . . . . . . . . . . . . . . . .credit up to $2,400 for one child or $4,800 for 2 children

**Form 1040EZ**

Department of the Treasury–Internal Revenue Service

Income Tax Return for Single and Joint Filers With No Dependents (T) **1993**

OMB No. 1545-0675

**Use the IRS label** (See page 10.) Otherwise, please print.

LABEL HERE

Print your name (first, initial, last)

If a joint return, print spouse's name (first, initial, last)

Home address (number and street). If you have a P.O. box, see page 11. Apt. no.

City, town or post office, state and ZIP code. If you have a foreign address, see page 11.

**Your social security number**

**Spouse's social security number**

See instructions on back and in Form 1040EZ booklet.

**Presidential Election Campaign** (See page 11.)

Note: *Checking "Yes" will not change your tax or reduce your refund.*

Do you want $3 to go to this fund? ▶

If a joint return, does your spouse want $3 to go to this fund? ▶

Yes   No

**Filing status**

1  ☐ Single   ☐ Married filing joint return (even if only one had income)

Dollars   Cents

**Report your income**

**Attach Copy B of Form(s) W-2 here.**

Attach any tax payment on top of Form(s) W-2.

Note: *You must check Yes or No.*

2  Total wages, salaries, and tips. This should be shown in box 1 of your W-2 form(s). Attach your W-2 form(s).   2

3  Taxable interest income of $400 or less. If the total is over $400, you cannot use Form 1040EZ.   3

4  Add lines 2 and 3. This is your **adjusted gross income.**   4

5  Can your parents (or someone else) claim you on their return?
☐ **Yes.** Do worksheet on back; enter amount from line G here.   ☐ **No.** If **single**, enter 6,050.00. If **married**, enter 10,900.00. For an explanation of these amounts, see back of form.   5

6  Subtract line 5 from line 4. If line 5 is larger than line 4, enter 0. This is your **taxable income.**   6

**Figure your tax**

7  Enter your Federal income tax withheld from box 2 of your W-2 form(s)   7

8  **Tax.** Look at line 6 above. Use the amount on **line 6** to find our tax in the tax table on pages 24-28 of the booklet. Then, enter the tax from the table on this line.   8

**Refund or amount you owe**

9  If line 7 is larger than line 8, subtract line 8 from line 7. This is your **refund.**   9

10  If line 8 is larger than line 7, subtract line 7 from line 8. This is the **amount you owe**. For details on how to pay, including what to write on your payment, see page 16.   10

**Sign your return**

Keep a copy of this form for your records.

I have read this return. Under penalties of perjury, I declare that to the best of my knowledge and belief, the return is true, correct, and accurately lists all amounts and sources of income I received during the tax year.

Your signature   Spouse's signature if joint return

Date   Your occupation   Date   Spouse's occupation

For IRS Use Only – Please do not write in boxes below.

For Privacy Act and Paperwork Reduction Act Notice, see page 4.   Cat. No. 11329W   Form

**1040EZ**

---

The following are samples of the forms to use when filing your federal income tax return.

Form 1040A (bottom) is used when you have deductions or dependents (exemptions) to claim. It is advisable to use an accountant or an income tax service when filing this form.

Choose form 1040EZ (left) when you do not have deductions or dependents. This form is simple and be completed without professional help.

For more information on deductions see page D-31.

---

**Form 1040A**

Department of the Treasury–Internal Revenue Service

**U.S. Individual Income Tax Return** (T) **1993**

IRS Use Only–Do not write or staple in this space.

OMB No. 1545-0675

**Label** (See page 15)

**Use the IRS label** Otherwise please print or type.

LABEL HERE

Your first name and initial   Last name

If a joint return, spouse's first name and initial   Last name

Home address (number and street). If you have a P.O. box, see page 6.   Apt. no.

City, town or post office, state, and ZIP code. If you have a foreign address, see page 16.

**Your social security number**

**Spouse's social security number**

For Privacy Act and Paperwork Reduction Act Notice, see page 4.

**Presidential Election Campaign Fund** (See page 16.)

Do you want $3 to go to this fund?

If a joint return, does your spouse want $3 to go to this fund?

Yes   No

Note: *Checking "Yes" will not change your tax or reduce your refund.*

**Check the box for your filing status** (See page 16.)

Check only one box.

1  ☐ Single

2  ☐ Married filing joint return (even if only one had income)

3  ☐ Married filing separate return. Enter spouse's social security number above and full name here. ▶

4  ☐ Head of household (with qualifying person). (See page 17.) If the qualifying person is a child but not your dependent, enter the child's name here. ▶

5  ☐ Qualifying widow(er) with dependent child (year spouse died ▶ 19 ). (See page 18.)

**Figure your exemptions** (See page 19.)

If more than seven dependents, see page 22.

6a  ☐ **Yourself.** If your parent (or someone else) can claim you as a dependent on his her tax return, **do not** check box 6a. But be sure to check the box on line 18b on page 2.

b  ☐ **Spouse**

c  Dependents:

| (1) Name (first, initial, and last name) | (2) Check if under age 1 | (3) If age 1 or older, dependent's social security number | (4) Dependent's relationship to you | (5) No. of months lived in your home in 1993 |
|---|---|---|---|---|
| | | | | |
| | | | | |
| | | | | |
| | | | | |
| | | | | |

No. of boxes checked on 6a and 6b

No. of your children on 6c who:
• lived with you
• didn't live with you due to divorce or separation (see page 22)

Dependents on 6c not entered above

d  If your child didn't live with you but is claimed as your dependent under a pre-1985 agreement, check here ▶ ☐

e  Total number of exemptions claimed.

Add number entered on lines above

**Figure your total income**

Attach Copy B of your Forms W-2 and 1099-R here.

If you didn't get a W-2, see page 24.

If you are attaching a check or money order, put it on top of any Forms W-2 or 1099-R.

7  Wages, salaries, tips, etc. This should be shown in box 1 of your W-2 form(s). Attach Form(s) W-2.   7

8a  **Taxable** interest income (see page 25). If over $400, also complete and attach Schedule 1, Part I.   8a

b  **Tax-exempt** interest. DO NOT include on line 8a.   8b

9  Dividends. If over $400, also complete and attach Schedule 1, Part II.   9

10a  Total IRA distributions   10a   10b  Taxable amount (see page 26)   10b

11a  Total pensions and annuities   11a   11b  Taxable amount (see page 26)   11b

12  Unemployment compensation (see page 30).   12

13a  Social security benefits   13a   13b  Taxable amount (see page 30).   13b

14  Add lines 7 through 13b (far right column). This is your **total income.** ▶   14

**Figure you adjusted gross income**

15a  Your IRA deduction (see page 32).   15a

b  Spouse's IRA deduction (see page 32).   15b

c  Add lines 15a and 15b. These are your **total adjustments.**   15c

16  Subtract line 15a from line 14. This is your **adjusted gross income.** If less than $23,050 and a child lived with you, see page 63 to find out if you can claim the "Earned income credit" on line 28c. ▶   16

Cat. No. 11327A   **1993 For 1040A page 1**

# METLIFE IS FISCALLY FIT.

Since security is the whole point of insurance, MetLife's top priority is to be financially secure, so we can be there when our customers need us, no matter what.

## GET MET. IT PAYS.®
✻ MetLife®

INSURANCE

# TABLE OF CONTENTS

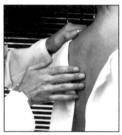

## INSURANCE

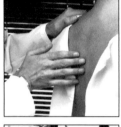

# INSURANCE

Insurance is protection against financial disaster. You pay a **premium** (scheduled payment) to an insurance company in return for the guarantee that you will be **indemnified** (paid in the event of a loss).

The major types of insurance are: life, health, automobile, and homeowners or renters.

## HEALTH INSURANCE

### Who needs it?

Everyone. The United States does not have a national health care plan. The cost of health insurance is the responsibility of the individual. Health insurance generally pays part or all of the costs of hospitalization, surgery, laboratory tests, medication, and doctors' bills. These medical services are very expensive. Without health insurance, you could lose your entire savings as a result of a serious illness.

Most health insurance policies carry a **deductible,** an amount of money you pay before an insurance provider begins coverage. Deductibles typically range from $100 to $1,000. The amount of your deductible is decided when you purchase your policy. Most health care policies pay only a percentage of the entire bill (80 percent is customary).

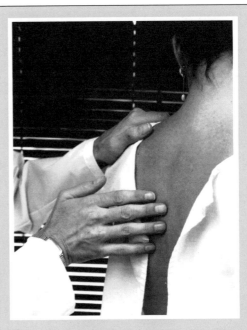

The Immigration and Naturalization Service (INS) does not require you to enter the United States with medical insurance unless you are a sponsored visitor (with a J-1 visa, for example). Some schools do insist on your obtaining insurance prior to registration. Ask your Association of International Educators (NAFSA) or your school itself for details.

### Who provides it?

#### Insurance companies

Private insurance companies (MetLife, for example) pay **cash benefits** (either a set amount or a percentage) to reimburse the policyholder for medical expenses. If those benefits do not cover the total costs of care, the policyholder is responsible for the difference.

#### Medical service plans

Medical service plans pay **service benefits** (direct payments to hospitals or doctors) for **reasonable and customary** (average) charges after the deductible has been paid. Medical service plans, unlike insurance companies, are nonprofit. Blue Cross and Blue Shield are the largest such plans in the United States.

### Health Maintenance Organizations (HMO)

An HMO is like a group medical practice (a medical office with a wide range of medical specialties). HMO members (patients) pay a fixed fee per month or per year. In return, the HMO doctors provide all necessary medical care at no additional cost. In most cases, the list of participating physicians is extensive. The HMO arrangement encourages doctors to provide preventative care and early treatment to avoid larger medical expenses later.

HMOs are sponsored by insurance companies, medical service plans, medical groups, foundations, employers, and communities. They provide a network of doctors and hospitals for participants to use. If you stay within that network, using the services of the participating doctors and hospitals, your expenses are usually fully paid without a deductible. If you go outside the network, coverage is limited. Some HMOs and PPOs charge a very small fee per visit to discourage unnecessary visits.

### Preferred Provider Organizations (PPO)

PPOs are similar to HMOs and are sponsored in the same way. They differ in that there are generally no central offices or owners. In a PPO, the insurance company has contracts with a large number and variety medical doctors and specialists. These medical professionals charge a negotiated (agreed upon) price for their services. In return for the negotiated price, the insurance company puts their name on the list of approved doctors that you may use and the insurance company will pay their fee. The list of approved doctors and medical professionals is usually very long and comprehensive.

### How do you get health coverage?

Most Americans who have health insurance receive it as an employment benefit. If you cannot get it that way, you can purchase it on your own. Independent coverage is the most expensive. The cost of a policy will depend on your age, your health, whether or not you smoke, the size of the deductible, and the number of dependents you include. Before you buy it, check to see if you are eligible for group health coverage. This is not only less costly to the individual but, it may cover dependents as well. Group plans are often available through associations or groups. Ask any association or group you belong to if they offer this benefit.

### What kinds of health care coverage are available?

Experts recommend that the following four types of coverage be included in your policy:

- **Hospital insurance** covers the cost of hospital room and board, operating room, laboratory tests, medication, X rays, and nursing service for a specified number of days annually.

- **Surgical insurance** covers a surgeon's operating fees – up to a reasonable and customary limit. Charges over that are the responsibility of the individual.

- **Outpatient insurance,** also called regular medical insurance or physician's expense insurance, covers physician fees for nonsurgical care in the doctor's office or hospital.

- **Major medical insurance** covers the costs of treatment for serious injuries or illnesses. Policies vary: some pay 80 percent of expenses; most have a deductible of $100 - $1,000 which you pay yourself. Anything over the deductible is paid by the insurance company.

*Optional coverages for dental, maternity, prescription drugs, and eyeglasses are also offered by various providers. Request these coverages if you anticipate the need.*

Your health care insurance carrier may provide you with an identification card which indicates the types of coverage you have as well as your policy number for billing purposes. Cards may also be issued to other members of the family covered under the policy. Carry your card at all times in case of emergency.

## PUBLIC HEALTH INSURANCE

- **Medicare** is government-provided health insurance for almost all persons 65 and older and for some disabled people. It provides hospital insurance (paid for through payroll taxes on both employees and employers). This helps cover the cost of hospital, rehabilitative nursing home, and at zhome care. It also provides supplementary medical insurance for doctors and additional medical costs. Medicare is financed through premiums paid by eligible recipients and by general tax dollars.

- **Medicaid** provides free government health coverage to the poor. Proof of need (low income and limited resources) is required.

## AUTOMOBILE INSURANCE

This insurance is required by law in most states. Those states that require insurance set a minimum level of coverage. You can choose to buy more. The amount and type of insurance coverage you should get depends on where you live and how much protection you want. There are five types of state liability insurance laws (featured to the right). Check with the Motor

## State Liability Insurance Laws for Automobiles

**Financial Responsibility Law** requires a minimum amount of liability insurance coverage applicable to death, injury, or property damage.

**Compulsory Insurance Law** requires proof of insurance as a condition of annual vehicle registration.

**No-fault Insurance Law** provides that if you are involved in an accident, you are automatically reimbursed for damages by your own insurance company regardless of who caused the accident. You do not need to go to court to prove that the other person caused the accident. This usually covers only bodily injury, not vehicle damage.

**Unsatisfied Judgment Funds Law:** Some states manage funds to cover pedestrians and others lacking no-fault insurance.

**Uninsured Motorists Law:** Some states require insurance companies to offer coverage against potential damage caused by motorists who are not insured.

**NOTE:** In states requiring it, you must have a valid insurance card in your possession in case of accident.

# WHAT TO DO IF YOU ARE INVOLVED IN AN ACCIDENT

If you are involved in an accident, call the police. They will get you any medical help needed. A police report is usually required for any insurance claim.

Remain at the scene of the accident. Anyone else involved should also stay. Write down what happened, including date, time, and road conditions. You have a right to see the insurance card of any other driver involved. Note the driver's name, address, insurance company and policy number. Then call your insurance agent as soon as possible.

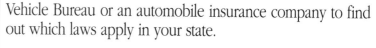

Vehicle Bureau or an automobile insurance company to find out which laws apply in your state.

## How do you get automobile insurance?

Look under that heading in the Yellow Pages for a listing of insurance companies. An agent will tell you about the minimum coverage required, if any, in your state. He may also recommend additional options.

## Types of automobile insurance

**Liability insurance** protects you (the policyholder) if you are responsible for an auto accident causing bodily injury or property damage. About half the states in the United States require you to have it to own or drive a car.

**Collision insurance** covers the car. It pays the cost of damage to your car if you hit something (another car or an object). Most people purchase it for newer cars.

**Comprehensive insurance** also covers the car, but for other kinds of damage (fire, flood, vandalism, theft, or other specified hazards).

**Medical payments insurance** pays for the medical expenses of the policyholder and passengers injured in an auto accident, regardless of fault.

Most companies offer a package policy that includes both property and liability coverage. Most also give you a discount if you purchase more than one kind of insurance with them (a policy for your car, for example, and another for your home).

The cost of automobile insurance (rate) varies from company to company and state to state. Rates depend on a number of factors: the age and type of the car you drive, where you live, how many people use the car, their ages and driving records, and your own age and driving record. The worse your driving record, the more you pay. The rates can go up if a driver causes an accident or is convicted of certain traffic violations such as speeding. Compare rates and benefits before you decide on a company. You can lower the cost of your premiums by taking a driver education course or by selecting a higher deductible (the amount you have to pay before the company does). A standard deductible for collision coverage is $250. You would pay that amount on any repair bill you claim; the company would pay the rest. If, instead, you chose a $1000 deductible, you would pay less for your collision insurance. Certain safety features in your vehicle, like anti-theft devices and airbags, can also qualify you for additional savings.

In states where insurance is required, your insurance company will provide you with a card that proves your coverage. Most states require you keep this card in the vehicle at all times.

### Drinking and driving

If you are found driving under the influence of alcohol or drugs, your auto insurance premiums will most likely be increased. Your license may also be suspended or revoked, you may be fined, required to attend a special educational program, or jailed. If you drink, do not drive. Appoint a "designated driver" for an evening out who will not drink.

### Seat belts

Wearing seat belts not only saves lives but is required by law in many states. In addition, children are often required to use state-approved child car seats. Laws may vary from state to state. Good judgment dictates that the driver and passenger should always wear their seat belts.

# HOMEOWNERS INSURANCE

### Who needs it?

You do, if you own a home, to protect your house and its contents. If you take out a mortgage (a loan to buy your home), the mortgage company will require you to have it. There are also homeowners policies for condominiums and co-operatives.

If you rent, you can also get a type of homeowners insurance called tenants or renters insurance to cover your personal property and provide liability coverage.

*Homeowners insurance protects your home and possessions from fire and theft.*

### What does it cover?

Homeowners property insurance policies vary. **Named perils** policies specify what they cover, such as loss from fire and theft. **Broad coverage** policies cover everything except what they explicitly exclude. Earthquake and flood damage are not generally covered, but can be for a larger premium. War damage, nuclear radiation, and "acts of God" are almost never covered. Special coverage can be obtained for valuables such as silverware, furs, jewelry, and other items. Homeowners insurance generally excludes coverage for liability of any criminal acts of the homeowner.

Homeowners liability insurance covers you in case of a lawsuit for damage or injury you may cause. It provides protection, for example, if someone is accidentally injured on your property. It may pay damages even if you are not sued. If you are sued, it pays the legal expenses and any damages awarded.

### How much coverage do you need?

Most insurance agents recommend that you insure for at least 80 percent of the replacement value of your home and possessions.

The cost of this insurance depends on the amount of coverage you want, the condition of your property, and where you live.

*Life insurance will help beneficiaries who survive your death.*

# LIFE INSURANCE

### What is it?

Life insurance is a way to replace the income lost to your family if you die. You pay premiums to the insurance company. After you die, the specified amount of money (the face value or death benefit) is paid to the beneficiary you have named. Some life insurance carries a double indemnity clause. This provides two or three times the face value of the policy if you die as a result of an accident.

### Who needs it?

You do, especially if you have people dependent on you for support. Businesses also buy it to cover essential employees or partners. In addition, some life insurance policies are used to save money.

### Types of Life Insurance

**Term life insurance** pays benefits only if the insured person dies within the term or period specified. It is the least expensive because it usually has no **cash value.** Cash value is the amount of money you can borrow against or collect if you turn in (surrender) the policy. Experts recommend it if you want coverage for a short time (perhaps until your children are grown) or if you have a limited budget. A major disadvantage is that if you develop a serious medical condition during the term, you may not be able to renew the insurance when the period is over.

The different types of term life insurance include:

• **Straight term insurance** which ends when the term is over.

• **Renewable term insurance** which lets you renew for additional terms. The cost increases with age. Compare it with **level premium** which is also renewable. Here, beginning premiums are higher, but they remain the same throughout the term.

• With **decreasing term insurance** the face value gets smaller throughout the policy period. You get most protection in the beginning years of the policy, less as you get older.

• **Convertible term insurance** enables you to switch a term insurance policy to whole life when the term expires.

• If you have a loan or a mortgage, consider getting **credit life insurance** to pay off the balance in the event of your death.

### Cash value insurance

• **Whole life insurance** provides coverage throughout your entire lifetime. Premiums do not increase with age as they can with term life; but they do cost more in the beginning. Whole life

## USING LIFE INSURANCE TO SAVE FOR IMPORTANT GOALS

Whether you are married or single, life insurance can be used as a way to save for the future. Whole life, universal life, and variable life, policies can accumulate cash value. The money is not usually taxable until you draw it out. It is often used as a supplement for retirement or for other purposes such as college tuition.

You can borrow from the existing cash value of your policy. The longer you have the policy, the more cash value it has. If you were to die before repaying the loan, your beneficiary would receive the face value of the policy minus the money owed.

policies can become significantly cheaper than term life over the years because the rates are fixed. Whole life insurance also has **cash value** which increases with the age of the policy. You can borrow against the policy or surrender it for that cash value.

- **Endowment life insurance** is primarily a means of saving. The policy matures (is paid in full) in 20 years or when you reach age 65. If you live until policy maturity, you collect the face value yourself; if you die, it goes to the beneficiary.

- **Universal life insurance** combines features of term and whole life insurance. It allows you to adjust coverage to fit your needs. You can change the proportion of term and whole life, the face value, and the amount you pay.

- **Variable life insurance** invests the cash value of your policy in one of the choices offered by the insurance company. The value of the policy reflects that of your investment. Usually a minimum death benefit is guaranteed regardless of market performance.

- **Universal variable life insurance** combines the last two types.

### HOW DO YOU CHOOSE AN INSURANCE COMPANY?

Check out the company's rating in Best's Insurance Reports. This is updated annually and is available in local libraries or by contacting:

A.M. Best Company
Ambest Road
Oldwick, NJ 08858
Phone:1- 908-439-2200

Look for a company with an "A" or "A+" rating.

## SOCIAL (GOVERNMENT) INSURANCE

Controlled by the government, social insurance provides benefits to the elderly; to unemployed, disabled, and sick workers and their families; and to families of deceased workers. It includes:

- **Medicare** – health insurance for almost all persons age 65 and older.

- **Social Security** which covers almost all U.S. workers. This provides benefits to retired and disabled workers and their dependents, and to survivors of workers who die.

- **Workers' compensation**, which all employers are required to provide, reimburses workers for job-related injuries and illness. It covers both medical costs and some income lost due to the accident or injury. It also provides death benefits.

- **Unemployment insurance** which is paid for by payroll tax on employers and employees. It provides cash benefits, usually for up to six months, to most workers who lose their jobs.

The process of deciding where to live and in what kind of housing must begin with an assessment of your income, your current and anticipated expenses, and your personal needs, including access to transportation.

The costs of housing vary greatly across the country, even within a given region. The same size house adjacent to a metropolitan area typically costs much more than the identical house in a rural area. This is true of both rental and real estate prices.

This chapter takes an in-depth look at those costs including mortgage, property taxes, and basic services.

# TABLE OF CONTENTS

## HOUSING

# HOUSING

Where you decide to settle may depend on where you enter the country, the location of friends and family, the work available, the type of climate, and the style of life you want. Life in a major city is vastly different from that in a small town or suburb. A city may offer greater intercultural sophistication, more work opportunity, and easier adjustment through its ethnic neighborhoods. Suburban areas may offer a more tranquil lifestyle, lower cost of living, and a faster way to becoming part of mainstream life.

Apartment

## BUYING A HOME

Part of the "American Dream" is owning your own home. In fact, about 60 percent of the estimated 100 million homes in the United States today are occupied by their owners. Over 50 percent of the immigrants who arrived here during the 1980s own their own homes. There are many psychological and financial benefits to owning your own home.

In addition to providing you a place to live, home ownership may be considered an investment. Your home's value usually rises over time. Also, the property taxes and the interest you pay on your mortgage is tax deductible.

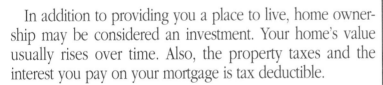
Duplex

While deciding where to live can be hard, the actual process of buying a home can be relatively simple. You will probably find a real estate agent invaluable, saving you time, matching your priorities to homes on the market, and assist-

Two story colonial

ing you in your transaction. The typical agency commission is six percent of the purchase price. This is paid by the seller and included in the selling price of the house. The typical real estate office has seller's agents. There are also buyer's agents who may work on retainer for the buyer, but this is not common.

A **real estate agent** is a professional licensed by the state to conduct transactions involving the buying, selling, and leasing of property. He is required to work for a **real estate broker** who is also licensed by the state. A broker has had more specific real estate education and is generally more experienced than an agent. A broker may

Split entry with integral garage

Two story with attached garage

Two story with attached garage

Ranch house with integral garage

Town Houses

be independent or work for a large real estate chain. He may have several agents working under him in either case.

In many states, you will need an attorney to review all documents and contracts before you sign them and to be present at the closing.

### Things to consider when buying a house

*In what type of neighborhood is the house located?* The location of the house significantly affects its current and future value. Things to consider are: access to quality schools, work, shopping, major roads, and transportation; noise levels; the value of other houses in the area; and zoning laws on the kind of building permitted (commercial or residential, for example) and their styles.

*What features should you look for in your house?* The size of what you want is often based on the size of your family. Consider the number and size of bedrooms and bathrooms you need to fit both your immediate and future needs, the room layout or floor plan, the overall appearance, the need for maintenance, and the possibilities for improvement or expansion. Do not consider houses in need of more than minor repair or extensive maintenance unless you are experienced in such areas.

**Property taxes** are a major consideration. They are a matter of public record on any house. While the amount can be disputed by legal means, it is not often lowered. Property taxes must be paid. Failure to do so can result in government seizure of the property.

### How to start looking for a house

The best way to start is by taking a ride through various towns you are considering. Pick up local Sunday and weekly newspapers and some of the free local booklets advertising homes in the area. These are often found in stores and supermarkets. These sources provide pictures and prices of many of the houses available for sale in the area and the names of real estate agencies **listing** (representing) them.

Next, call a real estate agent to make an appointment to see a particular house or two. You may also find an agency from the "For Sale" sign in front of a house. Once you meet with an agent, he will provide you with listings of other houses that might fit your needs.

In the real estate section of the newspaper you will also find houses that are listed with an "Open House" date. This means that the house is open to the public and that a real estate agent or the homeowner will be in the house to provide information. This is a good way to gain insight into housing in the area.

### How do you know what a house is worth?

The last price paid for a house is a matter of public record. However, it may have little bearing on what that house is worth today. What you need is a comparison of that house with others like it that have been recently sold. This can be provided by a real estate agent who looks at details on the size of the lot, the number of rooms, age, and other features, then arrives at a price range. This information is available in listing books and on computer for any houses currently put on the market by real estate agencies.

*Your bank or a mortgage broker can help you in obtaining a mortgage.*

### Mortgages

It is extremely rare for a buyer to pay in full for the purchase of a home. Typically, he takes out a mortgage, a loan made specifically for the purchase of real estate, using that real estate as collateral for the loan. The total cost of a mortgage depends on the amount of the loan (principal), the length of the loan (**term:** 15, 20, or 30 years are most often used), the interest rate (which may be fixed for the entire term or adjustable periodically), the points (prepaid interest: one point is one percent of the mortgage amount) paid at closing, and other fees the lender requires.

### Qualifying for a mortgage

The typical buyer can afford a house costing about two-and-a-half times his annual income. **Mortgage brokers** (who specialize in getting people such loans) often use a "28/36" qualifying ratio to determine if you can make the expected payments on a mortgage and keep up with your other expenses as well. The assumption behind the ratio is that you can spend 28 percent of your gross monthly income on the mortgage, and property taxes. The ratio also assumes that all of your monthly loan payments (car, mortgage, and personal loans for example) as well as credit card payments, are under 36 percent of your income.

### Where do you get a mortgage?

Your real estate agent can give you the names of mortgage brokers to help you find a mortgage. Your own bank or credit union may offer the best rates. A mortgage broker or company might make qualifying easier. If you buy a home in a development, the developer may be able to help. You can check advertisements or get a list of local mortgage lenders from HSH Associates. Call: 1-800-873-2837.

No lending institution will give you 100 percent of the purchase price of the house. You are required to have a

---

**Where to Live?**

There is no easy way to answer this question. However, the following reading list is recommended:

*The Top 300 Places to Live in the United States.* This is an annual survey and report conducted by Money Magazine. The most recent survey is published in their September, 1994 issue.

John Tepper Marlin, Ph.D., *The Livable Cities Almanac,* Harper Collins Publishers, 1992.

## Real Estate Terms

**Zoning.** Local governments have zoning rights. They use zoning laws to protect the value of the community and to determine how the land is to be used. The local government decides which areas of their town can be used exclusively for, or in any combination of, residential, commercial, industrial, or public purposes. Proposed changes must be presented at a town meeting, with proper notice of that meeting given. All people have the right to be heard and may legally challenge any decision.

**Development.** A developer (builder or financier) buys large pieces of land, sections it off, and builds homes for sale. These homes can be similar in design (to cost less) or custom built. They can be individual houses or condos. This group of homes is known as a development.

**Acre** An acre is a specific measure of land. It contains 43,560 square feet. This equals 4,407 square meters. Most land purchases are expressed in terms of acres (the house is on an acre of land or a half acre).

**down payment,** a cash amount of funds (generally five to 20 percent of the purchase price). The amount of down payment required varies with the lender. You must prove to the lending institution that you have the down payment available before it will consider you for a **mortgage.** Your mortgage is a loan for the remainder of the price.

The Federal Housing Administration (FHA) may give you a mortgage of up to 95 percent of the price of the house if it approves the total cost. Contact the FHA for details. In addition, some states have special mortgages available for qualified first-time buyers. Ask your real estate agent about this possibility.

National standards and guidelines are set by the Federal National Mortgage Association (FNMA, also called "FANNIE MAE") and the Federal Home Loan Mortgage Corporation ("Freddie Mac"). The Truth-in-Lending Statement on your mortgage will show the amount you are borrowing, the finance charges, and the annual percentage rate you will pay.

### Other costs

When you buy a house, there are other costs to consider besides the purchase price, property taxes, points, and mortgage.

An **engineering inspection** for structural safety, insect damage, and other potential hazards is advised before you buy. This way you can have the purchase price adjusted or require specific repairs be done prior to the closing. A similar written property **appraisal** is generally done or required by your insurance company or mortgage provider.

You also need to include the costs of any minor repairs, maintenance, and renovations needed in your personal household budget. Most homes are sold in move-in condition. Personal tastes and needs usually mean some expenses in these areas.

A written **survey** of the property diagraming the legal boundaries of the land is required.

**Title search and title insurance,** to be certain there are no claims against your house, generally cost several hundred dollars.

**Homeowners insurance** is required by the mortgage provider to protect the investment in your property. It covers the house and your possessions, protecting you against fire, theft, damage, and loss. It usually includes liability coverage to protect you against lawsuits if someone gets hurt on your property.

**Closing costs** are the payments you make on the day you actually legally purchase and take title to the house. They may cost an amount equivalent up to 10 percent of your mortgage. These normally include fees for filing and recording the deed, attorney's fees, state mortgage taxes, and points. You may be required to set up an **escrow** account, a reserve account holding the amount of your real estate taxes and your home insurance so the mortgage lender knows they will be paid. The closing is the final step in purchasing a home. Closings are typically done in an attorney's office or at a bank. You should not participate in the closing unless your attorney is present.

### Condominiums

When you buy a condo (condominium), you buy space in an individual housing unit. The association you buy the condo from owns the actual building and the land. You pay a mortgage, taxes, insurance on your unit, a monthly maintenance fee, and a share of taxes on the condominium property as a whole.

You can sell or rent your unit as you wish, generally without association approval.

### Co-operatives

With a co-op, (or co-operative housing) you buy a share in the corporation which owns the building and usually the land. This makes you a shareholder. You pay a monthly charge for your share of real estate taxes, insurance, loans, operating costs, repairs and maintenance.

As a prospective neighbor and shareholder, you will need to pass an interview with a board of owners prior to approval of your purchase. Your right to do as you please with your unit (renting or remodeling it for example) will be limited by the regulation of the ownership board. This type of housing is not widely in use and should only be considered if you have a good understanding of the benefits and liabilities associated with this type of real estate.

# RENTING

Renting a place to live is less complex and requires much less money than buying a home.

Apartments may or may not have complete facilities including laundry. However,

## Common Real Estate Ad Abbreviations:

Real estate listings often seem to have a language of their own. The following are common abbreviations and their meanings found in real estate listings for both houses and apartments:

| | |
|---|---|
| K | kitchen |
| DR | dining room |
| LR | living room |
| BR | bedroom |
| 2BR | two bedrooms |
| BATH | bathroom |
| 1 1/2 baths | one full bathroom and another with toilet and sink only. |
| GAR | garage |
| WD | washer/dryer |
| EA | eating area |
| FR | family room |
| FP | fireplace |
| EIK | eat-in kitchen |
| HW | hardwood floor |
| WW | wall-to-wall carpet |
| PAT | patio |
| CAC | central air conditioning |
| SCR POR | screened porch |
| MBR | master bedroom |

*The type of apartments vary widely. They range from private homes to large complexes.*

even unfurnished apartments generally provide a stove and a refrigerator.

Single rooms can be found in rooming houses. Ask about bathroom and kitchen facilities, they may be shared with the landlord or other tenants.

You cannot be denied rental access to an advertised place because of race or religion. You may be refused as a tenant for financial reasons. Your credit rating may be checked to see the extent of any outstanding debt you have. You may also have to prove your source of income. You will probably be asked to pay a **security deposit** (or damage deposit) to protect the landlord financially if you fail to pay the rent or damage the property. The equivalent of one to two months' rent in advance, this security deposit must be returned, usually with interest, when you leave if you have abided by the contract.

### Recommended Readings:

There are a large number of books available on how to buy a home. Try these:

Ilyce R. Glink, *100 Questions Every First-time Buyer Should Ask*, Time Books, a division of Random House, 1994.

Michael C. Thomsett, *How to Buy a House, Condo or Co-op*, Consumers Union, Yonkers NY, 1990.

Bill Adler, *The Home Buyers Guide*, A Fireside Book, Simon and Schuster, 1984.

### How do you find an apartment?

Check the newspapers for direct advertisements of rental property. Ads are placed by individual landlords as well as real estate agents.

Inquire locally. Look at bulletin boards, visit a supermarket, and pick up local apartment booklets, or inquire at a local real estate office. Ask friends in the neighborhood if they know of anything available. Universities post listings of available apartments in the area and usually have housing services to assist students.

### Leases

Not all landlords require a lease (written rental agreement). This can be an advantage if you are not sure how long you want to stay. You can end a verbal agreement with 30 days' notice in writing to the landlord – so can he. He can also raise the rent on short notice.

A lease stipulates a certain time period for the rental agreement. It may have a **break clause** in it that lets you get out of the agreement with sufficient notice, or a **sublet clause** that permits you to rent the premises to someone else. Unless stated in the lease, a lease prohibits raising the rent during the time it is in effect. It usually outlines the appliances (stove, refrigerator, washing machine, if any) and the services provided. Tenants are not usually responsible for major repairs and maintenance. Check your lease to see who is responsible for minor repairs.

A lease (rental agreement) is legally binding. It specifies your responsibilities and the landlord's. Before you sign it, be sure to understand what it includes. Who pays for utilities – electricity, water, and heat? Who controls the heating? Is the thermostat accessible to you so you can adjust the temperature as you wish? Is the heat seasonal – turned on at a specified date? What if it gets cold sooner? What are the bathroom, cooking, and laundry facilities? What about pest control? Are there any restrictions on pets, children, entertaining, parking?

Most states have enacted laws and regulations that protect the rights of tenants as well as landlords. Although these rights vary from state to state, information about your legal rights as a tenant may be furnished by your state department of housing.

### Renting with option to buy

You may not be able to buy a house now, but may want to be able to use part of your rent toward the eventual purchase of one. This option can be arranged with some owners who rent.

# BASIC SERVICES

Homes and apartments use different combinations of electricity, gas, and oil for heating and appliances. Electricity and natural gas are usually available only through a single company (utility) in a given area. Company rates are regulated by the state to prevent overcharging of customers and maintain standards. Utility companies are required to maintain gas and power lines and to provide high-quality service and safety to users. Household usage is monitored by meters for charges.

*Meters, which are usually on the outside of the building measure the amount of utilities used.*

Good quality water for drinking and general use is provided free to all homes in some areas of the country. In others, it is provided by the local government or utility for a reasonable fee. In these cases, water usage is monitored by meters and charged for accordingly. Private wells for individual homes exist in many rural areas. You should have well water tested before you buy or move into your home.

Heating oil is provided by companies competing for customers for oil delivery and service contracts. Check the Yellow Pages for company names in your area and compare companies.

Sewers for disposal of bodily waste are part of local government service, usually paid for by local taxes. In many rural areas individual houses have septic systems on the property, serviced by independent contractors.

Refuse collection for garbage and trash is usually provided by the town or city one or two specific days each week. In very rural areas, people may have to take their own refuse to a local dump for disposal. Mandatory recycling of garbage, paper, glass, and metal is increasingly common, requiring separate containers for each. There are

*Although you can sell your house on your own, it is generally advised to use a real estate agent.*

periodic collection days usually several times a year, for bulk trash, furniture, large appliances, and other such items.

## SELLING A HOME

Almost all homes in this country are sold through real estate agents. They provide such services as advertising, and multiple listing which gives you access to other real estate offices and a much broader market than you would have on your own. Your home is shown by professionals with no impact on your own time.

You can sell your home on your own; but what you save in commission you may lose in time, effort, and aggravation.

You may be required to pay a tax to the federal government if you make a profit when you sell your home. If you buy another house within two years, you may be able to defer the taxes. There is also a one time tax exclusion if you sell your house after you reach age 55. (For further information check with a tax professional.)

To be in the United States is to experience choice, especially with regard to food and shopping. The American demand for variety and availability is unequaled.

Restaurants of all kinds abound. Food markets of all sizes, from local grocery stores to supermarkets, are found in virtually every neighborhood.

Consumer goods, in astonishing array, are sold in a wide range of stores, from neighborhood shops to huge department stores and malls; even by television.

Enjoy it all.

# TABLE OF CONTENTS

# FOOD

The types of food available in the United States are as wide and varied as its people and cultures. No matter where you live, you will have not only a wide variety of food, but a wide variety of ways to purchase it. Each group of immigrants that comes here leaves its mark on the way we view and eat food. Recent immigrants have given us papaya, mango, chili peppers, cous-cous, pita bread, sushi, kim chee, tacos, and hundreds of other foods.

Americans are interested in food from many points of view: taste, nutrition, cooking convenience, (ease and speed of preparation) and even art. The cookbook section is often the largest section in many bookstores. You will also find interesting recipes featured in many newspapers and magazines.

It is important to note that there are strict public health laws regulating the sale of all food in this country, whether in a restaurant or in food stores.

Pizza and hamburgers with french fries top the list of our nationally favorite foods. No visit to the United States would be complete without sampling hot dogs, fried chicken, apple pie, chocolate chip cookies, or some of the two hundred different fla-

*Hot dogs, of German origin, are served with a variety of toppings, such as onions, sauerkraut and even chili.*

# WANT A TASTE OF AMERICA?

Throughout this chapter you will find recipes for popular regional American dishes. Either try them at home or order them at a restaurant if you happen to visit the area.

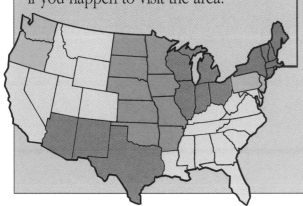

### New England Clam Chowder

| 2 dozen large clams | 2 medium onions |
| 1/4 cup salt pork | 3 cups water |
| 6 large white potatoes | 2 cups milk |
| 2 cups light cream | |

Begin with the clams. Steam them until their shells open. (You can do this in a strainer over a saucepan of boiling water.) Remove them from the shells and put them, together with their own liquid, into a small saucepan. Add the water and bring them to the boil. Remove and chop the clams, saving the liquid for flavor. Dice the salt pork and fry it in the bottom of a large heavy kettle (or Dutch oven, as a large iron pot is called). Add the onions and saute. Dice the potatoes. Add them, the reserved liquid, the pepper, and the clams to the kettle. Cook 15 minutes. Add the milk and cream. Reheat but do not boil. Serve with small round oyster crackers.

## Texas Barbecue Sauce

2 cloves garlic
1/2 cup vinegar
1/2 cup brown sugar
2 cups chili sauce
1/2 teaspoon Worcestershire sauce
2 dashes Tabasco sauce
2 tablespoons dry mustard
2 tablespoons oil

Crush the garlic into small saucepan. Add the other items and simmer, covered, an hour. Use as baste for barbecued spareribs (grilled over hot coals).

vors of ice cream. Regional favorites include grits (a southern cornmeal dish), fresh bagels and lox, Polish sausage, Philadelphia cheese steak, New England clam chowder, Cincinnati chili, Texas-style barbecued ribs, and California guacamole. While many regional favorites are available nationwide, they always seem to taste a little better in their place of origin.

A feast shared by family and friends is the focal point of several holidays. Perhaps the most noteworthy is Thanksgiving, celebrated each November to commemorate a special meal of thanks for a good harvest shared by the Indians and Pilgrims in 1621. The traditional meal features food originating in this country: roast turkey with stuffing, cranberry sauce, mashed potatoes, yams, yellow winter squash, and pumpkin pie.

Backyard barbecues are warm weather favorites. They usually consist of grilled ribs, hamburgers, hot dogs, or chicken. Side dishes include corn on the cob, tossed greens, potato salad, cole slaw, fruit salads, baked beans, and watermelon, all shared with family and friends.

Other festive holidays where food plays an important part include: New Year's Eve (plenty of hors d'oeuvres and snacks); Valentine's Day (chocolates and a special dinner for your wife or sweetheart, usually at a restaurant); Saint Patrick's Day (corned beef and cabbage); Easter (baked ham and dyed hard-boiled eggs); Memorial Day, the Fourth of July, and Labor Day (barbecues); Halloween (candy for children) and Christmas where dinner follows each family's special tradition. New tastes and traditions increase as our population grows more diverse.

# CHAIN RESTAURANTS

There are many nationwide chains of restaurants in America. They offer a large variety of foods to satisfy most any taste. The pictures on the left show a few of them. Chain restaurants usually specialize in either fast food or sit down table service.

Many nationwide chains have a selection of items on the menu for the health conscious customer (low calorie, low cholesterol, or low fat).

## RESTAURANTS

### Fast food

No matter where you live or travel in the United States you will find a wide selection of fast food restaurants. Perhaps easiest to find are: McDonald's, Burger King, Hardee's, Long John Silver's, and Wendy's. All specialize in rapidly cooked and served hamburgers, fish, and chicken sandwiches. Roy Roger's and Arby's restaurants feature roast beef sandwiches. The Kentucky Fried Chicken chain serves the chicken of its name. Taco Bell specializes in Mexican cooking.

All of these have a similar counter-service format. Customers place their orders at a counter in front of the kitchen and wait for the wrapped food and beverages to be put on a tray. They pay immediately and can either eat at a table or booth in the restaurant or take out the food. Drive-through service, where customers place orders at a window outside the restaurant, is a common feature, as are quick counter or table service, standardized food, low prices, and clean toilet facilities.

Two other styles of food that can be considered fast food but do not have a "chain" approach are chinese food and delicatessens (delis). Chinese restaurants are usually independently owned and offer both table service and take-out. Delicatessens are also usually independently owned, make sandwiches for take-out, and sell a small selection of grocery store items.

Soft ice cream is another favorite of American families. Dairy Queen and Carvel have large chains.

### Pizza

If pizza is your favorite, you will enjoy a trip to a pizzeria. Small family-owned "pizza parlors" can be found in almost every town. Chains (Pizza Hut, Domino's) may be seen nationwide. If you want your pizza delivered to your door, just check the Yellow Pages of the local phone directory and call. Home delivery of other fast foods is expanding rapidly across the country.

# DRIVE-THROUGH SERVICE

Many fast food restaurants offer drive-through service. You read the posted menu from your car, drive up to the speaker and place your order. You go on to the collection window, get your wrapped food and pay for it. You never need to get out of your car.

### Sauteed Maryland Softshell Crabs

1 dozen soft-shell crabs
1/2 cup flour
1 teaspoon salt
2 tablespoons lemon juice
1/4 cup butter
 parsley sprigs

A specialty of the Chesapeake Bay, soft-shell crabs are, in fact, so tender that they can be eaten shells and all.

They can be fried or broiled, but are most tender served this way:

Rinse crabs and pat dry. Sprinkle with lemon juice. Shake each crab individually in flour in a small paper bag with the salt and pepper. Saute lightly 5 minutes in butter. Serve with parsley garnish.

## Table service

Here you order your food from your table and are served there by a waiter or waitress. Food preparation usually takes longer than fast food service. Chefs can be more responsive to individual requests. Alcoholic beverages are more likely to be available. Even the most reasonable of these restaurants are usually more expensive than the fast food places.

The variety of food, price, service, and quality are for the most part very good. Virtually every town has good restaurants. Many specialize exclusively in a national cuisine (Italian, Chinese, Mexican, and Japanese are among the most popular).

Prices vary from region to region. However, the average family can afford a special night out with or without the children on a routine basis. Several fine dining magazines are sold where restaurants are reviewed and rated.

There are also many high-quality national, regional, and local chain restaurants run by major corporations. Each restaurant in the chain offers a similar type of menu and decor. You can enjoy your familiar favorite foods and be assured of a high degree of consistency in quality, service, and price. Howard Johnson, Denny's, Red Lobster, Chi-Chi's, Friendly's, and Pizza Hut are only a few representatives of such chains.

**Tipping:** A 15 percent tip is customary in all types of table service restaurants. It is generally not included in the bill. Parking lot attendants of a restaurant are usually tipped one or two dollars. Coat check attendants are usually tipped a dollar per item.

**Business meals:** If you entertain business clients at a restaurant, you may be able to deduct part of the cost from your taxes as a business expense. Keep all receipts if you plan to do so, and note the purpose of the meal and the names of your guests. Ask your accountant or supervisor for advice in this area.

**Credit cards:** It is never wise to carry large amounts of cash. It is rare that a restaurant does not accept a major credit card. Those that do not will typically have a sign stating so. This "no credit cards accepted" is found in only some small restaurants.

Look in the Yellow Pages of any town phone directory for a list of the restaurants in the area.

# FOOD STORES

Food is generally plentiful and available in great variety in this country. Most towns have one or more large general stores located within easy driving or walking distance.

There are over 300,000 supermarkets and grocery stores in the United States. This includes giant super stores that offer everything from food to prescription medicine and health care products to electronics to clothing - even tires for your automobile. It also includes small privately owned grocery stores that carry a small selection of food and over-the-counter medicines. The average supermarket has over 25,000 different types of items and at least several different brands and sizes made by various manufacturers. The choice is over-whelming at first. There is no national chain of supermarkets. However, there are a number of multi-billion dollar regional chains. You will find several major chains in almost every city competing for your shopping dollar. There will almost always be a good-sized supermarket in your neighborhood.

## Supermarkets

A typical supermarket offers a wide variety of domestic and imported fruits and vegetables, meat and fish (both frozen and fresh), dairy products, baked goods (breads and cakes), toiletries (shampoo and other personal hygiene products), candy, cereals, cold cuts (sliced meat for making sandwiches), canned goods (fruits, vegetables and sauces), frozen meals (ready to heat in an oven or microwave), condiments (mustard, ketchup, pickles), spices, ice cream, soda, baby food and diapers, food storage products, house-hold cleaning products, common small household items (light bulbs, tools, and electrical cords) and perhaps even a pharmacy for prescription drugs. All are available at reason-able prices.

Supermarkets, like most American stores, are self-service. Shoppers, using wheeled market carts supplied by the stores, select the items they want to buy from the shelves and pay for them at a check-out counter near the exit. Almost 85 percent of today's markets use check-out scanners (electronic devices to record prices). Increasing numbers of stores accept credit card payment. Many stores are open 24 hours a day.

All handling, preparation, packaging, and storage of food products is government regulated. Food labels listing ingredients in the order of their proportion are required. For example, you can tell from the ingredients listed on the label if a bottled juice is

In the home, large refrigerators with large freezer units are common. Many Americans shop only weekly, buying in large quantity especially on weekends and right before major holidays. Stores are often crowded then.

## Discounts for Shopping

There is a great deal of competition among the stores for your shopping dollar. Most offer special low prices on a wide range of products each week to entice you to their store. There is also a great deal of competition among the manufacturers of the products sold in supermarkets. Companies such as Coca Cola, Pepsi Cola, Kraft General Foods, Campbell Soup, Heinz and Nestles fight for your food dollar by offering coupons for reduced prices, special trial sizes, extra product in the package, rebates, a wide variety of sweep-stakes and other small rewards if you pur-chase their products. A wise shopper can save a significant amount on the food bud-get by carefully buying sale items.

### Apple Pie

The crust:
2 cups flour
1 teaspoon salt
2/3 cup shortening or oil
1/3 cup cold water
Sift together flour and salt. Cut in (or melt and add) shortening or oil. Add water. Knead briefly. Divide dough in half. Roll out one half in circular shape. If this is done between layers of plastic or wax paper, it is easy to peel top sheet back and transfer dough to pie plate. Repeat for top crust but do not transfer until ready to cover filling.
8 large apples, peeled and sliced
1/2 cup white sugar
1/4 cup brown sugar
1/2 teaspoon cinnamon
Place apples into bottom crust lined pie plate. Mix the sugars and cinnamon and sprinkle over the apples. (Add a teaspoon of lemon juice if you want to increase tartness.) Cover with top crust, sealing edges. Gash top crust in several places to vent steam. Bake at 450° F. for 10 minutes; reduce heat to 350° F. and bake 40 - 50 minutes longer.

really all juice or diluted with water or contains added sugar. In addition, a nutritional label is required by the Food and Drug Administration on each package. This allows you to easily follow a healthy well-balanced diet. (See chapter *Health Care*.)

All perishable products must carry a freshness date ("Sell before 10/2/94," for example). In addition, unit prices (how much you pay per quart or pound, for example) of all products are generally posted on the shelves for easy price comparison.

The prices marked on food store items are fixed and do not generally include sales tax, which varies by state.

### Specialized markets
Local butcher shops, bakeries, and produce (vegetables and fruit) stores are plentiful. Some, especially in urban neighborhoods, offer imported specialties or health food and organically raised products.

### Convenience stores
These are small local stores offering a variety of food items, beverages, and commonly needed items – flashlight batteries, health and beauty aids, snack foods, disposable diapers. Prices may be higher than in supermarkets, but these stores are usually close to home and always open – even on major holidays. Seven Eleven is the largest and only national chain of convenience stores. There are many large regional chains, including Cumberland Farms and Circle K. Convenience stores are also located in gasoline service stations in some states.

## MICROWAVE COOKING
No discussion of food in American life today can be considered complete without mentioning microwave cooking. Approximately 80 percent of homes now have a microwave oven and use it regularly. Microwave cooking is the fastest way to heat foods and is very simple to learn. It can boil water in one minute, bake a potato in five minutes and heat and cook foods significantly faster than in a regular oven. There are some important things that a microwave oven cannot do. It cannot brown foods. Also, certain foods such as eggs and frozen foods often require special attention. *Note: The use of anything metal inside a microwave oven is dangerous.*

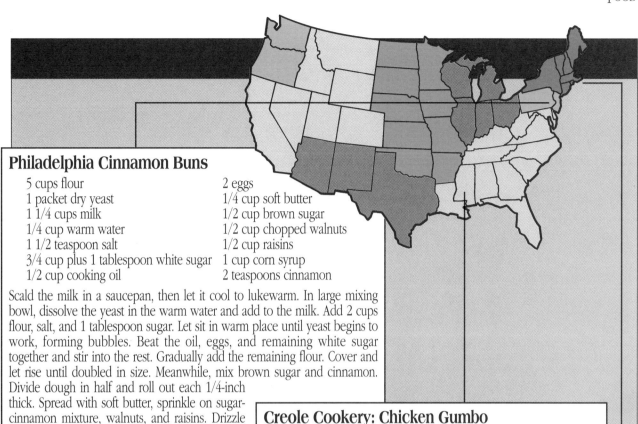

## Philadelphia Cinnamon Buns

| | |
|---|---|
| 5 cups flour | 2 eggs |
| 1 packet dry yeast | 1/4 cup soft butter |
| 1 1/4 cups milk | 1/2 cup brown sugar |
| 1/4 cup warm water | 1/2 cup chopped walnuts |
| 1 1/2 teaspoon salt | 1/2 cup raisins |
| 3/4 cup plus 1 tablespoon white sugar | 1 cup corn syrup |
| 1/2 cup cooking oil | 2 teaspoons cinnamon |

Scald the milk in a saucepan, then let it cool to lukewarm. In large mixing bowl, dissolve the yeast in the warm water and add to the milk. Add 2 cups flour, salt, and 1 tablespoon sugar. Let sit in warm place until yeast begins to work, forming bubbles. Beat the oil, eggs, and remaining white sugar together and stir into the rest. Gradually add the remaining flour. Cover and let rise until doubled in size. Meanwhile, mix brown sugar and cinnamon. Divide dough in half and roll out each 1/4-inch thick. Spread with soft butter, sprinkle on sugar-cinnamon mixture, walnuts, and raisins. Drizzle on 1/8 cup syrup. Roll dough into long "jelly roll" shapes. Cut into 1 1/2-inch sections. Butter two 2x9-inch pans and pour in syrup 1/4-inch deep. Stand buns in, cut sides up. Cover and let rise until doubled in size. Bake in preheated oven at 350°F. for 45 minutes. Remove from pan at once to avoid sticking.

## Creole Cookery: Chicken Gumbo

Originating in the bayous of Louisiana and New Orleans, Creole recipes combine cuisines from several cultures: Cajun (or Acadian refugee), French, Spanish, native Choctaw and Chickasaw, and African. This cookery revolves around the stock pot, blending game, fish, fowl, leftovers of all kinds in a traditional iron pot. Add to it a brown roux of butter and flour, herbs and spices, especially red pepper and file (pronounced fee-lay) powder, and alcoholic beverages made of almost any plant producing juice, and you get Creole.

| | |
|---|---|
| 1 four-pound chicken, cut up | 2 quarts water |
| 2 teaspoons salt | 2 cloves garlic |
| 1 teaspoon red pepper | 1 teaspoon thyme |
| 2 tablespoons fat | 8 sprigs parsley |
| 2 tablespoons flour | 2 dozen shelled oysters |
| 1 large onion | 1 1/2 tablespoons file powder |

Rub chicken with salt and pepper. Melt the fat in a large iron pot, brown the flour and then the chicken pieces. Slice and saute the onion. Add the water, garlic, and thyme. Cook 2 or more hours until chicken is tender. Add the oysters and simmer until they curl. Stir in the file powder but do not reheat. Garnish with parsley. Serve with cooked rice.

## Boston Brown Bread

| | |
|---|---|
| 2 cups buttermilk | 1/2 teaspoon salt |
| 2 teaspoons baking soda | 4 cups wholewheat flour |
| 4 tablespoons dark brown sugar | 4 tablespoons melted butter |
| 4 tablespoons molasses | |

In a large mixing bowl, dissolve the baking soda in the buttermilk. Add the brown sugar, molasses, and salt. Stir in the flour, a little at a time, and add the butter. Divide the dough into 2 brown bread tins (empty 1-pound coffee cans, sealed with aluminum foil will do). Steam for 2 1/2 hours. (This can be done on a rack over boiling water in a covered pot.) Place in 250°F. oven for 1/2 hour. Serve sliced with sweet butter (unsalted) or cream cheese.

*Recipes Continue on Page G-10*

Produce department

Frozen foods are abundant.

Bakery department

Signs listing items found in aisle assist shopper.

Wide variety of brands to choose from.

Packages clearly marked with weight, ingredients and purchase by date to ensure freshness.

Bags come in paper or plastic.

# WHAT YOU MAY FIND IN A SUPERMARKET

Scanner at check out to register price.

Pay with cash, check or credit card.

Safety seals on packages.

Shopping carts for convenience.

In addition to clean facilities, large selection, and competitive prices, you will find the following features in a supermarket:

## Bagging
Strong paper bags and plastic bags are at every check-out counter in the supermarket. The clerk or an assistant will usually put your purchases in bags for you. Some people do it themselves or help the store workers in bagging, especially if the store is very busy.

## Express Lines
Most supermarkets have an express line for people buying only a few (usually 10 to 12) items. This avoids waiting in a line with people purchasing large amounts of merchandise. Also in the interest of speed, express lines generally accept only cash.

## Check Cashing Cards
Most supermarkets allow you to pay by check and receive an additional amount of cash (usually up to $25) if you wish. You must apply for this service at the store manager's office. You are subsequently mailed a card that authorizes you to cash checks.

## Discount Cards (Store Cards)
Many supermarkets issue a plastic card that looks like a credit card or check cashing card. It is not. You present it when you check out to receive some special discounts because you are a regular customer.

## Safety Seals
Every prepackaged item in the store is required by law to have tamper-proof packaging, a highly visible protective seal. If the safety seal is broken, do not buy the item.

## Paying at the Check-out Counter
Supermarkets accept cash and authorized checks at the check-out area. If you are paying by check and do not have a check cashing privilege card from the store, speak with the store manager when you first arrive. He will ask you for identification, write it on your check and, if possible, mark it approved. If you wait until you are at the check-out counter, you will tie up the line until the store manager can come to the counter and check your identification. Needless to say, the people waiting in back of you will be very annoyed. Many supermarkets routinely accept major credit cards and debit cards. Make sure this is the case before you get in the check-out line.

## Shopping Carts
Shopping carts are available for your convenience at every supermarket. They have seats for small children. Exercise caution when you have a child in the cart. Do not leave a child unattended in a cart. Return your shopping cart to the proper area in the parking lot or front of the store as a courtesy to other customers.

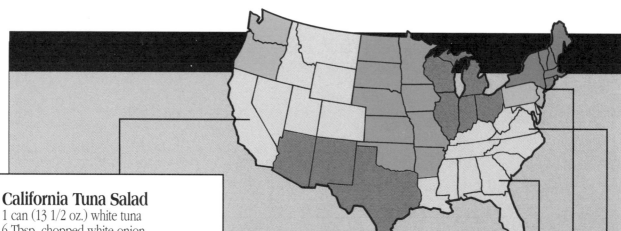

## California Tuna Salad

1 can (13 1/2 oz.) white tuna
6 Tbsp. chopped white onion
1/2 tsp. dried oregano
4 Tbsp. chopped canned green chilies
2 Tbsp. olive oil
1 ripe avocado, cubed, tossed in lime juice
Lettuce leaves
6 corn tortillas
oil for frying
parsley

Mix onion and lime juice. Set aside for 30 minutes. Drain tuna fish and flake. Combine with oregano, chilles, parsley, olive oil, avocado and the onion. Serve on a bed of lettuce. Cut tortillas into six pieces. Fry in oil and drain. Surround salad with chips.

## Baked Southern Grits

| | |
|---|---|
| 3 cups water | 4 eggs |
| 1 1/2 teaspoons salt | 1/4-pound butter |
| 1 cup grits | 1/2 cup grated cheese |
| 1 cup milk | |

Boil the water in a large pot. Sprinkle in the salt and grits. Cover and simmer an hour, stirring as needed to keep from sticking. (Add more butter, if necessary.) Blend in the milk, eggs, and butter. Pour into buttered casserole or baking dish and bake at 350°F. for 35 minutes. Sprinkle on the grated cheese and bake a final 10 minutes. Serve with fried bacon or sausage.

## New York Pot Roast

| | |
|---|---|
| 4-pound piece of beef (round, rump, or chuck) | |
| 1/4 cup flour | 2 carrots |
| 1 teaspoon salt | 1 parsnip |
| 1/2 teaspoon black pepper | 2 onions |
| 4 tablespoons cooking oil | 1 bay leaf |
| 1 clove garlic (or 1 teaspoon garlic powder) | 1 1/2 cups water |

Dredge the meat in the flour, salt, and pepper. Using a large heavy kettle (Dutch oven), brown evenly in the oil, with garlic. Add the water, bay leaf, and vegetables, cut into 1-inch chunks. (Turnips, tomatoes, and/or celery root can also be used.) Simmer covered for 3 1/2 hours, turning meat occasionally. Serve with gravy, made as follows:

**Gravy:**
2 cups of cooking liquid        2 tablespoons flour
Gradually blend flour into liquid and cook until thickened.

## Baked Virginia Ham

| | |
|---|---|
| 1 hickory-smoked ham | |
| 2 3/4 cups brown sugar | 2 bay leaves |
| 6 onions, quartered | 2 dozen whole cloves |
| 2 cups vinegar or wine | 2 teaspoons dry mustard |

Soak ham in cold water 2 days, changing water periodically. Rinse ham thoroughly, place in large kettle, and cover with fresh water. Add 2 cups brown sugar, quartered onions, vinegar or wine, 1 dozen cloves, and bay leaves. Cover and simmer about 20 minutes to the pound. (If you use a precooked ham, this step is not necessary.) Remove the ham and skin it, cutting off some of the fat. Score the remaining fat in diamond pattern and stud with remaining cloves. Pat remaining sugar and dry mustard on the fat. Bake at 425°F. about 30 minutes or until glazed and brown. (Bake at 350°F. for 1 1/2 hours if ham is precooked.)

# SHOPPING

No country offers more ways of distributing goods and services to customers than the United States. Whether you prefer old-fashioned one-to-one customer service, self-service, or even the ability to shop without leaving your home, it is easily available. Many stores also offer items not directly related to their primary business. For example, grocery (food) stores often carry health and beauty care products that were once only found in drug stores (pharmacies). Before you buy a major item or begin furnishing your household, check quality and price at several types of stores.

## DRUG STORES (PHARMACIES)

Where do you go to buy medicine? For doctor-prescribed medicine, go to a drug store (pharmacy). Look for the Rx sign; it means there is a licensed pharmacist at that location. You can find over-the-counter (non-prescription) items such as aspirin or cold remedies in supermarkets as well as drug stores. (See chapter *Health*

*There are over 50,000 drug stores, 10,000 department stores, 40,000 shopping centers or malls and over 150,000 clothing stores including over 37,000 shoe stores in the United States.*

Most stores use electronic scanners to register the price of the sale. In addition to being more accurate and creating a faster check out time, this information is used to monitor store inventories.

At times you may find the sales clerk asking for your zip code or telephone number. This information, as well the information obtained from the scanner is used to improve the distribution system of product thereby keeping costs low.

*Care.*) Drug stores also sell cosmetics, toiletries, camera supplies, watches, candy, stationery, newspapers, magazines, and in some cases a limited selection of grocery products.

## DEPARTMENT STORES

These are huge stores selling primarily clothes, shoes, cosmetics, and jewelry. Most also have bedding, hardware, small and large appliances (refrigerators, washers and dryers), books, electronics, compact discs (CDs), toys, kitchen utensils, and furniture.

## SPECIALIZED STORES

Almost every type of item sold in the United States is probably nearby. Look in the Yellow Pages, under the specific item you want, to find the places selling them. Specialized stores – sometimes large but often small and local – sell furniture, lamps, carpeting, clothing, shoes, sports equipment, hardware (nails, screws, tools, paint, wallpaper, fabric, tile, electrical supplies), major appliances (washers and dryers, refrigerators, and dishwashers), radios, televisions, tape and compact disc players, and toys. The variety is virtually unlimited.

Store sales are advertised on radio, television, in newspapers, and in specially mailed flyers. Prices are very competitive. You may be able to get a small discount (reduced price) on items slightly damaged or no longer in style.

## THE MALL SCENE:
The following are some of the sights commonly seen in malls.

## MALLS

Shopping malls, huge complexes of many kinds of stores, are a frequent part of the landscape. Some malls consist of factory outlets selling merchandise direct from the manufacturer at lower prices than retail stores.

## CATALOG SHOPPING

Some of the most famous stores in the United States operate by catalog. They send customers a catalog (magazine) describing their products. Customers dial a toll-free number and place an order. They can bill their credit card, send in a check, or pay Cash On Delivery (C.O.D), (see chapter *Mail Service)*. The merchandise is shipped directly to the customer, sometimes at no additional cost. Satisfaction is usually guaranteed. Items may sometimes be returned, even after use, if they prove unsatisfactory.

Virtually all types of merchandise are available through catalogs: clothing, vitamins, health and beauty care products, food, computers, office supplies, electronic equipment, and appliances. You can find offers for catalogs in national magazines. There are even catalogs of catalogs available. Once you purchase from a catalog you will generally receive new catalogs from that company as well as from other companies.

Prices in America are fixed. Bargaining is not generally done.

Keep all receipts. They prove you made the purchase. They are necessary if you want to return faulty or unsatisfactory merchandise.

Discount coupons for particular products are widely available in local newspapers and mail offerings.

## TELEVISION SHOPPING

A rapidly growing alternative to catalog and retail shopping is provided by television: home shopping channels. Products are displayed and described. Customers call to order them. These channels offer special programs on items such as jewelry, travel, clothing, cosmetics, toys, and electronics, among others. There are two major networks, *Home Shopping Network* and *QVC* which both offer 24-hour-a-day shopping. Customers generally pay by credit card. While there are pros and cons to this type of shopping, one thing is certain: this type of shopping will continue to grow and change.

## SECOND-HAND SHOPPING

Used furniture and clothing are available at local thrift shops at very low prices. You can also sell your own used items here. The store takes a percentage of the profit, often for a particular charity. The quality of the items is usually good for the price.

## GARAGE SALES

These are informal sales of personal items such as furniture, books, clothing, small appliances, toys and games, by private individuals. They are announced in local newspapers or by signs posted locally. They can be a pleasant way to spend time and save money, but there is no guarantee on the merchandise. People relocating or groups of neighbors often have garage sales, usually during the warmer seasons.

## CAR PURCHASE

One of the largest purchases you are likely to make is a car. Car prices, for both new and used cars, are seldom fixed. In deciding on the make and model of any car, new or used, think about why you want it and where you will be using it. Do you need front or four-wheel drive, for example, because you will be driving in snow? Consider price (and resale value), safety, and the costs of fuel, maintenance, and insurance.

The major automobile manufacturers in the United States are: the Chrysler Corporation (making Plymouth, Dodge and Chrysler); the Ford Motor Company (making Ford, Mercury, and Lincoln); General Motors Corporation (making Chevrolet, Geo, Pontiac, Oldsmobile, Buick, Cadillac, and Saturn); Volkswagon, Honda, Mazda, Nissan, Toyota, Mitsubishi, Mercedes Benz, Volvo, and Subaru.

### New cars

Shop around to learn the features and the prices of models available at different dealers and the delivery time if you order a car not currently in stock. Consider options (the extra equipment on the car) carefully. What is included in the purchase price? What extra features do you really need? Many can add to safety: power steering and power brakes on heavy cars, for example; or steel-belted radial tires which not only give better mileage, they give the best traction; adjustable seats, power seats, and a tilt steering wheel help prevent fatigue; electric door locks and power windows add security. Other options may directly affect resale value: air conditioning; radio, cassette, CD system; sun roof; air bags; and anti-theft devices.

The average price of a new car was $17,000 in 1994. How do you pay for it? Usually you pay an initial down payment and finance the rest. Financing your car using a dealer's plan, in general, will cost more than borrowing the same amount from a bank or credit union. Check with your bank and other lending companies.

## Recommended Reading

The editors of Consumer Reports with Bill Hartford, *New Car Buying Guide,* Consumer Reports Books, A Division of Consumers Union, Yonkers, NY.

### Leasing

This is a convenient method of financing but can often be more expensive than traditional financing. Why do it? The down payment and the subsequent monthly payments are very low. Factors you should consider are: any charges for mileage beyond a certain limit; scheduled maintenance you must pay for; penalty fees if you move from the lease location; and fees for early termination of the lease. Discuss the advantages, disadvantages, terms and conditions of the lease, the buyout cost, as well as your current financial situation, with a financial professional before you consider leasing.

### Used cars

Whether you are buying a used car privately or from a dealer, *The National Automobile Dealers Association Official Used Car Guide* is a good place to start. It will give you an estimate of both the regular retail value of the car and any options, and its wholesale or trade-in value (what a dealer would give you for the car when you trade it in as part of a purchase on a new model).

You may want to have the car examined by an independent mechanic before you buy; there may be a charge for this. If you buy from a reputable dealer, there is usually a guarantee available.

Buying a model that is no longer made or that is not common in the region where you expect to use it may be a mistake, regardless of price, as repair parts may be hard to find and expensive.

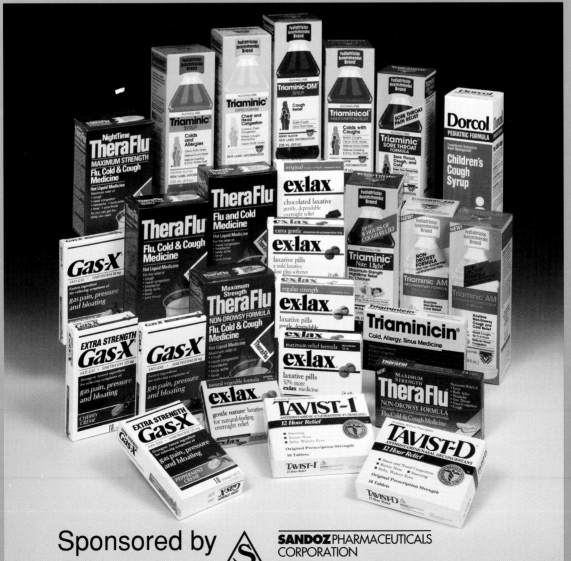

Sponsored by SANDOZ PHARMACEUTICALS CORPORATION
Consumer Pharmaceuticals Division

# TABLE OF CONTENTS

## HEALTH CARE

# HEALTH CARE

Overall, health care in the United States is among the best in the world. Our system provides many options for treatment. Most people have access to private health insurance through their place of employment. In this case the **premium** (the payment for the insurance) is shared by the employer and employee. Trade associations, schools, fraternal organizations, and unions also offer health care insurance. Finally, offered to individuals and families, are private health insurance plans provided by insurance companies such as MetLife and Blue Cross/Blue Shield. (See chapter *Insurance.*)

In virtually all communities there are volunteer organizations that sponsor free health screenings and evaluations. Most communities have hospital clinics for those without health insurance. Payment is on a sliding scale (fee schedule) based on what you earn. There are also several well-known specialized hospitals which charge no fees. These are supported entirely by charitable organizations and donations.

## PREVENTATIVE AND CURATIVE CARE

### How can you find a doctor?
One of the first things you should do when you arrive is to find a doctor who meets your needs. You may require a specialist who treats a specific disease, age group, or speaks your language.

Medical services are generally provided through private physicians and at public hospitals, community health centers, and clinics. The system is oriented toward **specialists,** (physicians focusing on a particular area of medicine). For every body part or disease, you are likely to find a specialist. Before going to one, you may want (or be required) to consult a "general practice" doctor for advice and to narrow

## WHAT YOU NEED TO KNOW ABOUT YOUR HEALTH CARE PROVIDER

As a patient, you have the right to know:

- The doctor's education and certification. Certification means that the doctor has received extra training in a particular area and has passed a national examination.

- In what hospitals he is allowed to practice. Doctors must receive authorization from a hospital before they are allowed to admit patients for treatment. While you may want the location of the hospital to be convenient, this may not be possible in cases of special treatment needs.

- What his fees are and what type of payment is required (cash, check, credit card, or direct payment from the insurance company). In many cases the insurance company payment is less than 100 percent. There is usually a deductible amount. (See chapter *Insurance.*)

All health care professionals must be licensed by the state in which they are practicing. You can call the licensing department in the state capital to inquire about a physician's credentials.

# TYPES OF HOSPITALS

There are over 7,000 hospitals in the United States. Four basic types of hospitals include:

**Teaching hospitals.** This type of hospital is often an extension of a medical school. In addition to the normal high quality of care, the patient is also seen by interns (recent medical school graduates) and residents (doctors who are past the intern level but want to gain additional experience).

**General hospitals**. A hospital that provides medical treatment for most types of medical problems. They are often found in local towns as they are generally community based.

**Private hospitals.** A hospital that is managed as a profit making business. They will generally not accept patients who cannot afford to pay.

**Voluntary hospitals.** This type of hospital cares for paying patients, private patients, and poor patients. They are often owned and run by religious orders. Included in this type of hospital are a small number of hospitals which care for serious burn victims, or persons with serious heart problems, or cancer at no charge. The money for these hospitals comes from donations and volunteer associations such as the Shriners.

down possible causes of your problem. Many specialists do not take patients except on referral.

Because of this, selecting a family physician is advised as a first step. A family practitioner (also known as a general practitioner or internist) will care for your routine needs and refer you to specialists. In case of emergency, your family doctor will provide instructions and meet you at the hospital if necessary.

There are several ways to find a physician. Ask your family or friends for recommendations, look in the Yellow Pages of a phone directory under "physician", or call a physician referral service at the nearest hospital or chamber of commerce. There are also regional toll-free 800 numbers for physician and dentist referrals.

## WHERE CAN YOU GET MEDICAL ATTENTION?

For routine problems or physical exams, visit your doctor's office (by appointment). He or she may be in a single practice, in a partnership, or in a group medical practice with a variety of specialists.

### HMOs (Health Maintenance Organizations)

HMOs, like group medical practices, offer a wide range of medical specialities (pediatrics, cardiology, and orthopedics, for instance). If you join an HMO, you must choose a doctor from it's list of participating physicians. In most cases, the list is extensive. Your HMO provides you a list of instructions in case of medical emergency. (See chapter *Insurance*.)

### PPOs (Preferred Provider Organizations)

PPOs are very similar but generally have no central office. (See the chapter *Insurance* for more information.)

### Hospitals

Private doctors and group practices are often based in hospitals. Most hospitals have an emergency room to handle urgent medical problems. Some people attempt to use emergency room services for minor problems instead of visiting a doctor. This is not advised as some hospitals refuse to handle non-emergency cases.

### Clinics and outpatient surgical centers

These can be part of a hospital or a separate facility. Often run by a group of doctors within the same area of specialization, they are used for medical problems that do not require hospitalization.

# MEDICATION (MEDICINE)

**Prescription drugs** (medicine ordered for you by a doctor) can only be obtained from a licensed pharmacist with a written prescription or phone call from a physician. Prescription medication can be paid for by your insurance carrier if that is included as a benefit in your insurance plan. Such medicine is strictly controlled by law. There are serious penalties for its improper distribution. Both pharmacists and physicians take extra care to insure that the proper procedures are followed.

**Over-the-counter medication** (OTC medication) can be purchased without a prescription. They are considered safe and effective for such minor health care problems as headaches, common colds, allergies, constipation, diarrhea, and intestinal gas.

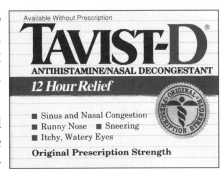

In recent years many medications that once required a prescription became available over the counter. For example, Tavist-D, a product for sinus and nasal congestion caused by sinusitis or allergies, was only sold by prescription until recently.

**Generic medicine** is sold by its chemical name as opposed to its "brand" name given by the manufacturer. Both prescription and OTC medications are usually available in generic form at lower cost than that sold under the equivalent brand label. The difference can be several dollars or several cents.

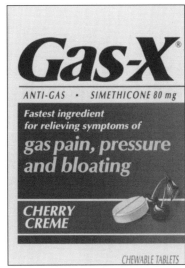

Some people feel there is a higher standard of quality with brand name products. Others prefer the lower-priced generics. Name brand manufacturers often give out coupons as incentives to purchase their products and reduce any price discrepancies. The choice is yours to make.

**The Food and Drug Administration (FDA)** All medicine sold in the U.S., whether prescription or not, must pass strict tests by the manufacturer and the Food and Drug Administration (FDA). The FDA is an independent government agency that regulates the way food and medicine are manufactured and sold. Even the writing on the package is regulated by the FDA to insure that it clearly states how to use the product and its purpose.

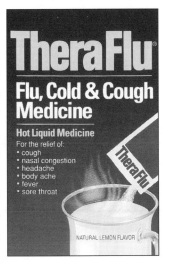

When manufacturers develop a new medication, they usually receive a patent, an exclusive legal right to make and sell a new product for a fixed number of years. This is done to allow the

developers of the product to recover the money they invested in the development and marketing of the product. After the set time period has passed the product is said to be "off patent" or generic. This means that any manufacturer can make and sell the product as long as it meets FDA requirements for manufacturing and safety and effectiveness when used as recommended. This is how generics and many competing brands are introduced.

### Tamper-proof packaging

All OTC products are required by law to be "safety-sealed," packaged in a way that the consumer will easily know if someone has opened the package. This is known as "tamper-proof packaging." Never buy or use a product whose safety seal has been broken.

*Child resistant caps (pictured above) help prevent children from opening medicine bottles. To open, you must push down while twisting or line up indicated marks.*

### Child resistant caps

All prescription drugs and over-the-counter medications are sold in bottles with child-resistant caps. These are tops that are extremely difficult for a child to remove. If you need an easier opening cap for a prescription medication, tell the pharmacist and he will provide it. Some OTC products also come with regular caps for people who need them.

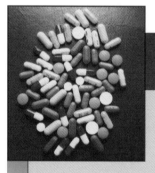

# TAKING MEDICATION

When the doctor prescribes a medication, his instructions and those of the pharmacist must be followed. Some common mistakes involving taking medication include:

**"I feel better so I don't need to take this medicine anymore."** Such failure to continue the medication often leads to a reoccurrence of the problem.

**"If I take twice as much medicine, I will get well sooner."** The dosage (amount of medicine to be taken) prescribed by your doctor takes into account your age, weight, stage of illness, and many other factors. You may seriously harm yourself if you overdose (take too much).

**"I think a drink of beer, wine, or other alcohol will help me feel better."** Do not drink alcoholic beverages while taking medication. In some cases it may seriously harm you or even be fatal. If you have any questions on this, ask your pharmacist or doctor to explain the risk.

**"This other medicine I have will probably also help me."** Be sure to advise the doctor and pharmacist of any other medications (both prescription and OTC) you are taking. They may cause serious side effects (bad reactions) when taken together. Whenever there is any doubt, call your physician or pharmacist.

# HOW TO READ AN OTC PACKAGE

**$1 REFUND OFFER** Printed on Inside Panel

**$1 REFUND OFFER** Printed on Inside Panel

**DIRECTIONS:** Children 6 to under 12 years: 2 teaspoons every 4 hours. Children 12 and over and adults: 4 teaspoons every 4 hours. Children under 6 years: consult physician.

**INDICATIONS:** Temporarily relieves cold and allergy symptoms, including runny nose; stuffy nose; sneezing; itching nose or throat; and itchy, watery eyes.

**EACH TEASPOONFUL (5ML) CONTAINS:** phenylpropanolamine hydrochloride, USP 6.25 mg and chlorpheniramine maleate, USP 1 mg.

**OTHER INGREDIENTS:** benzoic acid, edetate disodium, flavors, purified water, sodium hydroxide, sorbitol, sucrose, Yellow 6.

**WARNINGS:** Keep this and all drugs out of the reach of children. In case of accidental overdose, seek professional assistance or contact a Poison Control Center immediately.

Do not exceed recommended dosage because at higher doses nervousness, dizziness or sleeplessness may occur. Do not take this product for more than 7 days. If symptoms persist or are accompanied by fever, consult a doctor. Do not take this product: 1) if you have heart disease, high blood pressure, thyroid disease, diabetes, glaucoma, a breathing problem such as emphysema or chronic bronchitis, or difficulty in urination due to enlargement of the prostate gland, 2) if you are taking sedatives or tranquilizers, or 3) if you are presently taking another product containing phenylpropanolamine, unless directed by a doctor. May cause excitability, especially in children. May cause drowsiness. Alcohol, sedatives or tranquilizers may increase drowsiness. Avoid driving or operating machinery while taking this product.

As with any drug, if you are pregnant or nursing a baby, seek the advice of a health professional before using this product.

**Drug Interaction Precaution:** Do not use this product if you are now taking a prescription monoamine oxidase inhibitor [MAOI] (certain drugs for depression, psychiatric or emotional conditions, or Parkinson's disease) or for 2 weeks after stopping the MAOI drug. If you are uncertain whether your prescription drug contains an MAOI, consult a health professional before taking this product.

**STORE AT ROOM TEMPERATURE. CONTAINS NO ASPIRIN.**

0551-04

**SANDOZ** PHARMACEUTICALS CORPORATION
Consumer Pharmaceuticals Division

© 1994 Sandoz Consumer Pharmaceuticals Division, East Hanover, NJ 07936

## Triaminic© SYRUP

Triaminic offers you a complete system of effective and convenient cough and cold relief for your child.

- Great flavors children love
- True-Dose® dosing
- Alcohol-Free
- Trusted by two generations of parents
- And only Triaminic has eight different children's cough and cold formulas

**Choose the correct Triaminic product to relieve your child's symptoms.**

| | |
|---|---|
| | • Clears Stuffy Noses<br>• Relieves Runny Noses<br>• Relieves Sneezing & Itchy, Watery Eyes |
| | • Loosens Chest Congestion<br>• Makes Coughs Productive<br>• Clears Stuffy Noses |
| **Triaminic-DM®** SYRUP Cough Relief | • Quiets Coughs<br>• Clears Stuffy Noses |
| **Triaminicol®** MULTI-SYMPTOM RELIEF Colds with Coughs | • Quiets Coughs<br>• Clears Stuffy Noses<br>• Relieves Runny Noses<br>• Relieves Sneezing & Itchy, Watery Eyes |
| **Triaminic®** Nite Light Nighttime Coughs & Colds | • Quiets Coughs Up To 8 Hours<br>• Clears Stuffy Noses<br>• Relieves Sneezing & Runny Noses |
| **Triaminic®** SORE THROAT FORMULA | • Eases Sore Throat Pain<br>• Quiets Coughs<br>• Clears Stuffy Noses<br>• Reduces Fever |
| | • Quiets Coughs Up To 8 Hours<br>• Relieves Nasal Congestion |
| | • Relieves Nasal Congestion<br>• Clears Stuffy Noses<br>• Reduces Swollen Nasal Passages |

**PEDIATRICIAN RECOMMENDED**

Pediatrician Recommended Brand

ALCOHOL-FREE

## Triaminic© SYRUP

**Colds and Allergies**

Clears Stuffy Noses

Relieves Runny Noses

Relieves Sneezing & Itchy, Watery Eyes

PEDIATRICIAN RECOMMENDED

**ORANGE FLAVOR NEW LABEL INFORMATION**

**118 mL (4 fl oz)**

## Triaminic© SYRUP

Triaminic Syrup relieves children's cold and allergy symptoms, without alcohol.

Each dose of Triaminic Syrup contains:

- The maximum allowable level of phenylpropanolamine hydrochloride, USP—one of the most effective nasal/sinus decongestant agents available today...to relieve nasal congestion and help clear nasal airways fast.
- The ideal dosage of chlorpheniramine maleate, USP—a proven antihistamine... to quickly relieve sneezing, itchy, watery eyes and runny noses.

And kids will love its pleasant orange taste. When it comes to caring for your child, you want only the best. And Triaminic is the brand name that has been trusted by pediatricians, pharmacists and parents for over 30 years. Trust Triaminic Syrup.

**Easy accurate True-Dose® dosing**
FREE DOSAGE CUP ENCLOSED

READ LABEL DIRECTIONS
4 TSP
2 TSP
1 TSP

| Age | Weight | Dosage |
|---|---|---|
| Under 6 yrs. | Under 48 lbs. | Consult Physician |
| 6 to Under 12 yrs. | 48-95 lbs. | 2 Teaspoons |
| 12 yrs. to adult | 96+ lbs. | 4 Teaspoons |

The dose may be repeated every 4 hours.

During the past forty years people in the U.S. have been taking on more responsibility for their health care. This trend is expected to continue as the cost of medical care increases. New technologies and products now allow people to take care of select medical needs (such as monitoring blood pressure or cholesterol, testing for pregnancy, relief of occasional constipation or pain in the stomach from excess gas) by themselves.

Over-the-counter medication packages are designed to provide you clear, easy-to-read information that tells you what the product is and for what conditions it is recommended. It is important to always read the instructions on the package and those often included inside the package before you take any over-the-counter medicine.

Most large manufacturers of OTC products provide much more information and help than the FDA requires. They often can send you more detailed information in simple English. Some have special programs in which you can enroll to receive the latest information and advice on the problem and the product you are using to solve it. For example, the Triaminic brand publishes *Triaminic Parents Club*, a publication designed to help raise healthy happy families.

## Whenever you have a question about your medication, call a physician or medical professional.

## Self-Help Organizations and Support Groups.

Self-help organizations and support groups exist to help individuals (and their families) with particular health problems. Many provide toll-free phone numbers to make it easy to contact them. They are excellent sources of information on how to handle all aspects of the problem. They often provide help and support to family members who are having difficulty with an individual who is ill. The list of support groups is long and comprehensive. There is a group to help you deal with almost any difficult situation. Your doctor or a medical professional can usually provide details.

# HOW TO STAY WELL

People in the U.S. are becoming increasingly health conscious. Public and private educational programs, increases in the cost of health care, and a general desire to live longer, healthier lives are some of the factors that contribute to this trend. In fact, a new field of medicine called "wellness" is growing in demand. Its philosophy is that it is easier to stay well than to get well. Nutrition, exercise, and routine medical check-ups play an important role in maintaining good health.

### Nutrition

It is not difficult to find "healthy" foods such as vegetables, fruits, breads, low-fat meats, and dairy products. These products are readily available, usually at lower prices than most "junk foods" (processed foods with little or no nutritional value, generally high in sugar, salts, fats, and cholesterol).

The government has recently passed laws that require a chart of nutritional values to be on packages of manufactured or processed foods. This makes it easier to understand the nutritional value of your purchase. Manufacturers are now reformulating their products to provide foods with lower fat, sugar, salt, and cholesterol contents.

### Vitamins

A large and growing number of people routinely take vitamins to supplement their diet and help them stay healthy. Vitamins are most often sold without a prescription. While vitamins may be recommended, you should always check with a medical professional before you start taking them.

### Exercise

Americans young and old are discovering the benefits of including regular exercise in their lives. There are a number of ways to do it, some expensive and some not. Some programs involve the latest high-technology equipment and personal trainers. Other activities, like jogging, only require a good pair of running shoes.

There are also a number of in-home exercise programs that require purchasing expensive equipment. It is wise not to purchase any equipment until you are sure that it is right for your needs. The advertisements for these programs often imply results that are not easily attained.

# HOW TO READ THE NUTRITIONAL CONTENTS IN FOOD

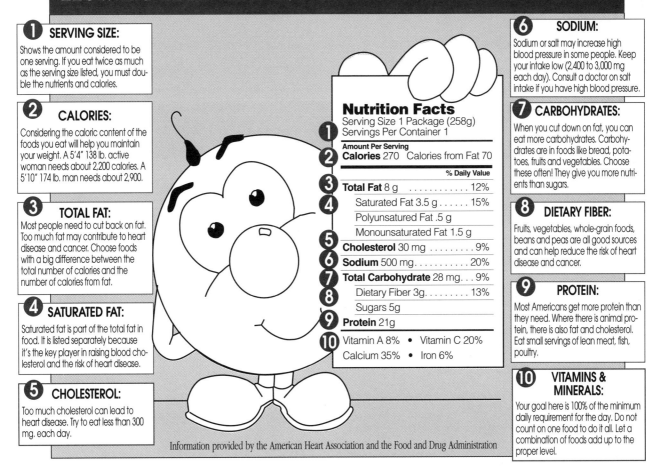

**1 SERVING SIZE:**
Shows the amount considered to be one serving. If you eat twice as much as the serving size listed, you must double the nutrients and calories.

**2 CALORIES:**
Considering the caloric content of the foods you eat will help you maintain your weight. A 5'4" 138 lb. active woman needs about 2,200 calories. A 5'10" 174 lb. man needs about 2,900.

**3 TOTAL FAT:**
Most people need to cut back on fat. Too much fat may contribute to heart disease and cancer. Choose foods with a big difference between the total number of calories and the number of calories from fat.

**4 SATURATED FAT:**
Saturated fat is part of the total fat in food. It is listed separately because it's the key player in raising blood cholesterol and the risk of heart disease.

**5 CHOLESTEROL:**
Too much cholesterol can lead to heart disease. Try to eat less than 300 mg. each day.

**6 SODIUM:**
Sodium or salt may increase high blood pressure in some people. Keep your intake low (2,400 to 3,000 mg each day). Consult a doctor on salt intake if you have high blood pressure.

**7 CARBOHYDRATES:**
When you cut down on fat, you can eat more carbohydrates. Carbohydrates are in foods like bread, potatoes, fruits and vegetables. Choose these often! They give you more nutrients than sugars.

**8 DIETARY FIBER:**
Fruits, vegetables, whole-grain foods, beans and peas are all good sources and can help reduce the risk of heart disease and cancer.

**9 PROTEIN:**
Most Americans get more protein than they need. Where there is animal protein, there is also fat and cholesterol. Eat small servings of lean meat, fish, poultry.

**10 VITAMINS & MINERALS:**
Your goal here is 100% of the minimum daily requirement for the day. Do not count on one food to do it all. Let a combination of foods add up to the proper level.

**Nutrition Facts**
Serving Size 1 Package (258g)
Servings Per Container 1

Amount Per Serving
**Calories** 270   Calories from Fat 70

% Daily Value

**Total Fat** 8 g . . . . . . . . . . 12%
Saturated Fat 3.5 g . . . . . . 15%
Polyunsaturated Fat .5 g
Monounsaturated Fat 1.5 g
**Cholesterol** 30 mg . . . . . . . . 9%
**Sodium** 500 mg. . . . . . . . . . 20%
**Total Carbohydrate** 28 mg. . . 9%
Dietary Fiber 3g. . . . . . . . 13%
Sugars 5g
**Protein** 21g

Vitamin A 8%  •  Vitamin C 20%
Calcium 35%  •  Iron 6%

Information provided by the American Heart Association and the Food and Drug Administration

There are dozens of different types of health clubs, community-based or privately owned and operated. Regardless of your age, sex, physical condition, or schedule, you should be able to find an exercise program that fits your needs. Before committing to an exercise program, discuss it with a medical professional. Talk to friends who have some experience in exercising. With a little effort, it is easy to find several acceptable programs that fit your exercise needs and budget.

## Routine Health Exams

Routine health examinations are an important way to safeguard your health. There are many community-based groups that provide periodic health screening at no cost. Many employers require passing a health examination as a condition of employment. Large companies often have a nurse or doctor available on call or on location to provide selected health services for employees.

Consult with your family doctor to determine the proper exam schedule for you and your family. For example, women with a certain medical background and age should be routinely given a breast examination. Men over a certain age should have a periodic prostate examination. Men and women after a certain age should have a routine blood pressure test.

# TOBACCO AND ALCOHOL

## Smoking

In recent years there has been a major movement to eliminate smoking in this country. There is now an overwhelming body of evidence that proves that the effects of smoking are extremely hazardous to your health.

Governments on a local, state, and national level are passing laws that limit the places a person can legally smoke.

There are a wide variety of programs to help people quit smoking. You can easily find out about these programs from your family doctor, local hospital, pharmacist, or even in magazine articles and advertisements.

## Alcohol

The amount of alcohol consumed by people in the U.S. is declining each year. In addition to the trend towards living a healthier life, there are harsh laws for drinking and driving. (See chapter *Insurance.*)

# LIVING WILL

A major factor to consider, in case of tragic accident or illness, is whether or not you want to be put on life-support systems. Life-support systems are mechanical means to keep your heart, lungs, or kidneys functioning. These systems can delay the time of your death, even maintain you in a state of permanent coma.

If you are unconscious and being kept alive only by artificial means (life support), a living will can take effect. You write your instructions (or advanced directives) before you are incapable of making your own decisions. Laws on and types of living wills and advance directives vary from state to state.

You can, in many states, appoint a medical proxy (health care agent) to carry out your wishes with regard to life-support systems. You may also give power of attorney to someone to make decisions on your behalf on any part of your medical treatment.

A conservator, appointed by state Probate Court, has comprehensive power, subject to the wishes expressed in a living will. The conservator takes responsibility for someone incapable of making his own decisions and must be consulted in areas covered by the living will. You can name in advance the person you want the court to appoint as your conservator.

For further information, consult an attorney, a local hospital, or an organization such as Choice in Dying, Inc. 1-212-246-6973.

# WHAT TO DO IN CASE OF AN EMERGENCY

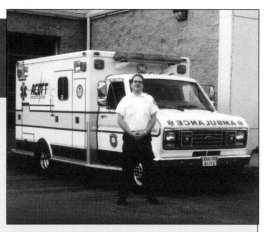

As soon as you move into your home there are some emergency phone numbers you should write down and put in a prominent place such as the front of the refrigerator door or near the telephone. These include the:

- Local Police Department
- Local Fire Department
- Local Poison Control Center
- Local Emergency Medical Service (EMS). The name for this service may be different depending on where you live. It may be called the Rescue Squad, Paramedics, or Ambulance Service.

There is no universal rule for emergency phone numbers. Look at the section on emergencies in your telephone book and write down the numbers you might need. Many communities are moving toward the 911 emergency call system. In others, you need to dial a seven-digit phone number for these services. **If you are not sure of what to do in an emergency, dial "0" for the operator.** Stay calm and ask for assistance. The operator should be able to connect you with the appropriate source of help.

## Emergency Medical Care

In case of an accident, injury, or sudden illness, call your local Emergency Medical Service (EMS) for help or go to the EMERGENCY ROOM of the nearest hospital. If possible, take along the health insurance identification card of the patient.

### CALL THE EMERGENCY MEDICAL SERVICE IF SOMEONE:

- has been or is unconscious
- has severe chest pain or pressure
- has difficulty breathing
- is bleeding heavily, vomiting excessively, or passing blood
- has continued severe abdominal (stomach) pain
- has head, neck, or back injuries, or any other injury or condition involving paralysis. Do not move anyone suspected of having such injuries
- might be poisoned or have taken a drug overdose. (Where available you should call your poison control center first.)

### TO GET HELP:

- Call: 911 or your local emergency number or the telephone operator (dial 0). Be sure to say that **"THIS IS A MEDICAL EMERGENCY"**,
- give the telephone number from which you are calling,
- your location and how to find it,
- what happened – (heart attack, injury, car crash, childbirth, or whatever); the victim's condition, and what help has already been given, and
- your name.

This helps dispatch an emergency vehicle or ambulance quickly to the scene.

*DO NOT HANG UP UNTIL THE OTHER PERSON DOES: more information may be needed or you may be provided with further instructions*

# MEDICAL PROFESSIONALS

There are numerous medical professionals who treat or assist in the treatment of specific medical conditions. The following provides a partial list of physicians (doctors) and other medical professionals you might need. You should use the recommendation of your family physician to guide you to an appropriate specialist.

**Allergist** A doctor who treats allergies and hypersensitivity to specific substances such as pollen or dust.

**Anesthetist** (anesthesiologist): A physician who administers anesthetics (drugs or gas) to eliminate pain during surgery.

**Cardiologist** A doctor who specializes in identification and treatment of problems related to the heart.

**Chiropractor:** A practitioner of chiropractic, a system of healing based on the theory that disease stems from lack of proper nerve function. Treatment involves manipulation of joints and spinal column rather than prescription

**Dentist:** A doctor who treats the teeth and gums, cleaning teeth, filling cavities, extracting teeth, and fitting dentures (false teeth) as necessary.

**Dermatologist** A doctor who specializes in identifying and treating diseases of the skin, hair, and nails.

**Endocrinologist** A physician specializing in the glands of internal secretion (thyroid, adrenal, pituitary, and others); often treats diabetes.

**Family Practitioner** (General Practitioner). A doctor who provides general medical care and advice for children, adults, and older persons. The family practitioner follows you and your family's health care and makes recommendations to insure you the best medical care. It is recommended that you make an appointment with a family practitioner to evaluate your family's health during the first month after your arrival. This is far less expensive than the cost of treating a medical problem that goes undiagnosed (not found) because an initial evaluation was not done.

**Gastroenterologist:** A physician specializing in the stomach and intestines.

**Hematologist:** A physician treating blood disorders.

**Internist:** A physician, often a family doctor, diagnosing and treating the internal organs.

**Nephrologist:** A physician specializing in the kidneys.

**Nurses** Nurses in this country are highly regarded and have a high degree of responsibility. There are two major classifications of nurses, RN (Registered Nurse) and LPN (Licensed Practical Nurse).

RNs are responsible for carrying out the doctors instructions and observing the patient's response to treatment. A degree in nursing from an approved school is required as well as passing a state examination.

LPNs do not have a degree and, therefore, cannot perform all the functions of RNs. They are typically assigned to basic patient care and work under the supervision of a doctor or RN.

Other types of nurses include: visiting nurse (visits patients in their home); nurse anesthetist; nurse practitioner (provides select services that a family practitioner does); and private duty nurse (provides care for a single patient).

**Obstetrician/Gynecologist** (OB/GYN): A physician specializing in prenatal care, childbirth, and the female reproductive system. Some doctors may specialize in only one of these areas.

**Oncologist** A doctor who identifies and treats tumors. Typically, those tumors related to cancer. Many oncologists specialize in a particular area such as breast cancer, prostate cancer, or lung cancer.

**Ophthalmologist:** A doctor who treats problems of the eye, including disease, glaucoma, cataracts, detached retina. He performs eye examinations, prescribes corrective lenses, and may perform surgery.

**Optometrist** a medical professional responsible for the measuring and fitting of corrective lenses. He may also perform basic eye examinations.

**Orthopedist** A doctor who specializes in problems relating to joints, muscles, tendons, ligaments, and the skeleton (bones).

**Osteopath:** A practitioner of osteopathy. (This places major emphasis on restoring the structural integrity of the body as the most important factor in disease through use of manipulation, medicine, diet, and other therapy.) An osteopath may hold both a Doctor of Osteopathy (D.O.) and a Doctor of Medicine (M.D.) degrees.

**Pediatrician** A doctor who specializes in children's (newborn to about fifteen to eighteen years old) health care. This includes treatment and prevention of disease. Your pediatrician or family practice doctor can provide the proper immunization for your child.

**Pharmacist** (Druggist): A highly educated professional licensed by the state to prepare and dispense medication as prescribed by a doctor. He provides the customer with information about the medicine: possible adverse reactions, how and when to take it. He can answer questions about it and advise on over-the-counter medications, as well.

**Podiatrist** A doctor who deals with problems of the foot and is usually licensed to prescribe medicine and perform surgery on the foot.

**Radiologist** A doctor who is involved in diagnosing illness with X-rays and other equipment such as ultrasound and magnetic resonance. He may also treat the patient with radioactive materials when it is recommended.

**Surgeon** A surgeon is the physician used when there is an injury or disease which requires an operation (entering the body by cutting). Many surgeons now use laser surgery, which does not involve entering the body by the traditional surgical means (cutting). In laser surgery the patient can often recover in a day or so. Some surgeons specialize in particular areas of the body; others are general surgeons.

**Urologist** A doctor who deals with diseases of the urinary tract. Some of the areas they evaluate and treat include kidney stones, frequent urination, inability to urinate, and urinary tract infections. They are also often surgeons who specialize in this area of the body.

# PRACTICE FIRE SAFETY

The following tips are provided as a general guideline of what you should know about fire and fire safety:

- Install smoke detectors on every floor in your house. These devices are designed to beep loudly if they sense smoke in the air. This alerts the occupant of a possible fire. The last Saturday in October is widely advertised as the day everyone should change the batteries in their smoke detector. Most states now have laws requiring that all houses and apartments have smoke detectors.
- Review escape routes with your family in the event of a fire. Make sure you have alternate plans in the event that fire blocks your main escape route.
- Teach your children what to do in the event of a fire. Young children tend to hide in closets and under beds in fear of the fire. Knowing what to do in a fire can save lives.
- If fire is blocking your escape route:
    Close the door in the room you are in, if possible
    Cover the bottom of the door with clothes or towels to prevent smoke from entering the room
    Stand by the window and alert someone that you are there.
- When exiting a fire in which there is thick smoke it is best to crawl on the floor to prevent smoke inhalation. (It is a fact that more people die from smoke inhalation than the fire itself).
- Call the fire department after you have safely exited the building.
- If you find that your clothes are on fire:
    **Stop** (do not run), **Drop** (to the floor) and, **Roll** (until the fire is out). Practice this as part of your fire drill.
- Pick a place outside the house that all family members will meet if the house is on fire. This spot should be away from the house but out of the way of where the fire trucks will arrive. This will enable you to know if any family members are trapped in the house.

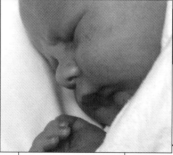

# IMMUNIZATIONS FOR CHILDREN

The following schedule reflects suggested immunizations for children in the United States. Virtually all schools require your child to be immunized before they are enrolled. It is advised to consult your family doctor about immunizations and what is necessary for your child.

| Disease | Vaccine | Birth | 1-2 Mo. | 2 Mo. | 4 Mo. | 6 Mo. | 6-18 Mo. | 12-15 Mo. | 15-18 Mo. | 4-6 Years | 11-12 Years | 14-16 Years |
|---|---|---|---|---|---|---|---|---|---|---|---|---|
| Hepatitis B | Hepatitis B | ✔ | ✔ | | | | ✔ | | | | ✔* | ✔* |
| Haemophilus Influenzae Type B | Hib | | | ✔ | ✔ | ✔ | | ✔ | | | | |
| Diptheria, Tetanus, Whooping Cough | DTP | | | ✔ | ✔ | ✔ | | | ✔ | ✔ | | |
| Polio | Polio | | | ✔ | ✔ | | ✔ | | | ✔ | | |
| Measles, Mumps German Measles | MMR | | | | | | | ✔ | | | ✔ | |
| Tetanus-Diptheria | Tetanus-Diptheria | | | | | | | | | | | ✔ |

Provided by the American Academy of Pediatrics     ✔* Previously unimmunized preadolescents/adolescents should be immunized.

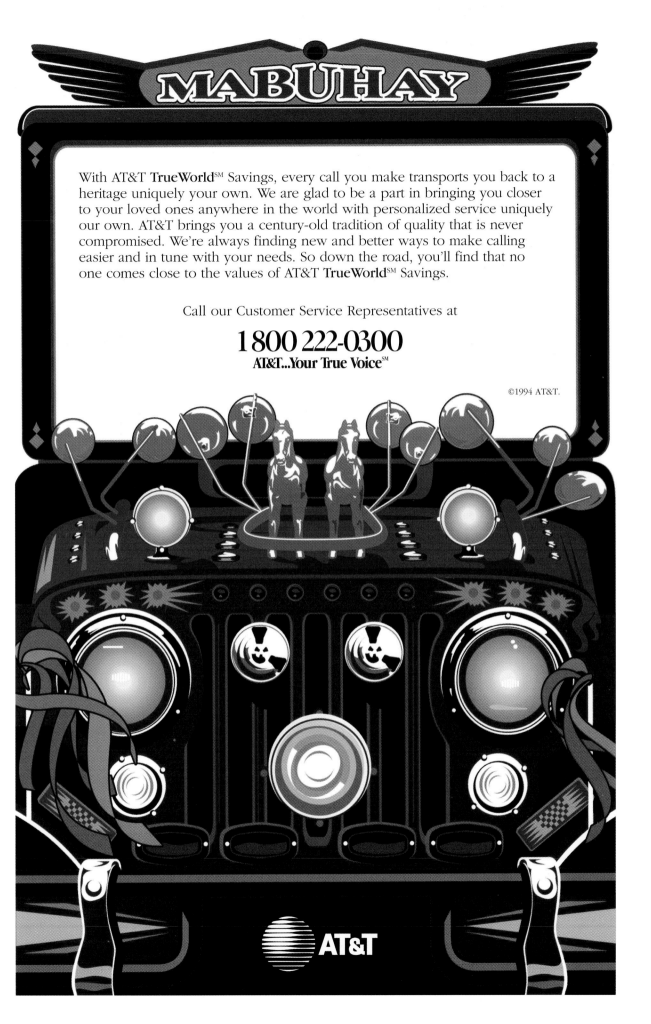

With AT&T TrueWorld[SM] Savings, every call you make transports you back to a heritage uniquely your own. We are glad to be a part in bringing you closer to your loved ones anywhere in the world with personalized service uniquely our own. AT&T brings you a century-old tradition of quality that is never compromised. We're always finding new and better ways to make calling easier and in tune with your needs. So down the road, you'll find that no one comes close to the values of AT&T TrueWorld[SM] Savings.

Call our Customer Service Representatives at

## 1 800 222-0300
### AT&T...Your True Voice[SM]

AT&T

# TABLE OF CONTENTS

## TELEPHONE

## MAIL AND TELEGRAPH SERVICE

# TELEPHONE

Telephone service in the U.S. is provided by private companies rather than the government. **Local service** (within the region surrounding you) is supplied by a designated company. **Long distance service** (for calls outside that immediate service area) is provided by competing companies (long distance carriers like AT&T). You choose the carrier.

*Telephones come in a wide variety of shapes, sizes and colors for both home and business use.*

## TELEPHONE EQUIPMENT

You can either rent or buy a telephone from AT&T or buy one from a retail store. Telephones come in a great variety of styles and colors and offer many features.

Rotary dial phones have been replaced by **touch tone** phones which allow access to many services not accessible by rotary dialing. Touch tone service offers faster switchboard response almost everywhere. Cordless, speaker, and headset features on phones also offer great convenience.

It can be less expensive over time to buy your phone - but the company is only responsible for repair service on the equipment that it owns. You will have to pay for repairs if you want the company to fix a phone you bought. Depending on the type of phone you purchase, there may be a **warranty** (promise to replace or repair something if it does not work within a specific period of time after its purchase).

## TELEPHONE SERVICE

To establish new service, call the local telephone company. The number is usually listed in the front of the telephone directory under new service. You can also call 411 or the operator (dial 0) for instructions. The company will charge you a monthly fee that will vary with the number and location of the calls you make, the type of service, and optional features you request.

Phone companies itemize their charges, the services they provide, and their rates per call. The cost to repair phone lines outside your home or business is included in the basic monthly charge. Repairs to wires within your home or office may not be. You can purchase repair service for wires within your home for a small monthly fee.

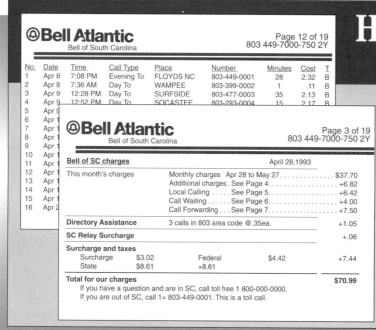

**⑥Bell Atlantic**
Bell of South Carolina

Page 12 of 19
803 449-7000-750 2Y

| No. | Date | Time | Call Type | Place | Number | Minutes | Cost | T |
|---|---|---|---|---|---|---|---|---|
| 1 | Apr 8 | 7:08 PM | Evening To | FLOYDS NC | 803-449-0001 | 28 | 2.32 | B |
| 2 | Apr 8 | 7:36 AM | Day To | WAMPEE | 803-399-0002 | 1 | .11 | B |
| 3 | Apr 9 | 12:28 PM | Day To | SURFSIDE | 803-477-0003 | 35 | 2.13 | B |
| 4 | Apr 9 | 12:52 PM | Day To | SOCASTEE | 803-293-0004 | 15 | 2.17 | B |
| 5 | Apr 9 | | | | | | | |
| 6 | Apr 9 | | | | | | | |
| 7 | Apr 1 | | | | | | | |
| 8 | Apr 1 | | | | | | | |
| 9 | Apr 1 | | | | | | | |
| 10 | Apr 1 | | | | | | | |
| 11 | Apr 1 | | | | | | | |
| 12 | Apr 1 | | | | | | | |
| 13 | Apr 1 | | | | | | | |
| 14 | Apr 1 | | | | | | | |
| 15 | Apr 1 | | | | | | | |
| 16 | Apr 2 | | | | | | | |

**⑥Bell Atlantic**
Bell of South Carolina

Page 3 of 19
803 449-7000-750 2Y

| Bell of SC charges | | April 28,1993 |
|---|---|---|
| This month's charges | Monthly charges  Apr 28 to May 27 . . . . . . . . . . . . . | $37.70 |
| | Additional charges . See Page 4 . . . . . . . . . . . . . . . . . | +6.82 |
| | Local Calling . . . . . See Page 5 . . . . . . . . . . . . . . . . . | +6.42 |
| | Call Waiting . . . . . . See Page 6 . . . . . . . . . . . . . . . . . | +4.00 |
| | Call Forwarding . . . See Page 7 . . . . . . . . . . . . . . . . . | +7.50 |

| Directory Assistance | 3 calls in 803 area code @ .35ea. | +1.05 |
|---|---|---|
| SC Relay Surcharge | | +.06 |

| Surcharge and taxes | | | | |
|---|---|---|---|---|
| Surcharge | $3.02 | Federal | $4.42 | +7.44 |
| State | $8.61 | +8.61 | | |

| Total for our charges | $70.99 |
|---|---|

If you have a question and are in SC, call toll free 1 800-000-0000.
If you are out of SC, call 1= 803-449-0001. This is a toll call.

# HOW TO READ YOUR PHONE BILL

Your monthly phone bill contains the details of every phone call and charge to your account. Because of this, your bill can be lengthy, you should review all pages for accuracy.

Send the indicated section of the bill with your payment in the envelope provided. If you think you have been charged in error (did not call a number listed) contact your phone company.

Two ways to pay for local calls are generally available:

•**Charge per call,** where you pay a set rate for each call, regardless of length, within the local calling area. This is recommended if you make very few local calls.

•**Unlimited calling,** where you pay a monthly basic service charge for all calls, regardless of number, within the local calling area. This is slightly more costly then the charge per call but is recommended if you make a more than a few calls a month.

You also pay a charge for calls outside your local calling area but within your area code. These are referred to as **toll calls.**

Optional service features may be available at additional cost. Review them carefully when you first establish service to avoid paying additional installment charges for adding features later. (See page 6 for some of the services available.)

## LONG DISTANCE SERVICE

You select your long distance carrier (choose from AT&T, Sprint, MCI, or others) when you set up local service. While you can always switch carriers later, you may pay another fee. Telephone companies offer a variety of money-saving calling plans. Contact them directly for details.

# IMPORTANT PHONE NUMBERS

| O | local operator |
|---|---|
| OO | long distance operator |
| 411 or 555-1212 | local directory assistance |
| 1 +area code + 555-1212 | long distance directory assistance |
| 1-800-555-1212 | directory assistance for toll-free numbers |
| 911 | emergency assistance *(Not yet available in all areas. Fire, police, and medical emergency numbers may be listed separately. Check your telephone directory.)* |

Important measures of service are the clarity of voice, the speed and reliability of long distance connection (including international), and customer service. AT&T, with the largest and most advanced telecommunications network, is the world technological leader. It has representatives available 24 hours a day, seven days a week – an important factor when considering international time zones. It also offers worldwide directory assistance to help you locate telephone numbers.

## OTHER TYPES OF CALLS

### Telephone charge cards

Provided by a telephone company, a phone card (or calling card) offers the convenience of charging a call automatically to your home number. This is easier than paying for it in coins at a pay phone or going through a slower voice procedure to charge the call to another number. You dial directly rather than going through an operator. This also gives you a substantial cost savings.

*Keep your phone card number secret; anyone knowing it can use it – and you may be responsible for the charges.*

Calling cards are used to make long distance telephone calls. You can use them at either public or private telephones.

### Collect calls

The call is charged against the account of the telephone called. The person answering that phone must agree to accept the charges before the call can go through.

## HOW DO YOU FIND A TELEPHONE NUMBER?

Your phone company gives you a free telephone book at least once a year. It is a directory of all listed telephone numbers in the region. (A person can keep his own number unlisted for a small fee.) The book also provides information about your local area, postal zip codes, area codes, emergency numbers, and phone services. Phone books vary somewhat with the size of the area served. Functions are categorized by colored sections. Standard white pages list residential and commercial numbers alphabetically. In highly populated regions, you may find separate white-page business listings (alphabetical, by company name). Yellow pages list commercial numbers alphabetically by the type of service provided. Blue pages, provided in some directories, give local, county, state, and federal government listings.

You can also get a phone number by calling directory assistance: (411) for local information or (1 + area code + 555-1212) for long distance. If you are not sure of the area code, you can find it in the phone directory or call the operator. There may be small charge for local and international directory assistance.

## RELATED EQUIPMENT

### Answering Machines

Answering machines have become essential to American life. An answering machine enables the caller to leave a recorded message if you are unable to answer.

*Answering machines*

*Fax machines*

*Modems*

*Cellular Phones*

*Beepers*

the phone. You can play back the message and return the call at your convenience. Telephones with built-in answering machines are widely available in retail stores.

### Voice Mail

Similar to answering machines, voice mail is offered as a service by specialized and private telephone companies. The difference is that the person receiving the call contacts the company to get the message.

### Facsimile (FAX)

In facsimile transmission (FAX), what is written on paper is converted into electrical signals and transmitted over telephone lines to a receiving fax machine. The signals, in turn, convert back to print. The copy (or facsimile) of the document is sent with the speed of a phone call.

FAX equipment is essential to business today. FAX transmission service is widely available (for a small fee) at many local stores. Inquire in any shopping area of your community for the fax service nearest you or check the Yellow Pages.

### Modem

The modem is a piece of equipment connecting a computer to a telephone line. It enables you to send information from one computer to another or to work from a small computer connected into a single machine. Both the fax and the modem can be combined in a single machine, the **FAX/modem.** With it, you can send data computer-to-computer. The receiving person can then print out the document from their computer.

### Electronic mail (E-mail)

E-mail also works between computers utilizing telephone lines. It is similar to regular mail except that you send the message (letter) using a network of computers. The message is received and stored for later reading in the recipients computer (rather than in a post office or mailbox).

### Cellular telephones

These battery-powered portable telephones are sold or rented by companies offering competing prices, guarantees, and services. As is the case with regular phone service, these companies bill you monthly; you choose your long distance carrier. Cellular phone service is available in most areas of the country. Companies are listed in the Yellow Pages.

### Beepers

A beeper is a small electronic device that enables the person carrying it to be contacted. Beepers have phone numbers like regular phones. When you call someone's beeper, you are asked to enter the phone number at which you can be reached. The beeper "beeps" or "vibrates." The person carrying it then knows he should return your call. A display on the beeper shows the phone number you entered.

# WHAT DO TELEPHONE DIRECTORY LISTINGS LOOK LIKE?

A phone directory provides a wide variety of useful information in addition to phone numbers. These are samples of pages found in a typical directory.

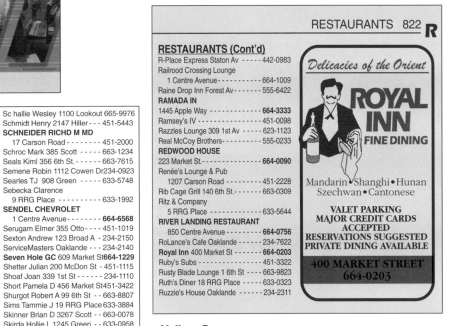

**REDWOOD–SANTOS    124**
©1994 Bell Atlantic 1994

**REDWOOD HOUSE**
223 Market St. - - - - - - - - - **664-0090**
Reginellis Sam 200 Lookout - 665-0987
Remington Don 2077 Hiller - - 451-7654
Renée's Lounge & Pub
    1207 Carson Road - - - - - - 451-2228
Reppert Jack 345 Scott - - - - - 663-4098
Rib Cage Grill 140 6th St. - - 663-0309
Richey Thos 404 Cowen Dr - - 234-5567
Riggles Brenda 111 Green- - - 633-9987
Ritz & Company
    5 RRG Place - - - - - - - - - 633-5644
**RIVER LANDING RESTAURANT**
    850 Centre Avenue - - - - - - **664-0756**
Robert Jack 244 Otto - - - - - - 451-0098
Roccart Wm E 45 Broad A - - - 234-9844
RoLance's Cafe Oaklande - - - 234-7622
**Royal Inn** 400 Market St - - - - **664-0203**
Ruby's Subs - - - - - - - - - - - - 451-3322
Rupp Walter 331 1st St - - - - - 234-1232
Rusch Richd 324 Market St - - 451-0094
Rusty Blade Lounge 1 6th St - 663-9823
Ruth's Diner 18 RRG Place - - 633-0323

Sc hallie Wesley 1100 Lookout 665-9976
Schmidt Henry 2147 Hiller - - - 451-5443
**SCHNEIDER RICHD M MD**
    17 Carson Road - - - - - - - - 451-2000
Schroc Mark 385 Scott - - - - - 663-1234
Seals Kiml 356 6th St. - - - - - - 663-7615
Semene Robin 1112 Cowen Dr234-0923
Searles TJ  908 Green  - - - - - 633-5748
Sebecka Clarence
    9 RRG Place - - - - - - - - - 633-1992
**SENDEL CHEVROLET**
    1 Centre Avenue - - - - - - - - **664-6568**
Serugam Elmer 355 Otto - - - - 451-1019
Sexton Andrew 123 Broad A - 234-2150
ServiceMasters Oaklande - - - 234-2140
**Seven Hole GC** 609 Market St**664-1229**
Shetter Julian 200 McDon St - 451-1115
Shoaf Joan 339 1st St - - - - - 234-1110
Short Pamela D 456 Market St451-3422
Shurgot Robert A 99 6th St - - 663-8807
Sims Tammie J 19 RRG Place 633-3884
Skinner Brian D 3267 Scott - - 663-0078
Skirda Hollie L 1245 Green - - 633-0958
Slate Dennis J 444 Market St- 451-2234
Smail Dee R 2 Princess Ave - 633-6996

## White Pages

*In the **white pages**, the listings are alphabetized by name (last name for individuals). Use the white pages when you know the name of the person or business you want to call. Some directories have a separate business section.*

*In the **yellow pages**, the listings are alphabetical by service. Many businesses also pay for display ads promoting the services offered. Use the yellow pages when you are looking for a particular kind of business. Some directories, especially in large metropolitan areas, use **blue pages** for all government listings.*

*Phone directories also contain many other pages of useful information. See the table of contents of your phone directory.*

**RESTAURANTS   822   R**

**RESTAURANTS (Cont'd)**
R-Place Express Staton Av - - - - - 442-0983
Railrood Crossing Lounge
    1 Centre Avenue - - - - - - - - - - 664-1009
Raine Drop Inn Forest Av - - - - - - 555-6422
**RAMADA IN**
1445 Apple Way - - - - - - - - - - - - **664-3333**
Ramsey's IV - - - - - - - - - - - - - - 451-0098
Razzles Lounge 309 1st Av - - - - 623-1123
Real McCoy Brothers- - - - - - - - - 555-0233
**REDWOOD HOUSE**
223 Market St.- - - - - - - - - - - - - **664-0090**
Renée's Lounge & Pub
    1207 Carson Road - - - - - - - - - 451-2228
Rib Cage Grill 140 6th St.- - - - - - 663-0309
Ritz & Company
    5 RRG Place - - - - - - - - - - - - 633-5644
**RIVER LANDING RESTAURANT**
    850 Centre Avenue - - - - - - - - **664-0756**
RoLance's Cafe Oaklande - - - - - - 234-7622
**Royal Inn** 400 Market St - - - - - - - **664-0203**
Ruby's Subs - - - - - - - - - - - - - - 451-3322
Rusty Blade Lounge 1 6th St - - - 663-9823
Ruth's Diner 18 RRG Place - - - - - 633-0323
Ruzzie's House Oaklande - - - - - - 234-2311

*Delicacies of the Orient*

**ROYAL INN**
**FINE DINING**

Mandarin • Shanghi • Hunan
Szechwan • Cantonese

**VALET PARKING**
**MAJOR CREDIT CARDS**
**ACCEPTED**
**RESERVATIONS SUGGESTED**
**PRIVATE DINING AVAILABLE**

**400 MARKET STREET**
**664-0203**

## Yellow Pages

## Customer Guide

*Table of Contents*

# POPULAR FEATURES AVAILABLE WITH MOST TELEPHONE SERVICE*

## CALL WAITING

Enables you to take incoming calls while you are already on the phone with someone else. A beep signals that you have another call.

## CALL FORWARDING

Transfers calls to a phone number you specify. This allows you to be reached at that number even if the calling party does not know where you are.

## REPEAT CALL

Redials the last number you called and will keep dialing that number each time you push the redial button for up to 30 minutes. This helps you to reach someone whose line is busy.

## RETURN CALL

Enables you to call back the last number that tried to reach you even if you do not know who it was.

## THREE-WAY CALLING

Lets you add a third person, at a different location, to your phone conversation.

## VOICE MAIL

Acts like a phone answering machine, answering for you and recording messages.

## CALLER IDENTIFICATION (I.D.)

Available in some areas, it lets you identify the caller before you pick up the phone. Special equipment is required that displays the caller's number when the phone rings.

## BLOCK OFF

Prevents the dialing of numbers which begin with 900. These numbers carry expensive charges. If you run a business or have children, you may want this service.

*Not all companies carry these services. Please check with your local phone company.

# SPECIAL SERVICES AVAILABLE THROUGH AT&T

**Language Line Services** offer operators who can interpret in over 140 languages. (Call 1-800-752-6096 for details.)

**World Plus Communications Service** gives you instant access to calling, interpretation, and voice and fax message services in the language of your choice. It operates 24 hours a day, in over 40 countries and locations around the world. By dialing the toll-free number, plus your account number (PIN), you can get help you with everything from local medical referrals and restaurant information to multipage faxes sent to countries worldwide. You can use this service no matter where you are or what language you speak.

**AT&T EasyReach 700** service gives you a permanent portable long distance phone number no matter where you live in mainland USA. It also provides call forwarding. (Call 1-800-982-8480 for information.)

**AT&T True Voice** creates clearer, closer, and more natural-sounding conversations. It captures the caller's voice so well you would think that the speaker was in the same room with you.

In addition to these innovative services, AT&T provides the following savings plans:

**AT&T True World Savings** can save you 25% on all international calls. Additional discounts apply to the one country that you call the most. These additional discounts can total 35% or more. The subscription rate is $3 a month.

**AT&T True USA Savings** offers a 20% savings if you spend $25 or more a month on domestic long distance calls.

**AT&T True Ties** provides you with a personal 800 number for your home use. This is especially important if you have family and friends who can not afford to call you as often as you wish. You are billed for these calls.

**AT&T True Rewards** earns you points on your long distance calls. These points can be exchanged for more long distance service or frequent flyer miles which are redeemable for airline tickets.

**800-CALL ATT** (1-800-325-5288) connects you to the AT&T network from any phone for services such as *collect calls, person-to-person calls, calling card calls, credit card calls,* and *customer service.*

**AT&T True Messages** allows you to leave a message for the person you are calling in the event that you can not get through. You can record a one minute message by dialing #123 (after calling the person and not being able to connect). AT&T will attempt to deliver that message every 1/2 hour for up to four hours.

For more detailed information or to enroll in any of these services, you may call the AT&T customer service line at 1-800-222-0300 at any time.

# MAIL SERVICE

The U.S. Postal Service is an agency of the federal government. It is managed by a board of governors appointed by the president and approved by Congress. The board elects a postmaster general who is responsible for the day-to-day operations of the Postal Service. Tampering (interfering) with the mail is a federal offense carrying stiff penalties.

In order to sort and deliver mail quickly, the nation is divided into small areas, each designated by a five-digit zip code. Always include the zip code in an address. Mail delivery may be delayed without it. Local zip codes are listed in the Yellow Pages. National zip code directories are available at the post office.

In 1983, the Postal Service began use of an expanded zip code system called zip + 4. It is composed of the original five-digit code plus a four-digit number. While use of this system is voluntary, it helps the Postal Service direct mail more efficiently. The zip + 4 is often used in business mailings to ensure faster delivery.

Postal delivery persons (mailmen) wear uniforms when delivering the mail to your home. They deliver mail Monday through Saturday except on federal holidays. (See chapter *Holidays.*) Post offices are generally open from 8:30 a.m. to 4:30 p.m. Monday through Friday and until noon on Saturdays.

## MAIL SERVICES

There are some 26,000 post offices across the country. They receive, sort, and deliver mail, sell postage stamps and the packing material required for parcels. They handle packages up to a certain size and weight. The size may not exceed 108 inches (274 centimeters) in combined girth (circumference) and length. The weight may not exceed 70 pounds (31.7 kilograms).

The cost of postage depends on the weight and features used. Mail services the post office provides include:

**First class mail** is used for letters, postcards, paying bills, sending checks or money orders and other types of general correspondences up to 11 ounces (312 grams). All first class mail is treated as airmail.

**Priority mail** is first class mail for heavier items, 11 ounces (312 grams) to 70

pounds (31.7 kilograms). Priority mail also treats all items as airmail service.

**Express mail** provides overnight delivery for letters and small packages in the United States. The price is currently $9.95 for a letter or package up to 1/2 pound (8 ounces, 227 grams); $13.95 up to two pounds (907 grams). For weights over two pounds and up to 70 pounds, ask the post office.

**Certified mail** provides a mailing receipt to the sender and a record of delivery at the recipients post office. It is for first class and priority mail only.

**Second class mail** is used by periodicals (newspapers and magazines).

**Third class mail** is a bulk business rate for authorized mailers only. It is used for circulars, catalogues, merchandise, and advertising material.

**Fourth class mail** (Parcel Post) is used for packages and printed matter, 16 oz. (454 grams) and over. There are special rates in this class for books. Always check the price between priority mail and parcel post.

**Registered mail** provides the greatest security. You declare the full value of what you are mailing. It is **insured** in amounts up to $25,000. Each postal worker who handles it must sign for while it is in his possession. A return receipt can be issued to the sender for an additional fee.

**International air letters (aerogrammes)** are single sheets of paper folded into envelope form, sealed, and mailed. They are sold for the price of an international air mail stamp.

**Collection on delivery (C.O.D.)** Some businesses will send you merchandise without requiring you to prepay for it. The payment is collected by the post office. At the time of delivery, you pay a C.O.D. fee added to the price of merchandise.

**Return receipts** are available for express mail, C.O.D., certified, insured, and registered mail. Request the return receipt (which is sent to you signed by the recipient) at the time of mailing.

For more information on services available ask for Publication 201, July 1992, entitled *A Consumer's Directory of Postal Services and Products.*

## POST OFFICE SERVICES

**Money orders,** purchased with cash from the post office, can be used like checks. They are signed by you and are accepted like cash.

Except in the case of money orders, the post office accepts personal checks up to the amount of the purchase. You must show two forms of identification. Usually, the checks must be drawn on a local or in-state bank. Out-of-state checks are often not accepted.

**Stamps** It is not always necessary to go to a post office to get stamps. They are often sold at local retail stores (supermarkets, drug, and convenience stores). Ask the cashier. Stamps can also be purchased by telephone using a credit card. Call: 1-800-782-6724.

*Post office boxes are typically located in the lobby of the post office.*

As long as it carries the correct postage, you can put mail directly into a public mailbox or have it collected by the mailman on his delivery route. If you are not sure of the postage go to the post office to get it weighed.

**Post office boxes** You can rent a post office box (a private mailbox) at the post office. Your mail is kept there until you collect it. Private carriers such as Fed Ex, UPS, or DHL will not deliver to a post office box.

**Change of address** If you are planning to move, get a free change-of-address kit from the post office. Once you send in the form, they will automatically forward your mail to your new address.

**Alien registration** Larger post offices also function as service points for registration of aliens, for passport application, for information about civil service employment, and obtaining tax forms. Check the federal government listings in your phone book to find the post office nearest you.

All mail from overseas is subject to **U.S. Customs Service** examination. Examinations are usually done when an item looks suspicious or there might be a customs duty (tax) involved.

## PRIVATE CARRIERS

The U.S. Post Office is not the exclusive provider of mail service. Competing private delivery companies offer a variety of options for express mail, parcel post, and freight service. Like the government service, private carriers deliver letters and packages directly to the address given. The zip code is also required as well as the recipients phone number. Carriers also offer pick-up service. Some of them do business strictly within U.S. borders. Others provide international service.

*Private carriers, like UPS, pick up and deliver packages and letters to your home or office. Before selecting a carrier call several and compare rates and services.*

International packages are subject to customs inspection and duties.

The prices and services of private carriers vary. Call for a rate schedule and service description before committing yourself. Prices are competitive. Carriers are listed under

"Mail Service" in the Yellow Pages. Some of the largest are: United Parcel Service (UPS), Federal Express (Fed Ex), Airborne, and DHL.

## TELEGRAPH SERVICE

Telegraph service is provided by competing private telegraph companies. These are listed under that title in your Yellow Pages. Rates and specialized services vary. Basic services provided are:

- **Telegrams,** sent locally and nationally (including Canada), are usually delivered to the recipient by hand within four to six hours. The message is telephoned to the recipient if hand delivery service is not available (or at the customer's request).

- **Mailgrams** are telegrams delivered through the post office.

- **Cables** are sent internationally via satellite (arriving in the country within two hours). How they are delivered to the addressee depends on the facilities available.

- **Telex** is also an international service. Messages require both sender and recipient to have telex equipment.

# TIPS TO KEEP THE MAIL MOVING

*The U.S. Postal Service moves over 500 million pieces of mail each day. You can help your own mail move more quickly and more safely by following these simple guidelines in addressing it.*

Return Address

YOUR NAME
YOUR ADDRESS
YOUR CITY STATE AND ZIP CODE

MR JOHN DOE
200 EASY STREET
ANYTOWN PA 15000-8349

Destination Address

## Addresses

- Use a return address in the upper left corner of the envelope in this format:

  Sender's name

  Sender's street (and apartment, suite, rural route, or P.O. box number, as needed)

  Sender's city, state, zip code

  Include "USA " on last line if mail is going to another country

- Use a complete destination address:

  Recipients name (person to whom you are sending the letter or package)

  Recipients street (and apartment, suite, rural route, or P.O. box number, if needed)

  Recipients city, state, and zip code

  Recipients country name and applicable foreign postal code for international mail

## To get the best service

- Print the destination address clearly in the center on one side only; print the return address in the upper left corner.

- Capitalize everything in the address.

- Omit punctuation marks.

- Use the common abbreviations found in the National Zip Code and Post Office Directory (available at post offices).

- Use the two-letter state abbreviations.

- Use complete and correct zip codes or zip + 4 codes when possible.

## Parcels and Packages

- Properly package and address parcels to prevent damage and loss:

  Use a container strong enough to protect contents during handling.

  Cushion contents inside container to protect them and prevent movement.

  Use pressure-sensitive reinforced tape for closing flaps and seams, not string.

  Use a plain box rather than wrapping paper.

• Print the destination address clearly in the center on one side only; print the return address in the upper left corner.

## U.S. Postal Service International Services

- **Intelpost (International Electronic Post)** is an international facsimile message service available between the United States and more than 40 other countries. Your message can be delivered at telephone speed.

- **Express Mail International Service** offers both speed and security for letters and merchandise to more than 120 countries. Rates depend on the country of destination.

- **International Money Orders** are an easy way to send money (up to $700) internationally. If the money is lost or stolen, it can be replaced when you present your customer receipt.

- **Recorded Delivery** service is similar to domestic certified mail service. It simply provides a record of delivery, useful in case of inquiry. For an additional fee, you can purchase a return receipt at the time of mailing.

- **International air letters (aerogrammes)** are single sheets of paper folded into envelope form, sealed, and mailed. They are sold for the price of an international air mail stamp.

## Domestic and International Postage Rates As of Jan. 1, 1995

| Weight not over (oz.) | POSTAGE RATES | | | |
|---|---|---|---|---|
| | Item Being Sent from U.S. to | | | |
| | U.S. | Canada | Mexico | Overseas |
| .05 | $ .32 | $ .40 | $ .35 | $ .50 |
| 1.0 | .32 | .40 | .45 | .95 |
| 1.5 | .55 | .63 | .55 | 1.34 |
| 2.0 | .55 | .63 | .65 | 1.73 |
| 2.5 | .78 | .86 | .90 | 2.12 |
| 3.0 | .78 | .86 | .90 | 2.51 |
| 3.5 | 1.01 | 1.09 | 1.15 | 2.90 |
| 4.0 | 1.01 | 1.09 | 1.15 | 3.29 |
| 4.5 | 1.24 | 1.32 | 1.40 | 3.68 |
| 5.0 | 1.24 | 1.32 | 1.40 | 4.07 |
| 5.5 | 1.47 | 1.55 | 1.65 | 4.46 |
| 6.0 | 1.47 | 1.55 | 1.65 | 4.85 |
| 6.5 | 1.70 | 1.78 | 1.90 | 5.24 |
| 7.0 | 1.70 | 1.78 | 1.90 | 5.63 |
| 8.0 | 1.93 | 2.01 | 2.15 | 6.41 |
| 9.0 | 2.16 | 2.24 | 2.40 | 7.19 |
| 10.0 | 2.39 | 2.47 | 2.65 | 7.97 |
| 11.0 | 2.62 | 2.70 | 2.90 | 8.75 |
| 12.0 | | 2.93 | 3.15 | 9.53 |
| 13.0 | | | | 10.31 |
| 14.0 | | | | 11.09 |
| 15.0 | | | | 11.87 |

*A free brochure entitled International Postal Rates and Fees is available at all post offices.*

## Postal Mark Cancellation

*This marking appears in the upper right hand corner of all packages and letters. It marks the postage used and also indicates the date and branch the letter was originally mailed from.*

Z 343 892 268

**Receipt for Certified Mail**

No Insurance Coverage Provided
Do not use for International Mail
(See Reverse)

UNITED STATES POSTAL SERVICE

PS Form **3800**, March 1993

| | | |
|---|---|---|
| Sent to | *Donald Machee* | |
| Street and No. | *Pitt Traffic Court* | |
| P.O., State and ZIP Code | *100 Grant St. Pitt. PA 15219* | |
| Postage | | $ .32 |
| Certified Fee | | 1.00 |
| Special Delivery Fee | | |
| Restricted Delivery Fee | | |
| Return Receipt Showing to Whom & Date Delivered | | 1.00 |
| Return Receipt Showing to Whom, Date, and Addressee's Address | | |
| TOTAL Postage & Fees | | $ 2.32 |
| Postmark or Date | | |

AUG 1 1994 BELLE VERNON

## ◀ Return Receipt Requested

*When you request a return receipt for certified mail as proof that the recipient received your letter this is what you will get back.*

*The recipient's signature will be on the top of the receipt as proof that he received the letter.*

## ▼ Delivery Notice/ Reminder/Receipt

*If you receive one of these forms in the mail it means that you have a certified letter waiting for you at your local post office. Usually the mail person would attempt to deliver this, however if you are not home he will leave this receipt notifying you of the letter.*

---

| • IMPORTANT: | Present this form to obtain your mail. ID required. Signature may be required. | ARTICLE NO. | | | |
|---|---|---|---|---|---|
| You may pick up your mail after _____ M. (Date) _____ _____ or notify carrier or Post Office for redelivery. | | | | **MAIL IS AT** ▶ | |

| ☐ Registered | ☐ Numbered Insured | ☐ Custom *(Omit Number)* | ☐ Letter | ☐ Flat |
| ☐ Certified | ☐ COD | ☐ Rtn Rcpt for Mdse | ☐ Postage Due | ☐ Parcel | ☐ Hold |
| ☐ Recorded Delivery Service (International only). | | | ☐ Restricted Delivery | |
| ☐ Special Delivery } For special deliveries Article | ☐ Placed Under Your Door. ☐ Placed in Your Letter Box. | ZIP of Origin | |
| Final Notice | Return Date | Amount Due $ | |
| Customer *(Please describe any visible damage)* | Addressee Name *(Print)* | | |
| | Address | | |
| Delivered by and Date | Received By X | | |

Thank you, we appreciate your business.

Left With Residential Unit Manager

**PS Form 3849,** Feb 1991    **Delivery Notice/Reminder/Receipt**

## Stamps

*Stamps come in a variety of types and denominations. Featured here are just a few of the most common.*

Education is given high priority in the United States. Public school is free and compulsory. While state laws vary in terms of ages of enrollment (five, six, or seven to 16, 17, or 18), children are required to attend, usually through high school. Many go on to university level and advanced degrees. Education, recognized as the key to personal growth and success is increasingly part of adult life as well. Vocational training opportunities are almost unlimited. Specialized training in the use of computers is widely available.

Essential to any education – and to your adaptation to this country – is an understanding of English. Affordable classes are available locally.

# TABLE OF CONTENTS

## EDUCATION

## LEARNING ENGLISH

# EDUCATION

The U.S. educational system is a product of national history. In colonial times, education was largely controlled by local religious groups. With the demands of a growing population and the formation of new secular (non-religious) colonies, it became a government function. A strong tradition of locally supported and publicly funded schools continues. There is no federally controlled or nationally administered school system; each state has its own system. There are, however, two principles: **universal compulsory education** and **locally-established schools.**

This evolution in education produced a system of both great diversity and remarkable sameness spread, over 50 states and some 15,500 local public school districts operating over 100,000 schools in the United States. Schools and districts differ by size, administrative structure, and the amount and source of financial support they receive. **Public schools** are paid for primarily by property taxes. **Private schools**, in contrast, are independently supported by student fees, often subsidized by a sponsoring church or group. **School boards,** which run the

*American culture widely encourages the practice of reading to children, no matter how young they are. This helps instill an enjoyment for books and education in the child. Public libraries are widely available in all areas of the country, providing a ready source of reading and reference materials. Reading programs, such as story hours for young children, are available, as are literacy programs for adults.*

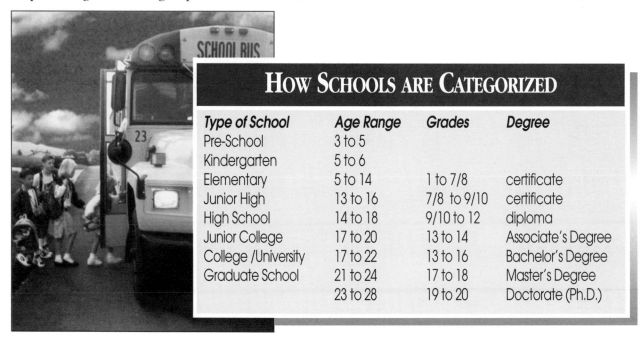

## HOW SCHOOLS ARE CATEGORIZED

| Type of School | Age Range | Grades | Degree |
|---|---|---|---|
| Pre-School | 3 to 5 | | |
| Kindergarten | 5 to 6 | | |
| Elementary | 5 to 14 | 1 to 7/8 | certificate |
| Junior High | 13 to 16 | 7/8 to 9/10 | certificate |
| High School | 14 to 18 | 9/10 to 12 | diploma |
| Junior College | 17 to 20 | 13 to 14 | Associate's Degree |
| College /University | 17 to 22 | 13 to 16 | Bachelor's Degree |
| Graduate School | 21 to 24 | 17 to 18 | Master's Degree |
| | 23 to 28 | 19 to 20 | Doctorate (Ph.D.) |

## Homework

Schools and teachers vary widely in their assignments. However, it is generally felt that regular homework significantly improves a child's learning and academic progress. You will need to visit with the teacher or teachers to find out what homework is required and how often it is assigned. You should also ask if the homework is checked by the teacher, graded, and returned.

## Report Cards

Almost all schools send report cards to parents. A parent is often required to sign the report card before it is returned to the teacher. Report cards are typically given six times a year. They are very important in terms of understanding the quality of the student's work.

Virtually all schools offer after-school clinics, tutoring programs, and other methods to help the student learn. A high degree of communication is encouraged between parent and teacher.

public schools, are elected by local communities. The schools reflect their attitudes. There are differences in the quality and the philosophy of education, as well as in the way schools are organized by age and grade.

School districts have similarities as well as differences in organizational structure, teaching method, instructional materials, curriculum control, and school experience. (*See Things to Consider When Evaluating a School,* on page J-7.) These similarities are fostered by the mobility of both students and teachers (Americans tend to relocate often), state-wide adoption of materials, major national educational publishers, national professional organizations, and both nationally and regionally standardized tests. Federal courts have made rulings on laws affecting such education-related issues as separation of church and state; freedom of speech for teachers and students; racial integration; and the right of state legislatures to regulate access to local schools.

# PRE-SCHOOL EDUCATION

American children are required to enter school, whether public or private, at the age of five, six or seven, depending on the state. Before that age, private pre-schools (or nursery schools) and day-care facilities are available. In major cities admission to pre-schools can be highly competitive and very expensive. Fees for day-care centers can also be costly.

### Nursery schools

Nursery schools are generally private and can be moderate to expensive in price. They provide educational and social training. They not only prepare the child with the basic education needed to start school but also lay the groundwork for future study habits and approach to learning. Hours range from four to eight hours per day, two to five days per week.

### Day-care centers

Day-care centers have a less academic and more practical emphasis; without them, many parents could not work. Day-care centers are typically open longer hours and provide more complete service (including meals) to the children. They may or may not provide educational training.

# PRIMARY AND SECONDARY EDUCATION

Typically, each state delegates authority for its schools to the local districts, but establishes guidelines for their operation. The state sets minimum standards, the number of hours in a school day and the number of school days in a year (approximately, 180 to 190 days per year – beginning in early September, and ending in June). There are often one or two major vacation periods, one in late December and the other in early spring. Summer school is often available for students needing additional help or accelerated work. Each state department of education certifies the professional school staff.

Public school students live at home, attending schools in their local area. Since public school choice is largely determined by neighborhood, the quality of schools in an area may be a factor in where you decide to live. Call the local school board to determine what public school your child would attend if you moved into a given area. Ask about the student records, if any, required for admission.

**Primary schools** include kindergarten and elementary schools (grammar schools). **Secondary schools** are com-

## Mainstreaming

The effort to provide equal services to the mentally or physically challenged within the public schools is common throughout the nation. The idea is to integrate the challenged (handicapped) individuals into normal social life rather than isolating them in subcultures based on their particular situation. Programs vary greatly from community to community.

# TECHNOLOGY IN THE CLASSROOM

PHOTO COURTESY THOMAS LONG

Technology has changed the way we practice education.

- The use of computers, video, and television is widespread and increasing in many areas.

- Classes are taught at the same time in several cities, via computer and video camera, that allow the teacher and students to see and speak with one another.

- The researching, by computer, through thousands of written sources on any subject can be carried out in minutes.

- Classroom televisions can "call up" any of a number of educational and instructional programs at any of a number of learning levels.

- Students can participate in "interactive learning" where they can progress at their own speed with a computer that adjusts to their personal learning level and ability, stimulates their interest, and cannot criticize or get angry.

Such changes are affecting the traditional roles of teachers, students, and schools.

## Student Government

Most schools maintain some form of student government on a classroom, school-wide basis, or both. The role of student government varies. It can be a very important experience in learning and establishing morals, values, ethics, management, leadership, and other qualities a student will need to be successful.

## Apprenticeship

Working directly with an experienced person in a particular trade is required in certain fields. It may consist of on-the-job experience as well as some classroom training. In some cases licenses are required. Check with trade unions or local tradespeople (electricians, plumbers) about opportunities.

prised of some combination of junior high and high school. Community variations include two or three grades in junior high and three or four in high school.

Private schools – which may be elementary only, high school only, or combined – operate under the general state laws for public schools but are chartered separately. They enroll less than 15 percent of the total U.S. school population. They usually finance their operations without tax monies and more heavily control the courses offered and educational policies. They may be **parochial schools** (religious – you do not necessarily have to belong to the religion to attend); **nonsectarian** (schools without religious affiliation); or **special needs** schools for physically or emotionally challenged (handicapped) or learning disabled students.

Most private schools cover the same subjects as public schools, differing primarily in teaching methodology, class size, and facilities available. Private schools generally offer smaller classes with greater individual attention than public. Some have rigorous entrance qualifications and standards. Some schools provide residential facilities or dormitories. Many private schools place an emphasis on cultural diversity.

It is possible to obtain a **Graduation Equivalency Diploma (GED),** equal to a high school diploma, outside the normal institutional pattern. This requires taking a course and passing a test. The local board of education can provide you information on how to earn it.

## POST-SECONDARY EDUCATION

There are a number of post-secondary opportunities in education. The institutions in each control their own procedures. Admission almost always requires prior completion of high school. Non-native English speakers are often required to take the Test of English as a Foreign Language TOEFL. (See chapter *Learning English.*)

**Technical schools,** both public and private, train students for specific occupations, technical services, or professions – usually over one to three years. They award certificates or associate degrees in many fields, including:

- **medical** – physical therapy, radiology, emergency medicine

EDUCATION

- **office** – secretarial skills, bookkeeping, stenography, word processing, and other computer skills

- **technical** – automobile mechanics, computer programming and repair, heating and air conditioning repair, and telephone system installation and repair

- **business** – accounting, hotel and restaurant management, sales and marketing.

Admission is not necessarily competitive. These schools usually offer both day and evening classes. Placement offices are usually available in these schools and can be helpful in assisting their graduates locate employment. The Yellow Pages list technical institutions under "Schools."

**Community colleges** (junior colleges), offer two-year programs of study and generally award the Associate of Arts degree (AA). Two-thirds of community colleges are public (tuition not free, but much lower than that at similar private institutions). They are often used to prepare for four-year colleges and universities.

**Four-year colleges** and universities admit students for undergraduate study. They consider academic grades, past courses of study, and student activities, interests, and accomplishments. Admission to the top-ranking colleges is very competitive. It usually requires the results of standardized tests such as the Scholastic Aptitude Test (SAT) or the American College Testing Program (ACT) and three achievement tests. Most colleges grant the Bachelor of Arts (BA) or Bachelor of Science (BS) degree. Students specialize in one of a great variety of fields, including liberal arts, various sciences or technical subjects, business, or pre-professional training for medicine or law.

There are over 3,400 colleges and universities, a little more than half of which are private rather than state-affiliated. Over six million students attend, 78 percent of them at public institutions where tuition rates are comparatively lower.

There has been a trend in recent years toward admission of older students, coinciding with the growth of community colleges and the increased availability of government financial assistance for tuition.

Advanced **(Graduate school)** study is available for selected students at several levels. There are also professional cer-

## College Entrance Exams

College entrance exams include the Scholastic Aptitude Test (SAT) or the American College Testing Program (ACT), and the Achievement Tests of the College Entrance Examination Board. Non-native English speakers are generally asked to take the Test of English as a Foreign Language (TOEFL).

Test scores can significantly affect the type of school the student can enter. These tests are given only by computer in some areas.

Students are advised to take advantage of the resources available to improve their scores. There are self-help books and computer programs. SAT preparation courses are available privately (for fees of $400-500) or free at many high schools.

## Translating academic and professional credentials

Before the state or other institution can review licenses, academic records, or degrees from foreign countries they may need to be professionally translated and evaluated. For further information contact World Education Services, Inc. at 1-212-966-6311

*Junior or community colleges also offering adult education courses are the fastest-growing segment of post-high school education.*

tificate programs to prepare students for external exams and licensing in state-certified occupations.

**Graduate school** admission requires another highly competitive process. Standardized exams depend on the field of study: the Graduate Record Exam (GRE) for most, the Medical College Admission Test (MCAT) or the Law School Admission Test (LSAT) as relevant.

The **masters** degree takes one to two years to complete depending on the degree and the graduate school.

The **doctorate** takes three to five years or more to complete. This includes the Doctor of Philosophy (Ph.D.), the Doctor of Medicine (M.D.), Doctor of Law (J.D.), and others.

### Adult Education

Large numbers of adults attend junior colleges, colleges, and graduate schools on a part-time basis in the evening. They may do so, while working full time in order to advance their careers or simply to learn more.

Most community schools and many community organizations offer classes on a wide variety of technical, practical, and interesting subjects for those who enjoy learning on an informal basis. It is common to have several community groups offering classes on hundreds of different topics, including English as a Second Language (ESL). Fees are typically very low. Catalogues are usually available a month before classes begin. There are generally no entrance requirements.

# THINGS TO CONSIDER WHEN EVALUATING A SCHOOL

Parents often make their decision concerning where to live based on the quality of the public schools in the area. Things to consider in a school are:

- The school's personality. What reputation does it have in the community, among the graduates, and among other learning institutions? How is a typical student described? What types of awards has the school won in academics and other areas?

- The school's educational philosophy and objectives. Parents should check to see that the school's ethics, morals, and values are in agreement with theirs.

- Are the teaching methods used by the school child-centered or subject-centered? Child-centered teaching methods are more focused on giving the child a wide degree of freedom in the classroom to create a positive atmosphere. Subject-centered classes are more focused on a strict set of rules that center on the subject being taught. Both systems have merits and drawbacks.

- The methods used when academic or behavioral problems occur. These should be consistent with your own values and approach to raising your child.

- What is the quality of the faculty? How long does the average teacher work for the school? What academic degrees do most of the faculty possess? How is the faculty selected? What type of training does the faculty receive? Do teachers pursue additional education to improve their skills? Is additional training encouraged by the school? How is it done – is it mandatory or suggested? Is the faculty made up of teachers who have studied primarily teaching methodology or the particular subjects they teach in depth?

- What are the physical facilities? What types and quality of equipment are available in areas such as visual aids, computers, printers, athletic equipment and facilities, auditorium, laboratories, transportation, musical instruments, security, and any other areas that you feel are important?

- What types of special facilities and programs are available for children who have either learning disabilities or are gifted (those possessing a special talent in areas such as mathematics or the arts)?

- What types of vocational and trade programs are offered for students who are not planning on attending college or university?

The best way to insure that the quality of education is high and that proper standards are in place is to take an active role in organizations designed to help manage the school. These include the Parent Teacher Association (PTA), the school board, and various volunteer committees that help guide the operation of the school.

You will find that most schools encourage this type of commitment from parents. Parental involvement is a very important part of a child's education. It is considered both a right and a responsibility for parents to take an active role in the educational process.

# THE LIBRARY

American libraries provide a wealth of information and services. They are usually staffed by people who are helpful, courteous, and knowledgeable.

Local public libraries reflect their local communities, often conducting a needs and interests survey in the local area to determine the basic collection of books, services, and hours of operation.

Typical hours are 9 AM to 8 PM weekdays. They are often open Saturdays and, in some cases, Sundays. Libraries generally provide:
- A formal education support center,
- An independent learning center,
- A pre-schooler's introduction to learning area,
- A research and information center for community and local businesses,
- A community activity center.

There are approximately 115,000 libraries (including smaller branch affiliates) in the United States. Library services vary. They usually include:
- The loaning of books,
- The use of reference materials, magazines, and newspapers,
- The loaning of video cassettes on topics not usually available in video stores and may also loan VCRs,
- The use of computers, printers, diskettes, and software. There are even courses available on selecting and buying a personal computer.

**On-line data bases** have largely replaced card catalogs. They can even be reached by home or office computer. Some even have a 24-hour bulletin board offering book and video cassette reviews, games, and other services.

**Programs for children** may include after-school enrichment programs such as help with homework, storytelling, writing, puppetry, arts and crafts, first aid, home safety, how to handle emergencies, health care, and simple meal preparation.

For pre-schoolers there are often toys and games available for loan that help them learn basic skills such as counting and recognizing shapes and textures. Bilingual story hours that promote language proficiency may also be available.

Children with special needs may check out toys adapted for their use. For example, some libraries have magnetic toys, Braille and large print games, and microcomputer add-on devices on loan.

**Business Services** – Many libraries have large business departments staffed by trained librarians who use a wide range of tools including: data bases of economic, legal, and financial information, business directories and corporate annual reports.

**Job Information Centers** are maintained by some large libraries to provide employment search assistance.

**Telephone Research Services** providing answers to most questions is widely available.

If any of these services are not available at your local library, discuss it with the librarian. Special loan arrangements with other libraries can often be made.

# LEARNING ENGLISH

A good, working knowledge of the English language is essential to your professional, social and personal success in this country. Command of the national language is your most vital tool for communication. It will help you earn the trust and respect of your new countrymen.

The study of English can also offer you invaluable insight into American culture. It enables you to participate in and enjoy all areas of that culture - business, science, education, recreation and the arts. It also gives you some protection against manipulation or deception by people trying to take advantage of your lack of language skills.

Typical American English is practical and flexible. It is clear and direct, and often very informal. Like the people who use it, the language is open to new words and idioms that help express ideas or changing conditions.

If you come to the United States with a textbook understanding of English grammar, but cannot use your English to order from a menu, to speak in a job interview, or to make a flight reservation on the telephone, consider a class in conversational English.

Your immediate objective should be learning to speak good, practical English. Later, you can go on to more advanced study, perhaps with specific focus on areas of professional, academic or personal interest.

*English is an important tool to use for your success and enjoyment in the United States.*

There are many places to learn English. The school you choose depends on its location, the flexibility of your schedule, your budget, your preference of teaching methods, and how quickly and thoroughly you want to master your new language and your new life.

## Home study

If you want to try studying on your own, books, audio and video cassette tapes are sold at book stores and are available at public libraries. They may also be available at foreign consulates here or U.S. consulates abroad.

PHOTOS COURTESY BERLITZ

# WHAT YOU SHOULD EXPECT FROM A LANGUAGE PROGRAM

A good program will offer English instruction at all levels and in all formats from the beginner level to the most advanced, and from individual and semi-private to small group classes of five to fifteen students. It should accommodate any schedule and budget. Classes should be available in the morning, afternoon and evening from Monday through Saturday. The instruction should be adaptable to fit the particular needs of the student.

Other program offerings may include:
- Intense, individual, day-long, Monday through Saturday lessons including lunch lessons with the teacher.
- Specially-designed classes for children to build both communication skills and cultural awareness.
- Cross-cultural training on social customs, beliefs and expressions.

### English as a Second Language (ESL) programs

Free ESL instruction is often available at local churches, organizations, elementary and high schools, vocational schools, and colleges. Contact Literacy Volunteers of America (under local municipal headings in the Yellow Pages) for details.

### Public schools

Some elementary and secondary schools offer ESL courses for their students. If you have children, you may want to call the local schools before moving into a particular district to find out if they offer ESL.

### Language schools

Language schools are listed under that heading in the Yellow Pages. Of these, Berlitz is the oldest, largest, and best known. There are over 320 Berlitz Language Centers in more than 30 countries. If there is one in your home country, you may want to begin your instruction there before you relocate. Once you get to the U.S., you may continue right where you left off to avoid problems often caused by interrupted instruction. These problems may include the waste of time and money due to placement in a class that is too easy or too difficult. To find the Berlitz Language Center nearest you, call (in the U.S.) 1-800-457-7958.

# HOW CAN I LEARN ENGLISH?

The way you choose to learn English may help or hinder your progress. There are a number of ways to learn a language. To protect your investment of time and money, consider the quality of your teachers and the method of instruction they use.

### The Berlitz Method

Since its founding in 1878, Berlitz has been a leader and innovator in language instruction. Its success is largely due to the use of its direct method, modeled on the natural process by which children learn their language – by hearing and speaking only that language. Berlitz students hear and speak only the language they are studying. Once considered experimental, this method has been accepted and imitated by the academic world. It works.

*How can students understand the instructor if they speak only the new language?*

The answer is demonstration. The teacher uses pictures, objects, and demonstration techniques to teach increasingly complex ideas. Lessons take the form of conversation (not boring lecture). Students talk as much or more than the teacher, asking questions, giving answers, and taking the initiative in conversation. They learn grammar by repetition, speaking the same way the teacher speaks. The teacher guides the conversation to introduce new material. Students and teacher role play (act out) common "real life" situations that students will encounter, such as checking into a hotel, or opening a bank account.

Berlitz action modules are similar, bringing students together in confrontational situations (negotiating the price of a car, for example). The acting students are tape recorded for analysis by the class as a whole.

Berlitz also offers special courses for:

- **Accent Reduction.** Live instruction, combined with audio tape programs, helps students reduce foreign accents. Some large American companies sponsor employees in these classes.

- **TOEFL** (Test of English as a Foreign Language). Berlitz can help you prepare for this standardized test. It is used by most American universities as part of the admission process for non-native English speakers.

- **TOEIC** (Test of English for International Communication). Corporations and government agencies use this test to assess the English proficiency of job applicants and current employees studying English. Berlitz both prepares students for and administers the TOEIC.

- **Self-Study.** A number of self-study programs are available for your home use. For example, "Berlitz and You" is an English course (on cassette or CD) designed for speakers of Arabic, French, German, Italian, Japanese, and Spanish. For information, call (in the U.S.) 1-800-526-8047; if abroad, call 1-609-461-2014.

PHOTO COURTESY BERLITZ

# TIPS TO LEARNING ENGLISH FASTER

- **Watch American TV.** It lets you hear the words and watch the faces and mouths of people as they speak. Public television stations are often the most educational and feature the best spoken English. If you have a video cassette recorder (VCR), record shows and re-play them as many times as you want. Go to the movies or rent videos to watch at home.

- **Listen to radio.** National Public Radio is best. It mixes music and news with intelligent political and cultural commentary in good, clear English. Try to imitate the pronunciation and speech patterns you hear. It will help your English as well as keep you informed about interesting ideas and news events.

- **Spend time with American friends.** You can learn a lot just by going with an American to a big supermarket or department store.

- **Do not be afraid to speak English, especially with children.** Most Americans will be delighted to talk with you.

- **Read American newspapers and magazines.** When you see a word you do not know, look it up in a dictionary.

- **Ask questions** when you do not understand something.

- **Play word games such as Scrabble® with your American friends.** (This is a board game which involves making words.) Do the crossword puzzles in the newspapers.

Leisure-time activities play a large part of life in American life. Whether you prefer indoor or outdoor recreation, whether your budget is large or small, there is something available for you. Radio and television programs, movies, videos and video games, concerts, theatre, books, newspapers, and magazines, hobbies, sports, associations, camping – the possibilities are almost unlimited.

Traditional holidays offer a focus for relaxation.

Travel is a favorite way to spend vacations here. Come visit our cities and seacoasts, our mountains and forests, and experience the great diversity of our culture.

# TABLE OF CONTENTS

## ENTERTAINMENT AND SOCIAL ACTIVITIES

# ENTERTAINMENT & SOCIAL ACTIVITIES

What do Americans do when they are not working? They enjoy themselves in an incredible number of ways. The entertainment industry is immense. There are movies, theaters, concerts, community programs, and sports events to attend; television, radio, videos, hobbies, and games of all types for home entertainment.

If you enjoy active participation, join in at all levels of sports, hobbies, camping, hunting, fishing, the arts, adult education courses (see chapter *Education),* and many forms of recreation on a community, state, or national basis.

Volunteer work is another important aspect of American life. Many people give some of their leisure time to helping churches or other non-profit organizations.

## TELEVISION

Television (TV) clearly dominates home entertainment in this country. It is estimated that 98 percent of households have a television set; over 64 percent have more than one. Virtually all television sets are color. The average American watches over 29 hours of television weekly. Sets are on in households an average of seven hours daily. Almost 100 million people watch television during prime time (8-11 PM weekdays including Saturday; 7-11 PM Sunday).

In virtually all areas of the nation there are a wide variety of programs to watch – feature films, comedy, suspense and mystery drama, general drama, news, documentaries, educational series, sports, and classical and contemporary music. Most shows are in English; however, foreign language programs are aired in many urban areas.

*Watching television is an integral part of American life.*

For example, one such service available for the new arrival is the Russian-American Broadcasting Company. You can subscribe to this television and radio network for Russian news and information, as well as programming that helps with your new life in America. This programming also provides a mix of entertainment and lifestyle programs such as movies, travel, and talk shows. To subscribe to this programming or for more information, call 1-800-742-9662.

What channels your home television can receive depends on your location and the type of reception you have. Television sets, usually with an attached antenna, are the simplest way to bring in regular television network programming. Major networks and local channels broadcast TV signals at no charge. The average city has six to eight major stations broadcasting free programming (paid for by advertisers). If you live in a rural part of the country or in an area with reception interference, you may get only a few stations. You can buy an inexpensive, additional antenna to bring in more or subscribe to cable television.

## Cable television

Cable television generally offers 30 to 60 different channels. It is subject to less interference than that of broadcast over the air because it brings TV signals directly into the home through wires from a central location. Cable TV service is provided by private companies to almost two-thirds of U.S. homes. A single company is licensed to operate in a given region. You pay a monthly charge for service.

Cable companies offer a variety of service plans. The more program options and channels, the more you pay. With a basic cable plan, there is generally a set monthly charge to receive all regular channels locally available over the airwaves and some additional channels. These additional channels most often include: sports, news, the arts, education, documentaries, general entertainment, home shopping, and local public access. By law, cable operators must offer free local air time and the facilities to produce programs to virtually anyone in the local community.

With a more expensive premium cable plan, you get additional channels. Typical programming on these channels include: recent movies, cultural events, and live sports events without interruption. These specialized channels generally do not accept the paid advertising common on regular network TV. You can pay for each premium channel separately or get several channels in a special offer.

There are also "Pay-Per-View" channels which show individual events and movies that have recently played exclusively in theaters, for a one-time fee. Special programs are listed in the monthly cable programming guide supplied with the service. You simply call the company and request the special program. You are billed at the end of the month with your regular statement.

To order cable TV, find the name and telephone number of your cable company in local advertisements or in the Yellow Pages under "Television."

## Satellite dishes

You can bring in the most channels with the use of a satellite dish antenna. This is a concave disc several feet in diameter used outside a home or building to receive the same satellite transmissions available to cable companies. The satellite dish might be a good idea if you live out of range of cable and regular broadcast television. However, it costs several thousand dollars to buy and install. It might also violate local zoning regulations. Check with local authorities before you make the investment.

### Video Cassette Recorders (VCRs)

Approximately 80 percent of households have at least one VCR. You can record television programs from your own TV with a video cassette recorder that operates with a television. What is the advantage? Saving programs for later viewing at a time of your own choosing. You can even set the VCR to record while you are away.

Most movies made today are soon released on video cassette after they have been shown in theaters. You can buy or rent these tapes (videos) at local video stores. The selection of tapes is wide, prices are reasonable, and length of rental time varies from one to three days. You can also take tapes out on loan from your public library.

*Renting videos to view at home is popular in America.*

# RADIO

The emergence of television as the dominant medium for communicating news, advertising, and entertainment has had enormous impact on radio.

Programming has been forced to shift emphasis from drama, comedy, and variety to music – aimed largely to a young listening audience. News, weather, and sportscasts continue to hold general interest. A trend toward talk shows (in which audience and announcer converse) has developed since the 1960s. Interest in public radio broadcasting, which has no commercial advertising, has also grown.

There are two major radio broadcast bands, AM and FM. Each has hundreds of stations across the United States, most of which are commercial. The average home has between six and seven radios. Virtually all cars have a radio.

# NEWSPAPERS

A free press, unlicensed and uncensored by any level of government, is a basic component of the nation's heritage and its daily life. Most Americans read at least one daily or weekly newspaper. There are also a number of foreign language newspapers published in the U.S. by ethnic organizations. Newspapers and magazines from your native country may also be available at newsstands in your local community or a library.

*Newspapers, as well as magazines are abundant. You can find information on almost anything of interest through them.*

## MAGAZINES

Magazines intended for the general and specialized reader are abundant. No matter what your interest, there will probably be several magazines for your reading pleasure. Magazines are purchased at newsstands, bookstores and grocery or convenience stores or by subscription (at a much lower rate). They cover an extensive variety of subjects – news, entertainment, sports, fashion, women, men, family life, intellectual life, science, crafts, home decorating, gardening, cooking, and virtually every hobby.

## SPORTS

Spectator (viewer) sports are a basic part of American entertainment. Major sports events, professional, and collegiate games are carried extensively on television and radio, widely featured in print, and commonly discussed. In addition, you will find all of these sports played by both children and adults as a means of recreation. Some familiarity with them might be useful in your cultural adjustment.

*Professional baseball, football, basketball and hockey are popular sports in America. Thousands of spectators come to the stadium to watch the game. The same games can also be viewed on television as well.*

### Baseball

Baseball dominates the summer airwaves from April to October. Twenty-eight professional teams in the U.S. and Canada play in the competing National and American Leagues. Each team has a home city full of loyal fans. Teams within each league compete with each other for the pennant (championship). The pennant winners from each league then compete in the World Series (world championship), won in both 1992 and 1993 by the Toronto Blue Jays of Canada. The 1994 World Series was not played for the first time since baseball was established in the late 1800s. The season was cut short by a player's strike.

Local high school, college, and semi-professional baseball is also watched. Many towns also offer baseball and softball (another variation of baseball played with a larger ball) leagues for amateur involvement.

### Football

Football is a game played with a large inflated oval leather ball on a field at either end of which there is a goal post. Each team, consisting of 11 players, tries to score touchdowns (by running or passing the ball over its opponents' goal line) and field goals (by kicking the ball over the crossbar of the opponents' goal post).

With the fall comes football, played between colleges (as well as most high schools), which dominates sports conversation. As is the case with other collegiate sports, teams play in divisions established on the basis of college size and location. There is no formal annual championship for college football. There are, how-

## Major College Football Bowl Games:

Rose Bowl (Pasadena, CA)

Orange Bowl (Miami, FL)

Sugar Bowl (New Orleans, LA)

Cotton Bowl (Dallas, TX)

Gator Bowl (Jacksonville, FL)

# PROFESSIONAL SPORTS TEAMS

## MAJOR LEAGUE BASEBALL TEAMS

| AMERICAN LEAGUE | NATIONAL LEAGUE |
| --- | --- |
| **Eastern Division** | **Eastern Division** |
| Baltimore Orioles | Atlanta Braves |
| Boston Red Sox | Florida Marlins |
| Detroit Tigers | Montreal Expos |
| New York Yankees | New York Mets |
| Toronto Blue Jays | Philadelphia Phillies |
| **Central Division** | **Central Division** |
| Chicago White Sox | Chicago Cubs |
| Cleveland Indians | Cincinnati Reds |
| Kansas City Royals | Houston Astros |
| Milwaukee Brewers | Pittsburgh Pirates |
| Minnesota Twins | St. Louis Cardinals |
| **Western Division** | **Western Division** |
| California Angels | Colorado Rockies |
| Oakland Athletics | Los Angeles Dodgers |
| Seattle Mariners | San Diego Padres |
| Texas Rangers | San Francisco Giants |

## PROFESSIONAL FOOTBALL TEAMS

| American Conference | National Conference |
| --- | --- |
| **Eastern Division** | **Eastern Division** |
| Buffalo Bills | Dallas Cowboys |
| Indianapolis Colts | New York Giants |
| Miami Dolphins | Philadelphia Eagles |
| New England Patriots | Phoenix Cardinals |
| New York Jets | Washington Redskins |
| **Central Division** | **Central Division** |
| Cincinnati Bengals | Chicago Bears |
| Cleveland Browns | Detroit Lions |
| Houston Oilers | Green Bay Packers |
| Pittsburgh Steelers | Minnesota Vikings |
| | Tampa Bay Buccaneers |
| **Western Division** | **Western Division** |
| Denver Broncos | Atlanta Falcons |
| Kansas City Chiefs | Los Angeles Rams |
| Los Angeles Raiders | New Orleans Saints |
| San Diego Chargers | San Francisco 49'ers |
| Seattle Seahawks | |

## PROFESSIONAL BASKETBALL TEAMS

### EASTERN CONFERENCE

| Atlantic Division | Central Division |
| --- | --- |
| Boston Celtics | Chicago Bulls |
| Philadelphia 76'ers | Detroit Pistons |
| New York Knicks | Milwaukee Bucks |
| Washington Bullets | Atlanta Hawks |
| New Jersey Nets | Indiana Pacers |
| Miami Heat | Cleveland Cavaliers |
| | Charlotte Hornets |

### WESTERN CONFERENCE

| Midwest Division | Pacific Division |
| --- | --- |
| San Antonio Spurs | Portland Trail Blazers |
| Utah Jazz | Los Angeles Lakers |
| Houston Rockets | Phoenix Suns |
| Orlando Magic | Golden State Warriors |
| Minnesota Timberwolves | Seattle Super Sonics |
| Dallas Mavericks | Los Angeles Clippers |
| Denver Nuggets | Sacramento Kings |

## PROFESSIONAL HOCKEY TEAMS

### EASTERN CONFERENCE

| Atlantic Division | North East Division |
| --- | --- |
| Florida Panthers | Boston Bruins |
| New Jersey Devils | Buffalo Sabres |
| New York Islanders | Hartford Whalers |
| New York Rangers | Montreal Canadiens |
| Philadelphia Flyers | Ottawa Senators |
| Tampa Bay Lightning | Pittsburgh Penguins |
| Washington Capitals | Quebec Nordiques |

### WESTERN CONFERENCE

| Central Division | Pacific Division |
| --- | --- |
| Chicago Blackhawks | Calgary Flames |
| Dallas Stars | Edmonton Oilers |
| Detroit Red Wings | Los Angeles Kings |
| St. Louis Blues | San Jose Sharks |
| San Jose Sharks | Vancouver Canucks |
| Winnipeg Jets | Mighty Ducks of Anaheim |

ever, national rankings by the sports press. Top teams are invited to play in "bowl" games at the end of the season. The major bowl games are enormously popular.

**Professional football** is played in the National Football League (NFL), divided into the American Football Conference (AFC) and the National Football Conference (NFC), each with Eastern, Western, and Central Divisions. Games are nationally broadcast and widely followed on radio and television. The Super bowl (national championship) is one of the major television events of the year. There are many super bowl parties where friends get together to watch the game. Food and drink are commonly served.

*Basketball teams are available for ladies as well as men on high school and college levels.*

### Basketball

Basketball is a game played, usually indoors, by two teams of five players each. Points are scored by throwing the ball through the baskets placed at either end of the oblong court.

About a hundred years ago, basketball began in the United States. Hundreds of college teams play a regular season, with the best competing for the national championship in a three-week-long tournament of the National Collegiate Athletic Association (NCAA). Major games are broadcast nationally; most others can be seen locally on cable TV.

**Professional basketball** is organized through the National Basketball Association (NBA), divided into Eastern and Western Conferences. Each professional team plays 82 games over the course of the regular season. The final play-off series matches the two top teams in a best-of-seven series. Games are widely followed in the media.

Tennis

### Hockey

Hockey is a game in which ice skaters on opposing sides seek, with curved sticks, (hockey sticks) to drive a disk (puck) into their opponent's goal.

Ice hockey is organized through the National Hockey League (NHL) in both the U.S. and Canada. It is followed in the U.S. by a small, but intensely interested audience.

### Other Popular Sports

**Tennis:** Both national and international tennis matches (the Davis Cup, the Federation Cup, Wimbledon, and U.S. Championships) and their champions occupy a prominent place in U.S. sports entertainment.

**Golf:** Particularly featured in the media are the Master's Tournament and the U.S. Open Tournaments.

**Boxing:** While amateur boxing (under Golden Gloves sponsorship) draws only a small audience, professional boxers hold claim to national attention during world title matches.

**Wrestling:** This sport has legitimate NCAA, World Cup, and National Championships. This should not be confused with theatrical wrestling, a commercial form of wrestling that is more entertainment than a professional sport.

**Soccer (football):** Soccer has not been regarded as a nationally popular sport. The United States' first national exposure was the 1994 World Cup games played in this country for the first time. Since then, it has been receiving much more attention.

*Golf*

### THE OLYMPIC GAMES

Americans love the Olympics. Even people who do not regularly follow sports can be found in front of the TV watching these games. Sporting events viewed during both the winter and summer games often increase in popularity after the games. Among Americans, popular sports featured in these games include:

**Figure skating:** U.S. figure skaters, both men and women, are highly rated in all facets of international competition, single and paired. Partly a result of nationwide interest in the Olympics, figure skating has gained increased media coverage and fans.

**Speed skating:** This also gets its share of national coverage, particularly when Americans are involved.

*Speed Skating*

**Skiing:** Amateur competition is organized for colleges through the NCAA for slalom, giant slalom, freestyle, and diagonal cross country; relatively little media coverage is provided. National and world championship alpine, nordic, and ski jumping events attract greater interest and publicity.

*Skiing*

**Track and field:** A major part of summer Olympics, track and field has gained popularity in this country over the last decade. The NCAA supervises collegiate track and field – running, walking, hurdling, and field events (high, long, and triple jumping; and throwing the shot-put, discus, hammer, and javelin). The Athletics Congress of the USA governs its amateur side.

**Swimming and diving:** These are largely school or club sports, attracting public attention at Olympic time and otherwise going rather unnoticed except by participants.

*Track and Field*

**Little League Baseball**

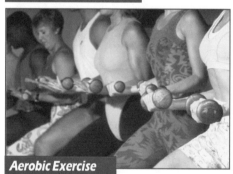

**Aerobic Exercise**

**Step Aerobics**

# RECREATIONAL SPORTS

Schools offer children a way to get involved in sports. Most schools have teams in baseball, softball, football, basketball, volleyball, soccer, tennis, swimming, skiing, lacrosse, hockey, and track.

Sports organizations offer children another opportunity for team play: the Police Athletic League (PAL), Little League, the American Youth Soccer Organization (AYSO), and the Young Men's and Young Women's Christian Associations (YMCA and YWCA) are particularly committed to providing youngsters with facilities and coaching support. YMCA's generally provide swimming pools for lessons and swim teams. YMCA's also offer facilities and programs for adults at all skill levels, including basketball, swimming, weight-lifting, aerobic classes, volleyball, squash, and racquetball.

**Fitness centers** or sports clubs are very popular today. You buy membership and use the services (swimming pools, weight-lifting, workout rooms, and aerobic exercise classes) under the guidance of skilled trainers. These clubs provide both social and physical benefit.

Sports associations can provide training and opportunity for participation in many other sports – fencing, gymnastics, bicycling, handball, archery, riflery, sailing, and scuba diving to name a few. The League of American Wheelmen, for example, organizes recreational bicycle rallies for two to 4,000 people.

Municipal (city or town) recreation departments offer children and adults opportunities for sports participation as well. This may include golf and tennis, and even sailing and fishing.

Sports stores – retail suppliers of sports equipment – often offer specialized training courses which teach you how to use the equipment and the techniques for a particular sport. Rental of scuba diving equipment, for example, requires a license. You can often obtain these from a store supplying the equipment. Mountaineering suppliers frequently have courses you can take to learn climbing skills. Competitive and recreational running is popular almost everywhere. All of these activities can give you a way to practice skills you already have, to meet people who share your interests, and to add to the quality of your life.

# MOTION PICTURES

To see the latest movies, go to a public movie theater (cinema). You can locate theaters and find out what is playing through the newspaper. The number of showings, times of shows, and the cost of admission vary. Typically, there are two evening shows for each film and several on weekend afternoons. There are also reduced price showings during weekday afternoons at some theatres. Snacks (popcorn, candy, and soda) are usually available. Smoking is usually not permitted.

Films are reviewed for quality in newspapers and magazines and on television and radio. They are rated by the Motion Picture Association of America (MPAA) as to their appropriateness for children and the age group for which they are designed.

### Movie ratings

A film rated "General" (G) is designed for all audiences. "Parental Guidance suggested" (PG) is a warning to parents that some part of a film might not be suitable for children. PG-13 means parents are strongly cautioned that some material may be inappropriate for children under 13. "Restricted" (R) rated films are limited to adults over 17 and children accompanied by adults; they may contain profanity, nudity, violence, and adult-oriented themes. "Not for Children" (NC-17) rates a film as inappropriate for a child to view even when accompanied by a parent.

# BOOKS

In addition to the 12,000 book stores in the United States, books are also sold at supermarkets, drug stores, newsstands, and other locations. Book stores carry the largest selection of current fiction and non-fiction, in both hardcover and paperback editions. Some larger chains have ongoing discounts of 10 to 20 percent on all purchases. You can find children's books, reference books, works on health, on hobbies, on business, and on every topic imaginable.

*Local libraries provide entertainment for young and old alike. (See page J-8 for details.)*

Public libraries generally contain a very complete selection of books. These libraries are free. The librarians will be glad to assist you. (See chapter *Education.*)

# MUSIC

Both classical and contemporary music (popular, jazz, blues, rock in all its various forms, folk, country and western, and the more recent rap) can be heard routinely on radio and television (particularly cable television's MTV, VH-1, VH-2, CMT and TNN). Recorded music compact discs (CDs) and cassettes are widely available for every type of music. For live concert information,

**Theatre**

classical or contemporary – what is on, where and how to get tickets – check the newspapers, magazines, or TV and radio ads.

# THEATER

American theater – musicals, dramas, and comedies, both professional and amateur – is widely developed. While New York and Broadway are still considered the best, Off-Broadway in the 1950s and Off-Off-Broadway in the 1960s emerged with experimental, unusual, and wonderful productions.

Throughout the country, particularly in the cities, you can find quality live theater productions announced in the weekend events sections of the newspapers.

# DANCE

Major cities and universities have some of the world's finest dance companies.

# SOCIAL CLUBS AND ORGANIZATIONS

A variety of special interest clubs exist, including organizations to welcome newcomers; hobby clubs focused on specific interests or crafts, garden clubs, drama clubs, film clubs, amateur choruses, bands, orchestras, and many others. These often facilitate friendship.

If you belonged to an international club such as the Kiwanis or the Elks in your home country, try the local lodges here. If you do not already have membership, you may find some private clubs difficult to get into; membership is typically by invitation only.

If you have school-aged children or are interested in educational issues, consider joining the local Parent Teacher Association (PTA). It offers a way to participate in and to meet other parents with common interests. Volunteer tutoring may be another option.

**Volunteering** (working without pay) for an organization or a cause is a long-standing tradition in this country. It provides a way to help others and to make new friends. Volunteers are needed to work in hospitals, hospices (specially equipped homes for the terminally ill), libraries, and social service agencies. Volunteers often assist in raising money for specific causes.

# ENVIRONMENTAL ORGANIZATIONS

Of particular note in this category are the National Audubon Society, the Sierra Club, the Appalachian Mountain Club, and the Wilderness Conservancy. Through these, you can learn about and act on ecological issues while participating in hiking, canoeing, skiing, or other forms of outdoor recreation. Both individuals and family memberships are available.

## SCOUTS

The Boy Scouts and the Girl Scouts of America offer children and adolescents the opportunity to learn practical and social skills in a supportive setting. Groups of children and adolescents are organized into volunteer troops under volunteer leaders. You may want to be involved as an adult leader. A system of merit badges fosters learning about camping, cooking, swimming, the outdoors, first aid, and any number of other disciplines. To advance in rank, scouts must also perform service projects and demonstrate leadership skills.

The Scouts run excellent residential summer camps with wide-ranging outdoor educational and achievement programs.

## Encyclopedia of Associations

If you are interested in joining any club or association, a trip to the library is in order to look in the Encyclopedia of Associations. It is a 3,000 page directory of every type of club or association in the United States.

It lists over 1,500 clubs for different hobbies; 1,000 sports organizations; 500 fraternal, national, and ethnic clubs; 2,000 social welfare organizations (children's rights, Planned Parenthood and animal rights, for example); 1,000 ecology and environmental organizations; and almost 2,000 cultural (literary, theatrical, musical, story-telling) groups.

## 4-H

More common in rural areas is the 4-H program aimed at developing skills in farming. The participating boys and girls learn about agriculture, dairy, and livestock production. They visit working farms, develop their own projects, and show them competitively at fairs.

## JUNIOR ACHIEVEMENT

This is run by local business people to introduce boys and girls to the basics of business. It helps them set up their own small businesses, taking ideas through production and marketing.

## RELIGION

Over 60 percent of adults in the United States state they belong to a religious group. There is a long tradition of religious tolerance in the United States. Religious freedom is a basic right guaranteed by the Constitution – "Congress shall make no law respecting an establishment of religion, or prohibiting the free exercise thereof.' This principle from the origins of the nation is considered sacred. While it has been often challenged in court, no laws or actions limiting the free practice of religion have succeeded.

# TOP 15 RELIGIONS IN THE UNITED STATES
## Christian and Non-Christian

1. Roman Catholic

2. Baptist

3. Protestant *(all denominations)*

4. Methodist

5. Lutheran

6. Christian *(all other denominations)*

7. Presbyterian

8. Jewish

9. Pentecostal

10. Episcopalian/Anglican

11. Mormon/LDS

12. Muslim/Islamic

13. Buddhist

14. Hindu

15. Bahai

## Patterns of Religious Development

Immigration and diversity of religious practice are inseparable. Our earliest immigrants came here in search of religious freedom. Primarily European Protestant Christians, they formed their settlements and generally ignored the religious practices of the million or so people they found here. By the time the new nation declared itself in 1776, some 450,000 Europeans of similar background had joined them. So had 150,000 West Africans, not of Christian origin, brought in as slaves. They worked in the fields of the Carolinas and Virginia; most eventually adopted Christianity.

The pattern of immigration of Christians from Europe continued, but beginning about 1820, it was no longer just Protestants. A wave of Irish came, fleeing the potato famine of the 1840s that established a large Roman Catholic influence.

Also during the 1840s, non-Christian Chinese began arriving, mainly in California. Because of a 1790 law limiting citizenship to whites, they were not allowed to vote. Had they been allowed to vote, a law to keep out Chinese workers might not have been written. (Passed in 1882, it was abolished in 1943.)

By 1870, thousands more German-speaking Protestants entered from northern Europe fleeing economic depression.

About 1880, the religious composition of immigrants changed again. Thirty million refugees came in from central and southeastern Europe (Italy, the Balkan states, Russia, and Poland). Two million of these were Jews fleeing Russia; most of the rest were Catholic.

The 1924 immigration law established an annual quota system of 150,000 immigrants from particular national origins (northern and western Europe), trying to preserve the ethnic (and therefore religious) mix of the era. Except in special cases such as the 38,000 Hungarians admitted in 1956, these quotas were not lifted for 40 years.

In 1965, Congress, reflecting the politics of the civil rights era, changed that law and eliminated quotas. Ninety percent of immigrants now come from Latin America, the Caribbean, and Asia. This trend is strengthening and increasing the religious diversity.

# HOLIDAYS

## LEGAL FEDERAL HOLIDAYS

Ten days have been designated by Congress as legal holidays to be observed by federal employees and the District of Columbia. While individual states have the authority to decide if they will celebrate them (and to proclaim state holidays), federal offices, banks, and schools are usually closed. Retail stores are often not only open but hold major sales. Several holidays such as Dr. Martin Luther King, Jr.'s birthday, George Washington's birthday and Memorial Day have been moved to Monday observances to create three day weekends.

### New Year's Day : January 1

Following the Roman calendar (set by Julius Caesar in 45 B.C.), the first day of the new year is always January 1. The big party happens December 31, New Year's Eve, in homes and public places everywhere. At the stroke of midnight, Americans cheer, drink to each other's health, and sing *"Auld Lang Syne."* Written in 1788 by Scottish poet Robert Burns, the song invokes the times of old. This is the most expensive bar and restaurant night of the year; higher rates are usually in effect. Millions watch in person or on television as an electric-light ball drops in New York's Times Square to mark the New Year. Many cities have begun lower cost and family-oriented "First Night" celebrations.

### Birthday of Dr. Martin Luther King, Jr.

The birthday of the great civil rights leader is January 15. It is observed the third Monday of that month. It was Reverend King (assassinated April 4, 1968) who roused the conscience of the nation in the 1960s. He worked for social justice for Black Americans and for racial harmony. His tools were non-violent protests, well-publicized marches, economic boycotts and his own extraordinary skills as leader and orator.

### George Washington's Birthday

A holiday since 1796, the birthday of the first president of the U.S. is actually February 22, but is observed the third Monday in the month.

### Memorial Day

Celebrated the last Monday in May, this holiday was established in 1868 to honor the soldiers who died in the Civil War. Now marked by large parades,

it honors all America's war dead and also signifies the start of the summer season.

### Independence Day - July 4

The Declaration of Independence was signed on this day in 1776. Its celebration as a holiday began the next year and typically features barbeques, picnics, family-get-togethers, public fireworks, and parades.

### Labor Day

First observed in New York in 1882 to honor the worker, this day is celebrated the first Monday in September. This three–day weekend marks the end of the summer season. Schools generally start their classes after this date.

### Columbus Day

The second Monday in October, it commemorates the 1492 discovery of America by Christopher Columbus. It is not celebrated in every state.

### Veterans Day - November 11

Also known as Armistice Day, it was established in 1926 to mark the end of World War I on that date in 1918. The day was renamed in 1954 to honor all Americans who served in the armed forces.

### Thanksgiving Day

Proclaimed by U.S. presidents annually until established in 1941 as the fourth Thursday in November, the day commemorates the first harvest and day of thanks at the Pilgrims' Plymouth Colony in New England, 1621. The traditional feast centers around sharing a turkey dinner with family and friends.

### Christmas Day - December 25

A Christian celebration of the birth of Jesus Christ, this is the only religious holiday that is also a legal one. Over 80 percent of Americans buy a Christmas tree and give each other cards and presents. Stores begin urging consumer buying, especially of toys, as soon as Thanksgiving is over. Towns and homes are festively decorated with greenery, lights, and other seasonal ornaments. A major figure in all the festivity is Santa Claus. With his red and white costume, this traditional jolly man (known internationally as St. Nicholas, Father Christmas, Le Père Nöel, or Sinterklaas) flies about in a reindeer-drawn sleigh distributing presents to children.

# OTHER HOLIDAYS AND FESTIVE OCCASIONS

### Lincoln's Birthday - February 12

The birthday of Civil War President Abraham Lincoln is a legal holiday in many states. Some observe it jointly with Washington's birthday as Presidents' Day.

### Valentine's Day - February 14

On this day, sweethearts traditionally exchange candy, flowers, and valentines (cards typically illustrated with hearts and Cupid, the naked cherub symbolizing love in Roman mythology). The practice may have to do with one of the several St. Valentines in history or with a pagan goddess of love. The message "I love you" has taken on a more general application, making this the second largest card-exchanging holiday in the year. Children, for example, give valentines to their teachers.

### St. Patrick's Day - March 17

This is the day of the Irish. Wear green, perhaps a shamrock, and pretend you are just a little bit Irish. It honors the patron saint of Ireland, famous for spreading Christianity across Ireland (and also, in myth, driving the snakes out of Ireland). The parade down New York's Fifth Avenue is a traditional event.

### Easter

An important Christian holiday, it falls between March 22 and April 25 (the first Sunday after the first full moon after March 21). It celebrates the resurrection of Jesus Christ (a basic belief of Christianity) from his death on earth to absolve believers from sin to eternal life in heaven.

Non-religious folk customs include the dyeing of eggs (perhaps a symbol of emerging life in spring), Easter baskets of candy brought by the Easter bunny, and the display of new clothes and Easter bonnets.

### Passover

Also falling in March or April, this eight-day Jewish holiday dates from 1300 B.C. when Moses asked the ruling Pharaoh of Egypt to let him lead the Israelites out of bondage. When the Pharaoh refused, God, the ancient tradition holds, sought to kill the firstborn sons of the Egyptians. He instructed the Israelites to mark their doors with the blood of a lamb in order to be "passed over." Afterwards, the Israelites left for the Promised Land, not taking time to wait for their bread to rise. Hence, the unleavened bread (matzo), symbolic, like most of the food at the first night Seder feast.

### April Fool's Day - April 1

A minor holiday, this day is known for practical jokes.

### Mother's Day

Celebrated the second Sunday in May, this holiday was first proclaimed by President Woodrow Wilson in 1914 to honor the country's mothers. It was the concept of the wealthy Anna M. Jarvis, who devoted her time and fortune to its establishment. Today, it is a day not just for mothers, but for anyone of maternal importance in the family. The traditional gifts include flowers, Sunday dinner at a restaurant, and other personal tokens of respect.

### Father's Day

Officially established by President Richard Nixon in 1972, the third Sunday in June is set aside to honor fathers.

### Rosh Hashanah/Yom Kippur

Celebrated in September or October (depending on the Jewish calendar), Rosh Hashanah, the Jewish New Year, begins the High Holy Days with the blowing of the shofar (ram's horn). Apples dipped in honey symbolize a sweet new year of hope. Long services go on at synagogues, culminating in Yom Kippur, the fasting Day of Atonement, ten days later.

### Halloween - October 31

This is purely a folk custom, the night of bats, witches, skeletons, black cats, and pumpkins made into jack-o'-lanterns. Hollow out the pumpkin, carve a face, and put a lighted candle inside to make one. Children go "trick-or-treating" in the neighborhoods, dressed in costume, asking for candy (treats) in return for not playing tricks.

### Hanukkah

The Jewish Festival of Lights (also spelled "Chanukah") occurs during November or December. It commemorates the rebellion against Syrian authority 21 centuries ago by Judas Maccabeus, the rededication of the Temple in Jerusalem and the rekindling of its lamp. According to the story, there was only enough oil to last a day; it lasted eight. Hence, the nine-branched menorah (candle holder) of today – a candle for each day and one to light them. Each night families give gifts, especially to children.

### Kwanzaa

Created in 1966, it is celebrated for seven days starting on December 26th. Each day is set aside for one of the following principles; unity, self-determination, collective work and responsibility, co-operative economics, purpose, creativity, and faith. It is based on the first harvest and celebrated by over 5 million African-Americans. Kwanzaa is Swahili for first fruits.

### Birthdays

A child's birthday is often celebrated at a party with other children. Small gifts are traditionally given to the child. The party may be at the child's home, a restaurant or other places specializing in children's activities. Games are often played, and birthday cake with ice cream is traditional.

Adult birthdays are also celebrated among friends and even in work settings. Presents are often given among close friends and relatives.

# TRAVEL

Each of the 50 states maintains its own independent department of travel and tourism. These departments provide free guides, maps, directories, calendars of events, information on attractions, and other data you need to plan a vacation. If you want information on any particular areas of interest, simply request it by telephone or in writing.

*The shore is a favorite place to travel for vacation.*

Tourist areas within states also provide free local information. You can get further details by:

- asking the state department of travel and tourism,
- telephoning or writing to the local department of travel and tourism in the nearest major city you plan to visit or,
- checking with a local travel agent.

## TOPOGRAPHICAL MAP OF THE UNITED STATES

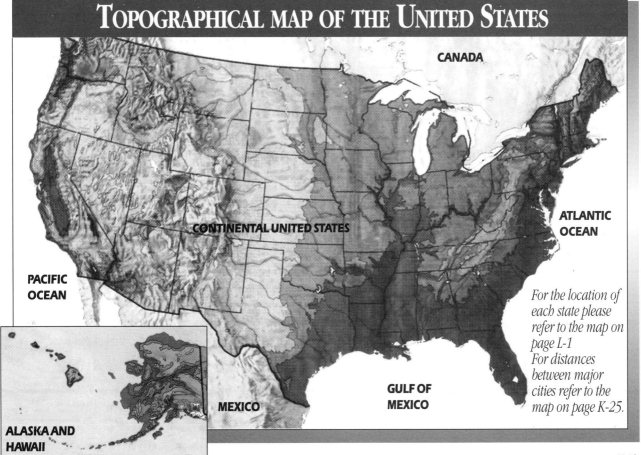

CANADA

ATLANTIC OCEAN

CONTINENTAL UNITED STATES

PACIFIC OCEAN

*For the location of each state please refer to the map on page L-1
For distances between major cities refer to the map on page K-25.*

MEXICO

GULF OF MEXICO

ALASKA AND HAWAII

*Yellowstone National Park*

*Americans like to camp. The national park system is designed to help them do it safely, with minimum impact on the environment.*

State departments of travel and tourism can give you a better understanding of the climate, lifestyle and features of an area that might influence your decision to move there.

A list of the state departments of travel and tourism departments is included at the end of this chapter.

# NATIONAL PARKS

There are over 165 national parks in the U.S., covering over 75 million acres (303,000 square kilometers) of land. There are also a large number of state parks. They offer accommodations ranging from campgrounds and cabins to hotels, motels, and lodges. Activities include: guided tours, fishing, boating, swimming, hiking, and horseback riding. Winter activities include skiing and snowmobiling. Each park offers different services, some of which include restaurants and snack areas, museums, special exhibits, groceries, bath facilities, and are generally equipped for the handicapped.

# TRAVEL AGENT

Do you need a travel agent to see America? No, but the professional advice one offers you is free, may save you time and money, and may provide you with a more rewarding and care-free trip than you could arrange on your own. A travel agent can help you plan a trip using any combination of air, rail, water, or road transportation, including driving your own car.

Travel agents are listed in the Yellow Pages. You can also find a reputable one through a professional travel association.

## Tolls

Some roads, tunnels, and bridges charge vehicle drivers a fee (or toll), payable at a toll booth along the way. There may be toll collectors to take your payment or mechanical bins where you toss in the correct amount in coins. A green light indicates when your payment is received and lets you proceed. Tokens are often used instead of cash. They are thrown in special bins which do not accept regular coins. Tokens are usually sold at one booth in a toll plaza. Read the signs carefully as you approach the toll booth to avoid getting in the wrong lane.

# TRANSPORTATION

## Cars

Americans like to travel, especially by car. Join in this favorite activity and drive across the country to get to know its varied regions and people. You have more than 3,900,000 miles (6,276,442 km) of roads to use. The 42,000-mile (67,592 km) Interstate Highway System connects 48 states and over 90 percent of cities with populations of 50,000 or more. You can drive from the Atlantic Coast to the Pacific Coast without stopping for a traffic light. Over 145 million automobiles, four million motorcycles, and 42 million trucks are registered in the United States.

### Car rental

Hertz, Avis, Budget, Alamo, and National are some of the dominant car rental companies. Rates can vary sharply from company to company and city to city. Check the Yellow Pages for listings. Compare rental plans, free mileage and service offered, models of cars available, and convenience. Most companies give you a choice of cars, ranging from sub-compacts for the budget conscious to luxury sedans. Be aware that discount rates may actually cost you more – they are usually offered on the larger and more expensive models. A smaller car might be all you need. Vans or four-wheel drive vehicles may be hard to locate and expensive.

*Rest areas are available on the interstate highways.*

Check your own auto insurance policy, it may cover car rentals. If not, consider buying the insurance offered by the car rental agency.

The car you rent generally comes with a full tank of gas. You are expected to return it full; if you do not, the company will fill it for you at a very high cost. Filling the tank just before you return the car is a lot cheaper.

To rent any vehicle, you usually must be age 25 or older, have a valid driver's license, and a major credit card. Your credit card may already cover the extra collision insurance the rental company offers.

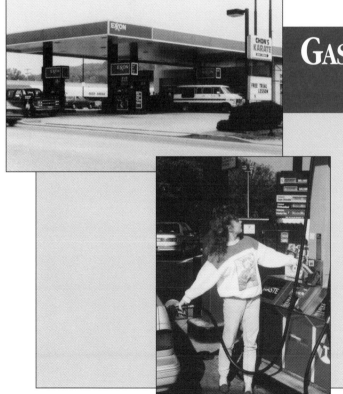

## GASOLINE STATIONS IN THE UNITED STATES

Gas stations in America are widely available. They sell not only gasoline, but maps and convenience foods as well.

Many gas stations offer **self-service** (you pump your own gas) in addition to **full service** (someone pumps it for you).

Most gas stations accept major credit cards for payment or supply customers with company credit cards for purchases.

Prices may differ for self-service or full service and cash payment or credit card payment. Be sure to check before purchasing.

*Recreational Vehicle*

## Travel Tips

Travel in the United States is no more or less dangerous than anywhere else in the world. Precautions are universal:

- Always be aware of your surroundings.
- Watch out for people watching you.
- Carry money separately from credit cards.
- Keep your purse closed and carry it close to your body.
- Carry your wallet in an inside coat pocket or front trouser pocket.
- Be aware of distractions such as a stumble into you or someone who spills something on you. They may be staging an event to divert your attention while stealing your wallet.
- Never count money or display expensive jewelry in public.
- Use credit cards and travelers checks. Avoid cash.
- If a situation does not feel right, it probably is not.

### In a hotel:

- Make sure you know where all the emergency exits are located in your hotel.
- Report any suspicious activity that concerns you to the front desk.
- Do not open your door to anyone you are not expecting. Always call the front desk to confirm anyone wishing to enter.
- Be sure all sliding doors have security bars in the tracks.

### Recreational Vehicles

Many Americans vacation in recreational vehicles (RV's) or trailers. These are mini-homes on wheels, complete with kitchens and bathrooms. There are designated areas for RV parking and sanitation services.

State laws regarding vehicle safety, insurance, and license requirements vary.

### Buses

Americans do most of their intercity travel in privately owned cars. However, public carriers (bus, subway, and rail commuter lines) are essential to some big-city work forces (especially in New York, Chicago, Boston, Washington, and Philadelphia).

There are public, charter, and rental bus lines – using some 625,000 buses – often with inexpensive fares. You can get details on the schedules and other information by calling the local bus depot, travel agent, or bus line listed in the Yellow Pages.

### Trains

Across the 3,000,000 square miles (7,770,000 square kilometers) of the continental USA are 300,000 miles (483,000 kilometers) of railway track. The nationwide railroad, owned by the federal government, is Amtrak. It runs "Great American Vacations," travel plans with a number of economical train-linked options that you can modify to suit yourself:

- "Hotel Packages" include hotel accommodations along your route. These are rated by their location and the services they provide.

- "Destination Vacations" include more features, offering sight-seeing tours as well.

- "National Parks Vacations" offer transportation to and accommodations at the nation's most popular parks (Yellowstone and the Grand Canyon, for example).

- The "Air-Rail Travel Plans," round-trip, let you see the country by train one way and save time by flying the other.

- "Rail/Sail Vacations" are yet another option: "cruise" by train and then by sea.

- "Ski Amtrak" offers winter tours to both eastern and western ski resorts.

There are also bus-linked options:

- "Amtrak Thruway Bus Service" connects cities where Amtrak trains do not stop.

- "City Escapades" offer day sight-seeing by bus at major cities through Gray Line.

- "Escorted Motorcoach Tour Vacations" offer sight-seeing by bus with a professional tour director, hotels, and meals, operated by Globus.

- "Tour America Pass" has seven different regional passes available, linking rail and bus lines through Amtrak and Gray Line.

- Amtrak's "USA Rail Pass" can be purchased outside the U.S. The fare (subject to change) for a 15-day unlimited use nationwide pass: $208; for a 30-day pass: $309.

All of these plans can be customized to your preference. Reservations are needed. You can save money by reserving outside peak seasons. Book vacation packages by calling 1-800-321-8684. Amtrak's general information telephone number is 1-800-872-7245.

### Airplanes

Airplane service in this country is provided by private competing airlines. Because many of them serve the same major cities, you have a variety of both flight times and fares. This is less true in the case of smaller cities. To make ticket reservations or get information, call a travel agent or the airline directly. Phone numbers are listed under Airlines in the Yellow Pages. Compare rates and any special fares offered. You may get a significant discount on your ticket by booking your reservation weeks ahead. However, the ticket may not be refundable.

Approximately 80 percent of airplane reservations are done via travel agents. There is no extra charge for their services. They can access all flight information by computer and tell you the schedules and rates of multiple airlines.

Because last minute cancellation and reservation changes by passengers is a common occurrence, it is legal for airlines to oversell tickets. This means there is a very small possibility you could "get bumped" from your flight (lose your seat and be rescheduled on another flight or be given a refund during peak travel seasons). Passengers that get bumped through no fault of their own often receive generous compensation for their inconvenience. Confirm your reservation a day or so ahead of departure. It is recommended that you check in at least half an hour ahead of departure time for domestic flights; two hours for international.

In some cases it can be a problem getting to the airport. There may or may not be public transportation; you may need to take a taxi or use a private or shared limousine (which may cost less than a taxi). To find a company, look under "Airport Transportation Service" in the Yellow Pages. Companies compete; call several to compare rates and services. Often the hotel you are staying at will offer free shuttle transportation to and from the airport. Inquire about this service when making your hotel reservations.

## ACCOMMODATIONS

There are a number of nationwide and regional chains of both hotels and motels. Styles, quality, and services vary greatly from chain to chain, but all maintain good basic quality. Prices can range from $30 to $40 a night outside a large city for a motel room to $75 to $150 or more a night for a larger city hotel room. Rates vary during the week and during conventions or other celebrations. There are often many special package arrangements that are available. You can make reservations yourself, look in the Yellow Pages under "Motels" and "Hotels", or call a travel agent.

Country inns are individual small hotels, usually of quaint antique style. Bathroom facilities are frequently shared with others on the same floor. Dining rooms are usually small, with meals served family style at common tables. A hearty breakfast is often the only meal served.

Bed and breakfast (B&B) places are frequently located in private homes, usually of some age and charm.

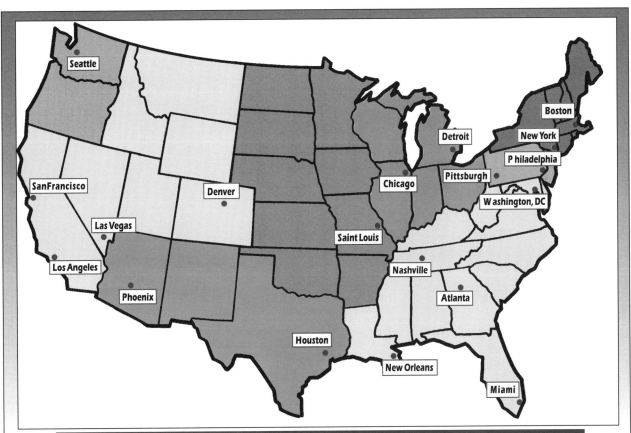

# DISTANCES TO MAJOR CITIES FROM LOS ANGELES AND NEW YORK IN HIGHWAY MILES

|  | From Los Angeles | | From New York | |
|  | Miles | Kilometers | Miles | Kilometers |
| --- | --- | --- | --- | --- |
| Atlanta | 2,280 | 3,669 | 870 | 1,400 |
| Boston | 3,015 | 4,852 | 210 | 338 |
| Chicago | 2,050 | 3,299 | 810 | 1,303 |
| Denver | 1,030 | 1,658 | 1,790 | 2,881 |
| Detroit | 2,280 | 3,669 | 650 | 1,046 |
| Houston | 1,550 | 2,495 | 1,630 | 2,623 |
| Las Vegas | 270 | 435 | 2,570 | 4,136 |
| Los Angeles | —— | —— | 2,790 | 4,490 |
| Miami | 2,750 | 4,426 | 1,340 | 2,157 |
| Nashville | 2,020 | 3,251 | 910 | 1,465 |
| New Orleans | 1,335 | 2,149 | 1,930 | 3,106 |
| New York | 2,790 | 4,490 | —— | —— |
| Philadelphia | 2,270 | 3,653 | 105 | 169 |
| Phoenix | 375 | 603 | 2,520 | 4,055 |
| Pittsburgh | 2,400 | 3,862 | 380 | 611 |
| Saint Louis | 1,835 | 2,953 | 990 | 1,593 |
| San Francisco | 385 | 620 | 2,925 | 4,707 |
| Seattle | 1,135 | 1,827 | 2,890 | 4,651 |
| Washington, D.C. | 2,665 | 4,289 | 235 | 378 |

# CLIMATE IN THE UNITED STATES

## SEASONAL TEMPERATURES

| Cities | | Summer Max° | Summer Min° | Fall Max° | Fall Min° | Winter Max° | Winter Min° | Spring Max° | Spring Min° |
|---|---|---|---|---|---|---|---|---|---|
| Atlanta | (F) | 86 | 45 | 72 | 52 | 53 | 34 | 70 | 50 |
| | (C) | 30 | 7 | 22 | 11 | 12 | 1 | 21 | 10 |
| Boston | (F) | 79 | 68 | 72 | 52 | 37 | 24 | 56 | 41 |
| | (C) | 26 | 20 | 22 | 11 | 3 | -4 | 13 | 5 |
| Chicago | (F) | 81 | 59 | 63 | 41 | 33 | 17 | 58 | 37 |
| | (C) | 27 | 15 | 17 | 5 | 1 | -8 | 14 | 3 |
| Denver | (F) | 84 | 56 | 66 | 37 | 45 | 18 | 60 | 34 |
| | (C) | 29 | 13 | 19 | 3 | 7 | -8 | 16 | 1 |
| Detroit | (F) | 81 | 61 | 62 | 45 | 34 | 21 | 56 | 38 |
| | (C) | 27 | 16 | 17 | 7 | 1 | -6 | 13 | 3 |
| Houston | (F) | 93 | 72 | 82 | 58 | 65 | 43 | 79 | 58 |
| | (C) | 34 | 22 | 28 | 14 | 18 | 6 | 26 | 14 |
| Las Vegas | (F) | 101 | 72 | 80 | 53 | 58 | 34 | 78 | 50 |
| | (C) | 38 | 22 | 27 | 12 | 14 | 1 | 26 | 10 |
| Los Angeles | (F) | 86 | 62 | 78 | 58 | 67 | 48 | 71 | 53 |
| | (C) | 30 | 17 | 26 | 14 | 19 | 9 | 22 | 12 |
| Miami | (F) | 89 | 75 | 84 | 70 | 76 | 59 | 82 | 67 |
| | (C) | 32 | 24 | 29 | 21 | 24 | 15 | 28 | 19 |
| Nashville | (F) | 89 | 67 | 72 | 49 | 49 | 30 | 70 | 48 |
| | (C) | 32 | 19 | 22 | 9 | 9 | -1 | 21 | 9 |
| New Orleans | (F) | 90 | 72 | 79 | 60 | 64 | 45 | 78 | 58 |
| | (C) | 32 | 22 | 26 | 16 | 18 | 7 | 26 | 14 |
| New York | (F) | 83 | 66 | 66 | 50 | 40 | 27 | 60 | 43 |
| | (C) | 28 | 19 | 19 | 10 | 4 | -3 | 16 | 6 |
| Philadelphia | (F) | 85 | 64 | 67 | 47 | 42 | 26 | 62 | 42 |
| | (C) | 29 | 18 | 19 | 8 | 6 | -3 | 17 | 6 |
| Phoenix | (F) | 103 | 74 | 87 | 57 | 67 | 39 | 84 | 52 |
| | (C) | 39 | 23 | 31 | 14 | 19 | 4 | 29 | 11 |
| Pittsburgh | (F) | 81 | 59 | 63 | 43 | 37 | 22 | 60 | 39 |
| | (C) | 27 | 15 | 17 | 6 | 3 | -6 | 16 | 4 |
| St. Louis | (F) | 87 | 67 | 68 | 48 | 42 | 25 | 65 | 45 |
| | (C) | 31 | 19 | 20 | 9 | 6 | -4 | 18 | 7 |
| San Francisco | (F) | 64 | 53 | 67 | 54 | 57 | 47 | 61 | 49 |
| | (C) | 18 | 12 | 19 | 12 | 14 | 8 | 16 | 9 |
| Seattle | (F) | 73 | 54 | 61 | 46 | 47 | 36 | 59 | 42 |
| | (C) | 23 | 12 | 16 | 8 | 8 | 2 | 15 | 6 |
| Washington, D.C. | (F) | 86 | 67 | 69 | 50 | 45 | 29 | 6 | 45 |
| | (C) | 30 | 19 | 21 | 10 | 7 | -2 | 1 | 7 |

**Summer Months
June, July, August**

**Fall Months
September, October,
November**

**Winter Months
December, January,
February**

**Spring Months
March, April, May**

# REGIONS OF THE UNITED STATES – A BRIEF TOUR

## The Northeast
(New England, Maine, Vermont, New Hampshire, Massachusetts, Rhode Island, Connecticut, and New York )

Start with the rocky seacoast of **Maine** and its scenic beaches. Explore the old docks and shops of Portland, sail off Bar Harbor, or take a Windjammer schooner out of Boothbay Harbor. If you are a good canoeist, run the 95-mile Allagash Wilderness Waterway. Maine, still almost 90 percent pine forest, draws those who love the wilderness to its 26 state parks, 2,600 lakes, and 5,000 streams. It grows most of the nation's blueberries – but is most famous for its lobster.

*Vermont Church*

In the Green Mountains of **Vermont** lies one of the nation's largest alpine and cross-country ski areas. Fishing and hunting are excellent. Dairy farms and great sugar maple orchards abound. Visit in April when the sap rises, the gathering buckets hang from the trees, and the rustic sugar house fires are burning to boil the sap down to maple syrup and sugar.

*New Hampshire Covered Bridge*

You will find great skiing, as well, in the White Mountains of **New Hampshire.** In summer, you can drive a car up Mt. Washington, or run whitewater in canoes or kayaks. Like the rest of New England, this is a year-round vacation state, perhaps most beautiful in its autumn foliage. It has historic towns along its seacoast and tucked into its valleys and 1,300 lakes and ponds.

**Massachusetts** has played a significant part in American history since the Pilgrims founded Plymouth Colony there in 1620. It was at Lexington and Concord that the Minutemen fired the first shots in the American Revolution (April 19, 1775). Take the Freedom Trail, a walking tour through Boston, for a quick course in history. Stay to experience the city's cultural life, watch whales, and see nearby Harvard University, the nation's oldest. Visit Old Sturbridge Village, preserved since colonial times. If you like beaches, try Cape Cod. It has 300 miles of coastline, as well as summer theater and an artists' colony.

*Salem, Massachusetts*

**Rhode Island,** tiniest state in the Union and one of the original 13 colonies, is noted for its summer resorts, the historic mansions and homes of Providence, and the yacht races and jazz festivals of Newport.

**Connecticut,** too, is a popular resort area, with 250 miles of shore along Long Island Sound, wooded rolling hills, and inland lakes. At Mystic, you will find a 19th century whaling port and the Marinelife Aquarium. On the Yale University campus in New Haven are the Gallery of Fine Arts and the Peabody Museum.

*Connecticut, Harbor*

*Niagara Falls, New York*

*Rockefeller Center, New York*

*City Skyline, New York*

*Cathedral, New York*

**New York**, largest of the northeastern states, has a great deal to offer beyond "The City." There are wilderness mountain areas with streams and lakes, including the six million acre Adirondack Park and the High Peaks; great rivers: the St. Lawrence with its Thousand Islands; the Hudson; the Mohawk; waterfalls: Ausable Chasm and Niagara Falls; and extensive beaches on Long Island. The U.S. Military Academy (Army) is located at West Point.

## New York City

Getting around in New York City (with its population of some 7,300,000) is an exercise in crowds. Over four million people use its bus and subway system every weekday. All traffic is heavy, especially during rush hour at each beginning and end of the 9 AM - 5:00 PM business day. The City is comprised of five boroughs, each with its own attractions:

- In Brooklyn, look for the Brooklyn Bridge, the Brooklyn Museum and the Children's Museum, the Brooklyn Botanical Garden, the New York Aquarium, and the Coney Island amusement park.

- The Bronx also has a Botanical Garden, the Bronx Zoo, and Yankee Stadium, home of baseball's NY Yankees.

- In Queens, you will find the site of two World's Fairs, as well as Shea Stadium, home of the New York Mets baseball team, and Aqueduct Race Track.

- Staten Island has rural areas, salt marshes, beaches, wildlife preserves, and Richmondtown, an 18th century restoration.

- Manhattan Island, 12 1/2 miles (20 kilometers) long by two and a half miles (four kilometers) wide, is generally regarded as the center of American culture, communications, and business. Areas to see include: Wall Street and the New York Stock Exchange, the World Trade Towers, South Street Seaport, the Empire State and the Chrysler Buildings, Times Square and the Theater District, Lincoln Center for the Performing Arts, Rockefeller Center, Radio City Music Hall, the United Nations, Central Park, Greenwich Village, Soho, Chinatown, Harlem, the Museum of Natural History, the Hayden Planetarium, Little Italy, the Diamond District, and the art museums (Metropolitan Museum of Art, Museum of Modern Art, the Cloisters, the Frick Collection, and many others).

## *The Mid-Atlantic*

(Pennsylvania, New Jersey, Delaware)

**Pennsylvania,** once famous for the coal mines and steel mills of Pittsburgh, today is rich in farms (nine million acres of them, with the largest rural population in the country) and history. In Philadelphia, once

principal home of the federal government, you can see the Liberty Bell, rung to proclaim Independence. Not far away is Valley Forge, major battleground of the Revolutionary War. Go to Gettysburg to see that battlefield, turning point of the Civil War.

**New Jersey,** despite its 15,000 factories and its oil refineries, still has many garden vegetable, poultry, and dairy farms. It remains about one-third forested. There is legalized casino gambling in Atlantic City. Tourists flock to the miles of ocean beach resorts. Outdoor enthusiasts prefer the Pine Barrens wilderness and the Delaware Water Gap, shared with Pennsylvania and New York. Princeton University, one of the nation's oldest, has one of the most beautiful campuses.

*Independence Hall, Philadelphia, PA*

**Delaware,** the "First State" is short on size but long on history. Despite a significant number of slave-owners at the time of the Civil War, the state did not secede from the Union. The DuPont gunpowder mills, established in 1802, supplied the armies of that war and led the way to today's great chemical industry in Wilmington. Geography has fostered a remarkably diverse economy. The agricultural southern tier is noted for chicken farms, while the eastern shore offers beaches, resorts, surfing, sailing, and deep sea fishing. Crabbing and clamming are popular in the bays of Rehoboth, Indian River, and Little Assawoman.

*New Jersey Shore*

### The South

(Maryland, District of Columbia, Virginia, West Virginia, North Carolina, South Carolina, Georgia, Tennessee, Kentucky, Florida, Alabama, Mississippi, Louisiana)

**Maryland,** founded by a British royal grant as a safe haven for Roman Catholics, made religious freedom law in 1649. Closely tied to both North and South in the Civil War, Maryland, occupied by Union troops, did not join the seceding Confederacy. Western Maryland, part of the Allegheny Mountains, today offers skiing, horseback riding, hunting and fishing (also popular along the coastal marshes), hiking, and camping. Half of the state lies on the Coastal Plain; tobacco is still grown there, and chicken farming thrives. But it is the Chesapeake Bay, with its crabs, clams, and oysters, that is most famous. The state is a center for science, engineering, and research, home to the National Institute of Health, the National Institute for Standards and Technology, the Goddard Space Flight Center, Johns Hopkins University and Hospital, and the U.S. Naval Academy in Annapolis.

*Washington Monument, Washington, D.C.*

**The District of Columbia,** the 67 square miles of the City of Washington, DC, is the seat of the federal government. Its urban influence extends to parts of Maryland and Virginia. 20 million tourists visit annually. Parking is a problem; public bus and subway transportation on the Metro system are excellent but require tokens, tickets, or exact

*White House, Washington, D.C.*

*Vietnam Veterans Memorial*

*Williamsburg, Virginia*

*West Virginia*

*Oceanliner, Louisiana*

*Farming in the South*

change. Famous sights include the White House, the Supreme Court, the Capitol, the Senate and House Office Buildings, the Washington Monument, the Lincoln and Jefferson Memorials, the Vietnam Veterans Memorial, the Museums of the Smithsonian Institution, the Library of Congress, the FBI building and the National Cathedral. Taking a sightseeing tour is recommended.

**Virginia,** in 1619, established the land's first representative legislative assembly – and received its first slaves from Africa (at Jamestown). It had exported its first tobacco only five years earlier. Today, it is still noted for that crop, and for turkey and Smithfield ham. Attractions include the restored colonial capital Williamsburg; the Courthouse at Appomattox where Confederate General Robert E. Lee surrendered to the Union's Ulysses S. Grant; Lee's home at Stratford; the homes of the first president, George Washington, at Mt. Vernon, and of Thomas Jefferson, author of the Declaration of Independence, at Monticello; Arlington National Cemetery; the 18-mile long Chesapeake Bay Bridge-Tunnel; the 470-mile Blue Ridge Parkway and the Skyline Drive; and the wild ponies of Chincoteague.

**West Virginia,** part of Virginia until its 40 counties refused to secede from the Union in 1861, ranks third in national coal production. Looking beyond its iron and steel mills, the state is finding new life as a recreation spot noted for its mountains and rafting rivers.

The old South is changing rapidly, with major industrial development in the cities called the Sunbelt. **North Carolina,** the most important industrial and agricultural producer in the southeast, is also now a major vacation and retirement center, noted for its mountains and beaches. **South Carolina,** too, has its beaches - and its peaches. Both states grow important crops of tobacco, cotton, peanuts, corn, sweet potatoes, and soy beans. Textiles and factories now outnumber South Carolina's farms, but not its traditional charms. Charleston, in particular, has preserved many of its old mansions.

**Tennessee** still grows some of the traditional southern crops (it is a major tobacco state) but is largely industrial today. Very diverse points of interest include the Museum of Atomic Energy at Oak Ridge, Chattanooga's Rock City Gardens, the Jack Daniel's Distillery at Lynchburg, and Nashville's Opryland.

**Kentucky** is most famous for its thoroughbred race horses and the blue grass they graze on. The Kentucky Derby is run each year at Churchill Downs in Louisville, also home to Kentucky State University, major cigarette manufacturers, and bourbon distilleries.

Atlanta, **Georgia,** once devastated by fire in the Civil War, is now the dominant and rapidly growing Sunbelt city. The state has extensive acreage under pine trees; supplies half the world with resins and turpentine. It also leads the country in producing paper and chicken. Tourism is on the increase; the beach at Sea Island and the Okefenokee Swamp are major attractions.

*Farming in America*

It is **Florida,** however, that really draws the tourists. Over 40 million people visit every year, seeking the tropical weather, the miles of beaches (most famous: Miami, Palm and Daytona Beaches, and Fort Lauderdale), the thousands of golf courses and resorts, and the theme parks: Sea World, Walt Disney World and Busch Gardens to name a few. The Kennedy Space Center and the Florida Keys, islands off the southern tip of the peninsula, are further attractions. Environmentalists celebrate the Manatee Rehabilitation Center at Homosassa Springs State Park, the Cedar Keys National Wildlife Refuge, and the Nature Conservancy's 70 miles of wetlands along the Gulf coast. Do not miss the Everglades National Park.

*Epcot Center, Disney World Florida*

The states from Florida to Texas that rim the Gulf of Mexico have been called America's third coast. They share salt marshes and fisheries, as well as the world's largest gas and oil fields. Major oil and petrochemical industries line the shore from Alabama to the Rio Grande River, extending to the continental shelf.

Montgomery, **Alabama,** saw the Confederacy founded in 1861 and the Civil Rights "Freedom March," led by Dr. Martin Luther King, a century later. Birmingham, now noted for its medical center, has long been a producer of coal, iron, and steel. The rest of the state relies on agriculture and such industries as paper, textiles, plastics, and chemicals. Huntsville is home to the Space and Rocket Center.

*Flamingos in Florida*

In **Mississippi,** cotton has been replaced by soybeans, and the John C. Stennis Space Center of the National Aeronautics and Space Administration (NASA) vies with Old South history, still visible in its mansions.

**Louisiana** was once a French crown colony, part of the Louisiana Purchase sold to the U.S. by Napoleon in 1803. That influence, mixed with Spanish, Caribbean, and African, lingers in the French Quarter of New Orleans, in its Creole cooking, Mardi Gras (the great carnival before Lent begins), and in the Cajun country by the Mississippi Delta. Louisiana's marshes are vital to the region's fisheries and shrimpers. Oil and petrochemical plants run up the Mississippi from Baton Rouge.

### The Southwest

(Texas, New Mexico, Arizona)

Think **Texas** and you think cowboy, with reason. This giant land, an

*Atlanta, Georgia*

*Rodeos, Texas*

*The Grand Canyon, Arizona*

*Farm lands in Ohio*

*Brickyard 400 Race, Indianapolis Speedway*

independent republic from 1836 to 1845, has huge cattle (and sheep) ranches, enormous natural resources, great industrial cities, the Lyndon B. Johnson Space Center in Houston, and a vibrant Mexican-influenced past. The state's oil industry, begun in Spindletop, Texas at the turn of this century, is today dominated by Houston and the Galveston refineries.

**New Mexico,** once part of Mexico and home of the Apache, is an important center in nuclear, geothermal, and solar research (Los Alamos Scientific Laboratories and Sandia Laboratories). It is rich in minerals: uranium, gold, silver, copper, zinc, lead, petroleum, and natural gas. You can find sheep ranches, skiing (at Taos, especially), and the Carlsbad Caverns, but perhaps the biggest tourist lure is Native American culture, both ancient (Gila Cliff Dwellings and Chaco Canyon) and contemporary (the crafts and resurgent customs of Taos and Santa Fe).

**Arizona,** ancestral home of the Chiricahua, Apaches, Cochise and Geronimo, today has the largest Native American population in the country. Fourteen tribes (the Najaho is largest) live on (and off) 19 reservations. Half of American copper comes from Arizona. This state is a "must see" it is where you find the Grand Canyon, the Petrified Forest, the Painted Desert, and London Bridge.

### The Midwest

(Ohio, Indiana, Illinois, Wisconsin, Michigan)

Lying in a triangle between the Ohio and the Mississippi Rivers are the flat and busy states once called the Rust Belt for their steel industry.

**Ohio** ranks third in U.S. manufactured products. Big cities are known for their industries: Akron for rubber; Cleveland for auto assembly and steel; Cincinnati for jet engines and machine tools; Dayton for office equipment, refrigeration, and heating; Youngstown and Steubenville for steel; Canton for roller bearings (and the Pro Football Hall of Fame). The state is also known for farming, mining, and the Indian burial mounds at Mound City.

Adjacent **Indiana** (think corn, its major crop; and car racing – the Indianapolis 500) has a great industrial center along its 41 miles of Lake Michigan coast.

Chicago, **Illinois,** great port city also on Lake Michigan, sits at the confluence of the transcontinental railways that built its industrial might. With a population of about three million, ranking it third behind Los Angeles and New York, Chicago is no longer "Hog Butcher to the world," as poet Carl Sandburg described it. Its famed slaughterhouses have moved to rural areas with the rise of refrigerated trucking. The new Comiskey Park sits in their place, home stadium to one of Chicago's two major league baseball teams, the White Sox. The Cubs are the other; the city is also home to the Bears professional football team, the Chicago Bullets basketball team, the Chicago Blackhawks hockey team, and also to the University of Chicago. A magnet for immigrants (110 languages are spoken there), the city is a vibrant grid of ethnic neighborhoods. It has a reputation as a workingman's city, a place where you can always get a job. Although half of its manufacturing jobs have disappeared since the 1960s, new service industry has developed, as have banking, finance, and architecture. This is where the skyscraper was invented. Over 75 new ones have been started since the 1980s. The 1974 Sears Tower is the tallest in the world. Ride the Loop (the elevated train around the downtown area) and visit the Art Institute, Field Museum, Museum of Science and Industry, Adler Planetarium, and Shedd Aquarium. Drive to Springfield to see the home of President Abraham Lincoln. Enjoy the countryside; Illinois is by no means just Chicago. It is the chief agricultural exporter of the U.S.

*Chicago Skyline*

If you like the outdoors, try **Wisconsin.** A seventh of this state is devoted to public wilderness recreation. It welcomes tourists to over 8,500 lakes and two Great Lakes (and its great city Milwaukee, of course).

**Michigan** borders on four Great Lakes. It has 11,000 lakes and 2,000 miles of shoreline. Needless to say, fishing (commercial and sport) is big here. So are summer resorts, farming - and, since its beginning, automobiles.

*Dairy Farming , Wisconsin*

### The Great Plains States

(Minnesota, North and South Dakota, Iowa, Nebraska, Missouri, Kansas, Arkansas, Oklahoma)

**Minnesota,** with the Boundary Waters it shares with Canada, the Minnehaha Voyageurs National Park, and its own 10,000 lakes, is definitely a place for canoeing and camping – in the summer. Winter here is long, cold, and very snowy. Visit Duluth to see the nation's biggest inland harbor; the Mesabi, Cuyana, and Vermillion iron ranges; and the Twin Cities, Minneapolis and St. Paul, divided by the Mississippi and dominating the old Northwest trade and culture. World famous Mayo Clinic is at Rochester.

*Michigan Lighthouse*

**North Dakota,** 90 percent farm, is America's most rural state. Fishing and hunting here are excellent. There are 20 parks and recreation areas, including the startling hills of the Badlands, shared with its southern neighbor. **South Dakota** has gold in its Black Hills, the highest mountains east of the Rockies. The Homestake Mine is the richest in the country. The faces of Presidents Washington, Jefferson, Lincoln, and Theodore Roosevelt are immortalized in granite at Mt. Rushmore.

*Livestock*

*Mt. Rushmore, South Dakota*

*Mansion, Oklahoma*

*Colorado Mountain Valley*

*Canyon Falls*

If you like endless fields of corn, livestock, and country fairs, go to **Iowa,** especially in August, to see the State Fair. You might stop at the communal Amana Colonies. Descendants of the original German idealists now own a major appliance corporation. Visit Marquette to see the prehistoric burial site, the Effigy Mounds and Fort Dodge for the Historical Museum and stockade.

**Nebraska** grows grain to feed its cattle and hogs. Dakota City and Lexington have become America's biggest meat-packers and cattle markets. This fits with the state's history, important to the development of the West. You can see it in the recreated pioneer village at Minden and the Stohr Museum of the Prairie Pioneer (57 original 19th century buildings) at Grand Island. The state has Agate Fossil Beds and Chimney Rock, by way of natural attractions, and the Sheldon Memorial Art Gallery and Lied Center for Performing Arts at the University of Nebraska in Lincoln.

If you are looking for the Old West, stop in **Kansas** to see Forts Larned, Leavenworth, and Riley; Dodge City has a recreated Front Street. For more recent history, visit Abilene, home of President Dwight D. Eisenhower.

**Oklahoma,** once reserved as Indian Territory in 1834, was opened to homesteaders in 1889. 50,000 entered the first day, according to history, opening a long conflict. That past is evident at the Cherokee Cultural Center and the restored Fort Gibson Stockade. Oil has played an even larger part in this state's history and economy.

The Ozark Mountains run through **Missouri** and **Arkansas,** each a home of Presidents (Harry S. Truman and Bill Clinton). Mark Twain, perhaps the most famous figure in American literature (author of Huckleberry Finn and Tom Sawyer) grew up in Hannibal, Missouri. Little Rock, Arkansas, has figured prominently – and negatively – in civil rights history. It holds a major folk festival each year (mid-April).

### The West

(Montana, Idaho, Wyoming, Colorado, Utah, Nevada, California)

**Montana** has cattle and sheep ranches, grainfields, mines (silver, copper, lead, zinc, and coal), and oil. Glacier National Park on the Continental Divide has some of the most important – and most visited – wilderness in the country. Cowboys and Indians are much in evidence here. Visit the Custer Battlefield where George A. Custer and 200 of his soldiers were killed by the Sioux and the Cheyenne in 1876. Practice cowboy skills on a dude ranch.

Next door in **Idaho** you can see mines and potato farms when you are not camping, boating, fishing, or hunting. (Idaho elk herds draw interna-

*Arches National Park*

tional hunters.) The state produces a fifth of the silver and a fourth of the potatoes of America. It is also noted for skiing, especially at Sun Valley.

If you are in **Wyoming** in late July, take in the Cheyenne Frontier Days. The state has great mountains and plains to see, as well as working and dude (tourist) ranches. (Only Texas and California raise more sheep.) Yellowstone National Park, largest in the nation, may also have the largest crowds of tourists. Camping permits must be obtained months ahead.

**Colorado,** center of the nation's greatest skiing, has over a thousand 10,000 foot-high (3,000 meter) peaks, 54 over 14,000 feet (4,300 meters). Here in the Rocky Mountains, wild bighorn sheep still roam – and so do wilderness lovers, who may also work in the state's advanced technology or defense industries. There is also desert here: the Great Sand Dunes. There are traces of an ancient past: the Indian cliff dwellings of Mesa Verde, and the Dinosaur Monuments.

*Las Vegas Nevada*

**Utah** shares oil shale deposits and a traditional farming, ranching and mining economy with Colorado and Wyoming. A newer computer-related and scientific industry is evident in Salt Lake City, founded by Mormons in 1847. Visit the Great Salt Lake and the Mormon Tabernacle. Join the skiers in the high mountains and campers in the national parks (Zion, Bryce Canyon, and Canyonlands).

**Nevada,** west of the Rockies, is a desert, alleviated at artificial Lake Mead by water from the Colorado River provided by giant Hoover Dam. Gold (and other minerals) from the Comstock Lode, discovered in 1859, is still mined. What do you do here? Gamble or get divorced (Nevada has unusually fast and simple divorce laws); in any case, be entertained – at Las Vegas, Reno and Nevada.

*Golden Gate Bridge*

**California** has the most and the wealthiest people in America. A land of extremes, it has Death Valley (the lowest point, 282 feet (84.6 meters) below sea level) and Mt. Whitney (at 14,491 feet, (4,347.3 meters) the highest in the 48 contiguous states). It takes in more immigrants than anywhere else – about a third of the U.S. annual total. It has Hollywood, Disneyland, the Golden Gate Bridge, Los Angeles and San Francisco, Pacific coastline, the peaks of the Sierra Nevadas and the Coast Range, an active volcano (Lassen Peak), giant redwood trees, and Yosemite National Park.

### The Pacific Northwest

(Washington, Oregon)

Both states have great forests and mountains (the Olympic and Cascade Ranges; Mt. Ranier; Mt. St. Helens, a volcano that erupted in

*Streetcar in San Francisco California*

*Hawaii*

*Hawaii Oceanview*

1980 in **Washington**; Mt. Hood in **Oregon**) on one side and the beautiful Pacific Coast on the other. Outdoor recreation of all kinds are available. You can visit over 90 dams, including the Grand Coulee. Commercial producers of lumber, fruit, and fish (most notably salmon), these states harness the Columbia and smaller rivers for electric power. In Seattle, on Puget Sound, some people commute by ferry. Take one yourself or have a meal in the revolving restaurant atop the Space Needle. Climb a mountain or visit spectacular Columbia River Gorge in Oregon.

### Alaska and Hawaii

If you are seeking wilderness and adventure, try the unspoiled beauty of **Alaska**. This is one area where getting tourist bureau advice is strongly recommended.

**Hawaii**, the last state to join the union (August, 1959). This group of islands are indeed vacation paradise. You can find volcanoes, Polynesian culture, and wonderful beaches, including internationally famous Waikiki, Diamond Head, and Black Sand.

# STATE DEPARTMENTS OF TOURISM

The following list provides the names, addresses, telephone numbers, and facsimile numbers of the state departments of travel and tourism. Allow four to six weeks for delivery of the materials after the department has received your request. Toll free 800 numbers, when available, can be used only in the United States.

## Alabama
Alabama Bureau of Tourism & Travel
401 Adams Avenue
P.O. Box 4309
Montgomery, Alabama 36103-4309

| | |
|---|---|
| Telephone | 1 800 252-2262 |
| | 1 205 242-4169 |
| Facsimile | 1 205 242-4554 |

## Alaska
Alaska Division of Tourism
PO Box 110801
Juneau, Alaska 99811-0801

| | |
|---|---|
| Telephone | 1 907 465-2010 |
| Facsimile | 1 907 465-2287 |

## Arizona
Arizona Office of Tourism
110 West Washington Street
Phoenix, Arizona 85007
3507 N. Central Ave. #506
Phoenix, Arizona 85012

| | |
|---|---|
| Telephone | 1 602 542-8687 |
| Facsimile | 1 602 542-4068 |

## Arkansas
Arkansas Department of Tourism
One Capitol Mall
Little Rock, Arkansas 72201

| | |
|---|---|
| Telephone | 1 800 628-8725 |
| | 1 800 828-8974 |
| | 1 501 682-7777 |
| Facsimile | 1 501 682-1364 |

## California
California Trade and Commerce Agency
Division of Tourism
801 K Street, Suite 1600
Sacramento, California 95814-3520

| | |
|---|---|
| Telephone | 1 800 862-2543 |
| | 1 916 322-2881 |
| Facsimile | 1 916 322-3402 |

## Colorado
Denver & Colorado Official Visitors Guide
Denver Metro Convention and Visitors Bureau
1555 California Street, Suite 300
Denver, Colorado 80202-4264

| | |
|---|---|
| Telephone | 1 800 645-3446 |
| | 1 303 892-1112 |
| Facsimile | 1 303 892-1636 |

## Connecticut
Connecticut Economic Development
Tourism Division
865 Brook Street
Rocky Hill, Connecticut 06067-3405

| | |
|---|---|
| Telephone | 1 800 282-6863 |
| | 1 203 258-4355 |
| Facsimile | 1 203 529-0535 |

## Delaware
Delaware Tourism Office
99 Kings Highway
P.O. Box 1401
Dover, Delaware 19903

| | |
|---|---|
| Telephone | 1 800 441-8846 |
| | 1 302 739-4271 |
| Facsimile | 1 302 739-5749 |

## Florida
Florida Division of Tourism
126 West Van Buren Street
Tallahassee, Florida 32399-2000

| | |
|---|---|
| Telephone | 1 904 487-1462 |
| Facsimile | 1 904 921-9158 |

## Georgia
Georgia Department of Tourism
285 Peachtree Center Avenue NE
Suite 1100
Atlanta, Georgia 30303-1230

| | |
|---|---|
| Telephone | 1 800 847-4842 |
| | 1 404 656-3590 |
| Facsimile | 1 404-651-9063 |

## Hawaii
Hawaii Visitors Bureau
2270 Kalakaua Avenue
Suite 801
Honolulu, Hawaii 96815

| | |
|---|---|
| Telephone | 1 808 923-1811 |
| Facsimile | 1 808 922-8991 |

## Idaho
Idaho Travel Council
700 West State Street
Boise, Idaho 83720-0093

| | |
|---|---|
| Telephone | 1 800 635-7820 |
| | 1 208 334-2470 |
| Facsimile | 1 208 334-2631 |

## Illinois
Illinois Bureau of Tourism
100 West Randolph Street
Chicago, Illinois 60601

| | |
|---|---|
| Telephone | 1 800 223-0121 |
| | 1 800 822-0292 |
| | 1 312 814-7179 |
| Facsimile | 1 312 814-6732 |

## Indiana
Indiana Department of Commerce
Tourism Division
1 North Capitol, Suite 700
Indianapolis, Indiana 46204-2288

| | |
|---|---|
| Telephone | 1 800 382-6771 |
| | 1 317 232-8860 |
| Facsimile | 1 317 233-6887 |

## Iowa
Iowa Division of Tourism
200 East Grand Avenue
Des Moines, Iowa 50309

| | |
|---|---|
| Telephone | 1 800 345-4692 |
| | 1 515 242-4705 |
| Facsimile | 1 515 242-4749 |

## Kansas
Kansas Travel and Tourism
Development
700 SW Harrison Street, Suite 1300
Topeka, Kansas 66603-3712

Telephone   1 800 252-6727
            1 913 296-2009
Facsimile   1 913 296-6988

## Kentucky
Kentucky Department of Travel
Development
Capitol Plaza Tower
500 Mero Street, Suite 2200
Frankfort, Kentucky 40601-1968

Telephone   1 800 225-8747
            1 502 564-4930
Facsimile   1 502 564-5695

## Louisiana
Louisiana Department Tourism
1051 North Third Street
Baton Rouge, Louisiana 70802

Telephone   1 800 334-8626
            1 504 342-8100
Facsimile   1 504 342-8390

## Maine
Maine Tourism Information Services
The Maine Publicity Bureau, Inc.
P.O. Box 2300
Hallowell, Maine 04347-2300

Telephone   1 800 533-9595
            1 207 623-0363
Facsimile   1 207 623-0388

## Maryland
Maryland Office of Tourism
217 East Redwood Street
Baltimore, Maryland 21202

Telephone   1 800 543-1036
            1 410 333-6611
Facsimile   1 410 333-6643

## Massachusetts
Massachusetts Office of Travel and
Tourism
100 Cambridge Street, 13th Floor
Boston, Massachusetts 02202

Telephone   1 800 447-6277
            1 617 727-3201
Facsimile   1 617 727-6525

## Michigan
Travel Bureau
Michigan Department of Commerce
P.O. Box 3393
Livonia, Michigan 48151-3393

Telephone   1 800 543-2937
            1 517 373-0670
Facsimile   1 517 335-0653

## Minnesota
Minnesota Office of Tourism
100 Metro Square
121 7th Place East
Saint Paul, Minnesota 55101-2112

Telephone   1 800 657-3700
            1 612 296-5029
Facsimile   1 612 296-7095

## Mississippi
Mississippi Division of Tourism
Development
P.O. Box 1705
Ocean Springs, Mississippi 39566

Telephone   1 800 927-6378
            1 601 875-0079
Facsimile   1 601 875-8198

## Missouri
Missouri Division of Tourism
Truman State Office Building
301 West High Street
Jefferson City, Missouri 65101

Telephone   1 800 877-1234
            1 314 751-4133
Facsimile   1 314 751-5160

## Montana
Travel Montana–Dept. of Commerce
PO Box 200533
Helena, Montana 59620-0533

Telephone   1 800 541-1447
            1 800 847-4868
            1 406 444-2654
Facsimile   1 406 444-2808

## Nebraska
Nebraska Tourism Office
P.O. Box 98913
Lincoln, Nebraska 68509-8913

Telephone   1 800 228-4307
            1 402 471-3796
Facsimile   1 402 471-3026

## Nevada
Nevada Commission on Tourism
Capitol Complex
Carson City, Nevada 89710

Telephone   1 800 237-0774
            1 702 687-4322
Facsimile   1 702 687-6779

## New Hampshire
New Hampshire Office of Travel and
Tourism
P.O. Box 1856
Concord, New Hampshire 03302-1856

Telephone   1 603 271-234
Facsimile   1 603 271-2629

## New Jersey
New Jersey Division of Travel and
Tourism
CN 826
20 West State Street
Trenton, New Jersey 08625-0826

Telephone   1 800 537-7397
            1 609 292-2470
Facsimile   1 609 633-7418

## New Mexico
New Mexico Department of Tourism
491 Old Santa Fe Trail
Santa Fe, New Mexico 87503

Telephone   1 800 545-2040
            1 505 827-7400
Facsimile   1 505 827-7402

## New York
New York State Department of
Economic Development
Division of Tourism
One Commerce Plaza
Albany, New York 12245

Telephone   1 800 225-5697
            1 518 474-4116
Facsimile   1 518 486-6416

## North Carolina
North Carolina Travel and Tourism
Division
430 North Salisbury Street
Raleigh, North Carolina 27611

Telephone   1 800 847-4862
            1 919 733-4171
Facsimile   1 919 733-8582

## North Dakota

North Dakota Tourism Promotion
Capitol Grounds
604 East Boulevard
Bismarck, North Dakota 58505

| | |
|---|---|
| Telephone | 1 800 435-5663 |
| | 1 701 224-2525 |
| Facsimile | 1 701 224-5878 |

## Ohio

Ohio Division of Travel and Tourism
PO Box 1001
77 South High Street, 29th Floor
Columbus, Ohio 43266-0101

| | |
|---|---|
| Telephone | 1 800 282-5393 |
| | 1 614 466-8844 |
| Facsimile | 1 614 466-6744 |

## Oklahoma

Oklahoma Tourism and Recreation
Department
2401 North Lincoln Boulevard
505 Will Rogers Building
Oklahoma City, Oklahoma 73105

| | |
|---|---|
| Telephone | 1 800 652-6552 |
| | 1 405 521-3981 |
| Facsimile | 1 405 521-3089 |

## Oregon

Oregon Economic Development
Tourism Division
775 Summer Street N.E.
Salem, Oregon 97310

| | |
|---|---|
| Telephone | 1 800 547-7842 |
| | 1 503 986-0000 |
| Facsimile | 1 503 986-0001 |

## Pennsylvania

Pennsylvania Office of Travel
Marketing
Department of Commerce
453 Forum Building
Harrisburg, Pennsylvania 17120

| | |
|---|---|
| Telephone | 1 800 847-4872 |
| | 1 717 787-5453 |
| Facsimile | 1 717 234-4560 |

## Rhode Island

Rhode Island Tourism Division
7 Jackson Walkway
Providence, Rhode Island 02903

| | |
|---|---|
| Telephone | 1 800 556-2484 |
| | 1 401 277-2601 |
| Facsimile | 1 401 277-2102 |

## South Carolina

South Carolina Tourism
1205 Pendleton Street
Columbia, South Carolina 29201

| | |
|---|---|
| Telephone | 1 803 734-0122 |
| Facsimile | 1 803 734-0133 |

## South Dakota

South Dakota Department of
Tourism
711 East Wells Avenue
Pierre, South Dakota 57501-3369

| | |
|---|---|
| Telephone | 1 800 732-5682 |
| | 1 605 773-3301 |
| Facsimile | 1 605 773-3256 |

## Tennessee

Tennessee Tourist Development
320 Sixth Avenue North, 5th Floor
Nashville, Tennessee 37219

| | |
|---|---|
| Telephone | 1 800 836-6200 |
| | 1 615 741-2159 |
| Facsimile | 1 615 741-7225 |

## Texas

Texas Department of Transportation
Division of Travel and Information
PO Box 5064
Austin, Texas 78763-5064

| | |
|---|---|
| Telephone | 1 800 452-9292 |
| | 1 512 483-3759 |
| Facsimile | 1 512 483-3766 |

## Utah

Utah Travel Council
Council Hall/Capitol Hill
Salt Lake City, Utah 84114

| | |
|---|---|
| Telephone | 1 800 200-1160 |
| | 1 801 538-1030 |
| Facsimile | 1 801 538-1399 |

## Vermont

State of Vermont
Department of Travel and Tourism
134 State Street
Montpelier, Vermont 05601-1471

| | |
|---|---|
| Telephone | 1 800 837-6668 |
| | 1 802 828-3236 |
| Facsimile | 1 802 864-9846 |

## Virginia

Virginia Division of Tourism
1021 East Cary Street
Richmond, Virginia 23219

| | |
|---|---|
| Telephone | 1 800 847-4882 |
| | 1 804 786-2051 |
| Facsimile | 1 804 786-1919 |

## Washington

Washington Tourism Development
Division
PO Box 42500
101 General Administration Building
Olympia, Washington 98504-2500

| | |
|---|---|
| Telephone | 1 800 544-1800 |
| | 1 206 753-5600 |
| Facsimile | 1 206 753-4470 |

## West Virginia

Division of Tourism and Parks
Telemarketing State Capitol Complex
Building 6  B564
1900 Kanawha Boulevard East
Charleston, West Virginia 25305

| | |
|---|---|
| Telephone | 1 800 225-5982 |
| | 1 304 558-2766 |
| Facsimile | 1 304 558-0077 |

## Wisconsin

Wisconsin Department of Tourism
123 West Washington Avenue
Madison, Wisconsin 53702

| | |
|---|---|
| Telephone | 1 800 432-8747 |
| | 1 608 266-2161 |
| Facsimile | 1 608 266-3403 |

## Wyoming

Wyoming Division of Tourism
I-25 College Drive
Cheyenne, Wyoming 82002-0240

Telephone    1 800 225-5996
                      1 307 777-7777
Facsimile    1 307 777-6904


Other important travel and tourism
information

## Washington D.C.

Washington D.C. Visitors Association
1212 New York Avenue
Suite 600
Washington D.C. 20005

Telephone    1 202 789-7000
Facsimile    1 202 789-7037


## U.S. National Parks Service

U.S. National Parks Service
P.O. Box 37127
Washington D.C. 20013-7127

Telephone    1 202 208-6985
Facsimile    1 202 219-0910

## New York City

New York City Visitors Bureau
2 Columbus Circle
New York, New York 10019

Telephone    1 212 484-1200
Facsimile    1 212 245-59431

# TABLE OF CONTENTS

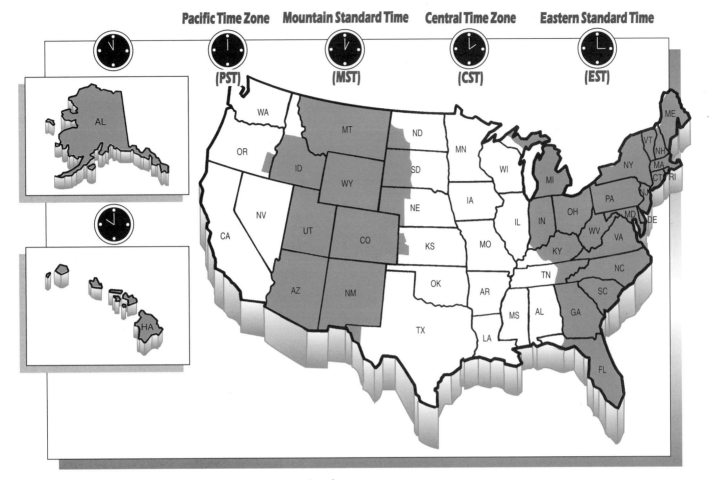

Pacific Time Zone    Mountain Standard Time    Central Time Zone    Eastern Standard Time

(PST)      (MST)      (CST)      (EST)

# U.S. STATES & THEIR ABBREVIATIONS

| | | | | | | | |
|---|---|---|---|---|---|---|---|
| Alabama | AL | Kentucky | KY | North Dakota | ND |
| Alaska | AK | Louisiana | LA | Ohio | OH |
| Arizona | AZ | Maine | ME | Oklahoma | OK |
| Arkansas | AR | Maryland | MD | Oregon | OR |
| California | CA | Massachusetts | MA | Pennsylvania | PA |
| Colorado | CO | Michigan | MI | Rhode Island | RI |
| Connecticut | CT | Minnesota | MN | South Carolina | SC |
| Delaware | DE | Mississippi | MS | South Dakota | SD |
| District of Columbia | DC | Missouri | MO | Tennessee | TN |
| Florida | FL | Montana | MT | Texas | TX |
| Georgia | GA | Nebraska | NE | Utah | UT |
| Hawaii | HI | Nevada | NV | Vermont | VT |
| Idaho | ID | New Hampshire | NH | Virginia | VA |
| Illinois | IL | New Jersey | NJ | Washington | WA |
| Indiana | IN | New Mexico | NM | West Virginia | WV |
| Iowa | IA | New York | NY | Wisconsin | WI |
| Kansas | KS | North Carolina | NC | Wyoming | WY |

# INTERNATIONAL TIME ZONES

# METRIC EQUIVALENTS

## LINEAR MEASURE

1 centimeter......................................................0.3937 inch
1 inch...............................................2.54 centimeters
1 decimeter.....................3.937 in ....................0.328 foot
1 foot.............................................3.048 decimeters
1 meter ......................39.37 inches................1.0936 yds.
1 yard...........................................0.9144 meter
1 dakameter...........................................1.9884 rods
1 rod ...........................................0.5029 dekameter
1 kilometer...........................................0.62137 mile
1 mile...........................................1.6094 kilometers

## SQUARE MEASURE

1 sq. centimeter.......................................0.1550 sq. inch
1 sq. inch ...............................6.452 sq. centimeters
1 sq. decimeter...........................................0.1076 sq. foot
1 sq. foot...........................................9.2903 sq. decimeters
1 sq. meter ...........................................1.196 sq. yards
1 sq. yard...........................................0.8361 sq. meter
1 hectare ...........................................2.471 acres
1 acre...........................................0.4047 hectare
1 sq. kilometer...........................................0.386 sq. mile
1 sq. mile...........................................2.59 sq. kilometers

## MEASURE OF VOLUME

1 cu. centimeter ...........................................0.061 cu. inch
1 cu. inch...........................16.39 cu. centimeters
1 cu. decimeter...........................................0.0353 cu. foot
1 cu. foot ...........................28.317 cu. decimeters
1 cu. yard...........................................0.7646 cu. meter
1 cu. meter...........................................0.2759 cord
1 cord...........................................3.625 steres
1 liter.......................0.908 qt. dry.........1.0567 qts. liq.
1 quart dry...........................................1.101 liters
1 quart liquid ...........................................0.9463 liter
1 dekaliter...................2.6417 gals .................1.135 pks.
1 gallon...........................................0.3785 dekaliter
1 peck...........................................0.881 dekaliter
1 hektoliter...........................................2.8378 bushels
1 bushel...........................................0.3524 hektoliter

## WEIGHTS

1 gram...........................................0.03527 ounce
1 ounce...........................................28.35 grams
1 kilogram ...........................................2.2046 pounds
1 pound...........................  ................0.4536 kilogram
1 metric ton............................  ...........0.98421 English ton
1 English ton ...........................................1.016 metric ton

# U.S. MEASURES

## LIQUID MEASURE

4 gills.................................................................1 pint
2 pints...............................................................1 quart
4 quarts ..............................................................1 gallon
31 1/2 gallons ......................................................1 barrel

## LONG MEASURE

12 inches ...........................................................1 foot
3 feet.............................................................. 1 yard
5 1/2 yards .........................................................1 rod
40 rods ...............................................................1 furlong
8 furlongs............................................................1 statute mile
3 nautical miles ...................................................1 league

## CUBIC MEASURE

1,728 cu. in .......................................................1 cu. ft.
27 cu. ft ............................................................1 cu. yd.
128 cu. ft .........................................................1 cord (wood)
40 cu. ft ...........................................................1 ton (shipping)
2,150.42 cu. in ...................................................1 standard bu.
231 cu. in...........................................1 U.S. standard gal.
1 cu. ft...........................................about 4/5 of a bushel

## DRY MEASURE

2 pints................................................................1 quart
8 quarts .............................................................1 peck
4 pecks..............................................................1 bushel
36 bushels .........................................................1 chaldron

# FAHRENHEIT CONVERSION CHART

| | | | | | | | | |
|---|---|---|---|---|---|---|---|
| 43 Far. | = | 6 | Cent. | 64 Far. | = | 18 | Cent. |
| 44 Far. | = | 7 | Cent. | 65 Far. | = | 18 | Cent. |
| 45 Far. | = | 7 | Cent. | 66 Far. | = | 19 | Cent. |
| 46 Far. | = | 8 | Cent. | 67 Far. | = | 19 | Cent. |
| 47 Far. | = | 8 | Cent. | 68 Far. | = | 20 | Cent. |
| 48 Far. | = | 9 | Cent. | 69 Far. | = | 21 | Cent. |
| 49 Far. | = | 9 | Cent. | 70 Far. | = | 21 | Cent. |
| 50 Far. | = | 10 | Cent. | 71 Far. | = | 22 | Cent. |
| 51 Far. | = | 11 | Cent. | 72 Far. | = | 22 | Cent. |
| 52 Far. | = | 11 | Cent. | 73 Far. | = | 23 | Cent. |
| 53 Far. | = | 12 | Cent. | 74 Far. | = | 23 | Cent. |
| 54 Far. | = | 12 | Cent. | 75 Far. | = | 24 | Cent. |
| 55 Far. | = | 13 | Cent. | 76 Far. | = | 24 | Cent. |
| 56 Far. | = | 13 | Cent. | 77 Far. | = | 25 | Cent. |
| 57 Far. | = | 14 | Cent. | 78 Far. | = | 26 | Cent. |
| 58 Far. | = | 14 | Cent. | 79 Far. | = | 26 | Cent. |
| 59 Far. | = | 15 | Cent. | 80 Far. | = | 27 | Cent. |
| 60 Far. | = | 16 | Cent. | 81 Far. | = | 27 | Cent. |
| 61 Far. | = | 16 | Cent. | 82 Far. | = | 28 | Cent. |
| 62 Far. | = | 17 | Cent. | 83 Far. | = | 28 | Cent. |
| 63 Far. | = | 17 | Cent. | 84 Far. | = | 29 | Cent. |
| | | | | 85 Far. | = | 29 | Cent. |

# U.S. CUSTOM TIPS FOR VISITORS

Upon entering the United States, residents must **declare all items in their possession and acquired abroad.** They may have to pay duty.

Written declaration is required only if the dutiable value of goods is over $1000, if the items are not for your personal or household use, or if customs duty or tax on any item is required. Using or wearing an article does not exempt it from duty. ($400 worth of duty-free items is allowed, as well as one liter of liquor, 200 cigarettes or 100 cigars.) These regulations do not apply to items from the U.S. Virgin Islands, American Samoa, or Guam.

Any currency over $10,000 in U.S. funds must be declared.

Prohibited or restricted are: narcotics and dangerous drugs; absinthe; obscene, seditious, or treasonable materials; liquor filled candy; fruits; hazardous articles (switchblade knives, fireworks, poisons, toxins, and others); various plant, pets and animal products.

Regulations do change. For details, contact the Department of the Treasury, U.S. Customs Service, Washington, DC, 20229.

# EMBASSIES AND CONSULATES

## Albania
**U.S. Embassy**
Rruga E. Elbansanit 103
Tirana
355-42-32875

## Algeria
**U.S. Embassy**
4 Chemin Cheikh Bachir
El-Ibrahimi
Algiers
213-2-601-425

**U.S. Consulate**
14 Square de Bamako
Oran
213-6-334-509

## Angola
**U.S. Embassy**
CP 6484
Luanda
244-2-345-481

## Antigua and Barbuda
**U.S. Embassy**
Queen Elizabeth
Highway
St. Johns
(809)462-3505

## Argentina
**U.S. Embassy**
4300 Colombia,
1425 Buenos Aires
Unit 4334
54-1-777-4533

## Armenia
**U.S. Embassy**
18 Gen Bagramian
Yerevan
7-8852-151-144

## Australia
**U.S. Embassy**
Moonah Place
Canberra A.C.T. 2600
61-6-270-5000

**U.S. Consulate**
59th Floor
MLC Center
19-29 Martin Place
Sydney, N.S.W. 2000
61-2-373-9200

**U.S. Consulate**
13th Floor,
16 St. George's Terrace
Perth, WA 6000
61-9-231-9400

**U.S. Consulate**
553 St. Kilda Road
Melbourne, Victoria 3004
61-3-526-5900

**U.S. Consulate**
383 Wickham Terrace
Brisbane,Queensland
4000
61-7-405-5555

## Austria
**U.S. Embassy**
Boltzmanngasse 16
A-1091, Unit 27937
Vienna
43-1-31-339

## Azerbaijan
**U.S. Embassy**
Hotel Intourist
Baku
7-8922-92-63-06

## Bahamas
**U.S. Embassy**
Mosmar Building
Queen Street
Nassau
809-322-1181

## Bahrain
**U.S. Embassy**
Bldg. # 979, Road # 3119
Zinj Dist., Manama
973-273-300

## Bangladesh
**U.S. Embassy**
Diplomatic Enclave
Madani Avenue
Baridhara,
Dhaka, 1212
880-2-884700-22

## Barbados
**U.S. Embassy**
Canadian Imperial Bank
of Commerce Bldg.
P.O. Box 302
Bridgetown
809-436-4950

## Belarus
**U.S. Embassy**
Starovilenskaya #46,
Minsk
7-01-72-34-65-37

## Belgium
**U.S. Embassy**
25 Boulevard du Regent
B-1000
Brussels
32-2-513-3830

**U.S. Consulate**
Ruebens Center
Nationalestraat 5,
B-200 Antwerp
03-225-0072

## Belize
**U.S. Embassy**
Gabourel Lane and
Hutson Street
Belize City
501-2-77161

## Benin
**U.S. Embassy**
Rue Caporal Anani
Bernard Anani
Cotonou
229-30-06-50

## Bermuda
**U.S. Consulate**
Crown Hill
16 Middle Road
Devonshire, Hamilton
809-295-1342

## Bolivia
**U.S. Embassy**
Banco Popular Del Peru
Bldg.
Corner of Calles Mercado
and Colon
La Paz
591-2-350251

## Bosnia/Herzegovina
**U.S. Embassy**
c/o Am. Embassy
Boltzmanngasse 16,
A-1091
Vienna
43-1-31-339

## Botswana
**U.S. Embassy**
P.O. Box 90
Gaborone
267-353-982

## Brazil
**U.S. Embassy**
Avenida das Nacoes
Lote 3
Brasilia
55-61-321-7272

**U.S. Consulate**
Avenida Presidente
Wilson, #147
Rio De Janeiro
55-21-292-7117

**U.S. Consulate**
Rua Padre Joao Manoel,
933
01411 Sao Paulo
55-11-881-6511

**U.S. Consulate**
9th Floor
Rua Coronel Genuino,
421, Porto Alegre
55-51-226-4288

**U.S. Consulate**
Rue Goncalves Maia,
163 Recife
55-81-221-1412-13

## Brunei
**U.S. Embassy**
3rd Floor, Teck Guan
Plaza
Jalan Sultan
Bandar Seri Begawan
673-2-229670

## Bulgaria
**U.S. Embassy**
1 Saborna Street
Sofia
359-2-88-48-01

## Burkina Faso
**U.S. Embassy**
01 B.P. 35
Ouagadougou
226-30-67-23

## Burma
**U.S. Embassy**
581 Merchant Street
(GPO 5Z1)
Rangoon
95-1-82055

## Burundi
**U.S. Embassy**
B.P. 34, 1720
Avenue des Etats-Unis
Bujumbura
257-223-454

## Cambodia
**U.S. Embassy**
27 EO Street 240
Phnom Penh
855-23-26436

## Cameroon
**U.S. Embassy**
Rue Nachtigal
Yaounde
237-234-014

## Canada
**U.S. Embassy**
100 Wellington Street
Ottawa, Ontario K1P 5T1
613-238-5335

**U.S. Consulate**
615 MacLeod Trail SE
Calgary, Alberta T2G-4T8
403-266-8962

**U.S. Consulate**
Cogswell Tower, Suite 910
Scotia Square
Halifax, Nova Scotia
B3J 3K1
902-429-2480

**U.S. Consulate**
P.O. Box 65
Postal Station Desjardins
Montreal, Quebec
H5B-1G1
514-398-9595

**U.S. Consulate**
2 Place Terasse Dufferin
Quebec, Quebec G1R 4T9
418-692-2095

**U.S. Consulate**
360 University Avenue
Toronto, Ontario M5G lS4
416/595-0228

**U.S. Consulate**
1095 West Pender Street
Vancouver, British
Columbia V6E 2M6
604-685-4311

## Cape Verde
**U.S. Embassy**
Rua Abilio Macedo 81
Praia
238-61-56-16

## Central African Republic
**U.S. Embassy**
Avenue David Dacko
Bangui, B.P. 924
236-61-02-00

## Chad
**U.S. Embassy**
Avenue Felix Eboue
N'Djamena, B.P.413
235-51-62-18

## Chile
**U.S. Embassy**
Codina Bldg.
1343 Agustinas
Santiago
56-2-671-0133

## China/Mainland
**U.S. Embassy**
Xiu Shui Bei Jie 3
Beijing, 100600
86-1-532-3831

**U.S. Consulate**
1 South Shamian Street
Shamian Island,
Guangzhou, 510133
86-20-888-8911

**U.S. Consulate**
1469 Huai Hai Middle Rd.
Shanghai, PSC 461
86-21-433-6880

**U.S. Consulate**
52, 14 Wei Road
Heping District, 110003
Shenyang PSC 451
86-24-282-0000

**U.S. Consulate**
Renmin Nan Lu-Duan 4
Lingshiquan Lu
Chengdu 610041
86-28-582-222

## Colombia
**U.S. Embassy**
Calle 38, No. 8-61
Apartado Aereo 3831
Bogota
57-1-320-1300

**U.S. Consulate**
Calle 77 Carrera 68
Centro Comercial
Mayorista
Apartado Aereo 51565
Barranquilla
57-58-45-8480

## Congo
**U.S. Embassy**
Avenue Amilcar Cabral
Brazzaville, B.P.1015
242-83-20-70

## Costa Rica
**U.S. Embassy**
Pavas Road
San Jose
506-2039-39

## Cote D'Ivoire
**U.S. Embassy**
5 Rue Jesse Owens
9th Floor
Abidjan, 01 B.P.1712
225-21-09-79

## Croatia
**U.S. Embassy**
Andrije Hebranga 2
Zagreb
38-41-444-800

## Cyprus
**U.S. Embassy**
Therissos St and
Dositheos Street
Nicosia
357-2-465151

## Czech Republic
**U.S. Embassy**
Trziste 15, 11B01
Prague 1
42-2-536641

## Denmark
**U.S. Embassy**
Dag Hammarskjolds
Alle 24
Copenhagen
45-31-42-31-44

## Djibouti, Republic of
**U.S. Embassy**
Plateau de Serpent Blvd.
Marechal Joffre
Djibouti
253-35-39-95

## Dominican Republic
**U.S. Embassy**
Corner of Calle Cesar
Nicolas Penson and Calle
Leopoldo Navarro
Santo Domingo
809-541-2171

## Ecuador
**U.S. Embassy**
Avenida 12 de Octubre y
Avenida Patria
Quito
593-2-562-890

**U.S. Consulate**
9 de Octubre y Garcia
Moreno
Guayaquil
593-4-323-570

## Egypt
**U.S. Embassy**
North Gate B
Kamal El-Din Salah Street
Garden City, Cairo
20-2-355-7371

## El Salvador
**U.S. Embassy**
Station Antiguo
Cuscatian
San Salvador
503-78-4444

## Equatorial Guinea
**U.S. Embassy**
Calle de Los Ministros
Malabo
240-9-2185

## Eritrea
**U.S. Embassy**
34 Zere Yocele St.
291-1-113-720

## Estonia
**U.S. Embassy**
Kentmanni 20, EE0001
Tallinn
001-372-6-312-021

## Ethiopia
**U.S. Embassy**
Entoto Street
Addis Ababa
251-1-550666

## Fiji
**U.S. Embassy**
31 Loftus Street
Suva
679-314-466

## Finland
**U.S. Embassy**
Itainen Puistotie 14A
SF-00140, Helsinki
358-0-171931

## France
**U.S. Embassy**
2 Avenue Gabriel
75382 Paris Cedex 08
33-1-42-96-12-02

**U.S. Consulate**
22 Cours du Marechal
Foch
33080 Bordeaux
Cedex
33-56-52-65-95

**U.S. Consulate**
12 Boulevard Paul Peytral
13285 Marseille
Cedex
33-91-549-200

**U.S. Consulate**
15 Avenue D'Alsace
67082 Strasbourg
Cedex
33-88-35-31-04

## Gabon
**U.S. Embassy**
Blvd. de la Mer
Libreville., B.P. 4000
241-762003

## Gambia
**U.S. Embassy**
Fajara (East)
Kairaba Avenue
Banjul. P.M.B. 19
220-392856

## Georgia
**U.S. Embassy**
No. 25 Antonely Street
Tbilisi, 380026
7-8832-98-99-68

## Germany
**U.S. Embassy**
Neustaedtische
Kirchstrasse 4-5
10117 Berlin
49-30-238-5174

**U.S. Consulate**
7 Urbanstrasse
70182 Stuttgart
49-711-21008-0

**U.S. Consulate**
Siesmayerstrasse 21
60323 Frankfurt
49-69-7530-0

**U.S. Consulate**
Alsterufer 27/28
20354 Hamburg
49-40-411-710

**U.S. Consulate**
Koeniginstrasse 5
80539 Muenchen
Munich
49-89-28880

**U.S. Consulate**
Deichmanns Aue 29
53170 Bonn 2
49-228-3391

**U.S. Consulate**
Wilhelm Seyfferth
Strasse 4
04107 Leipzig
37-41-211-7866

## Ghana
**U.S. Embassy**
Ring Road East
Accra
233-21-775348

## Greece
**U.S. Embassy**
91 Vasilissis Sophias
Boulevard
10160 Athens
30-1-721-2951

**U.S. Consulate**
59 Leoforos Nikis
GR-546-22 Thessaloniki
30-31-242-905

## Grenada
**U.S. Embassy**
P.O. Box 54
St. George's
809-444-1173

## Guatemala
**U.S. Embassy**
7-01 Avenida de la
Reforma
Zone 10
Guatemala City
502-2-31-15-41

## Guinea
**U.S. Embassy**
2nd Boulevard and 9th
Avenue
B.P.603 Conakry
224-44-15-20

## Guinea-Bissau
**U.S. Embassy**
Avenida Domingos Ramos
1067 Bissau Codex
Bissau
245-20-1139

## Guyana
**U.S. Embassy**
99-100 Young and Duke
Streets
Kingston, Georgetown
592-2-54900

## Haiti

**U.S. Embassy**
Harry Truman Boulevard
Port-au-Prince
509-22-0354

## The Holy See

**U.S. Embassy**
Villino Pacelli
Via Aurelia 294
Vatican City
00165 Rome
39646741

## Honduras

**U.S. Embassy**
Avenido La Paz
Tegucigalpa
504-36-9320

## Hong Kong

**U.S. Consulate**
26 Garden Road
Hong Kong
852-5-239011

## Hungary

**U.S. Embassy**
V. Szabadsag Ter 12
Budapest
36-1-112-6450

## Iceland

**U.S. Embassy**
Laufasvegur 21, Box 40
Reykjavik
354-1-629100

## India

**U.S. Embassy**
Shanti Path
Chanakyapuri 110021
New Delhi
91-11-600651

**U.S. Consulate**
Lincoln House
78 Bhulabhai Desai
Road 400026
Bombay
91-22-363-3611

**U.S. Consulate**
5/1 Ho Chi Minh Sarani
Calcutta 700071
91-33-242-3611

**U.S. Consulate**
220 Mount Road 600006
Madras
91-44-827-3040

## Indonesia

**U.S. Embassy**
Medan Merdeka Selatan 5,
Box 1
Jakarta
62-21-360-360

**U.S. Consulate**
Jalan Imam Bonjol 13
Medan
62-61-322200

**U.S. Consulate**
Jalan Raya Dr.
Sutomo 33
Surabaya
62-31-582287

## Iraq

**U.S. Embassy**
Opp. For. Ministry Club
Masbah Quarter
Baghdad
964-1-719-6138

## Ireland

**U.S. Embassy**
42 Elgin Road
Ballsbridge
Dublin
353-1-6687122

## Israel

**U.S. Embassy**
71 Hayarkon St.
Tel Aviv
972-3-517-4338

## Italy

**U.S. Embassy**
Via Veneto 119/A
00187 Rome
39-6-46741

**U.S. Consulate**
Via Principe Amedeo 2/10
20121 Milano
39-2-290-351

**U.S. Consulate**
Piazza della Repubblica
80122 Naples
Box 18
39-81-761-4303

**U.S. Consulate**
Via Vaccarini 1
90143 Palermo
39-91-343-532

**U.S. Consulate**
Lungarno Amerigo
Vespucci 38
50123 Firenza
Florence
39-55-239-6276

## Jamaica

U.S. Embassy
Jamaica Mutual Life
Center
2 Oxford Road
Kingston
809-929-4850

## Japan

**U.S. Embassy**
10-5 Akasaka 1-chome
Minato-ku
Tokyo, (107)
81-3-3224-5000

**U.S. Consulate**
2564 Nishihara
Urasoe City,
Naha Okinawa 90121
81-98-876-4211

**U.S. Consulate**
11-5 Nishitenma 2-chome
Kita-Ku
Osaka-Kobe (530)
81-6-315-5900

**U.S. Consulate**
5-26 Ohori 2-chome,
Chuo-ku
Fukuoka 810
81-92-751-9331

**U.S. Consulate**
Kita 1-Jo Nishi 28-chome
Chuo-ku
Sapporo 064
81-11-641-1115

## Jordan

**U.S. Embassy**
P.O. Box 354
Amman
962-6-820-101

## Kazakhstan

**U.S. Embassy**
99/97 Furmanova Street
Almaty 480012
7-3272-7-63-17-70

## Kenya

**U.S. Embassy**
Moi/Haile Selass Ave
Nairobi
254-2-334141

**U.S. Consulate**
Palli House
Nyerere Avenue
Mombasa
254-11-315101

## Korea

**U.S. Embassy**
82 Sejong-Ro
Chongro-ku
Seoul
82-2-397-4114

**U.S. Consulate**
242-Ka
Daechung Dong
Chung-ku
Pusan
82-51-246-7791

## Kuwait

**U.S. Embassy**
P.O. Box 77 SAFAT
13001 SAFAT Kuwait
965-242-4151

## Kyrgyzstan

**U.S. Embassy**
66 Erkindic Prospekt
Bishkek 720002
7-3312-22-29-20

## Laos
**U.S. Embassy**
Rue Bartholonie
Vientiane, B.P. 114
856-2220

## Latvia
**U.S. Embassy**
Raina Blvd 7
Riga 226050
011-469-882-0046

## Lebanon
Antelias
P.O. Box 70-840
Beirut
961-417774

## Lesotho
**U.S. Embassy**
P.O. Box 333
Maseru 100 Lesotho
266-312-666

## Liberia
**U.S. Embassy**
111 United Nations Drive
Monrovia
231-222991

## Lithuania
**U.S. Embassy**
Akmenu 6
Vilnius 232600
011-370-2223-031

## Luxembourg
**U.S. Embassy**
22 Blvd Emmanuel-
Servais
2535 Luxembourg
352-460123

## Madagascar
**U.S. Embassy**
14-16 Rue Rainitovo
Antsahavola
Antananarivo
261-2-212-57

## Malawi
**U.S. Embassy**
P.O. Box 30016
Lilongwe 3
265-738-166

## Malaysia
**U.S. Embassy**
376 Jalan Tun Razak
50400 Kuala Lumpur
60-3-248-9011

## Mali
**U.S. Embassy**
Rue Rochester NY and
Rue Mohamed V.,
Bamako
223-225470

## Malta
**U.S. Embassy**
2nd Floor, Development
House
St. Anne Street
Floriana, Malta
P.O. Box 535, Valletra
356-235960

## Marshall Islands
**U.S. Consulate**
P.O. Box 1379
Majuro 96960-1379
692-247-4011

## Mauritania
**U.S. Embassy**
B.P. 222
Nouakchott
222-2-52-660

## Mauritius
**U.S. Embassy**
4th Floor, Rogers House,
John Kennedy Street
Port Louis
230-208-9763

## Mexico
**U.S. Embassy**
Paseo de la Reforma 305
Colonia Cuauhtemoc
Mexico City, 06500
52-5-211-0042

**U.S. Consulate**
Chihuahua
924N Avenue Lopez
Mateos
Ciudad Juarez
52-16-134048

**U.S. Consulate**
Progreso 175
Guadalajara, Jalisco
52-3-625-2998

**U.S. Consulate**
Tapachula 96
Tijuana
52-66-81-7400

**U.S. Consulate**
Paseo Montejo 453
Merida, Yucatan
52-99-25-5011

**U.S. Consulate**
Avenida Constitucion
411 Poniente 64000
Monterrey, Neuvo Leon
52-83-45-2120

**U.S. Consulate**
Calle Allende 3330,
Col. Jardin
Nuevo Laredo,
Tamaulipas
52-871-4-05-12

**U.S. Consulate**
Monterrey 141
Hermosillo, Sonora
52-62-172375

**U.S. Consulate**
Tamaulipas Ave.
Primera 2002
Matamoros
52-891-6-72-70

## Micronesia
**U.S. Embassy**
P.O. Box 1286
Pohnpei, Kolonia 96941
691-320-2187

## Moldova
**U.S. Embassy**
Strada Alexei Mateevich
No. 103
Chisinau
373-2-23-37-72

## Mongolia
**U.S. Embassy**
c/o American Embassy
Beijing
Micro Region II
Big Rind Road
976-1-329095

## Morocco
**U.S. Embassy**
2 Ave de Marrakesh
Rabat
212-7-76-22-65

**U.S. Consulate**
8 Blvd. Moulay Youssef
Casablanca
212-2-26-45-50

## Mozambique
**U.S. Embassy**
Avenida Kenneth Kaunda
193,
Maputo
258-1-492-797

## Namibia
**U.S. Embassy**
Ausplan Building
14 Lossen Street
AusspannplatzWindhoek
264-61-221-601

## Nepal
**U.S. Embassy**
Pani Pokhari
Kathmandu
977-1-411179

## Netherlands
**U.S. Embassy**
Lange Voorhout 102
2514 EJ The Hague
3-70-310-9209

**U.S. Consulate**
Museumplein 19
1071 DJ Amsterdam
31-20-5755-309

**U.S. Consulate**
St. Anna Blvd. 19
Curacao
Netherlands Antilles
599-9-613066

### New Zealand
**U.S. Embassy**
29 Fitzherbert Terrace
Thordon, Wellington
64-4-472-2068

**U.S. Consulate**
4th Floor
Yorkshire General Bldg.
Shortland and O'Connell
Streets
Auckland
64-9-303-2724

### Nicaragua
**U.S. Embassy**
Km. 4-1/2 Carretera Sur
Managua
505-2-666010

### Niger
**U.S. Embassy**
Rue Des Ambassades
B.P. 11201
Niamey
227-72-26-61

### Nigeria
**U.S. Embassy**
2 Eleke Crescent
Lagos
234-1-2610097

**U.S. Consulate**
9 Maska Road
Kaduna
234-62-235990

### Norway
**U.S. Embassy**
Drammensveien 18
0244 Oslo 2
47-22-44-85-50

### Oman
**U.S. Embassy**
P.O. Box 202
Code No. 115
Muscat
968-698-989

### Pakistan
**U.S. Embassy**
Diplomatic Enclave
Ramna 5
Islamabad
92-51-826161

**U.S. Consulate**
8 Abdullah Haroon Road
Karachi
92-21-5685170

**U.S. Consulate**
11 Hospital Road
Peshawar, Cantt
92-521-279802

**U.S. Consulate**
Shara-E-Bin-Badees
50 Empress Road
Simla Hills, Labore K
92-42-6-365530

### Palau
**U.S. Embassy**
P.O. Box 6028
Koror, 96940
680-488-2920

### Panama
**U.S. Embassy**
Apartedo 6959,
Panama City 5
507-27-1777

### Papua NewGuinea
**U.S. Embassy**
Armit Street
Port Moresby
675-211-455

### Paraguay
**U.S. Embassy**
1776 Mariscal Lopez Ave.
Casilla Postal 402
Asuncion
595-21-213-715

### Peru
**U.S. Embassy**
Corner of Avenidas Inca
Garcilas de la Vega and
Espana
Lima
51-14-33-8000

**U.S. Consulate**
Grimaldo Del Solar 346
Miraflores, Lima 18
51-14-443621

### Philippines
**U.S. Embassy**
1201 Roxas Blvd.
Ernita, Manila 1000
63-2-521-7116

**U.S. Consulate**
PCI Bank, Gorordo Ave.,
3rd Floor
Lahug, Cebu City
63-32-311-261

### Poland
**U.S. Embassy**
Aleje Ujazdowskle 29/31
Warsaw
48-2-628-3041

**U.S. Consulate**
Ulica Chopina 4
61708 Poznan
48-51-551088

### Portutgal
**U.S. Embassy**
Avenida das Forcas
Arrnadas
1600 Lisbon
351-1-726-6600

**U.S. Consulate**
Avenida D. Henrique
Ponta Delgada,
Sao Miguel
Azores
351-96-22216

### Qatar
**U.S. Embassy**
149 Ali Bin Ahmed St.
Farig Bin Omran
Doha
0974-854701

### Romania
**U.S. Embassy**
Strada Tudor Arghezi 7-9
Bucharest
40-1-312-0149

### Russia
**U.S. Embassy**
Novinsky Bul Var
19/23 Moscow
7-095-252-2451

**U.S. Consulate**
Furshtatskaya Ulitsa 15,
St. Petersburg 191028
7-812-275-1701

**U.S. Consulate**
Ulitsa Mordovtseva 12
Vladivostok
7-4232-268-458

### Rvvanda
**U.S. Embassy**
Blvd de la Revolution
Kigali
250-75501

### Saudi Arabia
**U.S. Embassy**
Collector Road M
Riyadh Diplomatic
Quarter
Riyadh
966-1-488-3800

**U.S. Consulate**
Between Aramco Hqrs.
and Dhahran Int'l. Airport
Dhahran Airport 31932
966-3-891-3200

**U.S. Consulate**
Palestine Road
Ruwais, Jeddah 21411
966-2-667-0080

### Senegal
**U.S. Embassy**
Avenue Jean XXIII
Dakar
221-23-42-96

### Serbia-Montenegro
**U.S. Embassy**
Box 5070
Unit 25402
Belgrade
381-1-645-655

## Seychelles
**U.S. Embassy**
Box 148
Victoria
248-25256

## Sierra Leone
**U.S. Embassy**
Corner Walpole and Siaka
Stevens St.
Freetown
232-22-226481

## Singapore
**U.S. Embassy**
30 Hill Street
Singapore 0617
65-338-0251

## Slovakia
**U.S. Embassy**
Hviezdoslavovo
Namesite 4
81102 Bratislava
42-7-330861

## Slovenia
**U.S. Embassy**
Box 254
Prazakova 4,
61000 Ljubljana
386-61-301-427

## South Africa
**U.S. Embassy**
877 Pretorious Street
Pretoria
27-12-342-1048

**U.S. Consulate**
Broadway Industries
Center
Heerengracht, Foreshore
Cape Town
27-21-214-280

**U.S. Consulate**
Durban Bay House, 29th
Floor
333 Smith Street
Durban
27-31-304-4737

**U.S. Consulate**
11th Floor, Kine Center
Commissioner and Kruis
Streets
Johannesburg
27-11-331-1681

## Spain
**U.S. Embassy**
Serrano 75, 28006
Madrid
34-1-577-4000

**U.S. Consulate**
Reina Elisenda 23, 08034
Barcelona
34-3-280-2227

**U.S. Consulate**
Lehandakari Agirre
11-3, 48014 Bilbao
34-4-475-8300

## Sri Lanka
**U.S. Embassy**
210 Galle Rd.
Colombo 3
94-1-448007

## Sudan
**U.S. Embassy**
Sharia Ali Abdul Latif
Khartoum
74700

## Suriname
**U.S. Embassy**
Dr. Sophie Redmondstraat
129, Paramaribo
597-472900

## Swaziland
**U.S. Embassy**
Central Bank Building
Warner Street
Mbabane
268-46441

## Sweden
**U.S. Embassy**
Strandvagen 101
S-11589 Stockholm
46-8-783-5300

## Switzerland
**U.S. Embassy**
Jubilaeumstrasse 93
3005 Bern
41-31-437-011

**U.S. Consulate**
Zolliikerstrasse 141
8008 Zurich
41-1-422-2566

## Syria
**U.S. Embassy**
Abou Romaneh
Al Mansur St. No. 2
Damascus
963-332814

## Tajikistan
**U.S. Embassy**
Interim Chauncery
No. 39 Ainii Street
Dushanbe
7-3772-24-82-33

## Tanzania
**U.S. Embassy**
36 Laibon Rd.
Dar es Salaam
255-51-66010

## Thailand
**U.S. Embassy**
95 Wireless Rd.
Bangkok
66-2-252-5040

**U.S. Consulate**
Vidhayanond Rd.
Chiang Mai
66-53-252-629

**U.S. Consulate**
35/6 Supakitjanya Road
Udorn
66-42-244-270

## Togo
**U.S. Embassy**
Rue Pelletier Caventou &
Rue Vauban
Lome
228-21-29-92

## Trinidad and Tobago
**U.S. Embassy**
15 Queens Park West
Port of Spain
809-622-6372

## Tunisia
**U.S. Embassy**
144 Ave. de la Liberte
1002 Tunis-Belevedere
216-1-782-566

## Turkey
**U.S. Embassy**
110 Ataturk Blvd.
Ankara
90-312-468-6110

**U.S. Consulate**
Ataturk Caddesi
Adana
90-322-453-9106

**U.S. Consulate**
104-108 Mesrutiyet
Caddesi
Tepebasl, Istanbul
90-212-251-3602

## Turkmenistan
**U.S. Embassy**
Yubilenaya Hotel
Ashkabat
7/36320-2449-08

## Uganda
**U.S. Embassy**
Parliament Avenue
Kampala
256-41-259792

## Ukraine
Yuria Kotsyubinskovo
252053 Kiev 53
7-044-44-7349

## United Arab Emirates
**U.S. Embassy**
Al-Sudan St.
Abu Dhabi
971-2-4-336691

**U.S. Consulate**
21st Floor
Dubai International
Trade Center
Dubai
971-4-373115

### United Kingdom
**U.S. Embassy**
24/31 Grosvenor Square
London, W. 1A 2JB
499-1000

**U.S. Consulate**
Queen's House
14 Queen Street
B716EQ Northern Ireland
44-232-328239

**U.S. Consulate**
3 Regent Terrace
EH75B
Edinburgh, Scotland
44-31/556-8315

### Uruguay
**U.S. Embassy**
Lauro Muller 1776
Montevideo
598-2-23-6061

### Uzbekistan
**U.S. Embassy**
82 Chelanzanskaya
Tashkent
7-3712-77-14-07

### Venezuela
**U.S. Embassy**
Avenida Francisco de
Miranda and
Avenida Principal de la
Floresta
Caracas
58-2-285-2222

**U.S. Consulate**
Edificio Sofimara, Piso 3
Calle 77 Con Avenida 13
Maracaibo
68-61-84-253

### Western Samoa
**U.S. Embassy**
5th Floor Beach Road
Apia
685-21-631

### Yemen Arab Republic
**U.S. Embassy**
Dhahr Himyar Zone
Sheraton Hotel District
Sanaa
967-2-238-842

### Zaire
**U.S. Embassy**
310 Avenue des Aviateurs
Kinshasa
243-12-21532

**U.S. Consulate**
1029 Blvd. Kamanyoia
Lubumbashi
243-011-222324

### Zambia
**U.S. Embassy**
Corner of Independence
and United Nations
Avenues
Lusaka
260-1-228-595

### Zimbabwe
**U.S. Embassy**
172 Rhodes Ave
Harare
794-521

# INS REGIONAL SERVICE CENTERS

### EASTERN SERVICE CENTER
Immigration and
Naturalization Service
75 Lower Welden Street
St. Albans, VT 05478
802-527-1705

### NORTHERN SERVICE CENTER
Immigration and
Naturalization Service
Federal Building, U. S.
Courthouse
100 Centennial Mall,
Room 393
Lincoln, NE 65808
402-437-5218

### SOUTHERN SERVICE CENTER
Immigration and
Naturalization Service
7701 N. Stemmons
Freeway
Dallas, TX 75356
214-767-7769
214-767-7405 (fax)

### WESTERN SERVICE CENTER
Immigration and
Naturalization Service
24000 Avila Road
Laguna Hills, CA 92677
714-643-4236

# INS LOCAL OFFICES

### Alaska
New Federal Building
701 C Street
Anchorage, AL 99513
907-271-5029

### Arizona
Federal Building
230 N. First Avenue
Phoenix, AZ 85025
602-261-3122

Federal Building
300 W. Congress
Tucson, AZ 85701
602-629-6229

### California
U.S. Courthouse
1130 O Street
Fresno, CA 93721
209-487-5091

300 N. Los Angeles St.
Los Angeles, CA 90012
213-894-2780

650 Capital Mall
Sacramento, CA 95814
916-551-3116

880 Front Street
San Diego, CA 92188
619-557-5645

Appraisers Building
630 Sansome Street
San Francisco, CA 94111
415-704-4571

280 S. First Street
San Jose, CA 95113
(408) 291-7876

14560 Magnolia Street
Westminster, CA 92683

Telephone not published

### Colorado
Albrook Center
4730 Paris Street
Denver, CO 80239
303-844-4801

### Connecticut
3060 Ribcoff Federal Bldg.
450 Main Street
Hartford, CT 06103
203-240-3050

### Florida
400 W Bay Street
Jacksonville, FL 32202
904-791-2624

7880 Biscayne Boulevard
Miami, FL 33138
305-536-7642

4 East Port Road
Riviera Beach, FL 33404
(305) 844-4341

5509 W. Gray Street
Tampa, FL 33609
813-228-2131

### Georgia
77 Forsyth Street, S.W.
Room G-85
Atlanta, GA 30303
404-331-5158

### Guam
801 Pacific News Building
238 O'Hara Street Agana,
Guam 96910
671-472-6411

### Hawaii
595 Ala Moana Boulevard
Honolulu, HI 96809
808-541-1388

### Illinois
Dirksen Federal
Office Building
219 S. Dearborn Street
Chicago, Il 60604
312-353-7302

### Indiana
46 E. Ohio Street
Indianapolis, IN 46204
317-269-6009

### Kentucky
U.S. Courthouse W. 6th &
Broadway
Louisville, KY 40202
502-582-6375

### Louisiana
Postal Service Building
701 Loyola Avenue
New Orleans, LA 70013
504-589-6533

### Maine
739 Warren Avenue
Portland, ME 04103
207-780-3352

### Maryland
100 South Charles Street,
12th Floor
Baltimore, MD 21201
301-962-2120

### Massachusetts
Kennedy Federal Building
Government Center
Boston, MA 02203
617-565-3202

### Michigan
Federal Building
333 Mount Elliott Street
Detroit, MI 48207
313-226-3240

## Minnesota
2901 Metro Drive
Bloomington, MN 55325
612-725-3456

## Missouri
9747 N. Conant Avenue
Kansas City, MO, 64153
816-891-9318

1222 Spruce Street
St. Louis, MO 63102
314-539-2532

## Montana
Federal Building 301
South Park Helena,
MT 59626
406-449-5288

## Nebraska
3736 S. 32nd Street
Omaha, NE 68144
402-697-9152

## Nevada
Federal Building
U.S. Courthouse
300 Las Vegas Blvd. S.
Las Vegas, NV 89101
702-388-6251

712 Mill Street
Reno, NV 89502
702-784-5427

## New Jersey
Federal Building
970 Broad Street
Newark, NJ 07102
201-645-3350

## New Mexico
517 Gold Avenue, S.W.,
Room 1114
Albuquerque, NM 87102
505-766-2378

## New York
Post Office & Courthouse
Building 445 Broadway
Albany, NY 12207
518-472-2434

68 Court Street
Buffalo, NY 14202
716-849-6760

26 Federal Plaza
New York, NY 10278
212-264-5942

## North Carolina
6 Woodlawn Green,
Suite 138
Charlotte, NC 28210
704-523-1704

## Ohio
U. S. Post Office &
Courthouse
550 Main Street, Room
8525 Cincinnati, OH 45201
513-684-2930

Anthony J. Celebreeze
Federal Office Building
1240 E. 9th Street
Cleveland, OH 44199
(216) 522-4770

## Oklahoma
4149 Highline Boulevard,
Suite 300
Oklahoma City, OK 73108
405-231-5660

## Oregon
Federal Building
511 N.W. Broadway
Portland, OR 97209
503-326-2271

## Pennsylvania
U.S. Courthouse
Independence Mall West
601 Market Street
Philadelphia, PA 19106
215-597-7333

2130 Federal Building
1000 Liberty Avenue
Pittsburgh, PA 15222
412-644-3356

## Puerto Rico
Federal Building Chardon
Street Hato Ray, Puerto
Rico 00936
809-766-5329

## Rhode Island
John Pastore
Federal Building
Kennedy Plaza
U. S. Post Office
Exchange Terrace
Providence, RI 09203
401-528-5315

## South Carolina
Federal Building
334 Meeting Street
Charleston, SC 29403
803-371-6637

## Tennessee
814 Federal Building
167 N. Main Street
Memphis, TN 38103
901-521-3301

## Texas
810 N. Stemmons
Freeway
Dallas, TX 75247
214-655-3063

700 E. San Antonio
El Paso, TX 79984
915-543-6366

2102 Teege Avenue
Harlingen, TX 78550
512-425-7333

509 North Belt
Houston, TX 77060
713-847-7900

Federal Building
8940 Fourwinds Drive
San Antonio, TX 78239
512-229-5130

## Utah
230 W. 400 South Street
Salt Lake City, UT 84101
801-524-6272

## Vermont
Federal Building
St. Albans, VT 05478
802-524-6742

## Virgin Islands
P.O. Box 1270, Kingshill
Christiansted
St. Croix, Virgin Islands
809-773-7559

Federal Building
Charlotte Amalie,
St. Thomas
Virgin Islands 00801
809-774-1390

## Virginia
Norfolk Federal Building
200 Granby Mall
Norfolk, VA 23510
804-441-3081

## Washington
815 Airport Way, South
Seattle, WA 98134
206-442-5950

691 Federal Building
West 920 Riverside
Spokane, WA 99201
509-353-2129

## Washington, D.C.
4420 N. Fairfax Drive
Arlington, VA 22203
703-235-4055

## Wisconsin
Federal Building
517 E. Wisconsin Avenue
Milwaukee, WI 53202
414-291-3565

# STATE CHAMBERS OF COMMERCE

## Alabama
Alabama Development Office
135 S. Union Street
Montgomery, AL 36130
205-263-0048

## Alaska
Dept. of Commerce & Economic Development
P.O. Box D
Juneau, AK 99811
907-465-2500

## Arizona
Dept. of Commerce
3800 N. Central Ave.
Phoenix, AZ 85012
602-280-1306

## Arkansas
Industrial Development Comm.
1 Capitol Mall
Room 4C-300
Little Rock, AR 72201
501-682-1121

## California
Dept. of Commerce
801 K St., Ste. 1700
Sacramento, CA 95814
916-322-3962

## Conneticut
Dept. of Economic Development
865 Brook Street
Rocky Hill, CT 06067
203-258-4201

## Delaware
Dept. of State
Townsend Bldg.
P.O. Box 1401
Dover, DE 19901
302-739-4111

## Florida
510 C Collins Bldg.
107 W. Gaines Street
Tallahassee, FL 32399
904-488-3104

## Georgia
Industry, Trade & Tourism Dept.
285 Peachtree Ctr. Ave., NE, Ste, 1000
Atlanta, GA 30303
404-656-3573

## Hawaii
Dept. of Commerce & Consumer Affairs
1010 Richards St.
Honolulu, HI 96813
808-586-2850

## Idaho
Dept. of Commerce
700 W. State Street
Boise, ID 83720
208-334-2470

## Illinois
Dept. of Commerce & Community Affairs
620 E. Adams St., 3rd Fl.
Springfield, IL 62701
217-785-1032

## Indiana
333 State House
Indianapolis, IN 46204
317-232-4545

## Iowa
Dept. of Commerce
1918 SE Hulsizer
Ankeny, IA 50021
515-281-7401

## Kansas
Dept. of Commerce
400 SW Eighth, 5th Fl.
Topeka, KS 66612
913-296-3480

## Kentucky
Commerce Cabinet
Capital Plaza Tower
Frankfort, KY 40601
502-564-7670

## Louisiana
Dept. of Economic Development
P.O. Box 94185
Baton Rouge, LA 70804
504-342-5359

## Maine
Dept. of Economic & Community Development
State House Station # 59
Augusta, ME 04333
207-289-2656

## Maryland
Office of Business & Development
217 E. Redwood St.
Baltimore, MD 21202
301-333-6985

## Massachusetts
Executive Office of Economic Affairs
1 Ashburton Pl., Rm. 2101
Boston, MA 02108
617-727-8380

## Michigan
Dept. of Commerce
Law Bldg., 4th Fl.
P.O. Box 30004
Lansing, MI 48909
517-373-1820

## Minnesota
Dept. of Commerce
133 E. Seventh St.
St. Paul, MN 55101
612-296-4026

## Mississippi
Dept. of Economic & Community Development
P.O. Box 849
Jackson, MS 39205
601-359-3449

## Missouri
Dept. of Economic Development
P.O. Box 1157
Jefferson City, MO 65102
314-751-4962

## Montana
Dept. of Commerce
1424 Ninth Avenue
Helena, MT 59620
406-444-3797

## Nebraska
Dept. of Economic Development
301 Centennial Mall S.
P.O. Box 94666
Lincoln, NE 68509
402-471-3111

## Nevada
Dept. of Commerce
1665 Hot Spring Road
Carson City, NV 89710
702-687-4250

## New Hampshire
Dept. of Resources & Economic Development
105 Loudon Road
P.O. Box 856
Concord, NH 03301
603-271-2411

## New Jersey
Dept. of Commerce & Economic Development
20 W. State St., CN 820
Trenton, NJ 08625
609-292-2444

### New Mexico
Dept. of Economic
Development
1100 St. Francis Dr.
Santa Fe, NM 87503
505-827-0380

### New York
Dept. of Commerce
1 Commerce Plaza
Albany, NY 12245
518-474-4100

### North Carolina
Dept. of Economic &
Community Development
430 N. Salisbury St.
Raleigh, NC 27603
919-733-4962

### North Dakota
Economic Development
& Finance
State Capitol Grounds
604 E. Blvd.
Bismarck, ND 58505
701-224-2810

### Ohio
Dept. of Commerce
30 E. Broad Street
Columbus, OH 43266
614-466-3379

### Oklahoma
Dept. of Commerce
6601 Broadway Ext.
Oklahoma City, OK 73116
405-843-9770

### Oregon
Dept. of Insurance &
Finance
21 Labor & Industries
Bldg.
Salem, OR 97310
503-378-4120

### Pennsylvania
Dept. of Commerce
433 Forum Bldg.
Harrisburg, PA 17120
717-783-3840

### Rhode Island
Dept. of Economic
Development
7 Jackson Walkway
Providence, RI 02903
401-277-2601

### South Carolina
State Development Board
P.O. Box 927
Columbia, SC 29202
803-734-1400

### South Dakota
Dept. of Commerce &
Regulations
910 E. Sioux Avenue
Pierre, SD 57501
605-773-3563

### Tennesse
Dept. of Economic &
Community Development
320 Sixth Avenue, N.
Nashville, TN 37243
615-741-1888

### Texas
Dept. of Commerce
816 Congress, 12th Fl.
Austin, TX 78701
(512) 472-5059

### Utah
Dept. of Community &
Economic Development
6290 State Office Bldg.
Salt Lake City, UT 84114
801-538-8708

### Vermont
Dept. of Economic
Development
109 State Street
Montpelier, VT 05602
802-828-3221

### Virginia
Dept. of Commerce
3600 W. Broad St., 5th Fl.
Richmond, VA 23230
804-367-8519

### Washington
Dept. of Trade &
Economic Development
101 General
Administration Bldg.
M/S: AX-13
Olympia, WA 98504
206-753-7426

### West Virginia
Div. of Commerce
State Capitol Complex
2101 Washington St., E.
Charleston, WV 25305
304-348-2200

### Wisconsin
Dept. of Development
P.O. Box 7970
Madison, WI 53707
608-266-1916

### Wyoming
Dept. of Commerce
Barrett Bldg., 4th Fl.
Cheyenne, WY 82002
307-777-6303

### District of Columbia
Economic Development
1350 Pennsylvania, NW
Washington, DC 20004
202-727-6600

### American Samoa
Office of Economic
Development Planning
American Samoa
Government
Utulei
Pago Pago, AS 96799
684-633-5155

### Guam
Dept. of Commerce
590 S. Marine Dr., Ste. 601
Tamuning, GU 96911
671-646-6931

### Northern Mariana Islands
Dept. of Commerce &
Labor
Office of the Governor
Saipan, MP 96950
670-322-8711

### Puerto Rico
Dept. of Commerce
P.O. Box S
San Juan, PR 00905
809-724-1451

### U.S. Virgin Islands
Dept. of Economic
Development &
Agriculture
P.O. Box 6400
St. Thomas, VI 00804
809-774-8784

# SAMPLE IMMIGRATION FORMS

| Form # | Name | Use | Where Form Can Be Obtained | Filing Fee | Appendix Page # |
|---|---|---|---|---|---|
| I-130 | Petition for Alien Relative | Filed by citizen or lawful permanent resident to establish relationship of certain alien relatives who may wish to immigrate to the U.S. | INS office | $80 (U.S.) | M-5 |
| OF-230-I | Application for Immigrant Visa and Alien Registration–Biographic Information | Filed by the beneficiary abroad during the application process. Used to perform a security check of the applicant. | U.S. consulate | | M-10 |
| OF-169 | Certification of Documents | Filed by the beneficiary abroad during the application process. Certifies that the applicant possesses all documents needed to complete the application and to attend the immigration interview. | U.S. consulate | | M-12 |
| OF-230-II | Application for Immigrant Visa and Alien Registration | Filed by the applicant abroad at a U.S. consulate at the time of the immigration interview only. | U.S. consulate | | M-18 |
| I-134 | Affidavit of Support | Certifies that someone will assume financial responsibility for the applicant, or for his or her accompanying relatives. | U.S. consulate | | M-22 |
| I-485 | Application to Register Permanent Residence or Adjust Status | Used to apply to adjust permanent resident status or register for permanent residence while in the U.S. | INS office | $130[1] (U.S.) | M-25 |
| G-325-A | Biographic Information | Filed during the application process in the U.S. Used to compile personal background information. | INS office | | M-31 |
| I-94 | Departure Record | Records the entrance in and departure out of the U.S. by the foreign national. | INS office | | M-32 |
| I-765 | Application for Employment Authorization | Filed by applicant if he wishes to work before his green card has been approved. | INS office | $70 (U.S.) | M-33 |

[1] A fee of $100 (U.S.) is required if the applicant is under 14 years of age.

| Form # | Name | Use | Where Form Can Be Obtained | Filing Fee | Appendix Page # |
|---|---|---|---|---|---|
| OF-156 | **Application for Nonimmigrant Visa** | Application used to obtain a nonimmigrant visa. | U.S. consulate | | M-36 |
| I-20 A-B | **Certificate of Eligibility for Nonimmigrant Student Status** | This form is used to obtain a nonimmigrant visa for a student (category F). Usually filed by the academic institution. | INS office or academic institution | | M-37 |
| I-539 | **Application to Extend/Change Nonimmigrant Status** | Used by a nonimmigrant visa holder to apply for an extension or stay or change to another immigrant status. | INS office | $75[2] (U.S.) | M-40 |
| ETA-9029 | **Health Care Facility Attestation** | Filed by the U.S. institution seeking to hire foreign nurses to start the application process. | U.S. department of labor | | M-44 |
| I-129 | **Petition for a Nonimmigrant Worker** | Application used to file for nonimmigrant visa categories E, H, L, O, P, Q, or R. | INS office | $75[2] (U.S.) | M-46 |
| I-129 | **E Supplement to Petition for a Nonimmigrant Worker** | Supplement to be filed with I-129 when applying for an E-1 or E-2 nonimmigrant visa. | INS office | | M-48 |
| I-129 | **H Supplement to Petition for a Nonimmigrant Worker** | Supplement to be filed with I-129 when applying for an H-category nonimmigrant visa. | INS office | | M-49 |
| I-129 | **L Supplement to Petition for a Nonimmigrant Worker** | Supplement to be filed with I-129 when applying for a L-category nonimmigrant visa. | | | M-51 |
| I-129 | **O and P Supplement for Petition for a Nonimmigrant Worker** | Supplement to be filed with I-129 when applying for an O or P category nonimmigrant visa. | | | M-52 |
| I-129 | **Q and R Supplement for for a Nonimmigrant Worker** | Supplement to be filed with I-129 when applying for a Q or R category nonimmigrant visa. | | | M-53 |
| ETA-9035 | **Labor Condition Application for H-1B Nonimmigrants** | Filed by the prospective employer to start the immigration process for an H-1B visa. | U.S. department of labor | | M-55 |

[2] $10 each for any additional persons included on the application.

| Form # | Name | Use | Where Form Can Be Obtained | Filing Fee | Appendix Page # |
|---|---|---|---|---|---|
| OF-179 | **Biographic Data for Visa Purposes** | Collects biographic information of the applicant. | US consulate | | **M-56** |
| I-131 | **Application for Travel Document** | Used to apply for an INS travel document, reentry permit, refugee travel document or advance parole document. | INS office | $70 (U.S.) | **M-58** |
| I-360 | **Petition for Amerasian, Widow(er), or Special Immigrant** | Used to classify an alien as an Amerasian, widow(er) or special immigrant | INS office | $80 (U.S.) | **M-62** |
| I-526 | **Immigrant Petition by Alien Entrepreneur** | Used by an entrepreneur to petition for status as an immigrant to the U.S. | INS office | $155 (U.S.) | **M-68** |
| I-751 | **Petition to Remove the Conditions on Residence** | Used by a conditional resident who obtained such status through marriage to apply to remove the conditions on his/her residence. | INS office | $80 (U.S.) | **M-73** |
| I-140 | **Immigrant Petition for Alien Worker** | Filed by the sponsor, usually U.S. employer to petition for an immigrant based on employment. | INS office | $75 (U.S.) | **M-77** |
| N-400 | **Application for Naturalization** | Used to apply to become a naturalized citizen of of the U.S. | | $95 (U.S.) | **M-81** |
| I-485 Sup. A | **Supplement to Application to Register Permanent Residence or Adjust Status** | Used by a person already present in the U.S. who is applying for adjustment of status to that of lawful permanent resident. (Exceptions do apply). | | $650[3] (U.S.) | **M-87** |
| OF-167 | **Proof of financial support** | May be used instead of I-134 to determine that someone will assume financial responsibility for the applicant. | U.S. consulate | | **M-91** |
| I-129F | **Petition for Alien Fiancé(e)** | Used to obtain a category K visa for the fiancé(e) of a U.S. citizen and their children who intend to marry in the U.S. | | $75 | **M-97** |

3. Section 245 (i) of the Immigration and Nationality Act temporarily lifts certain restrictions of eligibility for adjustment of status to that of a lawful permanent resident of the U.S. It allows an otherwise eligible applicant to adjust status under Section 245 of the act without regard to manner of entry into the U.S. and without regard to most immigration status violations. A fee of $650 (U.S.) in addition to the fee paid when filing I-485 sums may be required or proof that Section 245 (i) of the act does not require the payment of the additional sum.

**U.S. Department of Justice**
Immigration and Naturalization Service (INS)          **Petition for Alien Relative**

## Instructions

**Read the instructions carefully. If you do not follow the instructions, we may have to return your petition, which may delay final action. If more space is needed to complete an answer continue on separate sheet of paper.**

1. **Who can file?**
   A citizen or lawful permanent resident of the United States can file this form to establish the relationship of certain alien relatives who may wish to immigrate to the United States. You must file a separate form for each eligible relative.

2. **For whom can you file?**
   A. If you are a citizen, you may file this form for:
      1) your husband, wife, or unmarried child under 21 years old
      2) your unmarried child over 21, or married child of any age
      3) your brother or sister if you are at least 21 years old
      4) your parent if you are at least 21 years old.
   B. If you are a lawful permanent resident you may file this form for:
      1) your husband or wife
      2) your unmarried child
   **Note:** If your relative qualifies under instruction A(2) or A(3) above, separate petitions are not required for his or her husband or wife or unmarried children under 21 years old. If your relative qualifies under instruction B(2) above, separate petitions are not required for his or her unmarried children under 21 years old. These persons will be able to apply for the same type of immigrant visa as your relative.

3. **For whom can you not file?**
   You cannot file for people in the following categories:
   A. An adoptive parent or adopted child, if the adoption took place after the child became 16 years old, or if the child has not been in the legal custody and living with the parent(s) for at least two years.
   B. A natural parent if the United States citizen son or daughter gained permanent residence through adoption.
   C. A stepparent or stepchild, if the marriage that created this relationship took place after the child became 18 years old.
   D. A husband or wife, if you were not both physically present at the marriage ceremony, and the marriage was not consummated.
   E. A husband or wife if you gained lawful permanent resident status by virtue of a prior marriage to a United States citizen or lawful permanent resident unless:
      1) a period of five years has elapsed since you became a lawful permanent resident; OR
      2) you can establish by clear and convincing evidence that the prior marriage (through which you gained your immigrant status) was not entered into for the purpose of evading any provision of the immigration laws, OR
      3) your prior marriage (through which you gained your immigrant status) was terminated by the death of your former spouse.
   F. A husband or wife if he or she was in exclusion, deportation, rescission, or judicial proceedings regarding his or her right to remain in the United States when the marriage took place, unless such spouse has resided outside the United States for a two-year period after the date of the marriage.
   G. A husband or wife if the Attorney General has determined that such alien has attempted or conspired to enter into a marriage for the purpose of evading the Immigration laws.
   H. A grandparent, grandchild, nephew, niece, uncle, aunt, cousin, or in-law.

4. **What documents do you need?**
   You must give INS certain documents with this form to prove you are eligible to file. You must also give the INS certain documents to prove the family relationship between you and your relative.
   A. For each document needed, give INS the original and one copy. However, because it is against the law to copy a Certificate of Naturalization, a Certificate of Citizenship or an Alien Registration Receipt Card (Form I-151 or I-551) give INS the original only. **Originals will be returned to you.**
   B. If you do not wish to give INS the original document, you may give INS a copy. The copy must be certified by:
      1) an INS or U.S. consular officer, or
      2) an attorney admitted to practice law in the United States, or
      3) an INS accredited representative (INS may still require originals).
   C. Documents in a foreign language must be accompanied by a complete English translation. The translator must certify that the translation is accurate and that he or she is competent to translate.

5. **What documents do you need to show you are a United States citizen?**
   A. If you were born in the United States, give INS your birth certificate.
   B. If you were naturalized, give INS your original Certificate of Naturalization.
   C. If you were born outside the United States, and you are a U.S. citizen through your parents, give INS:
      1) your original Certificate of Citizenship, or
      2) your Form FS-240 (Report of Birth Abroad of a United States Citizen).
   D. In place of any of the above, you may give INS your valid unexpired U.S. passport that was initially issued for at least 5 years.
   E. If you do not have any of the above and were born in the United States, see instruction under 8 below. *What if a document is not available?"*

6. **What documents do you need to show you are a permanent resident?**
   You must give INS your alien registration receipt card (Form I-151 or Form I-551). Do not give INS a photocopy of the card.

7. **What documents do you need to prove family relationship?**
   You have to prove that there is a family relationship between your relative and yourself.

   In any case where a marriage certificate is required, if either the husband or wife was married before, you must give INS documents to show that all previous marriages were legally ended. In cases where the names shown on the supporting documents have changed, give INS legal documents to show how the name change occurred (for example a marriage certificate, adoption decree, court order, etc.)

   Find the paragraph in the following list that applies to the relative for whom you are filing.

Form I-130 (Rev. 10/01/89) Y

If you are filing for your:

A. **husband or wife**, give INS
1) your marriage certificate
2) a color photo of you and one of your husband or wife, taken within 30 days of the date of this petition. These photos must have a white background. They must be glossy, unretouched, and not mounted. The dimension of the facial image should be about 1 inch from chin to top of hair in 3/4 frontal view, showing the right side of the face with the right ear visible. Using pencil or felt pen, lightly print name (and Alien Registration Number, if known) on the back of each photograph.
3) a completed and signed G-325A (Biographic Information) for you and one for your husband or wife. Except for name and signature, you do not have to repeat on the G-325A the information given on your I-130 petition.

B. **child** and you are the **mother**, give the child's birth certificate showing your name and the name of your child.

C. **child** and you are the **father or stepparent**, give the child's birth certificate showing both parents' names and your marriage certificate. **Child** born out of wedlock and you are the **father**, give proof that a parent/child relationship exists or existed. For example, the child's birth certificate showing your name and evidence that you have financially supported the child. (A blood test may be necessary).

D. **brother or sister**, your birth certificate and the birth certificate of your brother or sister showing both parents' names. If you do not have the same mother, you must also give the marriage certificates of your father to both mothers.

E. **mother**, give your birth certificate showing your name and the name of your mother.

F. **father**, give your birth certificate showing the names of both parents, and your parents' marriage certificate.

G. **stepparent**, give your birth certificate showing the names of both natural parents and the marriage certificate of your parent to your stepparent.

H. **adoptive parent or adopted child**, give a certified copy of the adoption decree, the legal custody decree if you obtained custody of the child before adoption, and a statement showing the dates and places you have lived together with the child.

**8. What if a document is not available?**
If the documents needed above are not available, you can give INS the following instead. (INS may require a statement from the appropriate civil authority certifying that the needed document is not available.)

A. Church record: A certificate under the seal of the church where the baptism, dedication, or comparable rite occurred within two months after birth, showing the date and place of child's birth, date of the religious ceremony, and the names of the child's parents.

B. School record: A letter from the authorities of the school attended (preferably the first school), showing the date of admission to the school, child's date and place of birth, and the names and places of birth parents, if shown in the school records.

C. Census record: State or federal census record showing the names, place of birth, and date of birth or the age of the person listed.

D. Affidavits: Written statements sworn to or affirmed by two persons who were living at the time and who have personal knowledge of the event you are trying to prove; for example, the date and place of birth, marriage, or death. The persons making the affidavits need not be citizens of the United States. Each affidavit should contain the following information regarding the person making the affidavit: his or her full name, address, date and place of birth, and his or her relationship to you, if any; full information concerning the event; and complete details concerning how the person acquired knowledge of the event.

**9. How should you prepare this form?**
A. Type or print legibly in ink.
B. If you need extra space to complete any item, attach a continuation sheet, indicate the item number, and date and sign each sheet.
C. Answer all questions fully and accurately. If any item does not apply, please write "N/A".

**10. Where should you file this form?**
A. If you live in the United States, send or take the form to the INS office that has jurisdiction over where you live.
B. If you live outside the United States, contact the nearest American Consulate to find out where to send or take the completed form.

**11. What is the fee?**
You must pay eighty dollars ($80.00) to file this form. **The fee will not be refunded, whether the petition is approved or not.** DO NOT MAIL CASH. All checks or money orders, whether U.S. or foreign, must be payable in U.S. currency at a financial institution in the United States. When a check is drawn on the account of a person other than yourself, write your name on the face of the check. If the check is not honored, INS will charge you $5.00.

Pay by check or money order in the exact amount. Make the check or money order payable to "Immigration and Naturalization Service". However,
A. if you live in Guam: Make the check or money order payable to "Treasurer, Guam", or
B. if you live in the U.S. Virgin Islands: Make the check or money order payable to "Commissioner of Finance of the Virgin Islands".

**12. When will a visa become available?**
When a petition is approved for the husband, wife, parent, or unmarried minor child of a United States citizen, these relatives do not have to wait for a visa number, as they are not subject to the immigrant visa limit. However, for a child to qualify for this category, all processing must be completed and the child must enter the United States before his or her 21st birthday.

For all other alien relatives there are only a limited number of immigrant visas each year. The visas are given out in the order in which INS receives properly filed petitions. To be considered properly filed, a petition must be completed accurately and signed, the required documents must be attached, and the fee must be paid.

For a monthly update on the dates for which immigrant visas are available, you may call (202) 647-0508.

**13. What are the penalties for committing marriage fraud or submitting false information or both?**
Title 8, United States Code, Section 1325 states that any individual who knowingly enters into a marriage contract for the purpose of evading any provision of the immigration laws shall be imprisoned for not more than five years, or fined not more than $250,000.00 or both.

Title 18, United States Code, Section 1001 states that whoever willfully and knowingly falsifies a material fact, makes a false statement, or makes use of a false document will be fined up to $10,000 or imprisoned up to five years, or both.

**14. What is our authority for collecting this information?**
We request the information on the form to carry out the immigration laws contained in Title 8, United States Code, Section 1154(a). We need this information to determine whether a person is eligible for immigration benefits. The information you provide may also be disclosed to other federal, state, local, and foreign law enforcement and regulatory agencies during the course of the investigation required by this Service. You do not have to give this information. However, if you refuse to give some or all of it, your petition may be denied.

**15. Reporting Burden.**
Public reporting burden for this collection of information is estimated to average 30 minutes per response, including the time for reviewing instructions, searching existing data sources, gathering and maintaining the data needed, and completing and reviewing the collection of information. Send comments regarding this burden estimate or any other aspect of this collection of information, including suggestions for reducing this burden, to: U.S. Department of Justice, Immigration and Naturalization Service (Room 2011), Washington, D.C. 20536; and to the Office of Management and Budget, Paperwork Reduction Project, OMB No. 1115-0054, Washington, D.C. 20503.

**It is not possible to cover all the conditions for eligibility or to give instructions for every situation. If you have carefully read all the instructions and still have questions, please contact your nearest INS office.**

**U.S. Department of Justice**

Immigration and Naturalization Service (INS)

OMB #1115-0054

**Petition for Alien Relative**

### DO NOT WRITE IN THIS BLOCK - FOR EXAMINING OFFICE ONLY

| Case ID# | Action Stamp | Fee Stamp |
|---|---|---|
| A# | | |
| G-28 or Volag # | | |

Section of Law:
- ☐ 201 (b) spouse    ☐ 203 (a)(1)
- ☐ 201 (b) child     ☐ 203 (a)(2)
- ☐ 201 (b) parent    ☐ 203 (a)(4)
-                  ☐ 203 (a)(5)

AM CON: _____

Petition was filed on: _____ (priority date)

- ☐ Personal Interview           ☐ Previously Forwarded
- ☐ Pet. ☐ Ben. "A" File Reviewed    ☐ Stateside Criteria
- ☐ Field Investigations         ☐ I-485 Simultaneously
- ☐ 204 (a)(2)(A) Resolved       ☐ 204 (h) Resolved

Remarks:

## A. Relationship

1. The alien relative is my
   ☐ Husband/Wife   ☐ Parent   ☐ Brother/Sister   ☐ Child

2. Are you related by adoption?
   ☐ Yes   ☐ No

3. Did you gain permanent residence through adoption?
   ☐ Yes   ☐ No

## B. Information about you

1. **Name** (Family name in CAPS)    (First)    (Middle)

2. **Address** (Number and Street)    (Apartment Number)

   (Town or City)    (State/Country)    (ZIP/Postal Code)

3. **Place of Birth** (Town or City)    (State/Country)

4. **Date of Birth** (Mo/Day/Yr)
5. **Sex**  ☐ Male  ☐ Female
6. **Marital Status**  ☐ Married  ☐ Single  ☐ Widowed  ☐ Divorced

7. **Other Names Used** (including maiden name)

8. **Date and Place of Present Marriage** (if married)

9. **Social Security Number**
10. **Alien Registration Number** (if any)

11. **Names of Prior Husbands/Wives**
12. **Date(s) Marriage(s) Ended**

13. If you are a U.S. citizen, complete the following:

   My citizenship was acquired through (check one)
   ☐ Birth in the U.S.
   ☐ Naturalization (Give number of certificate, date and place it was issued)

   ☐ Parents
      Have you obtained a certificate of citizenship in your own name?
      ☐ Yes    ☐ No
      If "Yes", give number of certificate, date and place it was issued.

14a. If you are a lawful permanent resident alien, complete the following:
   Date and place of admission for, or adjustment to, lawful permanent residence, and class of admission:

14b. Did you gain permanent resident status through marriage to a United States citizen or lawful permanent resident?   ☐ Yes  ☐ No

## C. Information about your alien relative

1. **Name** (Family name in CAPS)    (First)    (Middle)

2. **Address** (Number and Street)    (Apartment Number)

   (Town or City)    (State/Country)    (ZIP/Postal Code)

3. **Place of Birth** (Town or City)    (State/Country)

4. **Date of Birth** (Mo/Day/Yr)
5. **Sex**  ☐ Male  ☐ Female
6. **Marital Status**  ☐ Married  ☐ Single  ☐ Widowed  ☐ Divorced

7. **Other Names Used** (including maiden name)

8. **Date and Place of Present Marriage** (if married)

9. **Social Security Number**
10. **Alien Registration Number** (if any)

11. **Names of Prior Husbands/Wives**
12. **Date(s) Marriage(s) Ended**

13. Has your relative ever been in the U.S.?
   ☐ Yes    ☐ No

14. If your relative is currently in the U.S., complete the following: He or she last arrived as a (visitor, student, stowaway, without inspection, etc.)

   Arrival/Departure Record (I-94) Number    Date arrived (Month/Day/Year)

   Date authorized stay expired, or will expire, as shown on Form I-94 or I-95

15. Name and address of present employer (if any)

   Date this employment began (Month/Day/Year)

16. Has your relative ever been under immigration proceedings?
   ☐ Yes    ☐ No    Where _____  When _____
   ☐ Exclusion  ☐ Deportation  ☐ Recession  ☐ Judicial Proceedings

| INITIAL RECEIPT | RESUBMITTED | RELOCATED | | COMPLETED | | |
|---|---|---|---|---|---|---|
| | | Rec'd | Sent | Approved | Denied | Returned |
| | | | | | | |

Form I-130 (Rev. 10/01/89) Y

## C. (continued) Information about your alien relative

**16. List husband/wife and all children of your relative** (If your relative is your husband/wife, list only his or her children).

(Name)                          (Relationship)                     (Date of Birth)                          (Country of Birth)

**17. Address in the United States where your relative intends to live**

(Number and Street)                                    (Town or City)                          (State)

**18. Your relative's address abroad**

(Number and Street)          (Town or City)          (Province)          (Country)          (Phone Number)

**19. If your relative's native alphabet is other than Roman letters, write his or her name and address abroad in the native alphabet:**

(Name)                    (Number and Street)          (Town or City)          (Province)          (Country)

**20. If filing for your husband/wife, give last address at which you both lived together:**          **From**          **To**

(Name)          (Number and Street)          (Town or City)     (Province)     (Country)          (Month)   (Year)          (Month)   (Year)

**21. Check the appropriate box below and give the information required for the box you checked:**

☐ Your relative will apply for a visa abroad at the American Consulate in _____

(City)                              (Country)

☐ Your relative is in the United States and will apply for adjustment of status to that of a lawful permanent resident in the office of the Immigration and

Naturalization Service at _____ . If your relative is not eligible for adjustment of status, he or she will
                          (City)                    (State)

apply for a visa abroad at the American Consulate in _____
                                          (City)                              (Country)

(Designation of a consulate outside the country of your relative's last residence does not guarantee acceptance for processing by that consulate.
Acceptance is at the discretion of the designated consulate.)

## D. Other Information

1.  **If separate petitions are also being submitted for other relatives, give names of each and relationship.**

2.  **Have you ever filed a petition for this or any other alien before?**          ☐ Yes          ☐ No
    If "Yes," give name, place and date of filing, and result.

**Warning:** The INS investigates claimed relationships and verifies the validity of documents. The INS seeks criminal prosecutions when family relationships are falsified to obtain visas.

**Penalties:** You may, by law be imprisoned for not more than five years, or fined $250,000, or both, for entering into a marriage contract for the purpose of evading any provision of the immigration laws and you may be fined up to $10,000 or imprisoned up to five years or both, for knowingly and willfully falsifying or concealing a material fact or using any false document in submitting this petition.

**Your Certification:** I certify, under penalty of perjury under the laws of the United States of America, that the foregoing is true and correct. Furthermore, I authorize the release of any information from my records which the Immigration and Naturalization Service needs to determine eligibility for the benefit that I m seeking.

Signature _____      Date _____      Phone Number _____

## Signature of Person Preparing Form if Other than Above

I declare that I prepared this document at the request of the person above and that it is based on all information of which I have any knowledge.

Print Name _____    (Address) _____    (Signature) _____    (Date) _____

G-28 ID Number _____

Volag Number _____

## NOTICE TO PERSONS FILING FOR SPOUSES IF MARRIED LESS THAN TWO YEARS

Pursuant to section 216 of the Immigration and Nationality Act, your alien spouse may be granted conditional permanent resident status in the United States as of the date he or she is admitted or adjusted to conditional status by an officer of the Immigration and Naturalization Service. Both you and your conditional permanent resident spouse are required to file a petition, Form I-751, Joint Petition to Remove Conditional Basis of Alien's Permanent Resident Status, during the ninety day period immediately before the second anniversary of the date your alien spouse was granted conditional permanent residence.

Otherwise, the rights, privileges, responsibilities and duties which apply to all other permanent residents apply equally to a conditional permanent resident. A conditional permanent resident is not limited to the right to apply for naturalization, to file petitions in behalf of qualifying relatives, or to reside permanently in the United States as an immigrant in accordance with the immigration laws.

> **Failure to file Form I-751, Joint Petition to Remove the Conditional Basis of Alien's Permanent Resident Status, will result in termination of permanent residence status and initiation of deportation proceedings.**

**NOTE: You must complete Items 1 through 6 to assure that petition approval is recorded. Do not write in the section below item 6.**

1. **Name of relative** (Family name in CAPS)        (First)        (Middle)

2. **Other names used by relative** (including maiden name)

3. **Country of relative's birth**        4. **Date of relative's birth** (Month/Day/Year)

5. **Your name** (Last name in CAPS)    (First)    (Middle)    6. **Your phone number**

**Action Stamp**

| SECTION | DATE PETITION FILED |
|---------|---------------------|
| ☐ 201 (b)(spouse) | |
| ☐ 201 (b)(child) | |
| ☐ 201 (b)(parent) | |
| ☐ 203 (a)(1) | ☐ STATESIDE |
| ☐ 203 (a)(2) | CRITERIA GRANTED |
| ☐ 203 (a)(4) | SENT TO CONSUL AT; |
| ☐ 203 (a)(5) | |

**CHECKLIST**

**Have you answered each question?**

**Have you signed the petition?**

**Have you enclosed:**

☐ The filing fee for each petition?

☐ Proof of your citizenship or lawful permanent residence?

☐ All required supporting documents for each petition?

**If you are filing for your husband or wife have you included:**

☐ Your picture?

☐ His or her picture?

☐ Your G-325A?

☐ His or her G-325A?

Relative Petition Card
Form I-130A (Rev. 10/01/89) Y

OMB APPROVAL NO. 1405-0015
EXPIRES: 8-31-92
*ESTIMATED BURDEN: 1 HOUR

 **APPLICATION FOR IMMIGRANT VISA AND ALIEN REGISTRATION**

### PART I - BIOGRAPHIC DATA

INSTRUCTIONS: Complete one copy of this form for yourself and each member of your family, regardless of age, who will immigrate with you. Please print or type your answer to all questions. Questions that are Not Applicable should be so marked. If there is insufficient room on the form, answer on a separate sheet using the same numbers as appear on the form. Attach the sheet to this form.

**WARNING:  Any false statement or concealment of a material fact may result in your permanent explusion from the United States.**

This form is Part I of two parts which, together with Optional Form OF-230 PART II, constitute the complete Application for Immigrant Visa and Alien Registration.

1.  FAMILY NAME                    FIRST NAME                    MIDDLE NAME

2.  OTHER NAMES USED OR BY WHICH KNOWN *(If married woman, give maiden name)*

3.  FULL NAME IN NATIVE ALPHABET *(If Roman letters not used)*

| 4.  DATE OF BIRTH *(Day)   (Month)   (Year)* | 5.  AGE | 6.  PLACE OF BIRTH *(City or town)        (Province)        (Country)* |
|---|---|---|

| 7.  NATIONALITY *(If dual national, give both)* | 8.  SEX  ☐ Male  ☐ Female | 9.  MARITAL STATUS  ☐ Single *(Never married)*  ☐ Married  ☐ Widowed  ☐ Divorced  ☐ Separated  Including my present marriage, I have been married _____ times. |
|---|---|---|

10. PERSONAL DESCRIPTION
    a. Color of hair _____   c. Height _____
    b. Color of eyes _____   d. Complexion _____

11. OCCUPATION

12. MARKS OF IDENTIFICATION

13. PRESENT ADDRESS



    Telephone number : Home                    Office

14. NAME OF SPOUSE *(Maiden or family name)*          *(First name)*          *(Middle name)*


    Date and place of birth of spouse:

    Address of spouse *(If different from your own)*:

15. LIST NAME, DATE AND PLACE OF BIRTH, AND ADDRESSES OF ALL CHILDREN

| NAME | DATE AND PLACE OF BIRTH | ADDRESS (If different from your own) |
|---|---|---|
| _____ | _____ | _____ |
| _____ | _____ | _____ |
| _____ | _____ | _____ |
| _____ | _____ | _____ |
| _____ | _____ | _____ |
| _____ | _____ | _____ |
| _____ | _____ | _____ |

THIS FORM MAY BE OBTAINED GRATIS AT CONSULAR OFFICES OF THE UNITED STATES OF AMERICA          OPTIONAL FORM 230 I (ENGLISH)
NSN 7540-00- 149-0919

16. PERSON(S) NAMED IN 14 AND 15 WHO WILL ACCOMPANY OR FOLLOW ME TO THE UNITED STATES.

17. NAME OF FATHER, DATE AND PLACE OF BIRTH, AND ADDRESS  *If deceased, so state, giving year of death)*

18. MAIDEN NAME OF MOTHER, DATE AND PLACE OF BIRTH, AND ADDRESS *(If deceased, so state, giving year of death)*

19. IF NEITHER PARENT IS LIVING PROVIDE NAME AND ADDRESS OF NEXT OF KIN *(nearest relative)* IN YOUR HOME COUNTRY.

20. LIST ALL LANGUAGES YOU CAN SPEAK, READ, AND WRITE

| LANGUAGE | SPEAK | READ | WRITE |
|---|---|---|---|
| | | | |
| | | | |
| | | | |

21. LIST BELOW ALL PLACES YOU HAVE LIVED FOR SIX MONTHS OR LONGER SINCE REACHING THE AGE OF 16. BEGIN WITH YOUR PRESENT RESIDENCE.

| CITY OR TOWN | PROVINCE | COUNTRY | OCCUPATION | DATES (FROM-TO) |
|---|---|---|---|---|
| | | | | |
| | | | | |
| | | | | |
| | | | | |
| | | | | |

22. LIST ANY POLITICAL, PROFESSIONAL, OR SOCIAL ORGANIZATIONS AFFILIATED WITH COMMUNIST, TOTALITARIAN, TERRORIST OR NAZI ORGANI-ZATIONS WHICH YOU ARE NOW OR HAVE BEEN A MEMBER OF OR AFFILIATED WITH SINCE YOUR 16TH BIRTHDAY.

| NAME AND ADDRESS | FROM/TO | TYPE OF MEMBERSHIP |
|---|---|---|
| | | |
| | | |
| | | |

23. LIST DATES OF ALL PREVIOUS RESIDENCE IN OR VISITS TO THE UNITED STATES. *(If never, so states)* GIVE TYPE OF VISA STATUS IF ANY. GIVE I.N.S. "A" NUMBER IF ANY.

| LOCATION | FROM/TO | VISA | I.N.S. FILE NO. *(If known)* |
|---|---|---|---|
| | | | |
| | | | |
| | | | |
| | | | |

| SIGNATURE OF APPLICANT | DATE |
|---|---|
| | |

**NOTE: Return this completed form immediately to the consular office address on the covering letter. This form will become part of your immigrant visa an your visa application cannot be processed until this form is complete.**

* Public reporting burden for this collection of information is estimated to average 24 hours per response, including time required for searching existing data sources, gathering the necessary data, providing the information required, and reviewing the final collection. Send comments on the accuracy of this estimate of the burden and recommendations for reducing it to: Department of State (OIS/RA/DR) Washington, D.C. 20520-0264, and to the Office of Information and Regulatory Affairs. Office of Management and Budget, Paperwork Reduction Project (1405-0015), Washington, D. C. 20503.

Immigrant Visa Branch
United States Embassy

I   A.  FIRST      Complete and return immediately to this office the enclosed Optional Form 230-I (formerly DSP-70), Biographic Data for Visa Purposes.

      B.  SECOND    Obtain the documents listed in Part II. As you obtain each document check the box before each item listed in Part II.

      C.  THIRD      Notify this office when you have assembled the documents which are applicable to your case listed in Part II by completing Part III on page 4 and submitting the entire form to this office.

<u>All documents</u>, except passports and photographs, must be submitted in one copy, with the original. If you have only the original of your birth, marriage and/or other certificates you may submit one photostatic copy thereof but <u>you must bring the original(s) with you</u>, for inspection by the consular officer. The original(s) will be returned to you if you furnish one copy of each document in addition to the original.

<u>NOTICE</u>
DO NOT UNDER ANY CIRCUMSTANCES SEND ANY DOCUMENTS TO THIS OFFICE UNLESS YOU ARE SPECIFICALLY REQUESTED TO DO SO. A FINAL DETERMINATION CONCERNING THE ACCEPTABILITY OF DOCUMENTS CAN ONLY BE MADE AT THE TIME OF YOUR FORMAL INTERVIEW.

THIS WILL ALSO PREVENT LOSS OF DOCUMENTS AND YOUR HAVING TO OBTAIN DUPLICATES.

It is strongly recommended that you make and retain an additional certified copy of each document required in support of your immigrant visa application. The Embassy will not maintain copies of your documents and visa. If your issued immigrant visa is destroyed, lost, or otherwise rendered useless, you must present the original or certified copies of all supporting documents before we can reissue the visa or you can be admitted to the United States.

II

☐  1.  <u>PASSPORTS</u>: A passport must be valid for at least six months and be endorsed by the issuing authority for travel to the United States. Britain regular passports meet this consideration. Each child 16 years of age or older, who is included in the parent's passport but whose photograph does not appear in such passport must obtain his own separate passport.

☐  2.  <u>BIRTH CERTIFICATES</u>: One birth certificate* is required for each person, including children, applying for a visa. The certificate must state your date and place of birth and <u>names of both your parents</u> and be a certified copy of an original issued by the Registrar or other official keeper of the records. Alternatively, one photographic copy of an original or certified copy may be presented provided the original or certified copy is also produced for comparison purposes at the formal visa application.

In addition, you should assemble one long form birth certificate for any of your children under 21 who will be accompanying you to the United States. UNOBTAINABLE BIRTH CERTIFICATE: In rare cases, it may be impossible to obtain a birth certificate because records have been destroyed, or the government will not issue one. In such a case, a baptismal certificate may be submitted for consideration provided it contains the date and place of the applicant's birth and information concerning parentage and provided the baptism took place shortly after birth. Should a baptismal certificate be unobtainable, a close relative, preferably the applicant's mother, should prepare a notarized statement stating the place and date of the applicant's birth, the names of both parents and maiden name of the mother. The statement must be executed before an official authorized to administer oaths of affirmation.

☐  3.  <u>ADOPTION CERTIFICATE</u>: Obtain original and one copy of the certificate* in cases of applicants who have been adopted.

**SAMPLE DOCUMENT – NOT TO BE USED WHEN FILING.**

☐   4.   DEED POLL:  For applicants who have ever changed their names (except by marriage) original and one copy of the Deed Poll, or other legal evidence of the change in name should be furnished.

☐   5.   POLICE CERTIFICATES:  (Certificates of Good Conduct).
Please state below the name of the country or countries from which you or accompanying members of your family have obtained Police Certificates.

_____

Each visa applicant aged 16 years or over is required to submit a police certificate to cover any period of residence of six months or more since reaching the age of sixteen. The term "police certificate" as used in this paragraph means a certification by the appropriate police authorities stating either there is no record or what their records show concerning the applicant including any and all arrests, the reasons therefor and the disposition of each case of which there is a record. If you should reside anywhere for six months or more after submission of the completed Optional Form 230-I, Biographic Data for Visa Purposes (enclosed), please inform this office immediately.
Police certificates are not issued by the police in the United Kingdom. You need not concern yourself with this requirement (but see item 6, Court and Prison Records).

(SEE PAGE 2 OF SUPPLEMENT 1 TO THIS FORM 169 FOR ADDITIONAL INFORMATION CONCERNING APPLICATION FOR POLICE CERTIFICATES.)

☐   6.   COURT AND PRISON RECORDS:  Persons who have been convicted of a crime must obtain one certified copy of the court record relating to each offense for which they have been convicted. This is necessary regardless of the fact that they may have subsequently benefited from an amnesty, pardon or other act of clemency or a Rehabilitation of Offenders Act.

☐   7.   MILITARY RECORDS:  One certified copy of any military record should be obtained covering periods spent in military service including wartime or national service.

☐   8.   PHOTOGRAPHS:  Two color photographs for each visa applicant, including infants, regardless of age. The photographs must be color photographs with a white background. They must be glossy, unretouched and not mounted; the dimension of facial image should be about 1 inch from chin to top of hair; the subject should be shown in 3/4 frontal view showing right side of face with the right ear visible. No earrings should be worn. (See UK/2, attached, listing approved photographers.)

☐   9   EVIDENCE OF SUPPORT:  Any evidence which will show that you and the members of your family also immigrating are not likely to become a public charge while in the United States. This is required of all visa applicants including the spouse of a United States citizen. The enclosed information sheet, Optional Form 167 - formerly DSL-845, lists evidence which may be presented to meet this requirement of the law. Such evidence must be less than 1 year old.

☐   10.   MARRIAGE CERTIFICATE:  Present original and one copy of your marriage certificate*. (Two copies if husband and wife are planning to travel separately.)

☐   11.   DIVORCE OR DEATH CERTIFICATES:  Proof of the termination of any previous marriage must also be furnished in the form of a divorce, death or annulment certificate*. A decree nisi is not acceptable, it must be a final divorce decree.

☐   12.   TRANSLATIONS:  All documents not in English must be accompanied by certified translations into English. Translations must be certified by a qualified independent translator and sworn to before a Notary Public or Commissioner of Oaths.

*All civil documents furnished must be issued by a public authority. Those originating from the United States must have been obtained from either a State vital statistics office or a city, county, or other local office. Certified copies of British documents are obtainable from either the General Register Office, London, or from the local registrar's office in the district of registration.

III

    C.  THIRD:  As soon as you have obtained all of the documents listed in items 1 to 12 which are applicable to your case, read carefully the statement below then complete this form by giving the information requested below and return the entire form to this office.

Enclosures:
1. Optional Form 230-I (DSP-70)
2. Optional Form 167 (DSL-845)

I have in my possession and am prepared to present all of the documents listed in items 1 through 12 which apply to my case, as indicated by the check marks I have placed in the appropriate boxes. I fully realize that no advance assurance can be given that a visa will actually be issued to me and I also understand that I should NOT give up my job, dispose of property, nor make any final travel arrangements until a visa is actually issued to me. At such time as it is possible for me to receive an appointment to make formal visa application, I intend to apply:
(check appropriate box)

☐   1.  Alone          ☐  2. With my spouse

☐   3.  With my spouse & following minor children:
       (print full names of each child)

_____

_____

DATE OF INTENDED TRAVEL _____

_____
SIGNATURE

_____
NAME IN BLOCK LETTERS

_____
ADDRESS

_____

_____
CASE NUMBER

PLEASE QUOTE YOUR CASE NUMBER AND FULL NAME WHEN CORRESPONDING WITH THIS OFFICE.

SUPPLEMENT 1 TO OPTIONAL FORM 169

## BIRTH CERTIFICATES

<u>A person born in India or Pakistan</u> must present the registration certificate if his birth was registered. If it was not registered, either in the locality or, if a Christian, in a church, sworn affidavits may be submitted. Such an affidavit must be executed before an official authorized to take oaths (i.e., a magistrate, commissioner of oaths, justice of the peace or the like) by the mother. If she is deceased that father may swear to the affidavit. The affidavit should indicate:

(1) that the applicant's birth was not registered;

(2) the full maiden name of the mother of the applicant;

(3) the full name of the father of the applicant;

(4) the date of the applicant's birth;

(5) the place of the applicant's birth.

If neither parent is alive, the next closest relative, who was old enough and of such relationship as to have personal knowledge of the birth at the time and place it occurred, may execute the affidavit.

A statement from the High Commission concerning your birth is not acceptable.

<u>A person who has used a different name</u> from the one shown on the birth certificate, must produce a document explaining the use of such name.

The following documents are commonly available as evidence:

(1) Baptismal certificate

(2) Deed Poll

(3) School records showing early use of adopted name.

If none of the foregoing documents are available any other document, or combination of documents, which appear to resolve the difference in names will be considered. <u>Your personal sworn statement is not acceptable unless there is other evidence to substantiate it.</u>

SUPPLEMENT 2 TO OPTIONAL FORM 169

Every applicant for an immigrant visa who has a child or children is by regulation required to submit to the interviewing consular officer the birth and/or baptismal certificate for each child. If your wife or husband has a child or children by a previous marriage who had not attained the age of eighteen years at the time of your marriage, or a child born out of wedlock, the birth and/or baptismal certificate for each such child must also be obtained for examination by the consular officer. This requirement applies even though one or more of the children of either spouse has no current intention to apply for an immigrant visa to the United States.

A CHILD AS DEFINED IN THE IMMIGRATION AND NATIONALITY ACT IS AN UNMARRIED PERSON NOT YET 21 YEARS OF AGE.

I (we) have the following children who will NOT accompany me (us) to the United States:

FAMILY NAME          FIRST NAME          MIDDLE NAMES          DATE & COUNTRY OF BIRTH

_____

_____

_____

_____

_____

_____

I (we) have obtained birth and/or baptismal certificates for each child, and these will be retained in my (our) possession for presentation to the consular officer on the date of my (our) formal application for an immigrant visa.


_____          _____
(Signature of Principal Applicant)          (Signature of spouse)

PLEASE RETURN THIS FORM TO THE CONSULAR OFFICER WHEN YOU RETURN OPTIONAL FORM 169.

DO NOT SEND ANY DOCUMENTS TO THIS OFFICE UNLESS SPECIFICALLY REQUESTED TO DO SO.

POLICE CERTIFICATES

If you or accompanying member(s) of your family now applying for a visa have resided in another country or countries, certificates covering residences of six months or more must be obtained. Generally, application for such certificates should be made directly to police authorities in the district in which you resided. If you have any questions about where or how to apply for police certificates in other countries you may communicate directly with this office.

Do not attempt to obtain police certificates covering residence in any of the following countries or areas, as they either are not available or may be obtained only by this office:

| | |
|---|---|
| AFGHANISTAN | MALAYSIA |
| ALBANIA | MARSHALL ISLANDS |
| MEXICO | MONGOLIA |
| ARUBA | NEPAL |
| BERMUDA | NETHERLANDS |
| BRAZIL | NETHERLANDS ANTILLES |
| BRUNEI | NEW ZEALAND |
| BULGARIA | NICARAGUA |
| CAMBODIA | NORTHERN IRELAND |
| CHAD | ROMANIA |
| CHILE | SAUDI ARABIA |
| COMOROS | SCOTLAND |
| COSTA RICA | SIERRA LEONE |
| CUBA | SOMALIA |
| ENGLAND | SOUTH AFRICA |
| EQUATORIAL GUINEA | SOVIET UNION |
| ESTONIA | SRI LANKA |
| ETHIOPIA | SURINAME |
| FIJI | TOGO |
| GHANA | TURKEY |
| INDONESIA | UGANDA |
| IRAQ | UNITED ARAB EMIRATES |
| KOREA | UNITED KINGDOM |
| KUWAIT | UNITED STATES OF AMERICA |
| LAOS | VANUATU |
| LATVIA | VENEZUELA |
| LEBANON | VIETNAM |
| LITHUANIA | WALES |
| MALAWI | ZIMBABWE |

OMB APPROVAL 1405-0015
EXPIRES: 8-31-92
*ESTIMATED BURDEN: 23 hours

# APPLICATION FOR IMMIGRANT VISA AND ALIEN REGISTRATION

## 移 民 査 証 お よ び 外 国 人 登 録 申 請 書

## PART II - SWORN STATEMENT
### パートⅡ 宣誓供述書

INSTRUCTIONS: Complete one copy of this form for yourself and each member of your family, regardless of age, who will immigrate with you. Please print or type your answer to all questions. Questions that are Not Applicable should be so marked. If there is insufficient room on the form, answer on a separate sheet using the same numbers as appear on the form. Attach the sheet to this form. DO NOT SIGN this form until instructed to do so by the consular officer. The fee for filing this application is listed under tariff item No. 20. The fee should be paid in United States dollars or local currency equivalent, or by bank draft, when you appear before the consular officer.

**WARNING: Any false statement or concealment of a material fact may result in your permanent exclusion from the United States. Even though you should be admitted to the United States, a fraudulent entry could be grounds for your prosecution and/or deportation.**

This form is a continuation of Form OF-230 Part I, which together, constitute the complete Application for Immigrant Visa and Alien Registration.

記入にあたり、次の指示に従って下さい：この書式は、年齢にかかわらず、申請者本人、および移民する家族全員についてそれぞれ一枚（英語で）記入しなければなりません。すべての質問に回答し、記入にはタイプライターを使用するか、または活字体で書いて下さい。該当しない質問には、該当しない（Not Applicable）、と書いて下さい。紙面が足りない時は、別紙に質問番号を明記して回答を記入し、その別紙をこの書式に添付して下さい。領事の指示があるまでは、この用紙に署名しないで下さい。申請料は料金表の20番に記載されています。申請料は米ドル、または同額の現地通貨、あるいは銀行為替で、領事との面接の際に支払っていただきます。

注意：虚偽の供述をしたり事実を隠蔽すると、米国への入国を永久に拒否されることがあります。また入国が許可されても、不正に入国した場合、起訴されたり、強制送還を命ぜられることになります。

このパートⅡは、二部から成る書式の第二部で、書式ＯＦ－230パートⅠと合わせて完全な移民査証および外国人登録申請書になります。

---

24. FAMILY NAME 姓                    FIRST NAME 名                    MIDDLE NAME 中間名

---

25. ADDRESS (Local)   現住所（日本国内）

Telephone No. 電話番号

26. FINAL ADDRESS TO WHICH YOU WILL TRAVEL IN THE UNITED STATES
アメリカにおけるあなたの落ち着き先
*(Street address including ZIP Code)*
（番地、郵便番号まで記入する）

Telephone No. 電話番号

---

27. PERSON YOU INTEND TO JOIN *(Name, address, and relationship)*
あなたが身を寄せることになっている人の氏名、住所、続柄

28. NAME AND ADDRESS OF SPONSORING PERSON OR EMPLOYER
あなたの身元引受人である個人あるいは雇用主の氏名、住所

---

29. PURPOSE OF GOING TO THE UNITED STATES   渡米の目的

30. LENGTH OF INTENDED STAY *(If permanently, so state)*
滞在期間（永久の時は permanently と書く）

---

31. INTENDED PORT OF ENTRY   入国予定港

32. DO YOU HAVE A TICKET TO FINAL DESTINATION?
最終目的地までの切符を持っていますか？

☐ Yes はい          ☐ No いいえ

---

33. United States laws governing the isuance of visas require each applicant to state whether or not he or she is a member of any class of individuals excluded from admission into the United States. The excludable classes are described below in general terms. You should read carefully the following list and answer YES or NO to each category. The answers you give will assist the consular officer to reach a decision on your eligibility to receive a visa.

EXCEPT AS OTHERWISE PROVIDED BY LAW, ALIENS WITHIN THE FOLLOWING
CLASSIFICATIONS ARE INELIGIBLE TO RECEIVE A VISA.
DO ANY OF THE FOLLOWING CLASSES APPLY TO YOU?

査証の発行を規定するアメリカの法律により、査証申請者は自分が「アメリカ入国を拒否される人の部類に入るかどうかを述べなければなりません。入国を拒否される人の種類を次に説明します。下記の説明を良く読み、それぞれの項目についてYESかNOをチェックして下さい。あなたの回答は、領事があなたの査証取得資格を判断する材料となります。

法律で別に定められている場合を除き、次の部類に属する人は査証を取得する資格がありません。
あなたは下記のいずれかの項目に該当しますか。

---

THIS FORM MAY BE OBTAINED GRATIS AT CONSULAR OFFICES OF THE UNITED STATES OF AMERICA
この用紙は各地にある米国領事館で無料で入手できます。

OPTIONAL FORM 230 II (English/Japanese)
REVISED 4-91
DEPT. OF STATE

TKY-V-74B (10-91)          Previous editions obsolete

a.  An alien who has a communicable disease of public health significance, or has had a physical or mental disorder that poses, or is likely to pose a threat to the safety or welfare of the alien or others; an alien who is a drug abuser or addict. [212(a)(1)]

a. 公衆衛生上危険な伝染病にかかっている人、本人または他の人々の安全や福祉を脅かす、あるいは脅かす可能性のある身体的または精神的障害を現在持つ、あるいは過去に持ったことのある人、麻薬常習者または麻薬中毒者 (212(a)(1))       はい ☐   いいえ ☒

b.  An alien convicted of, or who admits committing a crime involving moral turpitude, or violation of any law relating to a controlled substance; an alien convicted of 2 or more offenses for which the aggregate sentences were 5 years or more; an alien coming to the United States to engage in prostitution or commercialized vice, or who has engaged in prostitution or procuring within the past 10 years; an alien who is or has been an illicit trafficker in any controlled substance; an alien who has committed a serious criminal offense in the United States and who has asserted immunity from prosecution. [212(a)(2)]

b. 破廉恥罪を犯して、または規制薬物に関する法律に違反して有罪判決を受けたことのある人、あるいはそれらの犯罪を犯したことを認める人、2つ以上の犯罪を犯して通算5年以上の禁固刑を宣告されたことのある人、売春をするため、または売春を商売するためにアメリカへ入国しようとする人、あるいは過去10年間に売春をした、または売春婦を斡旋したことのある人、規制薬物を不法に売買する人、または売買したことのある人、アメリカにおいて重大な犯罪を犯したことがあり、起訴を免れるために免責を主張したことのある人 (212(a)(2))       Yes はい ☐   No いいえ ☒

c.  Alien who seeks to enter the United States to engage in espionage, sabotage, export control violations, overthrow of the Government of the United States, or other unlawful activity; an alien who seeks to enter the United States to engage in terrorist activities; an alien who has been a member of or affiliated with the Communist or any other totalitarian party; an alien who under the direction of the Nazi government of Germany, or any area occupied by, or allied with the Nazi Government of Germany, ordered, incited, assisted, or otherwise participated in the prosecution of any person because of race, religion, national origin, or political opinion; an alien who has engaged in genocide. [212(a)(3)]

c. スパイ行為、破壊活動、輸出規制違反、米国政府の転覆を図る行為、その他の不法行為をすることを目的にアメリカに入国しようとする人、テロ活動をするために入国しようとする人、共産党またはその他の全体主義政党の党員だったことのある、またはそれらの活動にかかわったことのある人、ドイツ・ナチ政府の指示によってか、同政府の占領下にあったか、同政府と同盟関係にあったために、人種、宗教、出身国、政治的見解を理由に、いかなる人に対してであれ迫害を加えることを命令したり、扇動したり、幇助したり、その他の形で迫害に参加した人、大量虐殺をしたことのある人 (212(a)(3))       Yes はい ☐   No いいえ ☐

d.  An alien who is likely to become a public charge. [212(a)(4)]

d. アメリカで生活保護者となるおそれのある人 (       Yes はい ☐   No いいえ ☐

e.  An alien who seeks to enter for the purpose of performing skilled or unskilled labor who has not been certified by the Secretary of Labor; an alien graduate of a foreign medical school seeking to perform medical services who has not passed the NBME exam or its equivalent. [212(a)(5)]

e. 熟練または非熟練労働をするために入国しようとする人で、労働省長官から許可を得ていない人、外国の医学校を卒業し、アメリカで医療行為を行おうとする人で、NBMEまたは同等の試験に合格していない人 (212(a)(5))       Yes はい ☐   No いいえ ☐

f.  An alien previously deported within one year, or arrested and deported within 5 years; an alien who seeks or has sought a visa, entry into the United States, or any U.S. immigration benefit by fraud or misrepresentation; an alien who knowingly assisted any other alien to enter or try to enter the United States in violation of the law; an alien who is in violation of Section 274C of the Immigration Act. [212(a)(6)]

f. 過去一年以内に強制退去させられた人、あるいは5年以内にアメリカで逮捕され強制退去させられた人、不正にまたは虚偽の申請によって査証を取得しようとする、または取得しようとしたことのある人、あるいは不正にまたは虚偽の申請によってアメリカへ入国しようとする人、または入国したことのある人、不正にまたは虚偽の申請によってその他の移民法の恩恵を得ようとする、あるいは得ようとしたことのある人、他人が法律に違反してアメリカに入国しようとする、または入国したのを、不法と知りながら援助したことがある人、移民法の274条C項に違反する人 (212(a)(6))       Yes はい ☐   No いいえ ☐

g.  An alien who is permanently ineligible to U.S. citizenship, a person who has departed the United States to evade military service in time of war. [212(a)(8)]

g. 永久にアメリカの市民権をとる資格のない人、戦時に兵役を回避するためにアメリカを出国したことのある人 (212(a)8)       Yes はい ☐   No いいえ ☐

h.  An alien who is coming to the United States to practice polygamy; an alien who is a guardian required to accompany an excluded alien; an alien who withholds custody of a child outside the United States from a United States citizen granted legal custody.

h. 一夫多妻を実行するためにアメリカへ入国しようとする人、入国拒否された外国人に同行する必要のある保護者、アメリカ市民が親権を持つ子供をアメリカ国外で引き留めている人 (212(a)9)       Yes はい ☐   No いいえ ☐

i.  An alien who is a former exchange visitor who has not fulfilled the 2-year foreign residence requirements. [212(e)]

i. 元交流訪問者で、アメリカ国外に2年間滞在しなければならない条件を満たしてない人 (212(e))       Yes はい ☐   No いいえ ☐

If the answer to any of the foregoing questions if YES or if unsure, explain in the following space or on a separate sheet of paper.

上記いずれかの項目にあなたが該当する場合、あるいは該当するかどうか不明な方は、この余白あるいは別紙に、その旨を説明して下さい。

M-19

---

34. Have you ever been arrested, convicted or ever been in prison or almshouse; have you ever been the beneficiary of a pardon or an amnesty; have you ever been treated in an institution or hospital or other place for insanity or other mental disease. [222(a)]
あなたはこれまでに逮捕されたり、有罪判決を決けたり、禁固刑に処せられたり私設救貧院に入れられたことがありますか、これまでに恩赦や大赦を受けたことがありますか。精神病のため、あるいはその他の精神障害のために、病院またはなんらかの施設で治療を受けたことがありますか。
   (222(a))                                                                                                                はい 「   いいえ！

---

35. I am unlikely to become a public charge because of the following:
私はアメリカで生活保障者になるおそれはありません。その理由は、

☐ Personal financial resources *(describe)*          ☐ Employment *(attach)*                    ☐ Affidavits of Support *(attach)*
自己資産がある（説明して下さい）              就職口がある（添付して下さい）             扶養宣誓供述書がある（添付して下さい）

---

36. Have you ever applied for a visa to enter the United States?                                    Yes はい ☐  No いいえ☐
これまでアメリカへ行くために査証を申請したことがありますか。

*(If answer is Yes, state where and when, whether you applied for a nonimmigrant or an immigrant visa, and whether the visa was issued or refused.)*
（はいと答えた方は、いつどこで申請したか、移民査証か非移民査証か、査証は発給されたか、拒否されたか、を書いて下さい。

---

37. Have you been refused admission to the United States?                                          Yes はい ☐  No いいえ☐
これまでにアメリカへの入国を拒否されたことがありますか。
*(If answer is Yes, explain)*

（はいと答えた方は説明して下さい）

---

38. Were you assisted in completing this application?                                               Yes はい ☐  No いいえ☐
この申請書の記入を誰かに手伝ってもらいましたか。
*(If answer is Yes, give name and address of person assisting you, indicating whether relative, friend, travel agent, attorney, or other)*

（はいと答えた方は、その人の氏名、住所と、あなたとの関係、つまり親戚、友人、旅行代理業者、弁護士、その他のいずれであるか記入する）
NAME ：氏名                     ADDRESS 住所                              RELATIONSHIP 関係

---

39. The following documents are submitted in support of this application:
この申請書と共に提出する証明書

☐ Passport                        ☐ Military record                      ☐ Evidence of own assets
旅券                            軍務記録                             所有資産の証明書

☐ Birth certificate               ☐ Police certificate                   ☐ Affidavit of support
出生証明書                       警察証明書                           扶養宣誓供述書

☐ Marriage certificate            ☐ Medical records                      ☐ Offer of employment
結婚証明書                       健康診断書                           雇用主からの採用通知

☐ Death certificate               ☐ Photographs                          ☐ Other (describe)
死亡証明書                       写真                                 その他（説明して下さい）

☐ Divorce decree                  ☐ Birth certificates of all children who will not
離婚証明書                          be immigrating at this time. (List those for
                                    whom birth certificates are not available.)
                                 今回移民査証を申請して
                                 いない子供全員の出生証明書（出生証明書の
                                 ない場合、その子供たちの名前を書く）

## DO NOT WRITE BELOW THE FOLLOWING LINE
この線から下の項目には何も書かないで下さい。

### The consular officer will assist you in answering items 40 and 41.
40項から41項の回答にあたっては領事がお手伝いします。

40. I claim to be exempt from ineligibility to receive a visa and exclusion under item _____ in Part 33 for the following reasons:

私は次の理由により、33項の_____ 号に基づく査証受領不適格および入国拒否の適用免除を要請します。

212(a)(3)(a)(5)                        Beneficiary of a Waiver under:
免除を受ける場合

| | | | |
|---|---|---|---|
| ☐ Not Applicable　該当せず | ☐ 212(a)(3)(D)(ii) | ☐ 212(e) | ☐ 212(h) |
| ☐ Not Required　必要なし | ☐ 212(a)(3)(D)(iii) | ☐ 212(g)(1) | ☐ 212(i) |
| ☐ Attached　添付 | ☐ 212(a)(3)(D)(iv) | ☐ 212(g)(2) | |

41. I claim to be:                                                                I am subject to the following:
私は、                                                                                私は次の項目の対象です。

☐ A Family-Sponsored Immigrant
家族呼び寄せによる移民                              優先順位 ☐ Preference: _____

☐ An Employment Based-Immigrant
雇用に基づく移民                                     数の制限 ☐ Numerical limitation: _____

☐ A Diversity Immigrant                             (登録国)
永住者の国別均等化プログラムに基づく移民                          *(foreign state)*

☐ A Special Category *(Specify)*
特別部門（特定する）_____
*(Returning resident, Hong Kong, Tibetan, Private Legislative, etc.)*
(帰国居住者、香港、チベット人、個別救済法、その他)

☐ I derive foreign state chargeability under Sec. 202(b) through my _____
私は202条(b)項に基づき、私の_____ と同じ登録国に割り当てられます。

I understand that I am required to surrender my visa to the United States Immigration officer at the place where I apply to enter the United States, and that the posession of a visa does not entitle me to enter the United States if at that time I am found to be inadmissable under the immigration laws.

I understand that any willfully false or misleading statement or willful concealment of a material fact made by me herein may subject me to permanent exclusion from the United States and, if I am admitted to the United States, may subject me to criminal prosecution and /or deportation.

I, the undersigned applicant for a United States Immigrant visa, do solemnly swear (or affirm) that all statements which appear in this application, consisting of Optional Forms 230 PART I and 230 PART II combined, have been made by me, including the answers to Items 1 through 41 inclusive, and that they are true and complete to the best of my knowledge and belief. I do further swear (or affirm) that, if admitted into the United States, I will not engage in activities which would be prejudicial to the public interest, or endanger the welfare, safety, or security of the United States; in activities which would be prohibited by the laws of the United States, relating to espionage, sabotage, public disorder, or in other activities subversive to the national security; in any activity a purpose of which is the opposition to or the control, or overthrow of, the Government of the United States, by force, violence, or other unconstitutional means. I understand all the foregoing statements, having asked for and obtained an explanation on every point which was not clear to me.

アメリカへの入国を申請する場所で、移民官に査証を提出しなければならないこと、および移民法に基づき入国資格のないことが判明した場合、査証を持っていても入国できないことを承知しています。

この査証申請において、故意に虚偽のまたは誤解を招く供述をしたり、故意に事実を隠したりすると、永久にアメリカへの入国を拒否される場合があること、またたとえ入国を許可されても、刑事訴訟や強制過去の対象となり得ることを承知しています。

私は、ここに移民査証申請者として署名し、書式OF-230 パートⅠおよびパートⅡで成るこの申請書の1項から41項までの記述は、すべて私自身が行なったもので、これらの供述内容は、私の知るかぎりまた信じるかぎりにおいて、真実かつ完全であることを厳粛に宣誓（または断言）します。さらに、アメリカへの入国を許可されたら、一般市民の利益を侵害する、またアメリカ合衆国の福祉、安全、保安を危険に陥れるような行為、スパイ行為や破壊活動、社会混乱を引き起こす違法行為、その他国家の安全を覆すような活動、また武力や暴力、その他の非合法的手段により合衆国政府に反抗したり、同政府の制圧もしくは転覆を図ることを目的とした活動、に従事しないことを宣誓（または断言）します。不明な点についてはすべて質問をし、説明を受けたので、上述の事柄についてはすべて理解しています。

The relationship claimed in items 14 and 15 verified by
documentation submitted to consular officer except as noted:

_____
*(Signature of Applicant)* 申請者の署名

Subscribed and sworn to before me this _____ day of _____ ,19 _____ at: _____

TARIFF ITEM NO. 20.                                    _____
                                                       *(Consular Officer)*

– 4 –

*(Please tear off this sheet before submitting Affidavit)*

**U.S. Department of Justice**
Immigration and Naturalization Service

**Affidavit of Support**

## INSTRUCTIONS

**I. EXECUTION OF AFFIDAVIT.** A separate affidavit must be submitted for each person. You must sign the affidavit in your full, true and correct name and affirm or make it under oath. If you are **in the United States** the affidavit may be sworn or affirmed before an immigration officer without the payment of fee, or before a notary public or other officer authorized to administer oaths for general purposes, in which case the official seal or certificate of authority to administer oaths must be affixed. If you are **outside the United States** the affidavit must be sworn to or affirmed before a United States consular or immigration officer.

**II. SUPPORTING EVIDENCE.** The deponent must submit in duplicate evidence of income and resources, as appropriate:

A. Statement from an officer of the bank or other financial institution in which you have deposits giving the following details regarding your account:
1. Date account opened.
2. Total amount deposited for the past year.
3. Present balance.

B. Statement of your employer on business stationery, showing:
1. Date and nature of employment.
2. Salary paid.
3. Whether position is temporary or permanent.

C. If self-employed:
1. Copy of last income tax return filed or,
2. Report of commercial rating concern.

D. List containing serial numbers and denominations of bonds and name of record owner(s).

**III. SPONSOR AND ALIEN LIABILITY.** Effective October 1,1980, amendments to section 1614(f) of the Social Security Act and Part A of Title XVI of the Social Security Act establish certain requirements for determining the eligibility of aliens who apply for the first time for Supplemental Security Income (SSI) benefits. Effective October 1, 1981, amendments to section 415 of the Social Security Act establish similar requirements for determining the eligibility of aliens who apply for the first time for Aid to Families with Dependent Children (AFDC) benefits. Effective December 22, 1981, amendments to the Food Stamp Act of 1977 affect the eligibility of alien participation in the Food Stamp Program. These amendments require that the income and resources of any person who, as the sponsor of an alien's entry into the United States, executes an affidavit of support or similar agreement on behalf of the alien, and the income and resources of the sponsor's spouse *(if living with the sponsor)* shall be deemed to be the income and resources of the alien under formulas for determining eligibility for SSI, AFDC, and Food Stamp benefits during the three years following the alien's entry into the United States.

An alien applying for SSI must make available to the Social Security Administration documentation concerning his or her income and resources and those of the sponsor including information which was provided in support of the application for an immigrant visa or adjustment of status. An alien applying for AFDC or Food Stamps must make similar information available to the State public assistance agency. The Secretary of Health and Human Services and the Secretary of Agriculture are authorized to obtain copies of any such documentation submitted to INS or the Department of State and to release such documentation to a State public assistance agency.

Sections 1621(e) and 415(d) of the Social Security Act and subsection 5(i) of the Food Stamp Act also provide that an alien and his or her sponsor shall be jointly and severably liable to repay any SSI, AFDC, or Food Stamp benefits which are incorrectly paid because of misinformation provided by a sponsor or because of a sponsor's failure to provide information. Incorrect payments which are not repaid will be withheld from any subsequent payments for which the alien or sponsor are otherwise eligible under the Social Security Act or Food Stamp Act, except that the sponsor was without fault or where good cause existed.

These provisions do not apply to the SSI, AFDC or Food Stamp eligibility of aliens admitted as refugees, granted political asylum by the Attorney General, or Cuban/Haitian entrants as defined in section 501(e) of P.L. 96-422 and of dependent children of the sponsor or sponsor's spouse. They also do not apply to the SSI or Food Stamp eligibility of an alien who becomes blind or disabled after admission into the United States for permanent residency.

**IV. AUTHORITY/USE/PENALTIES.** Authority for the collection of the information requested on this form is contained in 8 U.S.C. 1182(a)(15), 1184(a), and 1258. The information will be used principally by the Service, or by any consular officer to whom it may be furnished, to support an alien's application for benefits under the Immigration and Nationality Act and specifically the assertion that he or she has adequate means of financial support and will not become a public charge. Submission of the information is voluntary. It may also, as a matter of routine use, be disclosed to other federal, state, local and foreign law enforcement and regulatory agencies, including the Department of Health and Human Services, the Department of Agriculture, the Department of State, the Department of Defense and any component thereof (if the deponent has served or is serving in the armed forces of the United States), the Central Intelligence Agency, and individuals and organizations during the course of any investigation to elicit further information required to carry out Service functions. Failure to provide the information may result in the denial of the alien's application for a visa, or his or her exclusion from the United States.

Form I-134 (Rev. 12-1-84) Y

U . S . GOVERNMENT PRINTING OFFICE : 1992 0 - 316-325

OMB No. 1115-0062

**U.S. Department of Justice**
Immigration and Naturalization Service                                      **Affidavit of Support**

*(ANSWER ALL ITEMS: FILL IN WITH TYPEWRITER OR PRINT IN BLOCK LETTERS IN INK.)*

I, _____ , residing at _____
            (Name)                                                    (Street and Number)

_____
    (City)                    (State)                 (Zip Code if in U.S.)              (Country)

**BEING DULY SWORN DEPOSE AND SAY:**

1. I was born on _____ at _____
                        (Date)                              (City)                         (Country)

   If you are ***not*** a native born United States citizen, answer the following as appropriate:
   a. If a United States citizen through naturalization, give certificate of naturalization number _____
   b. If a United States citizen through parent(s) or marriage, give citizenship certificate number _____
   c. If United States citizenship was derived by some other method, attach a statement of explanation.
   d. If a lawfully admitted permanent resident of the United States, give "A" number _____
2. That I am _____ years of age and **have** resided in the United States since (date) _____
3. That this affidavit is executed in behalf of the following person:

| Name | | Sex | Age |
|---|---|---|---|
| Citizen of—(Country) | Marital Status | Relationship to Deponent | |
| Presently resides at--(Street and Number) | (City) | (State) | (Country) |

   Name of spouse and children accompanying or following to join person:

| Spouse | Sex | Age | Child | Sex | Age |
|---|---|---|---|---|---|
| Child | Sex | Age | Child | Sex | Age |
| Child | Sex | Age | Child | Sex | Age |

4. That this affidavit is made by me for the purpose of assuring the United States Government that the person(s) named in item 3 will not become a public charge in the United States.

5. That I am willing and able to receive, maintain and support the person(s) named in item 3. That I am ready and willing to deposit a bond, if necessary, to guarantee that such person(s) will not become a public charge during his or her stay in the United States, or to guarantee that the above named will maintain his or her nonimmigrant status if admitted temporarily and will depart prior to the expiration of his or her authorized stay in the United States.

6. That I understand this affidavit will be binding upon me for a period of three (3) years after entry of the person(s) named in item 3 and that the information and documentation provided by me may be made available to the Secretary of Health and Human Services and the Secretary of Agriculture, who may make it available to a public assistance agency.

7. That I am employed as, or engaged in the business of _____ with _____
                                                              (Type of Business)                    (Name of concern)

   at _____
        (Street and Number)                    (City)                    (State)              (Zip Code)

   I derive an annual income of (*if self-employed, I have attached a copy of my last income tax
   return or report of commercial rating concern which I certify to be true and correct to the best
   of my knowledge and belief. See instruction for nature of evidence of net worth to be
   submitted.*)                                                                        $ _____

   I have on deposit in savings banks in the United States                              $ _____

   I have other personal property, the reasonable value of which is                     $ _____

Form I-134 (Rev. 12-1-84) Y                                  OVER

I have stocks and bonds with the following market value, as indicated on the attached list
which I certify to be true and correct to the best of my knowledge and belief.                    $ _____
I have life insurance in the sum of                                                                $ _____
With a cash surrender value of                                                                     $ _____
I own real estate valued at                                                                        $ _____
    With mortgages or other encumbrances thereon amounting to    $ _____

Which is located at _____
                        (Street and Number)              (City)                (State)           (Zip Code)

8. That the following persons are dependent upon me for support: *(Place an "X" in the appropriate column to indicate whether the person named is **wholly** or **partially** dependent upon you for support.)*

| Name of Person | Wholly Dependent | Partially Dependent | Age | Relationship to Me |
|---|---|---|---|---|
|  |  |  |  |  |
|  |  |  |  |  |
|  |  |  |  |  |

9. That I have previously submitted affidavit(s) of support for the following person(s). If none, state *"None"*
_____
                    Name                                                        Date submitted
_____
_____

10. That I have submitted visa petition(s) to the Immigration and Naturalization Service on behalf of the following person(s). If none, state none.
_____
                    Name                          Relationship                  Date submitted
_____
_____

11. *(Complete this block only if the person named in item 3 will be in the United States temporarily.)*
    That I ☐ do intend ☐ do not   intend, to make specific contributions to the support of the person named in item 3. *(If you check "do intend", indicate the exact nature and duration of the contributions. For example, if you intend to furnish room and board, state for how long and, if money, state the amount in United States dollars and state whether it is to be given in a lump sum, weekly, or monthly, or for how long.)*
_____
_____
_____

### OATH OR AFFIRMATION OF DEPONENT

*I acknowledge at that I have read Part III of the Instructions, Sponsor and Alien Liability, and am aware of my responsibilities as an immigrant sponsor under the Social Security Act, as amended, and the Food Stamp Act, as amended.*

*I swear (affirm) that I know the contents of this affidavit signed by me and the statements are true and correct.*

*Signature of deponent* _____

*Subscribed and sworn to (affirmed) before me this* _____ *day of* _____ *, 19* _____

*at* _____ *.My commission expires on* _____

*Signature of Officer Administering Oath* _____ *Title* _____
*If affidavit prepared by other than deponent, please complete the following: I declare that this document was prepared by me at the request of the deponent and is based on all information of which I have knowledge.*

_____
*(Signature)*                          *(Address)*                          *(Date)*

## U.S. Department of Justice
Immigration and Naturalization Service

OMB No. 1115-0053

Application to Register Permanent Residence or Adjust Status

### Purpose of this Form
This form is for a person who is in the United States to apply to adjust to permanent resident status or register for permanent residence while in the U.S. It may also be used by certain Cuban nationals to request a change in the date their permanent residence began

### Who May File.
**Based on an immigrant petition.** You may apply to adjust your status if:
- an immigrant visa number is immediately available to you based on an approved immigrant petition; or
- you are filing this application with a complete relative, special immigrant juvenile, or special immigrant military petition which if approved, would make an immigrant visa number immediately available to you.

**Based on being the spouse or child of another adjustment applicant or of a person granted permanent residence .** You may apply to adjust status if you are the spouse or child of another adjustment applicant, or of a lawful permanent resident, if the relationship existed when that person was admitted as a permanent resident in an immigrant category which allows derivative status for spouses and children.

**Based on admission as the fiance(e) of a U.S. citizen and subsequent marriage to that citizen.** You may apply to adjust status if you were admitted to the U.S. as the K-1 fiance(e) of a U.S. citizen and married that citizen within 90 days of your entry. If you were admitted as the K-2 child of such a fiance(e), you may apply based on your parent's adjustment application.

**Based on asylum status.** You may apply to adjust status if you have been granted asylum in the U.S. and are eligible for asylum adjustment (Note: In most cases you become eligible after being physically present in the U.S. for one year after the grant of asylum if you still qualify as a refugee or as the spouse or child of refugee.)

**Based on Cuban citizenship or nationality.** You may apply to adjust status if:
- you are a native or citizen of Cuba, were admitted or paroled into the U.S. after January 1, 1959, and thereafter have been physically present in the U.S. for at least one year; or
- you are the spouse or unmarried child of a Cuban described above, and you were admitted or paroled after January 1, 1959, and thereafter have been physically present in the U.S. for at least one year.

**Based on continuous residence since before January 1,1972.** You may apply for permanent residence if you have continuously resided in the U.S. since before January 1, 1972.

**Other basis of eligibility.** If you are not included in the above categories, but believe you may be eligible for adjustment or creation of record of permanent residence, contact your local INS office.

**Applying to change the date your permanent residence began.** If you were granted permanent residence in the U.S. prior to November 6, 1966, and are a native or citizen of Cuba, his or her spouse or unmarried minor child, you may ask to change the date your lawful permanent residence began to your date of arrival in the U.S. or May 2, 1964, whichever is later.

### Persons Who Are Ineligible.
Unless you are applying for creation of record based on continuous residence since before 1/1/72, or adjustment of status under a category in which special rules apply (such as asylum adjustment, Cuban adjustment, special immigrant juvenile adjustment, or special immigrant military personnel adjustment), **you are not eligible for adjustment of status if any of the following apply to you:**
- you entered the U.S. in transit without a visa;
- you entered the U.S. as a nonimmigrant crewman;
- you were not admitted or paroled following inspection by an immigration officer;
- your authorized stay expired before you filed this application, you were employed in the U.S. prior to filing this application, without INS authorization, or you otherwise failed to maintain your nonimmigrant status, other than through no fault of your own or for technical reasons; unless you are applying because you are an immediate relative of a U.S. citizen (parent, spouse, widow, widower, or unmarried child under 21 years old), a K-1 fiance(e) or K-2 fiance(e) dependent who married the U.S. petitioner within 90

days of admission, or an "H" or "I" special immigrant (foreign medical graduates, international organization employees or their derivative family members);
- you are or were a J-1 or J-2 exchange visitor, are subject to the two-year foreign residence requirement, and have not complied with or been granted a waiver of the requirement;
- you have A, E or G nonimmigrant status, or have an occupation which would allow you to have this status, unless you complete Form 1-508 (1-508F for French nationals) to waive diplomatic rights, privileges and immunities, and if you are an A or G nonimmigrant, unless you submit a completed Form 1-566;
- you were admitted to Guam as a visitor under the Guam visa waiver program;
- you were admitted to the U.S. as a visitor under the Visa Waiver Pilot Program, unless you are applying because you are an immediate relative of a U.S. citizen (parent, spouse, widow, widower, or unmarried child under 21 years old);
- you are already a conditional permanent resident;
- you were admitted as a K-1 fiance(e) but did not marry the U.S. citizen who filed the petition for you, or were admitted as the K-2 child of a fiance(e) and your parent did not marry the U.S. citizen who filed the petition.

### General Filing Instructions.
Please answer all questions by typing or clearly printing in black ink. Indicate that an item is not applicable with **"N/A"** If the answer is **"none"**, write **"none"**. If you need extra space to answer any item, attach a sheet of paper with your name and your alien registration number (A#), if any, and indicate the number of the item to which the answer refers. You must file your application with the required **Initial Evidence**. Your application must be properly signed and filed with the correct fee. If you are under 14 years of age, your parent or guardian may sign your application.

### Translations.
Any foreign language document must be accompanied by a full English translation which the translator has certified as complete and correct, and by the translator's certification that he or she is competent to translate from the foreign language into English.

### Copies
If these instructions state that a copy of a document may be filed with this application, and you choose to send us the original, we may keep the original for our records.

### Initial Evidence.
You must file your application with following evidence:
- **Birth certificate.** Submit a copy of your birth certificate or other record of your birth
- **Photos.** Submit two (2) identical natural color photographs of yourself, taken within 30 days of this application [Photos must have a white background, be unmounted, printed on thin paper, and be glossy and unretouched. They must show a three-quarter frontal profile showing the right side of your face, with your right ear visible and with your head bare. You may wear a headdress if required by a religious order of which you are a member. The photos must be no larger than 2 X 2 inches, with the distance from the top of the head to just below the chin about 1 and 1/4 inches. Lightly print your A# (or your name if you have no A#) on the back of each photo, using a pencil .]
- **Fingerprints.** Submit a complete set of fingerprints on Form FD 258 if you are between the ages of 14 and 75 [Do not bend, fold, or crease the fingerprint chart. You should complete the information on the top of the chart and write your A# (if any) in the space marked "Your n.o OCA" or "Miscellaneous no. MNU". You should not sign the chart until you have been fingerprinted, or are told to sign by the person who takes your fingerprints. The person who takes your fingerprints must also sign the chart and write his/her title and the date you are fingerprinted in the space provided on the chart. You may be fingerprinted by police, sheriff, or INS officials or other reputable person or organization. You should call the police, sheriff, organization or INS office before you go there, since some offices do not take fingerprints or may take fingerprints only at certain times. ]

Form I-485 (Rev. 09-09-92) N

- **Medical Examination.** Submit a medical examination report on the form you have obtained from INS [Not required if you are applying for creation of record based on continuous residence since before 1/1/72, or if you are a K-l fiance(e) or K-2 dependent of a fiance(e) who had a medical examination within the past year as required for the nonimmigrant fiance(e) visa.].
- **Form G-325A,** Biography Information Sheet. You must submit a completed G-325A if you are between 14 and 79 years of age.
- **Evidence of status.** Submit a copy of your Form 1-94, Nonimmigrant Arrival/Departure Record, showing your admission to the U.S. and current status, or other evidence of your status.
- **Employment letter/Affidavit of Support.** Submit a letter showing you are employed in a job that is not temporary, an affidavit of support from a responsible person in the U.S., or other evidence that shows that you are not likely to become a public charge [Not required if you are applying for creation of record based on continuous residence since before 1 /1 /72, asylum adjustment, or a Cuban or a spouse or unmarried child of a Cuban who was admitted after 1/1/59].
- **Evidence of eligibility.**
  - **Based on an immigrant petition.** Attach a copy of the approval notice for an immigrant petition which makes a visa number immediately available to you, or submit a complete relative, special immigrant juvenile, or special immigrant military petition which, if approved, will make a visa number immediately available to you.
  - **Based on admission as the K-1 fiance(e) of a U.S. citizen and subsequent marriage to that citizen.** Attach a copy of the fiance(e) petition approval notice and a copy of your marriage certificate.
  - **Based on asylum status.** Attach a copy of the letter or Form 1-94 which shows the date you were granted asylum.
  - **Based on continuous residence in the U.S. since before 1/1/72.** Attach copies of evidence that shows continuous residence since before 1/1/72.
  - **Based on Cuban citizenship or nationality.** Attach evidence of your citizenship or nationality, such as a copy of your passport, birth certificate or travel document.
  - **Based on you being the spouse or child of another adjustment applicant or person granted permanent residence based on issuance of an immigrant visa.** File your application with the application of that other applicant, or with evidence it is pending with the Service or has been approved, or evidence your spouse or parent has been granted permanent residence based on an immigrant visa and:
    - If you are applying as the spouse of that person, also attach a copy of your marriage certificate and copies of documents showing the legal termination of all other marriages by you and your spouse; or
    - If you ue applying as the child of that person, also attach a copy of your birth certificate, and, if the other person is not your natural mother, copies of evidence, (such as a marriage certificate and documents showing the legal termination of all other marriages, and an adoption decree), to demonstrate that you qualify as his or her child.
  - Other basis for eligibility. Attach copies of documents proving that you are eligible for the classification.

**Where To File.**
File this application at the local INS office having jurisdiction over your place of residence.

**Fee.** The fee for this application is $130, except that it is $100 if you are less than 14 years old. The fee must be submitted in the exact amount. It cannot be refunded. **DO NOT MAIL CASH.** All checks and money orders must be drawn on a bank or other institution located in the United States and must be payable in United States currency. The check or money order should be made payable to the Immigration and Naturalization Service, except that::
- If you live in Guam, and are filing this application in Guam, make your check or money order payable to the "Treasurer, Guam."

- If you live in the Virgin Islands, and are filing this application in the Virgin Islands, make your check or money order payable to the "Commissioner of Finance of the Virgin Islands."

Checks are accepted subject to collection. An uncollected check will render the application and any document issued invalid. A charge of $5.00 will be imposed if a check in payment of a fee is not honored by the bank on which it is drawn.

**Processing Information.**
Acceptance. Any application that is not signed, or is not accompanied by the correct fee, will be rejected with a notice that the application is deficient. You may correct the deficiency and resubmit the application. An application is not considered properly filed until accepted by the Service.

**Initial processing.** Once an application has been accepted, it will be checked for completeness, including submission of the required initial evidence. If you do not completely fill out the form, or file it without required initial evidence, you will not establish a basis for eligibility, and we may deny your application.

**Requests for more information.** We may request more information or evidence. We may also request that you submit the originals of any copy. We will return these originals when they are no longer required.

**Interview.** After you file your application you will be notified to appear at an INS office to answer questions about the application. You will be required to answer these questions under oath or affirmation. You must bring your Arrival-Departure Record (Form 1-94) and any passport to the interview.

**Decision.** You will be notified in writing of the decision on your application.

**Travel Outside the U.S.** If you plan to leave the U.S. to go to any other country, including Canada or Mexico, before a decision is made on your application, contact the INS office processing your application before you leave. In many cases, leaving the U.S. without advance written permission will result in automatic termination of your application. Also, you may experience difficulty upon returning to the U.S. if you do not have written permission to reenter.

**Penalties.**
If you knowingly and willfully falsify or conceal a material fact or submit a false document with this request, we will deny the benefit you are filing for, and may deny any other immigration benefit. In addition, you will face severe penalties provided by law, and may be subject to criminal prosecution.

**Privacy Act Notice.**
We ask for the information on this form, and associated evidence, to determine if you have established eligibility for the immigration benefit you are filing for. Our legal right to ask for this information is in 8 USC 1255 and 1259. We may provide this information to other government agencies. Failure to provide this information, and any requested evidence, may delay a final decision or result in denial of your request.

**Paperwork Reduction Act Notice.**
We try to create forms and instructions that are accurate, can be easily understood, and which impose the least possible burden on you to provide us with information. Often this is difficult because some immigration laws are very complex. The estimated average time to complete and file this application is computed as follows: (1) **20** minutes to learn about the law and form; (2) **25** minutes to complete the form; and (3) **270** minutes to assemble and file the application, including the required interview and travel time; for a total estimated average of **5** hours and **15** minutes per application. If you have comments regarding the accuracy of this estimate, or suggestions for making this form simpler, you can write to both the Immigration and Naturalization Service, 425 I Street, N.W., Room 5304, Washington, D.C. 20536; and the Office of Management and Budget, Paperwork Reduction Project, OMB No. 1115-0053, Washington, D.C. 20503.

## U.S. Department of Justice
Immigration and Naturalization Service

OMB No. 1115-0053

### Application to Register Permanent Residence or Adjust Status

### START HERE - Please Type or Print

## Part 1. Information about you.

| Family Name | Given Name | Middle Initial |
|---|---|---|

**Address** - C/O

| Street Number and Name | Apt # |
|---|---|

City

| State | ZIP Code |
|---|---|

| Date of Birth (month/day/year) | Country of Birth |
|---|---|

| Social Security # | A # (if any) |
|---|---|

| Date of Last Arrival (month/day/year) | I-94 # |
|---|---|

| Current INS Status | Expires on (month/day/year) |
|---|---|

## Part 2. Application Type. *(check one)*

**I am applying for adjustment to permanent resident status because:**

a. ☐ an immigrant petition giving me an immediately available immigrant visa number has been approved (attach a copy of the approval notice), or a relative, special immigrant juvenile, or special immigrant military visa petition filed with this application will give me an immediately available number if approved.

b. ☐ My spouse or parent applied for adjustment of status or was granted lawful permanent residence in an immigrant visa category which allows derivative status for spouses and children.

c. ☐ I entered as a K-1 fiance(e) of a U.S. citizen whom I married within 90 days of entry, or I am the K-2 child of such a fiance(e) (attach a copy of the fiance(e) petition approval notice and the marriage certificate).

d. ☐ I was granted asylum or derivative asylum status as the spouse or child of a person granted asylum and am eligible for adjustment.

e. ☐ I am a native or citizen of Cuba admitted or paroled into the U.S. after January 1, 1959, and therefore have been physically present in the U.S. for at least 1 year.

f. ☐ I am the husband, wife, or minor unmarried child of a Cuban described in (e) and am residing with that person, and was admitted or paroled into the U.S. after January 1, 1959, and therefore have been physically present in the U.S. for at least 1 year.

g. ☐ I have continuously resided in the U.S. since before January 1, 1972.

h. ☐ Other-explain _____

**I am already a permanent resident and am applying to have the date I was granted permanent residence adjusted to the date I originally arrived in the U.S. as a nonimmigrant or parolee, or as of May 2, 1964, whichever is later, and:** *(Check one)*

i. ☐ I am a native or citizen of Cuba and meet the description in (e), above.

j. ☐ I am the husband, wife or minor unmarried child of a Cuban, and meet the description in (f), above.

Form I-485 (Rev. 09-09-92) N                    *Continued on back.*

### FOR INS USE ONLY

| Returned | Receipt |
|---|---|
| | |

Resubmitted

Reloc Sent

Reloc Rec'd

☐ Applicant Interviewed

**Section of Law**
☐ Sec. 209(b), INA
☐ Sec. 13, Act Of 9/11/57
☐ Sec. 245, INA
☐ Sec. 249, INA
☐ Sec. 1 Act of 11/2/66
☐ Sec. 2 Act of 11/2/66
☐ Other _____

**Country Chargeable**

**Eligibility Under Sec. 245**
☐ Approved Visa Petition
☐ Dependent of Principal Alien
☐ Special Immigrant
☐ Other _____

**Preference**

**Action Block**

**To Be Completed by**
*Attorney or Representative, if any*
☐ Fill in box if G-28 is attached to represent the applicant

VOLAG#

ATTY State License #

## Part 3. Processing Information.

**A.** City/Town/Village of birth

Current occupation

Your mother's first name

Your father's first name

Give your name exactly how it appears on your Arrival /Departure Record (Form 1-94)

Place of last entry into the U.S. (City/State)

In what status did you last enter? *(Visitor, Student, exchange alien, crewman, temporary worker, without inspection, etc.)*

Were you inspected by a U.S. Immigration Officer?  ☐ Yes  ☐ No

Nonimmigrant visa Number

Consulate where Visa was issued

Date Visa was issued (month/day/year)    Sex: ☐ Male ☐ Female

Marital Status ☐ Married ☐ Single ☐ Divorced ☐ Widowed

Have you ever before applied for permanent resident status in the U.S? ☐ No ☐ Yes (give date and place of filing and final disposition):

**B.** List your present husband/wife, all of your sons and daughters (if you have none, write "none". If additional space is needed, use separate paper).

| Family Name | Given Name | Middle Initial | Date of Birth (month/day/year) |
|---|---|---|---|
| Country of birth | Relationship | A # | Applying with you? ☐ Yes ☐ No |
| Family Name | Given Name | Middle Initial | Date of Birth (month/day/year) |
| Country of birth | Relationship | A # | Applying with you? ☐ Yes ☐ No |
| Family Name | Given Name | Middle Initial | Date of Birth (month/day/year) |
| Country of birth | Relationship | A # | Applying with you? ☐ Yes ☐ No |
| Family Name | Given Name | Middle Initial | Date of Birth (month/day/year) |
| Country of birth | Relationship | A # | Applying with you? ☐ Yes ☐ No |
| Family Name | Given Name | Middle Initial | Date of Birth (month/day/year) |
| Country of birth | Relationship | A # | Applying with you? ☐ Yes ☐ No |

**C.** List your present and past membership in or affiliation with every political organization, association, fund, foundation, party, club, society, or similar group in the United States or in any other place since your 16th birthday. Include any foreign military service in this part. If none, write "none". Include the name of organization, location, dates of membership from and to, and the nature of the organization. If additional space is needed, use separate paper.

Form I-485 (Rev. 09-09-92) N          Continued On Next Page

**Sample Document – Not To Be Used When Filing.**

## Part 3.   Processing Information. *(Continued)*

Please answer the following questions. ( If your answer is **"Yes"** on any one of these questions, explain on a separate piece of paper. Answering **"Yes"** does not necessarily mean that you are not entitled to register for permanent residence or adjust status).

1.   Have you ever, in or outside the U. S.:
   a.   knowingly committed any crime of moral turpitude or a drug-related offense for which you haw not been arrested?
   b.   been arrested, cited, charged, indicted, fined, or imprisoned for breaking or violating any law or ordinance, excluding traffic violations?
   c.   been the beneficiary of a pardon, amnesty, rehabilitation decree, other act of clemency or similar action?
   d.   exercised diplomatic immunity to avoid prosecution for a criminal offense in the U. S.?     ☐ Yes  ☐ No

2.   Have you received public assistance in the U.S. from any source, including the U.S. government or any state, county, city, or municipality (other than emergency medical treatment), or are you likely to receive public assistance in the future?     ☐ Yes  ☐ No

3.   Have you ever
   a.   within the past 10 years been a prostitute or procured anyone for prostitution, or intend to engage in such activities in the future?
   b.   engaged in any unlawful commercialized vice, including, but not limited to, illegal gambling?
   c.   knowingly encouraged, induced, assisted, abetted or aided any alien to try to enter the U.S. illegally?
   d.   illicitly trafficked in any controlled substance, or knowingly assisted, abetted or colluded in the illicit trafficking of any controlled substance?     ☐ Yes  ☐ No

4.   Have you ever engaged in, conspired to engage in, or do you intend to engage in, or have you ever solicited membership or funds for, or have you through any means ever assisted or provided any type of material support to, any person or organization that has ever engaged or conspired to engage, in sabotage, kidnapping, political assassination, hijacking, or any other form of terrorist activity?     ☐ Yes  ☐ No

5.   Do you intend to engage in the U.S. in:
   a.   espionage?
   b.   any activity a purpose of which is opposition to, or the control or overthrow of, the Government of the United States, by force, violence or other unlawful means?
   c.   any activity to violate or evade any law prohibiting the export from the United States of goods, technology or sensitive information?     ☐ Yes  ☐ No

6.   Have you ever been a member of, or in any way affiliated with, the Communist Party or any other totalitarian party?     ☐ Yes  ☐ No

7.   Did you, during the period March 23, 1933 to May 8, 1945, in association with either the Nazi Government of Germany or any organization or government associated or allied with the Nazi Government of Germany, ever order, incite, assist or otherwise participate in the persecution of any person because of race, religion, national origin or political opinion?     ☐ Yes  ☐ No

8.   Have you ever engaged in genocide, or otherwise ordered, incited, assisted or otherwise participated in the killing of any person because of race, religion, nationality, ethnic origin, or political opinion?     ☐ Yes  ☐ No

9.   Have you ever been deported from the U.S., or removed from the U.S. at government expense, excluded within the past year, or are you now in exclusion or deportation proceedings?     ☐ Yes  ☐ No

10.  Are you under a final order of civil penalty for violating section 274C of the Immigration Act for use of fraudulent documents, or have you, by fraud or willful misrepresentation of a material fact, ever sought to procure, or procured, a visa, other documentation, entry into the U.S., or any other immigration benefit?     ☐ Yes  ☐ No

11.  Have you ever left the U.S. to avoid being drafted into the U.S. Armed Forces?     ☐ Yes  ☐ No

12.  Have you ever been a J nonimmigrant exchange visitor who was subject to the 2 year foreign residence requirement and not yet complied with that requirement or obtained a waiver?     ☐ Yes  ☐ No

13.  Are you now withholding custody of a U.S. Citizen child outside the U.S. from a person granted custody of the child?     ☐ Yes  ☐ No

14.  Do you plan to practice polygamy in the U.S.?     ☐ Yes  ☐ No

## Part 4.   Signature.   *(Read the information on penalties in the instructions before completing this section. You must file this application while in the United States.)*

I certify under penalty of perjury under the laws of the United States of America that this application, and the evidence submitted with it, is all true and correct. I authorize the release of any information from my records which the Immigration and Naturalization Service needs to determine eligibility for the benefit I am seeking.

| *Signature* | **Print Your Name** | *Date* | **Daytime Phone Number** |
|---|---|---|---|

*Please Note.* If you do not completely fill out this form, or fail to submit required documents listed in the instructions, you may not be found eligible for the requested document and this application may be denied.

## Part 5.   Signature of person preparing form if other than above. *(Sign Below)*

I declare that I prepared this application at the request of the above person and it is based on all information of which I have knowledge.

| **Signature** | **Print Your Name** | *Date* | **Day time Phone Number** |
|---|---|---|---|

Firm Name
and Address

Form I-485 (Rev. 09-09-92) N

**INSTRUCTIONS: USE TYPEWRITER. BE SURE ALL COPIES ARE LEGIBLE. Failure to answer fully all questions delay action. Do Not Remove Carbons: If typewriter is not available, print heavily in block letters with ball-point pen.**

U.S. Department of Justice

Immigration and Naturalization Service

## BIOGRAPHIC INFORMATION

OMB No. 1115-0066

| (Family name) | (First name) | (Middle name) | ☐ MALE ☐ FEMALE | BIRTHDATE (Mo-Day-Yr.) | NATIONALITY | FILE NUMBER A |
|---|---|---|---|---|---|---|

| ALL OTHER NAMES USED (Including names by previous marriages) | CITY AND COUNTRY OF BIRTH | SOCIAL SECURITY NO. (if any) |
|---|---|---|

|  | FAMILY NAME | FIRST NAME | DATE, CITY AND COUNTRY OF BIRTH (if known) | CITY AND COUNTRY OF RESIDENCE. |
|---|---|---|---|---|
| FATHER |  |  |  |  |
| MOTHER (Maiden name) |  |  |  |  |

| HUSBAND (If none, so state) OR WIFE | FAMILY NAME (For wife, give maiden name) | FIRST NAME | BIRTHDATE | CITY & COUNTRY OF BIRTH | DATE OF MARRIAGE | PLACE OF MARRIAGE |
|---|---|---|---|---|---|---|

FORMER HUSBANDS OF WIVES (If none, so state)

| FAMILY NAME (For wife, give maiden name) | FIRST NAME | BIRTHDATE | DATE & PLACE OF MARRIAGE | DATE AND PLACE OF TERMINATION OF MARRIAGE |
|---|---|---|---|---|
|  |  |  |  |  |
|  |  |  |  |  |

APPLICANT'S RESIDENCE LAST FIVE YEARS. LIST PRESENT ADDRESS FIRST.

| STREET AND NUMBER | CITY | PROVINCE OR STATE | COUNTRY | FROM MONTH | FROM YEAR | TO MONTH | TO YEAR |
|---|---|---|---|---|---|---|---|
|  |  |  |  |  |  | PRESENT TIME |  |
|  |  |  |  |  |  |  |  |
|  |  |  |  |  |  |  |  |
|  |  |  |  |  |  |  |  |
|  |  |  |  |  |  |  |  |

APPLICANT'S LAST ADDRESS OUTSIDE THE UNITED STATES OF MORE THAN ONE YEAR

| STREET AND NUMBER | CITY | PROVINCE OR STATE | COUNTRY | FROM MONTH | FROM YEAR | TO MONTH | TO YEAR |
|---|---|---|---|---|---|---|---|
|  |  |  |  |  |  |  |  |

APPLICANT'S EMPLOYMENT LAST FIVE YEARS. (IF NONE, SO STATE) LIST PRESENT EMPLOYMENT FIRST

| FULL NAME AND ADDRESS OF EMPLOYER | OCCUPATION (SPECIFY) | FROM MONTH | FROM YEAR | TO MONTH | TO YEAR |
|---|---|---|---|---|---|
|  |  |  |  | PRESENT TIME |  |
|  |  |  |  |  |  |
|  |  |  |  |  |  |
|  |  |  |  |  |  |
|  |  |  |  |  |  |

*Show below last occupation abroad if not shown above. (Include all information requested above.)*

|  |  |  |  |  |
|---|---|---|---|---|

| THIS FORM IS SUBMITTED IN CONNECTION WITH APPLICATION FOR: ☐ NATURALIZATION   ☐ OTHER (SPECIFY): ☐ STATUS AS PERMANENT RESIDENT | SIGNATURE OF APPLICANT | DATE |
|---|---|---|

**Are all copies legible?** ☐ Yes

IF YOUR NATIVE ALPHABET IS IN OTHER THAN ROMAN LETTERS, WRITE YOUR NAME IN YOUR NATIVE ALPHABET IN THIS SPACE:

PENALTIES: SEVERE PENALTIES ARE PROVIDED BY LAW FOR KNOWINGLY AND WILLFULLY FALSIFYING OR CONCEALING A MATERIAL FACT.

# APPLICANT:   BE SURE TO PUT YOUR NAME AND ALIEN REGISTRATION NUMBER IN THE BOX OUTLINED BY HEAVY BORDER BELOW.

| COMPLETE THIS BOX (Family name) | (Given name) | (Middle name) | (Alien registration number) |
|---|---|---|---|

Form G-325-A (Rev. 10-1-82) Y

**SAMPLE DOCUMENT – NOT TO BE USED WHEN FILING.**

**U.S. Department of Justice**
Immigration and Naturalization Service                OMB No. 1115-01-18

## Welcome to the United States

**I-94W Nonimmigrant Visa Waiver Arrival/Departure Form**

**Instructions**

This form must be completed by every nonimmigrant visitor not in possession of a visitor's visa, who is a national of one of the countries enumerated in 8 CFR 217. The airline can provide you with the current list of eligible countries.

Type or print legibly with pen in ALL CAPITAL LETTERS. USE ENGLISH!

This form is in two parts. Please complete both the Arrival Record, items 1 through 11 and the Departure Record, items 14 through 17. The reverse side of this form must be signed and dated. Children under the age of fourteen must have their form signed by a parent/guardian.

Item 7 - If you are entering the United States by land, enter LAND in this space. If you are entering the United States by ship, enter SEA in this space.

### Admission Number

**774219362 03**

Immigration and Naturalization Service
Form I-94W (05-29-91) - Arrival Record
**VISA WAIVER**

1. Family Name
2. First (Given) Name     3. Birth Date (day/mo/yr)
4. Country of Citizenship     5. Sex (male / female)
6. Passport Number     7. Airline and Flight Number
8. Country where you live     9. City where you boarded
10. Address While in the United States (Number and Street)
11. City and State

### Government Use Only

12.     13.

### Departure Number

Immigration and Naturalization Service
Form I-94W (05-29-91) - Departure Record
**VISA WAIVER**

14. Family Name
15. First (Given) Name     16. Birth Date (day/mo/yr)
17. Country of Citizenship

See Other Side                                 Staple Here

**Do any of the following apply to you?** *(Answer Yes or No)*

A. Do you have a communicable disease; physical or mental disorder; or are you a drug abuser or addict? ☐ Yes ☐ No

B. Have you ever been arrested or convicted for an offense or crime involving moral turpitude or a violation related to a controlled substance or been arrested or convicted for two or more offenses for which the aggregate sentence to confinement was five years or more; or been a controlled substance trafficker; or are you seeking entry to engage in criminal or immoral activities? ☐ Yes ☐ No

C. Have you ever been or are you now involved in espionage or sabotage; or in terrorist activities; or genocide; or between 1933 and 1945 were you involved, in any way, in persecutions associated with Nazi Germany or its allies? ☐ Yes ☐ No

D. Are you seeking to work in the U.S.; or have you ever been excluded and deported; or been previously removed from the United States; or procured or attempted to procure a visa or entry into the U.S. by fraud or misrepresentation? ☐ Yes ☐ No

E. Have you ever detained, retained or withheld custody of a child from a U.S. citizen granted custody of the child? ☐ Yes ☐ No

F. Have you ever been denied a U.S. visa or entry into the U.S. or had a U.S. visa cancelled? If yes, when?_____ where?_____ ☐ Yes ☐ No

G. Have you ever asserted immunity from prosecution? ☐ Yes ☐ No

IMPORTANT: If you answered "Yes" to any of the above, please contact the American Embassy BEFORE you travel to the U.S. since you may be refused admission into the United States.

Family Name *(Please Print)*          First Name

Country of Citizenship          Date of Birth

WAIVER OF RIGHTS: I hereby waive any rights to review or appeal of an immigration officer's determination as to my admissibility, or to contest, other than on the basis of an application for asylum, any action in deportation.

CERTIFICATION: I certify that I have read and understand all the questions and statements on this form. The answers I have furnished are true and correct to the best of my knowledge and belief.

Signature          Date

Public Reporting Burden - The burden for this collection is computed as follows: (1) Learning about the form 2 minutes; (2) completing the form 4 minutes for an estimated average of 6 minutes per response. If you have comments regarding the accuracy of this estimate, or suggestions for making this form simpler, you can write to INS, 425 I Street, N.W., Rm. 5304, Washington, D.C. 20536; and the Office of Management and Budget, Paperwork Reduction Project, OMB No. 1115-0148, Washington, D.C. 20603.

### Departure Record

Important Retain this permit in your possession; you must surrender it when you leave the U.S. Failure to do so may delay your entry into the U.S. in the future.

You are authorized to stay in the U.S. only until the date written on this form. To remain past this date, without permission from Immigration authorities, is a violation of the law.

Surrender this permit when you leave the U.S.:
-By sea or air to the transportation line;
- Across the Canadian border to a Canadian Official;
- Across the Mexican border to a U.S. Official.

WARNING:You may not accept unauthorized employment; or attend school; or represent the foreign information media during your visit under this program. You are authorized to stay in the U.S. for 90 days or less. You may not apply for: 1) a change of nonimmigrant status; 2) adjustment of status to temporary or permanent resident, unless eligible under Section 201 (B) of the INA; or 3) extension of stay. Violations of these terms will subject you to deportation.

Port:
Date:
Carrier:
Flight #/ Ship Name

**U.S. Department of Justice**
Immigration and Naturalization Service

Application for Employment Authorization

---

**How to File:**
A separate application must be filed by each applicant. Applications must be typewritten or clearly printed in ink and completed in full. If extra space is needed to answer any item, attach a continuation sheet and indicate your name, A-number (if any) and the item number.

**Note:** It is recommended that you retain a complete copy of your application for your records.

**Who should file this application?**
Certain aliens temporarily in the United States are eligible for employment authorization. Please refer to the ELIGIBILITY SECTION of this application which is found on page three. Carefully review the classes of aliens described in Group A and Group C to determine if you are eligible to apply.

This application should not be filed by lawful permanent resident aliens or by lawful temporary resident aliens.

**What is the fee?**
Applicants must pay a fee of $70.00 to file this form <u>unless</u> otherwise noted on the reverse of the form. Please refer to page 3. If required, the fee will not be refunded. Pay by cash, check, or money order in the exact amount. All checks and money orders must be payable in U.S. currency in the United States. Make check or money order payable to "Immigration and Naturalization Service." However, if you live in Guam make it payable to "Treasurer, Guam," or if you live in the U.S. Virgin Islands make it payable to "Commissioner of Finance of the Virgin Islands." If the check is not honored the INS will charge you $5.00.

**Where should you file this application?**
Applications must be filed with the nearest Immigration and Naturalization Service (INS) office that processes employment authorization applications which has jurisdiction over your place of residence. You must appear in person to receive an employment authorization document. **Please bring your INS Form I-94 and any document issued to you by the INS granting you previous employment authorization.**

**What is our authority for collecting this information?**
The authority to require you to file Form I-765, Application for Employment Authorization, is contained in the "Immigration Reform and Control Act of 1986." This information is necessary to determine whether you are eligible for employment authorization and for the preparation of your Employment Authorization Document if you are found eligible. Failure to provide all information as requested may result in the denial or rejection of this application.

The information you provide may also be disclosed to other federal, state, local and foreign law enforcement and regulatory agencies during the course of the investigation required by this Service.

**Basic Criteria to Establish Economic Necessity:**
Title 45 - Public Welfare, Poverty Guidelines, 45 CFR 1060.2 may be used as the basic criteria to establish eligibility for employment authorization when the applicant's economic necessity is identified as a factor. If you are an applicant who must show economic necessity, you should include a statement listing all of your assets, income, and expenses as evidence of your economic need to work.

**Note: Not all applicants are required to establish economic necessity.** Carefully review the ELIGIBILITY SECTION of the application. Only aliens who are filing for employment authorization under Group C, items (c)(3) (i), (c)(13), (c)(14) and (c) (18) are required to furnish information on economic need. This information must be furnished on attached sheet(s) and submitted with this application.

**What are the penalties for submitting false information?**
Title 18, United States Code, Section 1001 states that whoever willfully and knowingly falsifies a material fact, makes a false statement, or makes use of a false document will be fined up to $10,000 or imprisoned up to five years, or both.

Title 18, United States Code, Section 1546(a) states that whoever makes any false statement with respect to a material fact in any document required by the immigration laws or regulations, or presents an application containing any false statement shall be fined or imprisoned or both.

**Please Complete Both Sides of Form.**

---

**Reporting Burden:** Public reporting burden for this collection of information is estimated to average sixty (60) minutes per response, including the time for reviewing instructions, searching existing data sources, gathering and maintaining the data needed, and completing and reviewing the collection of information. Send comments regarding this burden estimate or any other aspect of this collection of information, including suggestions for reducing this burden, to: U.S. Department of Justice, Immigration and Naturalization Service, Room 2011, Washington, D.C. 20536; and to the Office of Management and Budget, Paperwork Reduction Project: OMB No. 1115-0163, Washington, D.C. 20503.

---

Form I-765 ( Rev. 12/7/90)N Page 1

**U.S. Department of Justice**                                OMB #1115-0163
Immigration and Naturalization Service (INS)         Application for Employment Authorization

| **Do Not Write In This Block** | | **Please Complete Both Sides of Form** |
|---|---|---|
| Remarks | Action Stamp | Fee Stamp |
| A# | | |
| Applicant is filing under 274a. 12 | | |

☐ Application Approved.  Employment Authorized / Extended (Circle One) _____ (Date).
                                  until _____ (Date).
    Subject to the following conditions: _____
☐ Application Denied.
    ☐  Failed to establish eligibility under 8 CFR 274a. 12 (a) or (c).
    ☐  Failed to establish economic necessity as required in 8 CFR 274a. 12(c) (13) (14) (18) and 8 CFR 214.2(f)

I am applying for:    ☐  Permission to accept employment
                      ☐  Replacement (of lost employment authorization document).
                      ☐  Extension of my permission to accept employment (attach previous employment authorization document).

1. Name (Family Name in CAPS)   (First)   (Middle)

2. Other Names Used (Include Maiden Name)

3. Address in the United Slates  (Number and Street)   (Apt. Number)

   (Town or City)   (State/Country)   (Zip Code)

4. Country of Citizenship/Nationality

5. Place of Birth (Town or City)  (State/Providence)   (Country)

6. Date of Birth (Month/Day/Year)   7. Sex
                                ☐ Male ☐ Female

8. Marital Status   ☐ Married   ☐ Single
                  ☐ Widowed   ☐ Divorced

9. Social Security Number (Include all Numbers you have ever used)

10. Alien Registration Number (A-Number) or I-94 Number (if any)

11. Have you ever before applied for employment authorization from INS?
    ☐  Yes  (if yes, complete below)        ☐  No
    Which INS Office?        Date(s)

    Results (Granted or Denied - attach all documentation)

12. Date of Last Entry into the U.S.  (Month/Day/Year)

13. Place of Last Entry into the U.S.

14. Manner of Last Entry (Visitor, Student, etc.)

15. Current Immigration Status  (Visitor, Student, etc.)

16. Go to the Eligibility Section on the reverse of this form and check the box which applies to you.  In the space below, place the letter and number of the box you selected from the reverse side:

    Eligibility under 8 CFR 274a. 12

    (    ) (    ) (    )

## Complete the reverse of this form before signature.

**Your Certification:** I certify, under penalty of perjury under the laws of the United States of America, that the foregoing is true and correct.   Furthermore, I authorize the release of any information which the Immigration and Naturalization Service needs to determine eligibility for the benefit I am seeking.  I have read the reverse of this form and have checked the appropriate block, which is identified in item #16, above.

*Signature*                        Telephone Number            Date

**Signature of Person Preparing Form if Other Than Above:**  I declare that this document was prepared by me at the request of the applicant and is based on all information of which I have any knowledge.

Print Name          Address          *Signature*          Date

| Initial Receipt | Resubmitted | Relocated | | Completed | | |
|---|---|---|---|---|---|---|
| | | Rec'd | Sent | Approved | Denied | Returned |
| | | | | | | |

Form I-765 (Rev. 12/7/90) N Page 2

        **SAMPLE DOCUMENT – NOT TO BE USED WHEN FILING.**

# Eligibility

## GROUP A

The current immigration laws and regulations permit certain classes of aliens to work in the United States. If you are an alien described below, you do not need to request that employment authorization be granted to you, but you do need to request a document to show that you are able to work in the United States. For aliens in classes (a) (3) through (a) (11) **NO FEE** will be required for the original card or for extension cards. A **FEE** will be required if a replacement employment authorization document is needed. A **FEE IS REQUIRED** for aliens in item (a) (12) who are over the age of 14 years and under the age of 65 years.

Place an **X** in the box next to the number which applies to you.

☐ (a) (3) - I have been admitted to the United States as a refugee.

☐ (a) (4) - I have been paroled into the United States as a refugee.

☐ (a) (5) - My application for asylum has been granted.

☐ (a) (6) - I am the fiance(e) of a United States citizen and I have K-1 nonimmigrant status; OR I am the dependent of a fiance(e) of a United States citizen and I have K-2 nonimmigrant status.

☐ (a) (7) - I have N-8 or N-9 nonimmigrant status in the United States.

☐ (a) (8) - I am a citizen of The Federated States of Micronesia or of the Marshall Islands.

☐ (a) (10) - I have been granted withholding of deportation.

☐ (a) (11) - I have been granted extended voluntary departure by the Attorney General.

☐ (a) (12) - I am an alien who has been registered for Temporary Protected Status (TPS) and I want an employment authorization document. **FEE REQUIRED.**

## GROUP C

The immigration law and regulations allow certain aliens to apply for employment authorization. If you are an alien described in one of the classes below you may request employment authorization from the INS and, if granted you will receive an employment authorization document. The instruction **FEE REQUIRED** printed below refers to your initial document, replacement, and extension.

Place an **X** in the box next to the number which applies to you.

☐ (c) (1) - I am the dependent of a foreign government official (A-1 or A-2). I have attached certification from the Department of State recommending employment. **NO FEE.**

☐ (c) (2) - I am the dependent of an employee of the Coordination Council of North American Affairs and I have E-1 nonimmigrant status. I have attached certification of my status from the American Institute of Taiwan. **FEE REQUIRED.**

☐ (c) (3) (i) - I am a foreign student (F-1). I have attached certification from the designated school official recommending employment for economic necessity. I have also attached my INS Form I-20 ID copy. **FEE REQUIRED.**

☐ (c) (3) (ii) - I am a foreign student (F-1). I have attached certification from the designated school official recommending employment for practical training. I have also attached my INS Form I-20 ID copy. **FEE REQUIRED.**

☐ (c) (3) (iii) - I am a foreign student (F-1). I have attached certification from my designated school official and I have been offered employment under the sponsorship of an international organization within the meaning of the International Organization Immunities Act. I have certification from this sponsor and I have also attached my INS Form I-20 ID copy. **FEE REQUIRED.**

☐ (c) (4) - I am the dependent of an officer or employee of an international organization (G-1 or G-4). I have attached certification from the Department of State recommending employment. **NO FEE.**

☐ (c) (5) - I am the dependent of an exchange visitor and I have J-2 nonimmigrant status. **FEE REQUIRED.**

☐ (c) (6) - I am a vocational foreign student (M-1). I have attached certification from the designated school official recommending employment for practical training. I have also attached my INS Form I-201D Copy. **FEE REQUIRED.**

☐ (c) (7) - I am the dependent of an individual classified as NATO-1 through NATO-7. **FEE REQUIRED.**

☐ (c) (8) - I have filed a non-frivolous application for asylum in the United States and the application is pending. **FEE REQUIRED FOR REPLACEMENT ONLY.**

☐ (c) (9) - I have filed an application for adjustment of status to lawful permanent resident status and the application is pending. **FEE REQUIRED.**

☐ (c) (10) - I have filed an application for suspension of deportation and the application is still pending. **FEE REQUIRED.**

☐ (c) (11) - I have been paroled into the United States for emergent reasons or for reasons in the public interest. **FEE REQUIRED.**

☐ (c) (12) - I am a deportable alien and I have been granted voluntary departure either prior to or after my hearing before the immigration judge. **FEE REQUIRED.**

☐ (c) (13) - I have been placed in exclusion or deportation proceedings. I have not received a final order of deportation or exclusion and I have not been detained. **I understand that I must show economic necessity and I will refer to the instructions concerning "Basic Criteria to Establish Economic Necessity."** **FEE REQUIRED.**

☐ (c) (14) - I have been granted deferred action by INS as an act of administrative convenience to the government. **I understand that I must show economic necessity and I will refer to the instructions concerning "Basic Criteria to Establish Economic Necessity."** **FEE REQUIRED.**

☐ (c) (16) - I entered the United States prior to January 1, 1972 and have been here since January 1, 1972. I have applied for registry as a lawful permanent resident alien and my application is pending. **FEE REQUIRED.**

☐ (c) (17) (i) - I am a (B-1) visitor for business. I am and have been (before coming to the United States) The domestic or personal servant for my employer who is temporarily in the United States. **FEE REQUIRED.**

☐ (c) (17) (ii) - I am a visitor for business (B-1) and am the employee of a foreign airline. I have B-1 nonimmigrant classification because I am unable to obtain visa classification as a treaty trader (E-1). **FEE REQUIRED.**

☐ (c) (18) - I am a deportable alien who has been placed under an order of supervision (OS). **I Understand that I must show economic necessity and I will refer to the instructions concerning "Basic Criteria to Establish Economic Necessity."** **FEE REQUIRED.**

☐ (c) (19) - I am an alien who is prima facie eligible for Temporary Protected Status (TPS) and (1) INS has not given me a reasonable chance to register during the first 30 days of the registration period **[FEE REQUIRED],** or (2) INS has not made a final decision as to my eligibility for TPS. **FEE REQUIRED.**

**SAMPLE DOCUMENT – NOT TO BE USED WHEN FILING.**                    M-35

## Page 1

PLEASE TYPE OR PRINT YOUR ANSWERS IN THE SPACE PROVIDED BELOW EACH ITEM.

1. SURNAMES OR FAMILY NAMES *(Exactly as in Passport)*

2. FIRST NAME AND MIDDLE NAME *(Exactly as in Passport)*

3. OTHER NAMES *(Maiden, Religious, Professional, Abases)*

4. DATE OF BIRTH *(Day, Month, Year)*       8. PASSPORT NUMBER

5. PLACE OF BIRTH
   City  Province       Country       DATE PASSPORT ISSUED *(Day, Month, Year)*

6. NATIONALITY       7. SEX
   ☐ MALE
   ☐ FEMALE       DATE PASSPORT EXPIRES *(Day, Month, Year)*

9. HOME ADDRESS *(Include apartment no., street, city, province, and postal zone)*

10. NAME AND STREET ADDRESS OF PRESENT EMPLOYER OR SCHOOL *(Postal box number unacceptable)*

11. HOME TELEPHONE NO.       12. BUSINESS TELEPHONE NO.

13. COLOR OF HAIR       14. COLOR OF EYES       15. COMPLEXION

16. HEIGHT       17. MARKS OF IDENTIFICATION

18. MARITAL STATUS
   ☐ Married  ☐ Single  ☐ Widowed  ☐ Divorced  ☐ Separated
   *If married, give name and nationality of spouse.*

19. NAMES AND RELATIONSHIPS OR PERSONS TRAVELING WITH YOU (NOTE: *A separate application must be made for a visa for each traveler, regardless of age.)*

20. HAVE YOU EVER APPLIED FOR A U.S. VISA BEFORE, WHETHER IMMIGRANT OR NONIMMIGRANT?
   ☐ No
   ☐ Yes  Where? _____
   When? _____  Type of visa? _____
   ☐ Vsa was issued       ☐ Visa was refused

21. HAS YOUR U.S. VISA EVER BEEN CANCELLED?
   ☐ No
   ☐ Yes  Where? _____
   When? _____  By whom? _____

22. Bearers of visitors visas may generally not work or study in the U.S.
   DO YOU INTEND TO WORK IN THE U.S.?  ☐ No  ☐ Yes
   *If YES, explain.*

23. DO YOU INTEND TO STUDY IN THE U.S.?  ☐ No  ☐ Yes
   *If YES, write name and address of school as it appears on form I-20.*

### DO NOT WRITE IN THIS SPACE

B-1/B-2 MAX       B-1 MAX       B-2 MAX

OTHER _____ MAX
Visa Classification

MULT OR _____
   Number Applications

MONTHS _____
   Validity

L.O. CHECKED _____

ISSUED/REFUSED

ON _____ BY _____

UNDER SEC. _____ INA

REFUSAL REVIEWED BY _____

24. PRESENT OCCUPATION *(If retired, state occupation)*

25. WHO WILL FURNISH SUPPORT, INCLUDING TICKETS?

26. AT WHAT ADDRESS WILL YOU STAY IN THE U.S.A.?

27. WHAT IS THE PURPOSE OF YOUR TRIP?

28. WHEN DO YOU INTEND TO ARRIVE IN THE U.S.A.?

29. HOW LONG DO YOU PLAN TO STAY IN THE U.S.A.?

30. HAVE YOU EVER BEEN IN THE U.S.A.?
   ☐ No
   ☐ Yes  When? _____
   For how long? _____

### NONIMMIGRANT VISA APPLICATION

COMPLETE ALL QUESTIONS ON REVERSE OF FORM

OPTIONAL FORM 156 (Rev. 4-91) PAGE 1       50156-106       NSN 7540-00-139-
Department of State

## Page 2

31. (a) HAVE YOU OR ANYONE ACTING FOR YOU EVER INDICATED TO A U.S. CONSULAR OR IMMIGRATION EMPLOYEE A DESIRE TO IMMIGRATE TO THE U.S.? (b) HAS ANYONE EVER FILED AN IMMIGRANT VISA PETITION ON YOUR BEHALF? (c) HAS LABOR CERTIFICATION FOR EMPLOYMENT IN THE U.S. EVER BEEN REQUESTED BY YOU OR ON YOUR BEHALF?
   (a) ☐ No  ☐ Yes       (b) ☐ No  ☐ Yes       (c) ☐ No  ☐ Yes

32. ARE ANY OF THE FOLLOWING IN THE U.S.? *(If YES, circle appropriate relationship and indicate that person's status in the U.S., i.e., studying, working, U.S. permanent resident, U.S. citizen, etc.)*
   HUSBAND/WIFE _____  FIANCE/FIANCEE _____  BROTHER/SISTER _____
   FATHER/MOTHER _____  SON/DAUGHTER _____

33. PLEASE LIST THE COUNTRIES WHERE YOU HAVE LIVED FOR MORE THAN 6 MONTHS DURING THE PAST 5 YEARS. BEGIN WITH YOUR PRESENT RESIDENCE.

   Countries       Cities       Approximate Dates

34. IMPORTANT: ALL APPLICANTS MUST READ AND CHECK THE APPROPRIATE BOX FOR EACH ITEM:

   A visa may not be issued to persons who are within specific categories defined by law as inadmissible to the United States (except when a waiver is obtained in advance). Are any of the following applicable to you?

   - Have you ever been afflicted with a communicable disease of public health significance, a dangerous physical or mental disorder, or been a drug abuser or addict? ......................................... ☐ Yes  ☐ No

   - Have you ever been arrested or convicted for any offense or crime, even though subject of a pardon, amnesty, or other such legal action? ......................................... ☐ Yes  ☐ No

   - Have you ever been a controlled substance (drug) trafficker, or a prostitute or procurer? ......................................... ☐ Yes  ☐ No

   - Have you ever sought to obtain or assist others to obtain a visa, entry into the U.S., or any U.S. immigration benefit by fraud or willful misrepresentation? ......................................... ☐ Yes  ☐ No

   - Were you deported from the U.S.A. within the last 5 years? ......................................... ☐ Yes  ☐ No

   - Do you seek to enter the United States to engage in export control violations, subversive or terrorist activities, or any unlawful purpose? ......................................... ☐ Yes  ☐ No

   - Have you ever ordered, incited, assisted, or otherwise participated in the persecution of any person because of race, religion, national origin, or political opinion under the control, direct or indirect, of the Nazi Government of Germany, or of the government of any area occupied by, or allied with, the Nazi Government of Germany, or have you ever participated in genocide? ......................................... ☐ Yes  ☐ No

   A YES answer does not automatically signify ineligibility for a visa, but if you answered YES to any of the above, or if you have any question in this regard, personal appearance at this office is recommended. If appearance is not possible at this time, attach a statement of facts in your case to this application.

35. I certify that I have read and understood all the questions set forth in this application and the answers I have furnished on this form are true and correct to the best of my knowledge and belief. I understand that any false or misleading statement may result in the permanent refusal of a visa or denial of entry into the United States. I understand that possession of a visa does not entitle the bearer to enter the United States of America upon arrival at port of entry if he or she is found inadmissible.

   DATE OF APPLICATION _____

   APPLICANT'S SIGNATURE _____

   If this application has been prepared by a travel agency or another person on your behalf, the agent should indicate name and address of agency or person with appropriate signature of individual preparing form.

   SIGNATURE OF PERSON PREPARING FORM
   *(If other than applicant)* _____

DO NOT WRITE IN THIS SPACE

37 mm x 37 mm

PHOTO

Glue or Staple
photo here

OPTIONAL FORM 156 (Rev. 4-91) PAGE 2

**SAMPLE DOCUMENT – NOT TO BE USED WHEN FILING.**

**U.S. Department of Justice**
Immigration and Naturalization Service
Please Read Instructions on Page 2

**Certificate of Eligibility for Nonimmigrant (F-1) Student Status - For Academic and Language Students**

OMB No. 1115-0051

Page 1

**This page must be completed and signed in the U.S. by a designated school official.**

1. Family Name (surname)

   First (given) name (do not enter middle name)

   Country of birth

   Date of birth (mo./day/year)

   Country of citizenship

   Admission number (Complete if known)

2. School (school district) name

   School official to be notified of student's arrival in U.S. (Name and Title)

   School address (include zip code)

   School code (including 3-digit suffix, if any) and approval date

   _____ 214F _____ approved on _____

**For Immigration Official Use**

Visa issuing post    Date Visa issued

Reinstated, extension granted to:

3. This certificate is issued to the student named above for:
   (Check and fill out as appropriate)
   a. ☐ Initial attendance at this school.
   b. ☐ Continued attendance at this school .
   c. ☐ School transfer.
      Transferred from _____ .
   d. ☐ Use by dependents for entering the United States.
   e. ☐ Other _____ .

4 Level of education the student is pursuing or will pursue in the United States
   (check only one)
   a. ☐ Primary          e. ☐ Master's
   b. ☐ Secondary        f. ☐ Doctorate
   c. ☐ Associate        g. ☐ Language training
   d. ☐ Bachelor's       h. ☐ Other

5. The student named above has been accepted for a full course of study at this school, majoring in _____ .
   The student is expected to report to the school not later than (date) _____ and complete studies not later than (date) _____
   The normal length of study is _____ .

6. ☐ English proficiency is required:
   ☐ The student has the required English proficiency.
   ☐ The student is not yet proficient, English instructions will be given at the school.
   ☐ English proficiency is not required because _____

7. This school estimates the student's average costs for an academic term of _____ (up to 12) months to be:
   a. Tuition and fees        $ _____
   b. Living expenses         $ _____
   c. Expenses of dependents  $ _____
   d. Other (specify):        $ _____
   Total    $ _____

8. This school has information showing the following as the student's means of support, estimated for an academic term of _____ months (Use the same number of months given in item 7).
   a. Student's personal funds    $ _____
   b. Funds from this school (specify type)    $ _____
   c. Funds from another source (specify type and source)    $ _____
   d. On-campus employment (if any)    $ _____
   Total    $ _____

9. Remarks: _____

10. School Certification: I certify under penalty of perjury that all information provided above in items 1 through 8 was completed before I signed this form and is true and correct; I executed this form in the United States after review and evaluation in the United States by me or other officials of the school of the student's application, transcripts or other records of courses taken and proof of financial responsibility, which were received at the school prior to the execution of this form; the school has determined that the above named student's qualifications meet all standards for admission to the school; the student will be required to pursue a full course of study as defined by 8 CFR 214.2(f)(6); I am a designated official of the above named school and I am authorized to issue this form.

Signature of designated school official    Name of school official (print or type)    Title    Date Issued    Place issued (city and state)

11. Student Certification: I have read and agreed to comply with the terms and conditions of my admission and those of any extension of stay as specified on page 2. I certify that all information provided on this form refers specifically to me and is true and correct to the best of my knowledge. I certify that I seek to enter or remain in the United States temporarily, and solely for the purpose of pursuing a full course of study at the school named on Page 1 of this form. I also authorize the named school to release any information from my records which is needed by the INS pursuant to 8 CFR 214.3(g) to determine my nonimmigrant status.

Signature of student    Name of student    Date

Signature of parent or guardian if student is under 18    Name of parent/guardian (Print or type)    Address (city)    (State or province)    (Country)    (Date)

Form I-20 A-B/I-201D (Rev 04-27-88)N

For official use only
Microfilm Index Number

I-20 SCHOOL

**SAMPLE DOCUMENT – NOT TO BE USED WHEN FILING.**

M-37

**Page 2**

Authority for collecting the information on this and related student forms is contained in 8 U.S.C. 1101 and 1184. The information solicited will be used by the Department of State and the Immigration and Naturalization Service to determine eligibility for the benefits requested.

### INSTRUCTIONS TO DESIGNATED SCHOOL OFFICIALS

**1. The law provides severe penalties for knowingly and willfully falsifying or concealing a material fact, or using any false document in the submission of this form.** Designated school officials should consult regulations pertaining to the issuance of Form 1-20 A-B at 8 CFR 214.3 (K) before completing this form. Failure to comply with these regulations may result in the withdrawal of the school approval for attendance by foreign students by the Immigration and Naturalization Service (8 CFR 214.4).

**2. ISSUANCE OF FORM 1-20 A-B.** Designated school officials may issue a Form I-20 A-B to a student who fits into one of the following categories, if the student has been accepted for full-time attendance at the institution: a) a prospective F-1 nonimmigrant student; b) an F-1 transfer student; c) an F-1 student advancing to a higher educational level at the same institution; d) an out of status student seeking reinstatement. The form may also be issued to the dependent spouse or child of an F-1 student for securing entry into the United States.

**When issuing a Form 1-20 A-B, designated school officials should complete the student's admission number whenever possible to ensure proper data entry and record keeping.**

**3. ENDORSEMENT OF PAGE 4 FOR REENTRY.** Designated school officials may endorse page 4 of the Form 1-20 A-B for reentry if the student and/or the F-2 dependents is to leave the United States temporarily. This should be done only when the information on the Form I-20 remains unchanged. If there have been substantial changes in item 4, 5, 7, or 8, a new Form I-20 A-B should be issued.

**4 REPORTING REQUIREMENT.** Designated school official should always forward the top page of the Form I-20 A-B to the INS data processing center at P.O. Box 140, London, Kentucky 40741 for data entry except when the form is issued to an F-1 student for initial entry or reentry into the United States, or for reinstatement to student status. (Requests for reinstatement should be sent to the Immigration and Naturalization Service district office having jurisdiction over the student's temporary residence in this country.)

**The INS data processing center will return this top page to the issuing school for disposal after data entry and microfilming.**

**5. CERTIFICATION.** Designated school officials should certify on the bottom part of page 1 of this form that the Form 1-20 A-B is completed and issued in accordance with the pertinent regulations. The designated school official should remove the carbon sheet from the completed and signed Form I-20 A-B before forwarding it to the student.

**6. ADMISSION RECORDS.** Since the Immigration and Naturalization Service may request information concerning the student's immigration status for various reasons, designated school officials should retain all evidence which shows the scholastic ability and financial status on which admission was based, until the school has reported the student's termination of studies to the Immigration and Naturalization Service.

### INSTRUCTIONS TO STUDENTS

**1. Student Certification.** You should read everything on this page carefully and be sure that you understand the terms and conditions concerning your admission and stay in the United States as a nonimmigrant student before you sign the student certification on the bottom part of page 1. The law provides severe penalties for knowlingly and willfully falsifying or concealing a material fact, or using any false document in the submission of this form.

**2. ADMISSION.** A nonimmigrant student may be admitted for duration of status. This means that you are authorized to stay in the United States for the entire length of time during which you are enrolled as a full-time student in an educational program and any period of authorized practical training plus sixty days. While in the United States you must maintain a valid foreign passport unless you are exempt from passport requirements.

You may continue from one educational level to another, such as progressing from high school to a bachelor's program or a bachelor's program to a master's program, etc., simply by invoking the procedures for school transfers.

**3.SCHOOL.** For initial admission, you must attend the school specified on your visa. If you have a Form I-20 A-B from more than one school, it is important to have the name of the school you intend to attend specified on your visa by presenting a Form I-20 A-B from that school to the visa issuing consular officer. Failure to attend the specified school will result in the loss of your student status and subject you to deportation.

**4. REENTRY.** A nonimmigrant student may be readmitted a temporary absence of five months or less from the United States, if the student is otherwise admissible. You may be readmitted by presenting a valid foreign passport, a valid visa, and either a new Form I-20 A-B or a page 4 of the Form I-20 A-B (the I-20 ID Copy) properly endorsed for reentry if the information on the I-20 form is current.

**5. TRANSFER.** A nonimmigrant student is permitted to transfer to a different school provided the transfer procedure is followed. To transfer school, you should first notify the school you are attending of the intent to transfer, then obtain a Form I-20 A-B from the school you intend to attend. Transfer will be effected only if you return the Form I-20 A-B to the designated school official within 15 days of beginning attendance at the new school. The designated school official will then report the transfer to the Immigration and Naturalization Service.

**6. EXTENSION OF STAY.** It you cannot complete the educational program after having been in student status for longer than the anticipated length of the program plus a grace period in a single educational level, or for more than eight consecutive years, you must apply for extension of stay. An application for extension of stay on a Form I-538 should be filed with the Immigration and Naturalization Service district office having jurisdiction over your school at least 15 days but no more man 60 days before the expiration of your authorized stay.

**7. EMPLOYMENT.** As an F-1 student, you are not permitted to work off-campus or to engage in business without specific employment authorization. After your first year in F-1 student status, you may apply for employment authorization on Form 1-538 based on financial needs arising after receiving student status, or the need to obtain practical training.

**8. Notice of Address.** If you move, you must submit a notice within 10 days of the change of address to the Immigration and Naturalization Service. (Form AR-11 is available at any INS office.)

**9. Arrival/Departure.** When you leave the United States, you must surrender your Form 1-94 Departure Record. Please see the back side of Form 1-94 for detailed instructions. You do not have to turn in the 1-94 if you are visiting Canada, Mexico, or adjacent islands other than Cuba for less than 30 days.

**10. Financial Support.** You must demonstrate that you are financially able to support yourself for the entire period of stay in the United States while pursuing a full course of study. You are required to attach documentary evidence of means of support.

**11. Authorization to Release Information by School.** To comply with requests from the United States Immigration & Naturalization Service for information concerning your immigration status, you are required to give authorization to the named school to release such information from your records. The school will provide the Service your name, country of birth, current address, and any omer information on a regular basis or upon request.

**12. Penalty.** To maintain your nonimmigrant student status, you must be enrolled as a full-time student at the school you are authorized to attend. You may engage in employment only when you have received permission to work. Failure to comply with these regulations will result in the loss of your student status and subject you to deportation.

**IF YOU NEED MORE INFORMATION CONCERNING YOUR F-1 NONIMMIGRANT STUDENT STATUS AND THE RELATING IMMIGRATION PROCEDURES, PLEASE CONTACT EITHER YOUR FOREIGN STUDENT ADVISOR ON CAMPUS OR A NEARBY IMMIGRATION AND NATURALIZATION SERVICE OFFICE.**

THIS PAGE, WHEN PROPERLY ENDORSED, MAY BE USED FOR ENTRY OF THE SPOUSE AND CHILDREN OF AN F-1 STUDENT FOLLOWING TO JOIN THE STUDENT IN THE UNITED STATES OR FOR REENTRY OF THE STUDENT TO ATTEND THE SAME SCHOOL AFTER A TEMPORARY ABSENCE FROM THE UNITED STATES.

**For reentry of the student and/or the F-2 dependents (EACH CERTIFICATION SIGNATURE IS VALID FOR ONLY ONE YEAR.)**

| Signature of Designated School Official | Name of School Official (print or type) | Title | Date |
|---|---|---|---|
| Signature of Designated School Official | Name of School Official (print or type) | Title | Date |
| Signature of Designated School Official | Name of School Official (print or type) | Title | Date |
| Signature of Designated School Official | Name of School Official (print or type) | Title | Date |
| Signature of Designated School Official | Name of School Official (print or type) | Title | Date |
| Signature of Designated School Official | Name of School Official (print or type) | Title | Date |

Dependent spouse and children of the F-1 student who are seeking entry/reentry to the U.S.

| Name family (caps)    first | Date of birth | Country of birth | Relationship to the F-1 student |
|---|---|---|---|
|  |  |  |  |
|  |  |  |  |
|  |  |  |  |
|  |  |  |  |

**Student Employment Authorization and other Records**

| | | |
|---|---|---|
| | | |
| | | |
| | | |
| | | |
| | | |
| | | |
| | | |
| | | |
| | | |
| | | |
| | | |
| | | |
| | | |
| | | |
| | | |
| | | |
| | | |
| | | |

**U.S. Department of Justice**

Immigration and Naturalization Service

OMB No.1115-0093

Application to Extend/Change Nonimmigrant Status

### Purpose Of This Form.

This form is for a nonimmigrant to apply for an extension of stay or change to another nonimmigrant status. However, an employer should file Form I-129 to request an extension/change to E, H, L, O, P, Q or R status for an employee or prospective employee. Dependents of such employees should file for an extension/change of status on this form, not on Form I-129. This form is also for a nonimmigrant F-1 or M-1 student to apply for reinstatement.

This form consists of a basic application and a supplement to list co-applicants.

### Who May File.

#### For extension of stay or change of status.

If you are a nonimmigrant in the U.S., you may apply for an extension of stay or a change of status on this form except as noted above. However, you may not be granted an extension or change of status if you were admitted under the Visa Waiver Program or if your current or proposed status is as:

- an alien in transit (C) or in transit without a visa (TWOV);
- a crewman (D); or
- a fiance(e) or dependent of a fiance(e) (K).

There are additional limits on change of status.

- A J-1 exchange visitor whose status was for the purpose of receiving graduate medical training is ineligible for change of status.
- A J-1 exchange visitor subject to the foreign residence requirement who has not received a waiver of that requirement, is only eligible for a change of status to A or G.
- An M-1 student is not eligible for a change to F-1 status, and is not eligible for a change to any H status if training received as an M-1 student helped him/her qualify for the H status.
- You may not be granted a change to M-1 status for training to qualify for H status.

#### For F-1 or M-1 student reinstatement.

You will only be considered for reinstatement if you establish when filing this application:

- that the violation of status was solely due to circumstances beyond your control or that failure to reinstate you would result in extreme hardship;
- you are pursuing, or will pursue, a full course of study;
- you have not been employed off campus without authorization or, if an F-1 student, that your only unauthorized off-campus employment was pursuant to a scholarship, fellowship, or assistantship, or did not displace a U.S. resident; and
- you are not in deportation proceedings.

### Multiple Applicants.

You may include your spouse and your unmarried children under age 21 as co-applicants in your application for the same extension or change of status if you are all in the same status now or they are all in derivative status.

### General Filing Instructions.

Please answer all questions by typing or clearly printing in black ink. Indicate that an item is not applicable with "N/A". If the answer is "none," please so state. If you need extra space to answer any item, attach a sheet of paper with your name and your alien registration number (A#), if any, and indicate the number of the item to which the answer refers. Your application must be filed with the required Initial Evidence. Your application must be properly signed and filed with the correct fee. If you are under 14 years of age, your parent or guardian may sign your application.

#### Copies.

If these instructions state that a copy of a document may be filed with this application and you choose to send us the original, we may keep that original for our records.

#### Translations.

Any foreign language document must be accompanied by a full English translation which the translator has certified as complete and correct, and by the translator's certification that he or she is competent to translate from the foreign language into English.

### Initial Evidence.

#### Form I-94, Nonimmigrant Arrival-Departure Record.

You must file your application with the original Form I-94, Nonimmigrant Arrival/Departure Record, of each person included in the application, if you are filing for:

- an extension as a B-1 or B-2, or change to such status;
- reinstatement as an F-1 or M-1 or filing for change to F or M status; or
- an extension as a J, or change to such status.

In all other instances, file this application with a copy of the Form I-94 of each person included in the application.

If the required Form I-94 or required copy cannot be submitted, you must file Form I-102, Application for Replacement/initial Nonimmigrant Arrival/Departure Document, with this application.

#### Valid Passport.

A nonimmigrant who is required to have a passport to be admitted must keep that passport valid during his/her entire nonimmigrant stay. If a required passport is not valid when you file this application, submit an explanation with your application.

#### Additional Initial Evidence.

An application must also be filed with the following evidence.

- If you are filing for an extension/change of status as the dependent of an employee who is an E, H, L, O, P, Q or R nonimmigrant, this application must be filed with:
  - the petition filed for that employee or evidence it is pending with the Service; or
  - a copy of the employee's Form I-94 or approval notice showing that he/she has already been granted status to the period requested in your application.
- If you are requesting an extension/change to A-3 or G-5 status, this application must be filed with:
  - a copy of your employer's Form I-94 or approval notice demonstrating A or G status;
  - an original letter from your employer describing your duties and stating that he/she intends to personally employ you; and
  - an original Form I-566, certified by the Department of State, indicating your employer's continuing accredited diplomatic status.
- If you are filing for an extension/change to other A or G status, you must submit Form I-566, certified by the Department of State to indicate your accredited diplomatic status.
- If you are filing for an extension/change to B-1 or B-2 status, this application must be filed with a statement explaining, in detail,:
  - the reasons for your request;
  - why your extended stay would be temporary including what arrangement you have made to depart the U.S.; and
  - any effect of the extended stay on your foreign employment and residency.
- If you are requesting an extension/change to F-1 or M-1 student status, this application must be filed with an original Form I-20 issued by the school which has accepted you. If you are requesting reinstatement to F-1 or M-1 status, you must also submit evidence establishing that you are eligible for reinstatement.
- If you are filing for an extension/change to I status, this application must be filed with a letter describing the employment and establishing that it is as the representative of qualifying foreign media.
- If you are filing for an extension/change to J-1 exchange visitor status, this application must be filed with an original Form IAP-66 issued by your program sponsor.
- If you are filing for an extension/change to N-1 or N-2 status as the parent or child of an alien admitted as a special immigrant under section 101(a)(27)(I), this application must be filed with a copy of that person's alien registration card.

### When To File.

You must submit an application for extension of stay or change of status before your current authorized stay expires. We suggest you file at least 45 days before your stay expires, or as soon as you determine you need to change status. Failure to file before the expiration date may be excused if you demonstrate when you file the application:

- the delay was due to extraordinary circumstances beyond your control;
- the length of the delay was reasonable;
- that you have not otherwise violated your status
- that you are still a bona fide nonimmigrant; and
- that you are not in deportation proceedings

Form I-539 (Rev. 12-2-91)

**Where To File.**
File this application at your local INS office if you are filing:
- for an extension as a B-1 or B-2, or change to such status;
- for reinstatement as an F-1 or M-1 or filing for change to F or M status; or
- for an extension as a J, or change to such status.

In all other instances, file your application at an INS Service Center, as follows:

If you live in Connecticut, Delaware, District of Columbia, Maine, Maryland, Massachusetts, New Hampshire, New Jersey, New York, Pennsylvania, Puerto Rico, Rhode Island, Vermont, Virgin Islands, Virginia, or West Virginia, mail your application to: USINS Eastern Service Center, 75 Lower Welden Street, St. Albans, VT 05479-0001.

If you live in Alabama, Arkansas, Florida, Georgia, Kentucky, Louisiana, Mississippi, New Mexico, North Carolina, Oklahoma, South Carolina, Tennessee, or Texas, mail your application to: USINS Southern Service Center, P.O. Box 152122, Dept. A, Irving, TX 75015-2122.

If you live in Arizona, California, Guam, Hawaii, or Nevada, mail your application to: USINS Western Service Center, P.O. Box 30040, Laguna Niguel, CA 92607-0040.

If you live elsewhere in the United States, mail your application to: USINS Northern Service Center, 100 Centennial Mall North, Room, B-26, Lincoln, NE 68508.

**Fee.**
The fee for this application is $75.00 for the first person included in the application, and $10.00 for each additional person. The fee must be submitted in the exact amount. It cannot be refunded. DO NOT MAIL CASH.

All checks and money orders must be drawn on a bank or other institution located in the United States and must be payable in United States currency. The check or money order should be made payable to the Immigration and Naturalization Service, except that:
- If you live in Guam, and are filing this application in Guam, make your check or money order payable to the "Treasurer, Guam."
- If you live in the Virgin Islands, and are filing this application in the Virgin Islands, make your check or money order payable to the "Commissioner of Finance of the Virgin Islands."

Checks are accepted subject to collection. An uncollected check will render the application and any document issued invalid. A charge of $5.00 will be imposed if a check in payment of a fee is not honored by the bank on which it is drawn.

**Processing Information.**
*Acceptance.* Any application that is not signed or is not accompanied by the correct fee will be rejected with a notice that the application is deficient. You may correct the deficiency and resubmit the application. An application is not considered properly filed until accepted by the Service.

*Initial processing.* Once the application has been accepted, it will be checked for completeness. If you do not completely fill out the form, or file it without required initial evidence, you will not establish a basis for eligibility, and we may deny your application.

*Requests for more information or interview.* We may request more information or evidence or we may request that you appear at an INS office for an interview. We may also request that you submit the originals of any copy. We will return these originals when they are no longer required.

*Decision.* An application for extension of stay, change of status, or reinstatement may be approved in the discretion of the Service. You will be notified in writing of the decision on your application.

**Penalties.**
If you knowingly and willfully falsify or conceal a material fact or submit a false document with this request, we will deny the benefit you are filing for, and may deny any other immigration benefit. In addition, you will face severe penalties provided by law, and may be subject to criminal prosecution.

**Privacy Act Notice.**
We ask for the information on this form, and associated evidence, to determine if you have established eligibility for the immigration benefit you are filing for. Our legal right to ask for this information is in 8 USC 1184, and 1258. We may provide this information to other government agencies. Failure to provide this information, and any requested evidence, may delay a final decision or result in denial of your request.

**Paperwork Reduction Act Notice.**
We try to create forms and instructions that are accurate, can be easily understood, and which impose the least possible burden on you to provide us with information. Often this is difficult because some immigration laws are very complex. The estimated average time to complete and file this application is as follows: (1) 10 minutes to learn about the law and form; (2) 10 minutes to complete the form; and (3) 25 minutes to assemble and file the application; for a total estimated average of 45 per application. If you have comments regarding the accuracy of this estimate, or suggestions for making this form simpler, you can write to both the Immigration and Naturalization Service, 425 I Street, N.W., Room 5304, Washington, D.C. 20536; and the Office of Management and Budget, Paperwork Reduction Project, OMB No. 1115-0093, Washington, D.C. 20503.

**Mailing Label--Complete the following mailing label and submit this page with your application if you are required to submit your original Form I-94.**

------------------------------------------------------------

## Name and address of applicant

Name _____

Street _____

City, State, & Zip Code _____

Your I-94 Arrival-Departure Record is attached. It has been amended to show the extension of stay/change of status granted.

Form I-539 (Rev. 12-2-91)

**U.S. Department of Justice**                                                OMB #1115-0093
Immigration and Naturalization Service                   Application to Extend/ChangeNonimmigrant Status

## START HERE - Please Type or Print

### Part 1. Information about you.

| Family Name | Given Name | Middle Initial |
|---|---|---|
| | | |

**Address** - In
Care of:

| Street # and Name | | Apt # |
|---|---|---|
| | | |

| City | State |
|---|---|
| | |

Zip Code

| Date of Birth (Month/Day/Year) | Country of Birth |
|---|---|
| | |

| Social Security # (if any) | A # (if any) |
|---|---|
| | |

| Date of Last Arrival Into the U.S. | I-94# |
|---|---|
| | |

| Current Nonimmigrant Status | Expires on (month/day/year) |
|---|---|
| | |

### Part 2.  Application Type.          (See instructions for fee.)

**1.  I am applying for:** (check one)
a.  ☐  an extension of stay in my current status
b.  ☐  a change of status. The new status I am requesting is: _____

**2.  Number of people included in this application:** (check one)
a.  ☐  I am the only applicant
b.  ☐  Members of my family are filing this application with me.
The Total number of people included in this application is _____
(complete the supplement for each co-applicant)

### Part 3.  Processing information.

1.  I/We request that my/our current or requested
status be extended until (month/day/year)          _____

2.  Is this application based on an extension or change of status already granted to our spouse,
child or parent?
☐  No          ☐  Yes (receipt # _____ )

3.  Is this application being filed based on a separate petition or application to give your spouse,
child or parent an extension or change of status?
☐  No   ☐  Yes, filed with this application   ☐  Yes, filed previously and pending with INS

4.  If you answered yes to question 3, give the petitioner or applicant name:

If the application is pending with INS, also give the following information.

Office filed at _____ Filed on _____ (date)

### Part 4.  Additional information.

1.  For applicant #1, provide passport information:

| Country of issuance | Valid to: (month/day/year) |
|---|---|
| | |

2.  Foreign address

| Street # and Name | Apt# |
|---|---|
| | |

| City or Town | State or Province |
|---|---|
| | |

| Country | Zip or Postal Code |
|---|---|
| | |

Form I-539 (Rev. 12-2-91 ) N          *Continued on back.*

---

### FOR INS USE ONLY

| Returned | Receipt |
|---|---|
| Date _____ | |
| _____ | |
| Resubmitted | |
| Date _____ | |
| _____ | |
| Reloc Sent | |
| Date _____ | |
| _____ | |
| Reloc Rec'd | |
| Date _____ | |
| Date _____ | |
| ☐ Applicant Interviewed | |

☐ *Extension Granted*
to (date): _____
☐ *Change of Status/Extension Granted*
New Class: _____   To (date): _____

If denied:
☐  Still within period of stay
☐  V/D to: _____
☐  S/D to: _____
☐  Place under docket control

**Remarks**

**Action Block**

**To Be Completed by**
***Attorney* or *Representative*, if any**
☐  Fill in box if G-28 is attached to represent the applicant

VOLAG#

ATTY State License #

## Part 4.  Additional Information.  *(continued)*

| 3. Answer the following questions. If you answer yes to any question, explain on separate paper. | Yes | No |
|---|---|---|
| a. Are you, or any other person included in this application, an applicant for an immigrant visa or adjustment of status to permanent residence? | | |
| b. Has an immigrant petition ever been filed for you, or any other person included in this application? | | |
| c. Have you, or any other person included in this application ever been arrested or convicted of any criminal offense since last entering the U.S.? | | |
| d. Have you, or any other person included in this application done anything which violated the terms of the nonimmigrant status you now hold? | | |
| e. Are you, or any other person included in this application, now in exclusion or deportation proceedings? | | |
| f. Have you, or any other person included in this application, been employed in the U.S since last admitted or granted an extension or change of status? | | |

If you answered YES to question 3f, give the following information on a separate paper: Name of person, name of employer, address of employer, weekly income, and whether specifically authorized by INS.

If you answered NO to question 3f, fully describe how you are supporting yourself on a separate paper. Include the source and the amount and basis for any income.

## Part 5.    Signature.    *Read the information on penalties in the instructions before completing this section.   You must file this application while in the United States.*

I certify under penalty of perjury under the laws of the United States of America that this application, and the evidence submitted with it, is all true and correct. I authorize the release of any information from my records which the Immigration and Naturalization Service needs to determine eligibility for the benefit I am seeking.

| Signature | Print you name | Date |
|---|---|---|
| | | |

***Please Note:*** *If you do not completely fill out this form, or fail to submit required documents listed in the instructions, you cannot be found eligible for the requested document and this application will have to be denied.*

## Part 6.    Signature of person preparing form if other than above.  *(Sign below)*

I declare that I prepared this application at the request of the above person and it is based on all information of which I have knowledge.

| Signature | Print Your Name | Date |
|---|---|---|
| | | |

Firm Name
and Address

*(Please remember to enclose the mailing label with your application)*

## Health Care Facility Attestation (H-1A)

**U.S. Department of Labor**
Employment and Training Administration
U.S. Employment Service

1. Name of Facility (Full Legal Name of Organization)

3. Telephone (Area Code and Number)

OMB Approval No.: 1205-0305
Expires: 11/91

2. Address (Number, Street, City or Town, State and Zip Code)

4. Facility's Federal Employer I.D. Number

5. Nature of Facility's Business Activity

6. Name of Chief Executive Officer

7. Kind of Facility (check appropriate item)

☐ a. Nurse contractor intending to petition for H-1A nurses. (Also complete item 8.g.)
☐ b. Other Facility intending to petition for H-1A nurses
☐ c. Facility intending to use H-1A nurses through a contractor only (check appropriate item: waivers of some of the elements in Item 8 may be requested, in writing, if Item 7.c.(i), 7.c.(ii), or 7.c.(iii) is checked; see the instructions for items 7. and 8.)
    ☐ (i) For no more than 15 workdays in any 3-month period to meet emergency needs on a temporary basis.
    ☐ (ii) For more than 15 but no more than 60 workdays in any 3-month period to meet temporary needs.
    ☐ (iii) For more than 60 workdays in any 3-month period due to a bona fide medical emergency. Describe on an attached sheet; see instructions.
    ☐ (iv) None of the above.

8. FACILITY ATTESTATION: Applicable in its entirety if Item 7.a. or Item 7.b. is checked. Item 8.g. required it Item 7.a. is checked.

☐ a. (i) This facility has not laid off any registered nurses within the past year; and
☐   (ii) Through no fault of this facility, there would be a substantial disruption in the delivery of health care services of the facility without the services of a nonimmigrant nurse(s), as demonstrated by (check one or more appropriate items):
    ☐ Current nurse vacancy rate of seven percent or more.
    ☐ Unutilized bed rate of seven percent or more.
    ☐ Elimination/Curtailment of essential health care services.
    ☐ Inability to implement established plans for needed new health care services.
    ☐ Other (Describe on an attached sheet; see instructions).

☐ b. The employment of the alien(s) will not adversely affect the wages and working conditions of registered nurses similarly employed.
☐ c. Alien(s) employed by the facility will be paid the wage rate for registered nurses similarly employed by this facility.
☐ d. (i) Check appropriate item:

    ☐ This facility has taken and is taking timely and significant steps designed to recruit and retain registered nurses who are United States citizens or immigrants who are authorized to perform nursing services in order to remove as quickly as reasonably possible our dependence on nonimmigrant nurses; or
    ☐ This facility is subject to an approved State plan for the recruitment and retention of nurses. (if checked, skip Item 8.d.(ii).)

(NOTE: 8. FACILITY ATTESTATION CONTINUES ON THE BACK OF THIS FORM.)

9. DECLARATION OF FACILITY:

Pursuant to 28 U.S.C. 1746, I declare under penalty of perjury that the information provided on this form is true and correct

_____
Signatue of Chief Executive Officer

_____
Date

FOR GOVERNMENT AGENCY USE ONLY:

By virtue of my signature below, I acknowledge that this attestation is accepted or filing on _____
(date) and will be valid through _____ (date twelve months from the date it is accepted for filing).

_____
Signature of Authorized Department of Labor Official

The Department of Labor is not the guarantor of the accuracy, truthfulness or adequacy of an attestation accepted for filing).

Public reporting burden for this collection of information is estimated to average _____ minutes per response, including the time for reviewing instructions, searching existing data sources, gathering and maintaining the data needed, and completing and reviewing the collection of information. Send comments regarding this burden, including estimates or any other aspect of this collection of information, including suggestions for reducing this burden, to the Office of Information Management, Department of Labor, Room N1301, 200 Constitution Avenue, N.W., Washington, D.C. 20210; and to the Office of Management and Budget, Paperwork Reduction Project (1205-0305) Washington, D.C. 20503.

ETA 9029 (Rev. Nov. 1990)

**SAMPLE DOCUMENT – NOT TO BE USED WHEN FILING.**

(8.   FACILITY ATTESTATION CONTINUATION)

(ii)  Timely and significant steps being taken by this facility include (Check two or more unless second step is unreasonable:
see Item 8.d.(iii) and instructions).

☐   Operating a training program for registered nurses at the facility or financing (or providing participation in) a training program for registered nurses elsewhere.
☐   Providing career development programs and other methods of facilitating health care workers to become registered nurses.
☐   Paying registered nurses at a rate higher than currently being paid registered nurses similarly employed in the geographic area.
☐   Providing adequate support services to free registered nurses from administrative and other nonnursing duties.
☐   Providing reasonable opportunities for meaningful salary advancement by registered nurses.
☐   Other (Describe on an attached sheet; see instructions.)

(iii)  Only one timely and significant step has been and is being taken by this facility. (Check Item below and attach explanation; see instructions.)

☐   Taking a second step is unreasonable.

(iv)  Alternative to criteria for each step for second and succeding years. (Check Item below and attach explanation; see instructions).

☐   This facility does not have a valid attestation on file with the Department of Labor. This facility will, within the next year, reduce the number if nonimmigrant nurses it utilizes by at least 10 percent without reducing the quality or quantity of services provided.

☐   This facility has a valid attestation on file with the Department of Labor. This facility will, within the next year, reduce the number of nonimmigrant nurses it utilizes by at least 10 percent without reducing the quality or quantity of services provided

☐   Pursuant to its prior attestation, this facility has reduced the number of nonimmigrant nurses it utilizes by 10 percent within one year of the date of such prior attestation, without reducing the quality or quantity of services provided.

e.  There is not a strike or lockout in the course of a labor dispute, and the employment of such an alien is not intended or designed to influence an election for a bargaining representative for registered nurses of this facility.

f.  A copy of this attestation and supporting documentation are available for examination by interested parties. Copies of all visa petitions filed by the facility with INS for H-1A nurses will also be available for examination at this facility. The facility will make this attestation, including supporting documentation and other records available to officials of the Department of Labor upon request during any investigation upon this attestation.

CHECK APPROPRIATE ITEM:

☐   (i) Notice of this filing has been provided to the bargaining representatives of the registered nurses at this facility; or
☐   (ii) Where there is no such bargaining representative, notice of this filing has been provided to registered nurses employed at this facility through posting in conspicuous locations.

g. For nurse contractors only.
☐   (i) H-1A nurses shall be referred only to facilities which themselves have valid and current attestations.
☐   (ii) This employer maintains copies of the valid attestation (Form ETA 9029) from each facility where its H-1A nurses are working.

**U.S. Department of Justice**
Immigration and Naturalization Service

OMB #1115-0168
Petition for a Nonimmigrant Worker

## START HERE - Please Type or Print

| | FOR INS USE ONLY |

**Part 1.  Information about the employer filing this petition.**
If the employer is an individual, use the top name line.  Organizations should use the second line.

| Family Name | Given Name | Middle Initial |

Company or Organization Name

**Address** - Attn:

| Street Number and Name | | Apt # |
| City | State or Province | |
| Country | | ZIP/Postal Code |

IRS Tax #

FOR INS USE ONLY

Returned

Receipt

Resubmitted

Reloc Sent

Reloc Rec'd

**Part 2.  Information about this Petition.**
(See instructions to determine the fee).

1. **Requested Nonimmigrant Classification:**
(write classification symbol at right) _____

2. **Basis for Classification** (check one)
   a. ☐  New employment
   b. ☐  Continuation of previously approved employment without change
   c. ☐  Change in previously approved employment
   d. ☐  New concurrent employment

3. **Prior petition.** If you checked other than "New Employment" in item 2. (above) give the most recent prior petition number for the worker(s): _____

4. **Requested Action**:  (check one)
   a. ☐  Notify the office in Part 4 so the person(s) can obtain a visa or be admitted (NOTE: a petition is not required for an E-1, E-2, or R visa).
   b. ☐  Change the person(s) status and extend their stay since they are all now in the U.S. in another status (see instructions for limitations). This is available only where you check "New Employment" in item 2, above.
   c. ☐  Extend or amend the stay of the person(s) since they now hold this status.

5. **Total number of workers in petition:** _____

(See instructions for where more than one worker can be included.)

Interviewed
☐  Petitioner
☐  Beneficiary

Class: _____
# of Workers: _____
Priority Number: _____
Validity Dates:  From _____
                        To _____

☐ **Classification Approved**
   ☐  Consulate/POE/PFI Notified

   At: _____
   ☐  Extension Granted
   ☐  COS/Extension granted

**Partial Approval (explain)**

**Action Block**

**Part 3.  Information about the person(s) you are filing for.**
Complete the blocks below. Use the continuation sheet to name each person included in this petition.

If an entertainment group, give their group name.

| Family Name | Given Name | Middle Initial |
| Date of Birth (Month/Day/Year) | Country of Birth | |
| Social Security # | A # | |

If in the United States, complete the following:

| Date of Arrival (Month/Day/Year) | I-94 # | |
| Current Nonimmigrant Status | Expires (Month/Day/Year) | |

**To Be Completed by Attorney or Representative, if any**
☐  Fill in box if G-28 is attached to represent the applicant

VOLAG#

ATTY State License #

Form I-129 (Rev. 12/11/91 ) N                  *Continued on back.*

## Part 4. Processing Information.

a.  If the person named in Part 3 is outside the U.S. or a requested extension of stay or change of status cannot be granted, give the U.S. consulate or inspection facility you want notified if this petition is approved.

Type of Office (check one):  ☐ Consulate                    ☐ Pre-flight inspection        ☐ Port of Entry

Office Address (City)                                                            U.S. State or Foreign Country

Person's Foreign Address

b.  Does each person in this petition have a valid passport?
    ☐ Not required to have passport        ☐ No - explain on separate paper  ☐ Yes

c.  Are you filing any other petitions with this one?                  ☐ No        ☐ Yes - How many? _____

d.  Are applications for replacement/Initial I-94's being filed with this petition?  ☐ No   ☐ Yes - How many? _____

e.  Are applications by dependents being filed with this petition?     ☐ No        ☐ Yes - How many? _____

f.  Is any person in this petition in exclusion or deportation proceedings?  ☐ No   ☐ Yes - explain on separate paper

g.  Have you ever filed an immigrant petition for any person in this petition?  ☐ No  ☐ Yes - explain on separate paper

h.  If you indicated you were filing a new petition in Part 2, within the past 7 years has any person in this petition:

    1)  ever been given the classification you are now requesting?    ☐ No        ☐ Yes - explain on separate paper

    2)  ever been denied the classification you are now requesting?   ☐ No        ☐ Yes - explain on separate paper

i.  If you are filing for an entertainment group, has any person in this petition not been with the group for at least 1 year?
                                                                        ☐ No        ☐ Yes - explain on separate paper

## Part 5.   Basic Information about the proposed employment and employer.
Attach the supplement relating to the classification you are requesting.

| Job Title | Nontechnical Description of Job |
|---|---|

Address where the person(s) will work
if different from the address in Part 1.

| Is this a full-time position? | | Wages per week or per year |
|---|---|---|
| ☐ No - Hours per week | ☐ Yes | |

| Other Compensation (Explain) | Value per week or per year | Dates of Intended employment From:            To: |
|---|---|---|

Type of Petitioner - check one: ☐ U.S. citizen or permanent resident     ☐ Organization     ☐ Other - explain on separate paper

| Type of business: | Year Established: |
|---|---|

| Current Number of Employees | Gross Annual Income | Net Annual Income |
|---|---|---|

## Part 6.   Signature.
*Read the information on penalties in the instructions before completing this section.*

I certify, under penalty of perjury under the laws of the United States of America, that this petition, and the evidence submitted with it, is all true and correct. If filing this on behalf of an organization, I certify that I am empowered to do so by that organization. If this petition is to extend a prior petition, I certify that the proposed employment is under the same terms and conditions as in the prior approved petition. I authorize the release of any information from my records, or from the petitioning organization's records, which the Immigration and Naturalization Service needs to determine eligibility for the benefit being sought.

| Signature and title | Print Name | Date |
|---|---|---|

**Please Note:** If you do not completely fill out this form and the required supplement, or fail to submit required documents listed in the instructions, then the person(s) filed for may not be found eligible for the requested benefit, and this petition may be denied.

## Part 7.   Signature of person preparing form if other than above.

I declare that I prepared this petition at the request of the above person and it is based on all information of which I have any knowledge.

| Signature | Print Name | Date | |
|---|---|---|---|

Firm Name
and Address

OMB #1115-0168

**U.S. Department of Justice**
Immigration and Naturalization Service

**E Classifications**
Supplement to Form I-129

Name of person or organization filing petition:

Name of person you are filing for:

Classification sought (check one):
☐ E-1  Treaty trader          ☐ E-2  Treaty investor

Name of country signatory to treaty with U.S.

**Section 1.    Information about the Employer Outside the U.S. (if any)**

Name

Address

Alien's Position - Title, duties and number of years employed

Principle Product, merchandise or service

Total Number of Employees

**Section 2.    Additional Information about the U.S. Employer.**

The U.S. company is, to the company outside the U.S. (check one)
☐ Parent          ☐ Branch          ☐ Subsidiary          ☐ Affiliate          ☐ Joint Venture

Date and Place of Incorporation or establishment in the U.S.

**Nationality of Ownership** (Individual or Corporate)

| Name | Nationality | Immigration Status | % Ownership |
|------|-------------|--------------------|-------------|
|      |             |                    |             |
|      |             |                    |             |
|      |             |                    |             |
|      |             |                    |             |
|      |             |                    |             |
|      |             |                    |             |

| Assets | Net Worth | Total Annual Income |
|--------|-----------|---------------------|

| **Staff in the U.S.** | Executive/Manager | Specialized Qualifications or Knowledge |
|-----------------------|-------------------|------------------------------------------|

Nationals of Treaty Country in E or L Status

Total number of
employees in the U.S.

Total number of employees the alien would supervise; or describe the nature of the specialized skills to the U.S. company.

**Section 3.    Complete if filing for an E-1 Treaty Trader**

Total Annual Gross Trade/Business of the U.S. company          For Year Ending
$

Percent of total gross trade which is between the U.S. and the country of which the treaty trader organization is a national.

**Section 4.    Complete if filing for an E-2 Treaty Investor**

| Total Investment: | Cash | Equipment | Other |
|-------------------|------|-----------|-------|
|                   | $    | $         | $     |
|                   | Inventory | Premises | Total |
|                   | $    | $         | $     |

Form I-129 Supplement E/L (12/11/91) N

**Sample Document – Not To Be Used When Filing.**

OMB #1115-0168

**U.S. Department of Justice**
Immigration and Naturalization Service

**H Classifications**
Supplement to Form I-129

---

Name of person or organization filing petition:       Name of person or total number of workers or trainees you are filing for:

List the alien's and any dependent family members; prior periods of stay in H classification in the U.S. for the last six years. Be sure to list only those periods in which the alien and/or family members were actually in the U.S. in an H classification. If more space is needed, attach an additional sheet.

---

Classification sought (check one):

☐ H-1A   Registered Professional nurse

☐ H-1B1   Specialty occupation

☐ H-1B2   Exceptional services relating to a cooperative research and development project administered by the U.S. Department of Defense

☐ H-1B3   Artist, entertainer or fashion model of national or international acclaim

☐ H-1B4   Artist or entertainer in unique or traditional art form

☐ H-1B5   Athlete

☐ H-1BS   Essential Support Personnel for H-1B entertainer or athlete

☐ H-2A   Agricultural worker

☐ H-2B   Nonagricultural worker

☐ H-3   Trainee

☐ H-3   Special education exchange visitor program

---

## Section 1. Complete this section if filing for H-1A or H-1B classification.

Describe the proposed duties

Alien's present occupation and summary or prior experience

*Statement for H-1B speciality occupations only:*

By filing this petition, I agree to the terms of the labor condition application for the duration of the alien's authorized period of stay for H-1B employment

Petitioner's Signature       Date

*Statement for H-1B specialty occupations and DOD projects:*

As an authorized official of the employer, I certify that the employer will be liable for the reasonable costs of return transportation of the alien abroad if the alien is dismissed from employment by the employer before the end of the period of authorized stay.

Signature of authorized official of employer       Date

*Statement for H-1B DOD projects only:*

I certify that the alien will be working on a cooperative research and development project or a coproduction project under a reciprocal Government-to Government agreement administered by the Department of Defense.

DOD project manager's signature       Date

---

## Section 2. Complete this section if filing for H-2A or H-2B classification.

Employment is: (check one)
☐ Seasonal
☐ Peakload
☐ Intermittent
☐ One-time occurrence

Temporary need is: (check one)
☐ Unpredictable
☐ Periodic
☐ Recurrent annually

Explain your temporary need for the alien's services (attach a separate paper if additional space is needed).

---

Form 1-129 Supplement H (12/11/91) N       *Continued on back.*

## Section 3. Complete this section If filing for H-2A classification.

The petitioner and each employer consent to allow government access to the site where the labor is being performed for the purpose of determining compliance with H-2A requirements. The petitioner further agrees to notify the Service in the manner and within the time frame specified if an H-2A worker absconds or if the authorized employment ends more than five days before the relating certification document expires, and pay liquidated damages of ten dollars for each instance where it cannot demonstrate compliance with this notification requirement. The petitioner also agrees to pay liquidated damages of two hundred dollars for each instance where it cannot be demonstrated that the H-2A worker either departed the United States or obtained authorized status during the period of admission or within five days of early termination, whichever comes first.

The petitioner must execute Part A. If the petitioner is the employer's agent, the employer must execute Part B. If there are joint employers, they must each execute Pat. C.

### Part A.  Petitioner:

By filing this petition, I agree to the conditions of H-2A employment, and agree to the notice requirements and limited liabilities defined in 8 CFR 214.2 (h) (3) (vi).

Petitioner's signature                                          Date

### Part B.  Employer who is not petitioner:

I certify that I have authorized the party filing this petition to act as my agent in this regard. I assume full responsibility for all representations made by this agent on my behalf, and agree to the conditions of H-2A eligibility.

Employer's signature                                          Date

### Part C.  Joint Employers:

I agree to the conditions of H-2A eligibility.

Joint employer's signature(s)                                 Date

Joint employer's signature(s)                                 Date

Joint employer's signature(s)                                 Date

Joint employer's signature(s)                                 Date

Joint employer's signature(s)                                 Date

## Section 4. Complete this section if filing for H-3 classification.

If you answer "yes" to any of the following questions, attach a full explanation.

| | | | |
|---|---|---|---|
| a. | Is the training you intend to provide, or similar training, available in the alien's country? | ☐ No | ☐ Yes |
| b. | Will the training benefit the alien in pursuing a career abroad? | ☐ No | ☐ Yes |
| c. | Does the training involve productive employment incidental to training? | ☐ No | ☐ Yes |
| d. | Does the alien already have skills related to the training? | ☐ No | ☐ Yes |
| e. | Is this training an effort to overcome a labor shortage? | ☐ No | ☐ Yes |
| f. | Do you intend to employ this person abroad at the end of this training, explain why you wish to incur the cost of providing this training, and your expected return from this training. | | |

OMB #1115-0168

**U.S. Department of Justice**
Immigration and Naturalization Service

**L Classifications**
Supplement to Form I-129

Name of person or organization filing petition:

Name of person you are filing for:

This petition is (check one):     ☐ An individual petition     ☐ A blanket petition

**Section 1.    Complete this section if filing an individual petition.**

Classification sought (check one):     ☐ L-1A manager or executive     ☐ L-1B specialized knowledge

List the alien's, and any dependent family members' prior periods of stay in an L classification in the U.S. for the last seven years.  Be sure to list only those periods in which the alien and/or family members were actually in the U.S. in an L classification.

Name and address of employer abroad

Dates of alien's employment with this employer. Explain any interruptions in employment.

Description of the alien's duties for the past 3 years.

Description of alien's propsed duties in the U.S.

Summarize the alien's education and work experience.

The U.S. company is, to the company abroad: (check one)
☐ Parent          ☐ Branch          ☐ Subsidiary          ☐ Affiliate          ☐ Joint Venture
Describe the stock ownership and managerial control of each company.

Do the companies currently have the same qualifying relationship as they did during the one-year period of the alien's employment with the company abroad?     ☐ Yes          ☐ No (attach explanation)

Is the alien coming to the U.S. to  open a new office?
☐ Yes (explain in detail on separate paper)          ☐ No

**Section 2.    Complete this section if filing a Blanket Petition.**

List all U.S. and foreign parent, branches, subsidiaries and affiliates included in this petition. (Attach a separate paper if additional space is needed.)
Name and Address                                                                                          Relationship

Explain in detail on separate paper.

Form I-129 Supplement E/L (12/11/91) N

**U.S. Department of Justice**
Immigration and Naturalization Service

OMB #1115-0168
**O and P Classifications**
Supplement to Form I-129

Name of person or organization filing petition:

Name of person or group or total number of workers you are filing for:

Classification sought (check one):

☐ O-1 Alien of extraordinary ability in sciences, art, eduction, or business.

☐ P-2 Artist or entertainer for reciprocal exchange program

☐ P-2S Essential Support Personnel for P-2

Explain the nature of the event

Describe the duties to be performed

If filing for O-2 or P support alien, dates of the alien's prior experience with the O-1 or P alien.

Have you obtained the required written consultations(s)?     ☐ Yes - attached          ☐ No - Copy of request attached
If not, give the following information about the organizations(s) to which you have sent a duplicate of this petition.

**O-1 Extraordinary ability**

| Name of recognized peer group | Phone # |
|---|---|
| Address | Date sent |

**O-1 Extraordinary achievement in motion pictures or television**

| Name of labor organization | Phone # |
|---|---|
| Address | Date sent |
| Name of management organization | Phone # |
| Address | Date sent |

**O-2 or P alien**

| Name of labor organization · | Phone # |
|---|---|
| Address | Date sent |

Form I-129 Supplement O/P/Q/R (12/11/91) N

**U.S. Department of Justice**
Immigration and Naturalization Service

OMB #1115-0168
**Q and R Classifications**
Supplement to Form I-129

Name of person or organization filing petition:

Name of person you are filing for:

**Section 1.**    **Complete this section if you are filing for a Q international cultural exchange alien.**

I hereby certify that the participant(s) in this international cultural exchange program:
- is at least 18 years of age,
- has the ability to communicate effectively about the cultural attributes of his or her country of nationality to the American public, and
- has not previously been in the United States as a Q nonimmigrant unless he/she has resided and been physically present outside the U.S. for the immediate prior year.

I also certify that the same wages and working conditions are accorded the particpants as are provided to similarly employed U.S. workers.

Petitioner's signature                          Date

**Section 2.**    **Complete this section if you are filing for an R religious worker.**

List the alien's, and any dependent family members, prior periods of stay in R classification in the U.S. for the last six years, Be sure to list only those periods in which the alien and/or family members were actually in the U.S. in an R classification.

Describe the alien's proposed duties in the U.S.

Describe the alien's qualifications for the vocation or occupation

Description of the relationship between the U.S. religious organization and the organization abroad of which the alien was a member.

Form I-129 Supplement O/P/Q/R (12/11/91) N

# Supplement-1

**Attach to Form I-129 when more than one person is included in the petition.** *(List each person separately. Do not include the person you named on the form).*

| Family Name | Given Name | Middle Initial | Date of Birth (month/day/year) |
|---|---|---|---|
| Country of Birth | Social Security No. | | A# |

| IF IN THE U.S. | Date of Arrival (month/day/year) | | I-94# |
|---|---|---|---|
| | Current Nonimmigrant Status: | | Expires on (month/day/year) |

| Country where passport issued | Expiration Date (month/day/year) | Date Started with group |
|---|---|---|

| Family Name | Given Name | Middle Initial | Date of Birth (month/day/year) |
|---|---|---|---|
| Country of Birth | Social Security No. | | A# |

| IF IN THE U.S. | Date of Arrival (month/day/year) | | I-94# |
|---|---|---|---|
| | Current Nonimmigrant Status: | | Expires on (month/day/year) |

| Country where passport issued | Expiration Date (month/day/year) | Date Started with group |
|---|---|---|

| Family Name | Given Name | Middle Initial | Date of Birth (month/day/year) |
|---|---|---|---|
| Country of Birth | Social Security No. | | A# |

| IF IN THE U.S. | Date of Arrival (month/day/year) | | I-94# |
|---|---|---|---|
| | Current Nonimmigrant Status: | | Expires on (month/day/year) |

| Country where passport issued | Expiration Date (month/day/year) | Date Started with group |
|---|---|---|

| Family Name | Given Name | Middle Initial | Date of Birth (month/day/year) |
|---|---|---|---|
| Country of Birth | Social Security No. | | A# |

| IF IN THE U.S. | Date of Arrival (month/day/year) | | I-94# |
|---|---|---|---|
| | Current Nonimmigrant Status: | | Expires on (month/day/year) |

| Country where passport issued | Expiration Date (month/day/year) | Date Started with group |
|---|---|---|

| Family Name | Given Name | Middle Initial | Date of Birth (month/day/year) |
|---|---|---|---|
| Country of Birth | Social Security No. | | A# |

| IF IN THE U.S. | Date of Arrival (month/day/year) | | I-94# |
|---|---|---|---|
| | Current Nonimmigrant Status: | | Expires on (month/day/year) |

| Country where passport issued | Expiration Date (month/day/year) | Date Started with group |
|---|---|---|

# Labor Condition Application for H-1B Nonimmigrants

## U.S. Department of Labor
Employment and Training Administration
U.S. Employment Service

1. Full Legal Name of Employer

2. Federal Employer I.D. Number

3. Telephone No.

   (     )

4. FAX No.

   (     )

5. Employer's Address
   (No., Street, City, State, and ZIP Code)

   OMB Approval No.: 1205-0310

6. Address Where Documentation Is Kept (If different than item 5)

7. OCCUPATIONAL INFORMATION (Use Attachment if additional space is needed)

| (a) Three-Digit Occupational Groups Code | (b) Job Title (Check (✔) if position is part-time) | (c) No. of Aliens | (d) Rate of Pay | (e) Period of Employment From   To | (f) Location(s) Where Alien(s) will work (see instructions) |
|---|---|---|---|---|---|
| _____ | _____ □ _____ | _____ | _____ | _____ _____ | _____ |
| _____ | _____ □ _____ | _____ | _____ | _____ _____ | _____ |
| _____ | _____ □ _____ | _____ | _____ | _____ _____ | _____ |
| _____ | _____ □ _____ | _____ | _____ | _____ _____ | _____ |

8. EMPLOYER LABOR CONDITION STATEMENTS (Employers are required to develop and maintain documentation supporting each labor condition statement except 8(c). Employers are further required to make available for public examination a copy of the labor condition application and supporting documentation within one (1) working day after the date on which the application is filed with DOL. Check each box to indicate that you will comply with each statement.)

□ (a)   H-1B nonimmigrants and other similarly employed workers will be paid the actual wage for the occupation at the place of employment or the prevailing wage level for the occupation in the area of employment, whichever is higher.

□ (b)   The employment of H-1B nonimmigrant workers will not adversely affect the working conditions of workers similarly employed in the area of intended employment.

□ (c)   On the date this application is signed and submitted, there is not a strike, lockout or work stoppage in the course of a labor dispute in the occupations at the place of employment.

□ (d)   As of this date, notice of this application has been provided to workers employed in the occupations in which H-1B workers will be employed: (check appropriate box)

   □ (i)    Notice of this filing has been provided to the bargaining representatives of workers in the occupations in which H-1B workers will be employed; or

   □ (ii)   There is no such bargaining representative; therefore, a notice of this filing has been posted in a conspicuous place where H-1B nonimmigrant workers will be employed.

9. DECLARATION OF EMPLOYER: Pursuant to 28 U.S.C. 1746, I declare under penalty of perjury that the information provided on this form is true and correct. In addition, I declare that I will comply with the Department of Labor regulations governing this program and, in particular, that I will make this application, supporting documentation, and other records, files and documents available to officials of the Department of Labor, upon such official's request, during any investigation under this application or the Immigration and Nationality Act.

Name and Title of Hiring or Other Designated Official          Signature                          Date

FOR U.S. GOVERNMENT AGENCY USE ONLY:  By virtue of my signature below, I acknowledge that this application is hereby approved and will be valid from _____ through_____

Signature and Title of Authorized DOL Official          ETA Case No.

Subsequent DOL Action:        Suspended_____ (date)  Invalidated_____ (date)  Withdrawn_____ (date)

The Department of Labor is not the guarantor of the accuracy, truthfulness or adequacy of an approved labor condition application.

Public reporting burden for this application of information is estimated to average 1 hour per response, including the time for reviewing instructions, searching existing data sources, gathering and maintaining the data needed, and completing and reviewing the collection of information. Send comments regarding this burden or any other aspect of this collection of information, including suggestions for reducing this burden, to the Office of Information Management, Department of Labor, Room N1301, 200 Constitution Avenue, N.W., Washington D.C. 20210; and to the Office of Management and Budget, Paperwork Reduction Project (1205-0310). Washington, D.C.  20503.

ETA 9035 (Oct. 1991)

**SAMPLE DOCUMENT – NOT TO BE USED WHEN FILING.**

Post Symbol:                          Department of State
L N D                        BIOGRAPHIC DATA FOR VISA PURPOSES

Complete this form for your entire family (yourself, spouse and unmarried children under 21 years of age).

1. NAME    (Family name)                    (First name)                    (Middle names)

OTHER NAMES, ALIASES (If married woman, maiden name and surname of any previous spouses)

2. PLACE OF BIRTH (City)                    (State or Province)              (Country)

DATE OF BIRTH   (Month) (Day) (Year)                    Sex ☐ Male        ☐ Female

PRESENT NATIONALITY                         PAST NATIONALITY

3. NAME OF FATHER                           4. MAIDEN NAME OF MOTHER

5. FATHER'S BIRTHPLACE (City)               (State or Province)             (Country)

6. MOTHER'S BIRTHPLACE (City)               (State or province)             (Country)

7. NAME OF SPOUSE (Maiden/family name)      (First name)                    (Middle name)

8. SPOUSE'S BIRTHPLACE (City)               (State or province)             (Country)

9. SPOUSE'S BIRTHDATE (Month) (Day) (Year) | 10. WILL SPOUSE IMMIGRATE WITH YOU?    ☐ Yes  ☐ No

11. NAME OF SPOUSE'S FATHER                 12. NAME OF SPOUSE'S MOTHER

13. BIRTHPLACE OF    (City)    SPOUSE'S FATHER    (State or province)    (Country)

14. BIRTHPLACE OF    (City)    SPOUSE'S MOTHER    (State or province)    (Country)

15. LIST UNMARRIED CHILDREN UNDER 21 YEARS. NOT U.S. CITIZENS WHO WILL ACCOMPANY YOU.

| NAME OF CHILD | PLACE OF BIRTH (City) | (State or province)   (Country) | SEX | BIRTHDATE |
|---|---|---|---|---|
| | | | | |
| | | | | |
| | | | | |
| | | | | |

16. IF YOU OR YOUR SPOUSE ARE NOW, OR HAVE BEEN IN THE UNITED STATES, STATE:

☐ APPLICANT        WHERE WAS VISA OBTAINED        WHEN WAS VISA GRANTED
☐ SPOUSE

CHECK TYPE OF VISA USED FOR SUCH ENTRY:
☐ Immigrant
☐ Visitor
☐ Exchange Visitor
☐ Other Nonimmigrant (Specify)

17. IF YOU OR YOUR SPOUSE WERE PREVIOUSLY IN THE UNITED STATES, STATE: ☐ Applicant ☐ Spouse

DATE ADMITTED                DATE DEPARTED                REASON FOR DEPARTURE

OF-179                                                                        /over

**SAMPLE DOCUMENT – NOT TO BE USED WHEN FILING.**

FORM OF-179   AUG 86                                                                 Page 2

18. Latest or Last Address in the United Kingdom.


19.   List Below in Date Order All Places Where You, Your Spouse and Unmarried Children Named on the Other Side Have Lived Since Reaching the Age of Sixteen.   You need not list those places where you have lived less than six months.

| First name of Family Member | Town, City, Province, Country | Occupation | From Month   Year | To Month   Year |
|---|---|---|---|---|
|  |  |  |  |  |
|  |  |  |  |  |
|  |  |  |  |  |
|  |  |  |  |  |
|  |  |  |  |  |
|  |  |  |  |  |
|  |  |  |  |  |
|  |  |  |  |  |
|  |  |  |  |  |
|  |  |  |  |  |

20.   On separate sheet, give following information on each family member who resided in:

| | | |
|---|---|---|
| ARGENTINA | - | Cedula number; date, place of issue and complete address in Argentina. |
| BERMUDA | - | Date of arrival in Bermuda, occupation and places of employment in Bermuda. |
| CAMEROON | - | Place of employment there. |
| HONDURAS | - | Passport number and date of insuance. |
| JERUSALEM | - | Israeli Identity Card number or passport number if non-Israeli; family and former names used in Jerusalem, family and former names used on arrival, date of arrival and exact address in Jerusalem. |
| JAPAN | - | Registered domicile in Japan and, if Japanese, Chinese or Korean, give name in Chinese (Kanji characters). |
| MALAYSIA | - | National Registration Identity Card number and, if Chinese, full name and parents names and parents' names in Chinese characters. |
| NETHERLANDS | | Full street addresses in the Netherlands. |
| SINGAPORE | - | Singapore Identity card number for Singapore citizens and permanent residents. If Chinese, full name and names of spouse and parents in Chinese characters. |

21. Membership or affiliation in organizations in each country named in item 19:
    Cultural, Social, Labor or Political

| ORGANIZATION | FROM | TO |
|---|---|---|
|  |  |  |
|  |  |  |
|  |  |  |
|  |  |  |

I certify that all information given is complete and correct.


DATE              SIGNATURE AND PRESENT ADDRESS                        PHONE NO.

NOTE: If space above is insufficient to answer any questions properly, the additional information may be printed on a separate sheet of paper and attached to this form.

**U.S. Department of Justice**

Immigration and Naturalization Service

OMB #1115-0005

Application for Travel Document

## INSTRUCTIONS

**Purpose of This Form.**
This form is used to apply for an INS travel document, reentry permit, refugee travel document, or advance parole document. Each applicant must file a separate application.

**Who May File.**
*Reentry permit.* If you are in the United States as a permanent resident or conditional resident, you may apply for a reentry permit. A reentry permit allows a permanent resident or conditional resident to apply for admission to the U.S. during the permit's validity without having to obtain a returning resident visa from an American Consulate. A reentry permit is not required for return from a trip of less than one year's duration.

Possession of a reentry permit does not relieve you of any of the requirements of the immigration laws except the necessity to obtain a visa from an American consulate. For the purpose of later naturalization, absence from the United States for 1 year or more will normally break the continuity of any required period of continuous residence in the United States and you will need to file an application to preserve residence for naturalization purposes. Inquire at your local INS office for further information.

*Refugee travel document.* If you are in the United States in a valid refugee or asylee status, or obtained permanent residence as a direct result of refugee or asylee status in the U.S. you may apply for a refugee travel document. A refugee travel document is a document issued by the Service in implementation of Article 28 of the U.N. Convention of July 28, 1951. You must have a refugee travel document to return to the United States after temporary travel abroad unless you are traveling to Canada to apply for a U.S. immigrant visa (see advance parole document below).

*Advance parole document. If you are outside the United States* and must travel to the United States temporarily for emergent business or personal reasons, you may apply for an advance parole document to be paroled into the U.S. on humanitarian grounds if you cannot obtain the necessary visa and any required waiver of excludability. Parole cannot be used to circumvent normal visa issuing procedures, and is not a means to bypass delays in visa issuance. Parole is an extraordinary measure, sparingly used to bring an otherwise inadmissible alien into the U.S. for a temporary period of time due to a very compelling emergency.

Another person who is in the U.S. may file this application in your behalf. He or she should complete Part 1 with Information about himself or herself.

*If you are in the United States* you may apply for an Advance Parole document if you:
- have an adjustment of status application pending which is only being held in abeyance because a visa number is not immediately available and you seek to travel abroad for bona fide business or emergent personal reasons;
- have an adjustment of status application pending for any other reason and you seek to travel abroad for emergent personal or bona fide business reasons;
- hold refugee or asylum status and intend to depart temporarily to apply for a U.S. immigrant visa in Canada; or
- seek to travel abroad temporarily for emergent personal or bona fide business reasons.

An advance parole document is issued solely to authorize the temporary parole of an individual into the United States. It may be accepted by a transportation company in lieu of a visa as authorization for the holder to travel to the United States. It is not issued to serve in lieu of any required passport.

**Additional Processing Criteria.**
*Reentry Permit or Refugee Travel Document.* A reentry permit or refugee travel document may not be issued to you if:

- you have already been issued such a document and it is still valid, unless the prior document has been returned to the Service or you can demonstrate it was lost; or
- due to national security, diplomatic or public safety reasons the government has published a notice in the Federal Register precluding issuance of such a document for travel to the area you intend to go to.

In addition, a reentry permit may not be issued if you have been a permanent resident for more than 5 years and have been outside the U.S. for more than 4 of the last 5 years, unless you are a crewman regularly serving abroad on an aircraft or vessel of American registry and the travel is in connection with your duties as a crewman, or your travel is on the orders of the United States government, other than exclusion or deportation order.)

*Advance Parole.* An advance parole may not be issued to a person who is in deportation proceedings, is the beneficiary of a private bill, or is subject to the 2 year foreign residence requirement due to having held J-1 nonimmigrant status.

**General Filing Instructions.**
Please answer all questions by typing or clearly printing in black ink. Indicate that an item is not applicable with "N/A". If an answer is "none," please so state. If you need extra space to answer any item, attach a sheet of paper with your name and your A#, if any, and indicate the number of the item. Every application must be properly signed and filed with the correct fee. You must file your application with the required Initial Evidence. If you are under 14 years of age, your parent or guardian may sign the application in your behalf.

A reentry permit or refugee travel document may be sent to a U.S. Consulate or INS office overseas for you to pick up if you request it when you file your application. However, you must be in the U.S. when you file the application.

**Initial Evidence.**
*Evidence of eligibility. If you are a permanent resident or conditional resident,* you must attach:
- a copy of your alien registration receipt card; or
- if you have not yet received your alien registration receipt card, a copy of the biographic page and the page indicating initial admission as a permanent resident of your passport, or other evidence that you are a permanent resident; or
- a copy of the approval notice of a separate application for replacement of your alien registration receipt card or temporary evidence of permanent resident status.

*If you are a refugee or asylee applying for a refugee travel document*, you must attach a copy of the document issued to you by the Service showing your refugee or asylee status and indicating the expiration of such status.

*If you are in the U.S. and are applying for an advance parole document for yourself* you must attach a copy of any document for yourself issued by the Service showing any present status in the United States, and an explanation or other evidence demonstrating the circumstances that warrant issuance of advance parole. If you are basing your eligibility for advance parole on your separate application for adjustment of status, you must also attach a copy of the filing receipt for that application. If you are traveling to Canada to apply for an immigrant visa, you must also attach a copy of the consular appointment.

*If the person to be paroled is outside the U.S.,* you must also submit:
- a statement of how, and by whom, medical care, housing, transportation, and other expenses and subsistence need will be met;
- an Affidavit of Support (Form 1-134), with evidence of the sponsor's occupation and ability to provide necessary support;

Form 1-131 (Rev. 12/10/91) N

**SAMPLE DOCUMENT – NOT TO BE USED WHEN FILING.**

- a statement of why a U.S. visa cannot be obtained, including when and where attempts were made to obtain a visa;
- a statement of why a waiver of excludability cannot be obtained to allow issuance of a visa, including when and where attempts were made to obtain a waiver, and a copy of any written decision;
- a copy of any decision on an immigrant petition filed for the person, and evidence regarding any pending immigrant petition; and
- a complete description of the emergent reasons why parole should be authorized and copies of any evidence you wish considered, and indicating the length of time for which parole is requested.

*Photographs.* You must submit 2 identical natural color photographs of yourself taken within 30 days of this application. The photos must have a white background, be unmounted, printed on thin paper and be glossy and unretouched. They should show a three quarter frontal profile showing the right side of your face, with your right ear visible and with your head bare (unless you are wearing a headdress as required by a religious order of which you are a member). The photos should be no larger than 2 X 2 inches, with the distance from the top of the head to just below the chin about 1 and 1/4 inches. Lightly print your A# on the back of each photo with a pencil. (If you are applying for an advance parole and are outside the U.S., keep these photographs. You will be instructed as to where to submit them if parole is approved. If you are applying for parole for another person, the required photographs are of the person to be paroled.)

*Copies.* If these instructions state that a copy of a document may be filed with this application and you choose to send us the original, we may keep that original for our records.

### Where to File.
*Reentry Permit or Refugee Travel Document.* Mail your application to: USINS, Northern Service Center, 100 Centennial Mall North, Room B-26, Lincoln, NE 68508.

*Advance Parole.* If the person being filed for is in the United States, file the application at the INS office with jurisdiction over the area in which you live. If he or she is not in the United States, mail it to: USINS, Office of International Affairs and Parole, 425 I Street N.W., Room 1203, Washington, DC 20536.

### Effect of Travel Before the Travel Document is Issued.
Departure from the United States before a decision is made on an application for a reentry permit or refugee travel document does not affect the application. Departure from the United States or application for admission to the United States before a decision is made on an application for an advance parole document shall be deemed an abandonment of the application.

### Fee.
The fee for this application is $70.00. The fee must be submitted in the exact amount. It cannot be refunded. DO NOT MAIL CASH. All checks and money orders must be drawn on a bank or other institution located in the United States and must be payable in United States currency. The check or money order should be made payable to the Immigration and Naturalization Service, except that:
- If you live in Guam, and are filing this application in Guam, make your check or money order payable to the "Treasurer, Guam."
- If you live in the Virgin Islands, and are filing this application in the Virgin Islands, make your check or money order payable to the "Commissioner of Finance of the Virgin Islands."

Checks are accepted subject to collection. An uncollected check will render the application and any document issued invalid. A charge of $5.00 will be imposed if a check in payment of a fee is not honored by the bank on which it is drawn.

### Processing Information.
*Acceptance.* Any application that is not signed or is not accompanied by the correct fee will be rejected with a notice that the application Is deficient. You may correct the deficiency and resubmit the application. However, an application is not considered properly filed until it is accepted by the Service.

*Initial processing.* Once the application has been accepted, it will be checked for completeness, including submission of the required initial evidence. If you do not completely fill out the form, or file it without required initial evidence, you will not establish a basis for eligibility, and we may deny your application.

*Requests for more information or interview.* We may request more information or evidence or we may request that you appear at an INS office for an interview. We may also request that you submit the originals of any copy. We will return these originals when they are no longer required.

*Decision.* You will be advised of the decision on your application. If it is approved, the document will be issued.

*Invalidation.* Any travel document obtained by making a material false representation or concealment in this application will be invalid. A document will also be invalid if you are ordered excluded or deported. In addition, a refugee travel document will be invalid if the U.N. Convention of July 28, 1951, shall cease to apply or shall not apply to you as provided in Article 1C, D, E, or F of the Convention.

### Effect of Claim to Nonresident Alien Status for Federal Income Tax Purposes.
An alien who has actually established residence in the United States after having been admitted as an immigrant or after having adjusted status to that of an immigrant, and who is considering the filing of a nonresident alien tax return or the non-filing of a tax return on the ground that he/she is a nonresident alien, should consider carefully the consequences under the immigration and naturalization laws if he/she does so.

If you take such action, you may be regarded as having abandoned residence in the United States and as having lost immigrant status under the immigration and naturalization laws. As a consequence, you may be ineligible for a visa or other document for which lawful permanent resident aliens are eligible; you may be inadmissible to the United States if you seek admission as a returning resident; and you may become ineligible for naturalization on the basis of your original entry or adjustment as an immigrant.

### Penalties.
If you knowingly and willfully falsify or conceal a material fact or submit a false document with this request, we will deny the benefit you are filing for, and may deny any other immigration benefit. In addition, you will face severe penalties provided by law, and may be subject to criminal prosecution.

### Privacy Act Notice.
We ask for the information on this form, and associated evidence, to determine if you have established eligibility for the immigration benefit you are filing for. Our legal right to ask for this information is in 8 USC 1203 and 1225. We may provide this information to other government agencies. Failure to provide this information, and any requested evidence, may delay a final decision or result in denial of your request.

### Paperwork Reduction Act Notice.
We try to create forms and instructions that are accurate, can be easily understood, and which impose the least possible burden on you to provide us with information. Often this is difficult because some immigration laws are very complex. The estimated average time to complete and file this application is as follows: (1) 10 minutes to learn about the law and form; (2) 10 minutes to complete the form, and (3) 35 minutes to assemble and file the application, for a total estimated average of 55 minutes per application. If you have comments regarding the accuracy of this estimate, or suggestions for making this form simpler, you can write to both the Immigration and Naturalization Service, 425 I Street, N.W., Room 5304, Washington, D.C. 20536; and the Office of Management and Budget, Paperwork Reduction Project, OMB No. 1115-0005, Washington, D.C. 20503.

---

**SAMPLE DOCUMENT – NOT TO BE USED WHEN FILING.**

**U.S. Department of Justice**
Immigration and Naturalization Service

OMB #1115-0005
Application for Travel Document

## START HERE - Please Type or Print

## Part 1. Information about you.

| Family Name | Given Name | Middle Initial |
|---|---|---|

**Address - C/O**

| Street Number and Name | | Apt # |
|---|---|---|
| City | State or Province | |
| Country | | ZIP/Postal Code |

| Date of Birth (Month/Day/Year) | Country of Birth |
|---|---|
| Social Security # | A # |

## Part 2. Application Type (check one).

a. ☐ I am a permanent resident or conditional resident of the United States and I am applying for a Reentry Permit.

b. ☐ I now hold U.S. refugee or asylee status and I am applying for a Refugee Travel Document.

c. ☐ I am a permanent resident as a direct result of refugee or asylee status, and am applying for a Refugee Travel Document.

d. ☐ I am applying for an Advance Parole to allow me to return to the U.S. after temporary foreign travel.

e. ☐ I am outside the U.S. and am applying for an Advance Parole.

f. ☐ I am applying for an Advance Parole for another person who is outside the U.S. *Give the following information about that person:*

| Family Name | Given Name | Middle Initial |
|---|---|---|
| Date of Birth (Month/Day/Year) | Country of Birth | |

**Foreign Address - C/O**

| Street Number and Name | | Apt. # |
|---|---|---|
| City | State or Province | |
| Country | | ZIP/Postal Code |

## Part 3. Processing Information.

| Date of Intended departure (Month/Day/Year) | Expected length of trip. |
|---|---|

Are you, or any person included in this application, now in exclusion or deportation proceedings?
☐ No  ☐ Yes, at (give office name) _____

*If applying for an Advance Parole Document, skip to Part 7.*

Have you ever before been issued a Reentry Permit or Refugee Travel Document?
☐ No        ☐ Yes (give the following for the last document issued to you)

| Date Issued | Disposition (attached, lost, etc.) |
|---|---|

### FOR INS USE ONLY

| Returned | Receipt |
|---|---|
| _____ | |
| _____ | |
| Resubmitted | |
| _____ | |
| _____ | |
| Reloc Sent | |
| _____ | |
| _____ | |
| Reloc Rec'd | |
| _____ | |
| _____ | |

☐ Applicant Interviewed on
_____

**Document Issued**
☐ Reentry Permit
☐ Refugee Travel Document
☐ Single Advance Parole
☐ Multiple Advance Parole
Validity to _____

**If Reentry Permit or Refugee Travel Document**
☐ Mail to Address in Part 2
☐ Mail to American Consulate
☐ Mail to INS overseas office
AT

**Remarks:**
☐ Document Hand Delivered
On _____ By

**Action Block**

**To Be Completed by *Attorney* or *Representative*, if any**
☐ Fill in box if G-28 is attached to represent the applicant

VOLAG# 

ATTY State License # 

Form I-131 (Rev. 12/10/91 ) N          ***Continued on back.***

**SAMPLE DOCUMENT – NOT TO BE USED WHEN FILING.**

## Part 3. Processing Information. (continued)

Where do you want this travel document sent? (check one)

a. ☐ Address in Part 2, above
b. ☐ American Consulate at (give City and Country, below)
c. ☐ INS overseas office at (give City and Country, below)
   City                                        Country

If you checked b. or c., above, give your overseas address:

## Part 4. Information about the Proposed Travel.

| Purpose of trip. *If you need more room, continue on a separate sheet of paper.* | List the countries you intend to visit. |
|---|---|
| | |

## Part 5. Complete only if applying for a Reentry Permit.

Since becoming a Permanent Resident (or during the past five years, whichever is less) how much total time have you spent outside the United States?

☐ less than 6 months   ☐ 2 to 3 years
☐ 6 months to 1 year   ☐ 3 to 4 years
☐ 1 to 2 years         ☐ more than 4 years

Since you became a Permanent Resident, have you ever filed a federal income tax return as a nonresident, or failed to file a federal return because you considered yourself to be a nonresident? (if yes, give details on a separate sheet of paper).   ☐ Yes   ☐ No

## Part 6. Complete only if applying for a Refugee Travel Document.

Country from which you are a refugee or asylee:

If you answer yes to any of the following questions, explain on a separate sheet of paper.

Do you plan to travel to tho above-named country?   ☐ Yes   ☐ No

Since you were accorded Refugee/Asylee status, have you ever: returned to the above-named country; applied for an/or obtained a national passport, passport renewal, or entry permit into this country; or applied for an/or received any benefit from such country (for example, health insurance benefits)?   ☐ Yes   ☐ No

Since being accorded Refugee/Asylee status, have you, by any legal procedure or voluntary act, re-acquired the nationality of the above-named country, acquired a new nationality, or been granted refugee or asylee status in any other country?   ☐ Yes   ☐ No

## Part 7. Complete only if applying for an Advance Parole.

*On a separate sheet of paper, please explain how you qualify for an Advance Parole and what circumstances warrant issuance of Advance Parole. Include copies of any documents you wish considered. (See instructions.)*

For how may trips do you intend to use this document?   ☐ 1 trip   ☐ More than 1 trip
*If outside the U. S., at right give the U S Consulate or INS office you wish notified if this application is approved.*

## Part 8. Signature.
*Read the information on penalties in the instructions before completing this section. You must file this application while in the United States if filing for reentry permit or refugee travel document.*

I certify under penalty of perjury under the laws of the United States of America that this petition, and the evidence submitted with it, is all true and correct. I authorize the release of any information from my records which the Immigration and Naturalization Service needs to determine eligibility for the benefit I am seeking.

Signature                          Date                    Daytime Telephone #
                                                           (        )

*Please Note: If you do not completely fill out this form, or fail to submit required documents listed in the instructions, you may not be found eligible for the requested document and this application will have to be denied.*

## Part 9. Signature of person preparing form if other than above. (sign below)

I declare that I prepared this application at the request of the above person and it is based on all information of which I have knowledge.

Signature                          Print Your Name          Date

Firm Name                                                   Daytime Telephone #
and Address                                                 (        )

*U.S. GPO:1992-312-328/51145

**U.S. Department of Justice**
Immigration and Naturalization Service

OMB #1115-0117
Petition for Amerasian, Widow(er), or Special Immigrant

## INSTRUCTIONS

### Purpose of This Form.

This petition is used to classify an alien as an Amerasian, Widow(er), or as a Special Immigrant (Juvenile, Religious Worker, based on employment with the Panama Canal Company, Canal Zone Government or U.S. government in the Canal Zone, Physician, International Organization Employee or family member).

### Who May File; Initial Evidence Requirements.

If these instructions state that a copy of a document may be filed with this petition, and you choose to send us the original, we may keep that original for our records. Any foreign language document must be accompanied by an English translation certified by the translator that he/she is competent to translate from the foreign language into English and that the translation is accurate.

*Amerasian.* Any person who is 18 or older, an emancipated minor, or a U.S. corporation may file this petition for an alien who was born in Korea, Vietnam, Laos, Kampuchea, or Thailand after December 31, 1950, and before October 22, 1982, and was fathered by a U.S. citizen.

The petition must be filed with:
- copies of evidence the person this petition is for was born in one of the above countries between those dates. If he/she was born in Vietnam, you must also submit a copy of his/her Vietnamese I.D. card, or an affidavit explaining why it is not available.
- copies of evidence establishing the parentage of the person, and of evidence establishing that the biological father was a U.S. citizen. Examples of documents that may be submitted are birth or baptismal records or other religious documents; local civil records; an affidavit, correspondence or evidence of financial support from the father; photographs of the father (especially with the child); or, absent other documents, affidavits from knowledgeable witnesses which detail the parentage of the child and how they know such facts.
- a photograph of the person;
- if the person is married, submit a copy of the marriage certificate, and proof of the termination of any prior marriages;
- if the person is under 18 years old, submit a written statement from his/her mother or legal guardian which:
  - o irrevocably releases him/her for emigration and authorizes the placing agencies to make necessary decisions for his/her immediate care until a sponsor receives custody;
  - o shows an understanding of the effects of the release, and states whether any money was paid or coercion used prior to obtaining the release;
  - o includes the full name, date and place of birth, and present or permanent address of the mother or guardian, and with the signature of the mother or guardian on the release authenticated by a local registrar, court of minors, or a U.S. immigration or consular officer.

The following sponsorship documents are also required. You may file these documents with the petition, or wait until we review the petition and request them. However, not filing them with the petition will add to the overall processing time.
- An Affidavit of Financial Support, executed by the sponsor, with the evidence of financial ability required by that form. Please note that the original sponsor remains financially responsible for the Amerasian if any subsequent sponsor fails in this area.
- Copies of evidence the sponsor is at least 21 years old and is a U.S. citizen or permanent resident.
- Fingerprints of the sponsor on Form FD-258.
- If this petition is for a person under 18 years old, the following documents issued by a placement agency must be submitted:
  - o a copy of the private, public or state agency's license to place children in the U.S., proof of the agency's recent experience in the intercountry placement of children and of the agency's financial ability to arrange the placement;
  - o a favorable home study of the sponsor conducted by a legally authorized agency;
  - o a pre-placement report from the agency, including information regarding any family separation or dislocation abroad that would result from the placement;
  - o a written description of the orientation given to the sponsor and to the parent or guardian on the legal and cultural aspects of the placement;

  - o a statement from the agency showing that the sponsor has been given a report on the pre-placement screening and evaluation of the child;
  - o a written plan from the agency to provide follow-up services, including mediation and counseling, and describing the contingency plans to place the person this petition is for in another suitable home if the initial placement fails.

### Widow(er) of a United States Citizen. You can file this petition on your own behalf if:
- you were married for at least two years to a U.S. citizen who is now deceased and who had been a U.S. citizen for at least two years at the time of death;
- your citizen spouse's death was less than two years ago;
- you were not legally separated from your citizen spouse at the time of death, and you have not remarried.

The petition must be filed with:
- a copy of your marriage certificate to the U.S. citizen and proof of termination of any prior marriages of either of you;
- copies of evidence that your spouse was a U.S. citizen, such as a birth certificate if born in the U.S.; Naturalization Certificate or Certificate of Citizenship issued by this Service; Form FS-240, Report of Birth Abroad of a Citizen of the United States, or a U.S. passport which was valid at the time of the citizen's death;
- a copy of the death certificate of your U.S. citizen spouse.

### Special Immigrant Juvenile. Any person, including the alien, can file the petition for an alien who:
- is unmarried;
- has been declared dependent upon a juvenile court in the U.S. and has been found eligible by that court for long-term foster care;
- is still a juvenile under the law of the state in which the juvenile court is located and is still dependent upon the court and eligible for long term foster care; and
- has been the subject of administrative or judicial proceedings in which it was determined that it would not be in his/her best interests to be returned to his/her country of nationality or last habitual residence, or to his/her parent's country of nationality or last habitual residence. However, after a person is admitted as a Juvenile, his/her parent may not receive any immigration benefit based on being his/her parent.

The petition must be filed with:
- copies of the court documents upon which your claim to eligibility is based.

### Special Immigrant Religious Worker. Any person, including the alien, can file this petition for an alien who for the past 2 years has been a member of a religious denomination which has a bona fide nonprofit, religious organization in the U.S.; and who has been carrying on the vocation, professional work, or other work described below, continuously for the past 2 years; and seeks to enter the U.S. to work solely:
- o as a minister of that denomination; or
- o in a professional capacity in a religious vocation or occupation for that organization;
- o in a religious vocation or occupation for the organization or its nonprofit affiliate.

A petition for a special immigrant for a person who is not a minister may only be filed until October 1, 1994.

The petition must be filed with:
- a letter from the authorized official of the religious organization establishing that the proposed services and alien qualify as above;
- a letter from the authorized official of the religious organization attesting to the alien's membership in the religious denomination and explaining, in detail, the person's religious work and all employment during the past 2 years and the proposed employment; and
- evidence establishing that the religious organization, and any affiliate which will employ the person, is a bona fide nonprofit religious organization in the U.S. and is exempt from taxation under section 501(c)(3) of the Internal Revenue Code of 1986.

Form I-360 (Rev. 09/19/91) N

**SAMPLE DOCUMENT – NOT TO BE USED WHEN FILING.**

***Special Immigrant based on employment with the Panama Canal Company, Canal Zone Government or U.S. government in the Canal Zone.*** Any person can file this petition for an alien who, at the time the Panama Canal Treaty of 1977 entered into force, either:

- was resident in the Canal Zone and had been employed by the Panama Canal Company or Canal Zone Government for at least 1 year; or
- was a Panamanian national and either honorably retired from U.S. Government employment in the Canal Zone with a total of 15 or more years of faithful service or so employed for 15 years and since honorably retired; or
- was an employee of the Panama Canal Company or Canal Zone government, had performed faithful service for 5 years or more as an employee, and whose personal safety, or the personal safety of his/her spouse or child, is in danger as a direct result of the special nature of his/her employment and as a direct result of the Treaty.

The petition must be filed with:
- a letter from the Panama Canal Company, Canal Zone government or U.S. government agency employing the person in the Canal Zone, indicating the length and circumstances of employment and any retirement or termination;
- copies of evidence to establish any claim of danger to personal safety.

***Special Immigrant Physician.*** Any person may file this petition for an alien who:
- graduated from a medical school or qualified to practice medicine in a foreign state;
- was fully and permanently licensed to practice medicine in a State of the U.S. on January 9, 1978, and was practicing medicine in a State on that date;
- entered the U.S. as an "H" or "J" nonimmigrant before January 9 1978; and
- has been continuously present in the U.S. and continuously engaged in the practice or study of medicine since the date of such entry.

The petition must be filed with:
- letters from the person's employers, detailing his/her employment since January 8, 1978, including the current employment;
- copies of relevant documents that demonstrate that the person filed for meets all the above criteria.

***Special Immigrant International Organization Employee or family member.*** Certain long-term "G" and "N" nonimmigrant employees of a qualifying international organization entitled to enjoy privileges, exemptions and immunities under the International Organizations Immunities Act, and certain relatives of such an employee, may be eligible to apply for classification as a Special Immigrant. To determine eligibility, contact the qualifying international organization or your local INS office. The petition must be filed with:
- a Letter from the international organization demonstrating that it is a qualifying organization and explaining the circumstances of qualifying employment and the immigration status held by the person the petition is for; and
- copies of evidence documenting the relationship between the person this petition is for and the employee.

### General Filing Instructions.
Please answer all questions by typing or clearly printing in black ink only. Indicate that an item is not applicable with "N/A". If an answer is "none," please so state. If you need extra space to answer any item, attach a sheet of paper with your name and your alien registration number (A#), if any, and indicate tho number of the item the answer refers to. Every petition must be properly signed, and accompanied by the proper fee. If you are under 14 years of age, your parent or guardian may sign the petition.

### Where to File.
If you are filing for a Special Immigrant Juvenile, file the petition at the local INS office having jurisdiction over the place he/she lives.

If you are filing for Amerasian classification and the person you are filing for is outside the United States, you may file this petition at the INS office that has jurisdiction over the place he/she lives or the office that has jurisdiction over the place he/she will live.

In all other instances file this petition at an INS Service Center, as follows:

If you live in Connecticut, Delaware, District of Columbia, Maine, Maryland, Massachusetts, New Hampshire, New Jersey, New York, Pennsylvania, Puerto Rico, Rhode Island, Vermont, Virgin Islands, Virginia, or West Virginia, mail this petition to USINS, Eastern Service Center, 75 Lower Weldon Street, St. Albans, VT 05479-0001.

If you in Alabama, Arkansas, Florida, Georgia, Kentucky, Louisiana, Mississippi, New Mexico, North Carolina, Oklahoma, South Carolina, Tennessee, or Texas, mail this petition to USINS, Southern Service Center, P.O. Box 152122, Dept. A, Irving, TX 75015-2122.

If you live in Arizona, California, Guam, Hawaii, or Nevada, mail this petition to USINS, Western Service Center, P.O. Box 30040, Laguna Niguel, CA 92607-0040

If you live elsewhere in the U.S., mail this petition to USINS, Northern Service Center, 100 Centennial Mall North, Room B-26, Lincoln, NE 68508.

### Fee.
The fee for this petition is $80.00, except that there is no fee if you are filing for an Amerasian. The fee must be submitted in the exact amount. It cannot be refunded. DO NOT MAIL CASH. All checks and money orders must be drawn on a bank or other institution located in the United States and must be payable in United States currency. The check or money order should be made payable to the Immigration and Naturalization Service, except that:
- If you live in Guam, and are filing this application in Guam, make your check or money order payable to the "Treasurer, Guam."
- If you live in the Virgin Islands, and are filing this application in the Virgin Islands, make your check or money order payable to the "Commissioner of Finance of the Virgin Islands."

Checks are accepted subject to collection. An uncollected check will render the application and any document issued invalid. A charge of $5.00 will be imposed if a check in payment of a fee is not honored by the bank on which it is drawn.

### Processing Information.
*Rejection.* Any petition that is not signed or is not accompanied by the correct fee will be rejected with a notice that the petition is deficient. You may correct the deficiency and resubmit the petition. However, a petition is not considered properly filed until accepted by the Service.

*Initial processing.* Once the petition has been accepted, it will be checked for completeness, including submission of the required initial evidence. If you do not completely fill out the form, or file it without required initial evidence, you will not establish a basis for eligibility and we may deny your petition.

*Requests for additional information or interview.* We may request additional information or evidence or we may request that you appear at an INS office for an interview. We may also request that you submit the originals of any copy. We will return these originals when they are no longer required.

*Decision.* If you establish that the person this petition is for is eligible for the requested classification, we will approve the petition. We will send it to the U.S. Embassy/Consulate for visa issuance unless he or she is in the U.S. and appears eligible and intends to apply for adjustment to permanent resident status while here. If you do not establish eligibility, we will deny the petition. We will notify you in writing of our decision.

### Penalties.
If you knowingly and willfully falsify or conceal a material fact or submit a false document with this request, we will deny the benefit you are filing for and may deny any other immigration benefit. In addition, you will face severe penalties provided by law, and may be subject to criminal prosecution.

### Privacy Act Notice
We ask for the information on this form, and associated evidence, to determine if you have established eligibility for the immigration benefit you are filing for. Our legal right to ask for this information is in 8 USC 1154. We may provide this information to other government agencies. Failure to provide this information, and any requested evidence, may delay a final decision or result in denial of your request.

### Paperwork Reduction Act Notice.
We try to create forms and instructions that are accurate, can be easily understood, and which impose the least possible burden on you to provide us with information. Often this is difficult because some immigration laws are very complex. Accordingly, the reporting burden for this collection of information is computed as follows: (1) learning about the law and form, 15 minutes; (2) completing the form, 20 minutes; and (3) assembling and filing the application, 55 minutes for an estimated average of 1 hour and 30 minutes per response. If you have comments regarding the accuracy ** to both the Immigration and Naturalization Service, 425 I Street, N.W., Room 5304, Washington, D.C. 20536; and the Office of Management and Budget, Paperwork Reduction Project, OMB No. 1115-0117, Washington, D.C. 20503.

**U.S. Department of Justice**
Immigration and Naturalization Service

OMB #1115-0117
Petition for Amerasian, Widow or Special Immigrant

## START HERE - Please Type or Print

**FOR INS USE ONLY**

**Part 1. Information about person or organization filing this petition.** (Individuals should use top name line; organizations should use the second line.) *If you are filing for yourself, skip to Part 2. A widow(er) must file for him/her self.*

| Family Name | Given Name | Middle Initial |
|---|---|---|
| | | |

Company or Organization Name

**Address - C/O**

| Street Number and Name | | Apt # |
|---|---|---|
| City | State or Province | |
| Country | ZIP/Postal Code | |

| U.S. Social Security # | A # | IRS Tax # (if any) |
|---|---|---|
| | | |

## Part 2. Classification Requested (check one):

a. ☐ Amerasian

b. ☐ Widow(er) of a U.S. citizen who died within the past 2 years

c. ☐ Special Immigrant Juvenile

d. ☐ Special Immigrant Religious Worker

e. ☐ Special Immigrant based on employment with the Panama Canal Company, Canal Zone Government or U.S. Government in the Canal Zone

f. ☐ Special Immigrant Physician

g. ☐ Special Immigrant International Organization Employee or family member

## Part 3. Information about the person this petition is for.

| Family Name | Given Name | Middle Initial |
|---|---|---|
| | | |

**Address - C/O**

| Street Number and Name | | Apt # |
|---|---|---|
| City | State or Province | |
| Country | ZIP/Postal Code | |

| Date of Birth (Month/Day/Year) | Country of Birth |
|---|---|
| | |

| U.S. Social Security # (if any) | A # (if any) |
|---|---|
| | |

Complete the items below if this person is in the United States:

| Date of Arrival (Month/Day/Year) | I-94 # |
|---|---|
| Current Nonimmigrant Status | Expires on (Month/Day/Year) |

### FOR INS USE ONLY (right column)

Returned

Receipt

Resubmitted

Reloc Sent

Reloc Rec'd

☐ Petitioner/ Applicant Interviewed

☐ Beneficiary Interviewed

☐ I-485 Filed Concurrently
☐ Bene "A" File Reviewed

Classification

Consulate

Priority Date

Remarks:

**Action Block**

| **To Be Completed by** |
|---|
| ***Attorney* or *Representative*, if any** |
| ☐ Fill in box if G-28 is attached to represent the applicant |
| VOLAG# |
| ATTY State License # |

Form I-360 (Rev. 09/19/91 ) N                    ***Continued on back.***

## Part   4.  Processing Information.

Below give the United States Consulate you want notified if this petition is approved and if any requested adjustment of status cannot be granted.

| *American Consulate*: City | Country |
|---|---|

If you gave a United States address in Part 3, print the person's foreign address below. If his/her native alphabet does not use Roman letters, print his/her name and foreign address in the native alphabet.

| Name | Address |
|---|---|

| | | |
|---|---|---|
| Sex of the person this petition is for. | ☐ Male | ☐ Female |
| Are you filing any other petitions or applications with this one? | ☐ No | ☐ Yes (How many? _____ ) |
| Is the person this petition is for in exclusion or deportation proceedings? | ☐ No | ☐ Yes (Explain on a separate sheet of paper) |
| Has the person this petition is for ever worked in the U.S. without permission? | ☐ No | ☐ Yes (Explain on a separate sheet of paper) |
| Is an application for adjustment of status attached to this petition? | ☐ No | ☐ Yes |

## Part 5. Complete only if filing for an Amerasian.

### Section A.   Information about the mother of the Amerasian

| Family Name | Given Name | Middle Initial |
|---|---|---|

Living? ☐ No (Give date of death _____ )   ☐ Yes (complete address line below)   ☐ Unknown (attach a full explanation)

Address

### Section B.   Information about the father of the Amerasian: If possible attach a notarized statement from the father regarding parentage. Explain on separate paper any question you cannot fully answer in the space provided on this form.

| Family Name | Given Name | Middle Initial |
|---|---|---|
| Date of Birth (Month/Day/Year) | Country of Birth | |

Living? ☐ No (give date of death _____ )   ☐ Yes (complete address line below)   ☐ Unknown (attach a full explanation)

Home Address

| Home Phone # | Work Phone # |
|---|---|

At the time the Amerasian was conceived:

☐   The father was in the military (indicate branch of service below - and give service number here): _____

    ☐ Army    ☐ Air Force    ☐ Navy    ☐ Marine Corps    ☐ Coast Guard

☐   The father was a civilian employed abroad. Attach a list of names and addresses of organizations which employed him at that time.

☐   If the father was not in the military and was not a civilian employed abroad. *(Attach a full explanation of the circumstances.)*

## Part 6. Complete only if filing for a Juvenile.

### Section A.   Information about the Juvenile

List any other names used.

| Marital Status: | ☐ Single | ☐ Married | ☐ Divorced | ☐ Widowed |
|---|---|---|---|---|

Answer the following questions regarding the person this petition is for. If you answer "no" explain on a separate sheet of paper.

Is he/she still a juvenile under the laws of the state in which the juvenile

| court upon which the alien has been declared dependent is located? | ☐ No | ☐ Yes |
|---|---|---|
| Does he/she continue to be dependent upon the juvenile court? | ☐ No | ☐ Yes |
| Does he/she continue to be eligible for long term foster care? | ☐ No | ☐ Yes |

*Continued on next page.*

## Part 7. Complete only if filing for a Widow or Widower.

**Section A. Information about the U.S. citizen husband or wife who died.**

| Family Name | Given Name | Middle Initial |
|---|---|---|

| Date of Birth (Month/Day/Year) | Country of Birth | Date of Death (Month/Day/Year) |
|---|---|---|

His/her U.S. citizenship was based on (check one)

☐ Birth in the U.S.          ☐ Birth abroad to U.S. citizen parent(s)          ☐ Naturalization

**Section B. Additional Information about you.**

| How many times have you been married? | How many times was the person in Section A married? |
|---|---|

Give the date and place you and the person In Section A were married.

Did you live with this U.S citizen spouse from the date you were married until he/she died?

☐ Yes          ☐ No (attach explanation)

Were you legally separated at the time of the United States citizen's death?

☐ Yes (attach explanation)          ☐ No

Give your address at the time of the United States citizens death.

## Part 8. Information about the children and spouse of the person this petition is for.
For a widow or widower, include any children of your deceased spouse

| A. Family Name | Given Name | Middle Initial | Date of Birth (Month/Day/Year) |
|---|---|---|---|
| Country of Birth | Relationship ☐ Spouse ☐ Child | | A # |

| B. Family Name | Given Name | Middle Initial | Date of Birth (Month/Day/Year) |
|---|---|---|---|
| Country of Birth | Relationship ☐ Spouse ☐ Child | | A # |

| C. Family Name | Given Name | Middle Initial | Date of Birth (Month/Day/Year) |
|---|---|---|---|
| Country of Birth | Relationship ☐ Spouse ☐ Child | | A # |

| D. Family Name | Given Name | Middle Initial | Date of Birth (Month/Day/Year) |
|---|---|---|---|
| Country of Birth | Relationship ☐ Spouse ☐ Child | | A # |

| E. Family Name | Given Name | Middle Initial | Date of Birth (Month/Day/Year) |
|---|---|---|---|
| Country of Birth | Relationship ☐ Spouse ☐ Child | | A # |

| F. Family Name | Given Name | Middle Initial | Date of Birth (Month/Day/Year) |
|---|---|---|---|
| Country of Birth | Relationship ☐ Spouse ☐ Child | | A # |

| G. Family Name | Given Name | Middle Initial | Date of Birth (Month/Day/Year) |
|---|---|---|---|
| Country of Birth | Relationship ☐ Spouse ☐ Child | | A # |

| H. Family Name | Given Name | Middle Initial | Date of Birth (Month/Day/Year) |
|---|---|---|---|
| Country of Birth | Relationship ☐ Spouse ☐ Child | | A # |

*Continued on back.*

**Part 9. Signature**

*Read the information on penalties in the instructions before completing this part. If you are going to file this petition at an INS office in the United States, sign below. If you are going to file it at a U.S. consulate or INS office overseas, sign in front of a U.S. INS or consulate official.*

I certify, or, if outside the United States, I swear or affirm, under penalty of perjury under the laws of the United States of America, that this petition, and the evidence submitted with it, is all true and correct. If filing this on behalf of an organization, I certify that I am empowered to do so by that organization. I authorize the release of any information from my records, or from the petitioning organization's records, which the Immigration and Naturalization Service needs to determine eligibility for the benefit being sought.

| *Signature* | Date |
|---|---|
| **Signature of INS or Consular Official** | Print Name | Date |

***Please Note:*** *If you do not completely fill out this form, or fail to submit required documents listed in the instructions, then the person(s) filed for may not be found eligible for a requested benefit, and it may have to be denied.*

## Part 10. Signature of person preparing form if other than above. (sign below)

I declare that I prepared this application at the request of the above person and it is based on all information of which I have knowledge.

| **Signature** | Print Your Name | Date |
|---|---|---|
| Firm Name and Address | | |

*U.S. Government Printing Office: 1991 - 303-532

**U.S. Department of Justice**                                   OMB #1115-0081
Immigration and Naturalization Service            Immigrant Petition by Alien Entrepreneur

## INSTRUCTIONS

### Purpose of This Form.
This form is for use by an entrepreneur to petition for status as an immigrant to the U.S.

### Who May File.
You may file this petition for yourself if you have established a new commercial enterprise
- in which you will engage in a managerial or policy-making capacity, and
- in which you have invested or are actively in the process of investing the amount required for the area in which the enterprise is located, and
- which will benefit the U.S. economy, and
- which will create full-time employment in the U.S. for at least 10 U.S. citizens, permanent residents, or other immigrants authorized to be employed, other than yourself, your spouse, your sons or daughters, or any nonimmigrant aliens.

The establishment of a new commercial enterprise may include:
- creation of a new business;
- the purchase of an existing business with simultaneous or subsequent restructuring or reorganization resulting in a new commercial enterprise; or
- the expansion of an existing business through investment of the amount required, so that a substantial change (at least 40%) in either the net worth, number of employees, or both, results.

The amount of investment required in a particular area is set by regulation. Unless adjusted downward for targeted areas or upward for areas of high employment, the figure shall be $1,000,000. You may obtain this information from an INS office or American consulate.

### General Filing Instructions.
Please answer all questions by typing or clearly printing in black ink. Indicate that an item is not applicable with **"N/A"**. If an answer to a question is "none," please so state. If you need extra space to answer any item, attach a sheet of paper with your name and your A#, if any, and indicate the number of the item. Your petition must be properly signed and filed with the correct fee.

### Initial Evidence Requirements.
The following evidence must be filed with your petition:
- Evidence that you have established a lawful business entity under the laws of the jurisdiction in the U.S. in which it is located, or, if you have made an investment in an existing business, evidence that your investment has caused a substantial (at least 40%) increase in the net worth of the business, the number of employees, or both. Such evidence shall consist of copies of articles of incorporation, certificate of merger or consolidation, partnership agreement, certificate of limited partnership, joint venture agreement, business trust agreement, or other similar organizational document; a certificate evidencing authority to do business in a state or municipality or if such is not required, a statement to that effect; or evidence that the required amount of capital has been transferred to an existing business resulting in a substantial increase in the net worth or number of employees, or both. This evidence must be in the form of stock purchase agreements, investment agreements, certified financial reports, payroll records or other similar instruments, agreements or documents evidencing the investment and the resulting substantial change.
- Evidence, if applicable, that your enterprise has been established in a targeted employment area. A targeted employment area is defined as a rural area or an area which has experienced high unemployment of at least 150% of the national average rate. A rural area is an area not within a metropolitan statistical area or not within the outer boundary of any city or town having a population of 20,000 or more.
- Evidence that you have invested or are actively in the process of investing the amount required for the area in which the business is located. Such evidence may include, but not be limited to copies of bank statements, evidence of assets which have been purchased for use in the enterprise, evidence of property transferred from abroad for use in the enterprise, evidence of monies transferred or committed to be transferred to the new commercial enterprise in exchange for shares of stock, any loan or mortage, promisory note, security agreement, or other evidence of borrowing which is secured by assets of the petitioner.
- Evidence that capital is obtained through lawful means, the petition must be accompanied, as applicable, by: Foreign business registration records, tax returns of any kind filed within the last five years in or outside the United States, evidence of other sources of capital, or certified copies of any judgment, pending governmental civil or criminal actions, or private civil actions against the petitioner from any court in or outside the United States within the past fifteen years.
- Evidence that the enterprise will create at least 10 full-time positions for U.S. citizens, permanent residents, or aliens lawfully authorized to be employed (except yourself, your spouse, sons, or daughters, and any nonimmigrant aliens). Such evidence may consist of copies of relevant tax records, Form I-9, or other similar documents, if the employees have already been hired, or a business plan showing when such employees will be hired within the next two years.
- Evidence that you are or will be engaged in the management of the enterprise, either through the exercise of day-to-day managerial control or through policy formulation. Such evidence may include a statement of your position title and a complete description of your duties, evidence that you are a corporate officer or hold a seat on the board of directors, or if the new enterprise is a partnership, evidence that you are engaged in either direct management or policy-making activities.

Form I-526 (Rev. 12-2-91)

**SAMPLE DOCUMENT – NOT TO BE USED WHEN FILING.**

### Copies.

**If** these instructions state that a copy of a document may be filed with this application, and you choose to send us the original, we may keep that original for our records.

### Where to File.

The petition must be filed with the INS Service Center having jurisdiction over the area in which the new commercial enterprise will be principally doing business.

If the enterprise is in Alabama, Connecticut, Delaware, District of Columbia, Florida, Georgia, Maine, Maryland, Massachusetts, New Hampshire, New Jersey, New York, North Carolina, Pennsylvania, Puerto Rico, Rhode Island, South Carolina, Vermont, Virgin Islands, Virginia, or West Virginia, mail this petition to USINS, Eastern Service Center, 75 Lower Welden Street, St. Albans, VT 05479-0001.

If the enterprise is in Arizona, California, Guam, Hawaii, or Nevada, mail this petition to USINS, Western Service Center, P.O. Box 30040, Laguna Nigel, CA 92607-0040.

If the enterprise is elsewhere in the U.S., mail this petition to USINS, Northern Service Center, 100 Centennial Mall North, Room, B-26, Lincoln, NE 68508.

### Fee.

The fee for this petition is $155.00. The fee must be submitted in the exact amount. It cannot be refunded. DO NOT MAIL CASH. All checks and money orders must be drawn on a bank or other institution located in the United States and must be payable in United States currency. The check or money order should be made payable to the Immigration and Naturalization Service, except that:

- If you live in Guam, and are filing this application in Guam, make your check or money order payable to the "Treasurer, Guam."
- If you live in the Virgin Islands, and are filing this application in the Virgin Islands, make your check or money order payable to the "Commissioner of Finance of the Virgin Islands."

Checks are accepted subject to collection. An uncollected check will render the application and any document issued invalid. A charge of $5.00 will be imposed if a check in payment of a fee is not honored by the bank on which it is drawn.

### Processing Information.

*Acceptance.* Any petition that is not signed or is not accompanied by the correct fee will be rejected with a notice that it is deficient. You may correct the deficiency and resubmit the petition. However, a petition is not considered properly filed until accepted by the Service. A priority date will not be assigned until the petition is properly filed.

*Initial processing.* Once the petition has been accepted, it will be checked for completeness, including submission of the required initial evidence. If you do not completely fill out the form, or file it without required initial evidence, you will not establish a basis for eligibility, and we may deny your petition.

*Requests for more information or interview.* We may request more information or evidence or we may request that you appear at an INS office for an interview. We may also request that you submit the originals of any copy. We will return these originals when they are no longer required.

*Approval.* If you have established that you qualify for investor status, the petition will be approved. If you have requested that the petition be forwarded to an American consulate abroad, the petition will be sent there unless that consulate does not issue immigrant visas. If you are in the U.S. and state that you will apply for adjustment of status, and the evidence indicates that you are not eligible for adjustment, the petition will be sent to an American consulate abroad. You will be notified in writing of the approval of the petition and where it has been sent, and the reason for sending it to a place other than the one requested, if applicable.

*Meaning of petition approval.* Approval of a petition shows only that you have established that you have made a qualifying investment. It does not guarantee that the American Consulate will issue the immigrant visa. There are other requirements which must be met before a visa can be issued. The American Consulate will notify you of those requirements. Immigrant status granted based on this petition will be conditional. Two years after entry the conditional investor will have to apply for the removal of conditions based on the ongoing nature of the investment.

*Denial.* If you have not established that you qualify, the petition will be denied. You will be notified in writing of the reasons for the denial.

### Penalties.

If you knowingly and willfully falsify or conceal a material fact or submit a false document with this request, we will deny the benefit you are filing for, and may deny any other immigration benefit. In addition, you will face severe penalties provided by law, and may be subject to criminal prosecution.

### Privacy Act Notice.

We ask for the information on this form, and associated evidence, to determine if you have established eligibility for the immigration benefit you are filing for. Our legal right to ask for this information is in 8 USC 1184, 1255 and 1258. We may provide this information to other government agencies. Failure to provide this information, and any requested evidence, may delay a final decision or result in denial of your request.

### Paperwork Reduction Act Notice.

We try to create forms and instructions that are accurate, can be easily understood, and which impose the least possible burden on you to provide us with information. Often this is difficult because some immigration laws are very complex. Accordingly, the reporting burden for this collection of information is computed as follows: (1) learning about the law and form, 15 minutes; (2) completing the form, 25 minutes; and (3) assembling and filing the application, 35 minutes, for an estimated average of 1 hour and 15 minutes per response. If you have comments regarding the accuracy of this estimate, or suggestions for making this form simpler, you can write to both the Immigration and Naturalization Service, 425 I Street, N.W., Room 5304, Washington, D.C. 20536; and the Office of Management and Budget, Paperwork Reduction Project, OMB No. 1115-0081, Washington, D.C. 20503.

Form I-526 (Rev. 12-2-91)

**U.S. Department of Justice**
Immigration and Naturalization Service

OMB No. 1115-0081
Immigrant Petition by Alien Entrepreneur

## START HERE - Please Type or Print

### Part 1. Information about you.

| Family Name | Given Name | Middle Initial |
|---|---|---|

**FOR INS USE ONLY**

| Returned | Receipt |
|---|---|

**Address** - in Care of:

| Street # and Name | Apt # |
|---|---|

Resubmitted

| City or town | State or Province |
|---|---|

| Country | ZIP or Postal Code |
|---|---|

Reloc Sent

| Date of Birth (month/day/year) | Country of Birth |
|---|---|

| Social Security # | A # |
|---|---|

Reloc Rec'd

If in the U.S.

| Date of Arrival (month/day/year) | I-94 # |
|---|---|
| Current Nonimmigrant Status | Expires on (month/day/year) |

☐ Applicant Interviewed

### Part 2. Application Type (check one).

a. ☐ This petition is based on an investment in a commercial enterprise in a targeted employment area for which the required amount of capital invested has been adjusted downward.

b. ☐ This petition is based on an investment in a commercial enterprise in an area for which the required amount of capital invested has been adjusted upward.

c. ☐ This petition is based on an investment in a commercial enterprise which is not in either a targeted area or in an upward adjustment area.

### Part 3. Information about your investment.

Name of Commercial Enterprise Invested In

Street Address

| Phone # | Business Organized as (Corporation, partnership, etc...) |
|---|---|

Kind of Business
*(Example: Furniture Manufacturer)*

| Date established (month/day/year) | IRS Tax # |
|---|---|
| Date of your initial Investment (month/day/year) | Amount of your Initial Investment $ |
| Your total Capital Investment in Enterprise to date $ | % of Enterprise you own |

**Action Block**

If you are not the sole investor in the new commercial enterprise, list on separate paper the names of all other parties (natural and non-natural) who hold a percentage share of ownership of the new enterprise and indicate whether any of these parties is seeking classifications as an alien entrepreneur. Include the name, percentage of ownership and whether or not the person is seeking classification under section 203(b)(5).

If you indicate in Part 2 that the enterprise was in a targeted employment area or in an upward adjustment area, give the location at right.

County _____   State _____

**To Be Completed by Attorney or Representative, if any**
☐ Fill in box if G-28 is attached to represent the applicant

VOLAG#

ATTY State License #

Form I-526 (Rev. 12-2-91) N            *Continued on back.*

**SAMPLE DOCUMENT – NOT TO BE USED WHEN FILING.**

## Part 4.  Additional Information about the enterprise.

**Type of enterprise** *(check one)*:
☐ new commercial enterprise resulting from the creation of a new business
☐ New commercial enterprise resulting from the reorganization of an existing business.
☐ New commercial enterprise resulting from a capital investment in an existing business.

| Assets: | | |
|---|---|---|
| Total amount in U.S. bank account | $_____ |
| Total value of all assets purchased for use in the enterprise | $_____ |
| Total value of all property transferred from abroad to the new enterprise | $_____ |
| Total of all debt financing | $_____ |
| Total stock purchases | $_____ |
| Other (explain on separate paper) | $_____ |
| Total | $_____ |

**Income:**  When you made investment    Gross $_____    Net $_____
Now    Gross $_____    Net $_____

**Net worth**   When you made investment   $_____    Now   $_____

## Part 5.  Employment creation information.

**# of full-time employees in Enterprise in U.S.** (excluding you, spouse, sons & daughters)

When you made your initial investment  _____    Now  _____    Difference  _____

How many of these new jobs    How many additional new jobs will be
were created by your investment?  _____    created by your additional investment?  _____

What is your position, office or title with the new commercial enterprise?
_____

Briefly describe your duties, activities and responsibilities.
_____
_____
_____

Your Salary                          Cost of Benefits

## Part 6.  Processing Information.

Below give the U.S. Consulate you want notified if the petition is approved and if any requested adjustment of status cannot be granted.
American Consulate:  **City**                          **Country**

If you gave a U.S. address in Part 1, print your foreign address below. If your native alphabet does not use Roman letters, print your name and foreign address in the native alphabet.

**Name**                          **Foreign Address**

| | | |
|---|---|---|
| Is an application for adjustment of status to this petition? | ☐ yes | ☐ no |
| Are you in exclusion or deportation proceedings? | ☐ yes (if yes, explain on separate paper) | ☐ no |
| Have you ever worked in the U.S. without permission? | ☐ yes (explain on separate paper) | ☐ no |

## Part 7.  Signature. *Read the information on penalties in the instructions before completing this section.*

I certify under penalty of perjury under the laws of the United States of America that this petition, and the evidence submitted with it, is all true and correct. I authorize the release of any information from my records which the Immigration and Naturalization Service needs to determine eligibility for the benefit I am seeking.

**Signature**                          Date

*Please Note:* If you do not completely fill out this form, or fail to submit required documents listed in the instructions,you may not be found eligible for the requested document and this application may be denied.

## Part 8.  Signature of person preparing form if other than above. *(Sign below)*

I declare that I prepared this application at the request of the above person and it is based on all information of which I have knowledge.
**Signature**                          Print You Name                          Date

Firm name
and Address

Form I-526 (Rev. 12-2-91) _____

# Supplement-1

**Attach to Form I-129 when more than one person is included in the petition.**  *(List each person separately.  Do not include the person you named on the form).*

| Family Name | Given Name | Middle Initial | Date of Birth (month/day/year) |
|---|---|---|---|
| Country of Birth | Social Security No. | | A# |

| IF IN THE U.S. | Date of Arrival (month/day/year) | | I-94# |
|---|---|---|---|
| | Current Nonimmigrant Status: | | Expires on (month/day/year) |

| Country where passport issued | Expiration Date (month/day/year) | Date Started with group |
|---|---|---|

| Family Name | Given Name | Middle Initial | Date of Birth (month/day/year) |
|---|---|---|---|
| Country of Birth | Social Security No. | | A# |

| IF IN THE U.S. | Date of Arrival (month/day/year) | | I-94# |
|---|---|---|---|
| | Current Nonimmigrant Status: | | Expires on (month/day/year) |

| Country where passport issued | Expiration Date (month/day/year) | Date Started with group |
|---|---|---|

| Family Name | Given Name | Middle Initial | Date of Birth (month/day/year) |
|---|---|---|---|
| Country of Birth | Social Security No. | | A# |

| IF IN THE U.S. | Date of Arrival (month/day/year) | | I-94# |
|---|---|---|---|
| | Current Nonimmigrant Status: | | Expires on (month/day/year) |

| Country where passport issued | Expiration Date (month/day/year) | Date Started with group |
|---|---|---|

| Family Name | Given Name | Middle Initial | Date of Birth (month/day/year) |
|---|---|---|---|
| Country of Birth | Social Security No. | | A# |

| IF IN THE U.S. | Date of Arrival (month/day/year) | | I-94# |
|---|---|---|---|
| | Current Nonimmigrant Status: | | Expires on (month/day/year) |

| Country where passport issued | Expiration Date (month/day/year) | Date Started with group |
|---|---|---|

| Family Name | Given Name | Middle Initial | Date of Birth (month/day/year) |
|---|---|---|---|
| Country of Birth | Social Security No. | | A# |

| IF IN THE U.S. | Date of Arrival (month/day/year) | | I-94# |
|---|---|---|---|
| | Current Nonimmigrant Status: | | Expires on (month/day/year) |

| Country where passport issued | Expiration Date (month/day/year) | Date Started with group |
|---|---|---|

**U.S. Department of Justice**                                      OMB No. 1115-0145

Immigration and Naturalization Service          Petition to Remove the Conditions on Residence

**Purpose Of This Form.**
This form is for a conditional resident who obtained such status through marriage to apply to remove the conditions on his or her residence.

**Who May File.**
If you were granted conditional resident status through marriage to a U.S. citizen or permanent resident, use this form to petition for the removal of those conditions. Your petition should be filed jointly by you and the spouse through whom you obtained conditional status if you are still married. However, you can apply for a waiver of this joint filing requirement on this form if:
- you entered into the marriage in good faith, but your spouse subsequently died;
- you entered into the marriage in good faith, but the marriage was later terminated due to divorce or annulment;
- you entered into the marriage in good faith, and remain married, but have been battered or subjected to extreme mental cruelty by your U.S. citizen or permanent resident spouse; or
- the termination of your status, and deportation, would result in extreme hardship.

You may include your conditional resident children in your petition, or they can file separately.

**General Filing Instructions.**
Please answer all questions by typing or clearly printing in black ink. Indicate that an item is not applicable with "N/A". If an answer is "none," write "none". If you need extra space to answer any item, attach a sheet of paper with your name and your alien registration number (A#), and indicate the number of the item to which the answer refers. You must file your petition with the required Initial Evidence. Your petition must be properly signed and accompanied by the correct fee. If you are under 14 years of age, your parent or guardian may sign the petition on your behalf.

*Translations.* Any foreign language document must be accompanied by a full English translation which the translator has certified as complete and correct, and by the translator's certification that he or she is competent to translate from the foreign language into English.

*Copies.* If these instructions state that a copy of a document may be filed with this petition, and you choose to send us the original, we may keep that original for our records.

**Initial Evidence.**
*Alien Registration Card.* You must file your petition with a copy of your alien registration card, and with a copy of the alien registration card of any of your conditional resident children you are including in your petition.

*Evidence of the relationship.* Submit copies of documents indicating that the marriage upon which you were granted conditional status was entered into in "good faith", and was not for the purpose of circumventing immigration laws. You should submit copies of as many documents as you wish to establish this fact and to demonstrate the circumstances of the relationship from the date of the marriage to date, and to demonstrate any circumstances surrounding the end of the relationship, if it has ended. The documents should cover as much of the period since your marriage as possible. Examples of such documents are:
- Birth certificate(s) of child(ren) born to the marriage.
- Lease or mortgage contracts showing joint occupancy and/ or ownership of your communal residence.
- Financial records showing joint ownership of assets and joint responsibility for liabilities, such as joint savings and checking accounts, joint federal and state tax returns, insurance policies which show the other as the beneficiary, joint utility bills, joint installment or other loans.
- Other documents you consider relevant to establish that your marriage was not entered into in order to evade the immigration laws of the United States.

- Affidavits sworn to or affirmed by at least 2 people who have known both of you since your conditional residence was granted and have personal knowledge of your marriage and relationship. (Such persons may be required to testify before an immigration officer as to the information contained in the affidavit.) The original affidavit must be submitted, and it must also contain the following information regarding the person making the affidavit: his or her full name and address; date and place of birth; relationship to you or your spouse, if any; and full information and complete details explaining how the person acquired his or her knowledge. Affidavits must be supported by other types of evidence listed above.

*If you are filing to waive the joint filing requirement due to the death of your spouse,* also submit a copy of the death certificate with your petition.

*If you are filing to waive the joint filing requirement because your marriage has been terminated,* also submit a copy of the divorce decree or other document terminating or annulling the marriage with your petition.

*If you are filing to waive the joint filing requirement because you and/or your conditional resident child were battered or subjected to extreme mental cruelty,* also file your petition with the following.
- Evidence of the physical abuse, such as copies of reports or official records issued by police, judges, medical personnel, school officials, and representatives of social service agencies, and original affidavits as described under *Evidence of the Relationship*; or
- Evidence of the extreme mental cruelty, and an original evaluation by a professional recognized by the Service as an expert in the field. These experts include clinical social workers, psychologists and psychiatrists. A clinical social worker who is not licensed only because the State in which he or she practices does not provide for licensing is considered a licensed professional recognized by the Service if he or she is included by the National Association of Social Workers or is certified by the American Board of Examiners in Clinical Social Work. Each evaluation must contain the professional's full name, professional address and license number. It must also identify the licensing, certifying or registering authority.
- A copy of your divorce decree if your marriage was terminated by divorce on grounds of physical abuse or mental cruelty.

*If you are filing for a waiver of the joint filing requirement because the termination of your status, and deportation would result in "extreme hardship",* you must also file your petition with evidence your deportation would result in hardship significantly greater than the hardship encountered by other aliens who are deported from this country after extended stays. The evidence must relate only to those factors which arose since you became a conditional resident.

*If you are a child filing separately from your parent,* also file your petition with a full explanation as to why you are filing separately, along with copies of any supporting documentation.

**When To File.**
*Filing jointly.* If you are filing this petition jointly with your spouse, you must file it during the 90 days immediately before the second anniversary of the date you were accorded conditional resident status. This is the date your conditional residence expires. However, if you and your spouse are outside the United States on orders of the U.S. Government during the period in which the petition must be filed, you may file it within 90 days of your return to the U.S.

Form I-751 (Rev. 12-4-91)

***Filing with a request that the joint filing requirement be waived.*** You may file this petition at any time after you are granted conditional resident status and before you are deported.

***Effect Of Not Filing.*** If this petition is not filed, you will automatically lose your permanent resident status as of the second anniversary of the date on which you were granted this status. You will then become deportable from the United States. If your failure to file was through no fault of your own, you may file your petition late with a written explanation and request that INS excuse the late filing. Failure to file before the expiration date may be excused if you demonstrate when you file the application that the delay was due to extraordinary circumstances beyond your control and that the length of the delay was reasonable.

### Effect of Filing.

Filing this petition extends your conditional residence for six months. You will receive a filing receipt which you should carry with your alien registration card (Form I-551). If you travel outside the U.S. during this period, you may present your card and the filing receipt to be readmitted.

### Where To File.

If you live in Connecticut, Delaware, District of Columbia, Maine, Maryland, Massachusetts, New Hampshire, New Jersey, New York, Pennsylvania, Puerto Rico, Rhode Island, Vermont, Virgin Islands, Virginia, or West Virginia, mail your petition to: USINS Eastern Service Center, 75 Lower Welden Street, St. Albans, VT 05479-0001.

If you live in Alabama, Arkansas, Florida, Georgia, Kentucky, Louisiana, Mississippi, New Mexico, North Carolina, Oklahoma, South Carolina, Tennessee, or Texas, mail your petition to: USINS Southern Service Center, P.O. Box 152122, Dept. A, Irving, TX 75015-2122.

If you live in Arizona, California, Guam, Hawaii, or Nevada, mail your petition to: USINS Western Service Center, P.O. Box 30111, Laguna Niguel, CA 92607-0111.

If you live in elsewhere in the U.S., mail your petition to: USINS Northern Service Center, 100 Centennial Mall North, Room B-26, Lincoln, NE 68508.

### Fee.

The fee for this petition is $80.00. The fee must be submitted in the exact amount. It cannot be refunded. **DO NOT MAIL CASH.**

All checks and money orders must be drawn on a bank or other institution located in the United States and must be payable in United States currency. The check or money order should be made payable to the Immigration and Naturalization Service, except that:

- If you live in Guam, and are filing this petition in Guam, make your check or money order payable to the "Treasurer, Guam".
- If you are living in the Virgin Islands, and are filing this application in the Virgin Islands, make your check or money order payable to the "Commissioner of Finance of the Virgin Islands".

Checks are accepted subject to collection. An uncollected check will render the application and any document issued invalid. A charge of $5.00 will be imposed if a check in payment of a fee is not honored by the bank on which it is drawn.

### Processing Information.

***Acceptance.*** Any petition that is not signed, or is not accompanied by the correct fee, will be rejected with a notice that the petition is deficient. You may correct the deficiency and resubmit the petition. A petition is not considered properly filed until accepted by the Service.

***Initial processing***. Once a petition has been accepted, it will be checked for completeness, including submission of the required initial evidence. If you do not completely fill out the form, or file if without required initial evidence, you will not establish a basis for eligibility, and we may deny your petition.

***Requests for more information or interview.*** We may request more information or evidence, or we may request that you appear at an INS office for an interview. We may also request that you submit the originals of any copy. We will return these originals when they are no longer required.

***Decision.*** You will be advised in writing of the decision on your petition.

### Penalties.

If you knowingly and willfully falsify or conceal a material fact or submit a false document with this request, we will deny the benefit you are filing for, and may deny any other immigration benefit. In addition, you will face severe penalties provided by law, and may be subject to criminal prosecution.

### Privacy Act Notice.

We ask for the information on this form, and associated evidence, to determine if you have established eligibility for the immigration benefit you are filing for. Our legal-right to ask for this information is in 8 USC 1184, 1255 and 1258. Failure to provide this information, and any requested evidence, may delay a final decision or result in denial of your request.

All the information provided on this form, including addresses, are protected by the Privacy Act and the Freedom of Information Act. This information will not be released in any form whatsoever to a third party, other than another government agency, who requests it without a court order, or without your written consent, or, in the case of a child, the written consent of the parent or legal guardian who filed the form on the child's behalf.

### Paperwork Reduction Act Notice.

We try to create forms and instructions that are accurate, can be easily understood, and which impose the least possible burden on you to provide us with information. Often this is difficult because some immigration laws are very complex. The estimated average time to complete and file this application is as follows: (1) 15 minutes to learn about the law and form; (2) 15 minutes to complete the form; and (3) 50 minutes to assemble and file the petition; for a total estimated average of 1 hour and 20 minutes per petition. If you have comments regarding the accuracy of this estimate, or suggestions for making this form simpler, you can write to both the Immigration and Naturalization Service, 425 I Street, N.W., Room 5304, Washington, D.C. 20536; and the Office of Management and Budget, Paperwork Reduction Project, OMB No. 1115-0145 Washington, D.C. 20503.

Form I-751 (Rev. 12-4-91)

**U.S. Department of Justice**
Immigration and Naturalization Service

OMB No. 1115-0145
Petition to Remove the Conditions on Residence

## START HERE - Please Type or Print

### Part 1. Information about you.

| Family Name | Given Name | Middle Initial |
|---|---|---|
| | | |

**Address** - C/O:

| Street Number and Name | | Apt # |
|---|---|---|
| City | State or Province | |
| Country | | ZIP/Postal Code |

| Date of Birth (month/day/year) | Country of Birth |
|---|---|
| | |

| Social Security # | A # |
|---|---|
| | |

Conditional residence expires on (month/day/year)

Mailing address if different from residence in C/O:

| Street Number and Name | | Apt # |
|---|---|---|
| City | State or Province | |
| Country | | ZIP/Postal Code |

### FOR INS USE ONLY

| Returned | Receipt |
|---|---|
| _____ | |
| Resubmitted | |
| _____ | |
| Reloc Sent | |
| _____ | |
| _____ | |
| Reloc Rec'd | |
| _____ | |
| ☐ Applicant Interviewed | |

**Remarks**

**Action**

### Part 2. Basis for petition (check one).

a. ☐ My conditional residence is based on my marriage to a U.S. citizen or permanent resident, and we are filing this petition together.

b. ☐ I am a child who entered as a conditional permanent resident and I am unable to be included in a Joint Petition to Remove the Conditional Basis of Alien's Permanent Residence (Form I-751) filed by my parent(s).

My conditional residence is based on my marriage to a U.S. citizen or permanent resident, but I am unable to file a joint petition and I request a waiver because: (check one)

c. ☐ My spouse is deceased.

d. ☐ I entered into the marriage in good faith, but the marriage was terminated through divorce/annulment.

e. ☐ I am a conditional resident spouse who entered in to the marriage in good faith, or I am a conditional resident child, who has been battered or subjected to extreme mental cruelty by my citizen or permanent resident spouse or parent.

f. ☐ The termination of my status and deportation from the United States would result in an extreme hardship.

### Part 3. Additional information about you.

| Other names used (including maiden name): | Telephone # |
|---|---|
| | |
| Date of Marriage | Place of Marriage |
| | |

If your spouse is deceased, give the date of death (month/day/year)

| Are you in deportation or exclusion proceedings? | ☐ Yes ☐ No |
|---|---|
| Was a fee paid to anyone other than an attorney in connection with this petition? | ☐ Yes ☐ No |

Form I-751 (Rev. 12-4-91) N      *Continued on back.*

**To Be Completed by Attorney or Representative, if any**
☐ Fill in box if G-28 is attached to represent the applicant

VOLAG#

ATTY State License #

## Part 3.    Additional Information about you. (con't)

Since becoming a conditional resident, have you ever been arrested, cited, charged, indicted, convicted, fined or imprisoned for breaking or violating any law or ordinance (excluding traffic regulations), or committed any crime for which you were not arrested?                                                                                     ☐ Yes  ☐ No

If you are married, is this a different marriage than the one through which conditional residence status was obtained?     ☐ Yes  ☐ No

Have you resided at any other address since you became a permanent resident?                               ☐ Yes  ☐ No *(If yes, attach a list of all addresses and dates.)*

Is your spouse currently serving employed by the U.S. government and serving outside the U.S.?            ☐ Yes  ☐ No

## Part 4.    Information about the spouse or parent through whom you gained your conditional residence

| Family Name | Given Name | Middle Initial | Phone Number (     ) |
|---|---|---|---|

Address

| Date of Birth (month/day/year) | Social Security # | A# |
|---|---|---|

## Part 5.    Information about your children. *List all your children.  Attach another sheet if necessary*

|  | Name | Date of Birth (month/day/year) | If in U.S., give A#, current immigration status and U.S. Address | Living with you? |
|---|---|---|---|---|
| 1 |  |  |  | ☐ Yes ☐ No |
| 2 |  |  |  | ☐ Yes ☐ No |
| 3 |  |  |  | ☐ Yes ☐ No |
| 4 |  |  |  | ☐ Yes ☐ No |

## Part 6.    Complete if you are requesting a waiver of the joint filing petition requirement based on extreme mental cruelty.

| Evaluator's ID Number    State: ☐☐   Number: ☐☐☐☐☐☐☐ | Expires on *(month/day/year)* | Occupation |
|---|---|---|
| Last Name | First Name | Address |

## Part 7.    Signature. *Read the information on the penalties in the instructions before completing this section. If you checked block "a" in Part 2 your spouse must also sign below.*

I certify, under penalty of perjury under the laws of the United States of America, that this petition, and the evidence submitted with it, is all true and correct. If conditional residence was based on a marriage, I further certify that the marriage was entered into in accordance with the laws of the place where the marriage took place, and was not for the purpose of procuring an immigration benefit. I also authorize the release of any information from my records which the Immigration and Naturalization Service needs to determine eligibility for the benefit being sought.

| Signature | Print Name | Date |
|---|---|---|
| Signature of Spouse | Print Name | Date |

**Please note**: If you do not completely fill out this form, or fail to submit any required documents listed in the instructions, then you cannot be found eligible for the requested benefit, and this petition may be denied.

## Part 8.    Signature of person preparing form if other than above.

I declare that I prepared this petition at the request of the person above and it is based on all information of which I have knowledge.

| Signature | Print Name | Date |
|---|---|---|

Firm Name and Address

Form I-751 (Rev. 12-4-91)                                                      * GPO : 1992 0 - 316-463

SAMPLE DOCUMENT – NOT TO BE USED WHEN FILING.

**U.S. Department of Justice**

Immigration and Naturalization Service

OMB No. #1115-0061

Immigrant Petition for Alien Worker

**Purpose Of This Form.**
This form is used to petition for an immigrant based on employment.

**Who May File.**
Any person may file this petition in behalf of an alien who:
- has extraordinary ability in the sciences, arts, education business, or athletics, demonstrated by sustained national or international acclaim, whose achievements have been recognized in the field; or
- is claiming exceptional ability in the sciences, arts, or business, and is seeking an exemption of the requirement of a job offer in the national interest.

*A U.S. employer may file this petition who wishes to employ:*
- an outstanding professor or researcher, with at least 3 years of experience in teaching or research in the academic area, who is recognized internationally as outstanding,
  - in a tenured or tenure-track position at a university or institution of higher education to teach in the academic area,
  - in a comparable position at a university or institution of higher education to conduct research in the area, or
  - in a comparable position to conduct research for a private employer who employs at least 3 persons in full-time research activities and has achieved documented accomplishments in an academic field;
- an alien who, in the 3 years preceding the filing of this petition, has been employed for at least 1 year by a firm or corporation or other legal entity and who seeks to enter the U.S. to continue to render services to the same employer or to a subsidiary or affiliate in a capacity that is managerial or executive;
- a member of the professions holding an advanced degree or an alien with exceptional ability in the sciences, arts, or business who will substantially benefit the national economy, cultural or educational interests, or welfare of the U.S.
- a skilled worker (requiring at least 2 years of specialized training or experience in the skill)- to perform labor for which qualified workers are not available in the U.S.;
- a member of the professions with a baccalaureate degree; or
- an unskilled worker to perform labor for which qualified workers are not available in the U.S.

**General Filing Instructions.**
Please answer all questions by typing or clearly printing in black ink. Indicate that an item is not applicable with "N/A". If an answer to a question is "none," write "none". If you need extra space to answer any item, attach a sheet of paper with your name and your A#, if any, and indicate the number of the item to which the answer refers. You must file your petition with the required Initial Evidence. Your petition must be properly signed and filed with the correct fee.

**Initial Evidence.**
*If you are filing for an alien or extraordinary ability in the sciences, arts, education, business, or athletics,* you must file your petition with:
- evidence of a one-time achievement (i.e., a major, internationally - recognized award), or
- at least three of the following:
  - receipt of lesser nationally or internationally recognized prizes or awards for excellence in the field of endeavor,
  - membership in associations in the field which require outstanding achievements as judged by recognized national or international experts,
  - published material about the alien in professional or major trade publications or other major media,
  - participation on a panel or individually as a judge of the work of others in the field or an allied field,
  - original scientific, scholarly artistic, athletic, or business-related contributions of major significance in the field,
  - authorship of scholarly articles in the field, in professional or major trade publications or other major media,
  - display of the alien's work at artistic exhibitions or showcases,
  - evidence that the alien has performed in a leading or critical role for organizations or establishments that have a distinguished reputation,
  - evidence that the alien has commanded a high salary or other high remuneration for services, or
  - evidence of commercial successes in the performing arts, as shown by box office receipts or record, casette, compact disk, or video sales.
- If the above standards do not readily apply to the alien's occupation, you may submit comparable evidence to establish the alien's eligibility.

*A U.S. employer filing for an outstanding professor or researcher* must file the petition with:
- evidence of at least 2 of the following:
  - receipt of major prizes or awards for outstanding achievement in the academic field
  - membership in associations in the academic field, which require outstanding achievements of their members,
  - published material in professional publications written by others about the alien's work in the academic field,
  - participation on a panel, or individually, as the judge of the work of others in the same or an allied academic field,
  - original scientific or scholarly research contributions to the academic field, or
  - authorship of scholarly books or articles, in scholarly journals with international circulation, in the academic field;
- evidence the beneficiary has at least 3 years of experience in teaching and/or research in the academic field; and
- if you are a university or other institution of higher education, a letter indicating that you intend to employ the beneficiary in a tenured or tenure-track position as a teacher or in a permanent position as a researcher in the academic field, or
- if you are a private employer, a letter indicating that you intend to employ the beneficiary in a permanent research position in the academic field, and evidence that you employ at least 3 full-time researchers and have achieved documented accomplishments in the field.

*A U.S. employer filing for a multinational executive or manager* must file the petition with a statement which demonstrates that:
- if the alien is outside the U.S., he/she has been employed outside the U.S. for at least 1 year in the past 3 years in a managerial or executive capacity by a firm or corporation or other legal entity, or by its affiliate or subsidiary; or
- if the alien is already in the U.S. working for the same employer, or a subsidiary or affiliate of the firm or corporation or other legal entity, by which the alien was employed abroad, he/she was employed by the entity abroad in a managerial or executive capacity for at least one year in the 3 years preceding his/her entry as a nonimmigrant;
  - the prospective employer in the U.S. is the same employer or a subsidiary or affiliate of the firm or corporation or other legal entity by which the alien was employed abroad;
  - the prospective U.S. employer has been doing business for at least one year; and
  - the alien is to be employed in the U.S. in a managerial or executive capacity and describing the duties to be performed.

*A U.S. employer filing for a member of the professions with an advanced degree or a person with exceptional ability In the sciences, arts, or business* must file the petition with:
- a labor certification (see GENERAL EVIDENCE) and either:
- an official academic record showing that the alien has a U S. advanced degree or an equivalent foreign degree, or an official academic record showing that the alien has a U.S. baccalaureate degree or an equivalent foreign degree and letters from current or former employers showing that the alien has at least 5 years of progressive post-baccalaureate experience in the specialty; or
- at least 3 of the following:
  - an official academic record showing that the alien has a degree, diploma, certificate, or similar award from an institution of learning relating to the area of exceptional ability;
  - letters from current or former employers showing that the alien has at least 10 years of full-time experience in the occupation for which he/she is being sought;
  - a license to practice the profession or certification for a particular profession or occupation;
  - evidence that the alien has commanded a salary, or other remuneration for services which demonstrates exceptional ability;
  - evidence of membership in professional associations; or
  - evidence of recognition for achievements and significant contributions to the industry or field by peers, governmental entities, or professional or business organizations.
- If the above standards do not readily apply to the alien's occupation, you may submit comparable evidence to establish the alien's eligibility.

*A U.S. employer filing for a skilled worker* must file the petition with:
- a labor certification (see GENERAL EVIDENCE); and requirement is 2 years of training or experience.
- evidence that the alien meets the educational, training, or experience and any other requirements of the labor certification (the minimum requirement is 2 years of training or experience).

Form I-140 (Rev. 12-02-91)

*A U.S. employer filing for a professional* must file the petition with:
- a labor certification (see GENERAL EVIDENCE);
- evidence that the alien holds a U.S. baccalaureate degree or equivalent foreign degree; and
- evidence that a baccalaureate degree is required for entry into the occupation.

*A U.S. employer filing for its employee in Hong Kong* must file its petition with a statement that demonstrates that:
- the company is owned and organized in the United States
- the employee is a resident of Hong Kong;
- the company, or its subsidiary or affiliate, is employing the person in Hong Kong, and has been employing him or her there for the past 12 months, or the company, or its subsidiary or affiliate, is employing him or her outside of Hong Kong during a temporary absence (i.e., of limited duration) and he or she had been employed in Hong Kong for 12 consecutive months prior to such absence(s), and that such employment is, and for that period has been, as an officer or supervisor, or in a capacity that is executive, managerial or involves specialized knowledge;
- the company employs at least 100 employees in the U.S. and at least 50 employees outside the U.S. and has a gross annual income of at least $50,000,000; and
- the company intends to employ the person in the United States as an officer or supervisor, or in a capacity that is executive, managerial or involves specialized knowledge, with salary and benefits comparable to others with similar responsibilities and experience within the company. A specific job description is required for immediate immigration; a commitment to a qualifying job is required for deterred immigration.

*A U.S. employer filing for an unskilled worker* must file the petition with:
- a labor certification (see GENERAL EVIDENCE); and
- evidence that the beneficiary meets any education, training, or experience requirements required in the labor certification.

### General Evidence.
*Labor certification.* Petitions for certain classifications must be filed with a certification from the Department of Labor or with documentation to establish that the alien qualifies for one of the shortage occupations in the Department of Labor's Labor Market Information Pilot Program or for an occupation in Group I or II of the Department of Labor's Schedule A. A certification establishes that there are not sufficient workers who are able, willing, qualified, and available at the time and place where the alien is to be employed and that employment of the alien if qualified, will not adversely affect the wages and working conditions of similarly employed U.S. workers. Application for certification is made on Form ETA-750 and is filed at the local office of the State Employment Service. If the alien is in a shortage occupation, or for a Schedule A/Group I or II occupation, you may file a fully completed, uncertified Form ETA-750 in duplicate with your petition for determination by INS that the alien belongs to the shortage occupation.

*Translations.* Any foreign language document must be accompanied by a full English translation which the translator has certified as complete and correct, and by the translator's certification that he or she is competent to translate from the foreign language into English.

*Copies.* It these instructions state that a copy of a document may be filed with this petition, and you choose to send us the original, we may keep that original for our records.

### Where To File.
File this petition at the INS Service Center with jurisdiction over the place where the alien will be employed.

If the employment will be in Alabama, Connecticut, Delaware, District of Columbia, Florida, Georgia, Maine, Maryland, Massachusetts, New Hampshire, New Jersey, New York, North Carolina, Pennsylvania, Puerto Rico, Rhode Island, South Carolina, Vermont, the Virgin Islands, Virginia, or West Virginia, mail your petition to: USINS Eastern Service Center, 75 Lower Welden Street, St. Albans, VT 05479-0001.

If the employment will be in Arizona, California, Guam, Hawaii, or Nevada, mail your petition to: USINS Western Service Center, P.O. Box 30040, Laguna Niguel, CA 92607-0040.

If the employment will be elsewhere in the U.S., mail your petition to: USINS Northern Service Center, 100 Centennial Mall North, Room, B-26, Lincoln, NE 68508.

### Fee.
The fee for this petition is $75.00. The fee must be submitted in the exact amount. It cannot be refunded. DO NOT MAIL CASH. All checks and money orders must be drawn on a bank or other institution located in the United States and must be payable in United States currency. The check or money order should be made payable to the Immigration and Naturalization Service, except that:
- If you live in Guam, and are filing this application in Guam, make your check or money order payable to the "Treasurer, Guam."
- If you live in the Virgin Islands, and are filing this application in the Virgin Islands, make your check or money order payable to the "Commissioner of Finance of the Virgin Islands."

Checks are accepted subject to collection. An uncollected check will render the application and any document issued invalid. A charge of $5.00 will be imposed if a check in payment of a fee is not honored by the bank on which it is drawn.

### Processing Information.
*Acceptance.* Any petition that is not signed or is not accompanied by the correct fee will be rejected with a notice that it is deficient. You may correct the deficiency and resubmit the petition. However, a petition is not considered properly filed until accepted by the Service. A priority date will not be assigned until the petition is properly filed.

*Initial processing.* Once the petition has been accepted, it will be checked for completeness, including submission of the required initial evidence. If you do not completely fill out the form, or file it without required initial evidence, you will not establish a basis for eligibility, and we may deny your petition.

*Requests for more information or interview.* We may request more information or evidence or we may request that you appear at an INS office for an interview. We may also request that you submit the originals of any copy. We will return these originals when they are no longer required. Decision. If you have established eligibility for the benefit requested, your petition will be approved. If you have not established eligibility, your petition will be denied. You will be notified in writing of the decision on your petition.

*Meaning of petition approval.*
Approval of a petition means you have established that the person you are filing for is eligible for the requested classification. This is the first step towards permanent residence. However, this does not in itself grant permanent residence or employment authorization. You will be given information about the requirements for the person to receive an immigrant visa, or to adjust status, after your petition is approved.

### Penalties.
If you knowingly and willfully falsify or conceal a material fact or submit a false document with this request, we will deny the benefit you are filing for, and may deny any other immigration benefit. In addition, you will face severe penalties provided by law, and may be subject to criminal prosecution.

### Privacy Act Notice.
We ask for the information on this form, and associated evidence, to determine if you have established eligibility for the immigration benefit you are filing for. Our legal right to ask for this information is in 8 USC 11854. We may provide this information to other government agencies. Failure to provide this information, and any requested evidence, may delay a final decision or result in denial of your request.

### Paperwork Reduction Act Notice.
We try to create forms and instructions that are accurate, can be easily understood, and which impose the least possible burden on you to provide us with information. Often this is difficult because some immigration laws are very complex. The estimated average time to complete and file this application is as follows: (1) 20 minutes to learn about the law and form; (2) 15 minutes to complete the form; and (3) 45 minutes to assemble and file the petition; for a total estimated average of 1 hour and 20 minutes per petition. If you have comments regarding the accuracy of this estimate, or suggestions for making this form simpler, you can write to both the Immigration and Naturalization Service, 425 I Street, N.W., Room 5304, Washington, D.C. 20536; and the Office of Management and Budget, Paperwork Reduction Project, OMB No. 1115-0061, Washington, D.C. 20503.

**U.S. Department of Justice**

Immigration and Naturalization Service

OMB #1115-0061

Immigrant Petition for Alien Worker

## START HERE - Please Type or Print

### Part 1. Information about the person or organization filing this petition

If an individual is filing, use the top Name line. Organizations should use the second line.

| Family Name | Given Name | Middle Initial |
|---|---|---|

Company or Organization

**Address** - Attn:

| Street Number and Name | Room # |
|---|---|

| City | State or Province |
|---|---|

| Country | ZIP/Postal Code |
|---|---|

| IRS Tax # | Social Security # |
|---|---|

### Part 2. Petition Type.    This petition is being filed for: (check one)

a. ☐ An alien of extraordinary ability
b. ☐ An outstanding professor or researcher
c. ☐ A multinational executive or manager
d. ☐ A member of the professions holding an advanced degree or an alien of exceptional ability
e. ☐ A skilled worker (requiring at least two years of specialized training or experience) or professional
f. ☐ An employee of a U.S. business operating in Hong Kong
g. ☐ Any other worker (requiring less than two years training or experience)

### Part 3. Information about the person you are filing for.

| Family Name | Given Name | Middle Initial |
|---|---|---|

Address - C/O

| Street # and Name | Apt. # |
|---|---|

| City | State or Province |
|---|---|

| Country | ZIP/Postal Code |
|---|---|

| Date of Birth (month/day/year) | Country of Birth |
|---|---|

| Social Security # (if any) | A # (if any) |
|---|---|

| if in the U.S. | Date of Arrival (month/day/year) | I-94# |
|---|---|---|
| | Current Nonimmigrant Status | Expires on (month/day/year) |

### Part 4. Processing Information.

Below give the U.S. Consulate you want notified if this petition is approved and if any requested adjustment of status cannot be granted.

| U.S. Consulate:   City | Country |
|---|---|

Form I-140 (Rev. 12-2-91)          ***Continued on back.***

---

### FOR INS USE ONLY

| Returned | Receipt |
|---|---|
| Resubmitted | |
| Reloc Sent | |
| Reloc Rec'd | |

☐ Petitioner Interviewed

☐ Beneficiary Interviewed

**Classification**
☐ 203(b)(1)(A) Alien Of Extraordinary Ability
☐ 203(b)(1)(B) Outstanding Professor or Researcher
☐ 203(b)(1)(C) Multi-national executive or manager
☐ 203(b)(2) Member of professions w/adv. degree or of exceptional ability
☐ 203(b)(3) (A) (i) Skilled worker
☐ 203(b)(3) (A) (ii) Professional
☐ 203(b)(3) (A) (iii) Other worker
☐ Sec. 124 IMMACT-Employee of U.S. business in Hong Kong

| Priority Date | Consulate |
|---|---|

**Remarks:**

**Action Block**

---

**To Be Completed by**
***Attorney*** or ***Representative***, if any

☐ Fill in box if G-28 is attached to represent the petitioner

VOLAG#

ATTY State License #

## Part   4.  Processing Information. (continued)

If you gave a U. S. address in Part 3, print the person's foreign address below. If his/her native alphabet does not use Roman letters, print his/her name and foreign address in the native alphabet.

Name                                                    Address

| | | | |
|---|---|---|---|
| Are you filing any other petitions or applications with this one? | | ☐ No | ☐ yes attach an explanation |
| Is the person you are filing for in exclusion or deportation proceedings? | | ☐ No | ☐ yes attach an explanation |
| Has an immigrant visa petition ever been filed by or in behalf of this person? | | ☐ No | ☐ yes attach an explanation |

## Part   5.  Additional Information about the employer.

Type of petitioner    ☐ Self           ☐ Individual U.S. Citizen        ☐ Company or organization
(check one)
                      ☐ Permanent Resident   ☐ Other explain _____

If a company, give the following:
   Type of business

| Date Established | Current #<br>of employees | Gross<br>Annual Income | Net Annual<br>Income |
|---|---|---|---|
| | | | |

| If an individual, give the following:<br>Occupation | Annual Income |
|---|---|
| | |

## Part   6.  BasIc Information about the proposed employment.

| Job<br>Title | Nontechnical<br>description of job |
|---|---|
| | |

Address where the person will work
if different from address in Part 1.

| Is this a full-time<br>position? | ☐ yes | ☐ No (hours per week _____ ) | Wages per<br>week |
|---|---|---|---|
| | | | |

Is this a permanent position?:    ☐ yes    ☐ No   │ Is this a new position?  ☐ yes   ☐ No

## Part   7.  Information on spouse and all children of the person you are filing for.

Provide an attachment listing the family members of the person you are filing for. Be sure to include their full name, relationship, date and country of birth, and present address.

## Part   8.  Signature. *Read the information on penalties in the instructions before completing this section.*

I certify under penalty of perjury under the laws of the United States of America that this petition, and the evidence submitted with it, is all true and correct. I authorize the release of any information from my records which the Immigration and Naturalization Service needs to determine eligibility for the benefit I am seeking.

**Signature**                                                                  Date

**Please Note:**  *If you do not completely fill out this form, or fail to submit required documents listed in the instructions, you cannot be found eligible for the requested document and this application may to be denied.*

## Part   9.  Signature of person preparing form if other than above. *(Sign below)*

I declare that I prepared this application at the request of the above person and it is based on all information of which I have knowledge.

**Signature**                                 Print Your Name                    Date

Firm Name
and Address

*US. GP0:1992-312-328/51143

Form 1-140 (Rev. 12-2-91)

**U.S. Department of Justice**

Immigration and Naturalization Service

OMB #1115-0009

Application for Naturalization

## INSTRUCTIONS

### Purpose of This Form.

This form is for use to apply to become a naturalized citizen of the United States.

### Who May File.

You may apply for naturalization if:

- you have been a lawful permanent resident for five years;
- you have been a lawful permanent resident for three years have been married to a United States citizen for those three years and continue to be married to that U.S. citizen;
- you are the lawful permanent resident child of United States citizen parents; or
- you have qualifying military service.

Children under 18 may automatically become citizens when their parents naturalize. You may inquire at your local Service office for further information If you do not meet the qualifications listed above but believe that you are eligible for naturalization you may inquire at your local Service office for additional information

### General Instructions.

Please answer all questions by typing or clearly printing in black ink. Indicate that an item is not applicable with "N/A". If an answer is "none," write "none". If you need extra space to answer any item attach a sheet of paper with your name and your alien registration number (A#), if any, and indicate the number of the item.

Every application must be properly signed and filed with the correct fee. If you are under 18 years of age, your parent or guardian must sign the application.

If you wish to be called for your examination at the same time as another person who is also applying for naturalization, make your request on a separate cover sheet. Be sure to give the name and alien registration number of that person.

### Initial Evidence Requirements.

You must file your application with the following evidence:

*A copy of your alien registration card.*

*Photographs.* You must submit two color photographs of yourself taken within 30 days of this application. These photos must be glossy, unretouched and unmounted, and have a white background. Dimension of the face should be about 1 inch from chin to top of hair. Face should be 3/4 frontal view of right side with right ear visible. Using pencil or felt pen, lightly print name and A#, if any, on the back of each photo. This requirement may be waived by the Service if you can establish that you are confined because of age or physical infirmity.

*Fingerprints.* If you are between the ages of 14 and 75, you must sumit your fingerprints on Form FD-258. Fill out the form and write your Alien Registration Number in the space marked "Your No. OCA" or "Miscellaneous No. MNU". Take the chart and these instructions to a police station, sheriff's office or an office of this Service, or other reputable person or organization for fingerprinting. You should contact the police or sheriff's office before going there since some of these offices do not take fingerprints for other government agencies. You must sign the chart in the presence of the person taking your fingerprints and have that person sign his/her name, title, and the date in the space provided. Do not bend, fold, or crease the fingerprint chart.

*U.S. Military Service.* If you have ever served in the Armed Forces of the United States at any time, you must submit a completed Form G-325B. If your application is based on your military service you must also submit Form N-426, "Request for Certification of Military or Naval Service."

*Application for Child.* If this application is for a permanent resident child of U.S. citizen parents, you must also submit copies of the child's birth certificate the parents' marriage certificate, and evidence of the parents' U.S. citizenship. If the parents are divorced, you must also submit the divorce decree and evidence that the citizen parent has legal custody of the child.

### Where to File.

File this application at the local Service office having jurisdiction over your place of residence.

### Fee.

The fee for this application is $95.00. The fee must be submitted in the exact amount. It cannot be refunded. DO NOT MAIL CASH.

All checks and money orders must be drawn on a bank or other institution located in the United States and must be payable in United States currency. The check or money order should be made payable to the Immigration and Naturalization Service, except that:

- If you live in Guam, and are filing this application in Guam, make your check or money order payable to the "Treasurer, Guam."
- If you live in the Virgin Islands, and are filing this application in the Virgin Islands, make your check or money order payable to the "Commissioner of Finance of the Virgin Islands."

Checks are accepted subject to collection. An uncollected check will render the application and any document issued invalid. A charge of $5.00 will be imposed if a check in payment of a fee is not honored by the bank on which it is drawn.

Form N-400 (Rev: 07/17/91) N

**Processing Information.**
Rejection. Any application that is not signed or is not accompanied by the proper fee will be rejected with a notice that the application is deficient. You may correct the deficiency and resubmit the application. However, an application is not considered properly filed until it is accepted by the Service.

*Requests for more information.* We may request more information or evidence. We may also request that you submit the originals of any copy. We will return these originals when they are no longer required.

*Interview.* After you file your application, you will be notified to appear at a Service office to be examined under oath or affirmation. This interview may not be waived. If you are an adult, you must show that you have a knowledge and understanding of the history, principles, and form of government of the United States. There is no exemption from this requirement.

You will also be examined on your ability to read, write, and speak English. If on the date of your examination you are more than 50 years of age and have been a lawful permanent resident for 20 years or more, or you are 55 years of age and have been a lawful permanent resident for at least 15 years, you will be exempt from the English language requirements of the law. If you are exempt, you may take the examination in any language you wish.

Oath of Allegiance. If your application is approved, you will be required to take the following oath of allegiance to the United States in order to become a citizen:

*"I hereby declare, on oath, that I absolutely and entirely renounce and abjure all allegiance and fidelity to any foreign prince, potentate, state or sovereignty, of whom or which I have heretofore been a subject or citizen; that I will support and defend the Constitution and laws of the United States of America against all enemies, foreign and domestic; that I will bear true faith and allegiance to the same, that I will bear arms on behalf of the United States when required by the law; that I will perform noncombatant service in the armed forces of the United States when required by the law; that I will perform work of national importance under civilian direction when required by the law; and that I take this obligation freely without any mental reservation or purpose of evasion; so help me God."*

If you cannot promise to bear arms or perform noncombatant service because of religious training and belief, you may omit those statements when taking the oath. "Religious training and belief" means a person's belief in relation to a Supreme Being involving duties superior to those arising from any human relation, but does not include essentially political, sociological, or philosophical views or merely a personal moral code.

*Oath ceremony.* You may choose to have the oath of allegiance administered in a ceremony conducted by the Service or request to be scheduled for an oath ceremony in a court that has jurisdiction over the applicant's place of residence. At the time of your examination you will be asked to elect either form of ceremony. You will become a citizen on the date of the oath ceremony and the Attorney General will issue a Certificate of Naturalization as evidence of United States citizenship.

If you wish to change your name as part of the naturalization process, you will have to take the oath in court.

**Penalties.**
If you knowingly and willfully falsify or conceal a material fact or submit a false document with this request, we will deny the benefit you are filing for, and may deny any other immigration benefit. In addition, you will face severe penalties provided by law, and may be subject to criminal prosecution.

**Privacy Act Notice.**
We ask for the information on this form, and associated evidence, to determine if you have established eligibility for the immigration benefit you are filing for. Our legal right to ask for this information is in 8 USC 1439, 1440, 1443, 1445, 1446, and 1452. We may provide this information to other government agencies. Failure to provide this information, and any requested evidence, may delay a final decision or result in denial of your request.

**Paperwork Reduction Act Notice.**
We try to create forms and instructions that are accurate, can be easily understood, and which impose the least possible burden on you to provide us with information. Often this is difficult because some immigration laws are very complex. Accordingly, the reporting burden for this collection of information is computed as follows:  (1) learning about the law and form, 20 minutes; (2) completing the form, 25 minutes; and (3) assembling and filing the application (includes statutory required interview and travel time, after filing of application), 3 hours and 35 minutes, for an estimated average of 4 hours and 20 minutes per response. If you have comments regarding the accuracy of this estimate, or suggestions for making this form simpler, you can write to both the Immigration and Naturalization Service, 425 I Street, N.W., Room 5304, Washington, D.C 20536; and the Office of Management and Budget, Paperwork Reduction Project, OMB No. 1115-0009, Washington, D.C. 20503.

**U.S. Department of Justice**
Immigration and Naturalization Service

OMB #1115-0009
Application for Naturalization

## START HERE - Please Type or Print

### Part 1. Information about you.

| Family Name | Given Name | Middle Initial |
|---|---|---|
| | | |

**U.S. Mailing Address** - Care of

| Street Number and Name | | Apt # |
|---|---|---|
| City | County | |
| State | | ZIP Code |

| Date of Birth (month/day/year) | Country of Birth |
|---|---|
| Social Security # | A # |

### Part 2. Basis for Eligibility *(check one).*

a. ☐  I have been a permanent resident for a least five (5) years.

b. ☐  I have been a permanent resident for at least three (3) years and have been married to a United States Citizen for those three years.

c. ☐  I am a permanent resident child of United States citizen parent(s).

d. ☐  I am applying on the basis of qualifying military service in the Armed Forces of this U.S. and have attached completed Forms N-426 and G-325B

e. ☐  Other. (Please specify section of law) _____ .

### Part 3. Additional information about you.

| Date you became a permanent resident (month/day/year) | Port admitted with an immigrant visa of INS Office where granted adjustment of status |
|---|---|

Citizenship

Name on alien registration card (if different than in Part 1)

Other names used since you became a permanent resident (including maiden name)

| Sex | ☐ Male  ☐ Female | Height | Marital Status | ☐ Single  ☐ Married | ☐ Divorced  ☐ Widowed |
|---|---|---|---|---|---|

Can you speak, read and write English?          ☐ No ☐ Yes.

**Absences from the U.S.:**

Have you been absent from the U.S. since becoming a permanent resident?     ☐ No ☐ Yes.

If you answered **"Yes"** , complete the following   Begin with your most recent absence. If you need more room to explain the reason for an absence or to list more trips, continue on separate paper.

| Date left U.S. | Date returned | Did absence last 6 months or more? | Destination | Reason for trip |
|---|---|---|---|---|
| | | ☐ Yes  ☐ No | | |
| | | ☐ Yes  ☐ No | | |
| | | ☐ Yes  ☐ No | | |
| | | ☐ Yes  ☐ No | | |
| | | ☐ Yes  ☐ No | | |
| | | ☐ Yes  ☐ No | | |

Form N-400 (Rev. 07/17/91 ) N                    *Continued on back.*

### FOR INS USE ONLY

| Returned | Receipt |
|---|---|
| _____ | |
| _____ | |
| **Resubmitted** | |
| _____ | |
| _____ | |
| **Reloc Sent** | |
| _____ | |
| _____ | |
| **Reloc Rec'd** | |
| _____ | |
| _____ | |

☐ Applicant Interviewed

**At interview**
☐   request naturalization ceremony at court

**Remarks:**

**Action**

**To Be Completed by**
***Attorney* or *Representative*, if any**
☐  Fill in box if G-28 is attached to represent the applicant

VOLAG#

ATTY State License #

## Part 4. Information about your residences and employment.

A   List your addresses during the last five (5) years or since you became a permanent resident, whichever is less. Begin with your current address. If you need more space, continue on separate paper:

| Street Number and Name, City, State, Country, and Zip Code | Dates (month/day/year) | |
| --- | --- | --- |
| | From | To |
| | | |
| | | |
| | | |
| | | |

B   List your employers during the last five (5) years. List your present or most recent employer first. If none, write "None". If you need more space, continue on separate paper.

| Employer's Name | Employer's Address Street Name and Number - City, State and ZIP Code | Dates Employed (month/day/year) | | Occupation/position |
| --- | --- | --- | --- | --- |
| | | From | To | |
| | | | | |
| | | | | |
| | | | | |
| | | | | |

## Part 5. Information about your marital history.

A .   Total number of times you have been married _____ . If you are now married, complete the following regarding your husband or wife.

| Family name | Given name | Middle initial |
| --- | --- | --- |

Address

| Date of birth (month/day/year) | Country of birth | Citizenship |
| --- | --- | --- |
| Social Security # | A# (if applicable) | Immigration status (if not a U.S. citizen) |

**Naturalization** (If applicable)
(month/day/year)                Place   (City, State)

If you have ever previously been married or if your current spouse has been previously married, please provide the following on separate paper: Name of prior spouse, date of marriage, date marriage ended, how marriage ended and immigration status of prior spouse.

## Part 6. Information about your children.

B.   Total Number of Children _____  Complete the following information for each of your children. If the child lives with you, state "with me" in the address column; otherwise give city/state/country of child's current residence. If deceased, write "deceased" in address column.   If you need more space, continue on separate paper.

| Full name of child | Date of birth | Country of Birth | Citizenship | A - Number | Address |
| --- | --- | --- | --- | --- | --- |
| | | | | | |
| | | | | | |
| | | | | | |
| | | | | | |
| | | | | | |
| | | | | | |
| | | | | | |

Form N-400 (Rev 07/17/91)N                *Continued on next page*

**SAMPLE DOCUMENT – NOT TO BE USED WHEN FILING.**

*Continued on back*

## Part 7. Additional eligibility factors.

Please answer each of the following questions. If your answer is **"Yes"**, explain on a separate paper.

1. Are you now, or have you ever been a member of, or in any way connected or associated with the Communist Party, or ever knowingly aided or supported the Communist Party directly, or indirectly through another organization, group or person, or ever advocated, taught, believed in, or knowingly supported or furthered the interests of communism?  ☐ Yes ☐ No

2. During the period March 23, 1933 to May 8, 1945, did you serve in, or were you in any way affiliated with, either directly or indirectly, any military unit, paramilitary unit, police unit, self-defense unit, vigilante unit, citizen unit of the Nazi party or SS, government agency or office, extermination camp, concentration camp, prisoner of war camp, prison, labor camp, detention camp or transit camp, under the control or affiliated with:

   a. The Nazi Government of Germany?  ☐ Yes ☐ No
   b. Any government in any area occupied by, allied with, or established with the assistance or cooperation of, The Nazi Government of Germany?  ☐ Yes ☐ No

3. Have you at any time, anywhere, ever ordered, incited, assisted, or otherwise participated in the persecution of any person because of race, religion, national origin, or political opinion?  ☐ Yes ☐ No

4. Have you ever left the United States to avoid being drafted into the U.S. Armed Forces?  ☐ Yes ☐ No

5. Have you ever failed to comply with Selective Service laws?  ☐ Yes ☐ No
   II you have registered under the Selective Service laws, complete the following information:
   Selective Service Number _____ Date Registered: _____
   If you registered before 1978, also provide the following:
   Local Board Number. _____ Classification: _____

6. Did you ever apply for exemption from military service because of alienage, conscientious objections or other reasons?  ☐ Yes ☐ No

7. Have you ever deserted from the military, air or naval forces of the United States?  ☐ Yes ☐ No

8. Since becoming a permanent resident, have you ever failed to file a federal income tax return?  ☐ Yes ☐ No

9. Since becoming a permanent resident, have you filed a federal income tax return as a nonresident or failed to file a federal return because you considered yourself to be a nonresident?  ☐ Yes ☐ No

10 Are deportation proceedings pending against you, or have you ever been deported, or ordered deported, or have you ever applied for suspension deportation?  ☐ Yes ☐ No

11. Have you ever claimed in writing, or in any way, to be a United States citizen?  ☐ Yes ☐ No

12. Have you ever:
    a  been a habitual drunkard?  ☐ Yes ☐ No
    b. advocated or practiced polygamy?  ☐ Yes ☐ No
    c. been a prostitute or procured anyone for prostitution?  ☐ Yes ☐ No
    d. knowingly and for gain helped any alien to enter the U.S. illegally?  ☐ Yes ☐ No
    e. been an illicit trafficker in narcotic drugs or marijuana?  ☐ Yes ☐ No
    f. received income from illegal gambling?  ☐ Yes ☐ No
    g. given false testimony for the purpose of obtaining any immigration benefit?  ☐ Yes ☐ No

13. Have you ever been declared legally incompetent or have you ever been confined as a patient in a mental institution?  ☐ Yes ☐ No

14. Were you born with, or have you acquired in same way, any title or order of nobility in any foreign State?  ☐ Yes ☐ No

15. Have you ever:
    a. knowingly committed any crime for which you have not been arrested?  ☐ Yes ☐ No
    b. been arrested, cited, charged, indicted, convicted, fined or imprisoned for breaking or violating any law or ordinance excluding traffic regulations?  ☐ Yes ☐ No

( If you answer yes to 15, in your explanation give the following information for each accident or occurrence the **city, state,** and **country**, where the offense took place, the **date** and **nature** of the offense, and the **outcome** or **disposition** of the case).

## Part 8. Allegiance to the U.S.

If your answer to any of the following questions is "NO", attach a full explanation:

1. Do you believe in the Constitution and form of government of The U.S.?  ☐ Yes ☐ No
2. Are you willing to take the full Oath of Allegiance to the U.S.? (see instructions)  ☐ Yes ☐ No
3. If the law requires it, are you willing to bear arms on behalf of the U.S.?  ☐ Yes ☐ No
4. It the law requires it, are you willing to perform noncombatant services in the Armed Forces of the U.S.?  ☐ Yes ☐ No
s. It the law requires it, are you willing to perform work of national importance under civilian direction?  ☐ Yes ☐ No

Form N-400 (Rev. 07/17/91)N

*Continued on back*

## Part 9. Memberships and organizations.

A.   List your present and past membership in or affiliation with every organization, association, fund, foundation, party, club, society, or similar group in the United States or in any other place. Include any military service in this part. If none, write "none". Include the name of organization, location, dates of membership and the nature of the organization. If additional space is needed, use separate paper.

_____

_____

_____

_____

## Part 10.  Complete only if you checked block "C" in Part 2.

How many of your parents are U.S. citizens?        ☐ One   ☐ Both      (Give the following about the U.S. citizen parent:)

| Family Name | Given Name | Middle Name |
|---|---|---|
| | | |

Address

Basis for citizenship:                Relationship to you (check one):   ☐   natural parent      ☐   adoptive parent
☐   Birth
☐   Naturalization Cert. No.                                   ☐   parent of child legitimated after birth

If adopted or legitimated after birth, give date of adoption or, legitimation: (month/day/year) _____

Does this parent have legal custody of you?        ☐ Yes   ☐ No

*(Attach a copy of relating evidence to establish that you are the child of this U.S. citizen and evidence of this parent's citizenship.)*

## Part 11. Signature.  *(Read the information on penalties in the instructions before completing this section).*

I certify or, if outside the United States, I swear or affirm, under penalty of perjury under the laws of the United States of America that this application, and the evidence submitted with it, is all true and correct. I authorize the release of any information from my records which the Immigration and Naturalization Service needs to determine eligibility for the benefit I am seeking.

*Signature*                                                                                     **Date**

_____

**Please Note:** *If you do not completely fill out this form, or fail to submit required documents listed in the instructions, you may not be found eligible for naturalization and this application may be denied.*

## Part 12. Signature of person preparing form if other than above. *(Sign below)*

I declare that I prepared this application at the request of the above person and it is based on all information of which I have knowledge.

Signature                          **Print Your Name**                          **Date**

Firm Name
and Address

### DO NOT COMPLETE THE FOLLOWING UNTIL INSTRUCTED TO DO SO AT THE INTERVIEW

I swear that I know the contents of this application, and supplemental
pages 1 through _____ , that the corrections , numbered 1
through _____ , were made at my request, and that this amended
application, is true to the best of my knowledge and belief.                    Subscribed and sworn to before me by the applicant.

_____                  _____
            *(Complete and true signature of applicant)*                    *(Examiner's Signature)*              *Date*

Form N-400 (Rev.  07/17/91)N                                              **FPI-LOM**

**U.S. Department of Justice**

Immigration and Naturalization Service

OMB No. 1115-0053

Supplement A to Form I-485

**Purpose of This Form.** This form is for use by a person in the United States who is applying for adjustment of status to that of a lawful permanent resident of the United States and who benefits from the provisions of section 245(i) of the Immigration and Nationality Act (the Act). It allows the applicant to determine whether he or she must file under this provision and whether an additional sum will be required. It also collects statistical information needed by the Immigration and Naturalization Service (INS).

Section 245(i) of the Act temporarily lifts certain restrictions on eligibility for adjustment of status to that of a lawful permanent resident of the United States. It allows an otherwise eligible applicant to adjust status under section 245 of the Act without regard to manner of entry into the United States and without regard to most immigration status violations. The applicant may be required to pay an additional sum when applying under this provision.

**Who May File.** An eligible applicant must:
- be physically present in the United States;
- have an immediately available immigrant visa number;
- be admissible to the United States for permanent residence;
- properly file an application for adjustment of status on or after October 1, 1994, and must adjust status under section 245 of the Act before October 1, 1997;
- pay the required additional sum, or show that section 245(i) of the Act does not require the payment of an additional sum; and

**NOT Be a Person Who:**
- is or was a J-1 or J-2 exchange visitor, is subject to the two-year foreign residence requirement, and has not complied with or been granted a waiver of the requirement;
- has A, E or G nonimmigrant status, or has an occupation which would allow such status, UNLESS Form I-508 (Form I-508F for French nationals) is filed to waive diplomatic rights, privileges and immunities, and, if in A or G nonimmigrant status, a completed Form I-566 is submitted;
- is already a lawful permanent resident;
- is applying for adjustment of status as an immediate relative or preference alien and is not the beneficiary of a valid unexpired immigrant visa petition; or
- was admitted as a K-1 fiance(e) but did not marry the U.S. citizen who filed the petition, or was admitted as the K-2 child of a fiance(e) and the alien fiance(e) parent did not marry the U.S. citizen who filed the petition.

See the Form I-485, "Application to Register Permanent Residence or Adjust Status" instructions for additional information about the immediate availability of immigrant visa numbers, admissibility and proper filing of an application for adjustment of status.

**General Filing Instructions.**

Each applicant for the benefits of section 245(i) of the Act, including a child, must complete and file:

- Form I-485, and the required supporting forms, documents and fee shown in the Form I-485 instructions; and
- Supplement A to Form I-485, and any additional sum required by Public Law 103-317.

First, complete Form I-485 following the instructions. Then, complete Supplement A to Form I-485 to determine whether you need to file Supplement A to Form I-485, and to determine whether you must pay the additional sum.

**Where to File.** File Form I-485 and Supplement A to Form I-485 with the office having jurisdiction over your place of residence.

**When to File.** To benefit from Public Law 103-317, you must file this form on or after October 1, 1994, and must adjust status before October 1, 1997.

**Additional Sum.** In addition to the fee required by Form I-485, you must pay the additional sum (if any) shown in Part II, # 13 of this form. The additional sum must be submitted in the exact amount. It cannot be refunded. **DO NOT MAIL CASH.** All checks and money orders must be drawn on a bank or other financial institution located in the United States and must be payable in United States currency. The check or money order should be made payable to the Immigration and Naturalization Service, except:

- If you live in Guam, and are filing this application in Guam, make your check or money order payable to the "Treasurer, Guam."

- If you live in the Virgin Islands, and are filing this application in the Virgin Islands, make your check or money order payable to the "Commissioner of Finance of the Virgin Islands."

Checks are accepted subject to collection. An uncollected check will render the application and any document issued invalid. A charge of $5.00 will be imposed if a check in payment of an additional sum under Public Law 103-317 is not honored by the bank on which it is drawn.

Form I-485 (09-30-94) Supplement A

Reports Control No.: HQADN-3-94

**Decision.** You will be notified in writing of the decision on your application for adjustment of status.

**Penalties.** If you knowingly and willfully falsify or conceal a material fact or submit a false document with the request, we will deny the benefit you are filing for, and may deny any other immigration benefit. In addition, you will face severe penalties provided by law, and may be subject to criminal prosecution.

**Privacy Act Notice.** We ask for the information on this form, and associated evidence, to determine if you have established eligibility for the immigration benefit you are filing for. Our legal right to ask for this information is in 8 U.S.C. 1255 and 1259. We may provide this information to other government agencies. Failure to provide this information, and any requested evidence, may delay a final decision or result in denial of your request.

Form I-485 (09-30-94) Supplement A

     **SAMPLE DOCUMENT – NOT TO BE USED WHEN FILING.**

**U.S. Department of Justice**

Immigration and Naturalization Service

OMB No. 1115-0053

Supplement A to Form I-485

### START HERE - Please Type or Print

## Part 1. Information about Applicant

| Family | First | Middle |
|---|---|---|
| Name | Name | Initial |

**Address** - C/O

| Street Number and Name | | Apt Suite |
|---|---|---|
| City | State or Province | |
| Country | ZIP/Postal Code | |

| INS A # | Date of Birth *(month/day/year)* | Country of Birth |
|---|---|---|

## Part 2. Basis for Eligibility *(check one):*

1. On Form I-485, Part 2, I checked application type (check one)

a. ☐ An immigrant petition …                Go to #2

b. ☐ My spouse or parent applied …          Go to #2.

c. ☐ I entered as a K-1 fiance …            Stop Here. Do Not File This Form.

d. ☐ I was granted asylum …                 Stop Here. Do Not File This Form.

e. ☐ I am a native or citizen of Cuba …     Stop Here. Do Not File This Form.

f. ☐ I am the spouse or child of a Cuban    Stop Here. Do Not File This Form.

g. ☐ I have continuously resided in the U.S..  Stop Here. Do Not File This Form.

h. ☐ Other …                                Go to #2

i. ☐ I am already a permanent resident …    Stop Here. Do Not File This Form.

j. ☐ I am already a permanent resident and  Stop Here. Do Not File This Form.
   am the spouse or child of a Cuban

2. I have filed Form I-360; and I am applying for adjustment of status as a special immigrant juvenile court dependent *(check one)*:

   ☐ Yes   Stop Here. Do Not File This Form        ☐ No   Go to #3.

3. I have filed Form I-360; and I am applying for adjustment of status as a special immigrant who has served in the United States Armed Forces (check one):

   ☐ Yes   Stop Here. Do Not File This Form        ☐ No   Go to #4.

4. I last entered the United States *(check one)*:

   ☐ Legally as a crewman (D-1/D-2 visa).   Go to #11.      ☐ Legally without a visa              Go to #5
   ☐ Without inspection.                    Go to #11.      ☐ Legally as a parolee.              Go to #5.
   ☐ Legally in transit without visa status. Go to #11.     ☐ Legally with another type of visa  (show type___ ) Go to #5.

5. I last entered the United States legally without a visa as a visitor for tourism or business; and I am applying for adjustment of status as the spouse, unmarried child less than 21 years old, parent, widow or widower of a United States citizen *(check one)*:

   ☐ Yes   Stop Here. Do Not File This Form        ☐ No   Go to #6.

6. I last entered the United States legally as a parolee, or with a visa (except as a crewman), or as a Canadian citizen without a visa: and I am applying for adjustment of status (check one):

   ☐ As the spouse, unmarried child less than 21 years old, parent, widow or widower of a United States citizen.
      Stop Here. Do Not File This Form.

   ☐ As a special immigrant retired international organization employee or family membe of an international organiation employee or as special immigrant physician; and I have filed Form I-360.   Stop Here. Do Not File This Form.

   ☐ Under some other category.  Go to #7.

### FOR INS USE ONLY

| Returned | Receipt |
|---|---|
| _____ | |
| _____ | |
| **Resubmitted** | |
| _____ | |
| _____ | |
| **Reloc Sent** | |
| _____ | |
| _____ | Family |
| **Reloc Rec'd** | Name |
| _____ | |
| _____ | |
| **Interviewed** ☐ ☐ | |
| *File Reviewed* ☐ ☐ | Class of Adjustment Code: _____ _____ _____ |

**To Be Completed by**
***Attorney or Representative***, if any

☐ Check if G-28 is attached showing you represent the petitioner

VOLAG#

ATTY State License #

---

Form I-485 (09/30/94)  Supplement A                    Reports Control No.: HQADN-3-94

## Part 2. continue.

7. I am a national of the (former) Soviet Union, Vietnam, Laos or Cambodia who last entered the United States legally as a public interest parolee after having been denied refugee status; and I am applying for adjustment of status under Public Law 101-167 *(check one)*:

     ☐ Yes   Stop Here. Do Not File This Form.     ☐ No   Go to #8.

8. I have been employed in the United States after 01/01/77 without INS authorization *(check one)*:

     ☐ Yes   Go To #9.           ☐ No   Go to #10.

9. I am applying for adjustment of status under the Immigration Nursing Relief Act (INRA); I was employed without INS authorization only on or before 11/29/90; and I have always maintained a lawful immigration status while in the United States after 11/05/86 *(check one)*:

     ☐ Yes   Stop Here. Do Not File This Form.     ☐ No   Go to #10.

10.   I am now in lawful immigration status; and I have always maintained a lawful immigration status while in the United States after 11/05/86 *(check one)*:

     ☐ Yes   Stop Here. Do Not File This Form.
     ☐ No, but I believe that INS will determine that my failure to be in or maintain a lawful immigration status was through no fault of my own or for technical reasons.   Stop Here. Do Not File This Form, and attach an explanation to your Form I-485 application.
     ☐ No   Go to #11.

11. I am unmarried and less than 17 years old *(check one)*:

     ☐ Yes   Stop Here. File This Form and Form I-485. Pay only the fee required with Form I-485.
     ☐ No   Go to # 12.

12. I am the unmarried child of a legalized alien and am less than 21 years old, or I am the spouse of a legalized alien; and I have attached a copy of my receipt or approval notice showing that I have properly filed Form I-817, Application for Voluntary Departure under the Family Unity Program *(check one)*:

     ☐ Yes   Stop Here. File This Form and Form I-485. Pay only the fee required with Form I-485.
     ☐ No   Go to #13.

13. **File This Form and Form I-485. You must pay the additional sum:**

     $130.00 - Fee required with Form I-485* and
     $650.00 - Additional sum under section 245(i) of the Act
     ————
     **$780.00** - Total amount you must pay.

*If you filed Form I-485 separately, attach a copy of your filing receipt and pay only the additional sum of $650.00. In # 11 and /or # 12, show the answer you would have given on the date you filed Form I-485.

## Part 3. Signature. Read the information on penalties in the instructions before completing this section. If someone helped you prepare this petition he or she must complete Part 4.

I certify, under penalty of perjury under the laws of the United States of America, that this application, and the evidence submitted with it, is all true and correct. I authorize the release of any information from my records which the Immigration and Naturalization Service needs to determine eligibility for the benefit I am seeking.

| Signature | Print Your Name | Date | Daytime Telephone No. |
|---|---|---|---|
| | | | |

**Please Note:** If you do not completely fill out this form or fail to submit required documents listed in the instructions, you may not be found eligible for the requested document and this application may be denied.

## Part 4. Signature of person preparing form if other than above. *(Sign Below)*

*I declare that I prepared this application at the request of the above person and it is based on all information of which I have knowledge.*

| Signature | Print Your Name | Date | Daytime Telephone No. |
|---|---|---|---|
| | | | |

Firm Name
and Address

Form I-485 (09/30/94) Supplement A

EMBASSY OF THE
UNITED STATES OF AMERICA

EVIDENCE WHICH MAY BE PRESENTED TO MEET THE
PUBLIC CHARGE PROVISIONS OF THE LAW

GENERAL

The Immigration and Nationality Act requires an applicant for a visa to establish to the satisfaction of the consular officer at the time of his application for a visa, and also to the satisfaction of the United States immigration officials at the time of his application for admission into the United States, that he is not likely at any time to become a public charge.

An applicant for an immigrant visa may generally satisfy this requirement of the law by the presentation of documentary evidence establishing that:

1. he has, or will have, in the United States funds of his own sufficient to provide for the support of himself and members of his family; or

2. he has employment awaiting him in the United States which will provide an adequate income for himself and members of his family; or

3. he is skilled in a profession or occupation which has been determined to be in short supply in the United States and can show that he has funds adequate for transportation to the United States and for the support of himself and members of his family until he is able to locate employment in his profession or occupation; or

4. relatives or friends in the United States will assure his support.

APPLICANTS OWN FUNDS

An applicant who expects to be able to meet the public charge provisions of the law under 1 or to present evidence of funds required under 3 above may submit to the consular officer one or more of the following items:

(a) statement from an officer of a bank showing present balance of applicant's account, date account was opened, and average balance during the year. If there have been recent unusually large deposits, an explanation therefor should be given;

(b) proof of ownership of property or real estate, in the form of a letter from a lawyer, banker or responsible real estate agent showing its present valuation. Any mortgages or leans against the property must be stated;

(c) letter or letters verifying ownership of stocks and bonds, with present market value indicated;

Optional Form 167
Formerly DSL-845
NOV 86                                                                          OVER...

(d) statement from insurance company showing policies held and present cash surrender value;

(e) proof of income from business investments or other sources.

## EMPLOYMENT

Applicants having prearranged employment should submit evidence thereof from the prospective employer on his business letterhead or if he has no letterhead in the form of a contract or affidavit. An applicant whose employment has been certified by the Department of Labor need not furnish a statement or contract of employment, unless specifically requested to do so by the consular officer.

The letter, contract or affidavit should:

(a) contain a definite offer of employment;

(b) state whether the employment will be immediately available upon the applicant's arrival in the United States;

(c) specify the location, type, and duration (whether seasonal, temporary, or indefinite) of the employment offered;

(d) specify the rate or range of compensation to be paid;

(e) be of recent date; and

(f) if the prospective employer is an individual rather than a firm, some evidence proving that the individual is in a financial position to carry out the offer of employment.

## AFFIDAVIT OF SUPPORT

Those persons who desire to furnish sponsorship in the form of an affidavit of support should complete the enclosed Form I-134. Additional copies of Form I-134 (Rev. 12.1.84) may be obtained from this office or from any Immigration and Naturalization Service office in the United States.

If the sponsor is married, the affidavit should be jointly signed by both husband and wife.

Affidavits of support should be of recent date when presented to the consular officer. They are unacceptable if more than a year has elapsed from the date of execution.

A sponsor may prefer to forward his affidavit of support directly to the consular officer where the visa application will be made, in which event the contents will not be divulged to the applicant.

IMPORTANT: An applicant who expects to meet the public charge provisions of the law through the presentation of an affidavit of support is encouraged to forward this information sheet to his sponsor so as to assist him in preparing his affidavit.

<u>IMPORTANT</u> - This document must be read and signed by persons wishing to submit an affidavit of support on behalf of an alien applying for an immigrant visa. A signed copy of this document must be attached to each copy of any affidavits of support submitted on behalf of an applicant.

The Social Security Act, as amended, establishes certain requirements for determining the eligibility of aliens for Supplemental Security Income (SSI) and Aid to Families with Dependent Children (AFDC) benefits. The Food Stamp Act, as amended, contains similar provisions. These amendments require that the income and resources of any person (and that person's spouse) who executes an affidavit of support or similar agreement on behalf of an immigrant alien, be deemed to be the income and resources of the alien under formulas for determining eligibility for SSI, AFDC, and Food Stamp benefits during the three years following the alien's entry into the United States.

The eligibility of aliens for SSI, AFDC, and Food Stamp benefits will be contingent upon their obtaining the cooperation of their sponsors in providing the necessary information and evidence to enable the Social Security Administration and/or State Welfare Agencies to carry out those provisions. An alien applying for SSI, AFDC, or Food Stamp benefits must make available to the Social Security Administration and/or State Welfare Agencies documentation concerning his income or resources or those of his sponsors, including information which he provided in support of his application for an immigrant visa or adjustment of status. The Secretary of Health and Human Services and/or State Welfare Agencies are authorized to obtain copies of any such documentation from other agencies.

The Social Security Act and the Food Stamp Act also provide that an alien and his or her sponsor shall be jointly and severally liable to repay any SSI, AFDC, and Food Stamp benefits which are incorrectly paid because of misinformation provided by sponsor or because of sponsor's failure to provide information. Also, any incorrect payments of SSI and AFDC benefits which are not repaid will be withheld from any subsequent payments for which the alien or sponsors are otherwise eligible under the Social Security Act.

These provisions do not apply to aliens admitted as refugees or granted political asylum by the Attorney General. They also will not apply to the SSI eligibility of aliens who become blind or disabled after entry into the United States. The AFDC provisions do not apply to aliens who are dependent children of the sponsor or sponsor's spouse.

I, _____ , residing at _____
              (name)                                             (number and street)

_____ , _____
(City)                                            (State)

acknowledge that I have read the above and am aware of my responsibilities as an immigrant sponsor under the Social Security Act, as amended, and the Food Stamp Act, as amended. This statement is submitted on behalf of the following persons:

| Name | Sex | Age | Country of Birth | Married or Single | Relationship to Sponsor |
|------|-----|-----|------------------|-------------------|-------------------------|
|      |     |     |                  |                   |                         |

_____
Signature of Sponsor(s)

OF-167A
Mar 83

OMB Approval No. 44-R1301

**U.S. DEPARTMENT OF LABOR**
**Employment and Training Administration**

# APPLICATION
# FOR
# ALIEN EMPLOYMENT CERTIFICATION

**IMPORTANT: READ CAREFULLY BEFORE COMPLETING THIS FORM**
*PRINT legibly in ink or use a typewriter. If you need more space to answer questions on this form, use a separate sheet. Identify each answer with the number of the corresponding question. SIGN AND DATE each sheet in original signature.*
*To knowingly furnish any false information in the preparation of this form and any supplement thereto or to aid, abet, or counsel another to do so is a felony punishable by $10,000 fine or 5 years in the penitentiary, or both (18 U.S.C. 1001)*

**PART A. OFFER OF EMPLOYMENT**

1. Name of Alien *(Family name in capital letters, First, Middle, Maiden)*

2. Present Address of Alien *(Number, Street, City and Town, State ZIP Code or Province, Country)*

3. Type of Visa *(If in U.S.)*

The following information is submitted as evidence of an offer of employment.

4. Name of Employer *(Full name of organization)*

5. Telephone *(Area Code and Number)*

6. Address *(Number, Street, City or Town, Country, ZIP Code)*

7. Address Where Alien Will Work *(If different from item 6)*

| 8. Nature of Employer's Business Activity | 9. Name of Job Title | 10. Total Hours Per Week | | 11. Work Schedule *(Hourly)* | 12. Rate of Pay | |
|---|---|---|---|---|---|---|
| | | a. Basic | b. Overtime | | a. Basic | b. Overtime |
| | | | | a.m. | $ | $ |
| | | | | p.m. | per ............ | per hour |

13. Describe Fully the Job to be Performed *(Duties)*

14. State in detail the MINIMUM education, training, and experience for a worker to perform satisfactorily the job duties described in item 13 above.

15. Other Special Requirements

| **EDU-CATION** *(Enter number of years)* | Grade School | High School | College | College Degree Required *(specify)* |
|---|---|---|---|---|
| | | | | Major Field of Study |

| **TRAIN-ING** | No. Yrs. | No. Mos. | Type of Training |
|---|---|---|---|

| **EXPERI-ENCE** | Job Offered | | Related Occupation | | Related Occupation (specify) |
|---|---|---|---|---|---|
| | Yrs. | Mos. | Number Yrs. | Mos. | |

16. Occupational Title of Person Who Will Be Alien's Immediate Supervisor ➤ ➤

17. Number of Employees Alien will Supervise ➤

◄ ENDORSEMENTS *(Make no entry in section - for government use only)*

Date Forms Received

| L.O. | S.O. |
|---|---|
| R.O. | N.O. |
| Ind. Code | Occ. Code |
| Occ. Title | |

*Replaces MA 7-5OA, B and C (Apr. 1970 edition) which is obsolete.*

ETA 750 (Oct. 1979)

**SAMPLE DOCUMENT – NOT TO BE USED WHEN FILING.**

| 18.   COMPLETE ITEMS ONLY IF JOB IS TEMPORARY | | | 19. IF JOB IS UNIONIZED *(Complete)* | |
|---|---|---|---|---|
| a.   No. of Openings To Be Filled By Aliens Under Job Offer | b. Exact Dates You Expect To Employ Alien | | a. Number of Local | b. Name of Local |
| | From | To | | |
| | | | | c. City and Status |

### 20. STATEMENT FOR LIVE-AT-WORK JOB OFFERS *(Complete for Private Household Job ONLY)*

| a. description of Residence | | b. No. Persons Residing at Place of Employment | | | | c.   Will free board and private room not shared with any-one be provided? | *("X" one)* |
|---|---|---|---|---|---|---|---|
| *("X" one)* | Number of Rooms | Adults | | Children | Ages | | ☐ YES ☐ NO |
| ☐ House | | | BOYS | | | | |
| ☐ Apartment | | | GIRLS | | | | |

**21: DESCRIBE EFFORTS TO RECRUIT U.S. WORKERS AND THE RESULTS.** *(Specify Sources of Recruitment by Name)*

22.   Applications require various types of documentation. Please read PART II of the instructions to assure that appropriate supporting documentation is included with your application.

### 23. EMPLOYER CERTIFICATIONS

*By virtue of my signature below, I HEREBY CERTIFY the following conditions of employment.*

a.   I have enough funds available to pay the wage or salary offered the alien.

b.   The wage offered equals or exceeds the prevailing wage and I guarantee that, if a labor certification is granted, the wage paid to the alien when the alien begins work will equal or exceed the prevailing wage which is applicable at the time the alien begins work.

c.   The wage offered is not based on commissions, bonuses, or other incentives, unless I guarantee a wage paid on a weekly, bi-weekly or monthly basis.

d.   I will be able to place the alien on the payroll on or before the date of the alien's proposed entrance into the United States.

e.   The job opportunity does not involve unlawful discrimination by race, creed, national origin, sex, religion, handicap, or citizenship.

f.   The job opportunity is not:

(1)   Vacant because the former occupant is on strike or is being locked out in the course of a labor dispute involving a work stoppage.

(2)   At issue in a labor dispute involving a work stoppage.

g.   The job opportunity's terms, conditions and occupational environment are not contrary to federal, States or local law.

h.   The job opportunity has been and is clearly open to any qualified U.S. worker.

### 24. DECLARATIONS

**DECLARATION OF EMPLOYER** ➤ *Pursuant to 28 U.S.C. 1746, I declare under penalty of perjury the foregoing is true and correct.*

| SIGNATURE | DATE |
|---|---|
| NAME *(Type or Print)* | TITLE |

**AUTHORIZATION OF AGENT OF EMPLOYER** ➤ *I HEREBY DESIGNATE the agent below to represent me for the purpose of labor certification and I TAKE FULL RESPONSIBILITY for accuracy of any representations made by my agent.*

| SIGNATURE OF EMPLOYER | DATE |
|---|---|
| NAME OF AGENT *(Type or Print)* | ADDRESS OF AGENT *(Number, Street, City, State, ZIP Code)* |

| PART B. STATEMENT OF QUALIFICATIONS OF ALIEN |
|---|

FOR ADVISE CONCERNING REQUIREMENTS FOR ALIEN EMPLOYMENT CERTIFICATION: *If alien is in the U.S., contact nearest office of Immigration and Naturalization Service. If alien is outside U.S., contact nearest U.S. Consulate.*
IMPORTANT: READ ATTACHED INSTRUCTIONS BEFORE COMPLETING THIS FORM.
*Print legibly in ink or use a typewriter. If you need more space to fully answer any questions on this form, use a separate sheet. Identify each answer with the number of the corresponding question. Sign and date each sheet.*

| 1. Name of Alien *(Family name in capital letters)* | First name | Middle name | Maiden name |
|---|---|---|---|
| | | | |

| 2. Present Address *(No., Street, City or Town, State or Province and ZIP Code* | Country | 3. Type of Visa *(if in U.S.)* |
|---|---|---|
| | | |

| 4. Alien's Birthday *(Month, Day, Year)* | 5. Birthplace *(City or Town, State or Province)* | Country | 6. Present Nationality or Citizenship *(Country)* |
|---|---|---|---|
| | | | |

7. Address in United States Where Alien Will reside

| 8. Name and Address of Prospective Employer If Alien has job offer in U.S. | 9. Occupation in which Alien is Seeking Work |
|---|---|
| | |

10. "X" the appropriate box below and furnish the information required for the box marked

| a. ☐ Alien will apply for a visa abroad at the American Consulates in ⟶ | City in Foreign Country | Foreign Country |
|---|---|---|

| b. ☐ Alien is in the United States and will apply for adjust-met of status to that of a lawful permanent resident in the office of the Immigration and Naturalization Service at ⟶ | City | Status |
|---|---|---|

| 11. Names and Addresses of Schools, Colleges and Universities Attended *(Include trade or vocational training facilities)* | Field of Study | FROM | | TO | | Degrees or Certificates Received |
|---|---|---|---|---|---|---|
| | | Month | Year | Month | Year | |
| | | | | | | |
| | | | | | | |
| | | | | | | |
| | | | | | | |
| | | | | | | |

## SPECIAL QUALIFICATIONS AND SKILLS

12. Additional Qualifications and Skills Alien Possesses and Proficiency in the use of Tools, Machines or Equipment Which Would Help Establish If Alien Meets Requirements for Occupation in item 9.

13. List Licenses *(Professional, journeyman, etc.)*

14. List Documents Attached Which are Submitted as Evidence that Alien Possesses the Education, Training, Experience, and Abilities Represented

| Endorsements | DATE REC. DOL |
|---|---|
| *(Make no entry in this section – FOR Government Agency USE ONLY)* | O.T.& C. |

*(Items continued on next page)*

**U.S. Department of Justice**

Immigration and Naturalization Service (INS)

## Petition for Alien Fiancé(e)

## Instructions

**Read the instructions carefully. If you need extra space to answer, attach a continuation sheet, indicate the item number, and date and sign the sheet.**

**1.  Who can file?**

A.  You are a United States citizen, and

B.  You and your fiancé(e) are both free to marry, and have met in person within two years before filing this petition unless:

(1)  The requirement to meet your fiancé(e) in person would violate strict and long-established customs of your or your fiancé(e),s foreign cultures or social practice; or

(2)  It is established that the requirement to personally meet your fiancé(e) would result in extreme hardship to you; and

C.  You and your fiancé(e) intend to marry within 90 days of your fiancé(e) entering the United States.

NOTE:  Unmarried children of your fiancé(e) who are under 21 years old and are listed on this form will be eligible to apply to accompany your fiancé(e).

**2.  What documents do you need?**

You must give INS certain documents with this form to show you are eligible to file.

A.  For each document needed, give INS the original and one copy. However, because it is against the law to copy a Certificate of Naturalization or a Certificate of Citizenship, give INS the original only. **Originals will be returned to you.**

B.  If you do not wish to give the original document, you may give INS a copy. The copy must be certified by:

(1)  an INS or U.S. consular officer, or

(2)  an attorney admitted to practice law in the United States, or

(3)  an INS accredited representative(INS) still may require originals).

C.  Documents in a foreign language must be accompanied by a complete English translation. The translator must certify that the translation is accurate and that he or she is competent to translate.

**3.  What documents do you need to show you are a United States citizen?**

A.  If you were born in the United States, give INS your birth certificate.

B.  If you were naturalized, give INS your original Certificate of Naturalization.

C.  If you were born outside the United States, and you are a U.S. citizen through your parents, give INS:

(1)  your original Certificate of Citizenship, or

(2)  your Form FS-240 (Report of Birth Abroad of a United States Citizen).

D.  In place of any of the above, you may give INS your valid unexpired U.S. passport that was initially issued for at least 5 years.

E.  If you do not have any of the above and were born in the United States, see the instructions under item 6, *"What if a document is not available?"*

Form I-129F (REV.  10-7-87)N

**4.  What documents do you need to prove you can legally marry?**

You must prove that you can legally marry your fiancé(e).

A.  If either of you is of an age that requires special consent or permission for you to marry in the jurisdiction in which your marriage will occur, give proof of that consent or permission.

B.  If either of you has been previously married, give INS documents to show that all previous marriages were legally ended. In cases where the names shown on the supporting documents have changed, give INS legal documents to show how the name change occurred (for example, a marriage certificate, adoption decree, court order, etc.)

**5.  What other documents do you need?**

A.  Give INS a color photo of you and one of your fiancé(e), taken within 30 days of the date of this petition. These photos must have a white background. They must be glossy, un-retouched, and not mounted. The dimension of the facial image should be about 1 inch from chin to top of hair in 3/4 frontal view, showing the right side of the face with the right ear visible. Using pencil or felt pen, lightly print name (and Alien Registration Number, if known) on the back of each photograph.

B.  Give a completed and signed Form G-325A (Biographic Information) for you and one for your fiancé(e). Except for name and signature, you do not have to repeat on the Biographic Information forms the information given on your I-129F petition.

**6.  What if a document is not available?**

If the documents needed above are not available, you can give INS the following instead. (INS may require a statement from the appropriate civil authority certifying that the needed document is not available.)

A.  Church record: A certificate under the seal of the church where the baptism, dedication, or comparable rite occurred within two months after birth, showing the date and place of child's birth, the date of the religious ceremony, and the names of the child's parents.

B.  School record: A letter from the authorities of the school attended (preferably the first school), showing the date of admission to the school, child's date and place of birth, and the names and places of birth of parents, if shown in the school records.

C.  Census record: State or federal census record showing the name , place of birth, and date of birth or the age of the person listed.

D. Affidavits: Written statements sworn to or affirmed by two persons who were living at the time, and who have personal knowledge of the event you are trying to prove; for example, the date and place of birth, marriage, or death. The persons making the affidavits need not be citizens of the United States. Each affidavit should contain the following information regarding the person making the affidavit: his or her full name, address, date and place of birth, and his or her relationship to you, if any; full information concerning the event; and complete details concerning how the person acquired knowledge of the event.

**7.  How should you prepare this form?**

A.  Type or print legibly in ink.

B.  If extra space is needed to complete any item, attach a continuation sheet, indicate the item number, and date and sign each sheet.

C.  Answer all questions fully and accurately. If any item does not apply, please write "N/A".

**8.  Where should you file this form?**

A.  If you live in the United States, send or take the form to the INS office that has jurisdiction over where you live.

B.  If you live outside the United States, contact the nearest American Consulate to find out where to send or take the completed form.

**9.  What is the fee?**

You must pay $75.00 to file this form. **The fee will not be refunded, whether the petition is approved or not.** DO NOT MAIL CASH. All checks or money orders, whether U.S. or foreign, must be payable in U.S. currency at a financial institution in the United States. When a check is drawn on the account of a person other than yourself, write your name on the face of the check. If the check is not honored, INS will charge you $5.00.

Pay by check or money order in the exact amount. Make the check or money order payable to "Immigration and Naturalization Service." However,

A.  If you live in Guam: Make the check or money order payable to " Treasurer, Gaum", or

B.  If you live in the U.S. Virgin Islands: Make the check or money order payable to " Commissioner of Finance of the Virgin Islands".

**10.  How does your alien fiancé(e) get his or her permanent resident status?**

Your alien fiancé(e) may apply for conditional permanent resident status after you have entered into a valid marriage to each other performed within ninety days of your fiancé's entry into the United States. Your new spouse should apply promptly to the Immigration and Naturalization Service for adjustment of status to conditional permanent resident using Form I-485. He or she will be a conditional permanent resident for a two-year period which begins on the date that he or she adjusts to conditional status.

The rights, privileges, responsibilities and duties which apply to all other permanent residents apply equally to a conditional permanent resident. For example, a conditional permanent resident has the right to apply for naturalization, to file petitions in behalf of qualifying relatives, or to reside permanently in the United States as an immigrant in accordance with the immigration laws.

**11.  How does your conditional permanent resident spouse become a lawful permanent resident without conditions?**

Both you and your conditional permanent resident spouse are required to file a petition, Form I-751, Joint Petition to Remove the Conditional Basis of Alien's Permanent Resident Status, during the ninety day period immediately before the second anniversary of the date your alien spouse was granted conditional permanent residence. Children who have been admitted as conditional permanent residents may be included in the joint petition to remove conditions.

FAILURE TO FILE FORM I-751, JOINT PETITION TO REMOVE THE CONDITIONAL BASIS OF ALIEN'S PERMANENT RESIDENCE STATUS, WILL RESULT IN TERMINATION OF PERMANENT RESIDENCE STATUS AND INITIATION OF DEPORTATION PROCEEDINGS.

**12.  What are the penalties for committing marriage fraud or submitting false information or both?**

Title 18, United States Code, Section 1001 states that whoever willfully and knowingly falsifies a material fact, makes a false statement, or makes use of a false document will be fined up to $10,000 or imprisoned up to five years, or both.

Title 8 United States Code, Section 1325 states that any individual who knowingly enters into a marriage contract for the purpose of evading any provision of the immigration laws shall be imprisoned for not more than five years, or fined not more than five years, or fined not more than $250,000.00, or both.

**13.  What is our authority for collecting this information?**

We request the information on this form to carry out the immigration laws contained in Title 8, United States Code 1184(d). We need this information to determine whether a person is eligible for immigration benefits. The information you provide may also be disclosed to other federal, state, local, and foreign law enforcement and regulatory agencies during the course of the investigation required by this Service. You do not have to give this information. However, if you refuse to give some or all of it, your petition may be denied.

**It is not possible to cover all the conditions for eligibility or to give instructions for every situation. If you have carefully read all the information and still have questions, please contact your nearest INS office.**

For sale by the Superintendent if Documents, U.S. Government Printing Office Washington, D.C. 20402

**U.S. Department of Justice**                                                    OMB No. 1115-0054
Immigration and Naturalization Service (INS)      **Petition for Alien Fiancé(e)**

| DO NOT WRITE IN THIS BLOCK |
|---|

| Case ID# | Action Stamp | Fee Stamp |
|---|---|---|
| A# | | |
| G-28 or Volag # | | |
| The petition is approved for status under Section 101(a)(15)(k). It is valid for four months from date of action | | AMCON: _____ <br> ☐ Personal Interview  ☐ Previously Forwarded <br> ☐ Document Check  ☐ Stateside Criteria <br> ☐ Field Investigations |

REMARKS:

## A. Information about you

1. **Name** (Family name in CAPS)          (First)          (Middle)

2. **Address** (Number and Street)          (Apartment Number)

   (Town or City)          (State/Country)          (ZIP/Postal Code)

3. **Place of Birth** (Town or City)          (State/Country)

4. **Date of Birth** (Mo/Day/Yr)   5. **Sex** ☐ Male ☐ Female   6. **Marital Status** ☐ Married ☐ Single ☐ Widowed ☐ Divorced

7. **Other Names Used** (including maiden name)

8. **Social Security Number**   9. **Alien Registration Number** (if any)

10. **Names of Prior Husbands/Wives**   11. **Date(s) Marriage(s) Ended**

12. **If you are a U.S. citizen, complete the following:**

    My citizenship was acquired through (check one)

    ☐ Birth in the U.S.

    ☐ Naturalization

      (Give number of certificate, date and place it was issued)

    ☐ Parents

      Have you obtained a certificate of citizenship in your own name?

        ☐ Yes          ☐ No

      If "Yes", give number of certificate, date and place it was issued.

13. **Have you ever filed for this or any other alien fiancé(e) or husband/wife before?** ☐ Yes ☐ No

    If you checked "yes," give name of alien, place and date of filing, and result.

## B. Information about your alien fiancé(e)

1. **Name** (Family name in CAPS)          (First)          (Middle)

2. **Address** (Number and Street)          (Apartment Number)

   (Town or City)          (State/Country)          (ZIP/Postal Code)

3. **Place of Birth** (Town or City)          (State/Country)

4. **Date of Birth** (Mo/Day/Yr)   5. **Sex** ☐ Male ☐ Female   6. **Marital Status** ☐ Married ☐ Single ☐ Widowed ☐ Divorced

7. **Other Names Used** (including maiden name)

8. **Social Security Number**   9. **Alien Registration Number** (if any)

10. **Names of Prior Husbands/Wives**   11. **Date(s) Marriage(s) Ended**

12. **Has your fiancé(e) ever been in the U.S.?**

    ☐ Yes          ☐ No

13. **If your relative is currently in the U.S., complete the following:**

    **He or she last arrived as a** (visitor, student, exchange alien, crewman, stowaway, temporary worker, without inspection, etc.)

    **Arrival/Departure Record (I-94) Number**          **Date arrived** (Month/Day/Year)

    **Date authorized stay expired, or will expire, as shown on Form I-94 or I-95**

| INITIAL RECEIPT | RESUBMITTED | RELOCATED | | COMPLETED | | |
|---|---|---|---|---|---|---|
| | | Rec'd | Sent | Approved | Denied | Returned |
| | | | | | | |

Form I-129F (Rev. 10-7-87) N

## B. (continued) Information about your alien fiancé(e)

**14.** **List all children of your alien fiancé(e)** (if any)

(Name)                          (Date of Birth)                    (Country of Birth)                        (Present Address)

**15.** **Address in the United States where your fiancé(e) intends to live**

(Number and Street)              (Town or City)              (State)

**16.** **Your fiancé(s) address abroad**

(Number and Street)              (Town or City)              (Province)              (Country)              (Phone Number)

**17.** **If your fiancé(e) native alphabet is other than Roman letters, write his or her name and address abroad in the native alphabet:**

(Name)          (Number and Street)              (Town or City)              (Province)          (Country)

**18.** **Your fiancé(e) is related to you.**          ☐ Yes          ☐ No
If you are related, state the nature and degree of relationship, e.g., third cousin or maternal uncle, etc.

**19.** **Your fiancé(e) has met and seen you.**          ☐ Yes          ☐ No
Describe the circumstances under which you met. If you have not personally met each other, explain how the relationship was established, and explain in detail any reasons you may have for requesting that the requirement that you and your fiancé(e) must have met should not apply to you.

**20.** **Your fiancé(e) will apply for a visa abroad at the American Consulate in** _____
                                                                 (City)                         (Country)

(Designation of a consulate outside the country of your fiancé(e)'s last residence does not guarantee acceptance for processing by that consulate. Acceptance is at the discretion of the designated consulate.)

## C. Other Information

If you are serving overseas in the armed forces of the United States, please answer the following:

I presently reside or am stationed overseas and my current mailing address is _____

I plan to return to the United States on or about _____

**PENALTIES: You may, by law be imprisoned for not more than five years, or fined $250,000, or both, for entering into a marriage contract for the purpose of evading any provision of the immigration laws and you may be fined up to $10,000 or imprisoned up to five years or both, for knowingly and willfully falsifying or concealing a material fact or using any false document in submitting this petition.**

### Your Certification

I am legally able to and intend to marry my alien fiancé(e) within 90 days of his or her arrival in the United States. I certify, under penalty of perjury under the laws of the United States of America, that the foregoing is true and correct. Furthermore, I authorize the release of any information from my records which the Immigration and Naturalization Service needs to determine eligibility for the benefit that I am seeking.

Signature _____          Date _____          Phone Number _____

### Signature of Person Preparing Form if Other than Above

I declare that I prepared this document at the request of the person above and that it is based on all information of which I have any knowledge.

Print Name                          (Address)                    (Signature)                        (Date)

G-28 ID Number _____

Volag Number _____

# GLOSSARY AND INDEX

# GLOSSARY

*The following glossary provides definitions of many terms used in this book. It is also referenced with page numbers from the book for additional information. Some of these terms have more than one meaning. For complete definitions, be sure to use a dictionary.*

**A-visas** Authorization granted to foreign nationals who are diplomats of foreign countries, their staff, spouses and children who wish to reside in the United States on a temporary basis. *(A-61)*

**Accountant** A person who keeps, audits, and inspects the financial records of a person or business. He may also prepare financial and tax reports. *(D-15, D-30)*

**Accumulate** To collect or gather over a period of time. In financial terms, you can accumulate interest, debt or assets.

**Acre** A measure of land containing 43,560 square feet (4,407 square meters). *(F-4)*

**Adjustable Rate Mortgage (ARM)** A type of loan used to purchase a home. The interest rate changes periodically (at regular intervals) to reflect the most recent rate of interest. *(F-3)*

**Aerobic exercise** Any type of exercise that conditions the heart and lungs by increasing the efficiency of oxygen intake by the body. Jogging, walking, swimming, and stair climbing are all examples of this type of exercise. *(K-8)*

**Alien registration receipt card** A card issued by the United States Department of Immigration and Naturalization certifying that a foreign national is a lawful permanent resident in the United States. It is also referred to as a *green card*. *(A-5)*

**Amend** To change, revise or add to a document or agreement.

**Amendment** A change (revision or addition) to a law (bill, constitution) or other legal document (contract). *(B-8, B-16)*

**Amortization** The gradual decrease of the principal and interest on a loan.

**Annual effective yield** The total amount of interest earned annually expressed as a percentage of the investment. *(D-2)*

**Annuities** Savings plans mainly sold by insurance companies to provide income for retirement. *(D-16)*

**Answering machine** A tape or digital device linked to a telephone to answer and record messages from callers. This machine is now being replaced by phone companies who offer this service without the need of a machine. *(I-3)*

**Appraisal** A written estimate of value by an expert in the field such as real estate or jewelry. Appraisals are usually required before you can purchase a home or certain types of insurance. *(F-4)*

**Appraised value** The amount of money an item (house, land, jewelry, car) is worth. There is usually little reason to dispute a written appraised value done by a professional.

**Articles of Confederation** This document, written in 1777, organized the colonies into a loose confederation of states. It created a legislative assembly and is the forerunner of the Constitution. *(B-8)*

**Assessed value** The worth of a property as established by a local tax assessor. It is used for calculating real estate taxes. It can be disputed in local courts if there is any disagreement.

**Asset management account** A bank account similar to a combined savings, checking, and investment account. It usually requires a high minimum balance ($5,000 or more) and may charge annual fees and investment fees. It typically offers unlimited no-charge check writing. This type of account is available at brokerage firms and some banks. *(D-5)*

**Assets** All property or resources a person owns that have a tangible (established) or legal value. *(D-11)*

**Attorney** Also called a *Lawyer* or *Counselor*. A person licensed by a state to practice law. They can be authorized to act on behalf of (represent) another person, group of persons, organization or company. Attorneys are required to have a specific educational background and pass certain state tests. It is illegal for persons not licensed to act as an attorney. *(B-17–B-18, F-2, F-5)*

**Automated Teller Machine (ATM)** Electronic banking machine that can dispense money, accept deposits, transfer money from one account to another account, and perform other routine banking services. They are used instead of a bank teller and can be found at many locations both inside and outside of banks, supermarkets, and shopping centers. They offer service to bank customers outside of normal banking hours. *(D-4)*

**Automatic withdrawal** Payment of routine bills automatically by a bank. This service must be authorized by filling out a form at the bank. *(D-4)*

**Automobile insurance** Insurance required by most states to cover the cost of injury and damages to people and property in the event of an automobile accident. *(E-3–E-4)*

**B-visas** Authorization granted to foreign nationals who wish to visit the United States on a temporary basis for the purpose of business or pleasure (tourism). *(A-61)*

**Balance** In financial terms, what is left in an account (savings, checking) after all deposits and withdrawals; the amount owed on a bill, loan, or credit card. *(D-3)*

**Bank card** Also called a *debit card*. These cards look like *credit cards*. They work the same way as checks. Instead of using a *check*, you give the merchant your bank card and the purchase amount is electronically deducted from your account. You can also use a bank card to withdraw money from your account at an *automated teller machine (ATM)*. *(D-22)*

**Barbecue** Any meat, fish or vegetables broiled on a spit or open flame. It usually refers to an informal outdoor party. *(G-2)*

**Base sticker price** In automobile sales, all new cars are required by law to display the manufacturer's suggested retail price. This is not the case with used cars. It is generally used as a basis for price comparison. In virtually all cases, you should pay less than the base sticker price.

**Bed and Breakfast (B&B)** An overnight room for rent – frequently located in a private home, usually with some age and charm. The term is also applied to a small country inn. *(K-24)*

**Beeper** Small battery-powered device that sounds a "beep" or vibrates to indicate that someone is trying to contact you. The phone number of the caller is displayed on the device so you can return the call. *(I-4)*

**Beneficiary** A recipient (a person who is to receive something). A person named by another to receive income or inheritance from a will, insurance policy, trust fund or other source. *(B-17– B-18, E-6)*

**Berlitz Method** Learning a language by hearing or speaking only that language. *(C-5, J-10–J-11)*

**Bicameral legislature** A two-chambered (two-house) system of legislation. In the federal government it consists of the House of Representatives and the Senate. All states, except Nebraska, also govern on a bicameral basis. *(B-11)*

**Bill consolidation loan** Combines unpaid bills into a single loan with one monthly payment, usually at a lower amount than the total of all the current bill payments. *(D-23)*

**Bill of Rights** The first ten amendments that were immediately added to the Constitution. They guarantee specific individual rights such as freedom of the press, freedom of religion, the right to bear arms, the right not to be searched or have property seized without legal approval and limitation by the court, the right to a speedy and public trial, the right to a trial by jury, the right that powers not specifically granted to the federal government remain with the states and the people. *(B-8, B-16)*

**Blue-chip stocks** High quality stocks. The term refers to stocks that are issued by well-established major corporations. *(D-12)*

**Blue-collar worker** A term meaning someone who works with their hands; craftsman, tradesperson, skilled or unskilled industrial worker or manual laborer. *(C-3)*

**Blue pages** Provided in some telephone books to give local, county, state, and federal government listings of phone numbers and addresses. *(I-3, I-5)*

**Bond** 1. In financial terms, an interest-bearing certificate, issued by a government or company, promising to pay the holder of the bond a specific sum (amount of money) on a specific date. It is a common way of raising money for businesses and federal, state, and local governments. *(D-13–D-14)* 2. In criminal matters, it is the amount of money pledged to guarantee that someone formally accused of a crime will return to the court on the assigned date. Failure to appear results in forfeiture (loss) of the money pledged. *(B-18)*

**Bookkeeper** A person who records the financial accounts and transactions of a person or business. A bookkeeper usually works for an accountant or in an accounting department.

**Bounced check** A check returned by the bank, unpaid, because of insufficient money in the account. Also referred to as bad checks *(D-4)*

**Budget** Spending plan based on income and expenses.

**Building codes** Government regulations on construction. These regulations may include local, county, state and federal laws. They may cover the use of the property as well as the types of materials used, safety requirements, and specific details on the installation of such things as electrical outlets and wiring.

**Business directories** Listings of companies under various headings such as The Fortune 500 (top 500 U.S. companies as noted by Fortune magazine), Forbes Magazine's Annual List of 2,500 Companies, or Standard and Poors directory. *(C-4)*

**Business periodicals** Magazines and newspapers such as Business Week, Barron's, The Wall Street Journal and Money Magazine. *(C-4)*

**Business plan** A written outline of long-term business goals, immediate objectives, and steps required to establish or run a business. *(C-12 – C-13)*

**Buyer's agent** Real estate agent working exclusively for the buyer. Buyer's agents are not commonly used. *(F-1)*

**C-visas** Authorization granted to foreign nationals who travel repeatedly through the United States to be in the United States for a temporary period of time. *(A-62)*

**Cabinet** A group of official or unofficial advisors. For example, as part of the federal government, the president appoints (officially names) his cabinet. This includes the Secretaries of State, Defense, Commerce, Transportation and Energy among others. He may also maintain a cabinet of unappointed, unofficial advisors which may include leaders from business, social services and former work colleagues. They may advise him on specific or general issues. *(B-9)*

**Cable television** A method of receiving television channels by wires brought directly into the home instead of over the air. Cable television is not free as is the case with over-the-air channels. Cable service also offers a much larger number of channels for viewing pleasure. The fees for cable service are reasonable. *(K-2)*

**Calling card** A card issued by a telephone company used by inserting the card into the telephone or by entering the card number and security code to charge the call to your account. Some calling cards come in predetermined amounts and can be used up to the limit printed on the face (front) of the card. *(I-3)*

**Canceled check** A written check, processed by the bank and returned to the person who wrote the check. It should be kept as a proof of payment. *(D-3)*

**Capital** In financial terms, it refers to money, assets, or wealth. *(D-11)*

**Capital gains tax** A tax on profits from the sale of real estate, stocks, or other financial transactions. The amounts as well as the names of this type of tax may vary. In some cases, the tax can be deferred. It is always best to consult a financial professional in these matters. *(D-28)*

**Cash advance** An amount of money you may borrow using your credit card, special checks from your credit card company, bank card, bank or other financial services companies. In many cases you may get a cash advance of several hundred dollars from an *Automated Teller Machine (ATM)* or a larger amount by simply writing out one of the special checks. The interest rates on these loans are generally higher than traditional loans.

**Cash benefits** In insurance terms, set (fixed) amounts paid by an insurance company for specific losses, medical benefits, or reimbursement for specific expenses such as automobile rental in case of an accident where your automobile cannot be used. *(E-1)*

**Cash flow** A record of the amount of income received and how it is spent.

**Cash value** The accumulated amount of money you can borrow against or collect (receive) if you turn in an insurance policy, bond, or other specific type of financial investment. *(E-6)*

**Cashier's check** This type of check is purchased from a bank and used to transfer large amounts of money (such as when purchasing a house). *(D-5)*

**Catalog shopping** Shopping done by sending the customer a catalog (magazine) describing the products, usually in pictures and words. The customer telephones or mails in the order and the merchandise is shipped directly to him. *(G-13)*

**Cellular phone** A battery powered portable telephone. *(I-4)*

**Census** An official periodic count of the population and the recording of their economic status, age, sex, and other statistical information. It is required by law as it is used to determine the appropriate amount of members of the House of Representatives for each state. *(B-10)*

**Certificate of Deposit (CD)** A form of investment bought from a bank or broker usually requiring a minimum of $500. It earns interest at a higher rate than a savings account because it is invested for a fixed minimum period of time (for example: six months, one year, or five years). There is usually a penalty fee on the interest if there is a withdrawal prior to the end of the fixed period. *(D-2, D-11)*

**Certified check** A personal check guaranteed by the bank. *(D-5)*

**Certified Financial Planner (CFP)** A professional who advises individuals on personal financial analysis and investment strategies. *(D-15)*

**Certified mail** A postal service that provides the sender a mailing receipt and a record of delivery at the recipient's (person receiving the mail) post office. The sender can also purchase a *return receipt* form to have a record of receipt with the signature of the person receiving the mail. *(I-10)*

**Certified Public Accountant (CPA)** A person licensed by the state to inspect, keep, adjust, and certify the records of money received and paid out for a person, organization, or business. They are also used to prepare federal, state, and local tax forms and filings as well as financial statements.

**Charge card** A type of credit card for use within a particular store or company. *(D-22)*

**Check** In financial terms, a written order (type of form) directing the bank to transfer an amount of money you specify to a person or company you specify. *(D-2, D-4)*

**Check cashing card** A type of identification used to allow you to cash or pay by a personal check at a specific store or business. *(D-22, G-9)*

**Check-out scanner** An electronic device used to register and total prices for payment at a store check-out counter. *(G-5, G-9, G-12)*

**Checks and Balances** A system established in the Constitution to balance the power of the executive (presidential), legislative, and judicial branches of government. *(B-8, B-10)*

**Classified advertisements** A section of a newspaper, divided by category, devoted to the sale of homes, apartment rentals, automobile sales, private sales of items, as well as employment opportunities.

**Closing costs** Payments of various fees made on the day ownership of a home is legally transferred to a new owner. *(F-5)*

**Cold calling** Telephoning to inquire about potential job opportunities or sell products and services when you do not specifically know the person you are calling or are not responding to an advertisement. *(C-5)*

**Collateral** Proven asset(s) that show ability to repay a loan, which in the event of **default** (inability to repay the loan) becomes the property of the lender. *(D-6)*

**Collect call** A telephone call where the charges are billed to the account of the phone receiving the call. The person answering the call is notified the call is collect and may refuse or accept the call. *(I-3)*

**College** A four-year academic institution or branch of an university offering courses that lead to a Bachelor's Degree. It may also refer to a school offering specialized instruction in a particular profession or occupation. *(J-4)*

**College placement services** Office at a college that solicits potential employers, lists job openings, provides employment counseling, has facilities for interviews, and other related services. *(C-6)*

**Collision insurance** A type of automobile insurance that pays for damages to your automobile in the event you hit another automobile or object.*(E-4)*

**Commodities** In investment terms, raw materials (oil, gas, precious metals, agricultural products) that are traded (bought and sold) on futures (commodity) markets. *(D-15)*

**Common stock** Ownership of a share (portion) of a company. *(D-12)*

**Community college** Also called a *junior college*. An academic institution which usually offers a two year program of study that leads to an Associate's Degree. *(J-5)*

**Comprehensive insurance** A type of automobile insurance that pays for specific losses such as theft, vandalism, fire, or flood. *(E-4)*

**Condominium (Condo)** A unit of privately owned housing similar to an apartment. *(F-5)*

**Conservator** A person, appointed by a court or named in a legal document, who has legal responsibility for caring for someone incapable of caring for himself. *(H-8)*

**Constitution of the United States of America (Constitution)** A single document, which is the foundation of the United States government in effect since 1788. *(B-7, B-8, B-10, B-16)*

**Continental Congress** Either of two assemblies of American colonists. The first, in 1774, was established to object to British policies. The second, in 1775, formed the Continental Army, issued the Declaration of Independence and the Articles of Confederation, and served as the law-making body. *(B-7–B-8)*

**Convenience store** A small store, usually open 24 hours a day and on holidays. It offers a selection of grocery items and other items that people often need. *(G-6)*

**Conventional mortgage** *See fixed rate mortgage.*

**Convertible term insurance** A type of life insurance that allows you to switch from a term policy (policy with a limited effective time period) to a whole life policy (which provides more benefits including an unlimited effective time period). *(E-6)*

**Co-operative apartment (Co-op)** A type of housing where you own a share of a corporation that owns the building and usually the land. Your rights to rent, sell, or make other than minor changes to your apartment are subject to approval by a board of owners. *(F-5)*

**Corporation** A legal entity having its own rights, privileges, and responsibilities. A corporation may be established for a wide variety of reasons. It is usually done to protect and limit the liability of the owners. This enables them to make business decisions on behalf of the corporation without fear of personal liability. *(C-11)*

**Counselor** *See attorney*

**Cover letter** In employment terms, an informal letter that accompanies a resume. It is used as an introduction and to highlight particular skills or qualifications in an informal way. *(C-3)*

**Credit bureaus** National and local services that collect information on a person's purchase and payment history and other relevant information such as income and home ownership. The information is sold to companies considering granting a person a loan, credit, or a line of credit. *(C-19)*

**Credit card** A personalized plastic card with a magnetic strip for electronic purposes. It is used instead of cash or a check to pay for an ever increasing wide variety of products and services. *(D-20 – D-21)*

**Credit history** The record of a person's borrowing and repayment. *(D-19, D-22)*

**Credit line** A set (fixed, limited) amount of money a lender is willing to allow a person to borrow (use). It is usually a predetermined amount for which a person has applied and been approved. *(D-22)*

**D-visas** Authorization granted to foreign nationals working on board international vessels and aircraft to be in the United States for a limited period of time. *(A-62)*

**Damages** Money claimed as a loss or paid as compensation for injury or loss.

**Day care center** Community or private facility caring for preschool and young school children. They are often used when both parents are working. *(J-2)*

**Death benefit** Money paid to beneficiaries of a life insurance policy upon the death of the insured person. *(E-6)*

**Debit card** *See bank card.*

**Declaration of Independence** Document that proclaimed the independence of the colonies from Britain on July 4, 1776. It is celebrated as a national holiday on July fourth each year. *(B-8)*

**Deductible** The amount of money an insurance *policyholder* must pay before the insurance company begins payment. *(E-1, E-2, E-4)*

**Deduction** In tax terms, the amount of money allowed by a federal, state, or local government to be deducted before income is considered taxable. *(D-31)*

**Default** Failure to make an agreed payment by the date specified.

**Delegate** To assign certain powers or rights to another person or entity such as a corporation or government.

**Delegated powers** Those powers given to the national (federal) government under the *Constitution*. All other powers belong to the states. *(B-8)*

**Democrat** A member of one of the two major political parties. *(B-11)*

**Department store** A large store selling a wide variety of merchandise including clothing, cosmetics, jewelry, electronics, furniture, appliances, and other household goods. *(G-12)*

**Deportation** The process of returning a person to their native country by court order. *(A-74 – A-75)*

**Development** In real estate terms, an area of land with homes of similar style built about the same time, often by the same builder or financier. *(F-4)*

**Direct deposit** The automatic electronic depositing of paychecks or other earnings into a person's bank account. This service requires authorized paperwork and is not yet available at all banks. *(D-4)*

**Directory assistance** A telephone company service to help provide telephone numbers. Dial 411 for local call assistance (in the area code you are located) and 1-area code-555-1212 for assistance outside your area code. *(I-3)*

**Discount brokerages** Licensed companies that sell stocks, bonds, and other financial services at significantly lower commissions (prices). Generally they do not provide the advisory services a full-service brokerage offers. *(D-13)*

**Down payment** A deposit, as security or to show intent, for a purchase that will be financed such as a home or car. *(F-4)*

**Drive-through service** Making purchases or conducting business without leaving your car such as when buying fast food or banking. (Also may be referred to as drive-in service.) *(D-5, G-3)*

**Drug store** A store which has a pharmacist to fill prescriptions for doctor-specified medicines. It usually carries a selection of non-prescription medicines and other health care related products. Many drug stores carry a selection of general merchandise including cosmetics, gifts, and food. *(G-11)*

**E-mail** Electronic mail used between computers over telephone lines. A device on each computer, called a *modem*, allows the users to transmit letters or other images on the computer screen to each other. *(I-4)*

**E-visas** Authorization issued to foreign nationals who are treaty traders or treaty investors, their spouses and children who wish to visit the United States on a temporary basis. *(A-62–63)*

**Electoral College** The system used to elect a president in the United States. A group of electors, one for each senator and representative in a state, are named. The presidential candidate with the highest number of popular votes (one vote per citizen) in each state wins all that state's electoral votes. *(B-9)*

**Emigrate** To leave a country in order to settle in another country.

**Employment agencies.** Private companies that provide professional employment services, usually not licensed or regulated for quality and costs. *(C-6)*

**Employment benefits** Employer paid benefits in addition to salary. They may include payment of all or part of health care insurance costs, pension and retirement plans, bonus programs, vacation time, and legal service plans among others. *(C-5)*

**Endorsement** The signing of a name on the back of a check to indicate approval and acceptance of the amount being paid. *(D-3)*

**Equity** The amount of money that you would receive if you sold an *asset* (house or car) and paid all loans made using the asset as security (*collateral*). *(D-23)*

**Escrow** placing money or documents with a third party (such as an attorney or bank) for safe-keeping until fulfillment of a particular condition. *(F-4)*

**Escrow account** In real estate terms, a reserve account usually at the mortgaging bank, to insure payment of specific expenses such as real estate taxes.

**Estate** In legal terms, the total of what a person owns including house, land, savings, and other personal property. *(B-18)*

**Exclusion** In immigration terms, the ability of the United States government to lawfully bar or prevent the entry of a foreign national to the U.S. when they fall within certain pre-established grounds. *(A-73 –A-74)*

**Execute** In business terms, to carry out or do in accordance with a predetermined agreement.

**Executive branch** The portion of government that deals with the powers and responsibilities of the president. *(B-9– B-10)*

**Executive recruiters** Also called executive search firms. Employment service companies that specialize in employment opportunities for business managers and other professionals. Their fees are virtually always paid by the employer and not the executive or professional. *(C-6)*

**F-visas** Authorization granted to foreign nationals who are academic students, their spouses and children who wish to visit the United States on a temporary basis. *(A-63–A-65)*

**Facsimile Transmission (FAX)** Conversion of what is written on paper into electrical signals by a transmitting fax machine and sent over telephone wires to a receiving fax machine. The receiving fax machine, in turn, converts the signals back into print, all within the speed of a phone call. *(I-4)*

**Factory outlet** A store selling merchandise directly from the manufacturer at a lower than retail price.

**Federal** Referring to the national government.

**Federal Deposit Insurance Commission (FDIC)** A government agency that regulates and insures bank deposits (usually up to a total of $100,000 per depositor) of its member banks. *(D-1)*

**Federal Income Tax** National tax required by law on income such as wages, profits, tips, and interest. *(D-27 – D-28)*

**Federal Insurance Contributions Act (FICA)** The law governing Social Security taxes and its *withholding* from your paycheck. *(D-28)*

**Federalism** A system of government where states give up a certain amount of rights, responsibilities, and powers to a central (federal) government. *(B-8)*

**Federal Reserve Bank** Any one of twelve district banks that make up the Federal Reserve System.

**Federal Reserve System** The banking system of the United States. It operates under the direction of a Board of Governors with supervisory powers over the twelve Federal Reserve Banks. Its role is to manage the financial stability of the United States. *(D-1)*

**Federal Trade Commission** A federal agency whose duty is to investigate and prosecute unfair methods of competition in business, fraudulent advertising, and other illegal commercial activities.

**Felony** Any of several major areas of crime such as burglary, rape, or murder which carry severe penalties.

**Financial plan** A written strategy to meet business or personal financial goals. *(C-12– C-13)*

**Financial Planner** *See Certified Financial Planner*

**First class mail** General mail used for letters, postcards, paying bills and sending checks. It is generally sent air mail when appropriate. *(I-9)*

**Fitness center** A business or club devoted to physical training. It usually has sophisticated training equipment and requires payment of membership fees. *(K-8)*

**Fixed rate mortgage** Also called a *conventional mortgage*. A home loan whose payment is based on a fixed interest rate that will not change over the term of the loan.

**Food and Drug Administration (FDA)** The government agency responsible for maintaining (enforcing) laws regarding food and medicines. It regulates areas such as manufacturing, testing, and sale of these types of products. *(H-3 – H-4)*

**Foreclosure** The legal taking of property by a lender for failure to make the agreed payments.

**Form 1099** A form received from a financial institution (bank, investment company, brokerage house) or company that indicates how much money was earned from an investment or how much income was paid to a company or person. *(D-30)*

**Form W-2** A form received from the employer, during January of each year, that states how much income was earned and taxes withheld for the previous year. *(D-29)*

**401(k) Plan** A type of company sponsored retirement plan. *(D-16)*

**403(b) Plan** A type of retirement plan for employees of the government or tax-exempt organizations. *(D-16)*

**4-H** A rural youth program that develops agricultural skills. *(K-11)*

**Franchise** A type of business where certain rights and responsibilities are purchased from a company (franchisor). The rights often include use of the company's name and instructions on how to start and operate the business. The responsibilities often include a fee, maintaining standards, and a percent of sales. *(C-14 – C-15)*

**Freshness date** Date stamped on perishable foods and drugs that indicates the last date it should be sold. "Sell before 10/30/94", for example. *(G-6)*

**G-visas** Authorization granted to international organization representatives, their spouses and children who wish to visit the United States on a temporary basis. *(A-65–A-66)*

**Garage sale** Sale of items out of the home by private individuals, announced in local newspapers or by signs posted locally, also known as tag sales. *(G-14)*

**Generic** In food, items that carry no particular manufacturer's name. In medicine, unpatented products that are sold by their chemical name rather than by a manufacturer's name. *(H-3)*

**Grace period** The amount of time you have to pay on a credit card purchase before interest is charged. *(D-20, D-21)*

**Graduate school** A college or university that offers a Master's Degree, the next highest degree after a Bachelor's Degree. *(J-5)*

**Graduation Equivalency Diploma (GED)** A certificate equal to a high school diploma. *(J-4)*

**Grand jury** Investigates and determines if there is sufficient evidence for trial. If there is sufficient evidence, the jury indicts (accuses). The case then goes on to a separate jury for trial; petit jury. *(B-13)*

**Green card** *see alien registration receipt card*

**Group health coverage** Health insurance available through an employer, professional association, or other type of group. *(E-2)*

**Growth stocks** Stock issued by companies who reinvest profits to expand (grow) their business. *(D-13)*

**H-visas** Authorization granted to foreign nationals who are qualified employees filling a temporary need of American workers, their spouse and children. *(A-66 – A-68)*

**Health insurance** Insurance that pays for part or all of the costs of hospitalization, surgery, laboratory tests, medications, and doctor's bills. It may be purchased privately or available through an employer or government agency. *(E-1, H-1)*

**Health Maintenance Organization (HMO)** A group of doctors, hospitals, and other medical service providers that perform general and select services for patients who are members of the organization. *(E-2, H-2)*

**Home equity credit line** A *line of credit* using your home as *collateral*. You may use only a portion of the amount of money available initially and more whenever you wish by writing special checks. *(D-23, D-24)*

**Home equity loan** A loan, using your home as collateral, with a fixed interest rate and fixed monthly payments. *(D-23, D-24)*

**Homeowners insurance** Insurance that provides protection against damage to the homeowners property and *personal liability* if someone is injured on their premises. *(E-5)*

**Hors d' oeuvres** Small appetizers usually served at the beginning of a meal.

**Hospice** A specially-equipped home for the terminally ill. It also provides extensive in-home care for terminally ill patients.

**Hospital expense insurance** Insurance that covers the cost of hospital room and board, operating room charges, laboratory charges, X-rays, nursing care, and other expenses associated with a stay in the hospital. *(E-2)*

**House of Representatives** The lower branch of legislature in the U.S. Congress. *(B-10)*

**I-visas** authorization granted to foreign media representatives, their spouses and children who wish to visit the United States on a temporary basis. *(A-68)*

**Immigrant visa** Authorization granted to foreign nationals who wish to remain in the United States on a permanent basis. There are many categories of immigrant visas and these categories may or may not be restricted by quotas. Once a foreign national qualifies for an immigrant visa, he is issued an *alien registration receipt card* or green card certifying his permanent residence. *(A-5–A-6)*

**Immigrate** To enter and settle in another country

**Income stocks** Stocks that generally provide a regular high dividend payment. *(D-12)*

**Indemnify** In insurance terms, to protect against or repay for financial loss. *(E-1)*

**Indians** A term, now considered offensive for the *Native Americans* who were living in the Americas prior to the arrival of the Europeans. *(B-7)*

**Individual Retirement Account (IRA)** A government designed program that provides financial incentives for retirement savings. *(D-1–D-2, D-15–D-16)*

**Inflation** In financial terms, the reduction of purchasing power over time. *(D-11)*

**Insufficient funds** The term for the reason a check is not processed when there is not enough money in the account to cover the amount specified on the check. *(D-4)*

**Insurance** Protection against financial loss. *(E-1–E-8)*

**Insurance agent** A licensed person who sells insurance.

**Insurance carrier** Insurance company that creates the policies and maintains the funds.

**Interest** The money a borrower pays for the use of the lender's money. *(D-1, D-2, D-13)*

**Internal Revenue Service (IRS)** The federal agency responsible for the collection of federal taxes, administration, and enforcement of tax laws. *(D-27)*

**International money order** Similar to checks, a written order to pay a person or company named, the face amount (value stated) on the money order. They can be purchased from a bank or U.S. Post Office. *(D-5, I-14)*

**International money transfer** A financial transaction where a bank wires the amount of money requested to an affiliated bank in a specified country. The affiliated bank converts the dollars into local currency and makes it available to the person you specified. *(D-5)*

**Interview** A meeting of people to question each other regarding a specific matter such as employment. *(C-4, C-8)*

**Investment** Commitment of money for a period of time in order to earn more money (financial return). *(D-11)*

**J-visas** Authorization granted to foreign nationals who are exchange visitors, their spouses and children wishing to visit the United States on a temporary basis. *(A-68)*

**Judicial branch** The portion of government that deals with the administration of justice. It may decide whether a law enacted (passed) by Congress or an action of the president is in agreement with the *Constitution of the United States*. If not, it can declare the law or action invalid. It is also in charge of all other federal (national) courts and can reverse decisions of state courts. *(B-12)*

**Junior Achievement** A youth organization that introduces boys and girls to the basics of developing and operating a business. It is run by local business people. *(K-11)*

**Junior college** *See community college*

**Junk bonds** High-risk corporate or municipal bonds that are rated low in terms of quality but carry high potential income. *(D-13)*

**K-visas** Authorization granted to the foreign national spouse of a U.S. citizen, and their children who wish to visit the United States on a temporary basis to marry the U.S. citizen. *(A-68)*

**Keogh plan** Retirement plan that provides tax deferred savings for the self-employed. *(D-16)*

**L-visas** Authorization granted to employees working for a foreign corporate subsidiary, affiliate or joint venture partner of a U.S. corporation who are being temporarily transferred to the U.S. as well as their spouse and children. *(A-69)*

**Lawyer** *See attorney*

**Lease** In real estate terms, a written legal agreement between a landlord (lessor) and tenant (renter, lessee). It usually includes the amount of rent to be paid, term (time period), and responsibilities of both the landlord and tenant. A lease can also apply to other financial situations. For example, you can lease a car or a piece of equipment and even have the right to buy it at an agreed price after the term of the lease is over. *(F-6 – F-7)*

**Legislative branch** The portion of government that deals with the establishment of laws. In the U.S. it is called "Congress". The U.S. Congress consists of two distinct houses or sections – the House of Representatives and the Senate – each with distinct authority and responsibility. *(B-10 – B-12)*

**Liabilities** In financial terms, the amounts of money you owe (debts). *(D-11)*

**Liability insurance** In automobile insurance, it pays benefits (money) on behalf of a *policyholder* if they are responsible *(liable)* for bodily injury or other damages to someone or something related to an automobile accident. There is also liability insurance available for other areas; for example, product liability insurance. Product liability insurance protects a manufacturer or distributor of a product in the event the product is claimed to have harmed someone or damaged something. *(E-4)*

**Liable (liability)** Legally responsible for someone or something.

**Lien** A legal claim against someone's personal property that must be paid when the property is sold.

**Life insurance** Insurance that pays a cash benefit upon the death of the *policyholder. (E-6 – E-7)*

**Life support systems** Machines that keep the heart, lungs, kidneys, and other vital organs operating. *(H-8)*

**Liquidity** The ease of which you can convert your assets into cash.

**Litigation** The act or process of carrying on a lawsuit.

**Living will** A set of legally approved instructions on life support systems and how you wish to be cared for in the event of being in an incapable or unconscious state with little hope of survival. *(B-18, H-8)*

**Load** In financial terms, a fee similar to a commission. **Front-end load** is a commission paid at the time you purchase a securities investment. **Back-end load** is a commission paid when you sell a securities investment. Both may be charged. *(D-14)*

**Local telephone service** For telephone billing purposes, the calling region in the immediate area (neighboring towns). *(I-1 – I-2)*

**Long distance carriers** Competing telephone companies that provide service for calls made outside of your area code. AT&T is by far the largest. Sprint, MCI and other small companies also provide service. *(I-2 – I-3)*

**M-visas** Authorization granted to foreign nationals who are vocational or other non-academic students, their spouses and unmarried children under 21 wishing to visit the United States on a temporary basis. *(A-69)*

**Mainstreaming** The effort to integrate physically or emotionally challenged (handicapped) individuals into everyday life. *(J-3)*

**Major medical insurance** Health insurance that covers the costs of treatment for serious illness or injury. *(E-3)*

**Margin account** A special account maintained at a stock brokerage firm that is used to purchase stocks on margin (for a percentage of their actual selling price). *(D-13)*

**Marital status** Whether you are single, married, divorced, or separated.

**Market value** The approximate price that a seller may expect to receive for merchandise, property, services, or securities available to appropriate buyers in an open market.

**Markup** The amount added to the cost of an item purchased by the seller to cover his expenses and profit.

**Mass mailing** The sending of printed material to a large number of potential customers or employers.

**Maturity** In financial terms, to become due (to be paid) at the end of an agreed time period.

**Medicaid** Government sponsored health insurance for the poor. *(E-2)*

**Medical payments insurance** In automobile insurance, insurance that pays for medical expenses of the *policyholder* and others involved in an automobile accident regardless of fault. *(E-4)*

**Medical service plans** Nonprofit companies that offer insurance to pay for medical services provided by doctors and hospitals. Blue Cross and Blue Shield are examples of the largest plans available. *(E-1)*

**Medicare** Government sponsored health insurance through *Social Security. (E-2)*

**Minimum balance** The lowest amount of money required on deposit by banks in order to earn interest or avoid service charges. *(D-1)*

**Minimum payment** The lowest payment required to be made on a monthly credit card bill or credit purchase. *(D-20)*

**Misdemeanor** A criminal offense of lesser seriousness than a felony. It may be punishable by a fine or brief imprisonment in a local jail.

**Modem** A piece of equipment that connects to the computer and telephone line. It makes it possible to transmit and receive information from one computer to another over telephone lines. *(I-4)*

**Money market** The financial system that deals with the supply and demand for money to loan on a short-term basis, usually for periods from six months to thirty months.

**Money market account** A type of interest paying savings and checking account with certain requirements (minimum balance, limited number of checks) that pays higher interest than a typical savings account. They are available through brokerage houses and banks. *(D-1 – D-2, D-4)*

**Money order** Purchased with cash from a post office or bank, it is used like a check and more widely accepted as cash. *(D-5, I-10 – I-11)*

**Mortgage** The pledging of property to a lender as security for the payment of a debt. Most often used as a loan from a financial institution to buy property. *(F-3 – F-4)*

**Mutual fund** A form of investment where the money from the shareholders (investors) is "pooled" (put together) to invest in a specific type of investment or range of investments. *(D-14)*

**N-visas** Authorization granted to foreign nationals of parents and children or special immigrants who wish to visit the United States on a temporary basis. *(A-7)*

**Name brand** Items manufactured or marketed by widely recognized companies or under well-known names for the product. *(H-3)*

**Native American** The term that refers to those who were living in America prior to the arrival of the Europeans.

**Negotiable Order of Withdrawal account (NOW account)** An interest paying checking account requiring a minimum balance. *(D-4)*

**Networking** Informally contacting social or work-related acquaintances to develop business contacts, get more information, or attain a goal. *(C-4 – C-5)*

**Net worth** The amount of money you have after all your *liabilities* (debts) are deducted from the value of all your *assets. (D-11)*

**Nonimmigrant visas** Authorization issued to foreign nationals who wish to remain in the United States temporarily. They are categorized A through R and permit a foreign national to enter the U.S. to perform a specific activity for a specified amount of time. *(A-5, A-7 – A-8, A-61 – A-70)*

**Nonsectarian school** A school that is not associated with any religious group. *(J-4)*

**Nursery school** Usually a private school, nursery schools provide education for pre-school children. *(J-2)*

**Nutrition** The process of using food to maintain life, growth, and replacement of tissues. *(H-6)*

**O-visas** authorization granted to foreign nationals of extraordinary ability in the arts, athletics, business and sciences, business and education their support staff and accompanying relatives who wish to visit the United States on a temporary basis. *(A-70)*

**Old age, survivors, and disability insurance** Government insurance covering workers as part of the *Social Security* system. *(D-28 – D-29)*

**Options** 1. In automobile sales, extra equipment or features available for purchase. *(G-15)* 2. In financial terms, investments that give you the right to buy or sell at a later date at an agreed price. *(D-15)*

**Ordinances**  Laws enacted by city governments. *(B-14)*

**Outpatient expense insurance**  The portion of your health insurance that covers the costs of doctor fees for nonsurgical care in the office or nonsurgical hospital visits. It is also called regular medical insurance or physician's expense insurance. *(E-3)*

**Overdraft protection**  Pays the full amount of the face value of checks written when you do not have sufficient funds in your checking account. This service must be applied for and approved by the bank. It is similar to a small loan or line of credit. *(D-2– D-4)*

**Over-the-counter medicine (OTC medicine)**  Medicine that can be purchased without a prescription. *(H-3)*

**Over-the-counter stock**  Stock that is not listed on the major stock exchanges.

**P-visas**  Authorization granted to foreign nationals who are outstanding athletes, members of athletic teams, artists, entertainers, or entertainment companies who wish to visit the United States on a temporary basis. *(A-70)*

**Package policy**  In insurance terms, an insurance policy that includes more than one type of insurance in a category. *(E-4)*

**Parent Teacher Association (PTA)**  Organization at the local school level that involves the parents and teachers working on common concerns. *(J-7, K-10)*

**Parochial school**  A school that has a religious affiliation. *(J-4)*

**Personal Identification Number (PIN)**  A number given by the bank or other electronic provider of services as a security measure in identifying your personal account. Anyone with your PIN can have access to your account. Therefore, it is extremely important not to share your PIN with anyone whom you do not want to have the ability to withdraw from or charge to your account. *(D-4, D-21)*

**Person-to-person call**  Telephone company service where, for an additional fee, the person calling is only charged if he is connected with the person he is trying to reach. This type of call can be combined with a collect call.

**Pharmacy**  The area of a store or medical facility where a pharmacist works and medication is dispensed (given out). See *drug store. (G-11)*

**Point-of-sale terminal**  A computer terminal used in retail stores for cash, credit card, or other electronic methods of payment.

**Points**  In real estate terms, prepaid interest payment to a lender made at the time of the closing. *(F-3, F-5)*

**Policyholder**  Individual who is named on the policy as the owner of the insurance. *(E-1, E-4)*

**Preferred Provider Organization (PPO)**  A listing of doctors and medical professionals authorized for use by an insurance company. *(E-2, H-2)*

**Preferred stock**  Stock that pays a fixed dividend (interest) and is generally not affected by the market value of the common stock. The dividend is paid before profits are made available to common stock holders. *(D-12)*

**Premium**  In insurance terms, the amount of money paid for an insurance policy. *(E-1)*

**Pre-school**  *See nursery school.*

**Prescription drug**  Medicine that can only be purchased from a pharmacist with a written order from a doctor. *(H-3)*

**Primary school**  Term used to refer to grades kindergarten through eighth grade (grammar school). *(J-3)*

**Prime time**  In television, the hours most heavily viewed. *(K-1)*

**Principal**  1. In financial terms, the amount borrowed in a loan or on deposit in a checking or savings account.  2. In educational terms, a senior director or head of a school.

**Priority mail**  First class mail for items weighing no more than two pounds (907 grams). *(I-9– I-10)*

**Private schools**  Schools paid for by independent (non-government) sources such as student fees or religious groups. *(J-1, J-4)*

**Property taxes**  Local taxes on land and buildings commonly used to support *public schools.*(D-30, F-2 –F-3)

**Public schools**  Local schools paid for primarily by property taxes. There is no charge for grades kindergarten through grade 12. *(J-1, J-3 – J-4)*

**R-visas**  Authorization granted to foreign nationals

who are religious workers and their accompanying relatives wishing to visit the United States on a temporary basis. *(A-70)*

**Ratify** To approve or give official permission to create or confirm an agreement or amendment. *(B-8)*

**Real estate agent** A person who has taken a real estate education course sponsored by a school or private organization and passed a state examination. He is then licensed by that state to conduct transactions involving real estate. In most states, a real estate agent must work for a *real estate broker*. *(F-1, F-3)*

**Real estate broker** A person who has been a *real estate agent* for a specified period of time, taken additional educational courses, and passed a state examination. He is then licensed by that state to operate a real estate office and employ real estate agents. *(F-1 – F-2)*

**Reasonable and customary charges** The usual fees for services based on the average charges nationally or regionally for the same services. *(E-1)*

**Renter's insurance** *See tenant's insurance.*

**Republican** A member of one of the two major political parties. *(B-11)*

**Resume** A written description of an employment applicant's work experience, education, and other general information. *(C-3, C-7)*

**Return** In financial terms, the amount of money received over and above the initial investment. *(D-11, D-12)*

**Return receipt mail** A post office service that provides the sender of mail a written receipt that it was delivered. *(I-10)*

**Rx** The symbol that indicates a licensed pharmacist area.

**Safety deposit boxes** Rented locked boxes in bank vaults for the secure storage of important papers or valuables. *(D-6)*

**Safety seal** *See tamper-proof packaging.*

**Savings account** A bank account established for the safe keeping of money for future needs. *(D-1 – D-2)*

**School boards** Usually elected by the community, school boards are responsible for running the schools in a local area.

**Secondary school** Term used to refer to grades nine through twelve (junior and senior high schools). *(J-3 – J-4)*

**Secured credit card** A type of credit card requiring that an amount equal to the line of credit available be kept in a related savings account. *(D-21)*

**Secured loan** A loan in which there is *collateral (asset)* pledged in case of *default* (inability to pay).

**Security deposit** In real estate terms, an amount of money held to pay for any damages to a rental property. *(F-6)*

**Seller's agent** In real estate terms, a real estate agent or broker representing the seller of a property. *(F-1)*

**Separation of powers** The principal that divides the U.S. government into three separate branches; the *executive*, the *legislative*, and the *judicial*. *(B-8)*

**Service benefits** In health insurance terms, money paid directly to the doctor, medical professional, or hospital. *(E-1)*

**Simplified Employee Pension Plans (SEPs)** Retirement plans for small businesses. *(D-16)*

**Social Security** A government insurance program that is paid for by payroll taxes. It provides some retirement income, health care benefits, and death benefits to surviving family members. *(D-17, D-28–D-29)*

**Stop payment** The halting of the processing of a check or other financial means of payment after it has been given to a person or company. There is usually a special procedure to follow which may involve a fee. *(D-2)*

**Straight life insurance** *See whole life insurance.*

**Supreme Court** The highest federal court. It consists of nine judges who are nominated by the president, approved by the Senate, and who serve for life. Its decisions are final and take precedence (priority) over those of all other courts in the country, presidential acts, and laws enacted by Congress. Individual states also have supreme courts. *(B-13)*

**Surgical insurance** Health insurance that pays a surgeon's fees. *(E-2)*

**Surrender** In financial terms, to turn in at or before an agreed time. *(E-6)*

**Tamper-proof packaging** Federal law requires that most food and health care products be packaged so that a consumer can easily see if someone has opened or otherwise possibly damaged the product. *(H-4)*

**Telephone book** A free directory routinely given out by a local telephone company that contains individual, business, and government office telephone numbers. It also contains emergency telephone numbers and instructions as well as other important information. See *Blue pages, White pages,* and *Yellow pages. (I-3, I-5)*

**Telephone card** *See calling card.*

**Temporary agency** An employment agency specializing in providing temporary employment. Also referred to as a temp agency. *(C-6)*

**Tenants insurance** A type of homeowners insurance for apartment renters. It provides protection for personal property and for liability if someone is injured in the apartment.

**Term life insurance** Life insurance that is for a specific period of time. It may or may not be renewed after that time period. *(E-6)*

**Title** In business terms, the legal certificate of ownership.

**Title insurance** In real estate terms, insurance that covers financial loss due to a dispute over the ownership (title) to a property. *(F-4)*

**Unemployment insurance** State sponsored insurance that pays benefits for a limited number of weeks if a person loses their employment for business or health reasons. It is usually financed through a state payroll tax.

**Universal compulsory education** Required schooling for all children, generally from ages six or seven to age sixteen. *(J-1)*

**Universal life insurance** Combines features of **term** and *whole life* insurance. It allows you to change the proportion of term and whole life, the face value, and the amount you pay. *(E-7)*

**Unsecured loan** A loan in which there is no *collateral (asset)* pledged in case of *default* (inability to pay).

**Utilities** Term used for basic public services such as gas, electricity, water, and telephone. *(F-7)*

**Variable life insurance** A type of life insurance policy that accumulates a cash value and offers investment options for the cash value. It typically pays a minimum death benefit regardless of the investment outcome. *(E-7)*

**Visa** authorizes a foreign national to enter and/or reside in the United States for a specific period of time.

**Warranty** A promise to repair or replace something if it does not work for a specified period of time after its purchase.

**White collar worker** A term designating an office worker. *(C-3)*

**White pages** Section of a telephone book that alphabetically lists residential, commercial, and governmental phone numbers. *(I-3, I-5)*

**Whole life insurance** Life insurance that has a fixed *premium* (payment) throughout the lifetime of the *policyholder* and *accumulates* a *cash value. (E-6 – E-7)*

**Will** A legal document that provides for the disposition (allocation) of your property *(estate)* after your death. It must meet certain legal requirements. Therefore, it is recommended that it be prepared by an appropriate legal professional. *(B-17–B-18)*

**Withholding** The amount of money deducted from a paycheck for taxes and *social security* sent by the employer to the appropriate government office.*(D-28)*

**Yellow pages** The section of the telephone book that contains listings of businesses and advertisements for those businesses. It is organized alphabetically by type of business.*(I-3, I-5)*

**Zip code** A five-digit number that identifies the local area to which you are mailing. It is an important part of any mailing address as it insures a prompt and speedy delivery. *(I-9)*

**Zip + 4** An expanded version of the zip code that adds four more numbers. It is primarily used in commercial mailings.*(I-9)*

**Zoning** The dividing of a city or town into areas by specific restrictions on usage and types of construction allowed such as residential or commercial. *(F-4)*

# RECEIVE YOUR FREE MEMBERSHIP
# IN
# ACCESS USA CLUB INTERNATIONAL[SM]

Included in the purchase price of your guidebook is your free first year's membership in Access USA Club International.

Free club membership provides you with valuable benefits and services that will make your adjustment to life in the United States easier and save you money. Some of these free benefits and services include:

- Information updates on immigration law and special programs

- Access to the club's helpline, a telephone number to call if you are not sure what to do in almost any situation

- Special information and discounts on products and services

- Qualification for you or one of your family members to be considered for one of ten annual $1,000 educational scholarships

- Enrollment in the club's **Gold Member Program** for $50.00 instead of the usual $100.00 fee.

The **Gold Member Program** includes the following additional benefits and services:

- A list of immigration attorneys based on your personal situation and needs

- Enrollment in the Green Card Lottery (where eligible, see page A-43) for you, your spouse, and any of your children under 21 years of age

- A quarterly newsletter containing the latest information on issues affecting immigration and articles on how to improve your quality of life in the United States as well as other special benefits.

N-21

# ENROLLMENT FORM

☐ **YES,** I want to receive a **FREE ONE-YEAR MEMBERSHIP** in Access USA Club International℠

Name: _____

Address: _____

_____

_____

Country: _____

Telephone: _____

☐ **YES,** I want to become a **GOLD MEMBER**

I am enclosing an international money order for $50.00 (U.S) annual membership fee as a Gold Member, made payable to Access USA, Inc.

You may also pay by Visa, MasterCard or American Express. Check method of payment:

☐ Visa          Account Number_____

☐ MasterCard          Expiration Date_____

☐ American Express

Cardholder's Name (Please Print)_____

Signature_____

Send to :  Access USA Club International
1761 Long Hill Road
Millington, NJ 07946-1344
USA

# ENROLLMENT INFORMATION QUESTIONNAIRE

Fill out this enrollment information questionnaire and send it in along with your enrollment form. You do not need to send in the questionnaire along with your enrollment form to begin receiving your benefits. You may send it in at a later date.

**Certification.** The information in this questionnaire is only to be used for benefits and services provided by Access USA, Inc. It is private information and not available to any government agency without the written permission of the club member.

Please Print or Type. If you are not sure of your answers, simply skip to the next question.

1. Your name, address, and phone number where we can send you information.

Your Name _____

Mailing Address _____

_____

_____

Phone number _____

2. How well do you understand English? Use the following ability ratings: very well; average (can do it but with some effort) or; not well.

| 2.1 Speaking Ability | 2.2 Reading Ability | 2.3 Writing Ability |
|---|---|---|
| ☐ Very Well ☐ Average ☐ Not Well | ☐ Very Well ☐ Average ☐ Not Well | ☐ Very Well ☐ Average ☐ Not Well |

3. In what language would you like us to send you information?

Please check all that apply.

☐ 3.1 English    ☐ 3.2 Spanish    ☐ 3.3 Portuguese    ☐ 3.4 Chinese

☐ 3.5 Korean    ☐ 3.6 Japanese    ☐ 3.7 Russian    ☐ 3.8 Other _____

CUT HERE AND RETURN

4. If you are not already in the United States, when do you plan to arrive for either a visit or immigration application? If you are not sure, use your best estimate.

4.1 MONTH (check one)

☐ January, February, March
☐ April, May, June
☐ July, August, September
☐ October, November, December

4.2 YEAR (check one)

☐ 1995 ☐ 1998
☐ 1996 ☐ 1999
☐ 1997

5. Of what country are you a citizen?_____

6. What is your marital status? (check one)

☐ 6.1 Married ☐ 6.2 Divorced ☐ 6.3 Single ☐ 6.4 Other _____

7. What are the names and relationship to you (wife, son, daughter, father, mother, brother or sister) of persons in your immediate family that you plan to have join you in the United States? If you need more room, please include their information on a separate piece of paper.

| | Name | Relationship | Date of Birth | Expected Month & Year of Arrival |
|---|---|---|---|---|
| 7.1 | _____ | _____ | _____ | _____ |
| 7.2 | _____ | _____ | _____ | _____ |
| 7.3 | _____ | _____ | _____ | _____ |
| 7.4 | _____ | _____ | _____ | _____ |
| 7.5 | _____ | _____ | _____ | _____ |
| 7.6 | _____ | _____ | _____ | _____ |

8. Do you have employment arranged for when you arrive?

8.1. ☐ Yes ☐ No (go to question 9)

8.2. Company name_____

8.3 Type of work _____

8.4 What will your annual salary be in US dollars? If you are not sure, please give your best estimate.

☐ Less than 10,000 ☐ $10,000 to $20,000 ☐ $20,001 to $30,000
☐ 30,001 to $40,000 ☐ $40,001 to $50,000 ☐ Over $50,000

(go to question 10)

9. Will you need help in finding employment?

      ☐ Yes           ☐ No (go to question 10)

  9.1 What type of employment?

_____

_____

_____

_____

  9.2.  If possible, please include a copy of your resume or, on a separate sheet of paper, include a description of your skills and areas of work you are seeking.

10. Do you wish to have a credit card?

      ☐ Yes           ☐ No

  Which of the following credit cards do you have?

  ☐ 10.1 Visa    ☐ 10.2 MasterCard  ☐ 10.3 American Express

  ☐ 10.4 Others _____    ☐ 10.5 None

11. Do you want an attorney who speaks languages other than English?

      ☐ Yes      What languages  _____

      ☐ No

                            _____

                            _____

12. In what city or state or area do you want your attorney to have an office?

_____

13. Please list any visa or visas for which you would like to receive more detailed information.

  13.1 _____

  13.2 _____

  13.3 _____

14. Are there any areas of special areas that you feel your attorney should have experience in handling (such as a family member with a serious illness or ethnic background or language ability).

_____

_____

_____

15. Please check any of the following areas to receive more information.  There is space available in each area for you to write in a request for any information not listed.

16.1 **INSURANCE**

☐ Health insurance

☐ Life insurance

☐ Automobile insurance

☐ Homeowners insurance

☐ General information

☐ Other _____

_____

17.1 **BANKING**

☐ Checking account

☐ Savings account

☐ Money market account

☐ International money transfer

☐ Other _____

_____

18.1 **TELEPHONE SERVICE**

☐ Calling cards

☐ Calling services

☐ Other _____

_____

19.1 **CARS**

☐ New cars

☐ Used cars

☐ Other _____

_____

20.1 **TRAVEL**

☐ Tourist information

☐ Travel agents

☐ Other_____

_____

21.1 **FOOD**

☐ Cookbooks

☐ Coupons for discounts

☐ Other_____

_____

22.1 **HEALTH CARE**

☐ Coupons for discounts

☐ Health care information

☐ Other _____

_____

23.1 **ENTERTAINMENT**

☐ Cable television

☐ Satellite dishes

☐ Other_____

_____

24.1 **INVESTMENTS**
- ☐ Mutual funds
- ☐ Stocks and bonds
- ☐ Educational information
- ☐ Other _____

_____

25.1 **REAL ESTATE**
- ☐ Buying a home
- ☐ Renting an apartment
- ☐ Obtaining a mortgage
- ☐ Other _____

_____

26.1 **TRANSLATION SERVICE**
- ☐ Academic credentials
- ☐ Professional credentials
- ☐ Business documents
- ☐ Legal documents
- ☐ Other _____

_____

27.1 **CREDIT CARDS**
- ☐ MasterCard
- ☐ Visa
- ☐ American Express
- ☐ Discover
- ☐ Other _____

_____

28. List any areas for which you would like to receive further information.

_____

_____

_____

_____

# GREEN CARD LOTTERY REGISTRATION

29. For **Gold Members** who are requesting submission to the "Green Card Lottery," you must send in the following information for you and your family members (spouse and children under 21 years of age) wishing submission. If you wish us to submit a separate green card lottery application for your spouse (at no additional charge) please include the information noted in question 29.1 on a separate piece of paper. Be sure to check eligibility requirements which are noted on page A-43.

29.1 Full name _____

Date of birth _____

Place of birth _____

Current mailing address_____

Last city and country of residence _____

Name of U.S. consulate where the case, if selected is to be processed _____

_____

Names, dates, and places of birth of spouse and children under 21 years of age expecting to immigrate.

29.2 Name _____

Date of Birth _____ Place of Birth _____

Relationship _____

29.3 Name _____

Date of Birth _____ Place of Birth _____

Relationship _____

29.4 Name _____

Date of Birth _____ Place of Birth _____

Relationship _____

29.5 Name _____

Date of Birth _____ Place of Birth _____

Relationship _____

29.6  Name _____

　　　Date of Birth _____Place of Birth _____

　　　Relationship_____


29.7  Name _____

　　　Date of Birth _____Place of Birth _____

　　　Relationship_____


29.8  Name _____

　　　Date of Birth _____Place of Birth _____

　　　Relationship_____


29.9  Name _____

　　　Date of Birth _____Place of Birth _____

　　　Relationship_____


29.10 Name _____

　　　Date of Birth _____Place of Birth _____

　　　Relationship_____


29.11 Name _____

　　　Date of Birth _____Place of Birth _____

　　　Relationship_____


29.12 Name _____

　　　Date of Birth _____Place of Birth _____

　　　Relationship_____